Photoshop
Elements 8
for Windows

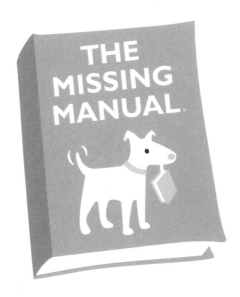

Barbara Brundage

POGUE PRESS™
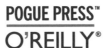
O'REILLY®

Beijing · Cambridge · Farnham · Köln · Sebastopol · Taipei · Tokyo

Photoshop Elements 8 for Windows: The Missing Manual
by Barbara Brundage

Published by O'Reilly Media, Inc., 1005 Gravenstein Highway North, Sebastopol, CA 95472.

O'Reilly books may be purchased for educational, business, or sales promotional use. Online editions are also available for most titles (*my.safaribooksonline.com*). For more information, contact our corporate/institutional sales department: (800) 998-9938 or *corporate@oreilly.com*.

Printing History:

September 2009:   First Edition.

 This book uses RepKover™, a durable and flexible lay-flat binding.

ISBN: 978-0-596-80347-6

[TI]

Table of Contents

Part Two: Elemental Elements

Part Three: Retouching

Chapter 7: Basic Image Retouching 205

Chapter 8: Elements for Digital Photographers 247

The Missing Credits

About the Author

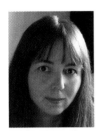

Barbara Brundage is the author of *Photoshop Elements 7: The Missing Manual*, and Adobe Community Expert, and a member of Adobe's prerelease groups for Elements 3, 4, 5, 6, 7, and 8. She's been teaching people how to use Photoshop Elements since it came out in 2001. Barbara first started using Elements to create graphics for use in her day job as a harpist, music publisher, and arranger. Along the way, she joined the large group of people finding a renewed interest in photography thanks to digital cameras. If she can learn to use Elements, you can, too! You can reach her at *bbrundage@me.com*.

About the Creative Team

Dawn Frausto (editor) is assistant editor for the Missing Manual series. When not working, she plays soccer, beads, and causes trouble. Email: *dawn@oreilly.com*.

Nellie McKesson (production editor) lives in Brighton, Mass., where she makes t-shirts for her friends (*http://mattsaundersbynellie.etsy.com*) and plays music with her band Dr. & Mrs. Van Der Trampp. Email: *nellie@oreilly.com*.

Jan Jue (copy editor) enjoys freelance copyediting, a good mystery, and the search for the perfect pot sticker.

Ron Strauss (indexer) is a full-time freelance indexer specializing in IT. When not working, he moonlights as a concert violist and alternative medicine health consultant. Email: *rstrauss@mchsi.com*.

Doug Nelson (technical reviewer) is the founder of RetouchPRO, a free online resource for anyone interested in digital imaging. He is also the host and moderator for RetouchPRO LIVE, an interactive, live webshow where you can watch professional retouchers at work and ask them questions. Website: *www.retouchpro.com*.

Barbara Olson (technical reviewer) volunteers at her local SeniorNet Learning Center where she teaches a class for beginning Photoshop Elements students.

Acknowledgments

Many thanks to Doug Nelson and Barbara Olson for reading this book and giving me the benefit of their advice and corrections. I'm also grateful for the help I received from everyone at Adobe, especially Bob Gager, Gaurav Jain, and Jim Mohan.

Special thanks also to graphic artist Jodi Frye (*lfrye012000@yahoo.com*) for allowing me to reproduce one of her Elements drawings to show what can be done by those with more artistic ability than I have. My gratitude also to Florida's botanical gardens, especially McKee Botanical Garden (*www.mckeegarden.org*), Historic Bok Sanctuary (*www.boktower.org*), Heathcote Botanical Gardens (*www.heathcotebotanicalgardens.org*), and Harry P. Leu Gardens (*www.leugardens.org*) for creating oases of peace and beauty in our hectic world. Finally, I'd like to thank everyone in the gang over at the Adobe Photoshop Elements support forum for all their help and friendship.

—Barbara Brundage

The Missing Manual Series

Missing Manuals are witty, superbly written guides to computer products that don't come with printed manuals (which is just about all of them). Each book features a handcrafted index; cross-references to specific pages (not just chapters); and RepKover, a detached-spine binding that lets the book lie perfectly flat without the assistance of weights or cinder blocks.

Recent and upcoming titles include:

Access 2007: The Missing Manual by Matthew MacDonald

AppleScript: The Missing Manual by Adam Goldstein

AppleWorks 6: The Missing Manual by Jim Elferdink and David Reynolds

CSS: The Missing Manual, Second Edition by David Sawyer McFarland

Creating a Web Site: The Missing Manual, Second Edition by Matthew MacDonald

David Pogue's Digital Photography: The Missing Manual by David Pogue

Dreamweaver 8: The Missing Manual by David Sawyer McFarland

Dreamweaver CS3: The Missing Manual by David Sawyer McFarland

Dreamweaver CS4: The Missing Manual by David Sawyer McFarland

eBay: The Missing Manual by Nancy Conner

Excel 2003: The Missing Manual by Matthew MacDonald

Excel 2007: The Missing Manual by Matthew MacDonald

Facebook: The Missing Manual by E.A. Vander Veer

FileMaker Pro 9: The Missing Manual by Geoff Coffey and Susan Prosser

FileMaker Pro 10: The Missing Manual by Susan Prosser and Geoff Coffey

Flash 8: The Missing Manual by E.A. Vander Veer

Flash CS3: The Missing Manual by E.A. Vander Veer and Chris Grover

Flash CS4: The Missing Manual by Chris Grover with E.A. Vander Veer

FrontPage 2003: The Missing Manual by Jessica Mantaro

Google Apps: The Missing Manual by Nancy Conner

The Internet: The Missing Manual by David Pogue and J.D. Biersdorfer

iMovie 6 & iDVD: The Missing Manual by David Pogue

iMovie '08 & iDVD: The Missing Manual by David Pogue

iMovie '09 & iDVD: The Missing Manual by David Pogue and Aaron Miller

iPhone: The Missing Manual, Third Edition by David Pogue

iPhoto '08: The Missing Manual by David Pogue

iPhoto '09: The Missing Manual by David Pogue and J.D. Biersdorfer

iPod: The Missing Manual, Eighth Edition by J.D. Biersdorfer and David Pogue

JavaScript: The Missing Manual by David Sawyer McFarland

Living Green: The Missing Manual by Nancy Conner

Mac OS X: The Missing Manual, Tiger Edition by David Pogue

Mac OS X: The Missing Manual, Leopard Edition by David Pogue

Microsoft Project 2007: The Missing Manual by Bonnie Biafore

Netbooks: The Missing Manual by J.D. Biersdorfer

Office 2004 for Macintosh: The Missing Manual by Mark H. Walker and Franklin Tessler

Office 2007: The Missing Manual by Chris Grover, Matthew MacDonald, and E.A. Vander Veer

Office 2008 for Macintosh: The Missing Manual by Jim Elferdink

Palm Pre: The Missing Manual by Ed Baig

PCs: The Missing Manual by Andy Rathbone

Photoshop Elements 7: The Missing Manual by Barbara Brundage

Photoshop Elements 6 for Mac: The Missing Manual by Barbara Brundage

PowerPoint 2007: The Missing Manual by E.A. Vander Veer

QuickBase: The Missing Manual by Nancy Conner

QuickBooks 2009: The Missing Manual by Bonnie Biafore

QuickBooks 2010: The Missing Manual by Bonnie Biafore

Quicken 2008: The Missing Manual by Bonnie Biafore

Quicken 2009: The Missing Manual by Bonnie Biafore

Switching to the Mac: The Missing Manual, Tiger Edition by David Pogue and Adam Goldstein

Switching to the Mac: The Missing Manual, Leopard Edition by David Pogue

Wikipedia: The Missing Manual by John Broughton

Windows XP Home Edition: The Missing Manual, Second Edition by David Pogue

Windows XP Pro: The Missing Manual, Second Edition by David Pogue, Craig Zacker, and Linda Zacker

Windows Vista: The Missing Manual by David Pogue

Windows Vista for Starters: The Missing Manual by David Pogue

Word 2007: The Missing Manual by Chris Grover

Your Body: The Missing Manual by Matthew MacDonald

Your Brain: The Missing Manual by Matthew MacDonald

Introduction

Photos are everywhere these days. Once upon a time, you only hauled out the camera to record important events that you wanted to remember forever. But in our digital era, when almost every cellphone has a camera, people take photos of everything from what they had for lunch to the weird faucet fitting they're trying to install so they can email it to friends for advice.

Photo sharing has become one of the basics of daily life, and Adobe is right there with you. Not only does Photoshop Elements 8 give you terrific tools for editing and improving your photos, but you also get a free account at Photoshop.com, making it incredibly easy to share photos on your personal Photoshop.com web page, back them up automatically, and sync them between your computers.

> **NOTE** For now, you have to be in the United States to use Photoshop.com. If you're in another country, you can create and share online albums at Adobe's Photoshop Showcase (*www. photoshopshowcase.com*), a site first created for folks using Elements 6. A few features are available only with Photoshop.com, so for now, these features are U.S.-only.

Why Photoshop Elements?

Adobe's Photoshop is the granddaddy of all image-editing programs. It's the Big Cheese, the industry standard against which everything else is measured. Every photo you've seen in a book or magazine in the past 15 years or so has almost certainly passed through Photoshop on its way to being printed. You just can't buy anything that gives you more control over your pictures than Photoshop does.

But Photoshop has some big drawbacks: It's darned hard to learn, it's horribly expensive, and many of the features in it are just plain overkill if you don't work on pictures for a living.

For several years, Adobe tried to find a way to cram many of Photoshop's marvelous powers into a package that normal people could use. Finding the right formula was a slow process. First came PhotoDeluxe, a program that was lots of fun, but that came up short when you wanted to fine-tune *how* the program worked. Adobe tried again with Photoshop LE, which many people felt just gave you all the difficulty of full Photoshop, but still gave too little of what you need to do top-notch work.

Finally—sort of like "The Three Bears"—Adobe got it just right with Photoshop Elements. It took off like crazy because it offers so much of Photoshop's power in a program that almost anyone can learn. With Elements, you, too, can work with the same wonderful tools that the pros use.

The earliest versions of Elements had something of a learning curve. It was a super program, but not one where you could expect to get perfect results right off the bat. In each new version, Adobe has added lots of push-button-easy ways to correct and improve your photos. Elements 8 brings you some really high-tech editing tools, new ways to arrange your workspace, and new ways to share your photos online more easily than ever.

What You Can Do with Elements 8

Elements not only lets you make your photos look great, but it also helps you organize your photos and gives you some pretty neat projects in which to use them. The program also comes loaded with lots of easy ways to share your photos. The list of what Elements can do is pretty impressive. You can use Elements to:

- Enhance your photos by editing, cropping, and color-correcting them, including fixing exposure and color problems.

- Add all kinds of special effects to your images, like turning a garden-variety photo into a drawing, painting, or even a tile mosaic.

- Combine photos into a panorama or montage.

- Move someone from one photo to another, and even remove people (your ex?) from last year's holiday photos.

- Repair and restore old and damaged photos.

- Organize your photos and assign keywords to them so you can search by subject or name.

- Add text to your images, and turn them into things like greeting cards and flyers.

- Create slideshows to share with friends, regardless of whether they use Windows, a Mac, or even just a cellphone.

- Automatically resize photos so that they're ready for email. Elements even lets you send your photos in specially designed emails.

- Create digital artwork from scratch, even without a photo to work from.

- Create and share incredible online albums and email-ready slideshows that will make your friends actually ask to see the pictures from your latest trip.

- Store your photos online so that you can get to them from any computer. You can organize your photos online, and upload new photos directly to your personalized Photoshop.com website. You can also keep an online backup of your photos, and even sync albums so that when you add a new photo from another computer, it automatically gets sent to your home computer, too.

- Create and edit graphics for websites, including making animated GIFs (pictures that move like cartoons).

- Create wonderful collages that you can print or share with your friends digitally. Scrapbookers—get ready to be wowed.

It's worth noting, though, that there are still a few things Elements *can't* do. While the program handles text quite competently, at least as photo-editing programs go, it's still no substitute for QuarkXPress, InDesign, or any other desktop-publishing program. And Elements can do an amazing job of fixing problems in your photos, but only if you give it something to work with. If your photo is totally overexposed, blurry, and the top of everyone's head is cut off, there's a limit to what even Elements can do to help you out. (C'mon, be fair.) The fact is, though, you're more likely to be surprised by what Elements *can* fix than by what it can't.

What's New in Elements 8

Elements 8 brings some really cool new editing features, as well as some helpful new organizing tools:

- **Recompose your photos** (page 297). You know how it is: You try and try to get a photo of all the kids together, but in the best one, there's an awkward gap between your son and daughter because they just wouldn't stand close together. Or you got a perfect shot of that mountain landscape, except for that pesky condo in the background. Wouldn't it be great if you could squeeze the edges of your photo together and get rid of the empty space or those unwanted objects? With the new Recompose tool you can. A couple of scribbles to tell Elements what to lose and what to keep, drag the edge of your picture, and presto!—a recomposed photo with no distortion. It's an awesome use of computer intelligence.

- **Exposure Merge** (page 267). Combine two or more different exposures of the same scene for one image that's well-exposed everywhere. This is similar to what you can do with the popular HDR (High Dynamic Range) tools found in Photoshop or from companies like Photomatix, only with Elements' classic ease of use. It's perfect for situations like night portraits, where properly exposing your subject can wash out the dramatic lighting of the skyline behind him.

- **New look** (page 24). Now you can view your images in the Editor as floating windows, as in previous versions of Elements, or as fixed tabs. You can arrange the Editor workspace to suit you, and you have far more options for doing so than you ever did before in Elements. What's more, you can quickly change it all if you decide you want a different setup for your current task.

- **Face recognition** (page 61). The Elements Organizer (the database where you keep track of your photos and organize them) has been able to search for human faces for some time now, but in Elements 8, it can recognize a face as Aunt Millie or Cousin Jobert and offer to tag it with the correct name.

- **Guides** (page 87). This has been one of the most-requested features missing from Elements: nonprinting guidelines you can position in your file to help you arrange any text or objects you're adding. They're finally here in Elements 8—a real boon for scrapbookers and other project makers.

- **Quick Fix previews** (page 119). If you're using the easy Quick Fix window in the Elements Editor, you can see thumbnail previews of different settings for the tool you're using. Click one of the thumbnails or drag back and forth on it with your cursor to see its effect on your image and to adjust its intensity.

- **Adjustments panel** (page 195). Experienced Elements folks will really appreciate the new Adjustments panel, which lets you see the settings for any of your Adjustment layers just by clicking the layer.

- **Sync your photos** (page 75). In Elements 7, you could sync your photos to an online backup at Photoshop.com (Adobe's online sharing service), but in Elements 8 you can also sync photos between two computers running Elements by means of Photoshop.com, so both computers always have the same photos available to them. (This feature is U.S.-only, for now.)

- **Better integration between the Organizer and Premiere Elements** (page 55). If you use both Photoshop Elements and Adobe's video-editing program Premiere Elements, you'll appreciate the increased number of options for sending film clips over to Premiere Elements and for analyzing your movies in the Elements 8 Organizer.

  NOTE One of the side effects of this better integration is that you'll see a lot of items pertaining to video editing in the Organizer's menus, even if you don't have Premiere Elements. You can turn most of these off if you don't care to see them. Page 55 tells you how. (Appendix A explains all the Organizer's menus.)

- **Tagging improvements** (page 58). The Organizer's Keyword Tag pane (where you assign keywords to your photos) has a handy new text box where you can just type in the name for a new tag, click Apply, and add that tag to all your selected photos. There's also a "cloud" view of your tags, like the keyword clouds you may have seen on websites.

- **Full Screen view** (page 56). Adobe has gussied up the Organizer's Full Screen view so you can edit and tag your photos while looking at them at full screen. You can even watch them as a slideshow, complete with music (page 525).

- **Activation** (page 608). You may not love this new feature, but Adobe only lets you use your copy of Elements 8 on two computers, so it's important to deactivate Elements on your old computer before installing it on a new one. Page 608 explains how.

If you've used Elements before and you're not sure which version you've got, a quick way to tell is to look for the version number on the CD. If the program is already installed, see page 16 for help figuring out which version you have.

Incidentally, all eight versions of Elements are totally separate programs, so you can run all of them on the same computer if you like, as long as your operating system is compatible. (Adobe doesn't recommend trying to have more than one version *open* at a time, though.) So if you prefer the older version of a particular tool, then you can still use it. If you've been using one of the earlier versions, then you'll feel right at home in Elements 8. You'll just find that it's easier than ever to get stuff done with the program.

If You Have a Mac

This book covers Elements 8 for Windows. Adobe is releasing Elements 8 for Mac a few weeks after the Windows version, and there's a separate version of this book, *Photoshop Elements 8 for Mac: The Missing Manual,* which you should get if you're using the Mac version. Editing is pretty much the same on both Windows and Mac computers, but the Mac version of Elements doesn't include the Organizer. Instead, you get Adobe Bridge (the deluxe photo-browser that comes with Photoshop), so the parts of this book about organizing your photos, using online services, and many of the projects are different from the Mac version.

Elements vs. Photoshop

You could easily get confused about the differences between Elements and the full version of Adobe Photoshop. Because Elements is so much less expensive, and because many of its more advanced controls are tucked away, a lot of Photoshop aficionados tend to view Elements as some kind of toy version of their program.

They couldn't be more wrong. Elements *is* Photoshop, but it's Photoshop adapted for use with a home printer, and for the Web. The most important difference between Elements and Photoshop is that Elements doesn't let you work or save in CMYK mode, which is the format used for commercial color printing. (CMYK stands for Cyan, Magenta, Yellow, and blacK. Your inkjet printer also uses those ink colors to print, but it expects you to give it an RGB file, which is what Elements creates. This is all explained in Chapter 7.)

Elements also lacks several tools that are basic staples in any commercial art department, like the ability to write actions or scripts (to help automate repetitive tasks), the extra color control you can get from Selective Color, and the Pen tool's special talent for creating vector paths. Also, for some special effects, like creating drop shadows or bevels, the tool you'd use—Layer styles—doesn't have as many settings in Elements as it does in Photoshop. The same holds true for a handful of other Elements tools.

And although Elements is all most people need to create graphics for the Web, it doesn't come with the advanced tools in Photoshop, which let you do things like automatically slice images into smaller pieces for faster web display. If you use Elements, then you have to look for another program to help out with that.

The Key to Learning Elements

Elements may not be quite as powerful as Photoshop, but it's still a complex program, filled with more features than most people ever use. The good news is that the Quick Fix window (Chapter 4) lets you get started right away, even if you don't understand every last option that Quick Fix presents you with. And you also get the Guided Edit mode (page 32), which provides a step-by-step walkthrough of some popular editing tasks, like sharpening your photo or cropping it to fit on standard photo paper.

As for the program's more complex features, the key to learning how to use Elements—or any other program, for that matter—is to focus only on what you need to know for the task you're currently trying to accomplish.

For example, if you're trying to use Quick Fix to adjust the color of your photo and crop it, don't worry that you don't get the concept of "layers" yet. You won't learn to do everything in Elements in a day or even a week. The rest will wait until you need it, so take your time; don't worry about what's not important to you right now. You'll find it much easier to master Elements if you go slowly and concentrate on one thing at a time.

If you're totally new to the program, then you'll find only three or four big concepts in this book that you really have to understand if you want to get the most out of Elements. It may take a little time for some concepts to sink in—resolution and layers, for instance, aren't the most intuitive concepts in the world—but once they click, they'll seem so obvious that you'll wonder why things seemed confusing at first. That's perfectly normal, so persevere. You *can* do this, and there's nothing in this book that you can't understand with a little bit of careful reading.

The very best way to learn Elements is just to dive right in and play with it. Try all the different filters to see what they do. Add a filter on top of another filter. Click around on all the different tools and try them. You don't even need to have a photo to do this. See page 50 to learn how to make an image from scratch in Elements, and read on to learn about the many downloadable practice images you'll find at this book's companion website, *www.missingmanuals.com*. Get crazy—you can stack up as many filters, effects, and Layer styles as you want without crashing the program.

About This Book

Elements is a cool program and lots of fun to use, but figuring out how to make it do what you want is another matter. Elements 8 comes only with a quick reference guide, and it doesn't go into as much depth as you might want. The Elements Help files are very good, but of course you need to know what you're looking for to use them to your best advantage. (The Help files that ship with Elements are sometimes incomplete, but you can download a more polished version from Adobe's Elements support pages at *www.adobe.com/support/photoshopelements/*.)

You'll find a slew of Elements titles at your local bookstore, but most of them assume that you know quite a bit about the basics of photography and/or digital imaging. It's much easier to find good intermediate books about Elements than books designed to get you going with the program.

That's where this book comes in. It's intended to make learning Elements easier by avoiding technical jargon as much as possible, and explaining *why* and *when* you'll want to use (or avoid) certain features of the program. That approach is as useful to people who are advanced photographers as it is to those who are just getting started with their first digital cameras.

> **NOTE** This book periodically recommends *other* books, covering topics too specialized or tangential for a manual about Elements. Careful readers may notice that not every one of these titles is published by Missing Manual parent O'Reilly Media. While we're happy to mention other Missing Manuals and books in the O'Reilly family, if there's a great book out there that doesn't happen to be published by O'Reilly, we'll still let you know about it.

You'll also find instructions throughout the book that refer to files you can download from the Missing Manual website (*www.missingmanuals.com*) so you can practice the techniques you're reading about. And throughout the book, you'll find several different kinds of short articles. The ones labeled "Up to Speed" help newcomers to Elements do things, or they explain concepts with which veterans are probably already familiar. Those labeled "Power Users' Clinic" cover more advanced topics that won't be of much interest to casual photographers.

NOTE Since Elements 8 works in both Windows Vista and Windows XP, you'll see screenshots from both operating systems in this book. It's also going to work with Windows 7 when Microsoft releases it (it wasn't out yet when this book was being written). Most things work exactly the same way in all three operating systems; only the styles of some windows are different. In a few instances, the file paths for certain program files aren't exactly the same. If that's the case, then you're given the directions for both Vista and XP. Also, since Elements has a setting that lets you choose between a dark and a light view of the program (see page 17), in the illustrations you'll see whichever one best displays the feature being discussed.

About the Outline

This book is divided into seven parts, each focusing on a certain kind of task you may want to do in Elements:

- **Part One: Introduction to Elements.** The first part of this book helps you get started with Elements. Chapter 1 shows how to navigate Elements' slightly confusing layout and mishmash of programs within programs. You'll learn how to decide which window to start from and how to set up Elements so it best suits your working style, and how to set up your Photoshop.com account. You'll also read about some important keyboard shortcuts, and where to look for help when you get stuck. Chapter 2 covers how to get photos into Elements, the basics of organizing them, and how to open files and create new images from scratch. You'll also find out how to save and back up your images, either on your home computer or using Photoshop.com. Chapter 3 explains how to rotate and crop photos, and includes a primer on that most important digital imaging concept—resolution.

- **Part Two: Elemental Elements.** Chapter 4 shows how to use the Quick Fix window to dramatically improve your photos. Chapters 5 and 6 cover two key concepts—making selections and layers—that you'll use throughout the book.

- **Part Three: Retouching.** Having Elements is like having a darkroom on your computer. In Chapter 7, you'll learn how to make basic corrections, such as fixing exposure, adjusting color, sharpening an image, and removing dust and scratches. Chapter 8 covers topics unique to people who use digital cameras, like Raw conversion and batch-processing your photos. In Chapter 9, you'll move on to some more sophisticated fixes, like using the clone stamp for repairs, making a photo livelier by adjusting the color intensity, and adjusting light and shadows in an image. Chapter 10 shows you how to convert color photos to black and white, and how to tint and colorize black-and-white photos. Chapter 11 helps you to use Elements' Photomerge feature to create a panorama from several photos, and to make perspective corrections to your images.

- **Part Four: Artistic Elements.** This part covers the fun stuff—painting on your photos and drawing shapes (Chapter 12), using filters and effects to create a more artistic look (Chapter 13), and adding text to images (Chapter 14).

- **Part Five: Sharing Your Images.** Once you've created a great image in Elements, you'll want to share it, so this part is about how to create fun projects like photo books (Chapter 15), how to get the most out of your printer (Chapter 16), how to create images for the Web and email (Chapter 17), and how to make slideshows and share them online (Chapter 18).

- **Part Six: Additional Elements.** You can get hundreds of plug-ins and additional styles, brushes, and other nifty tools to customize your copy of Elements and increase its abilities; the Internet and your local bookstore are chockfull of additional info. Chapter 19 offers a look at some of these, as well as information about using a graphics tablet in Elements, and some resources to turn to after you've finished this book.

- **Part Seven: Appendixes.** Appendixes A and B cover all the menu items in the Organizer and Editor, respectively. Appendix C helps you get your copy of Elements up and running, and suggests what to do if it starts misbehaving.

For Newcomers to Elements

This book holds a lot of information, and if you're new to Elements, then you don't need to digest it all at once, especially if you've never used any kind of photo-editing software before. So what do you need to read first? Here's a simple five-step way to use the book if you're brand-new to photo editing:

1. **Read all of Chapter 1.**

   That's important for understanding how to get around in Elements.

2. **If your photos aren't on your computer already, then read about the Photo Downloader in Chapter 2.**

   The Downloader gets your photos from your camera's memory card into Elements.

3. **If you want to organize your photos, then read about the Organizer (also in Chapter 2).**

   It doesn't matter where your photos are right now. If you want to use the Organizer to label and keep track of them, then read Chapter 2.

4. **When you're ready to edit your photos, read Chapters 3 and 4.**

   Chapter 3 explains how to adjust your view of your photos in the Editor. Chapter 4 shows you how to use the Quick Fix window to easily edit and correct your photos. Guided Edit (page 32) can also be very helpful when you're just getting started. If you skipped Chapter 2 because you're not using the Organizer, go back there and read the parts about saving your photos, so you don't lose your work.

5. **When you're ready to print or share your photos, flip to the chapters on sharing your images.**

   Chapter 16 covers printing, both at home and from online services. Chapter 17 explains how to email photos, and Chapter 18 teaches you how to post photos at Photoshop.com.

That's all you need to get started. You can come back and pick up the rest of the info in the book as you get more comfortable with Elements and want to explore more of the wonderful things you can do with it.

The Very Basics

This book assumes that you know how to perform basic activities on your computer like clicking and double-clicking your mouse buttons and dragging objects onscreen. Here's a quick refresher: to *click* means to move the point of your mouse or trackpad cursor over an object on your screen, and then to press the left mouse or trackpad button once. To *right-click* means to press the right mouse button once, which calls up a menu of special features. To *double-click* means to press the left button twice, quickly, without moving the mouse between clicks. To *drag* means to click an object and then to hold down the left button (so you don't let go of the object) while you use the mouse to move the object. Most selection buttons onscreen are pretty obvious, but you may not be familiar with *radio buttons*: To choose an option, click the little empty circle next to it. If you're comfortable with basic concepts like these, then you're ready to get started with this book.

In Elements, you'll often want to use keyboard shortcuts to save time, and this book tells you about keyboard shortcuts when they exist (and Elements has a lot). So if you see "Press Ctrl+S to save your file," that means to hold down the Control key while pressing the S key.

About → These → Arrows

Throughout this book (and the Missing Manual series, for that matter) you see sentences that look like this: "Go to the Editor and select Filter → Artistic → Paint Daubs." This is a shorthand way of helping you find files, folders, and menu items without having to read through excruciatingly long, bureaucratic-style instructions. So the sample sentence above is a short way of saying: "Go to the Editor component of Elements. In the menu bar at the top of the screen, click the Filter choice. In the menu that appears, choose the Artistic section, and then go to Paint Daubs in the pop-out menu." Figure I-1 shows you an example in action.

File paths are shown in the conventional Windows style, so if you see "Go to *C:\ Documents and Settings\<your user name>\My Documents\My Pictures*", that means you should go to your C drive, open the Documents and Settings folder, look for your user account folder, and then find the My Documents folder. In that folder, open the My Pictures folder that's inside it. When there are different file

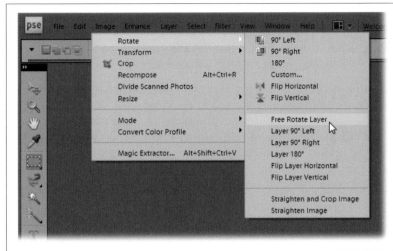

Figure I-1:
In a Missing Manual, when you see a sentence like "Image → Rotate → Free Rotate Layer," that's a quicker way of saying, "Go to the menu bar, click Image, slide down to Rotate, and then, from the pop-up menu, choose Free Rotate Layer."

paths for Vista and Windows XP, then you'll find them both listed. (Although Elements 8 works in Windows 7, you won't see any Windows 7 file paths listed, since Windows 7 hadn't been released as this book was being written.)

About MissingManuals.com

If you head over to this book's Missing CD page (*www.missingmanuals.com*), you'll find links to downloadable practice images mentioned throughout this book.

A word about these downloadable files: To make life easier for folks with slow Internet connections, the file sizes have been kept pretty small. So you probably won't want to print the results of what you create (since you'll end up with a print about the size of a match book). But that doesn't really matter because the files are really meant for onscreen use. You'll see notes throughout the book about which images are available to practice on for any given chapter.

At the website, you can also find articles, tips, and updates to this book. If you click the Errata link, then you'll see any corrections to the book's content, too. If you find something you think is wrong, feel free to report it by using that same link. Each time this book is printed, we'll update it with any confirmed corrections. If you want to be certain that your own copy is up to the minute, check the Missing Manuals website for any changes. And thanks for reporting any errors or suggesting corrections.

We'd love to hear your suggestions for new books in the Missing Manual line. There's a place for that on missingmanuals.com, too. And while you're online, you can also register this book at *www.oreilly.com* (you can jump directly to the registration page by going here: *http://tinyurl.com/yo82k3*). Registering means we can send you updates about this book, and you'll be eligible for special offers like discounts on future editions.

Safari® Books Online

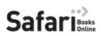 Safari® Books Online is an on-demand digital library that lets you easily search over 7,500 technology and creative reference books and videos to find the answers you need quickly.

With a subscription, you can read any page and watch any video from our library online. Read books on your cell phone and mobile devices. Access new titles before they are available for print, and get exclusive access to manuscripts in development and post feedback for the authors. Copy and paste code samples, organize your favorites, download chapters, bookmark key sections, create notes, print out pages, and benefit from tons of other time-saving features.

O'Reilly Media has uploaded this book to the Safari Books Online service. To have full digital access to this book and others on similar topics from O'Reilly and other publishers, sign up for free at *http://my.safaribooksonline.com*.

Part One: Introduction to Elements

Finding Your Way Around Elements

Photoshop Elements lets you do practically anything you want to your digital images. You can colorize black-and-white photos, remove demonic red-eye stares, or distort the facial features of people who've been mean to you. The downside is that all those options can make it tough to find your way around Elements, especially when you're new to the program.

This chapter helps get you oriented in Elements. You'll learn what to expect when you launch the program, how to use Elements to fix photos with just a couple of keystrokes, and how to sign up for and connect to all the goodies that await you on Photoshop.com. You'll also learn how to use Guided Edit mode to get started editing your photos. Along the way, you'll find out about some of Elements' basic controls, and how to get to the program's Help files.

The Welcome Screen

When you launch Elements for the first time, you're greeted by the Welcome screen (Figure 1-1). This is where you register Elements and sign up for your free Photoshop.com account (U.S. only). Page 607 explains how.

> NOTE   If you aren't in the U.S., the whole process of registering Elements works a bit differently—
> see page 607.

Interestingly, the Welcome screen isn't actually Elements. It's just a launching pad that starts up one of two different programs, depending on the button you click:

- **Organize button.** This starts the Organizer, which lets you store and organize your image files.

- **Edit button.** Click this for the Editor, which lets you modify your images.

You can easily hop back and forth between the Editor and the Organizer—which you might call the two halves of Elements—and you probably won't do much in one without eventually needing to get into the other. But in some ways, they function as two separate programs.

UP TO SPEED

Which Version of Elements Do You Have?

This book covers Photoshop Elements 8. If you're not sure which version you've got, the easiest way to find out is to look at the program's icon (the file icon you click to launch Elements). The icon for Elements 8 is actually pretty close to the icon for Elements 7—both use a blue square with the letters "PSE" (Elements' initials) on it, but the icon for version 8 is a lighter peacock blue than the icon for version 7. But if you're still not sure, click once on the Elements icon on your desktop, and the full name of the program, including the version number, appears below the icon, if it wasn't already visible. You can also check the Windows Start menu: Elements is listed along with its version number.

Or, if Elements is running, in the program's window, go to Help → About Photoshop Elements.

You can use this book if you have an earlier version of Elements because a lot of the basic editing procedures are the same. But Elements 8 is a little different, especially because of changes in how images are displayed in the program, so you'd probably feel more comfortable with a reference book for the version you have. There are Missing Manuals for Elements 3, 4, 5, 6, and 7, too, and you may prefer to track down the right book for your version of Elements.

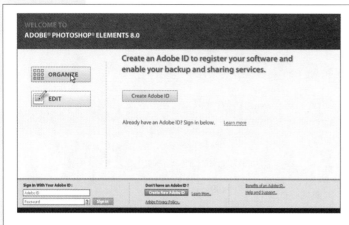

Figure 1-1:
Elements' Welcome screen. What you see in the right part of the window changes occasionally, so it may not be exactly the same as this illustration. The left part of the window always stays the same, though. There you can choose to start organizing or editing photos. The bottom of the screen always has links for signing onto Photoshop.com and displays info about your Photoshop.com account, if you have one. You can't bypass the Welcome screen just by clicking the upper-right Close (X) button. When you do, the screen goes away— but so does Elements. Fortunately, you've got options: The box on page 18 tells you how to permanently say goodbye to this screen.

If you start in the Organizer, then once you've picked a photo to edit, you have to wait a few seconds while the Editor loads. And when you have both the Editor and the Organizer running, just quitting the Editor doesn't close the Organizer—you have to close both programs independently. When both programs are running, you can switch back and forth between them by clicking the button at the upper right of the screen; the button reads "Organizer" when you're in the Editor and "Editor" when you're in the Organizer. (The Organizer button just takes a click, but the Editor button includes a drop-down menu where you choose the editing mode you want.) You can also just click the Editor or the Organizer icon in the Windows taskbar to switch from one to the other.

Adobe built Elements around the assumption that most people work on their photos in the following way: First, you bring photos into the Organizer to sort and keep track of them. Then, you open photos in the Editor to work on them and save them back to the Organizer when you've finished making changes. You can work differently, of course—like opening photos directly in the Editor and bypassing the Organizer altogether—but you may feel like you're always swimming against the current if you choose a different workflow. The next chapter has a few hints for disabling some of Elements' features if you find they're getting in your way.

The Welcome screen can also serve as your connecting point for signing onto *www.photoshop.com*. Page 20 has more about Photoshop.com, but for now you just need to know that a basic account is free if you're in the United States (it's not available yet in other countries), and it gives you access to all the interesting features in Elements 8 that require an Internet connection. If you're signed into Photoshop.com already, you can see how much of your online storage you've already used in the graph at the bottom of the Welcome screen. There's also a reminder of your personal URL at Photoshop.com and links to online help and to tips and tricks for using Elements. However, you can also get to all these things from within the Editor or the Organizer, so there's no need to keep the Welcome screen around for that.

WORKAROUND WORKSHOP

Turning the Lights On

You may find Elements' snazzy dark color scheme hard to see or just plain annoying. Elements 8 gives you a choice of a dark or light color scheme in both the Editor and the Organizer, although the "light" color scheme is more medium than light, really. In either part of the program, just go to Edit → Preferences → General → Appearance Options, and then use the radio buttons to choose Light or Dark. (The Organizer has one control for the overall window and its menus [User Interface] and a separate one for the background around your photo thumbnails [Grid].)

When you pick a new color scheme, the change takes effect immediately, so you don't need to restart Elements to see the difference. The Editor and Organizer adjustments are independent, so you can have each at a different brightness level if you like.

The images in this book include ones taken in both color schemes, so don't be alarmed if the graphics in these pages look darker or lighter than what you see on your screen.

TIP   After you create your Photoshop.com account, you may find you have trouble with the Welcome screen if your Internet connection isn't active when you start Elements. If the Welcome screen hangs while trying to gather your account info, just quit it (you may need to do this in Windows' Task Manager—press Ctrl+Alt+Del in XP or Ctrl+Shift+Esc in Vista to call it up), then follow the directions in the box below for starting the Editor or the Organizer directly from the program file.

Organizing Your Photos

The Organizer is where your photos come into Elements and go out again (when it's time to print or email them). The Organizer stores and catalogs your photos, and you automatically come back to it for any activities that involve sharing your photos, like printing a photo package (page 500) or making a slideshow (page 524). The Organizer's main window (Figure 1-2), which is sometimes called the *Media Browser,* lets you view your photos, sort them into albums, and assign keyword labels to them. (In previous versions of Elements it was called the *Photo Browser,* so you may hear that term, too.)

The Organizer has lots of really cool features you'll learn about throughout this book when they're relevant to the task at hand. The next chapter shows you how to use the Organizer to import and organize your photos, and Appendix A covers all the Organizer's different menu options. What's more, if you sign up for a Photoshop.com account (page 20), then you can access and organize your photos from any computer, not just at home.

FREQUENTLY ASKED QUESTION

Say Goodbye to the Welcome Screen

How do I get rid of the Welcome screen?

If you get to feeling welcomed enough, you probably want to turn off the Welcome screen so you don't have to click through it every time you start the program. In Elements 8, you can't: Every time you start Elements, you see the Welcome screen. There's a button in the upper-right corner of the Welcome screen that gives you some control over how it behaves, but only to say whether it should launch *along with* the Editor or Organizer (your choice), or simply let you choose which one to launch (its standard behavior). There's no option for "Don't show this screen again". If this is unwelcome news, don't fret: There's a workaround.

To directly launch the Editor or the Organizer, you just need to create a desktop shortcut. Go to *C:\Program Files\Adobe\Photoshop Elements 8.0,* and then find the actual application file (the one ending in *.exe*) for the Editor or the Organizer. Right-click it, and then choose Create Shortcut. Windows adds a direct shortcut to the component of your choice, right on the desktop. In the future, double-click the shortcut to launch your preferred part of Elements. (You can make shortcuts for both the Editor and the Organizer if you like.)

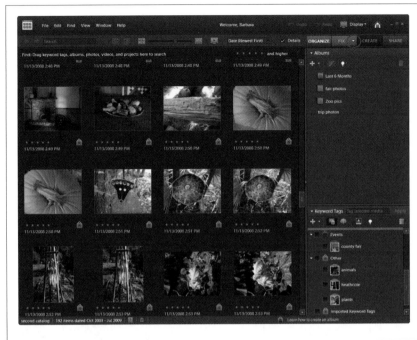

Figure 1-2:
The Media Browser is your main Organizer workspace. Click the Create tab and you can choose to start all kinds of new projects with your photos, or click the Share tab for ways to let other people view your images. Click the arrow at the right of the Fix tab (circled) for a menu that gives you a choice of going to Quick Fix, Guided Edit, or Full Edit. The Fix tab gives you access to some quick fixes right in the Organizer, too. The Organizer also gives you another way to look at your photos, Date view, which is explained in Chapter 2.

Photo Downloader

Elements has yet another component, which you may have seen already if you've plugged a camera into your computer after installing Elements: the Photo Downloader (Figure 1-3), which helps get photos straight into the Organizer directly from your camera's memory card.

If you've used older versions of Elements, then you'll be pleased to know that the Downloader is more polite than it used to be. In early versions of Elements, the Downloader ran constantly as a separate program (whether Elements was running or not), racing to be first on the scene whenever it detected any newly connected device that might have photos on it, and popping up its own window before the standard Windows dialog box could appear. For a few people, this was mighty convenient. But for the majority of folks (who didn't want to use the Downloader *every* time they plugged some photo-bearing device into their computers), it was a big nuisance. If you have an iPod, for instance, then you know how aggravating this was.

Now the Downloader appears as only one of your options in the regular Windows dialog box that you see when you connect a device. If you want to use the Downloader, then just choose it from the list. No more interfering with your iPod, and no extra dialog box to close every time you don't want to use the Downloader. It's a major improvement.

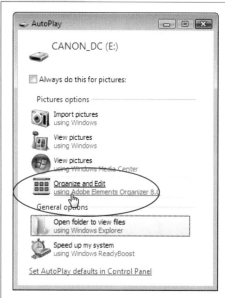

Figure 1-3:
Adobe's Photo Downloader is yet another program you get when you install Elements. Its job is to pull photos from your camera (or other storage device) into the Organizer. To use the Downloader, just click "Organize and Edit using Adobe Elements Organizer 8.0" (circled) in Windows Vista's AutoPlay dialog box. (If you use Windows XP, you'll see a dialog box with similar options.) After the Downloader does its thing, you end up in the Organizer.

UP TO SPEED

Where the Heck Did Elements Go?

If you've installed Elements but can't seem to figure out how to launch it, no problem. Windows automatically creates a shortcut to Elements on your desktop once you install the program. (If you need help installing Elements, turn to Appendix C.) You can also go to the Start menu, and then click the Adobe Photoshop Elements 8.0 icon. If you don't see Elements in the Start menu, then click the arrow next to All Programs, and you should find it in the pop-up menu.

You can read more about the Downloader in Chapter 2. If you plan to use the Organizer to catalog photos and assign keywords to them, then reading the section on the Downloader can help you avoid hair-pulling moments.

Photoshop.com

Adobe also gives you easy access to its *Photoshop.com* service as part of Elements. A basic account is free, and it's nicely integrated into Elements, making it very easy to use. With a Photoshop.com account, you can:

- **Create your own website.** You can make beautiful online albums that display your photos in elaborate slideshows—all accessible via your own Photoshop.com URL (web address). Great for dazzling friends and family. They can even download your photos or order prints, if you choose to let them (see page 519).

- **Automatically back up and sync your photos.** Frequent worriers and travelers, prepare to be amazed. You can set Elements to sync your PC-based photos to storage space on Photoshop.com, providing you with a backup, just in case. What's more, you can upload photos to your albums from *other* computers, and they automatically appear in the Organizer the next time you start Elements. See page 75 for more about how to use this nifty feature.

- **Access your photos from other computers.** When you're not at home, pop over to your Photoshop.com account to see and even organize your photos. That way, when you visit friends, you don't need to lug your computer along—just log into your account from their computers.

- **Download lots of extra goodies.** The Content panel (page 474) displays thumbnails for additional backgrounds, frames, graphics, and so on, that you can download right from Photoshop.com.

- **Get lots of great free advice.** Call up the Photoshop Inspiration Browser (page 34), and you can choose from a whole range of helpful tutorials for all sorts of Elements tasks and projects.

The bad news is that these Photoshop.com features are available only in the United States—for now. Adobe says it plans to expand this offering worldwide. As of this writing, folks outside the United States can get some of the same features, like the ability to create online albums and galleries, at Adobe's Photoshop Showcase site *http://photoshopshowcase.com*. (See page 607 for more about the regional differences.)

To sign up for a free account:

1. **Tell Adobe you want an account.**

   Just click the Create New Adobe ID button on the Welcome screen (page 15) or at the top of either the Organizer or the Editor's main window. This also registers Elements. If you've already got an Adobe ID (if you registered a previous version of Elements, for example), just sign in instead.

2. **In the window that opens, fill in your information to create your Adobe ID.**

   You need to fill in the usual address, phone, email, and so on, and pick what you'd like as your unique Adobe web address. (Hint: something like *http://johnspictures.photoshop.com* is probably already taken, so you may need to try a few alternatives. When you click Create Account, you get a message if the web address you chose is already in use.) Turn on the checkbox that says you agree to Adobe's terms and conditions. Finally, for security purposes, you need to enter the text you see in a box on the sign-up screen.

3. **Create your account.**

   Click the Create Account button. Adobe tells you if it finds any errors in what you submitted and gives you a chance to go back and fix them.

4. **Confirm your account.**

You'll get an email from Adobe that contains a link. Just click the link to confirm that you want to create an account, and you're all set. (You need to click the link within 24 hours of creating your account, or you may have to start the whole process again.)

Once you have an account, you can get to it by clicking Sign In at the top of the Editor or Organizer. After you sign in, you see "Welcome <your name>" instead of "Sign In", and you can click that to go to your account settings. (You can also look at the bottom of the Welcome screen to see how much free space you have left, as shown in Figure 1-4.)

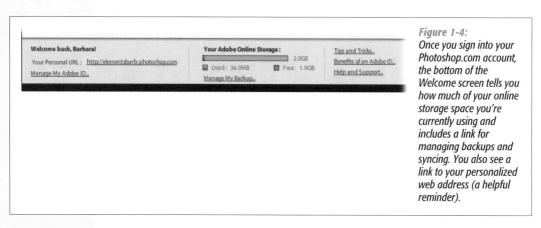

Figure 1-4:
Once you sign into your Photoshop.com account, the bottom of the Welcome screen tells you how much of your online storage space you're currently using and includes a link for managing backups and syncing. You also see a link to your personalized web address (a helpful reminder).

A free Photoshop.com account is a pretty nice deal. It even includes 2 GB of space on Adobe's servers for backing up and storing your photos. You can also upgrade to a paid account (called Plus), which gives you more of everything: more template designs for Online Albums, more downloads from the Content panel, more tutorials, and more storage space: 20–100 GB (depending on what level membership you choose). However, the Plus account costs $49.99 for 20 GB, and more as your storage amount increases, so you might want to try the free account first to see whether you'll really use it enough to justify the expense. Because this service has been available since Elements 7, you can also investigate Adobe's Photoshop.com support forum (*http://forums.adobe.com/community/photoshopdotcom*), as well as the independent forum sites (page 555) to see what people think about it.

NOTE   If you haven't bought Elements yet, Adobe tends to promote the combination of Elements and a Plus account on their website. You have to hunt around a bit to find where to purchase Elements with just the free account, so look carefully before you buy if you don't want to start off with the paid version.

Once you sign into your account, Elements logs you in automatically every time you launch the program. If you don't want that to happen, just click your name at the top of the Elements window (in either the Organizer or Editor), and then, in the window that opens, choose Sign Out.

Editing Your Photos

The Editor is the other main component of Elements (Figure 1-5). This is the fun part of the program, where you get to edit, adjust, transform, and generally glamorize your photos, and where you can create original artwork from scratch with the drawing tools and shapes.

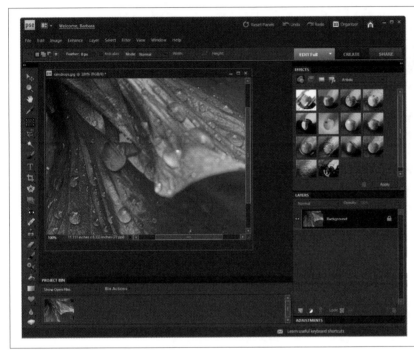

Figure 1-5:
The main Elements editing window, which Adobe calls Full Edit. In some previous versions of Elements it was known as the Standard Editor, something to keep in mind in case you ever try any tutorials written for Elements 3 or 4.

You can operate the Editor in any of three different modes:

- **Full Edit.** The Full Edit window gives you access to Elements' most sophisticated tools. You have far more ways to work on your photo in Full Edit than in Quick Fix, and if you're fussy, it's where you'll do most of your retouching work. Most of the Quick Fix commands are also available via menus in the Full Edit window.

- **Quick Fix.** For many beginners, Quick Fix (Figure 1-6) ends up being their main workspace. It's where Adobe has gathered together the basic tools you need to improve most photos. It's also one of the two places in Elements where you can choose to have a before-and-after view while you work. (Guided Edit, described below, is the other.) Chapter 4 gives you all the details on using Quick Fix.

- **Guided Edit.** This window can be a big help if you're a newcomer to Elements. It provides step-by-step walkthroughs for popular projects such as cropping your photos and removing blemishes from them. Like Quick Fix, Guided Edit offers a before-and-after view of your photo as you work on it (see page 32) and also offers some advanced features, like the Actions Player (page 421).

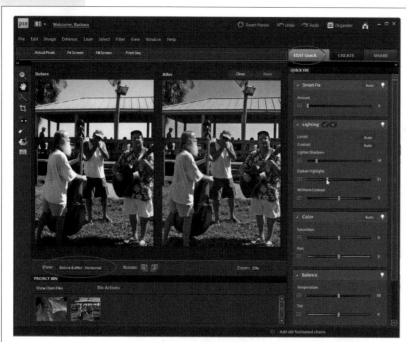

Figure 1-6:
The Quick Fix window. Use the drop-down menus in the tab at the top of the screen (circled, right) to navigate from Full Edit to the Quick Fix window (and to Guided Edit, if you like) and back again. To compare your fixes with the original photo, fire up Before & After view, which you get by clicking the View menu (circled, left).

The rest of this chapter covers some of the Editor's basic concepts and key tools.

NOTE   If you leave a photo open in the Editor, then when you switch back to the Organizer, you see a red band with a padlock across the photo's Organizer thumbnail as a reminder. To get rid of the lock and free up your image for Organizer projects, go back to the Editor and close the photo there.

Panels, Bins, and Tabs

When you first open the Editor, you may be dismayed at how cluttered it looks. There's stuff everywhere, and maybe not a lot of room left for the photos you're editing, especially if you have a small screen. Don't fret: One of Elements 8's best features is the way you can customize the Editor's workspace. There's practically no limit to how you can rearrange the Editor. You can leave everything the way it is if you like a cozy area with everything at hand. Or if you want a Zen-like empty workspace with nothing visible but your photo, you can move, hide, and turn off almost everything. Figure 1-7 shows two different views of the same workspace.

What's more, in Elements 8 you can hide *everything* in your workspace except for your images and the menu bar: no tools, panels, or Options bar. This is handy when you want a good, undistracted look at what you've just done to your photo. To do that, just press the Tab key; to bring everything back into view, press Tab again.

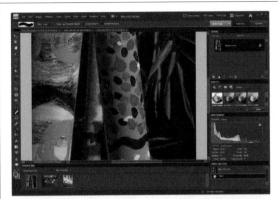

Figure 1-7:
Two different ways of working with the same images, panels, and tools. You can use any arrangement that suits you.

Top: The panels in the basic Elements arrangement, with the images in the new tabbed view (page 29).

Bottom: This image shows how you can customize your panels. Here the Project bin has been moved into the Panel bin, and the whole thing is collapsed to icons (they're to the right of the image being worked on). Click an icon and that panel pops out so you can work with it. The images here are in floating windows.

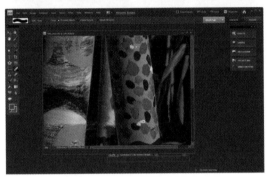

NOTE You may notice that Elements' menu bar at the very top of the program's window changes a little depending on the size of your monitor and whether you've got the Elements window maximized to fill your screen. You'll either see a single row above the Options bar (page 30) with the PSE logo at the left and the Arrange menu (page 99) and the Photoshop.com login area at the middle of the screen (as in Figure 1-7), or these items may be in a separate row *above* the menus that say File, Edit, Image, and so on (as in Figure 1-5). Both are perfectly normal, and you'll see both arrangements in this book's illustrations.

The Panel bin

When you're in Full Edit, the right side of the Elements window displays the *Panel bin*. Panels let you do things like keep track of what you've done to your photo (Undo History panel) and apply special effects to your images (Effects panel and Content panel). You'll learn about the various panels in detail throughout this book.

NOTE In previous versions of Elements and in older versions of Photoshop, panels were called "palettes." If you run across a tutorial that talks about the "Content palette" for example, that's exactly the same thing as the "Content panel."

You might like the Panel bin, but many people don't. If you don't have a large monitor, you may find it wastes too much desktop acreage, and in Elements, you need all the working room you can get. Fortunately, you don't have to keep your panels in the bin; you can close the bin and just keep your panels floating around on your desktop, or you can minimize them.

You can't close the bin completely when it has panels in it, but you can minimize it to just a narrow strip of icons by clicking the bin's very top bar, the one with the double arrows on it. To expand it again, click the top bar once more. (If you pull all the panels out of the bin so that it's empty, it disappears. To bring it back, click Reset Panels at the top of your screen, which resets all your panels, not just the bin.) You pull a panel out of the bin by dragging the panel's top tab; you've now got yourself a floating panel. Figure 1-8 shows how to make panels even smaller once they're out of the bin by collapsing them in one of two ways. You can also combine panels with each other, as shown in Figure 1-9; this works with both panels in the bin and freestanding panels.

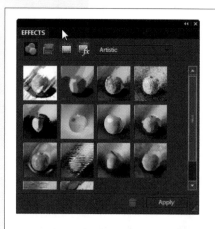

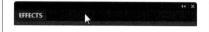

Figure 1-8:
You can free up even more space by collapsing your panels, accordion-style, once they're out of the bin.

Top: A full-sized panel.

Bottom left: A panel collapsed by double-clicking where the cursor is.

Bottom right: The same panel collapsed to an icon by clicking the very top of it (where the cursor is here) once. Click the top bar again to expand it.

When you launch Elements for the first time, the Panel bin contains only two panels: Layers and Effects. To see how many more panels Elements actually gives you, check out the Editor's main Window menu (the one at the top of your screen): Everything listed in the menu's middle section—from Adjustments to Undo History—is a panel you can put in the Panel bin.

When you select a new panel from the Window menu, it appears in the bin if you're using the bin, floating on the desktop if you don't have any panels in the bin, or right where it was when you closed it last time. In addition to combining panels as shown in Figure 1-9, you can also collapse the Panel bin or any group of panels into icons. Then, to use a panel, click its icon and it jumps out to the side of the group, full size. To shrink it back to an icon, click its icon again. To expand or shrink the Panel bin, click the double arrows at the panel's upper right. You can combine panels here by dragging their icons onto each other. Then those panels open as a combined group, like the panels in Figure 1-9. Clicking one of the icons in the group collapses the opened, grouped panel back to icons. (Combined panel icons don't show a dark gray line between them in the group the way separate icons do.) You can also separate combined panels in icon view by dragging the icons away from each other.

Adobe sometimes refers to floating panels as "tabs" in Elements' menus. To close a floating tab, click the Close button (the X) at its upper right, or below the X click the barely visible square (it's made up of four horizontal lines), and choose Close from the menu that appears. If you want to put a panel back in the bin, drag it over the bin and let go when you see a blue line, or drag onto the tab of a panel that's already in the bin to create a combined panel within the bin.

> **NOTE** If you lose panels or you move stuff around so much that you can't remember where you put things, you can always go home again by clicking the Reset Panels button at the top of your screen, which puts *all* your panels back in their original spots.

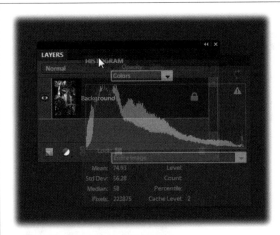

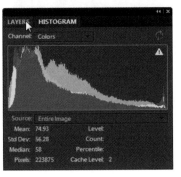

Figure 1-9:
You can combine two or more panels once you've dragged them out of the bin.

Top: The Histogram panel is being pulled into, and combined with, the Layers panel. To combine panels, drag one of them (by clicking on the panel's name tab) and drop it onto the other panel.

Bottom: To switch from one panel to another after they're grouped, just click the tab of the one you want to use. To remove a panel from a group, simply drag it out of the group. If you want to return everything to how it looked when you first launched Elements, click Reset Panels (not visible here) at the top of your screen.

The Project bin

In the Editor, the long narrow photo tray at the bottom of your screen is called the *Project bin*. It shows you what photos you have open, as explained in Figure 1-10, but it does a lot more than that. At the bin's upper left are two pull-down menus:

- **Show Open Files.** This menu lets you determine what the Project bin displays: the photos currently open in the Editor, selected photos from the Organizer, or any of the albums (page 62) you've made. If you send a bunch of photos over from the Organizer at once, you may think something went awry because no photo appears on your desktop or in the Project bin. If you switch this menu over to "Show Files from Elements Organizer", then you see the photos waiting for you in the bin.

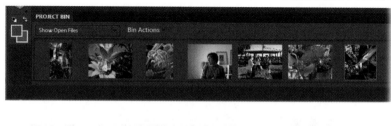
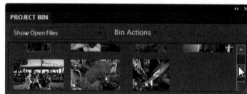

Figure 1-10:
The Project bin runs across the bottom of the Editor's screen. It holds a thumbnail of every photo you have open, as well as photos you sent over from the Organizer that are waiting to be opened. Here you see the bin three ways: as it normally appears (top), as a floating panel (bottom left), and collapsed to an icon (bottom right). You can also click the Close button (the X) at the bin's upper right, or right-click its tab and choose Close to hide it completely. To bring it back, go to Window → Project bin.

- **Bin Actions.** This is where the Project bin gets really useful. You can choose to use the photos in the bin in a project (via the Create tab), share them by any of the means listed under the Task panel's Share tab, print them, or make an album right there in the bin without ever going to the Organizer.

    TIP   If you don't use the Organizer, then the Project bin is a particularly great feature, because it lets you create groups of photos you can call up all together. Just put them in an album (page 62), and then, from the bin's Show Open Files menu, select the album's name to see that group again.

You can drag your photos' thumbnails in the bin to rearrange them if you want to use the images in a project.

The Project bin is useful, but if you have a small monitor, you may prefer to have the space it takes up for your editing work. In Elements 8, the Project bin behaves just like any of the other panels: you can rip it loose from the bottom of the screen and combine it with the other panels. You can even collapse it to an icon, like the other panels, or drag it into the Panel bin. (If you combine it with your other panels, the combined panel may be a little wider than it would be without the Project bin, although you can still collapse the combined group to icons.) If you've used the past couple of versions of Elements, you know this is a *great* improvement over the old, fixed Project bin.

Image windows

In Elements 8, you can choose how you want to see the images you're working on. Older versions of Elements have used floating windows, where each image appears in a separate window that you can drag around. Elements 8 starts you out with floating windows, but you can also put your images into a new, tabbed view, which is something like the tabs in a web browser, or the tabs you'd find on paper file folders. The advantage of tabbed view is that you have plenty of workspace around the image, which is handy when you're working near the edges of an image, or using a tool that requires you to be able to get outside the image's boundaries. All the things you can do with image windows are explained on page 97.

Incidentally, Clicking Reset Panels doesn't do anything to your image windows or tabs; it just resets your panels.

> NOTE   Because your view may vary, most of the illustrations in this book show only the image itself and the tool in use, without a window frame or tab boundary around it.

Elements' Tools

Elements gives you an amazing array of tools to use when working on your photos. You get almost two dozen primary tools to help select, paint on, and otherwise manipulate images, and many of the tools have as many as six subtools hiding beneath them (see Figure 1-11). Bob Vila's workshop probably isn't any better stocked than Elements' virtual toolbox.

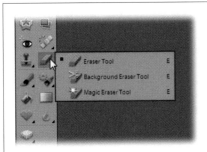

Figure 1-11:
Like any good toolbox, Elements' Tools panel has lots of hidden drawers tucked away in it. Many Elements tools are actually groups of tools, which are represented by tiny black triangles on the lower-right side of the tool's icon (you can see several of these triangles here). Right-clicking or holding the mouse button down when you click the icon brings out the hidden subtools. The little black square next to the regular Eraser tool means it's the active tool right now.

NOTE   To explore every cranny of Elements, you need to open a photo (in the Editor, choose File → Open). Lots of the menus are grayed out if you don't have a file open.

The long, skinny strip on the left side of the Full Edit window (shown back in Figure 1-5—page 23) is the Tools panel. It stays perfectly organized so you can always find what you want without ever having to lift a finger to tidy it up. If you forget what a particular tool does, just hover your cursor over the tool's icon, and a label (called a *tooltip*) appears telling you the tool's name. To activate a tool, click its icon. Any tool that you select comes with its own collection of options, as shown in Figure 1-12.

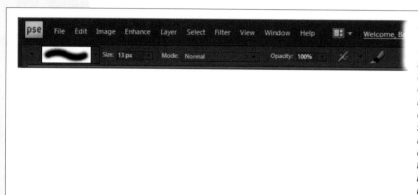

Figure 1-12:
When a tool is active, the Options bar changes to show settings specific to that tool. Elements' tools are highly customizable, letting you do things like adjust a brush's size and shape. Here you see the Brush tool's options. (The caterpillar-like thingy at the left is a sample of the brushstroke you'd get using the tool's current settings.)

As the box below explains, you can have either a single- or double-columned Tools panel.

Other windows in Elements, like Quick Fix and the Raw Converter (see page 248), also have toolboxes, but none is as complete as the one in Full Edit.

Doubling Up

If you have a single-column Tools panel and you'd prefer a double-columned version or vice versa (maybe you don't want your tools spread out so much, for example, or maybe the bottom of the Tools panel extends off the bottom of your screen), just click the double arrows at the top of the panel. If you had a single-row panel when you clicked, it changes to a nice, compact double-column panel with extra-large color squares (page 231). If you had two columns when you clicked, it becomes one long, svelte column.

Be careful, though—In Elements 8, you can close the Tools panel just like any other panel by clicking the Close button (the X) at the panel's upper-right corner. (To bring it back, go to Window → Tools.) You can also move the Tools panel like any other panel, but you can't combine it with other panels or collapse it. If you want to hide it temporarily, press the Tab key and it disappears along with your other panels; press Tab again to bring it back.

NOTE   If you've used Elements 5 or earlier, you'll notice an important difference in getting to subtools in Elements 8: You can't switch from one tool in a subgroup to another by using the Options bar anymore. Now you can choose a tool from a group only by using the tool's pop-out menu in the Tools panel, or by pressing its shortcut key repeatedly to cycle through the tool's subgroup. Stop tapping the key when you see the icon for the tool you want.

Don't worry about learning the names of every tool right now, but if you want to see them all, they're all on display in Figure 1-13. It's easier to remember what a tool is once you've used it. And don't be overwhelmed by all of Elements' tools. You probably have a bunch of Allen wrenches in your garage that you only use every year or so. Likewise, you'll find that you tend to use certain Elements tools more than others.

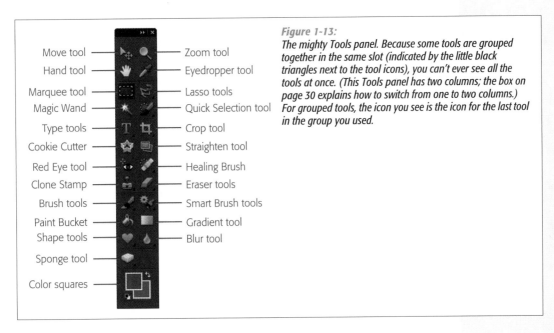

Move tool — Zoom tool
Hand tool — Eyedropper tool
Marquee tool — Lasso tools
Magic Wand — Quick Selection tool
Type tools — Crop tool
Cookie Cutter — Straighten tool
Red Eye tool — Healing Brush
Clone Stamp — Eraser tools
Brush tools — Smart Brush tools
Paint Bucket — Gradient tool
Shape tools — Blur tool
Sponge tool
Color squares

Figure 1-13:
The mighty Tools panel. Because some tools are grouped together in the same slot (indicated by the little black triangles next to the tool icons), you can't ever see all the tools at once. (This Tools panel has two columns; the box on page 30 explains how to switch from one to two columns.) For grouped tools, the icon you see is the icon for the last tool in the group you used.

TIP   You can save a *ton* of time by activating tools with their keyboard shortcuts, since you don't have to interrupt what you're doing to trek over to the Tools panel. To see a tool's shortcut key, hover your cursor over its icon. A label pops up indicating the shortcut key (it's the letter to the right of the tool's name). To activate the tool, just press the appropriate key. If the tool you want is part of a group, all the tools in that group have the same keyboard shortcut, so just keep pressing that key to cycle through the group until you get to the tool you want.

FREQUENTLY ASKED QUESTION

The Always-On Toolbox

Do I always need to have a tool selected?

Yes. When looking at the Tools panel, you'll probably notice that one tool icon is highlighted, indicating that the tool is active. You can deactivate it by clicking a different tool. But what happens when you don't want *any* tool to be active? How do you fix things so that you don't have a tool selected?

You don't. In the Editor, one tool always has to be selected, so you probably want to get in the habit of choosing a tool that won't do any damage to your image if you click it accidentally. For instance, the Pencil tool, which leaves a spot or line where you click, probably isn't a good choice. The Marquee selection tool (page 139), the Zoom tool (page 100), and the Hand tool (page 102) are all safe bets. When you open the Editor, Elements activates the tool you were using the last time you closed the program.

Getting Help

Wherever Adobe found a stray corner in Elements, they stuck some help into it. You can't move anywhere in this program without being offered some kind of guidance. Here are a few of the ways you can summon assistance if you need it:

- **Help menu.** Choose Help → Photoshop Elements Help, or press F1. Elements launches your web browser, which displays Elements' Help files, where you can search or browse a topic list and glossary. The Help menu also contains links to online video tutorials and Adobe's support forum for Elements.

- **Tooltips.** When you see a tooltip (page 31) pop up under your cursor as you move around Elements, if the tooltip's text is blue, that means it's linked to the appropriate section in Elements; Help. You can click blue-text tooltips for more information about whatever your cursor is hovering over.

- **Dialog box links.** Most dialog boxes have a few words of bright blue text somewhere in them. That text is actually a link to Elements Help. If you get confused about what Remove Color Cast does, for instance, then, in the Remove Color Cast dialog box, click the blue "color cast" text for a reminder.

Guided Edit

If you're a beginner, Guided Edit, shown in Figure 1-14, can be a big help. It walks you through a variety of popular editing tasks, like cropping, sharpening, correcting colors, and removing blemishes. It also includes some features that are useful even if you're an old Elements hand, like the Actions Player (page 421) and the new Exposure Merge (page 267).

Guided edit is really easy to use:

1. **Go to Guided Edit.**

   In the Editor, click the Edit tab → EDIT Guided.

2. **Open a photo.**

   Press Ctrl+O, and then, from the window that appears, choose your photo. If you already have a photo open, it appears in the Guided Edit window automatically. If you have several photos in the Project bin, then you can switch images by double-clicking the thumbnail of the one you want to work on.

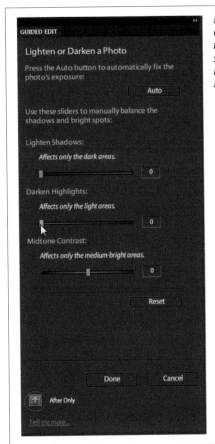

Figure 1-14:
Guided Edit gives you step-by-step help with basic photo editing. Just use the tools that appear in this panel once you choose an activity. After you've selected a task, you can change the view to Before & After. Keep clicking the little blue button (circled) at the bottom of the window to toggle views between After Only, Before & After–Horizontal, and Before & After–Vertical.

3. **Choose what you want to do.**

   Your options are grouped into major categories like Basic Photo Edits and Color Correction, with a variety of specific projects under each heading. Just click the task you want in the list on the right side of the window. The panel displays the relevant buttons and/or sliders for the task you selected.

4. **Make your adjustments.**

   Just move the sliders and click the buttons till you like what you see. If you want to start over, click Reset. If you change your mind about the whole project, click Cancel.

If several steps are involved, then Elements shows you just the buttons and slider you need to use for the current step, and then switches to a new set of choices for the next step as you go along.

If you need to adjust your view of your photo while you work on it, Guided Edit has a little toolbox with the Hand (page 102) and Zoom (page 100) tools to help you out.

5. **Click Done to finish.**

If there are more steps, then you may see another set of instructions. If you see the main list of topics again, you're all through. Don't forget to save your changes (page 67). To close your photo, press Ctrl+W, or leave it open and switch to another tab to share it or use it in a project.

> **NOTE**   Guided Edit shows you quick and easy ways to change your image, but you don't always get the best possible results. It's a great tool for starting out; just remember that what you see here isn't necessarily the best you can possibly make your images look. Once you're more comfortable in Elements, Quick Fix (Chapter 4) is a good next step.

The Inspiration Browser

You've probably noticed the little text alerts that zip in and out at the bottom of both the Editor and the Organizer windows, as shown in Figure 1-15. If you click one, then you get a pop-up window that suggests a tutorial explaining how to do whatever the text alert mentioned. Click the arrow where it says "Learn how", and up pops the Adobe Elements Inspiration Browser, a mini-program that lets you watch tutorials. You need a Photoshop.com account (available only for U.S. residents; see page 20) to use the Browser. (If you call up the Browser and you change your mind about using it, or if you don't have an account, press the Esc key to close it.) It's well worth checking out, because the Browser is a direct connection to a slew of tutorials for things you might want to do with Photoshop Elements or Premiere Elements (Adobe's movie-editing program).

The first time you start the Inspiration Browser, you see a license agreement for yet *another* program: Adobe AIR, which lets other programs show you content stored online; no need to get out a web browser and navigate to a website. (Adobe AIR got installed automatically along with Elements.)

This process may seem like a lot of work, but it's well worth the effort, since you can find tutorials on everything from beginner topics like creating albums to advanced subjects like working with Displacement Maps (a sophisticated technique used for things like making your photo look like it's painted on a brick wall, or making a page of text look like a crumpled newspaper). The tutorials are all in either PDF or video format. You'll see tutorials from well-known Elements gurus here, but *anyone* can submit a tutorial for the Inspiration Browser. So if you figure

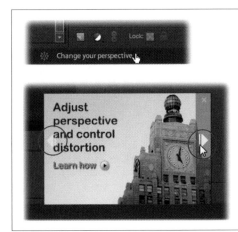

Figure 1-15:
Top: Click these little text banners for more information about the topic.

Bottom: In these pop-up windows you can either click "Learn how" to go directly to that particular tutorial, or click the faintly ghosted left and right arrows (circled; they get brighter when you mouse over them) in the pop-up window to read about other available tutorials. You can also get to the Inspiration Browser by going to Help → Photoshop Inspiration Browser. (Not all the pop-ups have these navigation arrows. Some have a single arrow that only takes you to the linked tutorial without letting you browse for others.)

out how to do a project you think might be useful to others, you can create a tutorial and send it in for approval by clicking the "Submit a Tutorial" button and entering the requested information in the window that appears. (You need to create your tutorial as either a PDF or, for a video, in the Flash FLV format.)

You can search for tutorials using the box on the Browser's left, or click All Tutorials and then filter them by category or product (so you don't have to see Premiere Elements topics if you have only Photoshop Elements, for example). You can also click on one of the column headings to see the available tutorials arranged by Title, Author, Difficulty, Date Posted, Category, Type (video or PDF), or the average star rating people have given it. Use the buttons at the window's upper right to change the view from a list to thumbnails (info about each tutorial appears below its thumbnail).

The Inspiration Browser is a wonderful resource and may well give you most of the help you need with Elements beyond this book.

> **TIP**   If the author of a tutorial has a website, then the tutorial's page has a link to it. Exploring these links can help you find lots of useful Elements-related resources, as well as useful add-on tools that extend Elements' capabilities (see Chapter 19).

Escape Routes

Elements has a couple of really wonderful features to help you avoid making permanent mistakes: the Undo command and the Undo History panel. After you've gotten used to them, you'll probably wish it were possible to use these tools in all aspects of your life, not just Elements.

Undo

No matter where you are in Elements, you can almost always change your mind about what you just did. Press Ctrl+Z, and the last change you made goes away. Pressing Ctrl+Z works even if you've just saved your photo, but only while it's still open—if you close the file, your changes are permanent. Keep pressing Ctrl+Z and you keep undoing your work, step by step.

If you want to *redo* what you just undid, press Ctrl+Y. These keyboard shortcuts are great for toggling changes on and off while you decide whether you really want to keep them. The Undo/Redo keystroke combinations work in the Organizer and the Editor.

> **TIP** You have a bit of control over the key combination you use for Undo/Redo, if you don't like Ctrl+Z/Ctrl+Y. Go to Edit → Preferences → General, where Elements gives you two other choices, both of which involve pressing the Z key in combination with the Control, Alt, and Shift keys.

Undo History panel

In the Full Edit window, you get even more control over the actions you can undo, thanks to the Undo History panel (Figure 1-16), which you open by choosing Window → Undo History.

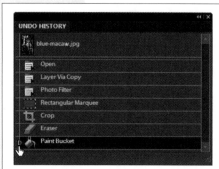

Figure 1-16:
For a little time travel, just slide the pointer (on the left, just above the cursor here) up and watch your changes disappear. You can go back only sequentially. Here, for instance, you can't go back to the Crop tool without first undoing what you did with the Paint Bucket and the Eraser. Slide the pointer down to redo your work. You can also hop to a given spot in the list by clicking the place where you want to go instead of using the slider.

This panel holds a list of the changes you've made since you opened your image. Just push the slider up and watch your changes disappear one by one as you go. Like the Undo command, Undo History even works if you've saved your file: As long as you haven't *closed* the file, the panel tracks every action you take. You can also slide the other way to redo changes that you've undone.

Be careful, though: You can back up only as many steps as Elements is set to remember. The program is initially set up to record 50 steps, but you can change that number by going to Edit → Preferences → Performance → History & Cache and adjusting the History States setting. You can set it as high as 1,000, but remembering even 100 steps may slow your system to a crawl if you don't have a superpowered processor, plenty of memory, and loads of disk space. If Elements runs slowly on your machine, then reducing the number of history states it remembers (try 20) may speed things up a bit.

The one rule of Elements

As you're beginning to see, Elements lets you work in lots of different ways. What's more, most people who use Elements approach projects in different ways. What works for your neighbor with her pictures may be quite different from how you'd work on the very same shots.

But you'll hear one suggestion from almost every Elements veteran, and it's an important one: *Never, ever work on your original. Always, always, always make a copy of your image and work on that instead.*

The good news is that if you store your photos in the Organizer, you don't need to worry about accidentally trashing your original. If you save your files as *version sets* (page 68), Elements automatically creates a copy when you edit a photo that's cataloged in the Organizer, so that you can always revert to your original.

If you're determined not to use the Organizer or version sets, then follow these steps to make a copy of your image in the Editor:

1. **Go to File → Duplicate.**

   The Duplicate Image dialog box appears.

2. **Name the duplicate and then click OK in the dialog box.**

   Elements opens the new, duplicate image in the main image window.

3. **Find the original image and click its Close button (the X).**

   If you have floating windows, the Close button is the standard Windows Close button you'd see at the upper right of any window. If you have tabs, the close X is on the right side of the image's tab. Now the original is safely tucked out of harm's way.

4. **Save the duplicate by pressing Ctrl+S.**

   Choose Photoshop (.psd) as the file format when you save it. (You may want to choose another format after you've read Chapter 3 and understand more about your different format options.)

Now you don't have to worry about making a mistake or changing your mind, because you can always start over.

> **NOTE** Elements doesn't have an autosave feature, so you should get into the habit of saving frequently as you work. Page 67 has more about saving.

Getting Started in a Hurry

If you're the impatient type and you're starting to squirm because you want to be up and doing something to your photos, here's the quickest way to get started in Elements: Adjust an image's brightness and color balance all in one step.

1. **In the Editor, open a photo.**

   Press Ctrl+O and navigate to the image you want, and then click Open.

2. **Press Alt+Ctrl+M.**

   You've just applied Elements' Auto Smart Fix tool (Figure 1-17).

Voilà! You should see quite a difference in your photo, unless the exposure, lighting, and contrast were almost perfect before. The Auto Smart Fix tool is one of Elements' many easy-to-use features. (Of course, if you don't like what just happened to your photo, no problem—simply press Ctrl+Z to undo it.)

If you're really raring to go, jump ahead to Chapter 4 to learn about using the Quick Fix commands. But it's worth taking the time to read the next two chapters so you understand which file formats to choose and how to make some basic adjustments to your images, like rotating and cropping them.

Don't forget to give Guided Edit a try if you see what you want to do in the list of topics. Guided Edit can be a big help while you're learning your way around.

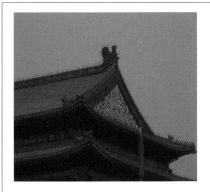
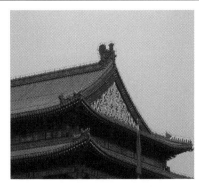

Figure 1-17:
Auto Smart Fix is the easiest, quickest way to improve the quality of your photos.

Top left: The original, unedited picture.

Top right: Auto Smart Fix makes quite a difference, but the colors are still slightly off.

Bottom: By using some of the other tools you'll learn about in this book (like Auto Contrast and Adjust Sharpness), you can make things look even better.

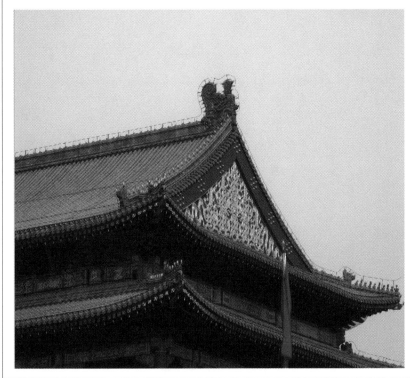

Importing, Managing, and Saving Your Photos

Now that you've had a look around Elements, it's time to start learning how to get photos *into* the program, and how to keep track of where these photos are stored. As a digital photographer, you don't have to deal with shoeboxes stuffed with prints, but you've still got to face the menace of photos piling up on your hard drive. Fortunately, Elements gives you some great tools for organizing your collection and quickly finding individual pictures.

In this chapter, you'll learn how to import photos from cameras, memory card readers, and scanners. You'll also find out how to import individual frames from videos, open files already on your computer, and create a new file from scratch. Then you'll be ready for a quick tour of the Organizer, where you can sort and find pictures once they're in Elements. Finally, you'll learn about photo preservation: saving and backing up your precious files.

Importing from Cameras

Elements gives you lots of different ways to get photos from camera to computer, but the simplest way is using Adobe's Photo Downloader. Even if you don't like the Downloader, read on. Later in this section, you'll learn about other ways to import your photos.

> **NOTE** Take a moment to carefully read the instructions from your camera's manufacturer. If those directions tell you to do something differently than anything you read here, follow the manufacturer's instructions.

The Photo Downloader

When you plug your camera or memory card reader into your Vista computer, you get a standard Windows dialog box (shown on page 20) asking what you want to do. To use the Photo Downloader to get your photos into Elements, just click "Organize and Edit using Adobe Photoshop Elements Organizer 8.0". (If you're using Windows XP, choose Elements Organizer 8.0 from the dialog box that appears.) The Downloader's job is pretty straightforward: to shepherd your photos as they make the trip from your camera to your PC and to make sure Elements knows where your new images are stored. Your job is to help it along by adjusting the following settings (on display in Figure 2-1).:

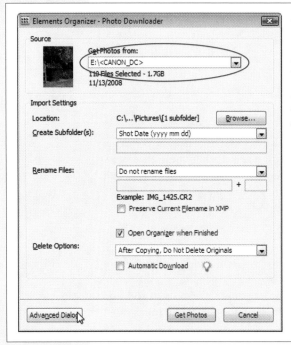

Figure 2-1:
When the Photo Downloader first launches, you see this dialog box, which lets you choose where Elements puts your photos and what it names them (say goodbye to names like IMG_0327.JPG). To start, choose your camera or card reader from the list of devices (circled). If you want to import only specific images, click the Advanced Dialog button so you can choose which photos to grab, and fine-tune other settings.

- **Get Photos From.** As your first step in downloading, choose your camera or card reader from the list of available devices. (You may see a more generic "Camera or Card Reader" choice rather than the name of your camera. If that's all you see, pick that option.) Just below this menu, the Downloader lists how many photos it found, and also how many duplicates (of images already in the Organizer) it plans to skip.

- **Location.** Your photos usually get stored in a folder named for the date you imported them. In Windows Vista, this folder lives in *C:\Users\<your user-name>\Pictures*; in XP, it's *C:\<your user name>\My Documents\My Pictures\Adobe\Digital Camera Photos*. (If you download more than one batch of photos on the same day, you get a second folder with the same name except with "-1" added to it, "-2" for the third one, and so on.) If you want to change where your photos are headed, click the Browse button and choose another location. You can permanently change the standard save location by opening the Organizer and going to Edit → Preferences → "Camera or Card Reader" and changing the Save Files In setting to a new location. From now on, the Downloader always puts your photos in the folder you chose.

- **Create Subfolder(s).** If you want to have more levels of organization, you can put your files into a subfolder *inside* the folder you chose in Location, with a name you pick (instead of the date). Or you can choose to have a subfolder named with a custom name or with today's date (with the date displayed in your choice of several different formats).

TIP When you name the subfolder, you can apply that name as a *tag* (label) to all the photos in the folder with just one click once you're in the Media Browser window. Page 58 has more about tags and how they can help you quickly find photos.

- **Rename Files.** You can choose to give all the files a custom name, if you like. So if you type in *obedience_school_graduation,* then you get photos named obedience_ school_graduation001, obedience_school_graduation002, and so on. Or you can use a combination of a custom name and the date you shot the photo, if you prefer. You can also use just the shot date or today's date, or the name of the subfolder. No matter which naming scheme you choose, Elements adds a three-digit number to the end of each file (as in the obedience-school example) to help you distinguish between them. You can also leave this setting at "Do not rename files", in which case you keep the camera's filenames and numbers.

- **Preserve Current Filename in XMP.** Turn this checkbox on if you want the photos' current filenames to be used as the filename stored in the photo's *metadata* (page 69).

- **Open Organizer when Finished.** If you're going to put your files in the Organizer, leave this checkbox turned on. But you can turn it off if you don't use the Organizer, or if you'd rather wait till later to get organized. (You won't see this option if the Organizer is already running when you import your photos.)

- **Delete Options.** You can have the Downloader delete your files off your camera's memory card when it's done importing them. Figure 2-2 explains more about this option.

- **Automatic Download.** If you like to live dangerously, you can turn on this checkbox, and Elements will download any new photos it detects without showing you the Downloader dialog box. It's almost always best to leave Automatic Download off so that you have some control over what's going on. (This checkbox appears only after you've selected a device in the "Get Photos from" menu.) If you decide to take this risky route, you can tell Elements where to put your photos and whether it should delete the originals by going to Organizer → Edit → Preferences → "Camera or Card Reader".

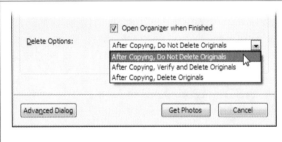

Figure 2-2:
The Photo Downloader offers to delete the files from your camera or memory card reader once it's imported them. This feature seems handy, but you may want to think twice about whether to actually delete the files. The Downloader is pretty reliable, but it's always good to wait until you've reviewed all your photos in Elements before deleting the originals. If you really want the Downloader to delete your files, at least choose "After Copying, Verify and Delete Originals", which forces Elements to check that it's copied your files correctly before vaporizing the originals.

The Downloader is smart enough to recognize any photos that it's already imported, and it doesn't reimport those. If you want to see your duplicates and for some reason download them again, or if you want to pick and choose which photos to import, then click the Advanced Dialog button at the bottom of the Downloader window to bring up the dialog box shown in Figure 2-3.

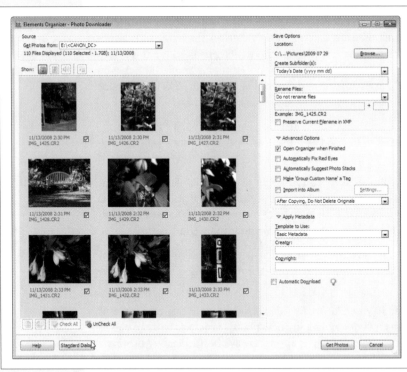

Figure 2-3:
When you want to select which photos to import, summon the Photo Downloader's advanced dialog box.

The advanced Downloader window gives you all the options found in the standard Downloader window, plus a few more. The advanced dialog box is divided into two main parts. On the left side are the thumbnails of your photos. The little checkmarks next to each image indicate which photos will be imported; just turn off the checkboxes for the ones you don't want to bring into the Organizer. (If you've already imported some of the images, the Organizer tells you so and doesn't import them again.) You can also import video and sound files. The four buttons above the preview area let you choose which files you see. From left to right, the buttons are:

- **Show/Hide Images.** If you want to temporarily hide your photos (so you can look at just your video files, for instance), click this button or press Ctrl+M.

- **Video files.** This button is grayed out unless Elements finds any movie or video files on your memory card. If it does, you can hide them by clicking this button. You might do that if, say, you're only interested in importing still photos right now. To see the video files again, click the button again.

- **Audio files.** This button works just like the video button, but it becomes active when Elements finds audio files you may want to import.

- **Show Duplicates.** If Elements has already imported some of the photos on your memory card, but you want to see those files again, click this button and you can reimport them (or just see them for comparison's sake). In the preview area, the thumbnails of the files you've already imported display an icon that looks just like the Show Duplicates button in their upper-right corners to indicate that they're duplicates.

NOTE   Although much of this chapter talks about importing pictures from a camera, most memory card readers work the same way. Use a card reader if you have one, since you'll spare your camera's batteries and subject your camera to less wear and tear.

The right side of the dialog box is where you can adjust the settings for where your pictures are stored on your PC and how their folders are named. Most of these choices are the same ones you get in the Photo Downloader's standard dialog box, but you also get a few extras:

- **Automatically Fix Red Eyes.** If you leave this checkbox turned on, Elements searches through all your newly imported photos looking for people with red eyes (caused by camera flash) and fixes them automatically. It sounds great, but it's not 100 percent reliable and tends to "fix" things like bright white teeth, as well. It's not destructive, because Elements makes a version set (page 68) with your original, so you can ditch the new version if you don't like what Elements did. But the extra time it takes while Elements analyzes all your photos and the time you waste looking for mistakes mean you're better off leaving this option turned off and using another method to fix red eyes later. See page 121 for more about Elements' Red Eye tool. (You may find you also need to turn off Automatically Fix Red Eyes in the Organizer by going to Edit → Preferences → "Camera or Card Reader" to keep this setting from turning itself back on again.)

- **Automatically Suggest Photo Stacks.** The Organizer lets you group related photos together into *stacks* (page 565). Turn this checkbox on to use the auto-stack feature, where Elements automatically finds photos that should be grouped together. This feature works best for photos taken in your camera's burst (rapid advance) mode—in other words, photos of the same subject, taken very close together in time.

- **Make 'Group Custom Name' a Tag.** If you chose a custom name for your images, you can assign the name as a tag here. (Tags are explained on page 58.)

- **Import into Album.** Turn this checkbox on and Elements automatically adds your current download to the album you choose. Click the Settings button to select an existing album or create a new one. This feature is especially useful if you've chosen albums to automatically sync to Photoshop.com (page 75).

- **Apply Metadata.** If you want to write your name or copyright info right into the file's *metadata* (page 69) so that anyone who views your file will know it's yours, you can do that here.

Once you're done adjusting the Downloader's settings, click Get Photos. The Downloader slurps down the photos and launches the Organizer so you can review your pictures.

TIP   You can tell the Organizer to "watch" folders that you often bring graphics—or even sound files or video—into. You can set your Pictures folder as a watched folder, for example, and Elements will find all the new photos that you put there. When you set a watched folder, Elements keeps an eye on it and lets you know when you have new photos there. Elements either imports the new files or tells you they're waiting for you, depending on which option you choose. In the Organizer, go to File → Watch Folders and click the Add button, and then browse to the folder you want Elements to watch. If you find that somehow Elements has started watching a folder and you don't want it to, this is also where you turn it off.

Opening Stored Images

If you've got photos already stored on your computer, you have several options for opening them with Elements. If the file format is set to open in Elements, then double-click the file's icon to launch Elements and open the image. (If you want to change which files open automatically in Elements, see the box on page 48.) You've also got a few ways to open files from within Elements:

- **From the Organizer, for files not yet in the Organizer:** Go to File → "Get Photos and Videos" → "From Files and Folders" or press Ctrl+Shift+G, navigate to your photo, and then select your file and click Get Media. The other options in the Get Photos menu (like fixing red eye and automatically suggesting photo stacks) are covered on page 45. Then follow the steps in the next bullet point for opening your photos in the Editor.

- **From the Organizer, for files already in the Organizer:** You can select an image that's stored in the Organizer and open it directly in the Editor. To do so, in the Organizer, click the file's thumbnail, and then press Ctrl+I; right-click and choose "Edit with Photoshop Elements"; or click the Fix button at the upper right of the screen, and select Full Photo Edit (if you'd rather go to Quick Fix [page 115] or Guided Edit [page 32], then select Quick Photo Edit or Guided Photo Edit instead). You can also Shift-click or Ctrl-click to select multiple photos before using any of these commands, and *all* those photos go to the Editor.

TIP   When your photo gets to the Editor, it should appear in the main editing space. If you don't see anything there, go down to the Project bin, and choose "Show Files from Elements Organizer". (If you send multiple images from the Organizer, they always appear in "Show Files from Elements Organizer", not Show Open Files.)

- **From the Editor, for files anywhere on your computer.** Go to File → Open or press Ctrl+O and select your file. You can also drop a file right onto the Editor's desktop and it'll open.

People who are new to Elements often get confused by the message shown in Figure 2-4. This appears in the Organizer when you leave a photo open in the Editor.

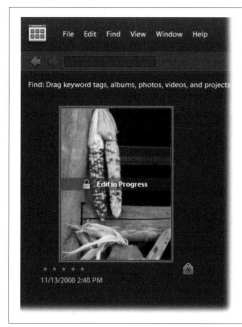

Figure 2-4:
This red "locked" band just means that you left your photo open in the Editor when you came back to the Organizer. To unlock it so that you have access to it in the Organizer, switch back to the Editor and close the photo.

FREQUENTLY ASKED QUESTION

Picking the File Types That Elements Opens

How do I stop Elements from opening all my files?

Many people are dismayed to discover that once they install Elements, it opens every time they double-click any kind of graphics file—whether they want the file to open in Elements or not. Windows makes it pretty easy to change that behavior. First, find a file of the type you want to change. Then:

1. Right-click the closed file's icon.

2. From the pop-up menu, in Vista choose Open With → Choose Default Program. In Windows XP, choose Open With → Choose Program.

3. Select the program you want to use to open the file. Turn on "Always use the selected program to open this kind of file" to set that program for all files of this type.

Working with PDF Files

If you open a PDF file in Elements, you'll see the Import PDF dialog box (Figure 2-5), which gives you lots of options for how Elements treats your file. You can choose to import whole pages or just the images on the pages, import multiple pages (if the PDF is more than one page), and choose the color mode (page 51) and the resolution of the imported files, as well as whether you want Elements to use anti-aliasing (page 151).

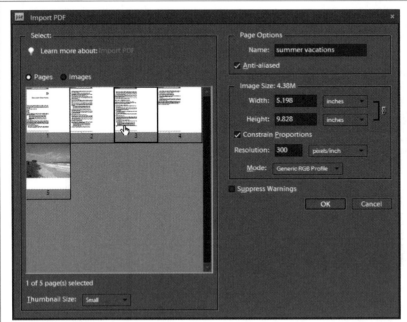

Figure 2-5:
You can open multipage PDF files in Elements. To open just one page of the file, double-click the page's thumbnail and Elements opens it. To open multiple pages of the file, Ctrl-click the pages you want, or Shift-click to select a page range before you double-click to open them. You can catalog PDF files in the Organizer, too.

Scanning Photos

Elements comes bundled with many scanners because it's the perfect software for making scans look their best. You have two main ways of getting scanned images into Elements. Some scanners come with a *driver plug-in,* a little program that lets you scan directly into Elements. Look on your scanner's installation software for info about Elements compatibility, or check the manufacturer's website for a Photoshop plug-in to download. (If you can scan into Photoshop, you should be able to scan into Elements.) You may also be able to scan into Elements if your scanner uses the *TWAIN interface,* an industry standard used by many scanner manufacturers.

To control your scanner from within Elements, you can scan from either the Editor or the Organizer. In the Editor, go to File → Import, and you'll see your scanner's name on the list that appears. In the Organizer, go to File → "Get Photos and Videos" → From Scanner, or press Ctrl+U. You should check out your available options for both locations because they're probably different. For instance, you may find that you have different file formats available to you in the Editor than you do in the Organizer.

If you don't have an Elements plug-in for your scanner and the Adobe TWAIN driver doesn't work for you, you'll need to use the scanning program that came with your scanner. Then, once you've saved your scanned image in a format that Elements understands, like TIFF (.tiff, .tif) or Photoshop (.psd), open the file in Elements like you'd open any other photo.

> **TIP**   If you do a lot of scanning, check out the Divide Scanned Photos command (page 81) for helpful tips on how to quickly scan in lots of photos at the same time. Also, you can save yourself a lot of drudgery in Elements if you make sure that both your scanner glass and the prints you're scanning are as dust-free as possible before you start.

Capturing Video Frames

Elements lets you snag a single frame from a video and use it the way you would any still photo. This feature works only on movies that are already on your computer (rather than one that's streaming to your PC from the Web).

Elements can read many popular video file formats, including .avi, .wmv, and .mpeg. But you do need to have a program on your computer (besides Elements) that's capable of viewing the video file to use this feature of Elements.

> **NOTE**   Elements' video-capture tool isn't really designed for use with long movies. You'll get the best results with clips that aren't more than a minute or two long.

To import a video frame, in the Editor, go to File → Import → Frame From Video, and then in the Frame From Video dialog box:

1. **Find the video that contains the frame you want to copy.**

   Click the Browse button and navigate to the movie you want. After you choose the movie, the first frame appears in the dialog box's preview window.

2. **Navigate to the frame you want.**

   Either click the Play button (the single triangle), or use the slider below the window to move through the movie until you see what you want.

3. **Copy the frame you want by clicking the Grab Frame button.**

   You can capture as many frames as you want. Each frame shows up in the Elements Editor as a separate file.

4. **When you have everything you need, click Done.**

While grabbing video frames is fun, it does have certain limitations. Most important, your video appears at a fairly low resolution, so don't expect to get a great print from a video frame.

Creating a New File

You may want to create a new, blank document when you're using Elements as a drawing program or when you're combining parts of other images together, for example.

To create a new file, go to the Editor, and choose File → New → Blank File or press Ctrl+N to bring up the New dialog box. You have lots of choices to make each time you start a new file, including what to name it. All your other options are covered in the following sections.

> **TIP** You can't create a new, blank file in the Organizer, but Elements gives you a quick shortcut from the Organizer to the Editor so you can open up a new file there. To open a new file, choose File → New → Photoshop Elements Image File, and Elements creates a virgin file for you and automatically hops you and the new blank file over to the Editor. If you want to create a new file based on a photo that's in the Organizer, select the thumbnail, press Ctrl+C to copy the image, and then choose File → New → "Image from Clipboard". Elements switches you to the Editor, where you'll see your copied photo awaiting you, all ready to work on.

Picking a File Size

The next thing you need to decide after you name your new file is how big you want it to be. There are two ways to do this:

- **Start with a Preset.** Preset, the second item in the New dialog box, lets you choose the general kind of document you want to create. If you want to create a file for printing, pick from the menu's second group. The third group contains choices for onscreen viewing. Once you make a selection in this menu, the next menu—Size—changes to show you suitable sizes for your choice. Figure 2-6 shows you how it works.

  > **TIP** If you're into scrapbooking, you'll be pleased to see that Elements offers some standard scrapbook page sizes as presets.

- **Enter the numbers yourself.** Just ignore the Preset and Size menus, and type what you want in the Width and Height boxes. You can choose inches, pixels, centimeters, millimeters, points, picas, or columns as your unit of measurement. Just pick the unit you want in the boxes' drop-down menus and then enter a number.

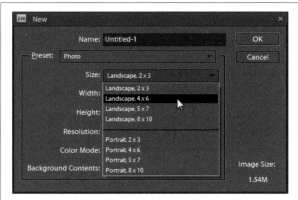

Figure 2-6:
Elements helps you pick an appropriate size when you use the Preset menu. Choose a general category—here, Photo is selected. The Size menu then changes to show you standard sizes for photo paper, each available in either landscape or portrait orientation. What Elements calls the "Default Photoshop Elements Size" is 4"×6" at 300 pixels per inch, which works well if you're just playing around and trying things out.

Choosing a Resolution

If you decide not to use one of the presets, you need to choose a resolution for your file. You'll learn a lot more about resolution in the next chapter (page 103), but a good rule of thumb is to choose 72 pixels per inch (ppi) for files that you'll look at only on a monitor, and 300 ppi for files you plan to print.

Selecting a Color Mode

Elements gives you lots of color choices throughout the program, but *color mode* is probably your most important one because it determines which tools and filters you can use in your document. Your options are:

- **RGB Color.** Choosing this mode (whose name stands for red, green, and blue) means that you're creating a color document, as opposed to a black-and-white one. You'll probably choose RGB Color mode most of the time, even if you don't plan on having color in your image, because RGB gives you access to all of Elements' tools. (Page 231 has more about color in Elements.) You can use RGB Color mode for black-and-white images—many people do, since it gives you the most options for editing your photo.

- **Bitmap.** Every pixel in a bitmap mode image is either black or white. Use Bitmap mode for true black-and-white images—shades of gray need not apply here.

- **Grayscale.** Black-and-white photos are called *grayscale* because they're really made up of many shades of gray. In Elements, you can't do as much editing on a grayscale photo as you can in RGB (for example, you can't use some of Elements' filters on a grayscale image).

NOTE Sometimes you may need to change the color mode of an existing file to use all of Elements' tools and filters. For example, there are quite a few things you can do only if your file is in the RGB color mode. So if you need to use a filter (page 405) on a black-and-white photo and your choice is grayed out, go to Image → Mode and select RGB Color. Changing the color mode won't suddenly colorize your photo; it just changes the way Elements handles the file. (You can always change back to the original color mode when you're done.) If you use Elements' "Convert to Black and White" feature (page 319), you still have an RGB mode photo afterward, not a grayscale mode image.

If you have a 16-bit file (page 263), you need to convert it to 8-bit color, or you won't have access to many of Elements' commands and filters. Make the change by choosing Image → Mode → 8 Bits/Channel. You're most likely to have 16-bit files if you import your images in Raw format (page 248); some scanners also let you create 16-bit files. JPEG files are always 8-bit.

Choosing Background Contents

The last choice you have to make when creating a new file is the file's *background contents*. Picking your file's background contents tells Elements what color to use for the empty areas of the file, like, well, the background. You can be a traditionalist and choose white (almost always a good choice), or choose a particular color or *transparency* (more about transparency in a minute).

To pick a color other than white, use the Background color square, as shown in Figure 2-7.

Figure 2-7:
To choose a new Background color, just click the Background color square (here, that's the red one) to bring up the Color Picker. Then select the color you want. Your new color appears in the square, and the next time you do something that involves using a Background color, that's the shade you get. The color-picking process is explained in much more detail on page 231.

"Transparent" is the most interesting option. To understand transparency and why it's such a wonderful invention, you need to know that *every* digital image is either rectangular or square. A digital image *can't* be any other shape.

But digital images can *appear* to be a different shape—sunflowers, sailboats, or German Shepherds, for example. How? By placing your object on a transparent background so that it looks like it was cut out and only its shape appears, as shown in Figure 2-8. The actual photo is still a rectangle, but if you placed it into another image, you'd see only the shell and not the surrounding area, because the rest of the photo is transparent.

To keep the clear areas transparent when you close your image, you need to save the image in a format that allows transparency. JPEGs, for instance, automatically fill transparent areas with solid white, so they're not a good choice. TIFFs, PDFs, and Photoshop files (.psd), on the other hand, let the transparent areas stay clear. Page 509 has more about which formats allow transparency.

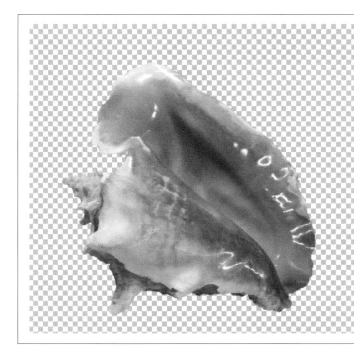

Figure 2-8:
This checkered background is Elements' way of indicating that an area is transparent. (It doesn't mean you've somehow selected a patterned background.) If you place this photo into another image, all you'll see is the seashell, not the checkerboard or the rectangular outline of the photo. If you don't like the size and color of the grid, you can adjust them in Edit → Preferences → Transparency.

Using the Organizer

The Organizer is where you keep track of your photos and start most of the projects that involve sharing photos with others (posting them online, for example). You can see thumbnails of all your photos in the Organizer, assign keywords (called *tags*) to make them easier to find, and search for them in lots of different ways. If you have a Photoshop.com account (page 20), that site also hosts a version of the Organizer that works just the way it does on your desktop.

The *Media Browser* is the Organizer's main window. *Date view* (Display → Date View, or press Ctrl+Alt+D) is a calendar-based system for looking at and searching for photos, as explained in Figure 2-9. But the Media Browser is more versatile: It's your main Organizer workspace, which is what the rest of this section is about.

The Organizer stores the information about your photos in a special database called a *catalog*. You don't have to do anything special—Elements creates your catalog (creatively named *My Catalog*) automatically the first time you import photos. It's possible to have more than one catalog, but most people don't because you can't search more than one catalog at a time. If you really want to have more than one catalog, or if you ever want to start over with a new catalog, in the Organizer go to File → Catalog, and click the New button. Enter a name and then click OK.

Your catalog can include photos stored anywhere on your computer, and even photos that you've moved to external hard drives and CDs or DVDs. There aren't any limits on where you can keep your originals. That's how it's supposed to work,

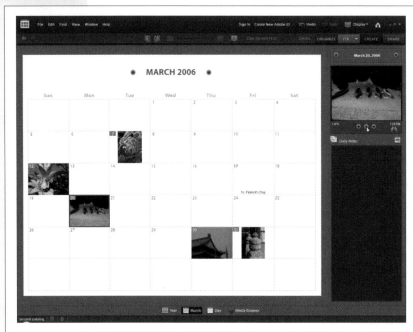

Figure 2-9:
Date view offers you the same menu options as the main Media Browser window, but instead of a contact sheet–like view of your photos, you see your images laid out on a calendar. Click a date (here, March 20 is selected), and in the upper-right corner of the screen, you can view or advance through a slideshow view of that day's pictures, by using the controls where the cursor is in the figure. Date view is fun, and sometimes handy for searching, but it doesn't offer many useful features that aren't also in the Media Browser.

anyway. But in practice, Elements sometimes has a tough time finding files stored on network drives and other externals, so you may run into trouble if you want Elements to find photos you've saved on such devices.

Once your photos appear in the Organizer, if you want to move them, you have to use the Organizer to do that—as opposed to using another method like Windows Explorer—if you want the Organizer to know where you put them. You aren't limited to photos, either—you can store videos and audio files in the Organizer as well.

> **TIP** If you want to edit photos in programs other than Elements, the Organizer lets you do that—just choose Edit → Preferences → Editing → Supplementary Editing Application. So if you want to supplement Elements with a program like Paint Shop Pro, it's easy to do. If you have Photoshop installed on your computer, it automatically appears as an editing option.

The Media Browser

Although the Media Browser (Figure 2-10) may look a little intimidating the first time you see it, it's really logical. By using the Media Browser's different menu options, you can import photos, print them, share them, create projects, edit your photos, or customize your view in various ways. The Media Browser displays thumbnails of all your images in the main part of the window (sometimes called the *image well*).

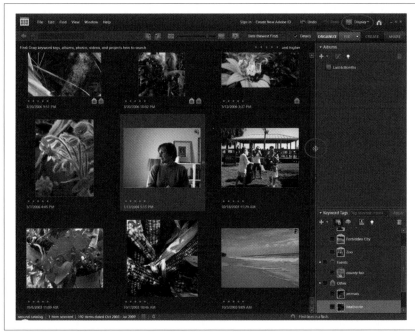

Figure 2-10:
The Media Browser is your main Organizer workspace. Click the divider (circled) to hide or show the Organize bin. (Notice how the cursor morphs into a double-headed arrow when you're in the correct spot for clicking.) If you want to change the way your photos are sorted, click the Display menu in the upper-right corner (also circled).

NOTE   In previous versions of Elements, the Media Browser was called the Photo Browser, in case you run across that term in any tutorials. Adobe changed the name to reflect the fact that now it's also meant for use with their Premiere Elements video-editing program, too. You may see a great many references to Premiere Elements in the Organizer menus. If you don't use Premiere Elements, you can get rid of most of them by going to the Organizer and choosing Edit → Preferences → Editing, and turning off the "Show Premiere Elements Options" checkbox.

On the right side of the Media Browser is the *Task pane,* which you also see in the Editor. It has the same Create and Share tabs as in the Editor, and two tabs unique to the Organizer. The first is the Organize tab, which is home to the *Organize bin,* where you *tag,* or label, your photos with keywords to make finding them easier. (Tagging is probably the first thing you'll want to do to your photos in the Organizer; you'll find directions on how to tag in the next section.) You can also group your photos together into collections, called *albums,* here.

To the right of the Organize tab is the Fix tab, where you can choose to send your photos over to the Editor or to an external editing program to work on them, or apply many basic quick fixes (see page 116).

If you'd like to see both your pictures and the folders on your PC where they're stored, go to Display → Folder Location. A new pane appears on the left side of the Media Browser's window, showing your computer's folder structure. If you click a thumbnail once you're in Folder Location view, the folder pane shows you exactly where the current batch of photos lives on your computer. Click a folder's icon to see its photos displayed in the image well.

Avoiding the Organizer

Nobody's neutral about Adobe's decision to include the Organizer with Elements: People either love the Organizer or they hate it. If you're in the latter group, try to see if you can come to terms with the Organizer, because it does have some useful features. You'll lose a lot if you give up the Organizer, because it's the only place in Elements where you get a visual preview of your images before opening them.

But if you find you just can't abide the Organizer, or if you prefer to use a different program like Lightroom or Vista's Windows Live Photo Gallery to organize your photos—or you just like to be disorganized—then you can sidestep the Organizer. Simply create a desktop shortcut, as described on page 18, so that you always start up in the Editor.

Remember to keep "Include in Organizer" and version sets turned off in the Save dialog box whenever you're saving a picture. Once you turn off the "Include in Organizer" setting, it stays off until you turn it back on, or until you open a photo from the Organizer (after which it turns itself back on). You may find you need to turn it off once every editing session (maybe not, if you're lucky) but you *don't* have to keep turning it off every time you save.

If you want to be extra sure that Elements doesn't interpret any of your photo-related activities as a call for the Organizer, go to Control Panel (if you're using Windows in Classic View) → Administrative Tools → Services and find *Adobe Active File Monitor V8.* (In Vista, you'll also see a dialog box or two asking for permission to continue.) This is a *service,* a small program that always runs in the background when your computer is on, even when Elements is closed. Click Adobe Active File Monitor, and then go to Action → Properties and set the "Startup type" option to Disabled.

There's a downside to disabling this service, though: The File Monitor also keeps track of the databases for the Content and Effects panels, so if you disable it, any new layer styles, effects, and so on, that you add to Elements (see Chapter 19) won't appear in their panels at all. The workaround is to turn Adobe Active File Monitor back on before the next time you start Elements after adding new material. Then you can disable it again till the next time you add something new.

> **NOTE** If you've used early versions of the Organizer and you miss the Timeline, you can still have it. Just go to Window → Timeline or press Ctrl+L to bring back your old friend. For folks new to Elements, the Timeline is explained on page 65.

You can also move your photos directly in this Folder view pane by dragging them between folders. Moving your photos this way is better than moving them by, say, using Windows Explorer, because it lets Elements keep track of where your photos are (Figure 2-11). But Folder view can be rather buggy, so your best bet is to just stop worrying about where your images are and to let the Organizer figure that out for you.

Full Screen view

One of the handiest new features in Elements 8 is the improved Full Screen view. Once you get your photos into the Organizer, you can use Display → "View, Edit, Organize in Full Screen" (keyboard shortcut: F11) or "Compare Photos Side by Side" (keyboard shortcut: F12) to see a larger, slideshow-like view of your photos (either singly or in pairs, depending on the option you select) and select the ones

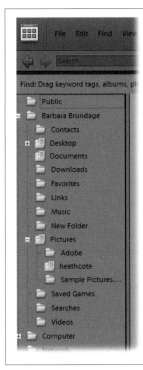

Figure 2-11:
If you want to move photos around on your PC after you've brought them into the Organizer, you can drag them within this pane of the Media Browser, but it's safer to go to File → Move (Folder view has a number of quirks and bugs). If you move photos around when you're not in the Organizer, Elements can't easily find them again. If Elements loses track of a photo, you can use the Reconnect command (File → Reconnect) to help Elements find it again.

you want to print or edit. You can even choose music to accompany them. (If you don't want anything that elaborate, just double-click a thumbnail in the Media Browser to see your photo enlarged to fit the available space. Double-click it again to go back to thumbnail view.)

Elements 8 also lets you apply many quick editing commands right in Full Screen or Side by Side view (see page 116). Just hover your cursor over the Quick Edit panel on the left side of your screen, and it pops out to give you access to all the one-button fixes available from the Editor's Quick Fix mode (page 115). You can also rate your photos here (page 60) by using the stars at the top of the panel. The Quick Organize panel (also on the left side of the screen) lets you apply keyword tags from the new Tag Cloud view (page 59), or put your photos into albums (page 62).

> **TIP** The Quick Edit and Quick Organize panels close back up each time a new image appears onscreen. If you want a panel to stay open, click the tiny pushpin icon on its right edge. To get rid of a panel entirely, click the Close button (the X). To bring it back, use the controls at the bottom of the screen, which are described in detail on page 525.

You can even use Full Screen view as a quick slideshow to show off your latest images—see page 525 to learn how. To get back to the regular Media Browser view, press Esc.

As if all these views aren't enough, Elements gives you yet another way to view your images: arranged on a Yahoo map. When you first import your photos, Elements gives you the option of assigning them to a location on a map of your choice, and you can assign any tag to a spot on a map, too. Page 541 explains more about using Yahoo maps in the Organizer, and also about sharing your maps with your friends.

Creating Categories and Tags

The Organizer has a great system for quickly finding photos, but it works only if you use special keywords, called *tags,* which the Organizer uses to track down your pictures.

A tag can be a word, a date, or even a rating (as explained in the box on page 60). When you import photos to the Organizer, the photos are automatically tagged with the date of import (and with any other tag choices you've made in the Photo Downloader—see page 46). But you may want to add more tags to make it easier to search for the subject of the photo later on. You can give a photo as many tags as you like.

Elements lets you group tags into *categories.* You get a few preset categories, like People, Places, and Events, and you can create your own, as well as make subcategories within categories. For example, you can make a Vacations category with China Trip and Cozumel as subcategories. Your photos in those categories could have tags like "Jim and Helen," "silk factory," or "snorkeling."

Working with tags and categories

Elements gives you a few generic tags to help you get started, but you'll want to learn how to create your own tags, too. After all, by the time you've got 5,000 or so photos in the Organizer, searching for "Family" probably isn't going to narrow things down much.

Creating a new tag in Elements 8 is easier than ever:

- **Just type it.** In the Organize bin, go to the box to the right of where it says Keyword Tags and start typing. At first you see a pop-up menu of all the existing tags, but if you keep typing, once Elements recognizes it as a new tag, the pop-up changes to say "Create new tag <text of your new tag>". Select the photo(s) you want to apply this new tag to and click Apply. Elements puts tags created this way in the Other category. If you'd like to put it somewhere else, just drag the tag's icon to the category where it belongs.

You can also create tags the way you did in earlier versions of Elements:

- **Keyboard shortcut.** Press Ctrl+N.

- **Menu.** In the Organize bin's Keyword Tags panel, click New (the green + sign) → New Keyword Tag. (You can also create a new category or subcategory from this same menu.)

When you create tags using either of these two methods, the Create Keyword Tag dialog box appears. Name the new tag by typing it in, and then assign it to a category by using the drop-down menu. (You can change the category later if you want.)

No matter which method you use, you can also edit the tag's icon, as explained in Figure 2-12.

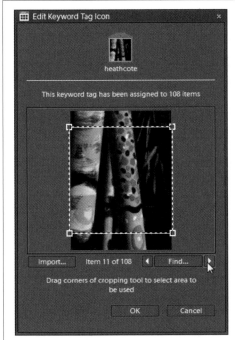

Figure 2-12:
Some people like to edit the icons that Elements uses to represent different tags to make it easy to search for a tag visually as well as by its name. To change the picture associated with a tag, right-click the tag in the Organize bin's Keyword Tags panel, and choose "Edit <name of tag> keyword tag". In the Edit Keyword Tag dialog box that appears, click Edit Icon. In the Edit Keyword Tag Icon dialog box (shown here), the arrows on either side of the Find button let you advance through all the photos that use that tag. (If you click the Find button, you see all those photos at once.) Or click the Import button to use a different image stored on your computer. Once you pick the picture you want, drag the dotted square to choose which part of your photo appears on the tag.

To assign the tag to a photo, just drag the tag's icon from the Organize bin onto the photo's thumbnail. It's as easy as that.

> **NOTE**   The Organizer also has a Tag Cloud view you can use for quick tagging and searching. In the Keyword Tags panel of the Organize bin, click the Tag Cloud icon (the blue cloud with the T on it) for the same kind of keyword list view you often see on web pages: all your tags listed in alphabetical order. The more images you've used a tag on, the bigger that tag's name is. You can drag a tag from here to an image to tag it.
>
> This view is really handy if you have only a few tags, but it's difficult to use if you have hundreds of different tags. To search by tags in this view, just click a tag. The text you click turns blue, and the Media Browser displays the photos with that tag assigned to them. To get back to regular Tag view, click the Tag Hierarchy icon (the little tagged photo rectangle) just to the left of the Tag Cloud icon.

You can rearrange the order of your tags by dragging them, and change tags to categories and categories to tags by right-clicking them and choosing from the pop-up menu. You can also drag tags from one category to another in the Organize bin.

Special Tags

Elements starts you off with two special kinds of tags:

- **Ratings.** These tags let you assign a one- to five-star rating to your photos. It's a good way to mark the ones you want to print or edit. Ratings are a great search tool because you can tell Elements to find, say, all your pictures rated four or more stars. (See page 64 for details on how to perform a search.) To assign ratings, just click the star under the photo's thumbnail that corresponds to your rating. In other words, to assign a three-star rating, click the third star from the left. To search by ratings, click the star you want at the top-right corner of the Media Browser (it works the same way as assigning tags—the second star from the left is the two-star rating, and so on) and then choose a qualifier (like "and higher") from the drop-down menu to the right of the stars. You can search for all photos rated four stars or higher, for instance, or those rated two stars or lower, and so on. To change or remove a photo's rating, right-click its thumbnail and choose Ratings from the menu that appears, and then pick the number of stars you want. You can also change a rating by clicking a different star under the thumbnail.

- **Hidden.** This tag is itself hidden when you start up the Organizer. You can only apply it by right-clicking a photo and choosing it from the menu that appears. When you apply this tag to a photo, the photo disappears from the Media Browser—once you select View → Hidden Files → Hide Hidden Files. The Hidden tag is useful for archiving photos that didn't come out quite right but that you're not ready to trash. You can save these pictures (just in case) without having them cluttering up your screen while you're working with your good photos. To assign the Hidden tag, right-click a photo and choose Visibility → "Mark as Hidden". To bring it back into the open, go to View → Hidden Files → Show All Files, which makes even your hidden files visible. Then right-click the photo again, and select Visibility → "Mark as Visible" to keep it in view. To put the rest of your hidden files back out of sight, choose View → Hidden Files. You can also see *only* your hidden files by going to View → Hidden Files → Show Only Hidden Files.

After you've assigned a tag to a photo, here's what to do if you decide you want to remove it:

- **From a single photo.** Right-click the photo's thumbnail and select "Remove <name of tag> Keyword Tag".

- **From a group of photos.** Select the photos, right-click one of them, select "Remove Keyword Tag from Selected Items", and then choose the tag you want to remove.

NOTE   When you first import images into the Organizer, the Media Browser displays only the photos in the batch you just imported. When you're in Folder view, you'll see an icon in the upper-right corner of the Browser called Instant Tag. Clicking it assigns the name of the folder where the photos are stored as a tag to all the photos in the group.

People Recognition

One of the interesting new features in Elements 8 is *face recognition*. In earlier versions of Elements you could tell the Organizer to find all the people in your photos, but that was as far as it went: the Organizer presented you with everything it thought looked like a human face, and it was up to you to sort it out. In Elements 8, the Organizer finds faces, and you help it out at first by naming the people it finds, and then it should be able to automatically recognize and tag Cousin Serafina and Great Uncle William in future photos without you having to identify them yourself.

To get started:

1. **Choose the photos you want Elements to analyze.**

   Select them in the Media Browser.

2. **Tell Elements to start evaluating them.**

   Click the People Recognition icon (the outline of a person's head and shoulders) in the Organize bin's Keyword Tags panel.

3. **Identify the people Elements finds.**

   After it analyzes your photos, Elements opens the People Recognition window. You see the first image where it located a person, with a square around the person's face and a little tag that says, "Who is this?" Click the tag and type a name. As you type, Elements suggests names based on the tags in your database. If you see the one you want, just click it to select it. To see all the photos of the person you've named, double-click the person's face in the image and Elements shows you all the photos definitely identified as that person (confirmed) and those it thinks might be that person (unconfirmed). That way you can tag them all at the same time.

   NOTE   Whether or not you use Elements' people recognition feature, you may notice "Who is this?" banners randomly appearing in your photos in the Media Browser. If you find this "fun" feature tiresome, you can disable it by opening the Organizer and going to Edit → Preferences → "Keyword Tags and Albums" and turning off "Display hints about people recognized".

4. **Give Elements some help with the people it didn't find and with any mistakes it made.**

   If Elements missed someone in your photo, click the Add Missing Person button, and drag a rectangle around the face or faces it missed. If Elements skipped a photo altogether, click the Name More People button to see more photos. If Elements found something that's not a face, click the rectangle's Close button (the X) to dismiss that outline. If Elements identified someone incorrectly, click the name it assigned and type the correct one. Use the arrows on either side of the preview area to step through your photos.

5. **When you're through tagging people, click Done.**

Any names you've added appear in the Organize bin's Keyword Tags panel under the People category. If you want to move a tag to another category, like Family, just drag it to the category you want.

Face recognition is fun to play with, and a pretty amazing thing for a computer to be able to do, but at this point it's more of a toy. It's not good at recognizing faces in profile, for example, and it can take quite a while to analyze everything in a large batch of images.

> **NOTE** You may want to disable the rest of the Auto-Analyzer features, described in the box on page 63. But to use People Recognition, go to Organizer → Edit → Preferences → Auto-Analyzer Options, and be sure that "Recognize People Automatically" is turned on. (If you aren't going to use People Recognition, you can save a little drain on your system's resources by turning it off.)

Albums and Smart Albums

You can group your photos into *albums*, which are great for gathering together pictures taken at a particular event. You can also use them to prepare groups of photos that you want to use in a Create project like a slideshow or photo collage (page 465).

When you create an album, you don't actually make a copy of all the photos you include in it; you just create a group of virtual "pointers" to each image so Elements knows where to find them. That means albums can hold lots of pictures without taking up much space and, even better, you can easily include the same pictures in different albums. Photos inside an album can appear in any order you choose, which is important, for instance, if you're preparing a slideshow.

Albums are particularly important if you're using Photoshop.com, since they give you a convenient way to upload, sync, and back up your photos without working with your whole catalog at once.

> **TIP** Albums are also good for gathering together groups of photos you want to export for use with another program.

Elements gives you several ways to create an album:

- **From the Organizer.** First Ctrl-click to select the photos you want to include. Then go to the Organize bin → Albums, click the New Album button (the green + sign), and choose New Album. Name your album and assign it to an album group (explained in a moment) if you wish, and then click Done. Your new album joins the list of albums. You can also choose to make an album from files anywhere on your computer, even if they're not in the Organizer, by selecting From File from the New Album button's pop-out menu.

Smart Tags

You may have noticed that the Organize bin has a category called Smart Tags. So what are these tags, and what makes them so smart?

If you right-click a photo's thumbnail in the Media Browser or select a group of images and then right-click one of them, the menu that appears includes a Run Auto-Analyzer option. Choose it, and Elements inspects all your files and assigns each image one or more *Smart tags* like High Quality, In Focus, High Contrast, and so on. Those are examples of what you'll get if you're lucky and a good photographer. You might also find that Elements considers an image to be Low Quality, Blurred, and Too Dark.

You can see the complete list of Smart tags at the bottom of the Organizer bin's Keyword Tags panel. Once it has applied these tags, Elements automatically writes them into each file, so if you send a photo to friends who have a way to view keywords, they can see right away that this is a Low Quality, Low Contrast, Shaky image.

Why does Elements include such a seemingly goofy feature? Actually, it's sometimes helpful if you have the Premiere Elements video-editing program, because it can analyze scenes within a movie clip to help you find the parts you want to edit. For still photos, you probably want to skip the Auto-Analyzer. But if you decide to give it a try, you can tell it what criteria to use by going to Edit → Preferences → Auto-Analyzer Options in the Organizer. If you feel like there's not enough criticism in your life already, there's even a checkbox in that window where you can tell Elements to analyze your photos automatically every time you start the Organizer.

- **From the Editor.** In the Editor, you can create an album in the Project bin's Bin Actions menu.

- **From the Share tab (Editor or Organizer).** To create an online album (one that you upload to Photoshop.com), just click Online Album in the list of projects.

NOTE   No matter which method you use to make your album, it will appear in the lists of albums in both the Organizer and the Project bin's Show menu.

In Elements 8, you can share any album online as you create it (see page 519 for more), or share existing albums by uploading them to your Photoshop.com account (just click Edit Album button at the top of the Organize bin's Album panel [the pencil]). You can also share your album in other ways by right-clicking its name in the list of albums and choosing the method you want to use. (Albums you create by clicking the Share tab's Online Album button are uploaded automatically.) Elements gives you lots of options for displaying your photos in a gallery and sharing them with friends. You can read more about working with online albums and sharing them in Chapter 18.

NOTE   You can also burn albums to a CD or DVD, or upload your slideshows and galleries to your own website. Page 523 explains how.

Once you've created an online album and shared it to Photoshop.com, you can edit it from any web browser, including adding or deleting photos, reorganizing photos, tagging them, and so on. The online Organizer looks just like the regular desktop Organizer on your computer, and you use it the same way. You can synchronize your online album(s) so that changes you make online are reflected in the album(s) stored on your computer, and vice versa. Page 75 explains more about how to do this. You can even sync albums between two desktop computers this way.

In the Organizer, to see the photos in an album, just click its name in the Albums panel. To return to viewing all your photos, click the binocular icon next to the album's name.

You can also create *album categories*, which are just what they sound like. If you have a lot of albums, you may want to group them into larger categories to make them easier to keep track of. To make an album category, go to the Organize bin's Albums panel, and click the New icon (the green + sign) → New Album Category. Name your category and it appears in the Albums list. To add albums to it, just drag their icons to the category's icon. To remove an album from it, click the flippy triangle to the left of the category name so you can see all the albums it contains. Then right-click the album you want to remove and choose Edit <album name>. In the window that opens, go to Album Category → None (Top Level) and then click Done. You can also create subcategories within categories. To do that, in the Albums panel, right-click a category and choose "Create new album category in <category name> category". The new category appears as a subcategory of the starting category.

Smart Albums are another useful feature. They automatically collect all the photos that meet the criteria you specify, as shown in Figure 2-13. To create a new Smart Album, in the Organizer, go to Albums → New (the green + sign) → New Smart Album.

Searching for Photos

Anyone who's been diligent enough to assign tags to all (or most) of their photos will be pleased to learn how easy Elements makes finding tagged photos. And as for the untagged masses? The good news is that Elements still gives you some helpful ways to find your pictures. The next few sections take you through all your options.

Browsing Through Photos

When you don't know exactly which photo you're looking for, Elements gives you a few ways to search through groups of pictures. These methods are also great if you don't want to look through your whole collection:

- **Text search.** You can just type what you're looking for into the Search box at the upper left of the Media Browser. Enter a filename, caption, date, tag, or anything that's in the file's *metadata* (see the box on page 69), and Elements will find it. As you type, Elements displays a pop-out list of your tags beginning with the letters you're typing. If you want to search for a tag, click one to select it.

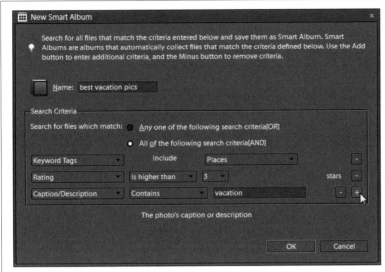

Figure 2-13:
When you create a Smart Album, this dialog box appears so you can choose criteria for it. Click the + sign button to add another search parameter. Here, the Smart Album "Best Vacation Pics" is set up to include photos with tags in the Places category, ratings of more than three stars, and the word "vacation" in the caption or description. All the photos that meet all three of these criteria automatically join the album.

You can also combine terms by using *and, or,* or *not.* You can also restrict what you want to search for; so if you enter, for example, *Tag:Birthday* in the Search box, you'll get photos with the Birthday tag attached to them.

- **Folders.** You can navigate through the folders stored on your computer, just as you do when using a program like Windows Explorer. First, turn on Folder view if you haven't already done so (Display → Folder Location or press Ctrl+Alt+3).

  TIP   Generally, you only see folders that contain photos the Organizer knows about. If you want to move photos to a folder the Organizer can't see, the workaround is to put a photo in the folder and then import it into Elements (page 46). After that, the Organizer will see the folder.

  Navigate by expanding the folders you want and working your way down to the ones that contain the photos you're looking for. When you reach a folder that contains photos, the pictures appear in the image well. (Be wary, though— Folder view has a number of bugs.)

- **Timeline.** Go to Window → Timeline, and the Timeline appears above the Find bar at the top of the image well. Each bar in the Timeline represents a group of photos. Click a bar, and you see the photos in that batch.

- **Date View.** You see your photos, listed by date, on a calendar page. Just click the date of the group you want to see. To get to Date view, go to Display → Date View.

- **Map.** If you've put your photos on a Yahoo map (page 541), go to Window → Show Map, and then click the various pins stuck in the map to see your photos.

TIP   The Find menu, covered on page 567, also lets you search for photos with similar colors. Choose Find → "By Visual Similarity with Selected Photo(s)". This option is great when you're looking for similarly toned graphics to use in a project.

Using Tags and Categories to Find Photos

When you're looking for a particular picture, you can use all the methods listed in the previous section and just keep clicking through groups of photos until you find the one you want. But searching by tags and categories is the easiest way to find a particular photo:

- **Keyword Tags panel.** In the Organize bin's Keyword Tags panel, click the empty square to the left of a tag or category, and Elements finds all the photos associated with that tag or category. (A pair of binoculars appears inside the square to indicate that tag or category is being used to search for photos.) Click as many tags and categories as you want, and Elements searches for them all.

  You can exclude a tag from a search by right-clicking the tag's name and, in the menu that appears, choosing the Exclude option. So you could search for photos with the tags "sports" and "rock-climbing," but not "broken leg," for instance.

  You can also search by switching to Tag Cloud view (page 59) and clicking a tag there.

- **Find bar.** The Organizer's *Find bar* gives you another way to perform a tag search. Figure 2-14 shows how to use it.

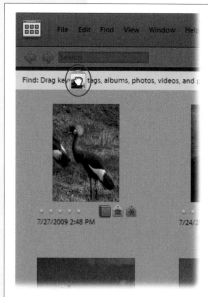

Figure 2-14:
To use the Find bar to search for pictures, just drag any tag, category, or photo from the Media Browser or the Organize bin onto the bar above the thumbnails (circled). When you get near the bar, it gets lighter so you can see it better. Your tag can hit the bar anywhere, not just where the lettering is. You can let go as soon as the bar changes color, and Elements will display your search results.

Searching by Metadata

As explained in the box on page 69, your camera stores lots of information about your images in the form of *metadata*. In the Organizer, you can search your photos by their metadata, looking for, say, all the photos you took with a particular camera model at a certain aperture and exposure. Figure 2-15 explains how. You can save your results as a Smart Album (page 62), so that any future files with the same characteristics will be grouped together.

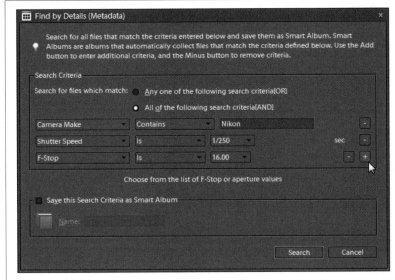

Figure 2-15:
To perform a search using your photos' metadata, go to Find → "By Details (Metadata)" to bring up this dialog box. Choose the category of metadata from the drop-down menu on the left, and enter your term or choose the exact setting in the box on the right. Click the + sign button to add additional search terms (up to 10). To remove a criterion, click the search term's – sign button.

TIP   If you want to share your tag information with people using the full version of Photoshop or Photoshop Elements for Mac, or even with other people using a Windows version of Elements, it's easy to do. Just select the photos you want, and then go to File → "Write Keyword Tag and Properties Info to Photos". This transforms your tags into metadata keywords, which can then be read by those programs, as well as by the old File Browser in Elements 2 and 3, if you have friends who still use those versions. You can also use the Organizer's Export command (File → "Export as New File(s)"), which also writes your tags into the metadata.

Saving Your Work

You've heard it before: save your files early and often. Saving your work is easy in Elements. You don't need to do anything special to save information like tags or collections in the Organizer; you need to save only images you've created or changed in the Editor. When you're ready to save a file, go to File → Save As or press Ctrl+Shift+S to bring up the Save As dialog box, shown in Figure 2-16.

The top part of the Save As dialog box is pretty much the same as it is for any program—you choose where you want to save your file, what you want to name it,

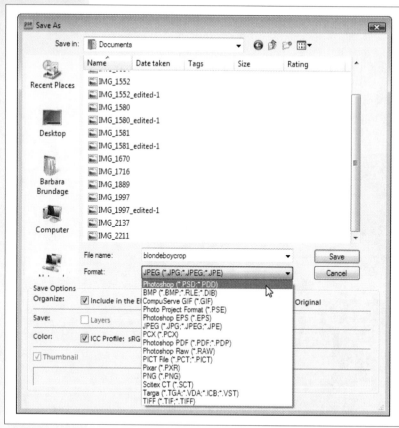

Figure 2-16:
Elements' Save As dialog box changes a little depending on what you're saving, but this example is pretty typical. When you click the Format drop-down menu (indicated by the cursor), you'll see a long list of file formats to choose from.

and the file format you want. (More about file formats in a moment.) You also get some important choices that are unique to Elements:

- **Include in the Organizer.** This checkbox is turned on the first time you use Elements. Leave it on and your photo gets saved in the Organizer. Turn it off if you don't want the new file to go to the Organizer (see page 56). If you turn it off, Elements should remember to *leave* it off, at least for this editing session or until you save a photo that came from the Organizer.

- **Save in Version Set with Original.** This option tells the Organizer to save your image (including any edits you've made) as a new *version,* separate from your original. Your photo gets the name of the original plus a suffix to indicate it's an edited version.

  You can create as many versions as you want. Then you can go directly to any state of your image that you've saved as a version, which is a really handy feature. When you turn on this checkbox to start a version set, from then on, you'll get the Save As dialog box every time you save (instead of being able to just save your changes). Elements does that to give you the chance to create a new version each time.

Viewing Data about Your Images

The Organizer is packed with information about your images. From captions you've written to statistics recorded by your camera, the Properties window is chockfull of interesting tidbits. To launch the Properties window, select any photo in the Organizer and then press Alt+Enter, or right-click any photo and choose Show Properties from the pop-up menu. You can choose from four different kinds of info by clicking one of the icons at the top of the window. From left to right they are:

- **General.** This includes the file's name, location on your PC, size, date you took the picture, caption (just put your cursor in the box and start typing to add one), and a link to any audio files associated with it (see page 535). You can also change the photo's filename here by highlighting its current name and typing in a new one.

- **Metadata.** The information about the photo that's stored in the photo's file is called *metadata*. Most notably, this is where you view your *EXIF* (Exchangeable Image Format) data, which is info your camera stores about your photos, including the camera you used, when you took the picture, the exposure, file size, ISO speed, aperture setting, and much more. By paying attention to your EXIF data, you can learn a lot about what works for making good shots…and what doesn't.

  The Metadata screen also includes many other kinds of info besides the EXIF data. Click the Complete radio button at the bottom of the window to see the full listing (click the Brief radio button to see only highlights).

- **Tags.** If you've assigned any tags to your photo, they're listed here.

- **History.** Look here to find out when the file was created, imported, and edited, and where you imported it from (your hard drive, for instance).

- **Layers.** If your image has *layers* (page 169), turn on this checkbox to keep them. When you turn off this setting, Elements usually forces you to save as a copy. To avoid having to save as a copy, *flatten* your image (page 193) before saving it; once you close a flattened image, you can't get your layers back again—flattening is a *permanent* change.

- **As a Copy.** When you save an image as a copy, Elements makes the copy, names it "Original filename. copy", and puts the copy away. The original version remains open. If you want to work on the copy, you have to open it. Sometimes Elements *forces* you to save as a copy—for instance, if you want to save a layered image and you turn off the layers option in the Save As dialog box. (See Chapter 6 for more about layers.)

- **ICC Profile.** Turn on this checkbox to make Elements embed a color profile (page 217) in your file.

- **Use Lower Case Extension.** This setting makes Elements save your file as yourfile.jpg rather than yourfile.JPG, for example. Leave this setting on unless you have a reason to turn it off.

Options for Saving Your Work

Elements gives you several ways to save files. Before choosing one, you need to consider whether you want to create version sets (page 68) of your photos.

To tell Elements how to react to the Save command, in the Editor, go to Edit → Preferences → Saving Files. In the Preferences dialog box that appears, under File Saving Options, you see the On First Save drop-down menu. By making a selection here, you can control (to some extent) when you'll see a dialog box offering you options for saving your file, and when Elements will behave like any other program and just save your changes without asking for any input from you.

For most people, it's fine to leave things as they are. (Elements selects the "Ask if Original" option—explained below—unless you change it.) But if you want more control over how Elements saves your photos (if you always want the option to create a new version set without your having to remember to choose Save As, for instance), you can configure Elements to suit you.

Here's what the three On First Save options do:

- **Always Ask.** Choose this setting and, when you press Ctrl+S to save, Elements brings up the Save As dialog box the first time you save—if it's the first time you've opened the file in this session of Elements. Close the file and reopen it while Elements is still running, and you won't see the Save As dialog box the next time you save. But once you exit Elements and launch it again, you get the Save As dialog box the first time you press Ctrl+S. You can think of this option as short for "Always ask the first time I save a file in an editing session and then don't bug me anymore."

- **Ask if Original.** If you're editing your original file (as opposed to a version) and don't have any version sets (page 68), Elements opens the Save As dialog box the first time you save the file. On subsequent saves, or if you already have a version set,

Elements just saves right over the existing version (unless you do a Save As to create a new version). This option is meant to help you avoid inadvertently creating dozens of versions of each file as you edit it.

- **Save Over Current File.** When you select this option, Elements overwrites your existing file when you press Ctrl+S, without offering you the Save As dialog box at all. This is the way most other programs behave when saving—if you save an existing file in Word, for instance, you don't get a dialog box; Word just saves your changes, writing over the previous version of the file. If you choose this menu option and then, while you're working, decide you want to Save As instead of Save, press Ctrl+Shift+S (or just choose Save As from the Editor's File menu).

There are certain situations where Elements presents you with the Save As dialog box no matter *what* you choose here. For instance, say you add layers (explained in Chapter 6) to a JPEG file; you can't save a JPEG with layers, so Elements brings up the Save As dialog box to let you choose a different file format for saving your work.

The File Saving Options section of the Saving Files Preferences dialog box has two other menus—Image Previews and File Extensions—but you probably won't ever need to change those settings.

You can also use the Saving Files Preferences dialog box to control how well your image file works with other programs. If you leave the Maximize PSD File Compatibility drop-down menu set to Always, Elements embeds a flattened image file for the benefit of programs that don't understand layers. That makes for a substantially larger file, but with disk space so cheap these days, it's usually best to let Elements maximize compatibility. If you choose Ask from this menu instead, you'll see the dialog box in Figure 2-17 when you save a layered PSD file.

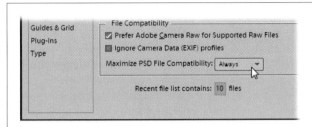

Figure 2-17:
Choose Always in the Maximum PSD File Compatibility menu if you want people who don't have Elements to be able to open your image. The downside: larger files.

File Formats Elements Understands

Elements gives you loads of file format options. Your best choice depends on how you plan to use your image.

- **Photoshop (.psd, .pdd).** It's a good idea to save your files as .psd files—the native file format for Elements or Photoshop—before you work on them. A .psd file can hold lots of information, and you don't lose any data by saving in this format. It also lets you keep layers, which is very important, even if you haven't used them for much yet.

- **Photo Project (.pse).** This special format is only for multipage Elements photo creations (see Figure 2-18 and page 474).

- **TIFF (.tif, .tiff).** This is another format that, like the Photoshop format, preserves virtually all your photo's info and lets you save layers. Also like Photoshop files, TIFFs can be really big. This format is used extensively in print production, and some cameras let you to choose TIFF as a shooting option.

- **JPEG (.jpg, jpeg, .jpe).** Almost everyone who uses a computer has run into JPEGs, and most digital cameras offer this format as an option. Generally, when you bring a JPEG into Elements, you want to use another format when you save it, to avoid losing data. Keep reading for more about why.

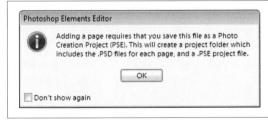

Figure 2-18:
If you add pages to a file (page 471), you see this warning. Elements is telling you it needs to save your multipage project in a format that almost no other programs can open. To learn more about working with the PSE format and how to get your project out of Elements for online printing or use by other programs, see the box on page 474.

- **PDF (.pdf, .pdp).** Adobe invented PDF, or Portable Document Format, which lets you send files to people with Adobe Reader (a free program formerly called Acrobat Reader) so they can easily open and view the files. Elements uses PDF files to create presentations like slideshows.

File Formats

After you've spent hours creating a perfect image, you want to share it with others. If everyone who wanted to view your images needed a copy of Elements, you probably wouldn't have a very large audience for your creations. So, Elements lets you save in lots of different *file formats.*

What does that mean? It's pretty simple, really. A file format is a way in which your computer saves information so that another program or another computer can read and use the file.

Because there are many different kinds of programs and several different computing platforms (Windows, Linux, and Mac, for example), the kind of file that's best for one use may be a really poor choice for doing something else. That's why many programs, like Elements, can save your work in a variety of different formats, depending on what you want to do with your image. There are many formats, like TIFF and JPEG, that lots of different programs can read. Then there are other formats—like the PUB files that Microsoft Publisher creates—which are easily read only by the program that created them.

- **CompuServe GIF (.gif).** (Everywhere except this menu, this format is known simply as GIF; Adobe adds "CompuServe" here because CompuServe invented and owns the code for this format.) This format is used primarily for web graphics, especially files without a lot of subtle shadings of color. For more on when to choose GIFs, see Chapter 17. GIFs are also used for web animations; page 511 explains how to create animated GIFs.

- **PICT (.pct).** PICT is an older Mac format that's still used by some applications. AppleWorks, for example, handles PICTs better than any other graphics format. Also, sometimes larger file formats like Mac-created TIFFs generate their thumbnail previews as PICT Resource files (the type of PICT used within the TIFF file).

- **BMP (.bmp).** This format is an old Windows standby. It's the file format used by the Windows operating system for many graphics tasks.

- **PNG.** Here's another web graphic format, created to overcome some of the disadvantages of JPEGs and GIFs. It has its own disadvantages, though. See page 509 for more about these files.

- **Photoshop EPS (.eps).** EPS (Encapsulated PostScript) format is used to share documents among different programs. You generally get the best results when the documents in this format are printed on a PostScript printer (some laser printers are PostScript printers; inkjets usually aren't).

- **Digital Negative (.dng).** This format was developed by Adobe to create a more universal way to store all the different Raw file formats (page 248). You can download a special DNG Converter from the downloads area of Adobe's support website (*www.adobe.com/downloads*) that lets you convert your camera's own Raw formatted photos into DNG files. DNG files aren't ready to use the way JPEG or TIFF files are—you have to run them through the Raw Converter before you can use them in projects. Page 265 has more about DNG files.

If you're wondering why JPEG 2000 isn't in this list, see the box on page 74.

Not-so-common file formats

Besides the garden-variety formats in the previous list, Elements lets you save in some formats you may never have heard of. Here's a list, and then you can forget all about them:

- **Filmstrip.** This format is designed for use with Premiere Elements, Adobe's video-editing program. You won't even see this option if Premiere isn't installed on your computer.

- **PIXAR.** Yup, *that* Pixar. This is the special format for the movie studio's high-end workstations, although if you're working on one of those, it's extremely unlikely that you're reading this book.

- **Scitex CT.** This format is used for prepress work in the printing industry.

- **Photoshop Raw.** No, it's not the same as your camera Raw file, but rather an older Photoshop format that consists of uncompressed data.

- **Targa TGA or Targa.** Developed for systems using the Truevision video board, this format has become a popular graphics format, especially for games.

- **PCX.** This format was popular for graphics back in the days of DOS (remember PC Paintbrush?). Nowadays it's mostly used by some kinds of fax systems and a few document management programs.

COMPATIBILITY CORNER

Opening Obscure File Formats

You may occasionally run into a file format that Elements doesn't understand. Sometimes you can fake Elements out and con it into opening the document by manually changing the file extension (the letters after the period near the end of the file's name, like "psd") to a more common one.

For the few file formats that make Elements throw up its hands in despair, try IrfanView (*www.irfanview.com*), a wonderful free program that can open almost any Windows-compatible format. You can sometimes even use IrfanView to salvage damaged files, especially if you get an "invalid JPEG marker" error. If Elements balks at one of your files, first try opening and resaving the photo in IrfanView. If you're lucky, that may be all you need to do to make Elements recognize your file again.

Very rarely, you'll run across a file that makes even Irfan-View give up. If that happens, try a Google search. (Use the file's three- or four-letter extension as your search term.) It's unlikely to help you open it, but if you can figure out what it is, you can probably figure out where it came from and ask whoever sent it to you to try again with a more standard format.

About JPEGs

In the next chapter, you'll read about how throwing away pixels can lead to shoddy-looking pictures (page 110). However, certain file formats are designed to make your file as small as possible—and they do that by throwing out information by the bucketful. These formats are known as *lossy* because they throw out, or lose, some of the file's data every time you save it, to help shrink the file.

Sometimes you want that to happen, like when you want a small (and hence, fast-loading) file for a website. So many of the file formats that were developed for the Web, most notably JPEG, are designed to favor smallness above all. They compress the file sizes by allowing some data to escape.

> **NOTE** Formats that preserve all your data are called *lossless.* (You may also run across the term *non-lossy*, which means the same thing.) The most popular file formats for people who are looking to preserve all their photos' data are PSD and TIFF.

If you save a file in JPEG format, every time you click the Save button and close the file, your computer squishes some of the data out of the photo. What kind of data? The info your computer needs for displaying and printing the fine details. You don't want to keep saving your file as a JPEG over and over again—every time you do, you lose a little more detail from your image. You can usually get away with saving as a JPEG once or twice, but if you keep it up, sooner or later you start to wonder what happened to your beautiful picture.

It's OK that your camera takes photos and saves them as JPEGs. Those are pretty enormous JPEGs, usually. Just importing a JPEG won't hurt your picture, and neither will opening it to look at it, as long as you don't make any changes. But once you get your files into Elements, save your pictures as Photoshop or TIFF files while you work on them. If you want the final product to be a JPEG, change the format back to JPEG *after* you're done editing it.

> **TIP** Your camera may give you several different JPEG compression options to help you fit more pictures on your memory card. Always choose the *least* compression possible. This makes the files slightly larger, but the quality is much, much better, so it's worth sacrificing the space.

MOMENT OF SILENCE

Bye-Bye, JPEG 2000

If you've been saving your files in the useful lossless JPEG 2000 format (.jpf, .jpx, .jp2), you may be perplexed to find that in Elements 8, you can't open those files in the Editor or import them to the Organizer (you can still *see* any existing JPEG 2000 files in an Organizer catalog—page 53—originally created in a previous version of Elements; you just can't *do* anything with them). That's right—Elements can no longer read these files. Back in Elements 2, when JPEG 2000 was a new format, you needed a special plug-in to work with them in Elements,

and today there's a special plug-in for Photoshop CS4 if you want to use this format there, but in Elements 8, you're out of luck.

Fortunately, there's a way around this: Download the free ImageMagick program (*www.imagemagick.org*) and use it to convert your JPEG 2000 images to another lossless format. Keep this in mind, because many books that include practice images on discs and a lot of downloadable artwork use the JPEG 2000 format.

Changing the File Format

It's super easy to change a file's format in Elements: Just press Ctrl+Shift+S or go to File → Save As and, from the Format drop-down menu, select the format you want. Elements makes a copy of your file in the new format and asks you to name it.

Backing Up Your Files

With computers, you just never know what's going to happen, so "Be prepared" is a good motto. If your computer crashes, it won't be nearly so painful if all your photos are safely backed up someplace else. Thanks to Elements' new Photoshop. com service, you can make that happen automatically. In the event of a problem with your home computer, you can restore your photos—or at least the ones you've chosen to sync to Photoshop.com.

The Photoshop.com-as-backup system has two main downsides: First, it only comes with 2 GB of space; if you want more than that, you have to pony up for more storage, as explained on page 22. You can back up your whole catalog (page 53) in Elements 8, but for most people that means a paid account. If you have a small catalog or a paid account, go to Organizer → Edit → Preferences → Backup/Synchronization, and click the "Backup/Sync Entire Catalog" button.

> NOTE   As of this writing, the Photoshop.com service is restricted to U.S. residents.

If those limitations turn you off, you'll be glad to know that Elements also makes it easy to save your files to any add-on storage device—like an external hard drive— or to a CD or DVD. All these options are covered in the pages ahead.

> TIP   Elements offers one frequently requested feature for making backups: You can create *multi-session* discs. That means you can tell Elements to leave your CD or DVD "open," so that you can come back later and use the disc again to add more files to it, instead of wasting a whole CD or DVD to burn a handful of pictures. To use this feature, in the Organizer, go to Edit → Preferences → Files and turn on the "Enable multisession burning to CD/DVD" checkbox.

Online Syncing and Backups

If you have a Photoshop.com account and you've created an online album (page 519), it's supersimple to set things up so that any changes you make to either your online album or the album on your computer appear in both places. If your catalog is small enough, you can even back up your whole catalog to your account. All you need to do is turn on the Backup/Synchronize checkbox when creating your album. After you do that once, Elements automatically syncs any additional albums you create. If you *don't* want that to happen, see Figure 2-19.

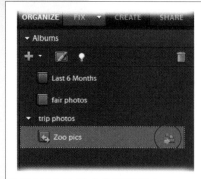

Figure 2-19:
When an album is set for syncing, its icon shows two arrows, like the ones on the "Zoo pics" album here. If you find you're syncing an album and you don't really want to, there are two ways to turn it off. Click the Share button (circled) and then turn off Backup/Synchronization in the Sharing pane of the Album Details panel, or just go to Edit → Preferences → Backup/ Synchronization and turn it off in the list of albums there.

You can control how syncing and automatic backups work from several places in Elements:

- **The Organizer's Albums panel.** Click the album's name. Then click the Share icon (the two people with an arrow) that appears on the right side of the panel and select Album Details → Sharing; or click the Edit Album button (the pencil), which also takes you to the Album Details panel.

- **The Welcome screen.** Just click Manage My Backup at the bottom of the window.

- **Organizer preferences.** Go to Edit → Preferences → Backup/Synchronization. (This is where you can tell Elements whether to back up your whole catalog.)

The last two options take you to the Organizer's Backup/Synchronization Preferences window, where you have a lot of control over what Elements does. You can turn off syncing altogether, turn off syncing for new albums, turn syncing on and off for particular albums, and choose a folder where you want Elements to put new photos it finds in your Photoshop.com account. You can also see how much of your Photoshop.com space you've used, and buy more if you want. If you're worried about space, you can tell Elements to skip syncing files over a certain size, too.

NOTE   Photoshop.com includes a few of Elements' editing tools. If you use these tools to edit one of your online photos, then Elements creates a version set (page 68) on your computer to preserve your original file. But be careful! Despite this, Photoshop.com doesn't really understand version sets. If you send a version set to Photoshop.com, you're only backing up the *top* version (the one that's visible in the Organizer when the set is collapsed). And if you edit a photo on your computer after backing up it up online (whether it's in a version set or not), your edited version replaces the original stored at Photoshop.com. The same goes for *stacks* (page 46)—only the top item in a stack gets synced.

Once you turn on syncing, Elements automatically makes backups of the albums you sync. A sync icon (a little gray safe) appears in the system tray/notification area at the bottom of your screen from now on. Right-click it and you can stop or start syncing from there, and tell Elements to sync your photos only when your computer is idle, rather than as soon as you make a change.

NOTE If you used Elements 7, you know how confusing it was that Elements didn't tell you whether it was doing anything once you set up syncing. In Elements 8, you can right-click the sync icon and select "View Backup/Sync Status" to see a window showing your current syncing situation, including a progress bar when Elements is in mid-sync.

You can also sync between two computers via Photoshop.com. Just create the same albums on both machines, set them to sync, and log into the same account. Then any changes you make on one computer get sent off to Photoshop.com and from there onto your other computer—very handy for keeping your laptop in sync with your desktop computer.

If you have photos on Photoshop.com and something happens to your computer, you can restore your online photos to your home machine—or any other computer—by turning on the sync settings in the preferences, as explained earlier (page 75). Of course you need to have Elements installed on the computer to set this up. Just turn on the Organizer's Backup/Synchronization preference for each album you want (or choose Select All for the whole kit and caboodle), log into your account, and then wait (it may take a while if you've got a lot of photos to restore).

If you're the sort of person who's not good about remembering to back up, Photoshop.com is a terrific, effortless way to get the job done. However, you shouldn't rely on this as your only backup. As mentioned above it has some limitations, so you'll probably want to make regular backups elsewhere, too. These backups are also easy, if not quite as automatic.

WARNING While online backups are swell, don't rely on them as your only backup. Make sure you have at least one other backup someplace else, because there's always a chance that things can happen to the computers that power online storage websites.

Organizer Backups

The Organizer offers a really helpful way to back up your photos. It's one of the best parts of Elements, and it's certainly thorough, even going so far as to remind you to label the disc you create. You can back up your whole catalog or just specific photos. Simply follow these steps:

1. **Make sure your catalog is in tip-top shape.**

   Go to File → Catalog and select your catalog in the list, then click Repair, just in case. It's also not a bad idea to go to File → Reconnect → All Missing Files, although the Organizer warns you if you have unconnected files when you start your backup. (An *unconnected file* is a cataloged item that the Organizer can't find.)

   TIP Organizer authority John Ellis has created Psedbtool, a special tool for editing and repairing your catalog. You can download it for free from *www.johnrellis.com/psedbtool/index.htm*. He also has a helpful set of Frequently Asked Questions with lots of helpful hints and useful suggestions for dealing with common Organizer problems at *www.johnrellis.com/psedbtool/photoshopelements-6-7-faq.htm*. They're for Elements 6 and 7, but most work for Elements 8, too.

2. **Call up the Backup dialog box, and let Elements make sure your catalog is in backup-ready shape.**

   Go to File → "Backup Catalog to CD, DVD, or Hard Drive", or press Ctrl+B.

3. **Tell Elements what kind of backup to make.**

   In the dialog box that opens, you have to decide whether to back up your whole catalog or to make an incremental backup. The Full Backup option backs up *everything* in your catalog. Pick that one the first time you make a backup, or if you're backing up everything to move to a new computer. The Incremental Backup option finds only the stuff that's new since the last time you made a backup, and that's all it copies—a major time- and space-saver. (You have to make a full backup at least once before Elements will let you do an incremental backup.)

   Your backup will have the same name as your catalog. You can see the name in the dialog box, but you can't change it. Click Next to continue.

   NOTE   If you have multiple catalogs (page 53), you can back up only one catalog at a time.

4. **Choose a destination for your files.**

   Your choices include a CD, a DVD, or any hard drive connected to your computer (either built-in or external). Choose by selecting from the list in the Select Destination Drive dialog box.

   If you're backing up to a hard drive, click the Backup Path Browse button to select where you want Elements to create your backup. Navigate through the folders in the window that appears, and create a new folder if you'd like to keep your backups tidy (a good idea). Once you're done, the folder's *path* (a roadmap to where it lives) appears in the Backup window.

   If you're making an incremental backup, you have to show Elements where to find your previous backup. Either insert the CD or DVD with the original full backup, or click the letter name of the drive where you made your previous backup and use the "Previous Backup file" Browse button to show Elements the existing backup file.

5. **If you're backing up to a CD or DVD, insert a disc in the drive when Elements asks you to. (If you're backing up to any other kind of media, including internal or external hard drives, skip ahead to step 6.)**

   Elements has to calculate how many discs you need to create your backup. As Elements burns each disc, it asks if you want it to verify the disc to be sure it's OK. You do. Elements prompts you to feed it more discs if your backup doesn't all fit on one disc.

   You can also change the write speed for your disc. (A slower speed takes longer but may be more reliable.) Just choose one of the other speed options from the drop-down menu. As Elements burns each disc, it asks if you want to verify the disc. Do this, so that Elements can check for any burn errors.

TIP   Always check your backup discs once you've burned them, even if you verified them during backup. Take a moment to put the disc in your computer and make sure that all your files are there. If there's an error, you want to know about it now, not six months from now.

6. **Create your backup.**

   Click Done, and Elements generates your backup. If you decide you don't want to make a backup, click Cancel instead.

   If you chose to burn CDs or DVDs, don't forget to label the discs when Elements finishes burning them, so you'll know what they are.

   NOTE   These directions cover how to back up your images and your catalog. Some people also like to back up their *catalog database* (the data file that the Organizer creates to keep track of where your photos are) every once in a while. To back up just the catalog information, use Windows Explorer to search for folders with the extension .pse8db, and burn those folders, including the files within them, to a CD, or copy them to an external hard drive.

At some point you may want to back up and then restore your catalog (if you have to reinstall Windows, for example.) To restore your catalog, in the Organizer, just go to File → "Restore Catalog from CD, DVD, or Hard Drive" and follow the onscreen directions. Elements asks for the last disc from your backup, not the first one as you might expect. Be aware that a backup made using these steps is for Element's use, not yours: If you open the discs in Windows Explorer, you'll see files with weird numerical names, and you can't just rummage around to find a particular photo you accidentally deleted. You have to let Elements handle restoring the files. Because you can't get individual files out of an official Elements backup, many people prefer to create their own backups, copying the catalog file (explained above) and their images to a regular data disc. That way you don't have to rely on Elements to retrieve lost photos for you.

   NOTE   If you have trouble restoring your catalog because your drive's letter name has changed (if you had to replace a hard drive, for example), try using Psedbtool (page 77) to fix things.

Making Quick CDs/DVDs

So far, you've learned how to back up your photos so that you can restore them to the Organizer with all your cataloging information intact. But what if you just want to burn a few photos or a project to a disc, and you don't care about the tags and such? Say you want to send your latest editing masterpieces to a friend, for instance. Here's what you do:

1. **Select the photos and/or projects you want to burn.**

   You can start from either the Editor or the Organizer, but if you're in the Editor, make sure you save your work first.

2. **Go to Share → Burn data CD/DVD.**

A dialog box pops up where you have to select the drive you want to use for burning. Just click the drive's name in the list. If you want, you can also name your disc here; if you don't type in a name, Elements names it today's date.

3. **Insert a blank CD or DVD when Elements asks you to, and then click OK.**

Elements has to see the disc to know how many photos will fit on it and to figure out how many discs you'll need, if all your photos won't fit on one. When the program is through figuring this out, you'll see the size and write time (how long it will take Elements to burn the disc) in the "Burn data CD/DVD" dialog box's Size area.

4. **Click OK to create your CD or DVD.**

When Elements is done, it asks if you want to verify the disc. This is always a good idea. When it finishes verifying your disc, it ejects it and reminds you to write its name on it so you'll know what it is.

When you make copies of just a few photos (rather than your whole catalog), you're copying only the photos, not all the catalog information about the photos. If you want to include your tags along with the photos, before you start, in the Organizer, go to File → "Write Keyword Tag and Properties Info to Photos". This makes your tags part of the files' EXIF data (see the box on page 69), so that if you send the photos to someone with Photoshop or another program that can read metadata, the tags appear as keywords in the file info.

> **NOTE** One drawback to including your tag and property info is that you can't use Elements to remove tags from the metadata later. So, for instance, if you attach a "stupid boss" tag to a photo and then have second thoughts, you can remove that tag from your catalog, but it will still exist in the files themselves, unless you use another program to edit the metadata. Psedbtool (*www.johnrellis.com/psedbtool/index.htm*) is a popular program is a popular program you can use to remove that "stupid boss" tag from the file's metadata before you email the photo to the editor of the company newsletter.

Rotating and Resizing Your Photos

In the last chapter, you learned how to get your photos *into* Elements. Now it's time to look at how to trim off unwanted areas and straighten crooked photos. You'll also learn how to change the overall size of your images and how to zoom in and out to get a better look at things while you're editing.

> **NOTE** From here through Chapter 14, you need to be in the Elements Editor. If you're still in the Organizer, press Ctrl+I to go to the Full Edit window.

Straightening Scanned Photos

Anyone who's scanned printed photos can testify about the hair-pulling frustration when the carefully placed pictures come out crooked onscreen. Whether you're feeding in precious memories one at a time or scanning batches of photos to save time, Elements can help straighten things out.

Straightening Two or More Photos at a Time

If you've got a pile of photos to scan, save yourself some time and lay as many of them as you can fit on your scanner. Thanks to Elements' wonderful Divide Scanned Photos command, you'll have individual images in no time.

Start by scanning in the photos (Figure 3-1). The only limit is how many can fit on your scanner at once. It doesn't matter whether you scan directly into Elements or use the scanner's own software. (See page 49 for more about scanning images into Elements.)

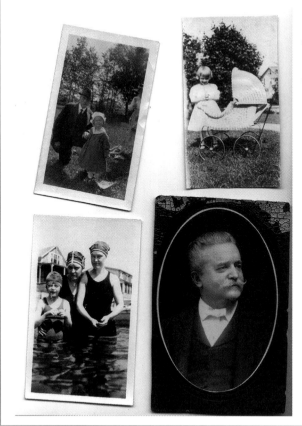

Figure 3-1:
*Consumer-grade flatbed scanners are generally
pretty slow, so it's a huge timesaver to scan four or
even six photos at a time. Elements can
automatically separate and straighten individual
photos in a group thanks to the Divide Scanned
Photos command.*

TIP   Sometimes it pays to be crooked. Divide Scanned Photos works best when your photos are
fairly crooked, so don't waste time trying to be precise when placing your pictures on the scanner.

When you're done scanning, follow these steps:

1. **Open your scanned image file in the Editor.**

    It doesn't matter what file format you used when saving your scanned group of
    photos: TIFF, JPEG, PDF, whatever. Elements can read 'em all (unless you used
    JPEG 2000, in which case see page 74).

2. **Divide, straighten, and crop the individual photos.**

    Go to Image → Divide Scanned Photos. Then just sit back and enjoy the view as
    Elements carefully calculates, splits, straightens out, and trims each image. You'll
    see the photos appear and disappear as Elements works through the group.

3. **Name and save each separated image.**

   When Elements is done, you'll have the original group scan as one image and a separate image file for each photo Elements carved out. Once you're done, import the cut-apart photos into the Organizer. To do that, just make sure that "Include in Organizer" is turned on in the Save As dialog box (see page 87).

Elements usually does a crackerjack job splitting photos, but once in a while it chokes, leaving you with an image file that contains more than one photo. Figure 3-2 shows you what to do when Elements doesn't succeed in splitting things up.

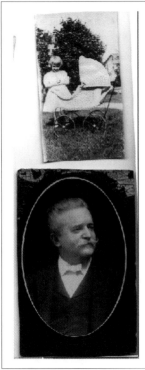

Figure 3-2:
Sometimes Elements just can't figure out how to split up photos, and you wind up with something like these two not-quite-split-apart images. Rescan the photos that confused Elements, but this time, make sure they're more crooked on the scanner and leave more space between them. Elements should then be able to split them correctly. Also, check for positioning problems like you see here, where Elements can't split the photos because it can't draw a straight line to divide these two without chopping off the corners. Put a little more space between the photos so Elements can split 'em.

TIP Occasionally you may find that Elements can't accurately separate a group scan, no matter what you do. In that case, use the Marquee tool (page 139) to select an individual image, paste it into its own document (File → New → "Image from Clipboard"), and then save it.

Straightening Individual Photos

Elements can also straighten and crop (trim) a single scanned image. Simply choose Image → Rotate → "Straighten and Crop Image", and Elements tidies things up for you. Or you can choose Straighten Image if you'd rather crop the edges yourself. Better still, you can use Divide Scanned Photos on a single image, as explained in the previous section. (Cropping is explained on page 89.)

Rotating Images

Owners of print photographs aren't the only ones who sometimes need a little help straightening their pictures. Digital photos sometimes have to be rotated because some cameras don't include data in their image files that tells Elements (or any other image-editing program) the correct orientation. Certain cameras, for example, send portrait-orientated photos out on their sides, and it's up to you to straighten things out.

Fortunately, Elements has rotation commands just about everywhere you go. If all you need to do is get Dad off his back and stand him upright, here's a list of where you can perform a quick 90-degree rotation on any open photo:

- **Quick Fix** (page 115). Click either of the Rotation buttons at the bottom of the preview area.

- **Full Edit.** Go to Image → Rotate → 90° Left (or Right).

- **Project bin.** Right-click a thumbnail and choose Rotate 90° Left (or Right).

- **Raw Converter** (page 248). Click the left or right arrow at the top of the Preview window.

- **Organizer** (page 53). You can rotate a photo almost anytime in the Organizer by pressing Ctrl plus the left or right arrow key. You can also choose Edit → Rotate 90° Left (or Right). There are Rotate buttons at the top of the Quick Edit panel in Full Screen view (page 56). Finally, there's a pair of Rotate buttons at the top of the Media Browser window.

Those commands all get you one-click, 90-degree changes. But Elements has all sorts of other rotational tricks up its sleeve, as the next section explains.

Rotating and Flipping Options

Elements gives you several ways to change your photo's orientation. To see what's available, in the Editor, go to Image → Rotate. You'll notice two groups of Rotate commands in this menu. For now, it's the top group you want to focus on. (The second group does the same things, only those commands work on layers, which are explained in Chapter 6.)

In the first group of commands, you'll see:

- **90° Left or Right.** These commands produce the same rotation as the rotate buttons explained earlier; use them to fix digital photos that come in on their sides.

- **180°.** This turns your photo upside down and backward.

- **Custom.** Selecting this command brings up a dialog box where, if you're mathematically inclined, you can type in the precise number of degrees you want to rotate the photo.

- **Flip Horizontal.** Flipping a photo horizontally means that if your subject was gazing soulfully off to the left, now she's gazing soulfully off to the right.

- **Flip Vertical.** This command turns your photo upside down *without* changing the left/right orientation like Rotate 180˚.

NOTE   When you're flipping photos around, remember you're making a mirror image of everything in the photo. So someone who's writing right-handed becomes a lefty, any text you can see in the photo is backward, and so on.

Figure 3-3 shows these commands in action.

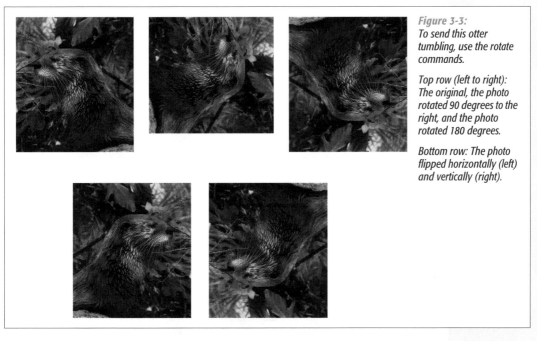

Figure 3-3:
To send this otter tumbling, use the rotate commands.

Top row (left to right): The original, the photo rotated 90 degrees to the right, and the photo rotated 180 degrees.

Bottom row: The photo flipped horizontally (left) and vertically (right).

If you want to position your photo at an angle (as you might in a scrapbook), use Free Rotate Layer, described on page 89.

Straightening the Contents of an Image

What about all those photos you've taken where the main subject (a person or a building, say) isn't quite straight? You can flip those pictures around forever, but if your camera was off-kilter when you snapped the shot, your subjects will still lean like a certain tower in Pisa. Elements has planned for this problem, too, by including a nifty Straighten tool that makes adjusting the horizon as easy as drawing a line.

NOTE   About 95 percent of the time, the Straighten tool does the trick. But in the few cases where you can't get things looking perfect, you can still use the old-school Elements method—the Free Rotate Layer command, described on page 89.

Straighten Tool

If you can never seem to hold a camera perfectly level, you'll love Elements' Straighten tool. It lives just below the Cookie Cutter tool (or next to it if you have two columns) in the Full Editor's Tools panel. To straighten a crooked photo:

1. **Open the photo, and then activate the Straighten tool.**

   Its icon is two little photos, one crooked and one not. Or, on the keyboard, just press P.

2. **Make any changes to the tool's Options bar settings tool before you use it.**

   Your choices are described after this list.

3. **Tell Elements where the horizon is.**

   Drag to draw a line in your photo to show Elements where horizontal *should* be. Figure 3-4 shows how—by drawing a line that traces the boundary between the ocean and the sky. Your line appears at an angle when you draw it. That's fine, because Elements is going to level out your photo, making your line the true horizontal plane.

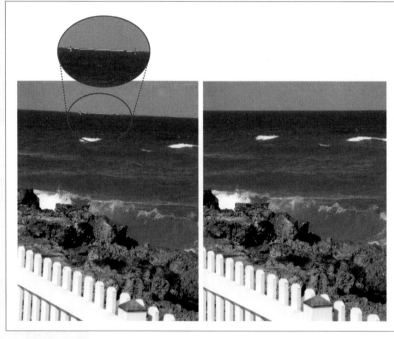

Figure 3-4:
Left: To correct the crooked horizon in this photo, just draw a line along the part that should be level. It's easiest to do this by choosing a clearly marked boundary like the horizon here, but you can actually draw a line across anything you want to make level.

Right: Elements automatically rotates the photo to straighten its contents.

4. **Elements responds by automatically straightening your photo. It also crops the photo if you chose that setting in the Options bar.**

If you don't like what Elements did, press Ctrl+Z to undo it and draw another line. If you're happy, you're all done, except for saving your work (Ctrl+S).

TIP   If you have a photo of trees, sailing ships, skyscrapers, or any other subject where you'd rather straighten vertically than horizontally, just hold down Ctrl while you drag. That way, the line you draw determines the *vertical* axis of your photo.

The Options bar gives you some control over how to handle the edges of your newly straightened photo. Once your picture's straightened, the edges are going to be a bit ragged, so you can choose what you want Elements to do about that:

• **Grow or Shrink Canvas to Fit.** Elements adds extra space around the edges of your photo to make sure that every bit of the original edges is still there. It's up to you to crop your photo afterward (see page 89).

ON THE SQUARE

Grids, Guides, and Rulers

Elements gives you plenty of help when it comes to getting things straightened and aligned. In the Editor, you can opt to turn on several features that make it really easy to create all kinds of projects in Elements:

• **Grid.** This option shows your entire image under a network of gridlines, as in Figure 3-5. This is really helpful when you're doing a free rotation (page 89) and you're not sure where straight is. Just go to View → Grid to toggle the grid on and off. You can adjust the grid's spacing in Edit → Preferences → Guides & Grid. You can also change the color of the grid to make it show up better. To do that, click the color square in the grid preferences window, and choose a color from the Color Picker (page 232).

• **Rulers.** If you want to measure in your image, go to View → Rulers, and rulers appear along the sides of your image. You can change the measurement unit by going to Edit → Preferences → Units & Rulers if you'd rather see, say, pixels or percents rather than inches.

• **Guides.** Guides are a new, much-requested feature in Elements 8. You can create as many guides as you want in your image. Just go to View → New Guide

and choose a horizontal or vertical line (you can't change the orientation of a guideline once you create it). You can also specify a position in your image, or you can just create it anywhere by clicking OK, and then use the Move tool to drag it where you want it. Once you get your guidelines set up, you can keep yourself from accidentally moving 'em by locking them (View → Lock Guides). To remove your guides, go to View → Clear Guides.

If you save your photo with guides in it and send it to someone else using a version of Elements that can display guides (Elements 6 and 7 can *see* guides; they just can't create guides) or using Photoshop, your guides will appear for them. If someone sends you a file with guides in it, you can see their guides if you turn them on in the View menu (View → Guides).

Guides are really handy, particularly for projects like scrapbooking, because you can make anything you add into your file *snap* (jump) right to the guide's location (View → Snap To → Guides). If you decide you'd rather move objects freely, just select the same menu option again to toggle off snapping. (You can also have objects snap to the grid, but you can only change this setting when the grid is visible.)

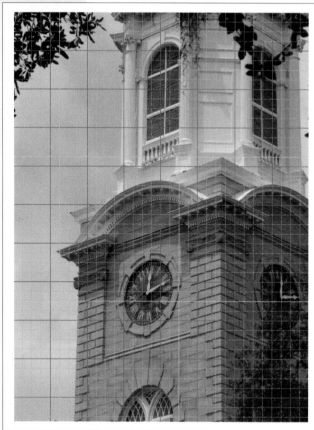

Figure 3-5:
If you need some help figuring out where straight is, in the Editor, you can add a grid or guidelines. The bright aqua lines are guides; the others are the grid. (Neither will show up when you print your photo.) Use the grid to help straighten your image. Guides are especially useful when you're adding things to your photo, since you can make things like text blocks (page 441) automatically line up by making them snap to the guidelines. The box on page 87 tells you how.

- **Crop to Remove Background.** Elements chops off the ragged edges to give you a nice rectangular image. The downside to this option is that you lose some of the perimeter of your photo—though just a bit, so usually it's not a big deal.

- **Crop to Original Size.** Elements makes sure your photo's dimensions stay exactly the same—even if that means including some blank space along the perimeter. You may also lose some of the edges of your image, particularly the corners.

If your photo has layers (see Chapter 6), you can use the Straighten tool to straighten just the active layer (page 173) by going to the Options bar and turning off the Rotate All Layers checkbox. If you want Elements to straighten your whole photo, leave this checkbox turned on.

The Straighten tool is best for photos where you were holding the camera crooked. If you try it and it makes things in your photo look very odd, perhaps straightening isn't what you need. Architectural photos, for instance, may look a bit crooked before you use this tool—but a lot worse afterward. If that house is *still* leaning even though you're sure the ground line has been leveled correctly, then most likely your real problem is *perspective distortion* (a visual warping effect). To fix that, use Correct Camera Distortion (see page 354).

TIP You can also straighten photos right in the Raw Converter. There's a Straighten tool in its toolbox, right between the Crop tool and the Red Eye tool. You use it just like the Editor's Straighten tool. Page 253 tells you more.

Free Rotate Layer

You can also use the Rotate commands to straighten your photos, or to turn them at angles for use in scrapbook pages or album layouts you create. The rotate command that's best for this is Free Rotate Layer, which lets you grab your photo and spin it to your heart's desire. And if you aren't sure where straight is, Elements can help you figure it out, as the box on page 87 explains.

NOTE You can use all the rotate commands on individual layers. Chapter 6 tells you all about layers, but you don't have to understand layers to use the Free Rotate Layer command.

To use the Free Rotate Layer command:

1. **Go to Image → Rotate → Free Rotate Layer.**

   If you have a Background layer, Elements automatically converts to a regular layer for you. (You'll learn about layers in Chapter 6, but for now it doesn't matter.)

2. **Use the handle or the curved two-headed arrow to adjust your photo (see Figure 3-6).**

   Your picture may look kind of jagged while you're rotating. Don't worry about that—Elements will smooth things out once you're done.

3. **When you've got your image positioned where you want it, click the Commit button or press Enter. (If you don't like what you did, click the Cancel button to cancel the rotation.)**

   If you were straightening your photo (rather than angling it), you've got a nice straight picture, but the edges are probably pretty ragged, since the original had slanted, unrotated sides. You can take care of that by cropping your photo as explained next.

Cropping Pictures

Whether or not you straightened your digital photos, sooner or later you'll probably need to *crop* them—trim them to a certain size. Most people crop their photos for one of two reasons: If they want to print on standard-size photo paper, they usually need to cut away part of the image to make it fit on the paper. Then there's the "I don't want *that* in my picture" reason. Fortunately, Elements makes it easy to crop away distracting background objects or people you'd rather not see.

A few cameras take photos that are proportioned exactly right for printing to a standard size like 4"×6" But most cameras create images that aren't the same proportions as any of the standard paper sizes like 4"×6" or 8"×10". (An image's width-to-height ratio is also known as its *aspect ratio*.)

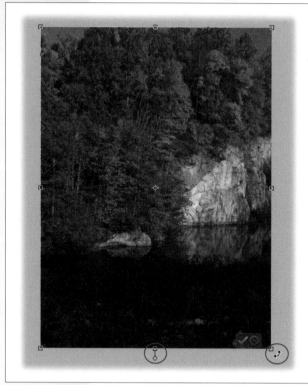

Figure 3-6:
You have two ways to straighten the contents of your photo—or even to spin it around in a circle. Just grab either the handle at the bottom center of your photo or a corner (both circled). (When you move your cursor near the image's corner, it turns into a curved, two-headed arrow.) Then drag to adjust your photo the way you'd straighten a crooked picture on the wall. Click the green checkmark Commit button when you're happy with what you've done, or the red Cancel button to cancel.

The extra area most cameras provide gives you room to crop wherever you like. You can also crop out different areas for different size prints (assuming you save your original photo). Figure 3-7 shows a photo that had to be cropped to fit on a 4"×6" piece of paper. If you'd like to experiment with cropping or changing resolution (explained on page 103), download the image in the figure (*river.jpg*) from the Missing CD page at *www.missingmanuals.com*.

If your photo isn't in the Organizer (which automatically protects your originals), it's best to crop a copy of the image, since cropping throws away the pixels outside the area you choose to keep. And you never know—you may want those pixels back someday.

The Crop Tool

You can use the Crop tool in either the Full Edit or Quick Fix window. The Crop tool includes a helpful list of preset sizes to make your job easier. In most cases the preset sizes are what you need, but if you do want to crop to a custom size, here's how:

1. **Activate the Crop tool.**

   Click the Crop icon in the Tools panel or press C. (If you can't find the Crop tool, it shares the same slot as the Recompose tool.)

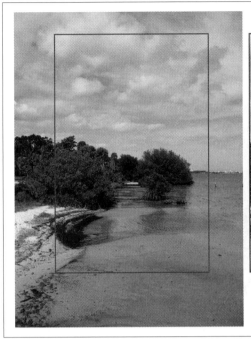

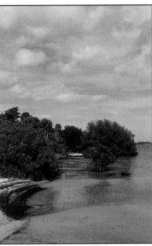

Figure 3-7:
When you print on standard-sized paper, you may have to choose the portion of your digital photo you want to keep.

Left: The photo as it came from the camera.

Right: After cropping–ready for a 4" × 6" print.

2. **Drag anywhere in your image to select the area you want to keep.**

The area outside the boundaries of your selection gets covered with a dark shield, indicating what you're discarding. To move the area you've chosen, just drag the *bounding box* (the outline) to wherever you want it.

You may find the Crop tool a little crotchety sometimes. See the box on page 92 for help making it behave.

3. **To resize your selection, drag one of the handles on the sides and corners.**

They look like little squares, as shown in Figure 3-8. You can drag in any direction, so you can also change the proportions of your crop if you want to.

TIP   You can rotate the crop area to any angle. This is a handy way to straighten *and* crop in one go. If you have a crooked image, turn the crop tool so that the outlines of the area are parallel to where straight should be in your photo and then crop. Elements straightens out your photo in the process.

4. **If you change your mind, click the Cancel button or press Esc.**

Elements undoes the selection so you can start over.

5. **When you're sure you've got the crop you want, press Enter or click the Commit button, or double-click inside the area you're going to keep, and you're done.**

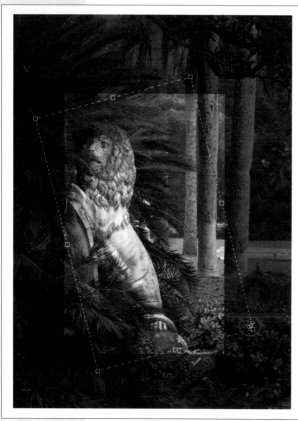

Figure 3-8:
If you want to change your selection from horizontal to vertical or vice versa, just move your cursor outside the cropped area and you'll see the rotation arrows (circled). Use them to rotate the crop's frame the same way you would a whole image. Rotating your selection doesn't rotate the photo—just the boundaries of the crop. When you're done, press Enter or click the Commit button to tell Elements you're satisfied. The Cancel button cancels your crop. (The symbols appear when you let go of the mouse button.)

TROUBLESHOOTING MOMENT

Crop Tool Idiosyncrasies

The Crop tool is cantankerous sometimes. People have called it "bossy," and that's a good word for it. Here are some settings that may help you control it better:

- **Turn off Snap To Grid.** You may find that you just can't position the crop selection exactly where you want it. Does the edge keep jumping slightly away from where you put it? Like most graphics programs, Elements uses a grid of invisible lines—called the *autogrid*—to help place things exactly (see the box on page 87 for details). Sometimes a grid is a big help, but in situations like this, it's a nuisance. If you hold down Ctrl, you can temporarily disable the autogrid. You can also get rid of the grid or adjust its spacing. To turn it off, first make the grid visible by going to View → Grid.

Then go to View → Snap To → Grid. You can adjust the grid's settings—things like the spacing, color, and whether you see a solid or dotted line—by going to Edit → Preferences → Guides & Grid.

- **Clear the Crop Tool.** Occasionally you may find that the Crop tool won't release a setting you entered, even after you clear the Options bar's boxes. For example, if the Crop tool won't let you drag where you want and keeps insisting on creating a particular-sized crop, you need to reset the Crop tool. Simply click the triangle at the left end of the Options bar, and then choose Reset Tool from the shortcut menu, as shown in Figure 3-9.

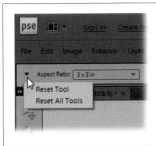

Figure 3-9:
If the Crop tool stops cooperating, there's an easy way to make it behave again: Click this tiny triangle in the Options bar, and then choose Reset Tool from the menu that appears. If you want all your tools to go back to their original settings, choose Reset All Tools.

Cropping an image to an exact size

You don't have to eyeball things when you're cropping a photo. You can enter any dimensions you want in the Options bar's Width and Height boxes or, from the Aspect Ratio menu, you can choose one of the presets, which automatically enters numbers for you. The Aspect Ratio menu includes several standard photo sizes, like 4"×6" and 8"×10". The No Restriction setting means you can drag freely. The Use Photo Ratio option lets you crop your image by using the same width/height proportions (the *aspect ratio*) as in the original. Figure 3-10 teaches you a time-saver: how to quickly swap the width and height numbers.

> **WARNING**   If you enter a number in the Resolution box that's different from your image's current resolution, the Crop tool resamples your image to match the new resolution. (Resolution is explained in the section on resizing, starting on page 103.) See page 110 to understand what resampling is and why it's not always a good thing.

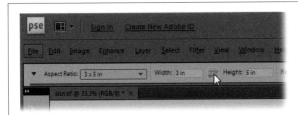

Figure 3-10:
If you want to change which number is the width setting and which is the height, just click these little arrows to swap them. So if you chose 3"×5" from the presets but want to switch to a landscape orientation, click the arrows (shown just above the cursor) to get 5"×3" instead.

Cropping with the Marquee Tool

The Crop tool is handy, but it wants to make decisions for you about several things you may want to control yourself. For instance, the Crop tool may decide to resample the image (see page 110) whether you want it to or not. It doesn't even warn you that it's resampling—it just does it.

For better control, you may prefer to use the Marquee tool. It's no harder than using the Crop tool, but you get to make all the decisions yourself.

There's one other big difference between using the Marquee tool and the Crop tool: With the Crop tool, all you can do to the area you selected is crop it. The Marquee tool, in contrast, lets you make lots of other changes to your selected area, like adjusting the color, which you may want to do before you crop.

To make a basic crop with the Marquee tool, follow these steps:

1. **Activate the Marquee tool.**

   Click the little dotted square in the Tools panel or press M. Figure 3-11 shows you the shape choices you get for the Marquee tool. For cropping, choose the Rectangular Marquee tool.

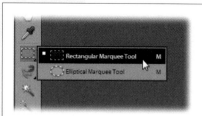

Figure 3-11:
Click the Marquee tool, and then choose the shape you want from this pop-out menu. The Tools panel icon shows you which shape is currently selected.

2. **Drag the selection marquee across the part of your photo you want to keep.**

   When you let go of the mouse button, your selected area is surrounded by the dotted lines shown in Figure 3-12. These are sometimes called "marching ants." (Get it? The dashes look like ants marching around your picture.) The area inside the marching ants is the part that you're keeping. (Chapter 5 has more about making selections.) If you make a mistake, press Ctrl+D to get rid of the selection and start over.

3. **Crop your photo.**

   Go to Image → Crop. The area outside your selection disappears, and your photo is cropped to the area you selected in step 2.

If you want to crop your photo to a particular aspect ratio, you can do that easily. Once the Marquee tool is active but before you drag, go to the Options bar. In the Mode menu, choose Fixed Ratio. Then enter the proportions you want in the Width and Height boxes. Finally, drag and crop as described in the previous list. Your photo will end up with exactly the proportions you entered in the Options bar.

You can also crop to an exact size with the Marquee tool:

1. **Check the resolution of your photo.**

   Go to Image → Resize → Image Size (or press Alt+Ctrl+I), and make sure the Resolution number is somewhere between 150 and 300 if you plan to print your cropped photo. You'll see that 300 is best, for reasons explained on page 107. If the number looks good, click OK and go to step 2.

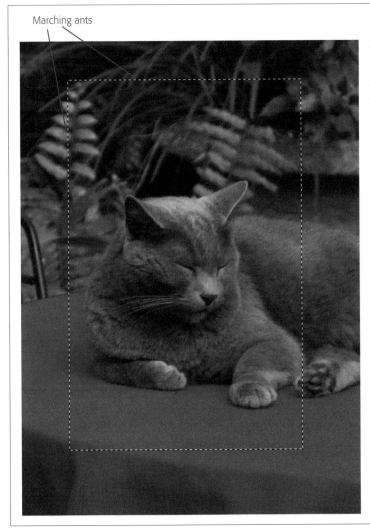

Marching ants

Figure 3-12:
When you let go after making your Marquee selection, you see the "marching ants" around the edge of your selection. You can reposition the marquee by dragging it—just put your cursor anywhere inside the selection marquee and then drag it.

If the resolution is too low, change the number in the Resolution box to what you want. Make sure that the Resample Image checkbox is turned off, and then click OK.

2. **Activate the Marquee tool.**

   Click the Marquee tool (the little dotted rectangle) in the Tools panel or press M. Choose the Rectangular Marquee tool.

3. **Enter your settings in the Options bar.**

   First, go to the Mode menu and choose Fixed Size. Next, enter the dimensions you want in the Width and Height boxes. (You can also change the unit of measurement from pixels to inches or centimeters if you want.)

4. **Drag anywhere in your image.**

You get a selection the exact size you chose in the Options bar. You can reposition it by dragging or using the arrow keys.

5. **Crop your Image.**

Go to Image → Crop.

The Cookie Cutter tool also gives you a way to create really interesting crops, as shown in Figure 3-13.

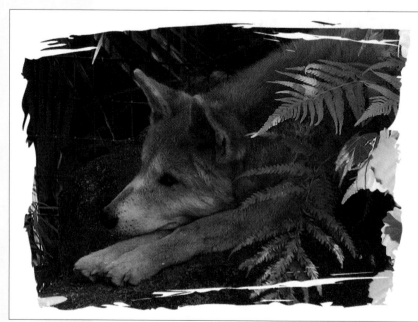

Figure 3-13:
With Elements' Cookie Cutter tool, you don't have to be square. The tool lets you crop your images to various shapes, from the kind of abstract border you see here, to heart- or star-shaped outlines. There's more on how to use the Cookie Cutter tool in Chapter 12.

TIP   If you're doing your own printing, there's no reason to restrict yourself to standard photo sizes like 4" × 6"—unless, of course, you need the image to fit a frame of that size. But most of the time, your images could just as well be square, or long and skinny, or whatever proportions you want. You can be especially inventive when sizing images for the Web. So don't feel that every photo you take has to be straitjacketed into a standard size.

Zooming and Repositioning Your View

Sometimes, rather than changing the size of your photo, all you want to do is change its appearance in Elements so you can get a better look at it. For example, you may want to zoom in on a particular area, or zoom out so you can see how edits you've made have affected your photo's overall look.

This section is about how to adjust your view of images. Nothing you do with the tools and commands covered in this section changes anything about your actual photo. You're just changing the way you see it. Elements gives you lots of tools and keystroke combinations to help with these new views; soon you'll probably find yourself making these changes without even thinking about them.

Image Views

Before you start changing your view of your photos, Elements gives you several different ways to position your image. Back in Chapter 1, you learned how to manage panels and bins. This section is just for image windows, which behave a little differently. In Elements 8, you have more choices than ever before, because you can choose between viewing your images as tabs or in their own windows. Elements automatically starts out using windows, but sometimes you may prefer to work with tabs. For instance, if you want to use the Transform commands (page 359), putting your image into a tab gives you plenty of room to pull the handles. There are a bunch of options for either view, and even if you're an Elements veteran, you should read this section in case you accidentally wind up in a view you didn't want, until you get the hang of the new system. Figure 3-14 shows the difference between tabs and windows.

To give yourself maximum viewing flexibility, go to Edit → Preferences → General and be sure that "Allow Floating Documents in Full Edit Mode" is turned on. When it's off, you're stuck with tabs no matter what you choose in the Editor's menus. When it's on, you can quickly switch back and forth between windows, tabs, or even a combination of the two.

Since accurate image viewing is crucial in Elements, Adobe gives you three main menus to control how your images display: the Window and View menus (logically enough), as well as the Arrange menu, which is the gray square to the right of the Help menu or to the right of the Elements logo (the blue "pse" square), depending on the size of the main Editor window. When you go to Window → Images, you get several choices of how to display your images:

- **Tile.** Your image windows or tabs appear edge to edge so they fill the available desktop space. For example, with two photos open, each gets half the workspace; with four photos, each gets one quarter of it, and so on. With tabs, you have a lot of additional options when you use the Arrange menu, described in Figure 3-15.

- **Cascade.** Your image windows appear in overlapping stacks (see Figure 3-14). Most people find Cascading windows the most practical view when they want to compare or work with two images. (This option is grayed out if you're working with tabs.)

- **Float in Window.** If you want to make a single image's tab into a window, click it to make it the active tab, and then choose this option.

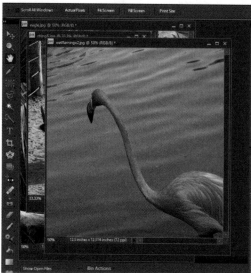

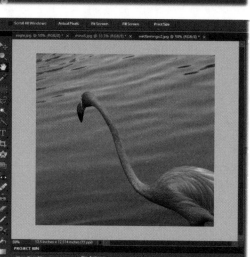

Figure 3-14:

Top: Three floating windows in Cascade view.

Bottom: The same three images as tabs. Notice that you only really see one image, with the others tucked away out of sight. You can change which image you see by clicking the tab of the image you want. (The workspace shown here is really small, so there's not much gray space around the image. But on your screen, the tab's background will fill all of the Elements desktop that isn't occupied by bins, however large the area may be.) The active image has a slightly darker tab, though that can be hard to see no matter which color-scheme you're using.

- **Float All in Windows.** If you have a bunch of tabs, choose this to make them all into floating windows.

- **Consolidate All to Tabs.** Got a lot of windows that you want to switch back to tabs? Here's the one-step command to turn all the windows back into tabs.

- **New Window.** Choose this command and you get a separate, duplicate window for your active image. This view is a terrific help when you're working on fine details. You can zoom way in on one view while keeping the other window in a regular view, so you don't lose track of where you are in the photo. (Don't worry about version control or remembering which window you're working in—both windows just show different views of the same image.)

- **Match Zoom.** All your windows get the same magnification level as the active window (the photo you're currently working on).

- **Match Location.** You see the same part of each image window, like the upper-right corner or the bottom-left edge. Elements makes all your windows match the active window.

Some of these commands are also in the new Arrange menu, but the Arrange menu includes a lot of options found nowhere else, as explained in Figure 3-15.

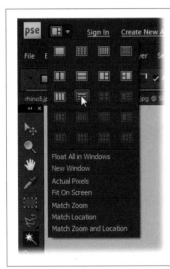

Figure 3-15:
To arrange your tabs to work with multiple images, just click the thumbnail for the layout you want. The top row shows general arrangements you can apply no matter how many images you have open. The lower section only offers arrangements possible for the number of images you have open (three, in this case). The rest are grayed out, since they don't pertain. If you have floating windows, clicking a thumbnail consolidates them all into tabs in the layout you chose.

The bottom section of the Arrange menu contains most of the commands described above, plus one additional choice:

- **Match Zoom and Location**. Select this option to see the same part of each of your tabs at the same zoom level.

Elements also gives you six handy commands for adjusting the view of your active image window. Go to the View menu, and you see:

- **New Window for.** This is the same as the New Window command in the Window menu, described above.

- **Zoom In/Out.** Zooming is explained on page 100. These menu commands are an alternative to using the actual Zoom tools.

TIP   You can zoom in or out using the View menu, but it's much faster to use the keyboard shortcuts so you don't have to keep trekking up to the menu. The short version: press Ctrl+= to zoom in and Ctrl+– (that's the Ctrl key plus the minus sign) to zoom out. The next section explains the Zoom tool in detail.

- **Fit on Screen.** This command makes your photo as large as it can be while still keeping the whole photo visible. You can also press Ctrl+0 to get this view.

- **Actual Pixels.** For the most accurate look at the onscreen size of your photo, go with this option. If you're creating graphics for the Web, this view shows how big your image will be in a web browser. Keyboard shortcut: Ctrl+1.

- **Print Size.** This view is really just a guess by Elements because it doesn't know exactly how big a pixel is on your monitor. But it's a rough approximation of the size your image would be if you printed it at its current resolution. (Resolution is explained on page 103 in the section on resizing photos.)

To adjust your view of a particular image, Elements gives you three useful tools: The Zoom tool, the Hand tool, and the Navigator panel, all of which are explained in the following sections. While you may find the whole tab vs. window business a little confusing at first, it gives you lots of ways to stay organized while you work. The box below has some additional tips for keeping things under control.

ORGANIZATION STATION

Window Management Hints

In addition to the various menu commands discussed in this section, there's another way to control whether you have tabs or windows without trekking up to the menu bar: dragging. Here are a few shortcuts:

- **Turn a tab into a window.** Just grab the tab's title bar and drag down. The tab pops off into a floating window.

- **Turn a window into a tab.** Drag up toward the Options bar till you see a blue outline around the desktop. The blue outline is Elements' way of telling you that if you let go of the mouse button, it'll consolidate your window with the outlined area, just like it consolidates panels (see page 27).

- **Create tabs in a floating window.** If you want to put two images in one floating window (say you're working on combining elements from many different images, and it's getting hard to know which is where), just drag one window's title bar to another

window's title bar, and let go when you see the blue outline. You now have a floating window with two tabs. (Repeat this trick as many times as you want for a multitabbed window.)

- **Avoid making tabs.** When you're working with floating windows, if the tops of the windows move too close together, Elements wants to combine them. If you're dragging windows around and you see the telltale blue outline, just keep going till it disappears.

- **Undo accidental tabs.** If you create a tab you didn't mean to, just grab the top of the image you want to free, and drag it loose from the tab group.

Just remember that in Elements 8, anytime you're dragging something and a blue outline appears, what you're dragging is going to consolidate with something if you let go. Keep moving till the outline disappears if you don't want that to happen.

The Zoom Tool

Some of Elements' tools require you to get a really close look at your image to see what's going on. Sometimes you need to see the actual pixels as you work, as shown in Figure 3-16. The Zoom tool makes it easy to zoom your view in and out.

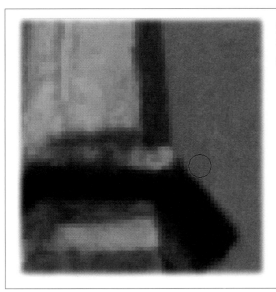

Figure 3-16:
There are times when you want to zoom way, way in.
You may even need to go pixel by pixel in tricky spots, as
shown here.

The Zoom tool's Tools panel icon is a little magnifying glass. Click it or press Z to activate the tool. Once you do that, you see circle icons at the left end of the Options bar. If you want to zoom in, click the one with the + sign on it. To use the Zoom tool, just click the spot in your photo where you want the zoom to focus. The point you click becomes the center of your view, and the view size increases again each time you click.

You can also select the Zoom Out tool in the Options bar by clicking the circle with the minus (–) sign on it.

> TIP   If you hold Alt as you click, the selected Zoom tool zooms in the opposite direction; for instance, the Zoom In tool zooms out rather than in.

The Zoom tool has several Options bar settings:

- **Zoom percent.** Enter a number here and the view immediately jumps to that percentage. The maximum is 3200 percent, and the minimum is 1 percent.

- **Resize Windows To Fit.** Turn this checkbox on and your image windows get larger and smaller as you zoom, along with the view size of the image. The image always fills the whole window with no gray space around it.

- **Zoom All Windows.** If you have more than one image window, turn this option on and the view changes in all the windows simultaneously when you zoom in one window. (This option works with tabs, too, so be careful. You may be zooming a hidden image when you don't want to.)

> TIP   If you hold down the Shift key while zooming in, all your windows zoom together. You don't need to go to the Options bar to activate this feature.

- **Actual Pixels.** This button (which is labeled "1:1") has the same effect as choosing Actual Pixels from the View menu. It's explained on page 100.

- **Fit Screen.** This button does the same thing as the View menu's "Fit on Screen" command—see page 100.

- **Fill Screen.** This makes your photo fill the whole viewing area, even if it doesn't all fit onscreen at once.

- **Print Size.** Another duplicate of a View menu command. See page 100 for the lowdown.

> **TIP** You don't need to bother with the Zoom tool at all—you can use your keyboard instead. Press Ctrl+= to zoom in and Ctrl+– (that's the Ctrl key plus the minus sign) to zoom out. Just hold down Ctrl and keep tapping the equal or minus sign until you see what you want. (You can zoom to 100 percent by double-clicking the Zoom tool's Tools panel icon.) It doesn't matter which tool you're using—you can always zoom in or out this way. Because you'll do a lot of zooming in Elements, these keyboard shortcuts are ones to remember.
>
> If you have a mouse with a scroll wheel, you can use that to zoom, too. Go to Edit → Preferences → General and turn on the "Zoom with Scroll Wheel" checkbox.

The Hand Tool

With all that zooming, sometimes you can't see your whole image at once. Elements includes the Hand tool to help you change which part of your image appears onscreen. It's super easy to use: Just click the little hand in the Tools panel or press H to activate it.

When the Hand tool is active, your cursor turns into the little hand shown in Figure 3-17. Drag with the hand to move your photo around in the window. This tool is really helpful when you're zoomed way in or working on a large image.

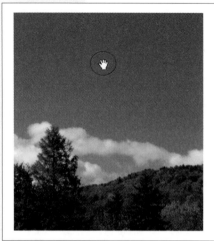

Figure 3-17:
The easiest way to activate the Hand tool is to press the space bar on your keyboard. You can tell the Hand tool is active by seeing this little white-gloved cursor. No matter what you're doing in Elements, pressing the space bar calls up the Hand tool. When you let go of the space bar, Elements switches back to the tool you were previously using.

The Hand tool gives you the same All Windows option you get with the Zoom tool (page 100), but you don't have to use the Options bar to activate it. Just hold down Shift while using the Hand tool, and all your windows scroll in sync. The Hand tool also gives you the same three buttons (Actual Pixels, Fit Screen, and Print Size) as the Zoom tool. Once again, they're the same as the menu commands described on page 100.

Figure 3-18 shows the Hand tool's somewhat more sophisticated assistant, the Navigator panel, which is really useful for working on big photos or when you want to have a slider handy for micromanaging the zoom level. Go to Window → Navigator to call it up.

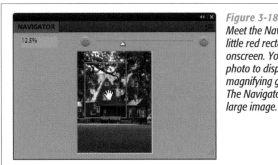

Figure 3-18:
Meet the Navigator. You can travel around your image by dragging the little red rectangle—it marks the area of your photo that you see onscreen. You can also enter a percentage for the size you want your photo to display at, move the slider, or click the zoom in/out magnifying glasses on either side of the slider to change the view. The Navigator is perfect for keeping track of where you are in a large image.

Changing the Size of an Image

The previous section explained how to resize your *view* of an image—how it appears on your monitor. But sometimes you need to change the actual size of your image, and that's what this section is about.

Resizing photos brings you up against a pretty tough concept in digital imaging: *resolution,* which measures, in pixels, the amount of detail your image can show. Where it gets confusing is that resolution for printing and for onscreen use (like for email and the Web) are quite different.

For example, you need many more pixels to create a good-looking print than you do to view a photo clearly onscreen. A photo that's going to print well almost always has too many pixels in it to display easily onscreen, and as a result, its file is usually pretty hefty for emailing. So you often need two copies of your photo for the two different uses. If you want to know more about the nitty-gritty of resolution, a good place to start is *www.scantips.com.*

This section gives you a brief introduction to both screen and print resolution, especially in terms of what decisions you'll need to make when using the Resize Image dialog box. You'll also learn how to add more canvas (more blank space) around your photos. You can add canvas to make room for a caption below your image, for instance, or when you want to combine two photos.

To get started, open a photo you want to resize and go to Image → Resize → Image Size (Figure 3-19).

Resizing Images for Email and the Web

It's important to learn how to size your photos so that they show up easily and clearly onscreen. Have you ever gotten an emailed photo that was so huge you could see only a tiny bit of it on your monitor at once? That happens when someone sends an image that isn't optimized to view onscreen. It's easy to avoid that problem—once you know how to correctly size your photos for onscreen viewing.

The Image Size dialog box has two main sections: Pixel Dimensions and Document Size. You'll use the Pixel Dimensions settings when you know your image is only going to be viewed onscreen. (Document Size is for printing, which is covered in the next section.)

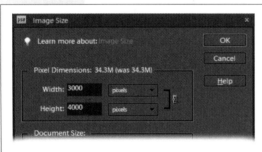

Figure 3-19:
The Image Size dialog box gives you two different ways to change the size of your photo. Use the Pixel Dimensions section (shown here) when preparing a photo for onscreen viewing. (The number next to Pixel Dimensions–here, 34. 3M–tells you the current size of your file in megabytes [as in this example] or in kilobytes.) Before you can make any changes here, you have to turn on the Resample Image checkbox at the bottom part of the dialog box (not visible here), since changing pixel dimensions always involves resampling (see page 110).

A monitor is concerned only with the size of a photo as measured in pixels, known as the *pixel dimensions*. On a monitor, a pixel is always the same size (unlike a printer, which can change the size of the pixels it prints). Your monitor doesn't know anything about pixels per inch (ppi), and it can't change the way it displays a photo even if you change the photo's ppi settings, as shown in Figure 3-20. (Graphics programs like Elements can change the size of your onscreen view by, say, zooming in, but most programs, like web browsers, can't.)

All you have to decide is how many pixels long and how many pixels wide you want your photo to be. You control those measurements in the Pixel Dimensions section of the Image Size dialog box.

What dimensions should you use? That depends a little on who's going to see your photos, but as a general rule, small monitors today are usually 1024 pixels wide by 768 pixels high. Some monitors, like the largest Dell and Apple models, have many more pixels than that, of course. Still, if you want to be sure that people who see your photo won't have to scroll, a good rule of thumb is to choose no more than 650 pixels for the longer side of your photo, whether that's the width or the height.

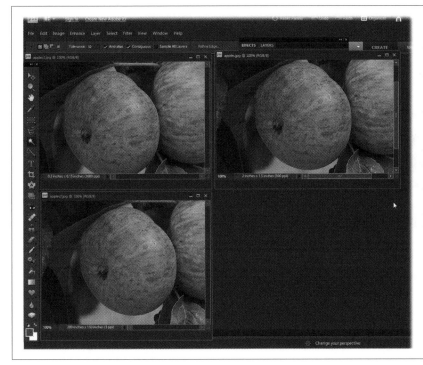

Figure 3-20:
This shows that your monitor doesn't care about the ppi settings you enter. One of these apple photos was saved at 3000 ppi, another at 300 ppi, and one at 3 ppi. Can you tell which is which? Nope. They all look exactly the same on your monitor because they all have exactly the same pixel dimensions, which is the only resolution setting your monitor understands.

If you want people to be able to see more than one image at a time, you may want to make your photos even smaller than that. Also, some people still set their monitors to display only 800 pixels wide by 600 pixels high, so you may want to make even smaller images to send to them.

On the other hand, if you send really small pictures to people with deluxe, high-resolution monitors where the individual pixels are miniscule, they're likely to complain that the photos are too tiny to see in detail. So if you send to a varied group of folks, you may need to make different copies for different audiences. On the whole, it's better to err on the side of caution—nobody will have trouble receiving and opening an image that's too small, while an overly large attachment can cause problems for people with small mailboxes.

TIP   To get the most accurate look at how your photo displays on a monitor, go to View → Actual Pixels.

Also, although a photo is always the same pixel dimensions, you really can't control the exact inch dimensions at which those pixels display on other people's monitors. A pixel is always the same size on any given monitor (as long as you don't change the monitor's screen resolution), but different monitors have different-sized pixels these days. Figure 3-21 may help you grasp this concept.

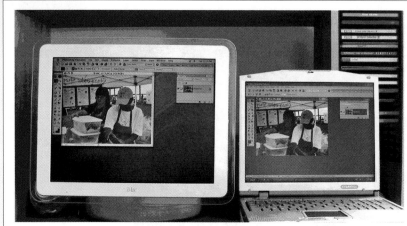

Figure 3-21:
Both these monitors have a resolution of 1024 × 768 pixels, and the photo they're displaying takes up exactly the same percentage of each screen. But the picture on the left is larger because the monitor is physically larger—in other words, the individual pixels are bigger.

NOTE In the following sections, you'll learn what to do when you want to *reduce* the size of an image. It's much easier to get good results making a photo smaller than larger. Elements does let you *increase* the size of your image, using a technique called upsampling (explained on page 110), but you often get mediocre results. The section on resampling (page 110) explains why.

To resize your photos, start by making extra sure you're not resizing your original. You're going to be shedding pixels that you can't get back, so if your photo's not already in the Organizer, resize a copy (File → Duplicate) rather than the original. Here's what you do:

1. **Call up the Image Size dialog box.**

   Go to Image → Resize → Image Size, or press Alt+Ctrl+I.

2. **Turn on Resample Image at the bottom of the dialog box.**

   You won't be able to make any changes to the pixel dimensions in the top part of the window until you do this.

3. **In the Pixel Dimensions area, enter the dimension you want for the longer side of your photo.**

   Usually you want 650 pixels or less, unless you know for sure that your recipients have up-to-date equipment and broadband Internet connections. Be sure to choose pixels as the unit of measurement. You just need to enter a number for one dimension. Elements automatically figures the other dimension as long as Constrain Proportions is turned on down near the bottom of the dialog box.

4. **Check the settings at the bottom of the dialog box.**

   Scale Styles doesn't matter, so leave it off. Constrain Proportions and Resample Image should be turned on. (*Resampling* means changing the number of pixels in your image.) The Resample Image menu lists the different resampling methods.

Adobe recommends Bicubic Sharper when you're making an image smaller, but you may want to experiment with the other menu options if you don't like the results Bicubic Sharper gives you. (In Elements 8, you'll see the suggested use for each method in parentheses after its name in the menu.)

5. Click OK.

Elements resizes your photo, although you may not immediately see a difference onscreen. (Go to View → Actual Pixels before and after you resize and you'll see the difference.) Save your resized photo to make your changes permanent.

Sometimes Elements resizes an image automatically—for example, when you use the Organizer's E-Mail command (see page 512). But the method described here gives you more control than letting Elements make all the decisions for you.

TIP   If you're concerned about file size, use "Save for Web" (see page 504), which helps you create smaller files.

Resizing for Printing

If you want great prints, you need to think about your photo's resolution quite differently than you do for images that you email. For printing, as a general rule, the more pixels your photo has, the better. That's the reason camera manufacturers keep packing more megapixels into their new models—the more pixels you have, the larger you can print your photo and still have it look terrific.

TIP   Even before you take your photos, you can do a lot toward making them print well if you always choose the largest size and the highest quality setting on your camera (typically Extra Fine, Superfine, or Fine).

When you print, you need to think about two things: the photo's size in inches (or whatever your preferred unit of measurement is) and its resolution in pixels per inch (ppi). Those settings work together to control the quality of your print.

Your printer is a virtuoso that plays your pixels like an accordion. It can squeeze the pixels together and make them smaller, or spread the pixels out and make them larger. Generally speaking, the denser the pixels (the higher the ppi), the higher the resolution of your photo and the better it looks.

If you don't have enough pixels in your photo, the print will look *pixelated*—very jagged and blurry. The goal is to have enough pixels in your photo so that they'll be packed fairly densely—ideally about 300 ppi.

You usually don't get a visibly better result if you go over 300 ppi, though—you just have a larger file. And depending on your tastes, you may be content with your results at a lower ppi. For instance, some photos taken with Canon cameras come into Elements at 180 ppi, and you may be happy with how they print. But 200 ppi is usually considered about the lowest density for an acceptable print. Figure 3-22 illustrates why it's so important to have a high ppi setting.

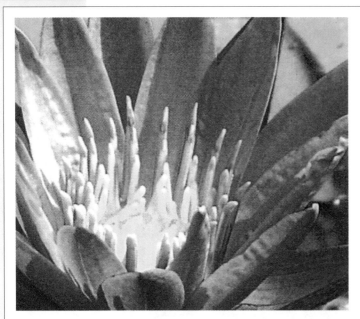

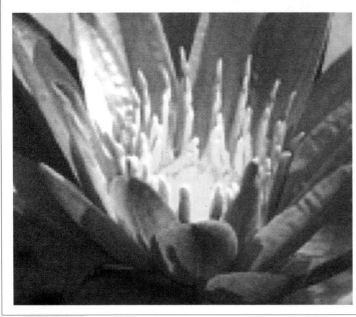

Figure 3-22:
Different resolution settings can dramatically alter the quality of a print. These photos have been printed and then scanned so you can see the results of printing them.

Top: A photo with a resolution of 300 ppi.

Bottom: The same photo with a resolution of 72 ppi. Too few pixels stretched too far causes this kind of blocky, blurry print. When you can see individual pixels, a photo is said to be pixelated.

To set the size of an image for printing:

1. **Call up the Image Size dialog box.**

   Go to Image → Resize → Image Size, or press Alt+Ctrl+I.

2. **Check your image's resolution.**

   Take a look at the Document Size section of the dialog box (see Figure 3-23). Start by checking the ppi (pixels/inch) setting. If it's too low, like 72 ppi, go to the bottom of the dialog box and turn off Resample Image. Then enter the ppi you want in the Document Size area. The dimensions should become smaller to reflect the greater density of the pixels. If they don't, click OK, and then open the dialog box again.

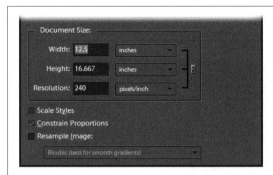

Figure 3-23:
Crop your image to the shape you want (see page 89), and then use this section of the Image Size dialog box to set its size for printing.

3. **Check the physical size of your photo.**

   Look at the Width and Height numbers in the Document Size area. Are they what you want? If so, you're all done. Click OK.

4. **If the size numbers aren't right, resize your photo.**

   If the proportions of your image aren't what you want, crop the photo (page 89) and then come back to the Image Size dialog box. (Don't try to reshape an image using this dialog box.)

   Once you've cropped the image and opened the dialog box again, turn on Resample Image and choose Bicubic Smoother from the drop-down menu. (This setting is Adobe's recommendation, but you may find that you prefer one of the other resampling choices.)

   Make sure that Constrain Proportions is turned on, and then enter the size you want for the width or height. (Elements calculates the other dimension for you.) Scale Styles doesn't matter, so leave it off.

5. **Click OK.**

   Your photo is resized and ready for printing.

Resampling

Resampling is an image-editing term for changing the number of pixels in an image. When you resample, the results are permanent, so you want to avoid resampling an original photo if you can help it. As a rule, it's easier to get good results when you *downsample* (make your photo smaller) than when you *upsample* (make your photo larger).

When you upsample, you're *adding* pixels to your image. Elements has to get them from somewhere, so it makes them up. Elements is pretty good at this, but these pixels are never as good as the pixels that were in your photo to begin with, as you can see from Figure 3-24. You can download the figure (*russian_box.jpg*) from the Missing CD page at *www.missingmanuals.com* if you'd like to try this yourself. Zoom in really close so you can see the pixels.

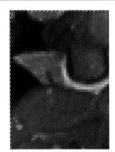
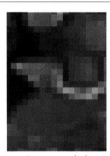
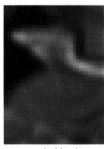

Figure 3-24:
Here's a closeup look at what happens to a photo when you resample it.

The photo as it came from the camera.

Downsampled to 72 ppi.

Upsampled back to the original resolution. See how soft the pixels look compared to the original?

When you enlarge an image to more than 100 percent of its original size, you'll definitely lose some of the original quality. So, for example, if you try to stretch a photo that's 3" wide at 180 ppi to an 8" × 10" print, don't be surprised if the results look pretty bad.

Elements offers several resampling methods, and they do a really good job when you find the right one for your situation. You select them from the Resample Image menu in the Image Size dialog box. Adobe recommends choosing Bicubic Smoother when you're upsampling (enlarging) images and Bicubic Sharper when you're downsampling (reducing) photos, but you may prefer one of the others. It's worth experimenting with them all to see which you like.

Adding Canvas

Just like the works of Monet and Matisse, your photos appear in Elements on digital "canvases." Sometimes you'll want to add more canvas to make room for text or to combine photos into a collage.

You can add canvas in either tabbed or window views. To make your canvas larger, go to Image → Resize → Canvas Size. You can change the canvas size using a variety of measurements. If you don't know exactly how much more canvas you want, choose "percent" from the Width and Height drop-down menus. Then you can guesstimate that you want, say, 2 percent more canvas or 50 percent more. Figure 3-25 shows how to get your photo into the right place on the new canvas.

Changing the size of your canvas doesn't change the size of your picture any more than pasting a postcard onto a full-size sheet of paper changes the size of the postcard. In both cases, all you get is more empty space around your picture.

> NOTE   If you just want to add canvas to the bottom of your image for a caption, check out the action in Guided Edit (page 32).

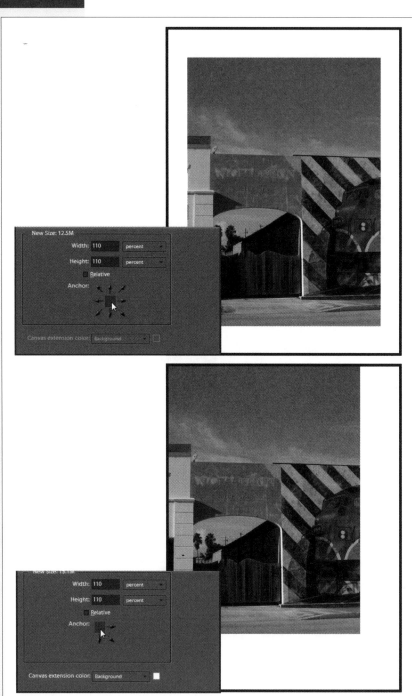

Figure 3-25:
The Canvas Size dialog box isn't as complicated as it looks. The strange little Anchor grid with arrows pointing everywhere lets you decide exactly where to add new canvas to your image. The Anchor box represents your photo's current position, and the arrows surrounding it show where Elements will add canvas. By clicking any of the surrounding arrows, you tell Elements where to position your photo on the newly sized canvas. In the top pair of images, the canvas was added equally around all sides of the image. In the bottom pair, the new canvas was added below and to the right of the image.

Part Two:
Elemental Elements

2

The Quick Fix

With Elements' Quick Fix tools, you can dramatically improve the appearance of a photo with just a click or two. The Quick Fix window gathers easy-to-use tools that help adjust the brightness and color of your photos and make them look sharper. You don't even need to understand much about what you're doing—just click a button or slide a pointer, and then decide whether you like how it looks.

Even if you *do* know what you're doing, you may still find yourself using the Quick Fix window for things like shadows and highlights because Quick Fix gives you a before-and-after view as you work. Also, the Temperature and Tint sliders can come in very handy for advanced color tweaking, like finessing the overall color of your otherwise finished photo. You also get two tools—the Selection brush and the Quick Selection tool—to help make changes to only a certain area of your photo. Besides making general fixes, do you want to whiten teeth, make the sky more blue, or even make part of a picture black and white? It's a snap to do any of these in the Quick Fix window. And in Elements 8, Adobe has made it easier to decide just what to do by adding a number of *presets* to the adjustments; you'll learn about them on page 119. You can pick one of the presets as a starting point if you need extra help.

In this chapter, you'll learn how (and in which order) to use the Quick Fix tools. If you have a newish digital camera, you may find that Quick Fix gives you everything you need to take your photos from pretty darn good to dazzling.

NOTE   If a whole chapter on Quick Fix is frustratingly slow, you can start off by trying out the ultrafast Auto Smart Fix—a quick-fix tool for the truly impatient. Page 38 tells you everything you need to know. Also, Guided Edit may give you enough help to accomplish what you want to do; page 32 has the full story.

The Quick Fix Window

Getting to the Quick Fix window from the Editor is easy: Just click the Edit tab's down arrow and choose EDIT Quick. If you're in the Organizer, click the Fix tab → Quick Photo Edit.

NOTE   In Elements 8, Adobe has made it a lot easier to apply many quick fixes right from the Organizer, even in Full Screen view. See the box below for details.

GEM IN THE ROUGH

Quick Fixes from the Organizer

The Organizer gives you several ways to apply the Quick Fix's Auto fixes without even launching the Editor. The Fix tab has buttons that let you automatically fix red eye, apply Auto Smart Fix, Auto Color, Auto Levels, Auto Contrast, Auto Sharpen, or crop your photo right in the Organizer. For more selective editing, you'll still want the Editor, but if Auto's your thing, you'll be very happy staying in the Organizer. If you use the Organizer, you get the added benefit of having your fixes automatically made on a copy, which Elements saves in a *version set* (page 68) with your original. Read on for more about what these tools do. They work the same way regardless of where you are when you use them.

There are two ways to get to the Organizer fixes:

• **Just click it.** In the main Organizer window, click the Fix tab to start auto-fixing.

• **Use Full Screen View.** In the Elements 8 Organizer, when you press F11 (for Full Screen view) or F12 (for side-by-side comparisons), a new Quick Edit panel appears at the left of your screen (it tends to hide itself, so you may need to click its edge to pop it open). Each icon is a button for one of the auto fixes. Just click one to apply that fix while you've got a large view of your photo—very handy for fixing as you preview a newly imported batch of photos, for example. (You can also get to these views from the Display button in the menu bar.)

The Quick Fix window looks like a stripped-down version of the Full Edit window (see Figure 4-1).

Your tools are neatly arranged on both sides of the image: On the left, there's an eight-item toolbox; on the right, there's a collection of quick-edit panels (Figure 4-2) stored inside the Panel bin. First, you'll take a quick look at the tools Quick Fix offers. Later in the chapter, you'll learn how to actually use them.

TIP   If you need extra help, check out Guided Edit (page 32), which walks you step by step through a lot of basic editing projects.

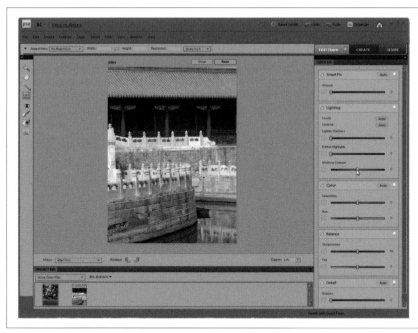

Figure 4-1:
The Quick Fix window. If you have several photos open when you launch this window, you can use the Project bin (page 28) at the bottom of the window to choose the one you want to edit. Just double-click an image's thumbnail, and that photo becomes the active image—the one that appears front and center in the Quick Fix preview area. See Figure 4-2 for a close-up view of the right-side quick-edit panels.

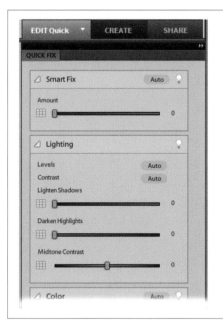

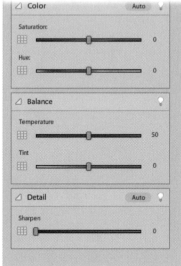

Figure 4-2:
A close-up look at all the ways you can enhance your photos with Quick Fix. The left figure shows the top part of the Panel bin; the right, the bottom part. Besides these handy tools, you can also use most of the Full Edit menu commands if you need something more than the Panel bin provides.

The Quick Fix Toolbox

The toolbox holds an easy-to-navigate subset of the Full Edit window's larger tool collection. All the tools work the same way in both modes, and you can also use the same keystrokes to switch tools here. From top to bottom, here's what you get:

- **The Zoom tool** lets you telescope in and out on your image—perfect for getting a good close look at details or pulling back to see the whole photo. (See page 100 for more on how this tool works.) You can also zoom by using the Zoom drop-down menu in the lower-right corner of the image preview area.

- **The Hand tool** helps move your photo around in the image window—just like grabbing it and moving it with your own five fingers. You can read more about this tool on page 102.

- **The Quick Selection tool** lets you apply Quick Fix commands to select portions of your image. You can also use the regular Elements Selection brush in Quick Fix. To get to the Selection brush, in the toolbox, just click the Quick Selection tool's icon and hold down your mouse button; then choose the Selection brush from the menu that appears. What's the difference between the two tools? The Selection brush lets you paint a selection exactly where you want it (or mask out part of your photo to keep it from getting changed), while the Quick Selection tool makes Elements figure out the boundaries of your selection based on your much less precise marks on the image. The Quick Selection tool is much more automatic than the regular Selection brush. You can read more about these brushes beginning on page 143. To get the most out of both these tools, you need to understand the concept of selections. Chapter 5 tells you everything you need to know, including the details of using these brushes.

- **The Crop tool** lets you change the size and shape of your photo by cutting off the areas you *don't* want (see page 89).

- **The Red Eye tool** lets you darken those demonic-looking red flash reflections in people's eyes. It's explained on page 121.

> **TIP** If the contents of your photo need straightening (see page 85), usually it's easier to do that in Full Edit before bringing it into the Quick Fix window, since the Quick Fix toolbox doesn't include the Straighten tool. However, there's a sneaky way to straighten with the Crop tool that you can use in Quick Fix, too—see page 91.

All the tools just listed are ones you also see in Full Edit, but the bottom part of the Quick Fix toolbox includes three tools you won't find anywhere else in Elements:

- **Touch Up tools.** From top to bottom, these buttons let you whiten teeth, make the sky more blue, or turn part of a photo to black and white. Their icons make it clear which is which, and you'll learn how to use them beginning on page 130.

The Quick Fix Panel Bin

When you switch to Quick Fix, the Task panel presents you with the Quick Fix Panel bin. The Panel bin is where you make the majority of your adjustments. Elements helpfully arranges everything into five panels—Smart Fix, Lighting, Color, Balance, and Detail—listed in the order you'll typically use them. In most cases, it makes sense to start at the top and work your way down until you get the results you want. (See page 133 for more suggestions on what order to work in.)

> **NOTE** There's one exception to this top-to-bottom order of operations—if you need to fix red-eye problems (page 121). The Red Eye tool is in the toolbox on the left of the window. You may want to jump over there first and use the Red Eye tool before you do your other editing.

The Panel bin always fills the right side of the Quick Fix screen. You can't drag the panels out of the Panel bin as you can in Standard Edit mode, but you can collapse the bin by clicking the double arrows in its upper-right corner. And you can expand and collapse the individual panels within the bin, as explained in Figure 4-3.

> **NOTE** If you go into Quick Fix mode *before* opening a photo, you won't see the pointers in the sliders, just empty tracks. Don't worry—they'll automatically appear as soon as you open a photo and give them something to work on.

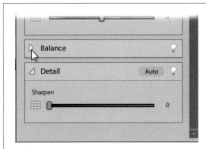

Figure 4-3:
Clicking any of these flippy triangles collapses or expands that section of the Panel bin. If you have a small screen, the Detail section at the bottom of the Panel bin may not show, so you can collapse one of the other sections you're not using to bring it into view. You can also use the slider on the right to scroll through the panels.

Using presets

Elements 8 has a new feature to help the undecided—presets. To the left of the sliders in the Panel bin are little grid-like squares (see Figure 4-4). If you think you need to use a particular slider but you aren't sure, click its square, and a grid of nine tiny thumbnails appears below the slider. Each thumbnail represents a different preset for that slider. There are presets for all the Quick Fix sliders.

If you don't have super-micro vision, you probably think these thumbnails are too darn small for you to be able to tell the difference—but not so fast: Run your cursor over a thumbnail, and Elements previews that setting on your image itself, so you can get a view as large as you need. You can even adjust the slider right from the thumbnail as explained in Figure 4-4. Once you like what you see, just click to apply the change to your photo. To reset your image to when you began using the current group of presets, click the thumbnail with the curved arrow on it.

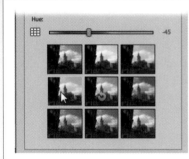

Figure 4-4:
Hover your cursor over any of the thumbnails to see the effect displayed on your photo. To adjust the strength of the effect, just click the thumbnail that's closest to what you want, and then drag left or right (this is called "scrubbing") and watch as your image changes. Click the thumbnail with the curved arrow to return your photo to when you opened that preset group.

Different Views: After vs. "Before and After"

When you open an image in Quick Fix, your picture first appears by itself in the main window with the word "After" above it to let you know that you're in After Only view. Elements keeps the Before view—your original photo—tucked out of sight. But you can pick from three other layouts, which you can choose anytime: Before Only, "Before and After—Horizontal", and "Before and After—Vertical". Both of the "Before and After" views are especially helpful when you're trying to figure out if you're improving your picture—or not—as shown in Figure 4-5. Switch between views by picking the one you want from the View pop-up menu just below your image.

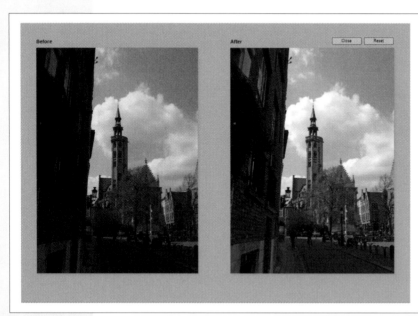

Figure 4-5:
The "Before and After" views in the Quick Fix window make it easy to see how you're changing your photo. Here you see "Before and After—Horizontal", which displays the views side by side. To see them one above the other, choose "Before and After—Vertical". If you want a more detailed view, use the Zoom tool (page 100) to focus on just a portion of your picture.

NOTE   Quick Fix limits the amount of screen space available for your image. If you want a larger view while you work, click over to Full Edit.

Editing Your Photos

The tools in the Quick Fix window are pretty easy to use. You can try one or all of them—it's up to you. And whenever you're happy with how your photo looks, you can leave Quick Fix and go back to the Full Edit window or the Organizer.

If you want to rotate your photo, click either of the Rotate buttons below the image preview area. (See page 84 for more about rotating photos.)

> **TIP** If you click the Reset button just above your image, you'll return your photo to the way it looked *before* you started working in Quick Fix. This button undoes *all* Quick Fix edits, so don't use it if you want to undo a single action only. For that, just use the regular Undo command: Edit → Undo or Ctrl+Z.

Fixing Red Eye

Everyone who's ever taken a flash photo has run into the dreaded problem of *red eye*—those glowing, demonic pupils that make your little cherub look like someone out of an Anne Rice novel. Red eye is even more of a problem with digital cameras than with film, but luckily, Elements has a simple and terrific Red Eye tool for fixing it. All you need to do is click the red spots with the Red Eye Removal tool, and your problems are solved. This tool works the same whether you use it in Quick Fix or Full Edit.

To use the Quick Fix Red Eye tool:

1. **Open a photo.**

2. **Zoom in so you can see where you're clicking.**

   Use the Zoom tool to magnify the eyes. You can also switch to the Hand tool if you need to drag the photo so that the eyes are front and center.

3. **Activate the Red Eye tool.**

   Click the Red Eye icon in the toolbox or press Y (this keystroke works in Full Edit, too).

4. **Click the red part of the pupil (see Figure 4-6).**

   That's it. Just one click should fix it. If a single click doesn't fix the problem, you can press Ctrl+Z to undo it, and then try dragging the Red Eye tool over the pupil. Sometimes one method works better than the other. And as explained in a moment, you can also adjust two settings on the Red Eye tool: Darken Amount and Pupil Size.

5. **Click in the other eye.**

   Repeat the process on the other eye, and you're done.

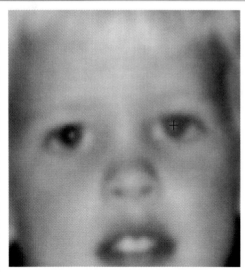

Figure 4-6:
Zoom in when using the Red Eye tool so you get a good look at the pupils. The eye on the left side of the picture has already been fixed. Don't worry if your photo looks so magnified that it loses definition—just make the red area large enough so you can hit it right in the center. Notice what a good job the Red Eye tool does of keeping the highlights (called catch lights) in the eye that's been treated.

NOTE   You can also apply the Organizer's Auto Red Eye Fix in either the Quick Fix or Full Edit window. In either window, just press Ctrl+R or go to Enhance → Auto Red Eye Fix. In Full Edit you can also activate the Red Eye tool, and click the Auto button in the Options bar. The only tradeoff to using the Auto Red Eye Fix in the Editor is you don't automatically get a version set (as you do when using the tool from in the Organizer). But you can create a version set when you save your changes, as explained on page 68.

POWER USERS' CLINIC

Another Red Eye Fix

The Red Eye tool does a great job most of the time, but it doesn't always work, and it doesn't work on animals' eyes. Elements gives you a couple of other ways to fix red eye that work in almost any situation. Here's one:

1. **Zoom way, way in on the eye.** You want to be able to see the individual pixels.

2. **Use the Eyedropper tool (page 234) to sample the color from a good area of the eye, or from another photo.** Confirm that you've got the color you want by checking the Foreground color square (page 231).

3. **Get out the Pencil tool (page 378) and set its size to 1 pixel.**

4. **Now click the bad or empty pixels of the eye to replace the color with the correct shade.** Remember to leave a couple of white pixels for a catch light (the pupil's glinting center highlight).

This solution works even if the eye is *blown out* (that is, all white with no color information left).

If you're a layers fan, you can also fix red eye by selecting the bad area, creating a Hue/Saturation Adjustment layer (page 196), and desaturating the red area. (This method doesn't work so well if the eye is blown out.)

If you need to adjust how the Red Eye tool works, the Options bar gives you two controls, although 99 percent of the time you can ignore them:

- **Darken Amount.** If the result is too light, increase the percentage in this box.

- **Pupil Size.** Increase or decrease the number here to tell Elements how much area to consider part of a pupil.

TIP   You can also fix red eye right in the Raw converter (page 248) if you're dealing with Raw format photos.

Smart Fix

The secret weapon in the Quick Fix window is the Smart Fix command, which automatically adjusts a picture's lighting, color, and contrast, all with one click. You don't have to figure anything out. Elements does it all for you.

You'll find the Smart Fix in the aptly named Smart Fix panel, and it's about as easy to use as hitting the speed dial button on your phone: Click the Auto button, and if the stars are aligned, your picture will immediately look better. (Figure 4-7 gives you a glimpse of its capabilities. If you want to see for yourself how this fix works, download this photo—*iris.jpg*—from this book's Missing CD page at *www. missingmanuals.com*.)

TIP   You'll find Auto buttons scattered throughout Elements. The program uses them to make a best-guess attempt to implement whatever change the Auto button is next to (Smart Fix, Levels, Contrast, and so on). It never hurts to at least try clicking these Auto buttons; if you don't like what you see, you can always perform the magical undo: Edit → Undo or Ctrl+Z.

If you're happy with Auto Smart Fix's changes, you can move onto a new photo, or try sharpening your photo a little (see page 129) if the focus appears a bit soft. You don't need to do anything to accept the Smart Fix changes. But if you're not thrilled with the results, take a good look at your picture. If you like what Auto Smart Fix did but the effect is too strong or too weak, press Ctrl+Z to undo it, and try playing with the Smart Fix Amount slider instead. Or click the little grid to the left of the slider to try out one of the tool's presets.

The Amount slider does the same thing Auto Smart Fix does, only *you* control the degree of change. Watch the image as you move the slider to the right. If your computer is slow, there's a certain amount of lag, so go slowly to give it a chance to catch up. If you happen to overdo it, sometimes it's easier to click the Reset button above your image and start again. Use the checkmark and X buttons (which appear next to the Smart Fix label; they look like the ones shown in Figure 4-8) to accept or reject your changes.

TIP   Usually you get better results with a lot of little nudges to the Smart Fix slider than with one big sweeping movement.

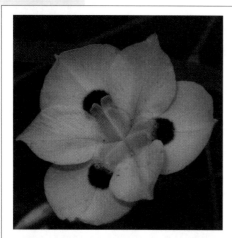
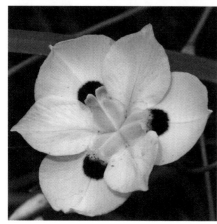

Figure 4-7:

Top: This photo, taken in the shade, is pretty dark.

Bottom: The Auto Smart Fix button improved it significantly with just one click. You might want to use the tools in the Balance section (page 128) to really fine-tune the color.

Incidentally, these are the same Smart Fix commands you see in the Editor's Enhance menu: Enhance → Auto Smart Fix (Alt+Ctrl+M), and Enhance → Adjust Smart Fix (Shift+Ctrl+M).

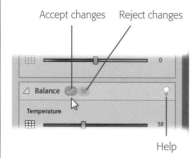

Accept changes   Reject changes

Balance

Temperature

Help

Figure 4-8:
When you move a slider in any of the Quick Fix panels, accept and cancel buttons appear in the panel you're using. Clicking the accept (checkmark) button applies the change to your image, while clicking the cancel (X) button undoes the last change you made. If you make several slider adjustments, the cancel button undoes everything you've done since you clicked accept. (Clicking the light bulb icon takes you to the Elements Help Center.)

Sometimes Smart Fix just isn't smart enough to do everything you want, and sometimes it does things you *don't* want. (It works better on photos that are underexposed than overexposed, for one thing.) Fortunately, you still have several other editing choices, covered in the following sections. If you don't like the effect Smart Fix has had, undo it before making other changes.

NOTE   Auto Smart Fix is one of the commands you can apply from within the Organizer, so there's no need to launch the Editor at all if you want just this tool. See the box on page 116 for more about making fixes from the Organizer.

Adjusting Lighting and Contrast

The Lighting panel lets you make sophisticated adjustments to the brightness and contrast of your photo. Sometimes problems you thought stemmed from exposure or even focus can be fixed with these commands.

Levels

If you want to understand how Levels really works, you're in for a long, technical ride. But if you just want to know what it can do for your photos, the short answer is that it adjusts the brightness of your image by redistributing the color information. Levels changes (and hopefully fixes!) both brightness and color at the same time.

If you've never used any photo-editing software before, this may sound rather mysterious, but photo-editing pros will tell you that Levels is one of the most powerful commands for fixing and polishing your pictures. To find out if its magic works for you, click the Auto button next to the word "Levels". Figure 4-9 shows what a big difference it can make. Download this photo (*ocean.jpg*) from the Missing CD page at *www.missingmanuals.com* if you'd like to try this.

What Levels does is complex. Chapter 7 has loads more details about what's going on behind the scenes and how you can apply this command much more precisely.

FREQUENTLY ASKED QUESTION

Calibrating Your Monitor

Why do my photos look awful when I open them in Elements?

You may find that when you open photos in Elements, they look really terrible even though they look decent in other programs. Maybe your photos look all washed out, or reddish or greenish, or even black and white.

If that's the case, you need to calibrate your monitor, as explained on page 215. It's easy to do and it makes a big difference.

Elements is what's known as a *color-managed* program. You can read all about color management on page 215.

For now, you just need to know that color-managed programs pay much more attention to the settings for your monitor than regular programs like word processors do.

Color-managed programs like Elements are a little more trouble to set up initially, but the advantage is that you can get truly wonderful results if you invest a little time and effort when you're getting started.

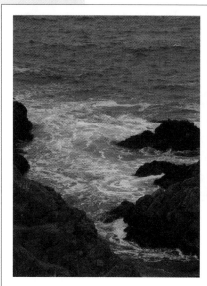
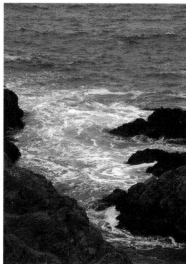

Figure 4-9:
A quick click of the Auto button for Levels can make a dramatic difference.

Left: The original photo isn't bad, and you may not realize that the colors could be better.

Right: This image shows how much more effective your photo is once Auto Levels has balanced the colors.

Contrast

The main alternative to Auto Levels in Quick Fix is Auto Contrast. Most people find that their images tend to benefit from one or the other of these options. Contrast adjusts the relative darkness and lightness of your image without changing the color, so if Levels made your colors go all goofy, try adjusting the contrast instead. You activate Contrast the same way you do the Levels tool: just click the Auto button next to its name.

> **TIP** After you use Auto Contrast, look closely at the edges of the objects in your photo. If your camera's contrast was already high, you may see a halo or a sharp line around the photo's subject. If you do, the contrast is too high and you need to undo Auto Contrast (Ctrl+Z) and try another fix instead.

Shadows and Highlights

The Shadows and Highlights tools do an amazing job of bringing out details that are lost in the shadows or in bright areas of your photo. Figure 4-10 shows what a difference these tools can make.

The Shadows and Highlights tools are a collection of three sliders, each of which controls a different aspect of your image:

- **Lighten Shadows.** Nudge the slider to the right, and you'll see details emerge from murky black shadows.

- **Darken Highlights.** Use this slider to dim the brightness of overexposed areas.

- **Midtone Contrast.** After you've adjusted your photo's shadows and highlights, your photo may look flat and not have enough contrast between the dark and light areas. This slider helps you bring a more realistic look back to your photo.

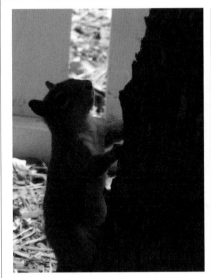 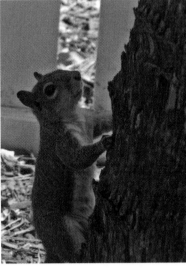

Figure 4-10:
Left: This image has highlights that are too bright and shadows that are much too dark.

Right: After a little shadows and highlights adjusting, you can see there's plenty of detail there. (Use the color sliders–described next– to get rid of the orange tone.)

TIP   You may think you need only lighten shadows in a photo, but sometimes just a smidgen of Darken Highlights may help, too. Don't be afraid to experiment by using this slider even if you've got a relatively dark photo.

Go easy: Getting overenthusiastic with these sliders can give your photos a washed-out, flat look.

Color

The Color panel lets you—surprise, surprise—play around with the colors in your image. In many cases, if you've been successful with Auto Levels or Auto Contrast, you won't need to do anything here.

Auto Color

Once again, there's another one-click fix available: Auto Color. Actually, in some ways Auto Color should be up in the Lighting section. Like Levels, it simultaneously adjusts color and brightness, but it looks at different information in your photos to decide what to do with them.

When you're first learning to use Quick Fix, you may want to try all three—Auto Levels, Auto Contrast, and Auto Color—to see which generally works best for your photos. Undo between each change and compare your results. Most people find they like one of the three most of the time.

Auto Color may be just the ticket for your photos, but you may also find that it shifts your colors in strange ways. Click it and see what you think. Does your photo look better or worse? If it's worse, just click Reset or press Ctrl+Z to undo it, and go back to Auto Levels or Auto Contrast. If they all make your colors look a little wrong, or if you want to tweak the colors in your photo, move on to the Color sliders, explained next.

Using the Color sliders

If you want to adjust the colors in your photo without changing the brightness, check out the Color sliders. For example, your digital camera may produce colors that don't quite match what you saw when you took the picture; you may have scanned an old print that's faded or discolored; or you may just want to change the colors in a photo for the heck of it. Whatever the case, the sliders below the Auto Color button are for you.

You get two ways to adjust colors here:

- **Saturation** controls the intensity of your image's color. For example, you can turn a color photo to black and white by moving the slider all the way to the left. Move it too far to the right, and everything glows with so much color that it looks radioactive.

- **Hue** changes the color from, say, red to blue or green. If you aren't looking for realism, you can have fun with your photos by really pushing this slider to create funky color changes.

You probably won't use both these sliders on a single photo, but you can if you like. Remember to click the accept checkmark that appears in the Color panel if you want to accept your changes. For fine-tuning your color, you may want to move on to the next panel: Balance. In fact, in many cases you'll only need the Balance sliders.

> **TIP** If you look at the color of the slider's track, it shows what happens if you move in that direction. So there's less and less color as you go left in the Saturation track, and more and more to the right. Looking at the tracks can help you figure out where to move the slider.

Balancing color

Photos often have the right amount of saturation, and moving the Hue slider makes everything look pretty funky, but suppose there's something about the color balance that just isn't right. The Balance panel contains two very useful controls for adjusting the overall colors in your image:

- **Temperature** lets you adjust colors from cool (bluish) on the left to warm (orangeish) on the right. Use this slider for things like toning down the warm glow you see in photos taken in tungsten lighting, or just for fine-tuning your color balance.

- **Tint** adjusts the green/magenta balance of your photo, as shown in Figure 4-11.

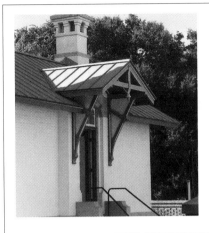
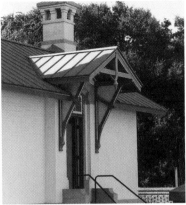

Figure 4-11:

Left: The greenish tint in this photo is a typical example of a common problem caused by many digital cameras.

Right: A little adjustment of the Tint slider clears it up in a jiffy. It's not always as obvious as it is here that you need a tint adjustment. If you aren't sure, the sky can be a dead giveaway: Is it robin's egg blue like in the left photo here? If so, tint is what you need.

NOTE   In previous versions of Elements, these sliders were grouped with the Color sliders, since you'll often use a combination of adjustments from both groups. Chapter 7 has lots more info about how to use the full-blown Editor to really fine-tune your image's colors.

Sharpening

Now that you've finished your other corrections, it's time to *sharpen* your photo, so move down to the Detail tab. Sharpening gives the effect of better focus by improving the edge contrast of objects in your photo. Most digital-camera photos need some sharpening because the sharpening the camera applies is deliberately conservative. Once again, a Quick Fix Auto button is at your service: Click the Detail panel's Auto button to get things started. Figure 4-12 shows what you can expect.

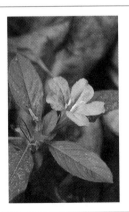
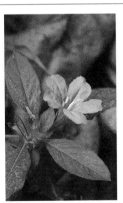
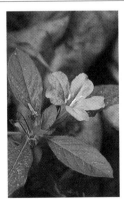

Figure 4-12:

Left: The original image. Like most digital photos, it could stand a little sharpening.

Middle: What you get by clicking the Detail panel's Auto button.

Right: The results of using the Sharpen slider to get stronger sharpening than Auto Sharpen applies.

The sad truth is that there really isn't any way to actually improve the focus of a photo once it's taken. Software sharpening just increases the contrast where the program perceives edges, so using it first can have strange effects on other editing tools you apply later and on their ability to understand your photo.

If you don't like what Auto Sharpen does (you very well may not), you can undo it (press Ctrl+Z) and try the slider instead. If you thought the Auto button overdid things, go gentle on the slider. Changes vary from photo to photo, but usually Auto's results fall at around the 30 to 40 percent mark on the slider.

> **TIP** If you see funny halos around the outlines of objects in your photos, or strange flaky spots (making your photo look like it has eczema), those are artifacts from too much sharpening; reduce the Sharpen settings till they go away.

Always look at the actual pixels (View → Actual Pixels) when you sharpen, because that gives you the clearest idea of what you're actually doing to your picture. If you don't like what the button does, undo it, and then try the slider. Zero sharpening is all the way to the left; moving to the right increases the amount of sharpening applied to your photo.

As a general rule, you want to sharpen photos you plan to print more than images for Web use. You can read lots more about sharpening on page 237.

> **NOTE** If you've used photo-editing programs before, you may be interested to know that the Auto Sharpen button applies Adjust Sharpness (page 239) to your photo. The difference is that you don't have any control over the settings, as you would if you applied it from the Enhance menu. But the good news is that if you want it, or if you prefer to use Unsharp Mask (page 237), you can get this control—even from within Quick Fix. Just go to the Enhance menu and choose the sharpener of your choice.

At this point, all that's left is cropping your photo, if you'd like to reduce its size. Page 89 tells you everything you need to know about cropping. However, you can also give your photo a bit more punch by using the Touch Up tools explained in the next section.

Touch-Ups

The bottom section of the Quick Fix toolbox contains four special tools to help improve your photos. You've already learned how to use one of them—the Red Eye Removal tool—earlier in this chapter (page 121). Here's what you can do with the other three:

- **Whiten Teeth.** As you probably guessed from the name, use this tool to make teeth look brighter. What's especially nice is that it doesn't create a fake, overly white look, as shown in Figure 4-13.

- **Make Dull Skies Blue.** It's a common problem with digital cameras: Your exposure for the subject is perfect, but the sky is all washed-out looking. Unfortunately, if your sky is really gray or blown out (white looking), this tool won't help much. It should probably have been called "Make Blue Skies Bluer." It is useful for creating more dramatic skies, though.

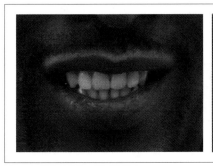 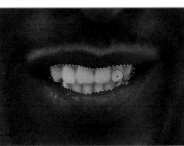

Figure 4-13:
Just a quick swipe across the teeth selects and whitens them, while keeping a realistic look.

- **Black and White – High Contrast.** You're probably wondering what the heck *that* means. It's Adobe's way of saying, "Transform the area I choose from color to black and white." This tool's a great timesaver when you want to create a photo where only part of the picture is in color. (High Contrast refers to the style of black-and-white conversion this tool uses.)

All three tools work pretty much the same way—just draw a line over the area you want to change, and Elements makes a detailed selection of the area and applies the change for you:

1. **Open a photo and make your other corrections first.**

   If you're an old hand at using Elements, use the Touch Up tools before sharpening. But if you're a beginner and not comfortable with layers (see Chapter 6), sharpen first. (See the note on page 132 for more about why.)

2. **Click the icon for the tool you want to use.**

   Hover your cursor over the icons for pop-up tooltips text if you aren't sure which is which.

3. **Draw a line over the area you want to change.**

   When you click one of the Touch Up tools, your cursor turns to a circle with crosshairs in it. Just drag that over the area you want to change. Elements automatically expands the area to include the entire object it thinks you want. (It works just like the Quick Selection tool, only it also applies the changes to your image. Page 143 has more about using the Quick Selection tool.) You'll see the marching ants appear (page 95) around the area Elements is changing.

4. **If Elements included too much or too little, tweak the size of the selected area.**

   In the Options bar, you'll see three little brush icons. Click the left icon to start another new selection, click the right one and drag over an area you want to remove, or click the middle one and drag to add to the area. You can also just drag to extend your selection, or Alt-drag if Elements covered too much area and you need to remove some of it, without going to the Options bar at all.

5. Once you're happy with the area covered by the change, you're done.

You can back up by pressing Ctrl+Z to undo your changes step by step. Just keep going to eliminate the change completely if you don't like it. (Clicking the Reset button doesn't undo the Touch Up changes.)

The Touch Up tools can be very helpful, but they work based on the colors in your photo, so they may not always give you exactly the results you want, as you can see in Figure 4-14. If you want to use the Color sliders (page 128) to adjust things, you'll need to switch away from the Touch Up tools and use the Selection brush to re-select the area. That's because the sliders aren't available when the Touch Up tools are active.

NOTE   The Touch Up tools create a layered file. If you understand layers, you can also go back to Full Edit and make changes after the fact, like adjusting the opacity or blend mode of the layer. (See Chapter 6 to learn about layers.) You can always discard your Touch Up changes by discarding the layer they're on. And you can even edit the area affected by the changes by editing the layer mask, as explained on page 329, or use the Smart Brush tool (page 211) in Full Edit. (The one exception is the "Black and White – High Contrast" tool [page 132]: You can't change the settings for the adjustments it makes. You just see a weird message telling you that your layer was created in the full version of Photoshop, even though you know it wasn't.)

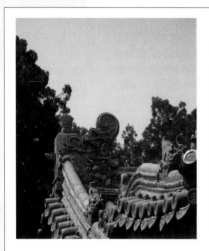
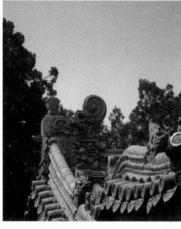

Figure 4-14:
Blue Skies can help punch up the sky color in your photos—sometimes.

Left: Smog makes the sky in this photo look really dull.

Right: One quick drag across the sky with the "Make Dull Skies Blue" tool produces a much more vivid sky—maybe too vivid (and a tad green). Elements used a gradient (see page 427) to give a more realistic shading to the new sky color.

Also, if there isn't enough color to begin with, the Touch Up tools may not produce any visible result in your photo. Whiten Teeth may not do anything if your subject has super white dentures, and Make Dull Skies Blue may prove to be a dud if your sky is solid gray or completely overexposed.

You may find that after using a Touch Up tool, nothing happens when you try to make *other* changes to your photo. As mentioned above, after you work with one of the Touch Up tools (except for the Red Eye Removal tool), Elements leaves you with a layered file. That isn't normally a problem, even if you don't know anything about layers, but once in a while you may find nothing happens when you try to make further changes to your photo. In that case, click the Edit tab at the top of the page, and select EDIT Full to go back to Full Edit. Then find the Layers panel. It should be in the Panel bin unless you've removed it. (If you can't find it, go to Window → Layers to bring it back.)

In the Layers panel, look for the word "Background" and click it. That part of the panel should be a lighter or darker gray (depending on your brightness settings—see page 17) than the rest of the panel (the area that says Blue Skies, Pearly Whites, or whatever). If it isn't, click it again. Then you can go back to the Quick Fix window (click the Edit tab and choose EDIT Quick), and do whatever you want to your photo. However, the part you used the Touch Up tools on may behave differently from the rest of the photo. If that happens and you haven't closed the photo since using the Touch Up tools, use Undo History (page 36) to back up to before you used the Touch Up tools.

Quick Fix Suggested Workflow

There are no hard-and-fast rules for what order you need to work in when using the Quick Fix tools. As mentioned earlier, Elements lays out the tools in the Panel bin, from top to bottom, in the order that usually makes sense. But you can pick and choose whichever tools you want, depending on what you think your photo needs. If you're the type of person who likes a set plan for fixing photos, here's one order in which to apply the commands:

1. **Rotate your photo (if needed).**

   Use the buttons below the image preview.

2. **Fix red eye (if needed).**

   See page 121.

3. **Crop the image.**

   If you know you want to crop your photo, now's the time. That way, you get rid of any problem areas before they affect other adjustments. For example, say your photo has a lot of overexposed sky that you want to crop out. If you leave it in, that area may skew the effects of the Lighting and Color tools on your image. So if you already know where you want to crop, do it before making other adjustments for more accurate results. (It's also okay to wait till later to crop if you aren't sure yet about what you'll want to trim.)

4. **Try Auto Smart Fix and/or the Smart Fix slider. Undo if necessary.**

   Pretty soon you'll get a good idea of how likely it is that this fix will do a good job on your photos. Some people love it; others think it makes their pictures too grainy.

5. **If Smart Fix didn't do the trick, work your way down through the other Lighting and Color commands until you like the way your photo looks.**

   Read the sections earlier in this chapter to understand what each command does to your photo.

6. **Sharpen.**

   Try to make sharpening your last adjustment, because other commands can give you funky results on photos you've already sharpened. But if you're a beginner and not comfortable with layers, you can sharpen *before* using Whiten Teeth, Make Dull Skies Blue, or "Black and White – High Contrast" in the Touch Up panel. (See page 132 for more about why you'd wait to use these.)

   TIP   When you're in Quick Fix mode, you can switch back to Full Edit at any point if you want tools not available in Quick Fix. If you want to close your photo from the Quick Fix window, use the Close button above the preview area or press Ctrl+W.

Adjusting Skin Tones

If you're like most amateur photographers, your most important photos are pictures of people: your family, your friends, or even just fascinating strangers. Elements gives you yet another tool for making fast fixes—one that's designed especially for correcting photos with people in them: The "Adjust Color for Skin Tone" command, available in both the Quick Fix and Full Edit windows.

The name "Adjust Color for Skin Tone" is a bit confusing. What this command actually does is adjust your *whole* image based on the skin tone of someone in the photo. The idea behind the command is that you may well be much more interested in the way the people in your photos look than in how the background looks. "Adjust Color for Skin Tone" gives the highest priority to creating good skin color. It's an automatic fix, but there's a dialog box where you can tweak the results once you've previewed Elements' suggested adjustments. To use the "Adjust Color for Skin Tone" command:

1. **Call up the "Adjust Color for Skin Tone" dialog box.**

   In either Quick Fix or Full Edit, go to Enhance → Adjust Color → "Adjust Color for Skin Tone". The dialog box shown in Figure 4-15 appears. You may need to move it out of the way of your photo so you can see what's happening.

2. **Show Elements an area of skin to sample for calculating the color adjustments.**

   Once the dialog box appears, your cursor turns to an eyedropper. Just find a portion of your photo where your subject's skin has relatively good color, and click it.

3. **Tweak the results.**

Elements is often a bit overenthusiastic in its adjustments. Use the sliders in the dialog box to get a more pleasing, realistic color. The Ambient Light slider works just like the Temperature slider in the Quick Fix Panel bin (page 128). Blush increases the rosiness of the skin as you move the slider to the right and decreases it to the left. Tan increases or decreases the browns and oranges in the skin tones. You may get swell results with your first click, or have to use all the sliders to get a truly realistic result. It all depends on the photo.

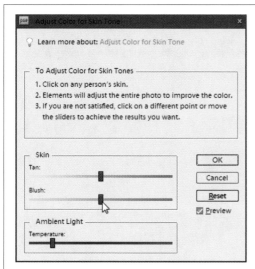

Figure 4-15:
When this dialog box appears, your cursor turns into a little eyedropper when you move it over your photo. Just click the best-looking area of skin you can find. You won't see any sliders in the tracks until you click. After Elements adjusts the photo based on your click, the sliders appear and you can use them to fine-tune the results. Clicking different spots gives different results, so you may want to experiment by clicking various places.

You can preview the changes right in your photo as you work. If you mess up and want to start again, click Reset. If you decide you'd rather be using another tool instead, click Cancel.

TIP   The "Adjust Color for Skin Tone" sliders are like the Quick Fix sliders in that you can get an idea of which way to move them by looking at the colors in the sliders' tracks.

4. **When you like what you see, click OK.**

Elements applies your changes. If you want to undo them, press Ctrl+Z.

"Adjust Color for Skin Tone" seems to work best on fair skin, and not so well on darker skin tones. And it's most suited for making fairly subtle adjustments, so you may have to reduce the amount of change from what Elements first did.

Also, notice that not just the skin tones change. Elements adjusts *all* the colors in the photo in sync with the skin tones (Figure 4-16). You may find your image has acquired quite a color cast by the time you've got the skin just right (see page 227). If this bothers you, try a different tool. On the other hand, you can create some very nice late-afternoon light effects with this command.

While "Adjust Color for Skin Tone" is really meant as a kind of alternative fast fix, you may find it's most useful for making small final adjustments to photos you've already edited using other tools.

> **TIP** If you understand layers (explained in Chapter 6), you may want to make a duplicate layer and apply this command to the duplicate. Then you can adjust the intensity of the result by adjusting the layer's opacity (see page 180).

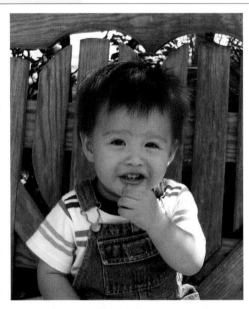

Figure 4-16:
Top: This photo has a slight greenish cast, giving the little boy a somewhat unappealing skin tone.

Bottom: "Adjust Color for Skin Tone" warms up his skin tones, and even removes the greenish tinge to the bench he's sitting on.

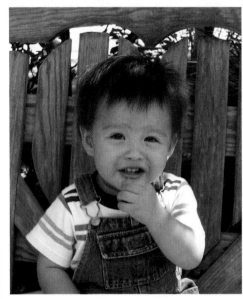

Making Selections

One of Elements' most impressive talents is its ability to let you *select* part of your image and make changes only to that area. Selecting something tells Elements, "Hey, *this* is what I want to work on. Don't touch the rest of it." You can select your entire image or any part of it.

Using selections, you can fine-tune your images in very sophisticated ways. You can change the color of just one rose in a whole bouquet, for instance, or change your nephew's festive purple hair back to something his grandparents would appreciate. Graphics pros will tell you that good selections make the difference between shoddy, amateurish work and a slick professional job.

Elements offers you a whole bunch of different selection tools to work with. You can draw a rectangular or a circular selection with the Marquee tools, for instance; paint a selection on your photo with the Selection brush; or just draw a line with the Quick Selection tool and let Elements figure out the exact boundaries of your selection. When you're looking to pluck a particular object (a beautiful flower, say) from a photo, the Magic Extractor works wonders. And Elements 8 introduces a new tool, Transform Selection, which lets you resize your selections in a snap.

For most jobs, there's no right or wrong tool; with experience, you may find you prefer working with certain tools more than others. Often you'll use more than one tool to create a perfect selection. Once you've read this chapter, you'll understand all the different selection tools and how to use each one.

> **TIP** It's much easier to select an object that's been photographed against a plain, contrasting background. So, if you know you're going to want to select a bicycle, for example, shoot it in front of a blank wall rather than, say, a hedge.

Selecting Everything

Sometimes you just want to select your whole photo, like when you want to copy and paste it, for example. Elements gives you some useful commands that help you easily make basic selections:

- **Select All** (Select → All or Ctrl+A) tells Elements to select your whole image. You'll see the "marching ants" (Figure 5-1) around the outer edge of the picture.

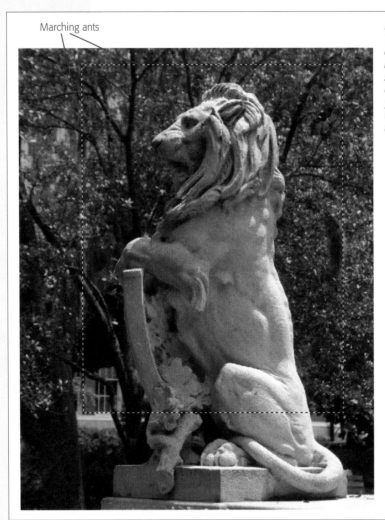

Marching ants

Figure 5-1:
The popular name for these dotted lines is "marching ants" because they march around your selections to show you where the edges lie. When you see the ants, your selection is active, meaning what you do next happens only to the selected area.

If you want to copy your image into another picture or program, Select All is the fastest way to go. If the photo contains layers, which you'll learn about in Chapter 6, you may not be able to get everything you want with the Select All command. In that case, use Edit → Copy Merged, or press Shift+Ctrl+C.

NOTE   If you're planning on pasting an image into another program like Microsoft Word or
PowerPoint, make sure you've got Export Clipboard turned on in Edit → Preferences → General.

• **Deselect Everything** (Select → Deselect, Esc, or Ctrl+D) removes any current
  selection. Remember the keystroke combination because it's one you'll probably use over and over.

• **Reselect** (Select → Reselect or Shift+Ctrl+D) tells Elements to reactivate the
  selection you just canceled. Use Reselect if you realize you still need a selection
  you just got rid of. Or you can just press Ctrl+Z to back up a step.

• **Hide/View a Selection** (Ctrl+H) keeps your selection active while hiding its
  outline. Sometimes the marching ants make it hard to see what you're doing, or
  they can be distracting. To see the ants again, press Ctrl+H a second time.

TIP   Sometimes it's easy to forget you have a selection. When a tool acts goofy or won't do anything, start your troubleshooting by pressing Ctrl+H to be sure you don't have a hidden selection
you forgot about.

If you want to quickly select an irregular area, try the Quick Selection tool,
explained on page 143.

Selecting Rectangular and Elliptical Areas

Selecting your whole picture is all well and good, but many times your reason for
making a selection is precisely because you *don't* want to make changes to the
whole image. How do you select just part of the picture?

The easiest way is to use the Marquee tools. You already met the Rectangular Marquee tool back in Chapter 3, in the section on cropping (page 89). If you want to
select a block, circle, or oval from your image, the Marquee tools are the way to go.
As the winners of the Most Frequently Used Selection Tools award, they get top
spot in the Selection area of the Editor's Tools panel. You can modify how they
work, like telling them to create a square instead of a rectangle, as explained in
Figure 5-2.

To use the Marquee tools to make a selection:

1. **Press M or click the Marquee tool's icon in the Tools panel to activate it.**

   The Marquee tool is the little dotted rectangle right below the Eyedropper icon
   in a single-row Tools panel, or below the Hand tool if you have two rows. (It
   may appear as a little dotted oval if you used the Elliptical Marquee tool last.)

2. **Choose the shape you want to draw: rectangle or ellipse.**

   In the Tools panel's pop-out menu for the Marquee tools, choose the rectangle
   or the ellipse to set the shape.

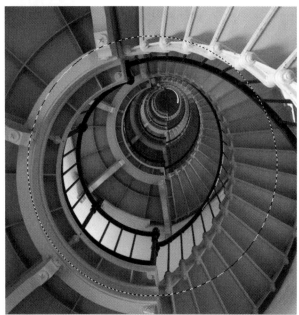

Figure 5-2:
*To make a perfectly circular or square selection,
hold down the Shift key while you drag. You can
reposition your selection after it's drawn by using
the arrow keys or by dragging it. You can also
adjust it by using Transform Selection, explained
on page 161.*

3. **Enter a feather value in the Options bar if you want one.**

   Feathering makes the edges of your selection softer or fuzzier for better blending (when you're trying, say, to replace Brad Pitt's face with yours). See the box on page 151 for a look at how feathering (and anti-aliasing) work.

4. **Drag within your image to make your selection.**

   Wherever you initially place your mouse becomes one of the corners of your rectangular selection or a point just beyond the outer edge of your ellipse (you can also draw perfectly circular or square selections, as shown in Figure 5-2). The selection outline expands as you drag your mouse.

   If you make a mistake, just press Esc. You can also press either Ctrl+D to get rid of *all* current selections, or Ctrl+Z to remove the most recent selection.

The mode choices in the Options bar give you three ways to control the size of your selection: Normal lets you manually control the size of your selection; Fixed Aspect Ratio lets you enter proportions in the Width and Height boxes; and Fixed Size lets you enter specific dimensions in these boxes. The Anti-alias checkbox is explained in the box on page 151.

Once you've made your selection, you can move the selected area around in the photo by dragging it, or you can use the arrow keys to nudge your selection in the direction you want to move it. And Elements 8's new Transform Selection command lets you drag your selection larger or smaller, or change its shape. Page 161 tells you how.

Selecting Irregularly Sized Areas

It would be nice if you could always get away with making simple rectangular or elliptical selections, but is life really ever that neat? You won't always want to select a geometric-shaped chunk of your image. If you want to change the color of one fish in your aquarium picture, selecting a rectangle or square just isn't going to cut it.

UP TO SPEED

Paste vs. Paste Into Selection

Newcomers to Elements are often confused by the fact that the program has two Paste commands: Paste and Paste Into Selection. Knowing what each one does will help you avoid problems.

- **Paste.** Ninety-nine percent of the time, Paste is the one you want. This command simply places your copied object wherever you paste it. Once you've pasted your object, you can move whatever you've pasted by moving the selected area.

- **Paste Into Selection.** This is a special command for pasting a selection into *another* selection. Your pasted object appears only *within* the bounds of the selection you're pasting into.

When you use Paste Into Selection, you can still move what you paste, but it won't be visible anywhere outside the edges of the selection you're pasting into. This command is very handy if you want to do something like putting a beautiful mountain view outside your window: Select the window, copy the mountain (Ctrl+C), and then use Paste Into Selection to add the view. Then you can maneuver the mountain photo around till it's properly centered. But if you move it outside the boundary of your window selection, it just disappears. Once you deselect, your material is permanently in place; you can't move it again.

If you understand layers (see Chapter 6), Paste creates a new layer, while Paste Into Selection puts what you paste on the existing layer.

Thankfully, Elements gives you other tools that make it easy for you to make very precise selections—no matter their size or shape. In this section, you'll learn how to use the rest of the selection tools. But first you need to understand the basic controls that they (almost) all share.

Controlling the Selection Tools

If you never make mistakes and never change your mind, you can skip this section. If, on the other hand, you're human, you need to know about the mysterious little squares you see in the Options bar when the selection tools are active (Figure 5-3).

These selection squares don't look like much, but they tell the selection tools how to do their job: whether to start a new selection with each click, to add to what you've already got, or to remove things from your selection. They're available for all the selection tools except the Selection brush and the Quick Selection tool, which have their own sets of options. From left to right, here's what they do:

- **New Selection** is the standard selection mode that you'll probably use most of the time. When you click this button and start a new selection, your previous selection disappears.

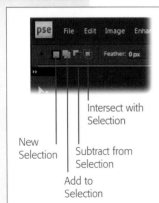

Figure 5-3:
These cryptic squares can save you hours once you understand how to use them to control the selection tools.

New Selection

Add to Selection

Subtract from Selection

Intersect with Selection

- **Add to Selection** tells Elements to add what you select to whatever you've already selected. Unless you have an incredibly steady mouse hand, this option is a godsend, because it's not easy to get a perfect selection on the first try. (Holding down the Shift key while you use any selection tool is another way to add to a selection.)

- **Subtract from Selection** removes what you select next from any existing selection. (Holding down Alt while selecting the area you want to remove accomplishes the same thing.)

- **Intersect with Selection** is a bit confusing. It lets you take a selected area, make a new selection, and wind up with only the area where the selections overlap, as shown in Figure 5-4. (The keyboard equivalent is Alt+Shift.) Most people don't need this one much, but it can be useful for things like creating special shapes. If you need a selection shaped like a quarter of a pie, for instance, do a circle selection, then switch to "Intersect with Selection" and drag a rectangular selection from the circle's center point. You'll wind up with an arc-shaped area where they intersect.

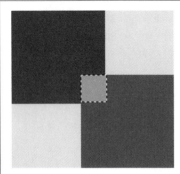

Figure 5-4:
"Intersect with Selection" lets you take two separate selections and select only the area where they intersect. If you have an existing selection, when you select again, your new selection includes only the overlapping area. Here, the top blue square is the first selection, and the bottom pink square is the second. The bright green area shows the final selection after you let go of the mouse button.

Selecting with a Brush

Elements also gives you two very special brushes to help make selections. The Selection brush has been around since Elements 2, so if you've used Elements before, you probably know how handy it is. These days it often takes a back seat to the amazing Quick Selection tool, which makes even the trickiest selections as easy as doodling. The Quick Selection tool automatically finds the bounds of the objects you drag it over, while the Selection brush only selects the area directly under the brush cursor.

The Quick Selection tool and the Selection brush are grouped together in the Tools panel, and they appear in both Full Edit and Quick Fix because they're so useful. You may well find that with these two tools you rarely need the other selection tools.

It couldn't be easier to use the Quick Selection tool:

1. **Activate the Quick Selection tool.**

   Click it in the Tools panel or press A, and then choose it from the Tools panel's pop-out menu. It shares a Tools panel slot with the regular Selection brush. Their icons are very similar, so look carefully—the Quick Selection tool looks more like a wand than a brush and it points up, while the regular Selection brush points down.

2. **Drag within your photo.**

   As you move the cursor, Elements calculates where it thinks the selection edges should be, and the selection outline jumps out to surround that area. It's an amazingly good guesser. There's no need to try to cover the entire area or to go around the edges of your object—Elements does that for you.

   There are a few Options bar controls, which are explained below, but you mostly won't need to think about them, at least not till you make your selection. Then you'll probably want to try Refine Edge (explained in the next section).

3. **Adjust the selection.**

   Odds are that you won't get a totally perfect selection that includes everything you wanted on the first click. To increase the selection area, drag in the direction where you want to add to the selection. A small move usually does it, and the selection jumps outward to include the area that Elements thinks you want, as shown in Figure 5-5.

   To remove an area from the selection, hold Alt and drag, or click in the area you don't want.

   Once you're happy with your selection, that's it, unless you want to tweak the edges by using Refine Edge (see the next section)—and you probably do.

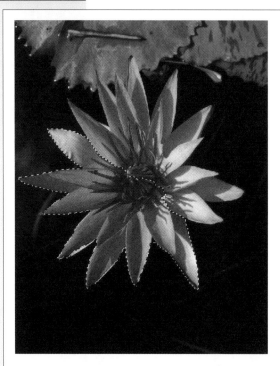

Figure 5-5:

Top: It would be a nuisance to select this water lily by hand because of the many pointy-edged petals. The first drag with the Quick Selection tool produced this partial selection. Notice how well the tool found the edges of the petals.

Bottom: Another drag across the lily told Elements to select the whole blossom. The whole selection took less than 5 seconds to complete. (Notice that the tool missed a little bit on the edges in a couple of spots. Reduce the brush size when dragging to add those, or switch to the regular Selection brush to finish up.)

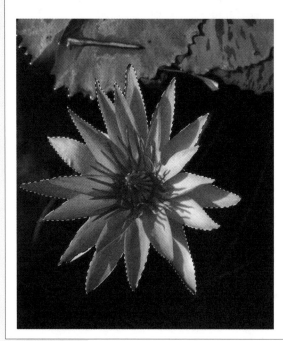

The Quick Selection tool has a few Options bar choices, but you really don't need most of them:

- **New Selection, Add to Selection, Subtract from Selection.** These three brush icons work just like the equivalent selection squares in selection tools (page 141), but you don't need to use them. The Quick Selection tool automatically adds to your selection if you drag toward an unselected area. Shift-drag to select multiple areas that aren't contiguous, or Alt-drag to remove areas from your selection.

- **Brush.** You can make all kinds of adjustments to your brush by clicking this pull-down menu, including choosing from many of the Additional Brush Options palette (see page 372), although you'll rarely need to tweak any of these except maybe the brush size once in a while.

- **Sample All Layers.** Turn this checkbox on, and the Quick Selection tool selects from all visible layers in your image, rather than just the active layer. (Chapter 6 tells you all about layers.)

- **Auto-Enhance.** This tells Elements to automatically smooth out the edges of the selection. It's a more automated way to make the same sort of edge adjustments that you make manually with Refine Edge.

- **Refine Edge.** This option lets you tweak the edges of your selection so that you'll get more realistic results when changing the selected area or copying and pasting it. (Refine Edge is grayed out until you actually make a selection.) It's explained in detail in the next section.

> **TIP** Depending on what you plan to do with your selection, you may want to check out the Smart Brush tool. It works just like Quick Selection, but it goes further than simply completing your selection for you; it also automatically applies the color correction or special effect you choose from its pull-down menu. See page 211 for more about working with the Smart Brushes.

The Quick Selection tool doesn't work every time for every selection, but it's a wonderful tool that's worth grabbing first for any irregular selection. You can use the Selection brush or one of the other selection tools to clean up afterward, if needed.

Refine Edge

This is another tremendously helpful Elements feature. It lets you create smooth, feathered, plausible edges on any selection—a must when you want to realistically blend edited sections into the rest of an image. It appears in the Options bar for some of the tools that let you make irregular selections (like Quick Selection), or you can use it on any active selection by going to Select → Refine Edge. To use it, first make a selection, and then:

1. **Call up Refine Edge.**

   If it's not currently available from the Options bar (it's not there when you use the Marquee tool, for example), go to Select → Refine Edge to call up the Refine Edge dialog box.

2. **Adjust the edges of your selection.**

   Use the sliders, explained in the list that follows, to tweak and polish the edges of your selection. The view buttons let you see your selection in either of two different ways, and you can zoom to 100 percent or more too see exactly how you're changing the selection.

3. **When you like what you've done, click OK.**

   If you decide not to refine your edges, then click Cancel. To start over, Alt-click the Cancel button to turn it into a Reset button. If you play with the sliders and then decide you want to put them back where you started, click Default.

You get three sliders in Refine Edge; you may need to use only one, or any combination of them to improve your selection. Your choices are:

- **Smooth.** This removes the jagged edges around your selection. Type a value in pixels, or use the slider (move it to the right for more smoothing, to the left for less). Be careful: You can go as high as 100 pixels, which is almost certainly much *more* smoothing than you need.

- **Feather.** Feathering is explained on page 151.

- **Contract/Expand.** You can use this to adjust the size of your selection. Move the slider to the left to contract the selection, or to the right to expand it.

It's easy to refine *too* much, so go in small increments, and keep checking your selection. Elements makes it easy to monitor things by giving you a choice of views. The buttons above the Description area of the dialog box give you two different ways to see your selection:

- **Standard** shows the regular marching ants around your selection.

- **Custom Overlay** shows the red mask overlay you'd get when using the Selection brush in Mask mode (see page 147). The red area *is the unselected* part of your image. Using this view is a good way to check for holes and jagged edges.

   TIP   Double-click the Custom overlay button to change the color and opacity of the overlay. You can hide the selection altogether by pressing X. Press X again to bring back the mask or the marching ants, or press F to toggle between Standard and Overlay views.

You also get icons for the Zoom (page 100) and Hand (page 102) tools, so you can adjust the view to see more or different details.

The Selection Brush

The Selection brush is one of the greatest tools in Elements. Making complex selections and cleaning up selections are really easy with this tool. You can use it on its own or as a complement to the Quick Selection tool, described in the previous section. The Quick Selection tool is awesome, but sometimes it doesn't stop your selection exactly where you want. The Selection brush gives you total control because it only selects the area you cover with your brushstroke.

With the Selection brush, you simply paint what you want to select by dragging over that area. You can let go of the mouse button, and each time you drag again, Elements automatically adds to your selection. There's no need to change modes in the Options bar or to hold down the Shift key as with other selection tools.

The Selection brush also has a Mask mode, in which Elements highlights what *isn't* part of your selection. Mask mode is great for finding tiny spots you may have missed and for checking the accuracy of your selection outline. In Mask mode, anything you paint over gets *masked* out; in other words, it's protected from being selected.

Masking is a little confusing at first, but you'll soon see what a useful tool it is. Figure 5-6 shows the same selection made with and without Mask mode.

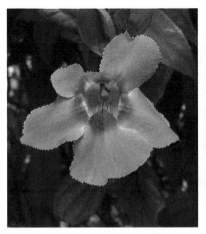 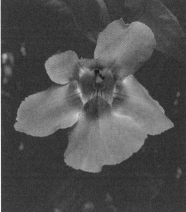

Figure 5-6:
Left: This flower was selected by painting with the Selection brush in Selection mode. It looks like a completed selection that you can make using any of the selection tools.

Right: The same selection in Mask mode. The red covers everything that's not part of the selection.

The Selection brush is pretty simple to use:

1. **Click the Selection brush in the Tools panel or press A.**

    The Selection brush is located in the Tools panel along with the Quick Selection tool. The Selection brush is the brush that looks like it's painting—the brush points down.

2. **In the Options bar, choose either Selection mode or Mask mode and the brush size you want.**

    Your Options bar choices are explained in the list below.

3. **Drag over the area you want.**

    If you're in Selection mode, the area you drag over becomes part of your selection. If you're in Mask mode, the area you drag over is excluded from becoming part of your selection.

The Selection brush gives you several choices in the Options bar:

• **Brush Thumbnail.** You can use many different brushes depending on whether you want a hard- or soft-edged selection. If you want a different brush, just choose it from the menu here. (For more about brushes, see page 369.)

• **Size.** To change the brush size, type a size in the box, or click the arrow and then use the slider. Or just press the close bracket key (]) to increase the size (keep tapping it until you get the size you want). The open bracket key ([) decreases the size. You can also just put your cursor on the word "Size", and scrub to the left or right to make the brush smaller or larger. (Don't know how to scrub? For more on this nifty Elements feature, see page 370.)

> TIP The bracket key shortcuts work with any brush, not just the Selection brush.

• **Mode.** This option is where you tell Elements whether you're creating a selection (Selection) or excluding an area from being part of a selection (Mask).

• **Hardness.** This option controls the sharpness of the edge of your brush, which affects your selection. See Figure 5-7.

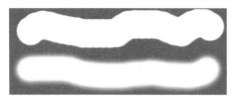

Figure 5-7:
These two Selection brushstrokes show the way the Hardness setting affects the edges of your selection. Here, two different selections were made in the green rectangle. The top selection was made at 100-percent hardness, and the bottom one at 50 percent. (The selected area was then deleted to show you the outline more clearly.)

Switching between Selection and Mask mode is a good way to see how well you've done when you finish making your selection. In Mask mode, the parts of your image that *aren't* part of your selection have a red film over them, so that you can clearly see the selected area.

> TIP You don't have to live with a red mask. To change the mask's color, click the Overlay Color box in the Options bar while the Selection brush is active and in Mask mode. Then use the Color Picker (page 232) to choose a color you prefer. You can also use the Overlay Opacity setting (called simply Overlay in the Options bar) to adjust how well your image shows through the mask.

You can temporarily make the Selection brush do the opposite of what it's been doing, by holding down Alt while you drag. This can save a lot of time in a tricky selection, since you don't have to keep jumping up to the Options bar to change what's happening, and you can keep the view (either your selection or the mask) the same. For example, if you're in Selection mode and you've selected too large an area, Alt-drag over the excess to remove it. If you're masking out an area, Alt-drag to add an area to the selection. This may sound confusing, but it'll make sense once you try it. Some things are easier to learn just by doing them.

TIP   The Selection brush is useful for fine-tuning selections you've made with the other selection tools. Quickly switching to the Selection brush in Mask mode is a great way to check for spots you may have missed—the red makes it really easy to spot them.

The Magic Wand

The Magic Wand is a slightly temperamental—and occasionally highly effective—tool for selecting an irregularly shaped, but similarly colored, area of an image. If you have a big area of a particular color, the Magic Wand can find its edges in one click. It's not actually all that magical: All it does is search for pixels with similar color values. But if it works for you, you may decide it should keep the "magic" in its name because it's a great timesaver when it cooperates, as Figure 5-8 shows.

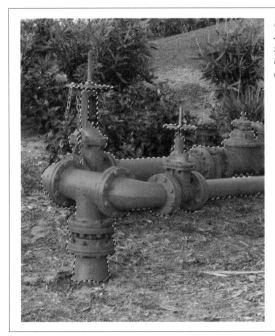

Figure 5-8:
Just one click with the Magic Wand created this nearly perfect selection. If there isn't a big difference between the color of the area you want to select and the colors of neighboring areas, the wand isn't as effective as it is here.

Using the Magic Wand is pretty straightforward: You just click anywhere in the area you want to select. Depending on your *tolerance* setting (explained in the following list), you may nail the selection right away, or it may take several clicks to get everything. If you need to click more than once, remember to hold down Shift so that each click adds to your selection.

The Magic Wand does best when you offer it a good solid block of color that's clearly defined and doesn't have a lot of different shades in it. But it's frustrating when you try to select colors that have any shading or tonal gradations—you have to click and click and click.

Elements gives you some special Options bar settings that you can adjust to help the Wand do a better job:

- **Anti-alias is explained in the box on page 151.**

- **Tolerance** adjusts the number of different shades that the tool selects at once. A higher tolerance includes more shades (resulting in a larger selection area), while a lower tolerance gets you fewer shades (and a more precise selection area). If you set the tolerance too high, you'll probably select a lot more of your picture than you want.

- **Contiguous** makes the Magic Wand select only colored areas that actually touch each other. It's on by default, but sometimes you can save a lot of time by turning it off, as Figure 5-9 explains.

- **Sample All Layers.** If you have a layered file (you'll learn about layers in the next chapter), turn this checkbox on if you want to select the color in all the layers of your image. If you want to select the color only in the active layer, leave it turned off.

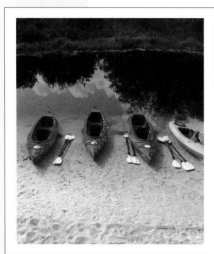
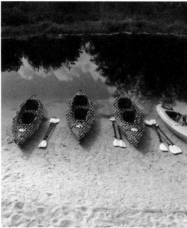

Figure 5-9:
In the left photo, the Contiguous checkbox has been turned on. By turning it off, as in the photo at right, you can select all the red canoes with just one click. If you want to quickly clean up the selection afterward, use the Selection brush (covered on page 146).

You also get access to the Refine Edge command for fixing up the edges of your selection, as explained on page 145.

The big disadvantage to the Magic Wand is that it tends to leave you with unselected contrasting areas around the edge of your selection that are a bit of a pain to clean up. You may want to try out the Quick Selection tool (page 143) before trying the Magic Wand, especially if you want to select a range of colors. If you put a Magic Wand selection on its own layer (see Chapter 6 to understand how layers work), you can use Refine Edge (page 145) or the Defringe command (page 159) to help clean up the edges.

The Lasso Tools

The Magic Wand is pretty good, but it works well only when your image has clearly defined areas of color. A lot of the time, you'll want to select something from a cluttered background that the Magic Wand just can't cope with. Sometimes the easiest way would be if you could just draw around the object you want to select.

Enter the Lasso tool. There are actually three Lasso tools: the Lasso tool, the Polygonal Lasso tool, and the Magnetic Lasso tool. Each tool lets you select an object by tracing around it.

UP TO SPEED

Feathering and Anti-Aliasing

If you're old enough to remember what supermarket tabloid covers looked like before there was Photoshop, you probably had a good laugh at the obviously faked photos. Anyone could see where the art department had physically glued a piece cut from one photo onto another picture.

Nowadays, of course, the pictures of Brad and Angelina's vampire baby from Mars are *much* more believable looking. That's because with Photoshop (and Elements) you can add *anti-aliasing* and *feathering* whenever you make selections.

Anti-aliasing is a way of smoothing the edges of a digital image so that it's not jagged-looking. When you make selections, the Lasso tools and the Magic Wand let you decide whether to use anti-aliasing. It's best to leave anti-aliasing on unless you want a really hard-looking edge on your selection.

Feathering blurs the edges of a selection. When you make a selection that you plan to move to a different photo, a tiny feather can do a lot to make it look like it's always been part of the new photo. Some selection tools, like the Marquee tools, let you set a feather value before using them. You can feather existing selections by going to Select → Feather. Generally, a 1- or 2-pixel feather gives your selection a more natural-looking edge without visible blurring.

If you apply a feather value that's too high for the size of your selection, you see a warning that reads "No pixels are more than 50% selected". Reduce the feather number to placate Elements.

A larger feather gives a soft edge to your photos, as you can see in Figure 5-10.

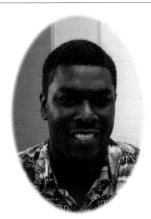

Figure 5-10:
Old-fashioned vignettes like this one are a classic example of when you'd want a fairly large feather. In this figure, the feather is 15 pixels wide. The higher the feather value, the softer the edge effect is.

You activate the Lasso tools by clicking their icon in the Tools panel (it's just below or next to the Marquee tool) or by pressing L, and then selecting the particular variation you want in the Tools panel's pop-out menu. Then drag around the outline of an object to make your selection. The following sections cover each Lasso tool. All the Lasso tools let you apply feathering and anti-aliasing as you make your selection (see the box on page 151), and the basic Lasso and the Polygonal Lasso give you access to Refine Edge (page 145) right in their Options bar settings.

The basic Lasso tool

The theory behind the basic Lasso tool is simple: Click the tool and your cursor changes to the lasso shape shown in Figure 5-11. Just click your photo, and then drag around the outline of what you want to select. When the end of your selection gets back around to join up with the beginning, you've got a selection.

The end of the rope controls
where your selection gets drawn.

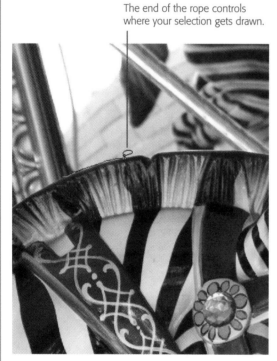

Figure 5-11:
The end of the "rope," not the lasso's loop, is the selection-drawing part of the basic Lasso tool. If the cursor's shape bothers you, change it to crosshairs by pressing the Caps Lock key anytime as you select.

It's not always easy to make an accurate selection with the Lasso, especially if you're using a mouse. A graphics tablet is a big advantage when using this tool, since tablets let you draw with a pen-shaped pointer. (Page 549 has more about graphics tablets.) But even if you don't happen to have a graphics tablet lying around, you can make all the tools work just fine with your mouse once you get used to their quirks.

It helps to zoom the view way in and go very slowly when using the Lasso. (See page 96 for more info on changing your view.) Many people use the regular Lasso tool to quickly select an area that roughly surrounds their object, and then go back with the other selection tools, like the Selection brush or the Magnetic Lasso, to clean things up.

> **TIP**   If you want to save time when you need to draw a straight line for part of your border, hold down Alt and click the points where you want the line to start and end. So if you're selecting an arched Palladian window, for instance, once you get around the curve at the top of the window and reach the straight side, press Alt and click at the bottom of the side to get the straight part of the side all in one go.

Once you've created a selection, you can use the Refine Edge command in the Options bar to adjust and feather the edges (see page 151). Press Esc or Ctrl+D to get rid of your selection if you decide you don't want it anymore.

The Magnetic Lasso

The Magnetic Lasso is a very handy tool, especially if you were the kind of kid who never could color inside the lines or cut paper chains out neatly. The Magnetic Lasso snaps to the outline of any clearly defined object you're trying to select, so you don't have to follow the edge exactly.

As you might guess, the Magnetic Lasso works best on objects with clearly defined edges. You won't get much out of it if your subject is a furry animal, for instance. The Magnetic Lasso also likes a good strong contrast between the object and the background. (You can change the cursor's shape with the Caps Lock key, just as with the basic Lasso.)

Click to start a selection, and then move your cursor around the perimeter of what you want to select. Click again back where you began to finish your selection. You can also Ctrl-click at any point, and the Magnetic Lasso will immediately close up whatever area you've surrounded. You can also adjust how many points the Magnetic Lasso puts down and how sensitive it is to the edge you're tracing, as shown in Figure 5-12.

In addition to Feathering and Anti-aliasing (explained in the box on page 151), the Magnetic Lasso comes with four additional settings in the Options bar:

- **Width** tells the Magnetic Lasso how far away to look when it's trying to find the edge. The value is in pixels, and you can set it as high as 256.

- **Contrast** controls how sharp a difference the Magnetic Lasso should look for between the outline and the background. A higher number looks for sharper contrasts, and a lower number looks for softer ones.

- **Frequency** controls how often Elements puts down the fastening points you see in Figure 5-12.

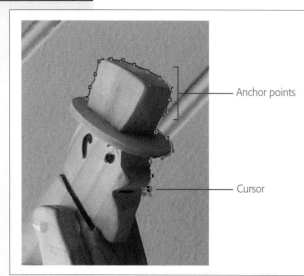

Figure 5-12:
One nice thing about the Magnetic Lasso is that it's easy to back up as you're creating your selection. As you go, it lays down tiny boxes called anchor or fastening points, as shown in this figure. If you make a mistake, pressing Backspace takes you back one point each time you press the key. (If you want to completely get rid of a Magnetic Lasso selection you've begun but not completed, just press Esc.) If the Magnetic Lasso skips a spot or won't grab onto a spot you want it to, you can force it to put down an anchor point by clicking once where you want the anchor to go.

Anchor points

Cursor

- **Use tablet pressure to change pen width**—the little button with a pen at the right of the Options bar—only works if you have a graphics tablet (page 549). When you turn this setting on, how hard you press controls how Elements searches for the edge of objects you're trying to select. When you bear down harder, it's more precise. When you press more lightly, you can be a bit sloppier, and Elements will still find the edge.

Many people live full and satisfying lives paying no attention whatsoever to these settings, so don't feel like you have to fuss with them all the time. You can usually ignore them unless the Magnetic Lasso misbehaves.

TIP   You get better results with the Magnetic Lasso if you go more slowly than if you speed around the object. Like most people, the Magnetic Lasso does better work if you give it time to be sure where it's going.

The Polygonal Lasso

At first, this may seem like a totally stupid tool. It works something like the Magnetic Lasso in that it puts down anchor points, but it creates only perfectly straight segments. So you may think, "That's great if I want to select a Stop sign, but otherwise, what's the point?"

Actually, if you're one of those people who just plain *can't* draw, and you even have a hard time following the edge of an object that's already on the screen, this is the tool for you. The trick is to use very short distances between clicks. Figure 5-13 shows the Polygonal Lasso in action.

The big advantage of the Polygonal Lasso over the Magnetic Lasso is that it's much easier to keep it from getting into a snarl. Your only options for this tool are Feathering and Anti-aliasing (which are explained in the box on page 157) and Refine Edge (page 145).

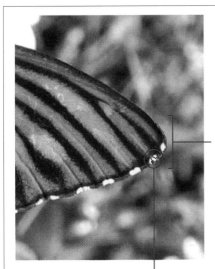

Figure 5-13:
If you have limited dexterity, the Polygonal Lasso tool and a lot of clicks eventually get you a nice accurate selection. You need to zoom way, way in to use this tool to select an object that doesn't have totally straight sides. Here, the Polygonal Lasso easily made it around the curve of the wing by clicking to make extremely short segments.

The selection path drawn
by the Polygonal Lasso

Polygonal Lasso cursor

Removing Objects from an Image's Background

Ever feel the urge to pluck an object out of your photo's background? For example, maybe you want to take an amazing shot you got of the moon and stick it in another photo. The traditional procedure is to make your selection, invert it (page 160), and then delete the rest of the image. But Elements streamlines this process with another "magic" tool—the Magic Extractor. It works much like the Quick Selection tool in that you just give Elements a few hints and let it do the rest. When the Magic Extractor's done, your selection is isolated in all its lonely glory, surrounded by transparency and ready for use on its own. Like the Quick Selection tool, this tool does a surprisingly good job—most of the time. To conduct your own experiments, download the practice photo (*figurine.jpg*) from the Missing CD page at *www.missingmanuals.com*.

> **TIP**   You may find it faster to use the Quick Selection tool (page 143), followed by inverting and deleting the background area as explained on page 160. If that doesn't work, then it's time to try the Magic Extractor.

The Magic Extractor has an elaborate dialog box with tools found nowhere else in Elements. To see it, go to Image → Magic Extractor (see Figure 5-14). You see a full-screen dialog box that includes a toolbox on the left side, instructions across the top, a preview of your image, and a set of controls at right. It looks complicated, but it's really just a bunch of easy-to-use options for tweaking what you've got before Elements extracts your object. Here's how to use this timesaving tool:

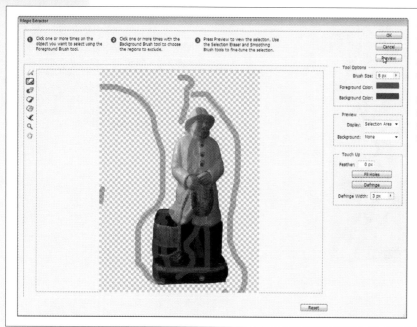

Figure 5-14:
*Manually removing this
figurine from its
background would be a
mighty long process.
With the Magic Extractor,
these few marks are all
the help Elements needs
to make the selection
for you.*

1. **Go to Image → Magic Extractor, or press Alt+Shift+Ctrl+V.**

   Your image appears in the preview area of the Magic Extractor dialog box
   (Figure 5-14).

   TIP   The Magic Extractor sometimes has problems with very large files. If you need to extract an
   object from a hefty image, you may get better results if you crop away any big, unnecessary areas
   first. See page 89 for more about cropping.

2. **If necessary, change the marker colors.**

   On the right side of the dialog box are two color squares. Usually, you'll see red
   for the Foreground brush (the one you use to mark what to keep) and blue for
   the Background brush (the one that tells Elements what to discard from your
   image). To make the brush tools easier to see, you can click the squares to bring
   up the Color Picker (page 232) and choose new colors.

3. **Use the Foreground brush to tell Elements what you want to extract.**

   Make some marks on the object you want to keep. You can draw lines, as shown
   in Figure 5-14, but making dots on your object may work just as well. With a
   little practice, you'll soon get the hang of knowing what kind of marks you need
   for each object.

4. **Click the Background brush and tell Elements what to exclude.**

   Similarly, make some marks in the areas you *don't* want Elements to include in
   your selection.

5. **Click the Preview button.**

The Preview area shows what Elements thinks you want to do. If what you see isn't even close, click Reset and start over.

6. **If necessary, use the various tools to adjust the boundaries of your selection.**

For example, if Elements left off an area you want, usually just one click with the Foreground brush is enough to tell Elements to add it. If there are spots missing within the selection, click the Fill Holes button. If you need to get a better view of your work, use the Zoom and Hand tools (both of which are explained in more detail starting on page 100).

7. **Fine-tune the edges of your selection if you wish.**

Add a feather (page 151), defringe (page 159), or smooth the edges of the selection with the Smoothing brush.

8. **When you like what you see, click OK.**

If you want to give up and try another method, click the Cancel button instead. Figure 5-15 shows what the Magic Extractor can do.

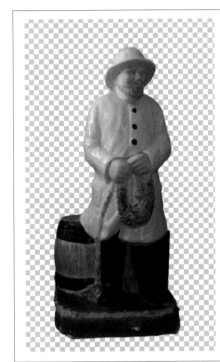

Figure 5-15:
Just the few marks you saw in Figure 5-14 produce this perfectly extracted selection, all ready to move to another image.

TIP   Once you understand layers (Chapter 6), you'll know that the Magic Extractor works only on the active layer of your photo. If you want to extract an object without wrecking the rest of your photo, make a duplicate layer (page 177) and work on that new layer.

The Magic Extractor gives you lots of ways to make sure Elements creates a perfect selection. The toolbox contains a whole set of special tools just for the Extractor, as you can see in Figure 5-16. Each has its own keyboard shortcut to make it easy to switch tools while you work (given in parentheses after the tool's name in the list below). From top to bottom, you get:

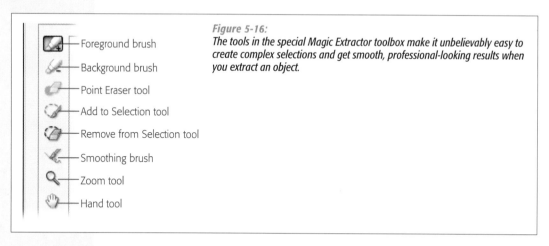

Foreground brush
Background brush
Point Eraser tool
Add to Selection tool
Remove from Selection tool
Smoothing brush
Zoom tool
Hand tool

Figure 5-16:
The tools in the special Magic Extractor toolbox make it unbelievably easy to create complex selections and get smooth, professional-looking results when you extract an object.

- **Foreground brush (Keyboard shortcut: B).** Use this brush to mark what you want to include in your extracted object. You can change the brush color by choosing a different foreground color in the square on the dialog box's right side.

- **Background brush (P).** This brush tells Elements what you want to cut away from your selection. Like the Foreground brush, this brush has a color square on the dialog box's right side where you can choose a different marker color.

- **Point Eraser tool (E).** If you mark something by mistake with the Foreground or Background brush, use this tool to erase the marks.

- **Add to Selection tool (A).** For adding to the selection you already have.

- **Remove from Selection tool (D).** Whatever you paint over with this tool gets removed from your selection.

- **Smoothing brush (J).** Once you've previewed your selection, you can use this brush to even out any ragged edges. Try the Touch Up commands from the right side of the dialog box (they're explained in a moment) first because you may not need this brush.

- **Zoom tool (Z)** and **Hand tool (H).** These are the same trusty standbys you use to adjust your view elsewhere in Elements. See page 100 for more about using the Zoom tool and page 102 for the Hand tool.

TIP   Some of the fine-tuning tools, like the Smoothing brush, work much better if you zoom in pretty close before using them.

So you can see exactly what you're doing, Elements gives you several ways to adjust the tools and your view of the image. These are found on the right side of the dialog box:

- **Tool Options.** You can use the color squares to choose different colors for the Foreground and Background brushes by clicking these squares and using the Color Picker (page 232). You can also adjust the brush size, but that's hardly ever necessary, unless the brush is too big for the area you want to select.

- **Preview.** Choose whether to see just the selected area or your entire image. You can also choose what kind of background you want to see your selection against to get a clearer view. For example, you can choose None (the standard transparency grid), or a black, gray, or white matte, which puts up a temporary solid background to make it easier to check the edges of your selection. Mask is just like the black-and-white view of a layer mask (see page 330). You can paint more of a mask or remove the mask to reveal a larger selection. (Remember that what's masked *isn't* selected.) Rubylith (the brand name of the original red masking film) is just a fancy name for the red mask view as opposed to the black-and-white view you get with Mask.

Once you've previewed your selection, you also get some very helpful options for making sure your selection is absolutely perfect. Most of these options are on the right side of the dialog box, under Touch Up:

- **Feather.** Enter the amount, in pixels, to feather the edge of your selection. (The box on page 151 explains feathering.)

- **Fill Holes.** If Elements left some gaps in your selection, you may be able to fill them by clicking this button. This tool works only for holes that are completely surrounded by selected material, though. If the edges of your selection have bites out of them, use the Smoothing brush instead, or give the area an extra click with the Foreground brush.

- **Defringe.** If your selection has a rim of contrasting pixels around it, this command can usually eliminate them. Figure 5-17 shows what a difference defringing can make. You can choose a different number of pixels for Elements to consider when defringing, but the standard setting is usually fine. Actually, Elements is pretty good about making clean selections, so you probably won't need this button very often.

    TIP If the edges of your selection are ragged but not contrasting, or if defringing alone doesn't clean things up enough, try the Smoothing brush (page 158). Just run it along the edge of your selection to polish it until it's smooth.

Extracting objects used to be a very time-consuming process, often involving expensive third-party plug-ins to make the job easier. Now the Magic Extractor is all you need in most situations.

Rough, jagged edges

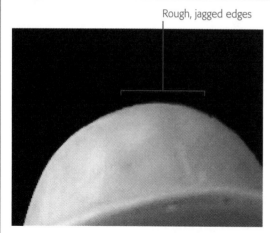

Smoother edges

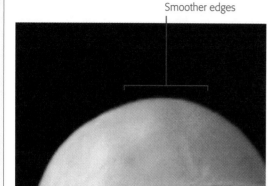

Figure 5-17:
Defringing is a big help in cleaning up the edges of your selections.

Top: Here's a closeup of the top of the little mariner's hat. The matte black background makes the ragged edges stand out. If you look closely, you can see the ragged edges of the yellow hat. If you place this image into another graphic, it'll look like you cut it out with very dull nail scissors.

Bottom: The edges will blend into another image much more believably after you apply defringing. Here you can see how much softer the edges are after defringing. Now you can place the figurine into another file without getting the cut-out effect.

You don't need the Extractor to defringe. You can also use this command on any layer by going to Layer → Defringe Layer.

Changing and Moving Selections

Now that you know all about making selections, it's time to learn some of the finer points about using and manipulating them. Elements gives you several handy options for changing the areas you've selected and for moving images around once they're selected. You can even save a tough selection so you don't have to do *that* again.

Inverting a Selection

One thing you often want to do with a selection is *invert* it. That means telling Elements, "Hey, you know the area I've selected? I want you to select everything *except* that area."

Why would you want to do that? Sometimes it's easier to select what you *don't* want. For example, suppose you have an object with a complicated outline, like the building in Figure 5-18. Say you want to use just the building in a scrapbook of your trip to Europe; it's going to be difficult to select. But the sky is just one big block of color. It's a lot faster to select the sky with the Magic Wand than to try to get an accurate selection of the building.

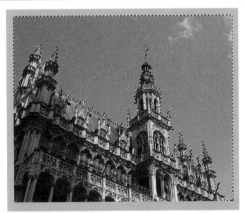

Figure 5-18:
Top: Say you want to make some adjustments to just this building. You could spend half an hour meticulously selecting all that Gothic detail, or just select the sky with a couple of clicks of the Magic Wand and invert your selection to get the building. Here, the sky has the marching ants around it to show that it's the active selection—but that's not what you want.

Bottom: Inverting the selection (Select → Inverse) gives you the ants around the buildings without the trouble of tracing over all the elaborate lacy details of the roofline.

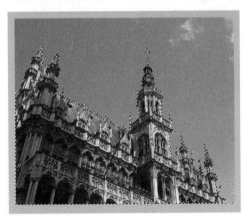

To invert a selection:

1. **Make a selection.**

   Usually, you select what you *don't* want if you're planning to invert your selection. You can select with any tool that suits your fancy.

2. **Go to Select → Inverse, or press Shift+Ctrl+I.**

   Now the part of your image that you *didn't* select is selected.

Making a Selection Larger or Smaller

What if you want to tweak the size of your selection? Sometimes you may want to move the outline of a selection outward a few pixels to expand it. Elements 8 gives you a really handy way to do this: the new Transform Selection command.

With Transform Selection, you can easily drag any selection larger or smaller, rotate it, squish it narrower or shorter, or pull it out longer or wider (think of smooshing a circular selection into an oval, for instance). As its name implies, Transform Selection does all these things to the *selection,* not to the object you've selected. (If you want to distort an object, you can use the Move tool [page 165] or the Transform tools [page 359].) This is really handy, as you can see in Figure 5-19.

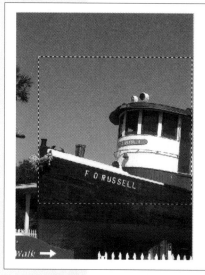
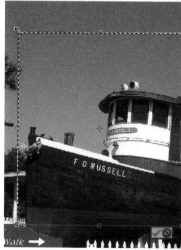

Figure 5-19:
Left: Sometimes it's really hard to draw exactly the selection you want. Here, attempting to avoid the sign and the palm fronds led to part of the rope bumper on the boat's bow being cut off.

Right: After you've decided that it would be easier to clone out any small unwanted details (see page 290 to learn how to clone), Transform Selection makes it easy to resize the selection to include all the rope.

To use Transform Selection:

1. **Make a selection.**

   Use the tools of your choice. Transform Selection is especially handy when you've used one of the Marquee tools and didn't hit the selection quite right, but you can use it on any selection.

2. **Go to Select → Transform Selection.**

   A bounding box with little square handles appears around your image, as shown in Figure 5-19. The Options bar changes to show the settings for this tool, which are the same as those for the Transform tools (page 359), but most of the time you won't need to worry about these settings.

3. **Use a handle to adjust the area covered by your selection.**

   The different ways you can adjust a selection are explained in the list below.

4. **When you get everything just right, click the checkmark or press Enter to accept your changes.**

   If you mess up or change your mind about the whole thing, click Cancel (the red No symbol) to revert to your original selection.

You can change your selection in most of the same ways you learned about back in the section on cropping (page 89):

- **To make your selection wider or narrower,** drag one of the side handles in or out.

- **To make your selection taller or shorter,** drag a top or bottom handle.

- **To make your selection larger or smaller,** drag a corner handle. Before you start, take a quick look at the Options bar to be sure Constrain Proportions is turned on if you want to be sure the selection's shape stays exactly the same. If you want the shape to change, then turn it off.

- **To rotate your selection,** move your mouse near a corner handle till you see the curved arrows, and spin the selection's outline to the angle you want.

Transform Selection is a great tool, but it only expands or contracts your selection in the same ways the Transform tools can change things: in other words, you can change the selection's width and its height as well as its proportions, but you can't change a star-shaped selection into a dog-shaped one, for example. You can use a number of other ways to adjust the size of a selection, which may work better for you in certain situations, although in most cases Transform Selection is probably the easiest. But what do you do if you don't want to keep the selection's shape, but just want to enlarge the selection to include surrounding areas of the same color, for instance? Elements has you covered.

Figuring out which of the following commands to use confuses people because Elements offers two similar-sounding ways to enlarge a selection: Grow and Expand. They sound like they should do the same thing, but there's a slight but important difference between them:

- **Grow** (Select → Grow) moves your selection outward to include more similar contiguous colors, no matter what shape your original selection was. Grow doesn't care about shape; it just finds more matching contiguous pixels.

- **Expand** (Select → Modify → Expand) preserves the shape of your selection and just increases the size of it by the number of pixels you specify.

- **Similar** (Select → Similar) does the same thing as Grow but looks at all pixels, not just the adjacent ones.

- **Contract** (Select → Modify → Contract) shrinks the size of a selection by the number of pixels you specify.

So what's the big distinction between Grow and Expand? Figure 5-20 shows how differently they behave.

Moving Selected Areas

So far you've learned how to move your selections themselves, but often you make selections because you want to move *objects* around—like putting that dreamboat who wouldn't give you the time of day next to you in your class photo.

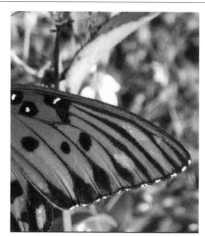

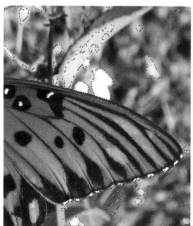
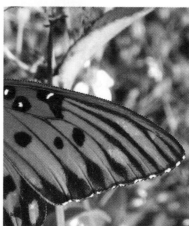

Figure 5-20:
Top: In the original selection, the butterfly's wing has been selected, but the selection missed some small areas on the edge.

Bottom left: If you use Grow to enlarge the selection, you also get parts of the background that are similar in tone. As a result, your selection isn't wing-shaped anymore.

Bottom right: If you use Expand instead, the selection still has the exact shape of the wing, only now the edges of the selection move outward to include the dark border area you missed the first time.

You can move a selection in several ways. Here's the simplest, tool-free way to move something from one image to another:

1. **Select it.**

   Make sure you've selected everything you want. It's really annoying when you paste a selection from one image to another and find you missed a spot.

2. **Press Ctrl+C to copy it.**

   You can use Ctrl+X if you want to cut it out of your original; just remember that Elements leaves a hole if you do that.

3. **If you want to dump the selection into its very own document, choose File → New → "Image from Clipboard".**

   Doing so creates a new document with just your selection in it. If you want to place the selection into an existing photo, follow the instructions in the next step instead.

4. **If you want to add the selection to another photo, then use Ctrl+V to paste it into another image in Elements.**

Once your selection is where you want it, you can use the Move tool (below) to position it, rotate it, or scale it to fit the rest of the photo. You can even paste your selection into a document in *another* program. Just be sure you've turned on Export Clipboard in Edit → Preferences → General.

TIP   If you copy and paste a selection and then notice it's got partially transparent areas in it, back up and go over your selection again with the Selection brush using a hard brush. Then copy and paste again.

Smoothing and Bordering

You'll probably use Refine Edge (page 145) most of the time, but Elements gives you other ways to tweak the edges of your selections:

- **Smoothing** (Select → Modify → Smooth) is a not-always-dependable way to clean up ragged spots in a color-based selection (like you'd make with the Magic Wand, for instance). You enter a pixel value, and Elements evens out your selection based on the number you entered by searching for similarly colored pixels.

  For example, if you enter 5 pixels, Elements looks at a 5-pixel radius around each pixel in your selection. In areas where most of the pixels are already selected, it adds in the others. Where most pixels aren't selected, it deselects the ones that are selected to get rid of the jagged edges and holes in the selection.

This is handy, but smoothing is sometimes hard to control. Usually it's easier to clean up your selection by hand with the Selection brush than to use Smoothing.

- **Bordering** (Select → Modify → Border) adds an anti-aliased, transparent border to your selection. You might say it selects the selection's outline. You might use it when your selection's edges are too hard and you want to soften them, although you're probably better off using Refine Edge. Choose a border size and then click OK. Only the border is selected, so you can also apply a slight Gaussian blur (see page 415) to soften that part of the photo more if you like.

The Move tool

You can also move things around *within* your photo using the Move tool, which lets you cut or copy selected areas. Figure 5-21 shows how to use the Move tool to conceal distracting details.

The Move tool lives at the very top of the Full Edit Tools panel. To use it:

1. **Make a selection.**

   Make sure your selection doesn't have anything in it that you don't want to copy.

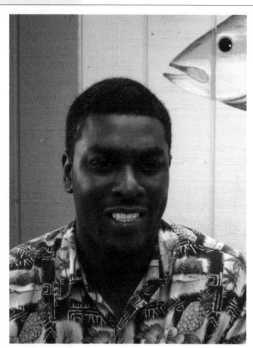

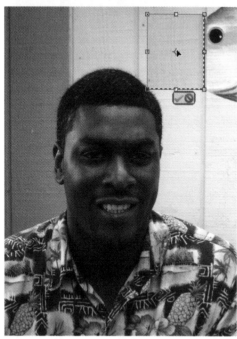

Figure 5-21:

Top: Here's the original version of the photo used for the feathered vignette on page 151. There's a distracting fish painted on the wall behind the man. By copying and moving a piece of the wall, you can cover up the fish and create a simpler background to put the focus on him rather than the background. You select the area prior to moving it.

Bottom: Hold down the Alt key while using the Move tool to copy a selected area. The piece of wall slides into its new position as a fish concealer. (If you use the Move tool without holding down the Alt key, Elements cuts away the selection, leaving a hole in your photo.)

2. **Switch to the Move tool.**

   Click the Move tool or press V. Your selection stays active but is now sur-rounded by a rectangle with square handles on the corners.

3. **Move the selection and press Enter when you're satisfied with its position.**

   As long as your selection is active, you can work on your photo in other ways and then come back and reactivate the Move tool. If you're worried about los-ing a complex selection, save it as described in the next section. If you're not happy with what you've done, just press Ctrl+Z (as many times as needed) to back up and start over again.

You can move a selection in several different ways:

- **Move it.** If you simply move a selection by dragging it, you leave a hole in the background where the selection was. The Move tool *truly* moves your selection. So unless you have something under it that you want to show through, that's probably not what you want to do.

- **Copy it and then move the copy.** If you press the Alt key as you're moving, you'll copy your selection, so the original stays where it is. But now you have a duplicate to move around and play with, as in Figure 5-21.

- **Resize it.** You can drag the Move tool's handles to resize or distort your selected material, which is great when you need to change the size of your selection. The Move tool lets you do the same things you can do with Free Transform (see page 359).

- **Rotate it.** The Move tool lets you rotate your selection the same way you can rotate a picture using Free Rotate (see page 89): Just grab a corner and turn it.

   TIP   You can save a trip to the Tools panel and move selections without activating the Move tool. To move a selection without copying it, just place your cursor in the selection, hold down Ctrl, and move the selection. To move a copy of a selection, do the same thing, but hold down the Alt key as well. You can drag the copy without damaging the original. To move multiple copies, just let go, press Ctrl+Alt again, and drag once more.

The Move tool is also a great way to manage and move objects that you've put on their own layers (Chapter 6). Page 186 explains how to use the Move tool to arrange layered objects.

Saving Selections

You can tell Elements to remember the outline of your selection so that you can reuse it again later on. This is a wonderful, easy timesaver for particularly intricate selections.

NOTE Elements' saved selections are the equivalent of Photoshop's *alpha channels*. Keep that in mind if you decide to try tutorials written for the full-featured Photoshop. Incidentally, alpha channels saved in Photoshop show up in Elements as saved selections, and vice versa.

To save a selection:

1. **Make your selection.**

2. **Choose Select → Save Selection, name your selection, and then click OK to save it.**

   When you want to use the selection again, go to Select → Load Selection, and there it is waiting for you.

   TIP When you save a feathered selection (see page 151) and then change your mind about how much feather you want, use the Refine Edge command (page 145) to adjust it. You can also save a hard-edged selection, load it, and then go to Select → Feather to add a feather if you need one. That way you can change the amount each time you use the selection, as long as you remember not to save the change to the selection.

Making changes to a saved selection

It's probably just as easy to start your selection over if you need to tweak a saved selection, but you can make changes if you want. This can save you time if your original selection was really tricky to create.

Say you've got a full-length photo of somebody, and you've created and saved a selection of the person's face (called, naturally enough, "Face"). Now, imagine that after applying a filter to the selection, you decide it would look silly to change only the face and not the person's hands, too. So you want to add the hands to your saved selection.

You have a couple of ways to do this. The simplest is just to load up "Face," activate your selection tool of choice, put the tool in "Add to Selection" mode, select the hands, and then save the selection again with the same name.

But what if you've already selected the hands and you want to add *that* new selected area to the existing facial selection? Here's what you'd do:

1. **Go to Select → Save Selection.**

   Choose your saved "Face" selection. All the radio buttons in the dialog box become active.

2. **Choose "Add to Selection".**

   What you just selected (the hands) is added to the original selection and saved, so now your "Face" selection includes the hands, too.

Layers: The Heart of Elements

If you've been working mostly in the Quick Fix window so far, you've probably noticed that once you close your file, the changes you've made are permanent. You can undo actions while the file's still open, but once you close it, you're stuck with what you've done.

In Elements, you can keep your changes (most kinds, anyway) and still revert to the original image if you use *layers,* a nifty system of transparent sheets that keeps each component of your image on a separate sliver that you can edit. Layers are one of the greatest image-editing inventions ever. By putting each change you make on its own layer, you can constantly rearrange your image's composition, and add or subtract changes whenever you want.

If you use layers, then you can save your file and quit Elements, come back days or weeks later, and *still* undo what you did or change things around some more. There's no statute of limitations for the changes you make using layers.

Some people resist learning about layers because they fear layers are too complicated. But they're actually really easy to use once you understand how they work. And once you get started with layers, you'll realize that using Elements without them is like driving a Ferrari in first gear. This chapter gives you the info you need to get comfortable working with layers.

Understanding Layers

Imagine you've got a barebones drawing of a room you're thinking about redecorating. To get an idea of your different decorating options, imagine that you've also got a bunch of transparent plastic sheets, each containing an image that changes the room's look: a couch, a few different colors for the carpet, a standing lamp, and so on. Your decorating work is now pretty easy, since you can add, remove, and mix and match the transparencies with ease.

Layers in Elements work pretty much the same way. With layers, you can add and remove objects, and make changes to the way your image looks. And you can modify or discard any of these changes later on.

Figure 6-1 shows an Elements file that includes layers. Each object in the flyer is on a different layer, so you can easily remove or rearrange things. (If you want to follow along and work with a layers-heavy file, you can download a version of this file—*gardenpartywin.psd*—from this book's Missing CD page at *www.missingmanuals.com.*)

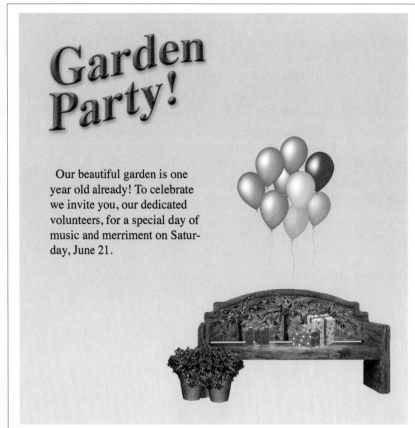

Figure 6-1:
Every object in this flyer—the background, the bench, the balloons, each block of text—is on its own layer, which makes changing things a snap. Want to change the background, get rid of the balloons, or change the date? Layers make changes like that easy.

NOTE   It's important to understand that photos from your camera start out with just one layer. That means if you've got a photo like the one in Figure 6-2, top, the individual objects—the two people, the ground they're standing on, and so on—all exist on the same layer. At least they do until you select a particular object and place it on its own layer.

That said, Elements often generates layers for you when you need them. For example, Elements automatically creates layers when you do things like move an object from one photo to another, or use the Smart Brush tool (page 211), which thoughtfully puts the changes it makes on their own layer.

You can also use layers for many adjustments to your photos, which lets you tweak or eliminate those changes later on. For instance, say you used Quick Fix's Hue slider, but the next day decide you don't like what you did—you're stuck (unless you can dig out a copy of your original). But if you'd used a *Hue/Saturation Adjustment layer* (page 196) to make the change, you could just throw out that layer and keep all your other changes intact. You can also use layers to combine parts of different photos, as shown in Figure 6-2.

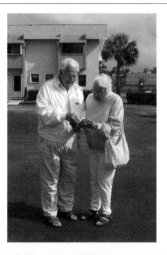

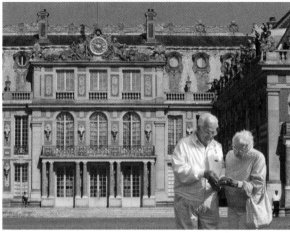

Figure 6-2:
Layers make it easy to combine elements from different images. Maybe you can't afford to send your grandparents on a real trip to Europe, but once you understand layers, you can give them a virtual vacation. When you copy part of one photo into another image, as was done here, Elements automatically places the pasted-in material on its own layer. You don't have to do anything special to create the layer—it just happens. Page 197 has more about combining elements from different photos.

Once you understand how to use layers, you'll feel much more comfortable making radical changes to an image, because any mistakes will be much easier to fix. Not only that, but by using layers, you can easily make lots of sophisticated changes that are otherwise very difficult and time-consuming. But the main reason to use layers is for creative freedom: Layers let you easily create lots of special effects that would be tough to get otherwise.

The Layers Panel

The Layers panel is your control center for any layer-related action you want to perform, like adding, deleting, or duplicating layers. Figure 6-3 shows you the Layers panel for an image with lots of layers. You see each layer's name and a little thumbnail of the layer's contents. You can adjust the size of the thumbnails or turn them off altogether, as explained in Figure 6-4.

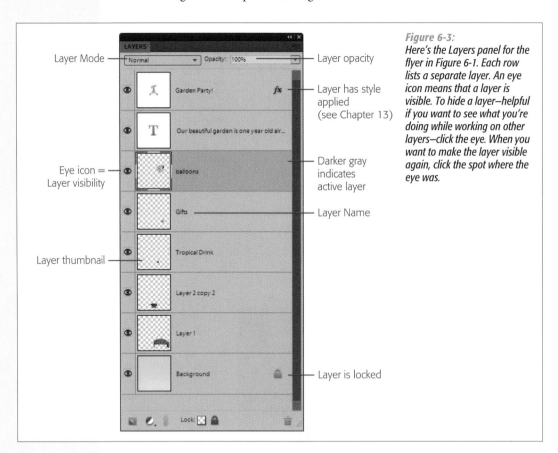

Figure 6-3:
Here's the Layers panel for the flyer in Figure 6-1. Each row lists a separate layer. An eye icon means that a layer is visible. To hide a layer—helpful if you want to see what you're doing while working on other layers—click the eye. When you want to make the layer visible again, click the spot where the eye was.

Labels in figure:
- Layer Mode
- Layer opacity
- Layer has style applied (see Chapter 13)
- Eye icon = Layer visibility
- Darker gray indicates active layer
- Layer Name
- Layer thumbnail
- Layer is locked

TIP   It helps to keep the Layers panel handy whenever you work with layers, not only for the info it gives you, but also because you can usually manipulate layers more easily from the panel than directly in your image. And many changes, like renaming a layer, you can make *only* in the panel.

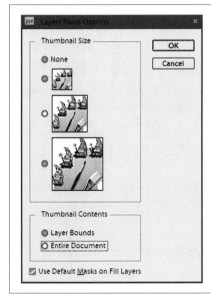

Figure 6-4:
If you want to change the size of the thumbnails in the Layers panel, in the panel's upper-right corner, click the almost invisible little square made of horizontal lines (above the Opacity setting) to open the panel's pop-out menu. Near the bottom of the menu, choose Panel Options, and the dialog box shown here appears. In this case, medium-sized icons are selected.

The Layers panel usually contains one layer that's *active,* meaning that any action you take, like painting, is going to happen on that layer (and that layer only). You can tell which layer is active by looking at the Layers panel—the active one is darker than the others (see Figure 6-3).

> **NOTE**   If you use the layer selection tricks described on page 184, then you can wind up with multiple active layers or none, but you generally want to have only one active layer.

When you look at a layered image, you're looking down on the stack of layers from the top, just the way you would with overlays on a drawing. The layers appear in the same order as in the Layers panel—the top layer of your image is the top layer in the Layers panel. (Layer order is important because what's on top can obscure what's beneath it.)

Elements lets you do lots of different maneuvers right in the Layers panel. You can make a layer's contents invisible and then visible again, change the order in which layers are stacked, link layers together, change layers' opacity, add and delete layers—the list goes on and on. The rest of this chapter covers all these options and more.

> **NOTE**   The Layers panel is really important, so most people like to keep it around. Use any of the panel management techniques described on page 24 to put it where it's easy to get to while you work.

The Background

The bottom layer of any image is a special kind of layer called the *Background.* When you first open an image or photo in Elements, its one existing layer is called

"Background". (That's assuming that nobody else has already edited the file in Elements and changed things.) The name Background is logical because whatever else you do will happen on top of this layer.

> **NOTE** There are two exceptions to the first-layer-is-always-the-Background rule. First, if you create a new image by copying something from another picture, then you just have a layer called "Layer 0." Second, Background layers can't be transparent, so if you choose the Transparency option (page 52) when creating a file from scratch, then you have a Layer 0 instead of a Background layer.

As for content, the Background can be totally plain or busy, busy, busy. A Background layer doesn't mean that it literally contains the background of your photograph—your whole photo can be a Background layer. It's entirely up to you what's on your Background layer, and what you place on other, newly added layers. With photographs, people often keep the basic photo on the Background layer, and then perform adjustments and embellishments (like adding type) on other layers.

You can do a lot to Background layers, but there are a few things you *can't* do: Change their blending modes (see page 182), opacity (page 180), or position in the layer stack. If you want to do any of those, then you need to convert the Background into a regular layer first.

> **TIP** The Background Eraser and Magic Eraser automatically turn a Background layer into a regular layer when you click a background with them. For example, say you have a picture of an object on a solid background and you want transparency around the object. One click with the Magic Eraser turns the Background layer into a regular layer, eliminates the solid-colored background, and replaces it with transparency. (There's more on the Eraser tools on page 387.)

You can change a Background layer into a regular layer by double-clicking the layer in the Layers panel, or going to Layer → New → Layer From Background. Or, if you try to make certain kinds of changes to the background (like using the Transform commands [page 359]), then Elements prompts you to change the Background layer into a regular layer.

You can also transform a regular layer into a Background layer if you want. One reason to do this is to send a layer zipping down to the bottom of the stack in a many-layered file. To do so:

1. **In the Layers panel, click the layer you want to convert to a Background layer.**

2. **Select Layer → New → "Background from Layer".**

   It may take a few seconds for Elements to finish calculating and to respond. When it's done thinking, the layer you've changed moves down to the bottom of the layer stack in the Layers panel and Elements renames it "Background."

COMPATIBILITY CORNER

Which File Types Can Use Layers?

You can add layers to any file you can open in Elements, but not every file format lets you *save* layers.

For instance, if your camera shoots JPEGs, you can open those JPEGs in Elements and add lots of layers to them. But when you try to save these files, Elements presents you with the Save As dialog box instead of just saving. If you turn off the dialog box's Save Layers checkbox, a warning tells you that you have to save as a copy. That's because you can't have layers in a JPEG file, and Elements is reminding you that you need to save in another format to keep the layers.

You usually want to choose either Photoshop (.psd) or TIFF as your format when saving an image with layers, because they both let you keep your layers. (PDF files can also have layers.) But if you don't need the layers, then just save your JPEG as a copy, close the original file, and say No when asked if you want to save changes.

If someone using the full-featured Photoshop sends you a layered image, then you see the layers in the Layers panel when you open the file in Elements. Likewise, Photoshop folks can see layers you create in Elements.

If you open a Photoshop file with a layer that says "indicates a set" when you move your cursor over it in the Layers panel, you have what Photoshop calls a Layer Group or *layer set* (a way to group *layers* into what are essentially folders in the Layers panel), depending on which version of Photoshop created the file. Elements doesn't understand layer sets, so ask the sender to expand the sets and send you the file again. Alternatively, you can use Layer → Simplify to convert the set to a single layer, which may or may not be editable.

Creating Layers

As you learned earlier in the chapter, your image doesn't automatically have multiple layers. Lots of newcomers to Elements expect the program to be smart enough to put each object in a photo onto its own layer. It's a lovely dream, but Elements isn't that brainy. To experience the joy of layers, you first need to add at least one layer to your image; you'll learn how in the next few sections.

> TIP   It may help you to follow along through the next few sections if you get out a photo of your own or create a new file to use for practice. (See page 50 for details on how to create a new file; if you do that, choose a white background.) Or, you can download either *gardenpartywin.psd* or *daisies.jpg* from the Missing CD page at *www.missingmanuals.com*.

Adding a Layer

Elements gives you several ways to add new layers. You can use any of the following methods:

- Choose Layer → New → Layer.

- Press Shift+Ctrl+N.

- In the Layers panel, click the "Create a new layer" icon (the little square shown in Figure 6-5).

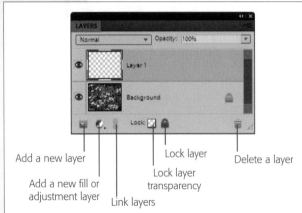

Figure 6-5:
More controls in the Layers panel. At the bottom left of the panel, click the little "Create a new layer" icon when you want to quickly add a new layer.

Add a new layer

Add a new fill or adjustment layer

Link layers

Lock layer transparency

Lock layer

Delete a layer

When you create a new layer using any of these commands, the layer starts out empty. You don't see a change in your image until you use the layer for something (painting on it, for example). If you look at the Layers panel, then you see that the new layer you added is just above the layer that was active when you created it. New layers get added directly above the active layer. So if you want a new layer at the top of the stack, click the current top layer to make it active before creating the new layer.

> **NOTE** The only practical limit to the number of layers your image can have is your computer's processing power. But if you find yourself regularly creating projects with upwards of 100 layers, you may want to upgrade to Photoshop, which has tools that make it easier to manage lots of layers.

Some actions create new layers automatically. For instance, if you copy and paste an object from another photo (see page 197 for instructions) or add artwork from the Content panel, then the object automatically arrives on its own layer. That's really handy because it lets you put the new item just where you want it, without disturbing the rest of your composition.

Sometimes you have to manually create new layers, but you don't always need a blank layer. An example of when you'd make a layer first is when you want to clone something (page 290). If you don't make a separate layer to clone on, your changes go right onto your Background layer, and you can't undo them after closing the file.

Deleting Layers

If you decide you don't want a particular layer anymore, you can easily delete it. Figure 6-6 shows the simplest method.

Elements also gives you a few other ways to delete a layer. You can:

- Select Layer → Delete Layer.

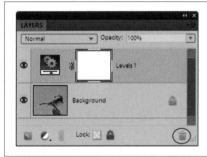

Figure 6-6:
To make a layer go away, either drag it to the trashcan icon on the Layers panel or select the layer and then click the trashcan (circled). Elements asks if you want to delete the active layer. Say yes, and it's history. Once you delete a layer, you can get it back by using one of the Undo commands (page 36), but once you close the file, the layer is gone forever.

- Right-click the layer in the Layers panel, and then, from the pop-up menu, choose Delete Layer.

- Click the Layers panel's upper-right square made of horizontal lines, and then, from the pop-up menu, choose Delete Layer.

Duplicating a Layer

Duplicating a layer can be really useful. Many Elements features, like filters or color-modification tools, don't work on brand-new, *empty* layers. This poses a problem because if you apply such changes to the layer containing your main image, then you alter it in ways you can't undo later. The workaround is to create a *duplicate* of the image layer and make your changes on the copy. Then you can ditch the duplicate later if you change your mind, and your original layer is safely tucked away unchanged.

If all this seems annoyingly theoretical, try going to Enhance → Adjust Color → Adjust Hue/Saturation, for example, when you're working on a new blank layer. You get the stern dialog box shown in Figure 6-7.

> **NOTE** Very rarely, you may encounter the dreaded "no pixels are more than 50% selected" warning. Several things can cause this, but the most common are too large a feather value on a selection (see the box on page 151) or trying to work in the empty part of a layer that contains objects surrounded by transparency.

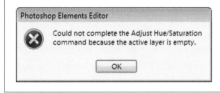

Figure 6-7:
Elements is usually pretty helpful when you try to do something that just isn't going to work, like applying a Hue/Saturation adjustment to an empty layer. The solution here is just to switch the Layers panel's focus to a layer that has something in it.

Elements gives you a few ways to duplicate a layer and its content. Select the layer you want to copy to make it the active layer, and then do one of the following:

- Press Ctrl+J. (Be sure you don't have any active selections when you do this, or Elements only copies the selection to the new layer.)

- Choose Layer → Duplicate Layer.

- In the Layers panel, drag the layer you want to copy to the "Create a new layer" icon.

- In the Layers panel, right-click the Layer, and then, from the pop-up menu, choose Duplicate Layer.

- Click the little four-lined square at the upper right of the Layers panel, and then choose Duplicate Layer.

All of these methods copy everything in the active layer into the new layer. You can then mess with the duplicate as much as you want without damaging the original.

GEM IN THE ROUGH

Naming Layers

You may have noticed that Elements isn't terribly creative when it comes to naming layers: You get Layer 1, Layer 2, and so on. Fortunately, you don't have to live with those titles. You can easily rename your layers.

Maybe renaming layers sounds like a job for people with too much time on their hands, but if you're working on a project that has lots of layers, you may find that you can pick out the layers you want more quickly if you give them descriptive names.

Incidentally, you can't rename a Background layer; you have to change it into a regular layer first. Also, Elements helps you out with Text layers (see page 446) by naming them using the first few words of the text they contain. To rename a layer:

1. **Double-click its name in the Layers panel.** The name becomes an active text box.

2. **Type in the new name.** You don't even need to highlight the text—Elements does that for you automatically.

As with any other change, you have to save your image afterward if you want to keep the new name.

Copying and Cutting from Layers

You can also make a new layer that consists of only a *piece* of an existing layer. (This is helpful for things like applying a Layer style to one object from the layer, for instance.) But first you need to decide whether you want to *copy* your selection or *cut* it out and place it on the new layer.

What's the difference? It's pretty much the same as copying versus cutting in your word processing program. When you make a "New Layer via Copy", the area you select appears in the new layer and remains in the old layer, too. On the other hand, "New Layer via Cut" removes the selection from the old layer and places it on a new layer, leaving a corresponding hole in the old layer. Figure 6-8 shows the difference.

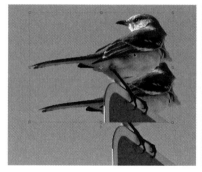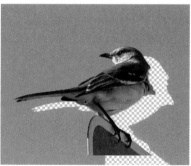

Figure 6-8:
The difference between "New Layer via Copy" and "New Layer via Cut" is obvious when you move the new layer to see what's beneath it.

Left: With "New Layer via Copy", the original bird is still in place in the underlying layer.

Right: When you use "New Layer via Cut", the excised bird leaves a hole behind.

Once you've selected what you want to copy or cut, your new layer is only a couple of keystrokes away:

- **New Layer via Copy.** You can most easily copy your selection to a new layer by pressing Ctrl+J. (You can also go to Layer → New → "Layer via Copy".) Either way, if you don't select anything beforehand, your *whole* layer gets copied, making this a good shortcut for creating a duplicate layer.

- **New Layer via Cut.** To cut your selection out of your old layer and put it on a layer by itself, press Shift+Ctrl+J (or go to Layer → New → "Layer via Cut"). Just remember that you leave a hole in your original layer when you do this. (On a Background layer, the hole is filled with the current background color.) If you want to cut and move everything in a layer, you can press Ctrl+A first, although usually it's easier just to move your layer instead. Just drag it up or down the stack in the Layers panel to put it where you want it.

TIP   If you want to use a layer as the basis for a new document, Elements gives you a quick way to do so. Instead of copying and pasting, you can create a new document by going to Layer → Duplicate Layer. You get a dialog box containing a drop-down menu that gives you the option of placing the duplicate layer into your existing image, into any image currently open in the Editor, or into a new document of its own. (This maneuver works only from the Layer menu; pressing Ctrl+J doesn't bring up the dialog box.) You can also create a new document with only part of a layer by pressing Ctrl+C to copy the part you want and then going to File → New → "Image from Clipboard".

Managing Layers

The Layers panel lets you manipulate your layers in all kinds of ways, but first you need to understand a few more of the panel's cryptic icons. Some of the things you can do with layers may seem obscure when you first read about them, but once you actually use layers, you'll quickly see why many of these options exist. The next few sections explain how to manipulate layers in several different ways: hide them, group them together, change the way you see them, and combine them.

Making Layers Invisible

You can turn the visibility of layers off and on at will. This feature is tremendously useful. If the image you're working on has a busy background, for example, it's hard to see what you're doing when working on a particular layer. Making the Background layer invisible can really help you focus on the layer you're interested in. To turn off visibility, in the Layers panel, click the eye icon to hide the layer. Click the eye once more to make the layer visible again.

> **TIP** If you have a bunch of hidden layers and decide you don't want them anymore, click the Layers panel's little four-line square in the upper right, and choose Delete Hidden Layers to get rid of them all at once.

Adjusting Opacity

Your choices for layer visibility aren't limited to on and off. You can create immensely cool effects by adjusting the *opacity* of layers. In other words, you can make a layer partially transparent so that what's underneath it shows through.

To adjust a layer's opacity, click the layer in the Layers panel, and then either:

- Double-click the Opacity box, and then type in the percentage of opacity you want.
- Click the triangle to the right of the Opacity percentage and adjust the pop-out slider, or just put your cursor on the word "Opacity" and "scrub" (drag) left for less opacity or right for more. (Figure 6-9 explains the advantage of scrubbing.) If you'd like to experiment with creating Fill and Adjustment layers (page 193) and changing their modes and opacity, download *daisies.jpg* from the Missing CD page at *www.missingmanuals.com*.

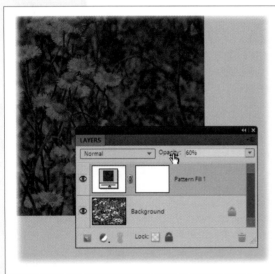

Figure 6-9:
You can watch the opacity of your layer change on the fly if you drag your cursor back and forth over the word "Opacity". Different blend modes (see page 182) often give the best effect if you adjust the opacity of their layers.

When you create a new layer using either the keyboard shortcut (Shift+Ctrl+N) or the menu (Layer → New → Layer), you can set the opacity right away in the New Layer dialog box. If you create a new layer by clicking the Layers panel's New Layer icon, then you need to Alt-click the New Layer icon to bring up the New Layer dialog box so you can change the opacity.

NOTE   You can't change a Background layer's opacity. You have to convert it to a regular layer first; page 174 explains how.

Locking Layers

You can protect your image from yourself by *locking* any of the layers. Locking keeps you from changing a layer's contents. You can also lock just the transparent parts of a layer—helpful when you want to modify an object that sits atop a transparent layer, like the seashell in Figure 6-10. When you do that, the transparent parts of your layer stay transparent no matter what you do to the rest of it. (You're actually locking the pixels' current transparency level, so if you have pixels that are only partly transparent, then they stay at their current transparency level, too.)

To lock the transparent parts of a layer, select the layer, and then, in the Layers panel, click the little "Lock transparent pixels" checkerboard. (Its grayed out if you have no transparency in your photo.) When you lock the transparency, a light gray padlock appears in the Layers panel to the right of the layer's name. The checkerboard icon shows a tiny border when a layer's transparency is locked. To unlock it, just click the checkerboard again.

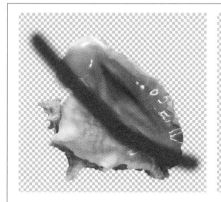 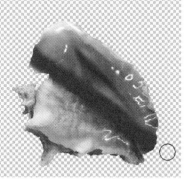

Figure 6-10:
After you've isolated an object on its own layer, sometimes you want to paint only on the object—and not on the transparent portion of the layer. Elements lets you lock the transparent part of a layer, making it easy to paint just the object.

Left: On a regular layer, paint goes wherever the brush does.

Right: With the layer's transparency locked, the stroke stops at the edge of the seashell, even though the brush (the circle) is now on the transparent part of the layer.

To lock *everything* in a layer so you can't make any changes to it, click the "Lock all" icon (the dark gray padlock in the Layers panel next to the checkerboard). A dark gray padlock appears in the Layers panel to the right of the layer's name, and the "Lock all" icon shows a dark gray outline around it. Now if you try to paint on that layer or use any other tools on it, your cursor turns into a universal No symbol (a red circle with a diagonal line through it) as a reminder that you can't edit that layer. You'll also see a lock icon next to the layer's name in the Layers panel. To unlock the layer, just click the "Lock all" icon again.

> **NOTE** Locking only preserves the layer from edits. It doesn't stop you from merging it into another layer or flattening it, or from cropping your image.

Blend Mode

In the Layers panel, you see a little menu that says "Normal" or, in the New Layer dialog box, "Mode: Normal". This is your *blend mode* setting. When used with layers, blend modes control how the objects in a layer combine, or *blend,* with the objects in the layer beneath it. By using different blend modes, you can make your image lighter or darker, or even make it look like a poster, with just a few bold colors in it. Blend modes can also control how some tools—those with Blend Mode settings—change your image. Changing a tool's blend mode can sometimes dramatically change your results.

Blend modes are an awful lot of fun once you understand how to use them. They can help you fix under- or overexposed photos and create all kinds of special visual effects. You can also use some tools, like the Brush tool, in different blend modes to achieve different effects. The most common blend mode is Normal, in which everything you do behaves just the way you'd expect: An object shows its regular colors, and paint acts just like, well, paint.

Page 382 has lots more about how to use blend modes. For now, take a look at Figure 6-11, which shows how you can totally change the way a layer looks just by changing its blend mode.

> **TIP** The blend modes are grouped together in the menu according to the way they affect your image.

Not every blend mode makes a visible change in every circumstance. Some of them may seem to do nothing—that's to be expected. It just means that you don't have a condition in your current image that's responding to that particular mode change. See page 242 for one example of a situation where a mode change makes an enormous difference.

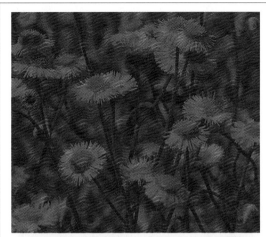

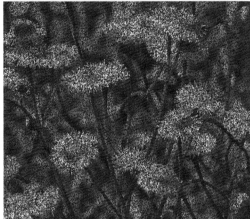

Figure 6-11:
This photo of fleabane flowers has a Pattern Fill layer over it, showing three different modes. In normal mode at 100-percent opacity, the pattern would completely hide the leaves, but by changing the blend mode and opacity of the pattern layer, you can create very different looks. (There's more about Pattern layers on page 195.) From top to bottom, the modes are Normal, Dissolve, and Hard Mix. Notice how Dissolve gives a grainy effect and Hard Mix produces a vivid, posterized effect.

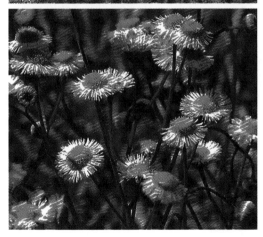

Fading in Elements

One great thing you get in the full-featured Photoshop that Elements lacks is the ability to *fade* special effects and filters. Fading gives you fine control over how much these tools change an image. (Often, filters generate harsh-looking results, and Photoshop's Fade command helps adjust a filter's effect until it's what you intended.)

In Elements, you can approximate the Fade tool: First, apply filters, effects, or layer styles to a duplicate layer. Then, reduce the layer's opacity till it blends in with what's below (and change the blend mode if necessary) to get exactly the result you want.

Rearranging Layers

One of the truly amazing things you can do with Elements is move your layers around. You can change the order in which layers are stacked so that different objects appear in front of or behind each other. For example, you can position one object behind another if they're both on their own layers. In the Layers panel, just grab the layer and drag it to where you want it.

> **TIP** Remember, you're always looking down onto the layer stack when you look at your image, so moving something up in the Layers panel's list moves it toward the front of the picture.

Figure 6-12 shows the early stages of the garden party invitation from Figure 6-1. The potted plants are already in place, and the bench was brought in from another image. The bench came in at the top of the stack, in front of the flowers. To put the bench behind the plants, simply drag the bench layer below the plants layer in the Layers panel.

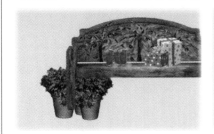 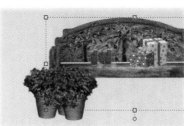

Figure 6-12:
Left: When you bring a new element into an image, it comes in on top of the active layer. In this case that move made the bench the front object.

Right: Move the new layer down in the stack, and the new object appears behind the objects on layers above it, just as the bench moves behind the plants here.

> **NOTE** Background layers are the only kind of layer you *can't* move. If you want to bring a Background layer to another spot in the layer stack, first convert it to a regular layer (page 174), and then move it.

You can also move layers by going to Layer → Arrange, and then choosing one of these commands:

- **Bring to Front** (Shift+Ctrl+]) sends the selected layer to the top of the stack so the layer's contents appear in the foreground of your image.

- **Bring Forward** (Ctrl+]) moves the layer up one level in the Layers panel, so it appears one step closer to the front of your image.

- **Send Backward** (Ctrl+[) moves the layer down one level so it's sent back one step in the image.

- **Send to Back** (Shift+Ctrl+[) puts the layer directly above the Background layer so it appears as far back as you can move anything.

- **Reverse** (no keyboard shortcut) switches two layers' locations in the stack. You have to select two layers in the panel (by Ctrl-clicking, for example) before using this command.

> **TIP** These commands (except Reverse) are also available from the Move tool's Options bar or by right-clicking in your photo when the Move tool is active. As a matter of fact, the Move tool can be a great way to rearrange layers in your image, as the next section explains.

Arranging layers with the Move tool

Using the Move tool, you can select and arrange layers right in the image window, without trekking all the way over to the Layers panel. (If you need a refresher on Move tool basics, flip to page 165.) To arrange layers with the Move tool:

1. **Activate the Move tool.**

   Click its icon in the Tools panel or press V.

2. **Select the layer(s) you want to move.**

   As soon as you activate the Move tool, you see a bounding box (the dotted lines) around the active layer in your image. As you move your cursor over the image, you see a blue outline around the layer the cursor is over—no matter how far down the layer stack the object is (see Figure 6-13). When you click to select the layer you want to move, a dotted-line bounding box appears around that layer. Shift-click to select multiple layers, and the bounding box expands to include everything you've selected. You can also drag a selection around multiple layers and choose them that way. (For instance, you could drag over all the balloons to move them as a group, so you don't have to rearrange them afterward.)

3. **Move the Layer.**

   For example, choose Layer → Arrange, or click the Options bar's Arrange Menu, or right-click inside the bounding box in the image. You see all the choices described in the previous section ("Bring to Front", Bring Forward, and so on) except for Reverse, which is available only from the Layer menu. You can also use keyboard shortcuts (again, except for Reverse).

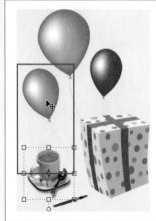

Figure 6-13:
The Move tool lets you select objects from any layer, not just the active one. When you move the cursor over an object, you see a blue outline around its layer. Here, the coffee cup is the active layer (you can see the bounding box around it), but the Move tool is ready to select the pink balloon, even though it's not on the active layer. If all these outlines annoy you, then you can turn them off in the Options bar (via the Show Bounding Box or "Show Highlight on Rollover" checkboxes). If you want to force the Move tool to concentrate only on the active layer, then turn off Auto Select Layer in the Options bar. (Incidentally, everything in this image came from the Content panel [page 474].)

NOTE   If you selected multiple layers, you may find that some of the commands are grayed out (that is, you can't choose them). If that's a problem, just click elsewhere in the image to deselect the layers, and then move the layers one at a time instead of as a group.

Aligning and Distributing Layers

You can easily arrange objects in an image thanks to the Move tool. The tool's *aligning* feature arranges the items on each layer so that they line up straight along their top, bottom, left, or right edges, or through their centers. So, for example, if you align the top edges of your objects, then Elements makes sure that the top of each object is exactly in line with the others.

TIP   Don't forget that in Elements 8 you can set guidelines (page 87) to help you position objects just so in your image.

You'll also find it a breeze to evenly distribute the *spacing* between multiple objects. The Move tool's *distributing* feature spaces out objects, also letting you choose edges or centers as a guide. If you distribute the top edges, for example, Elements makes sure there's an even amount of space from the top edge of one object to another.

TIP   Distributing objects is especially handy when you're creating projects like those described in Chapter 15.

Aligning and distributing layers with the Move tool works much like rearranging layers:

1. **Activate the Move tool.**

   Click its icon in the Tools panel or press V.

2. **Select the objects you want to align.**

   This maneuver works only if each object is on its own layer. If you have multiple objects on one layer, then move them to their own layers one at a time by selecting each object, and then pressing Ctrl+Shift+J.

   Shift-click inside the blue outline to select each layer you want to work with, or Shift-click or Ctrl-click in the Layers panel to select the layers you want.

3. **Choose how you want to align or distribute the objects by selecting from the Options bar menus.**

   The Align and Distribute menus both give you the same choices: Top Edges, Vertical Centers, Bottom Edges, Left Edges, Horizontal Centers, and Right Edges. The little thumbnails next to each option show you exactly how your objects will line up.

   TIP   You can apply as many different align and distribute commands as you like, as long as the layers you're working with are still inside the bounding box. Figure 6-14 also gives you an example of how these commands work.

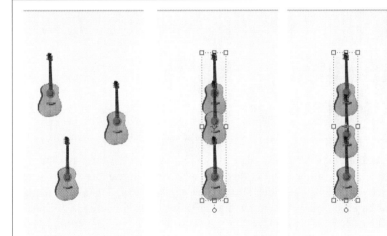

Figure 6-14:
Left: Each of these guitars is on its own layer, but they need to be tidied up if you want them in a neat stack.

Center left: Here's the result of selecting the guitars with the Move tool and then picking Align → Horizontal Center. As you see, the centers of the guitars are aligned, but they're not evenly distributed.

Right: The guitars after a trip to Distribute → Vertical Centers. Note that they're evenly spaced but still overlapping. That's because Distribute doesn't add any additional space between the outermost objects. If you want wider spacing between objects, then make sure they're farther apart before you distribute them.

Grouping and Linking Layers

What if you want to move several layers at once? For instance, in the garden party image back on page 170, two layers have potted plants in them. It's kind of a pain to drag each one individually if you need to move them in front of the bench. Fortunately, you don't have to; Elements gives you a way to keep your layers united.

Linking layers

You can *link* two or more layers together so they travel as a unit, as shown in Figure 6-15.

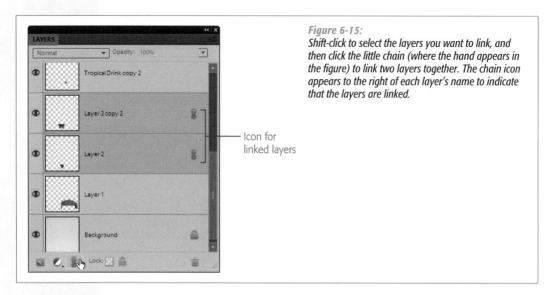

Figure 6-15:
Shift-click to select the layers you want to link, and then click the little chain (where the hand appears in the figure) to link two layers together. The chain icon appears to the right of each layer's name to indicate that the layers are linked.

Icon for
linked layers

If you want to unlink layers, then select the linked layers by clicking one, and then clicking the same chain icon you clicked to link them. You can always merge the layers (covered in the next section) into one layer if you want. Sometimes, though, you'll want to keep layers separate, while still being able to move the layers as a group, so linking is the way to go. You can also use the layer selection choices, described in the box on page 189, and skip the linking. As long as your layers all stay selected, they travel as a group. Linking's advantage is that your layers stay associated until you unlink them. There's no need to worry about accidentally clicking somewhere else in the panel and losing your selection group.

Grouping layers by clipping

An even more powerful way to combine layers is to group them together using a *clipping mask*. While this technique sounds complex, it's actually quite easy and very powerful. With this kind of grouping, one layer (the clipping mask layer) influences the other layers it's grouped with.

Selecting Layers

You can quickly choose multiple layers when you want to do things like link, move, or delete layers. For your quick-selection pleasure, Elements gives you a whole group of layer-selection commands, which you'll find in the Select menu. Here's what they do:

- **All Layers.** Choose this command, and every layer except the Background layer gets selected. Even if you've turned off a layer's visibility (page 180), that layer still gets selected.

- **Deselect Layers.** When you're done working with layers as a group, choose this option and you won't have any layers selected until you click one.

- **Similar Layers.** This command is the most useful. Choose this option and every layer that's the same type as the active one gets selected, no matter where it is in the stack. So, for example, if you have a Text layer active when you choose Similar Layers, Elements selects *all* your Text layers. Or if you have an Adjustment layer active, all the Adjustment layers get selected. You can use this command to quickly select a stack of Adjustment layers you want to drag to another image, for instance, using the technique described on page 198.

You can also Shift-click to select multiple layers that are next to each other in the Layers panel, or Ctrl-click to select layers that are separated. That way, you can avoid the Select menu altogether. Once you're done, you can either use the Deselect Layers command, or just click another layer to make it the active layer.

NOTE   This technique used to be called simply "grouping" layers in Elements, but with Elements 8 it's called "clipping," just as it is in Photoshop. The behavior is exactly the same as the old grouped layers—only the name is different.

Clipping layers isn't anything like linking them. You can probably understand the process most easily by looking at the example shown in Figure 6-16, which shows how to crop an image on one layer using the shape of an object on another layer.

TIP   If you clip two layers together, the bottom layer determines the opacity of both layers.

Once the layers are clipped together, you can still slide the top layer around with the Move tool to reposition it so that you see exactly the part of it that you want. So in Figure 6-16, the ocean layer was maneuvered around till the breaking wave showed in the bottom of the shell shape.

To clip two layers together, make the top layer (of the two you want to group) the active layer. Position the two layers one above the other in the Layers panel by dragging. (Put the one you want to act as the mask *below* the other image.)Then choose Layer → Create Clipping Mask or press Ctrl+G.

You can also clip right in the Layers panel. Hold down Alt, and then, in the panel, move your cursor over the dividing line between the layers. Click when two linked circles appear by your cursor. Now your layers are grouped together with a clipping mask.

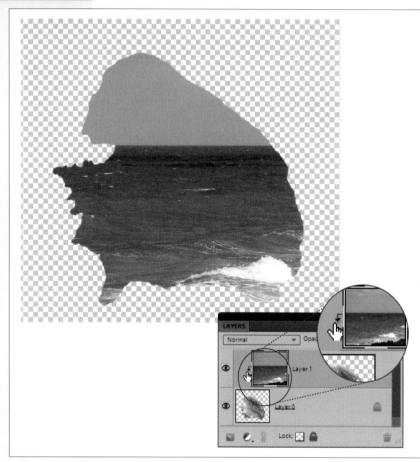

Figure 6-16:
This image began life as a picture of a seashell on one layer and an ocean scene on the layer above it. At first, the ocean image totally hid the shell, but interesting things happen when you clip the layers together. The ocean layer automatically gets cropped to the shape of the bottom layer, the seashell. The fancy way to say that is the shell now acts as the clipping mask for the ocean image. The tiny downward-bent arrow just above the cursor in the Layers panel indicates that the ocean layer is clipped.

If you get tired of the layer grouping or you want to delete or change one of the layers, then select Layer → Release Clipping Mask or press Shift+Ctrl+G to undo the grouping.

> **TIP** You have an even easier way to group layers: The New Layer dialog box has a checkbox for "Use Previous Layer to Create Clipping Mask". Turn it on, and your new layer is pre-clipped with the layer below it.

Merging and Flattening Layers

By now, you probably have some sense of how useful layers are. But there's a downside to having layers in your image: They take up a lot of storage space, especially if you have lots of duplicate layers. In other words, layers make files bigger. Fortunately, you don't have to keep layers in your file forever. You can reduce your file size quite a bit—and sometimes also make things easier to manage—by merging layers or flattening your image.

Merging layers

Sometimes you may have two or more separate layers that really could be treated as one layer, like the plants shown in Figure 6-1. You aren't limited to linking those layers together; once you've got everything arranged just right, you can *merge* them together into one layer. Also, if you want to copy and paste your image, many times the standard copy and paste commands (page 138) copy only the top layer. So it helps to get everything into one layer, at least temporarily.

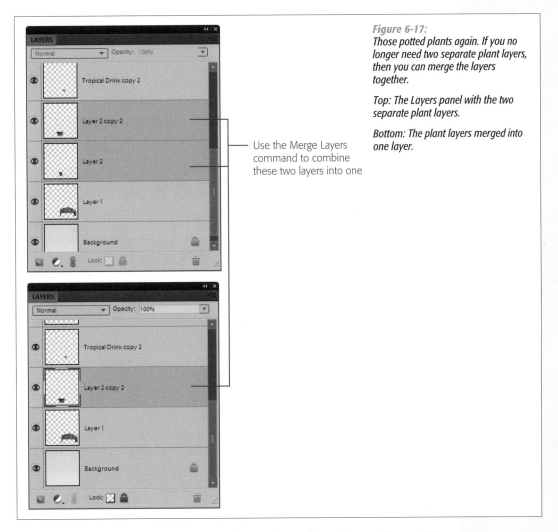

Use the Merge Layers command to combine these two layers into one

Figure 6-17:
Those potted plants again. If you no longer need two separate plant layers, then you can merge the layers together.

Top: The Layers panel with the two separate plant layers.

Bottom: The plant layers merged into one layer.

You'll probably merge layers quite often when you're working with multilayered files (for example, when you've got multiple objects that you want to edit simultaneously).

To merge layers, you have a few different options, depending on what's active in your image. You can get to any of the following commands from the Layers menu, or from the Layers panel's upper-right four-lined square, or by using keyboard shortcuts:

- **Merge Down** (Ctrl+E). This command combines the active layer and the layer immediately beneath it. If the layer just below the active layer is hidden, then you don't see this option in the list of choices.

- **Merge Visible** (Shift+Ctrl+E). This command combines all the visible layers into one layer. If you want to combine layers that are far apart, then just temporarily turn off the visibility for the ones in between, and any other layers that you don't want to merge, by clicking their eye icons (page 180).

- **Merge Linked** (Ctrl+E, just like Merge Down). Click any of your linked layers, and you can use this command, which joins those layers into one layer.

- **Merge Clipping Mask** (also Ctrl+E). You need to select the bottom layer of a layer group (page 188) to use this command, which combines the grouped layers into one layer.

POWER USERS' CLINIC

Stamp Visible

Sometimes you want to perform an action on all your image's visible layers without permanently merging them together. You can do this easily and quickly—even if you have dozens of layers in your file—by using the Stamp Visible command. This command combines the contents of all your layers into a new layer at the top of the stack.

Stamp Visible lets you work away on the new combined layer while preserving your existing layers untouched, in case you want them back later on.

Just press Ctrl+Shift+Alt+E or hold down Alt while selecting the Merge Visible command from the Layers menu or from the Layers panel's menu, which you open by clicking the square made of four horizontal lines. Elements creates a new top layer for you and fills it with the combined contents of all your other layers.

If you want to keep a layer or two from being included in this new layer, then just turn off the visibility of the layers you don't want to include before using Stamp Visible.

It's important to understand that once you merge layers and then save and close your file, you can't just unmerge them. While your file is still open, of course, you can use any of the undo commands (page 36). But once you've gotten past the undo limit you've set in Preferences (page 36), you're stuck with your merged layers.

> **TIP** The box above shows you another way to combine all your layers, while still keeping separate copies of the individual layers.

Sometimes, when your layer contains type or shapes drawn with the Shape tool, you can't merge the layer right away. Elements asks you to *simplify* the layer first. Simplifying means converting its contents to a *raster object*. In other words, now it's just a bunch of pixels, subject to the same resizing limitations as any photo. So, for example, if you have a Text layer, then you can apply filters to the text or paint on it, but you can no longer edit the words. (See page 395 for more about simplifying and working with shapes, and Chapter 14 for working with text.)

Flattening an image

While layers are simply swell when you're working on an image, they're a headache when you want to share your image, especially if you're sending it to a photoprinting service (their machines usually don't understand layered files). Even if you're printing at home, the large size of a layered file can make it take forever to print. And if you plan to use your image in other programs, very few non-Adobe programs are totally comfortable with layered files, so you may get some odd results if you feed them a layered file.

In these cases, you may want to squash everything in your picture into a single layer. You can do this easily in Elements by *flattening* your image: Go to Layer → Flatten Image, or in the Layers panel, click the four-lined-square and choose Flatten Image. Or, to keep your original intact, go to File → Save As, and in the Save As dialog box, turn off the Layers checkbox and turn on the "As a Copy" checkbox before clicking the Save button.

> TIP   Saving your image as a JPEG file automatically gets rid of layers, too.

There's no keyboard shortcut for flattening because it's something you don't want to do by accident. Like merging, flattening is a permanent change. Cautious Elements veterans always do a Save As, instead of a plain Save, before flattening. That way you have a flattened copy *and* a working copy with the layers intact, just in case. Organizer version sets (page 68) can help you here, too, because they let you save different states of your image. So, you could have both a version with layers and a flattened version.

> TIP   Flattening creates a Background layer out of the existing layers in your image, which means that you lose transparency, just as with a regular Background layer. If you want to create a single layer with transparency, then use Merge Visible (page 192) instead of Flatten Image.

Adjustment and Fill Layers

Adjustment layers and *Fill layers* are special types of layers. Adjustment layers let you manipulate the lighting, color, or exposure of the layers beneath them. If you're mainly interested in Elements to spruce up your photos, then you'll probably use Adjustment layers more than any other kind of layer. Adjustment layers are great because they let you undo or change your edits later on if you want to.

You can also use Adjustment layers to take the changes you've made to one photo and apply those same changes to another photo (see the Note on page 194). And after you've created an Adjustment layer, you can limit future edits so they change only the area of your photo affected by the Adjustment layer.

You'll find out about all the things you can do with Adjustment layers in the next few chapters. For now, you just need to learn how to create and manipulate them.

Fill layers are just what they sound like: layers filled with color, pattern, or *gradient* (a rainbow-like range of colors—see page 427).

TIP   Digital photographers should check out the Photo Filter Adjustment layers, which let you make the sort of adjustments to photos that you used to do by putting a colored piece of glass over your camera's lens. Page 243 has more about what you can do with photo filters.

GEM IN THE ROUGH

Adjustment Layers for Batch Processing

Page 274 shows you how to perform *batch* commands: simultaneously applying adjustments to groups of photos, by using the Process Multiple Files command. The drawback of Process Multiple Files is that it only gives you access to some of the auto commands, so your editing options are really limited. So what if you're a fussy photographer who's got 17 shots that are all pretty much the same, and you'd like to apply the same fixes to all of them? Do you have to edit each one from scratch?

Not in Elements. You can open the photos you want to fix, and then drag an Adjustment layer from the first photo onto each of the other photos (page 197 shows you how to drag layers between images). The new photo gets the same adjustments at the same settings. It's not as fast as true batch processing, but it saves a *lot* of time compared with editing each photo from scratch.

Adding Fill and Adjustment Layers

Creating an Adjustment or Fill layer is easy. In the Layers panel, just click the black-and-white circle to display the menu shown in Figure 6-18. The menu has all your Adjustment and Fill layer options (the first three items are Fill layers; the rest are Adjustment layers).

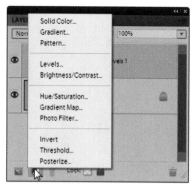

Figure 6-18:
To create a new Adjustment or Fill layer, click the black-and-white circle to see this menu, and pick the type of Adjustment or Fill layer you want. If you'd rather work from the menu bar, then go to Layer → New Adjustment Layer (or Layer → New Fill Layer), and choose the layer type you want.

Fill layers

When you create a Fill layer, you get a dialog box that lets you tweak the layer's settings. After you make your choices, click OK, and the new layer appears. Elements gives you three Fill layer choices: Solid Color, Gradient (a rainbow-like range of colors), and Pattern. See more about patterns on page 294, and gradients on page 427.

You can change a Fill layer's settings by selecting the layer in the Layers panel, and then going to Layer → Layer Content Options, or, in the Layers panel, double-clicking the left thumbnail icon for the layer. The layer's dialog box reappears, and you can adjust its settings.

Adjustment layers

In Elements 8, when you create an Adjustment layer, the layer automatically appears in your image, and the new Adjustments panel appears in the Panel bin so that you can adjust the layer's settings. (The exception is an Invert Adjustment layer—if you create one of those, you see the Adjustments panel, but it doesn't give you any settings to change.) Figure 6-19 shows the Adjustments panel.

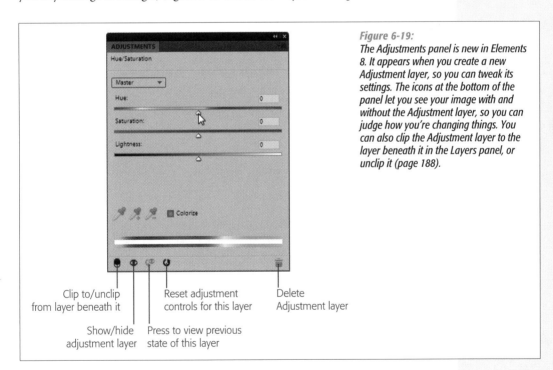

Figure 6-19:
The Adjustments panel is new in Elements 8. It appears when you create a new Adjustment layer, so you can tweak its settings. The icons at the bottom of the panel let you see your image with and without the Adjustment layer, so you can judge how you're changing things. You can also clip the Adjustment layer to the layer beneath it in the Layers panel, or unclip it (page 188).

Clip to/unclip from layer beneath it

Reset adjustment controls for this layer

Delete Adjustment layer

Show/hide adjustment layer

Press to view previous state of this layer

The Adjustments panel is really handy, because it lets you see the settings for any Adjustment layer anytime. In the Layers panel, just click the icon on the left (the one with the gears on it) for the layer you want to change. The Adjustments panel changes to show the settings for that layer. Click on a different Adjustment layer to see its settings instead—very useful, and less distracting than having dialog boxes popping up all the time.

Here are the kinds of Adjustment layers you can select from:

- **Levels.** This is a much more sophisticated way to apply Levels than using the Auto Levels button in Quick Fix or the Auto Level command from the Enhance menu. Page 221 has more about using Levels. For most people, Levels is *the* most important Adjustment layer.

- **Brightness/Contrast.** This does pretty much the same things as the Quick Fix adjustment (covered on page 126).

- **Hue/Saturation.** Again, this is much like the Quick Fix command (page 128), only with slightly different controls.

- **Gradient Map.** This one is tricky to understand and is explained in detail on page 438. It maps each tone in your image to a new tone based on the gradient (page 427) you select. That means you can apply a gradient so that the colors aren't just distributed in a straight line across your image.

- **Photo Filter.** Use this type of layer to adjust the color balance of your photos by adding warming, cooling, or special effects filters, just like you might attach to the lens of a film camera. See page 273.

- **Invert.** This reverses the colors of your image to their opposite values, for an effect similar to a film negative. See page 316.

- **Threshold.** Use this kind of layer to make everything in your photo pure black and white (with no shades of gray). See page 317.

- **Posterize.** Reduces the numbers of colors in your image to create a poster-like effect. See page 317.

Deleting Adjustment layers is a tad different from deleting regular layers, as explained in Figure 6-20. (Elements deletes Fill layers just like regular layers.)

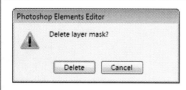

Figure 6-20:
When you click the Layers panel's "Delete layer" icon (the trashcan), Elements asks if you want to "Delete layer mask?" (The next section has more about layer masks.) Click Delete. Then you have to click the trashcan icon again to fully delete the layer. Or if you want to get rid of the layer in one step, you can go to the Layer menu, right-click the layer in the Layers panel, click the Layers panel's square made of four horizontal lines, or click the Adjustments panel's trashcan icon. All of these routes give you a Delete Layer option.

Layer Masks

Adjustment and Fill layers use something called a *layer mask*, which determines which parts of the layer are affected when you make your changes (see Figure 6-21). By changing the area covered by the layer mask, you can control which part of your image the adjustments affect.

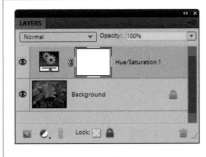

Figure 6-21:
Adjustment and Fill layers, like the Hue/Saturation layer shown here, always have two icons in the Layers panel. The gear icon indicates that the layer is making an adjustment (Hue/Saturation, in this case). With Fill layers, you can double-click that icon to bring up the dialog box to make changes to your settings. With Adjustment layers, just click the layer you want to change to make it the active layer, and then go to the Adjustments panel. (Fill Layers have a unique icon for each type of layer, but all Adjustment layers use the little gear icon you see here.) The right-hand icon (the white rectangle) is for the Layer Mask; you can use it to control the area that's covered by the adjustment.

The full version of Photoshop uses layer masks for all kinds of things, but in Elements, Adjustment and Fill layers are the only place you encounter them. The great thing about layer masks is that you can edit them by painting on them, as explained on page 329. In other words, you can go back later and change the part of your image that the Adjustment layer affects.

The term *layer mask* may be a bit confusing if you're thinking about masking with the Selection brush. With the Selection brush, masking prevents something from being changed. Layer masks really work the same way, but by definition, they start out empty. In other words, you can use a layer mask to prevent your adjustment from affecting parts of the layer, but not until you mask out parts of your image by painting on the layer mask. So to begin with, your whole layer is affected by your change. Don't worry—this will make sense once you see it in action. Page 329 explains how to edit layer masks.

Moving Objects Between Images

If you use layers, then you can easily combine parts of different photos. In Elements 8, if you're using tabs (page 29), the easiest way to do this simply copying and pasting: Select what you want to move (press Ctrl+A if you want to move the whole photo); then press Ctrl+C to copy it. Then make the destination image the active image by double-clicking it in the Project bin, and then press Ctrl+V to paste. The pasted material comes in on its own layer, and you can use the Move tool (page 165) to rearrange it in its new home.

You can also move objects by dragging. To do this, you need to choose one of the tiled views (see page 99) if you're using tabs, or Tile or Cascade (Window → Images → Tile or Cascade) if you're using floating windows. Just put what you want from photo A into its own layer, and then drag it onto photo B. You can use the Move tool (page 165) to move the object from one image to another, or you can just drag it. The trick is that you have to drag the layer from photo A *from the Layers panel.* If you try to drop one photo directly onto another photo's window, then you'll just wind up with a lot of windows stacked on top of each other. Figure 6-22 shows you how to move a layer between photos this way.

TIP   You can also drag a photo directly from the Project bin onto another image. This didn't work in Elements 6 and 7, so if you've used those versions, you'll find this is a welcome change in Elements 8. It's really useful for projects like scrapbooking where you have many objects, each in its own file, to add to a page in Elements.

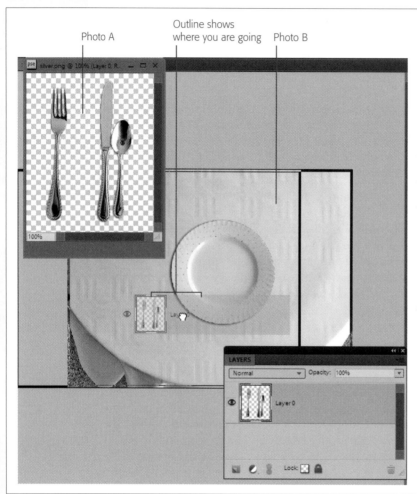

Photo A

Outline shows
where you are going   Photo B

Figure 6-22:
This figure shows how to move objects from one photo to another, working from the Layers panel. Here, the goal is to get the silverware from photo A (whose Layers panel is visible) onto the tablecloth in photo B. You always drag from the Layers panel onto a photo window when combining parts of different images into a composite. (If you try to drag from a photo to a photo, then it doesn't work unless you click the Move tool first.) Use the Move tool to adjust your object's placement once you've dropped it into the image.

But what if, rather than moving a whole layer, you just want to move a particular object—say, a person—to another photo? Just follow these steps:

1. **Open both photos in Full Edit.**

   You can pull off this maneuver by using a tabbed view, but most people find it easier to use floating windows when working with several images. To create floating windows, go to the Arrange menu → Float All in Windows, and then go to Window → Images and choose Tile or Cascade. If you want to use tabs, go to the Arrange menu (page 99), and choose a layout that gives you a view of all your images.

2. **Prepare both photos for combining.**

Go to Image → Resize → Image Size, and then make sure both photos have the same Resolution (ppi) setting before you start (see page 103 if you need a refresher on resizing and resolution). Why? If one photo is way bigger than the other, then the moved object could easily blanket the entire target image. You don't absolutely have to do this size balancing, but it'll make your life a lot easier, since it helps avoid having an enormous or tiny pasted object. (Keep reading for more advice about resolution when moving objects and layers.)

3. **Select what you want to move.**

Use the selection tools of your choice (see Chapter 5 if you need help making selections). Add a one- or two-pixel feather to your selection (see page 151) to avoid a hard, cut-out-looking edge.

4. **Move the object.**

There are several ways to move what you selected from one image to another:

- **Copy and paste.** Press Ctrl+C to copy the object from the first photo. Next, click the second photo to make it the active photo, and then press Ctrl+V to paste what you copied.

- **Use the Move tool.** Activate the Move tool (page 165), and then drag from one photo to the other. As you're moving, you may see a hole in the original where the selection was, but as long as you don't let go till you get over the second photo, this fixes itself after you let go. (If seeing this bothers you, just Alt-drag to move a copy of the selection.)

- **Drag the layer.** If the object you want to move is already on its own layer, surrounded by transparency, then you can just drag the layer from the first photo's Layers panel into the destination photo's main image window or tab.

It doesn't matter which method you use—whatever you move appears on its own layer in the combined image.

5. **If necessary, use the Move tool to position or scale the object after you've moved it, as shown in Figure 6-23.**

See page 165 for more about using the Move tool; Figure 6-23 explains scaling objects.

6. **Save your work.**

If you may want to make further adjustments to the moved object, then save your file as a TIFF or Photoshop (.psd) file to keep the layers. Remember that if you save your file as a JPEG, then you lose the layers, and you can't easily change or move the new object anymore.

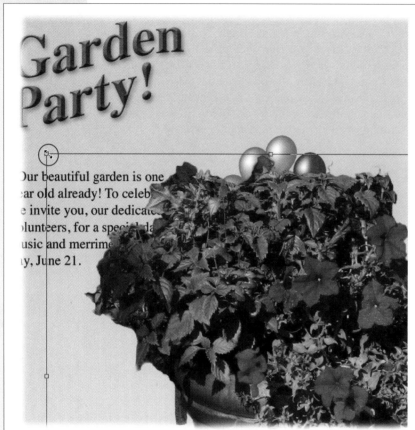

Figure 6-23:
If you forget to balance out the relative sizes and resolutions of the photos you're combining, then you can wind up with a giant object in your photo, like these flowers. The solution is simple: Just Shift-drag a corner of the oversized item (circled). You may need to drag the new object around a bit in order to expose the size-adjusting corner. Don't forget that you can use all the Move tool's features on your new object.

Here are a few things to keep in mind when copying from one image to another:

- **Watch out for conflicting resolution settings (see page 103).** The destination image (that is, the one receiving the moved layer or object) controls the resolution. So if you bring in a layer that's set to 300 pixels per inch (ppi), and place it on an image that's set to 72 ppi, then the object you're moving is now set to 72 ppi; its overall apparent size will increase proportionately as the pixels get spread out more.

NOTE   It's tricky to work with multiple images in tabs. Instead, try creating floating windows (Arrange menu → "Float All in Windows"), and then go to Window → Images and choose Tile or Cascade. Cascade gives you the most flexibility for positioning your photos.

- **Lighting matters.** Objects that are lit differently stand out if you try to combine them. If possible, plan ahead and use similar lighting for photos you're thinking about combining.

- **Center your moved layer.** If you're dragging a layer and want it to center itself in the new image, then Shift-drag the layer.

- **Feather with care.** A little feathering (page 151) goes a long way toward creating a realistic result.

If you'd like more practice using layers and moving objects between photos, visit the Missing CD page at *www.missingmanuals.com*, and download the table tutorial, which walks you through most of the basic layer functions.

_3_

Part Three: Retouching

Basic Image Retouching

You may be perfectly happy using Elements only in Quick Fix mode. And that's fine, as long as you understand that you've hardly scratched the surface of what the program can do. Sooner or later, though, you'll probably run across a photo where your best Quick Fix efforts just aren't enough. Or you may just be curious to see what else Elements has under its hood. That's when you finally get to put all your image-selecting and layering skills to good use.

Elements gives you loads of ways to fix your photos beyond the limited options in Quick Fix. This chapter guides you through fixing basic exposure problems, shows you various ways of sharpening your photos, and most importantly, helps you understand how to improve the colors in your photos. You'll also learn how to use the amazing Smart Brush tool that lets you apply many common fixes by just brushing over the area you want to correct.

If you want to get the most out of Elements, you need to understand a little about how your camera, computer, and printer think about color. Along with resolution, color is one of the most important concepts in Elements. After all, almost all the adjustments that image-editing programs make consist of changing the color of pixels. So quite a bit of this chapter is about understanding how Elements—and by extension, you—can manipulate your image's color.

> **TIP** Most of Elements' advanced-fixes dialog boxes have a Preview checkbox that lets you watch what's happening as you adjust the settings. It's a good idea to keep these checkboxes turned on so you can decide if you're improving things. And for a handy "before" and "after" comparison, toggle the checkbox on and off.

Fixing Exposure Problems

Incorrectly exposed photos are *the* number one problem that photographers face. No matter how carefully you set up your shot and how many different settings you try on your camera, it always seems like the picture you really want to keep is the one that's over- or underexposed.

The Quick Fix commands (page 115) can really help your photo, but if you've tried to bring back a picture that's badly over- or underexposed, you've probably run into the limitations of what Quick Fix can do. Similarly, the Shadows/Highlights command (page 209) can do a lot, but it's not intended to fix a photo whose exposure is totally botched—just ones where the contrast between light and dark areas needs a bit of help. And if you push Smart Fix to its limits, your results may be a little strange. In those situations, you need to move on to some of Elements' more powerful tools to help improve the image's exposure.

> **TIP**   In this section, you'll learn about the more traditional ways of correcting exposure in Elements, as well as how to use the Smart Brush tool for corrections. But be sure to also check out the Elements Camera Raw Converter (page 248), which can help with your JPEG and TIFF photos, too. Your results with non-Raw photos may vary, but the Raw Converter just might turn out to be your best choice.

UP TO SPEED

Understanding Exposure

What exactly *is* exposure, anyway? You almost certainly know a poorly exposed photo when you see one: It's either too light or too dark. But what exactly has gone wrong?

Exposure refers to the amount of light your film (or the sensor in your digital camera) received when you released the shutter.

A properly exposed photo shows details in *all* parts of the image—light and dark. Shadows aren't just pits of blackness, and bright areas show more than washed-out splotches of white.

Deciding Which Exposure Fix to Use

When you open a poorly exposed photo in Elements, the first thing to do is figure out what's wrong with it, just like a doctor diagnosing a patient. If the exposure's not perfect, what exactly is the problem? Here's a list of common symptoms to help figure out where to go next:

- **Everything is too dark.** If your photo is really dark, try adding a Screen layer, as explained on page 207. If it's just a bit too dark, try using Levels (page 221).

- **Everything is too light.** If the whole photo looks washed out, try adding a Multiply layer (explained on page 207). If it's just a bit too light, try Levels (page 221).

- **The photo is mostly OK, but your subject is too dark, or the light parts of the photo are too light.** Try the Shadows/Highlights adjustment (page 209) or the Smart Brush tool (page 211).

Of course, if you're lucky (or a really skilled photographer), you may not see any of these problems, in which case, skip to page 221 if you want to do something to make your colors pop. If you're lucky enough to have *bracketed* exposures (multiple exposures of exactly the same image), check out the new Exposure Merge feature (page 267), which makes it simple to blend those into one properly exposed image.

> **NOTE** You may have noticed that Brightness/Contrast wasn't mentioned in the previous list. A lot of people jump for the Brightness/Contrast controls when facing a poorly exposed photo. That's logical—after all, these dials usually help improve the picture on your TV. But in Elements, about 99 percent of the time, you've got a whole slew of powerful tools—like Levels and the Shadows/Highlights command—that can do much more than Brightness/Contrast can. However, in recent versions of Elements, Brightness/Contrast is much improved from earlier versions, so feel free to give it a try when you only need to make very subtle changes.

Fixing Major Exposure Problems

If your photo is completely over- or underexposed, you need to add special layers to correct the problems. You follow the same steps to fix either problem. The only difference is the layer blend mode (page 182) you choose: *Multiply* darkens your image's exposure while *Screen* lightens it. Figure 7-1 shows Multiply in action (and gives you a sense of the limitations of this technique if your exposure is *really* far gone). You can download the file *brickwindow.jpg* from the Missing CD page at *www.missingmanuals.com* if you'd like to try the different exposure fixes for yourself.

Be careful, though: If only part of your photo is out of whack, using Multiply or Screen can ruin the exposure of the parts that were OK to start with, because these layers increase or decrease the exposure of the whole photo. Your properly exposed areas may blow out (see the box on page 209) and lose the details if you apply a Screen layer, for example. So, if your exposure problem is spotty (as opposed to problems that affect the entire image), try the Smart Brush (page 211) or Shadows/Highlights (page 209) first. If your whole photo needs an exposure correction, here's how to use layers to fix it:

1. **Create a duplicate layer.**

   Open your photo and press Ctrl+J or go to Layer → Duplicate Layer. Check to be sure the duplicate layer is the active layer.

2. **In the Layers panel, change the mode for the new layer.**

   Use the drop-down menu in the panel's upper-left corner to choose Multiply if your photo is overexposed or Screen if it's underexposed. (Make sure you change the duplicate layer's mode, not the original layer's.)

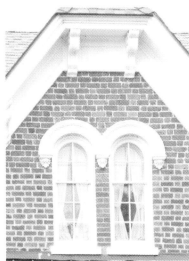

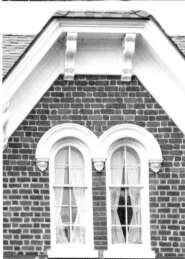

Figure 7-1:
In photography terms, each Multiply layer you add is roughly equivalent to stopping your camera down one f-stop, at least as far as the dark areas are concerned.

Top: This photo is totally overexposed, and it looks like there's no detail there at all. Multiply layers darken things enough to bring back a lot of the washed-out areas and bring out quite a bit of detail.

Bottom: As you can see in the corrected photo, even Elements can't do much in areas where there's no detail at all, like the sky and the white framing around the windows.

3. **Adjust the opacity of the layer if needed.**

   If the effect of the new layer is too strong, in the Layers panel, move the Opacity slider to the left to reduce the new layer's opacity.

4. **Repeat as necessary.**

   You may have to use as many as five or six layers if your photo is in really bad shape. If you need extra layers, you'll probably want them at 100 percent opacity, so you can just keep pressing Ctrl+J, which will duplicate the current top layer.

You're more likely to need several layers to fix overexposure than you are for underexposure. And, of course, there are limits to what even Elements can do for a blindingly overexposed image. Overexposure is usually tougher to fix than under-exposure, especially if the area is blown out, as explained in the box below.

Avoiding Blowouts

An area of a photo is *blown out* when it's so overexposed that it appears as just plain white—in other words, your camera didn't record any data at all for that area. (Elements isn't all that great with total black, either, but that doesn't happen quite so often. Most underexposed photos have some tonal gradations in them, even if you can't see them very well.)

A blowout is as disastrous in photography as it is when you're driving. Even Elements can't fix blowouts, because there's no data for it to work from. So, you're stuck with the fixes discussed in this chapter, which are never as good as a good original.

When you're taking pictures, remember that it's generally easier to correct underexposure than overexposure. Keep that in mind when choosing your camera settings. If you live where there's really bright sunlight most of the time, you may want to make a habit of backing your exposure compensation down a hair. Depending on your camera, your subject, and the average ambient glare, you should try starting at –.3 and adjusting from there.

You can also try *bracketing* your shots—taking multiple shots of exactly the same subject with different exposure settings. Then you can combine the two exposures for maximum effect using Elements' new Exposure Merge (page 267).

The Shadows/Highlights Command

The Shadows/Highlights command is one of Elements' best features. It's an incredibly powerful tool for adjusting only the dark or light areas of your photo without messing up the rest of it. Figure 7-2 shows what a great help it can be.

The Shadows/Highlights command in Full Edit works pretty much the same way it does in Quick Fix (page 126). The single flaw in this great tool is that you can't apply it as an Adjustment layer (page 193), so you may want to apply Shadows/Highlights to a duplicate layer. Then, later on, you can discard the changes if you want to take another whack at adjusting the photo. In any case, it's easy to make amazing changes to your photos with Shadows/Highlights. Here's how:

1. **Open your photo and duplicate the layer (Ctrl+J) if you want to.**

   If you haven't edited your photo before, this is usually the Background layer, but you can use this command on any layer. Duplicating the layer makes it easier to undo Shadows/Highlights later if you change your mind.

2. **Go to Enhance → Adjust Lighting → Shadows/Highlights.**

   Your photo immediately becomes about 30 shades lighter. Don't panic. As soon as you select the command, the Lighten Shadows setting automatically jumps to 25 percent, which is *way* too much for most photos. Just shove the slider back to 0 to undo this change before you start making your corrections.

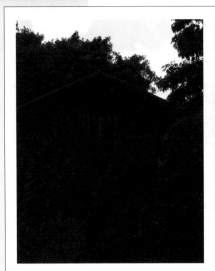 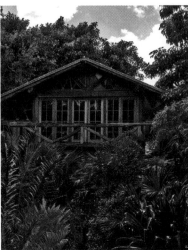

Figure 7-2:
The Shadows/Highlights command can bring back details in photos where you were sure there was no information at all—but sometimes at a cost.

Left: You might think there's no hope for this extremely backlit photo with its overly bright sky and murky foreground.

Right: A dose of Shadows/Highlights unearths plenty of details, although the overall effect is a bit flat when you push the tool this far. This photo needs lots more work, but at least now you can see what you're doing.

3. **Move the sliders in the Shadows/Highlights dialog box around until you like what you see.**

   The sliders do exactly what they say: Lighten Shadows makes the dark areas of your photo lighter, and Darken Highlights makes the light areas darker. (Midtone Contrast is discussed in a moment.) Pushing the sliders to the right increases their effect.

4. **Click OK when you're happy.**

The Shadows/Highlights tool is a cinch to use, because you just make decisions based on what you're seeing. Keep these tips in mind:

- You may want to add a smidgen of the opposite tool to balance things out a little. In other words, if you're lightening shadows, you may get better results by giving the Darken Highlights slider a teeny nudge, too.

- Midtone Contrast is there because your photo may look kind of flat after you're done with Shadows/Highlights, especially if you've made big adjustments. Move the Midtone Contrast slider to the right to increase the contrast in your photo. It usually adds a bit of a darkening effect, so you may need to go back to one of the other sliders to tweak your photo after you use it.

- You can overdo the Shadows/Highlights tool. When you see halos around the objects in your photo, you've pushed the settings too far.

TIP   If the Shadows/Highlights tool washes out your photo's colors—making everyone look like they've been through the laundry too many times—adjust the color intensity with one of the Saturation commands, either in Quick Fix or in Full Edit (as described on page 306). Watch people's skin tones when increasing the saturation—if the subjects in your photo start looking like sunless-tanning-lotion disaster victims, you've gone too far. Also check out the Vibrance slider in the Raw Converter (page 260), or try adjusting colors with Elements' Color Curves feature (page 302).

Correcting Part of an Image

Shadows/Highlights is great if you want to adjust *all* the light or dark areas of a photo, but what if you want to tweak the exposure only in certain areas? Or what if you like the photo's background just fine, but you want to tweak the subject a little? Of course, you can always make a selection in your photo (see Chapter 5 for more about selecting), or copy the selected area to a new layer, and then make adjustments to that layer. But Elements gives you a super simple way to apply a correction to just the area you want, by using the Smart Brush tools.

Correcting color with a brush

The Smart Brush is actually two different tools (the Smart Brush and the Detail Smart Brush) that work just like the Quick Selection tool and the regular Selection brush, respectively. Only instead of merely selecting part of your photo, they also edit it as you brush. So you may be able to make targeted adjustments to different areas of your photo just by drawing a line over them. (The Smart Brushes don't *always* work, but they're truly amazing when they do.)

In this section you'll learn how to use the Smart Brush to correct exposure, but you have a whole menu of different things you can choose to do with the Smart Brush: Change the color of someone's jacket, apply different special effects, put a little lipstick on people, convert an area to black and white—the list goes on and on. As a matter of fact, if you've been using Quick Fix, you may well have met the Smart Brush already, although it doesn't go by that name there: The Touch Up tools (page 130) in Quick Fix all use the Smart Brush to apply their effects.

Here's how to put this nifty pair of tools to work:

1. **Open a photo in Full Edit, and then activate the Smart Brush.**

   Click its icon in the Tools panel (it's the brush with the gears next to it) or press F. Use the fly-out menu to be sure you have the regular Smart Brush. It shares its Tools panel slot with the Detail Smart Brush, which works like the Selection brush in that it changes only the area directly under the brush, instead of automatically expanding your selection to include the whole object you brush over. For now, see if the regular Smart Brush is smart enough to select the area you want.

2. **Choose the correction you want to apply.**

   Go to the Options bar, and then choose from the pull-down menu. (Both Smart Brushes have the same Options bar settings, discussed below. The important one is explained in Figure 7-3.) Adobe calls these choices Smart Paint.

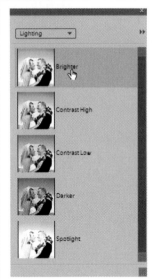

Figure 7-3:
Your Smart Paint options (the things you can do with the Smart Brush) are grouped into the categories listed in the pull-down menu. Each thumbnail image shows that option applied to a photo. For exposure issues, start by looking at the choices in the Lighting section (choose Lighting from the drop-down menu at the top of the list). You can choose to make the area darker, brighter, make the contrast low or high, or even put a spotlight effect on it. Just scroll through the list to find the effect you want, click it, and then click somewhere outside your photo to hide the menu. You can also drag the menu loose from the Options bar and put it where you want, if you'd like to keep it available and out of the way of your photo.

3. **Drag over the area you want to change.**

   This step is just like using the Quick Selection tool—you don't need to make a careful selection, since Elements calculates the area it thinks you want to include and creates the selection for you. A simple line should do it.

4. **Tweak the selection, if necessary.**

   If Elements didn't quite select everything you want, then add to the selection by brushing again. If you still need to modify the selection, then use the selection editing tools explained in Figure 7-4. If you're really unhappy with the Smart Brush's selection talents, then head back to the Tools panel and try the Detail Smart Brush.

   You can invert a selection (page 160) by turning on the Options bar's Inverse checkbox. Then what you select with the brush is *excluded* from your selection, and everything else is included. You can turn on the checkbox before or after using the Smart Brush, as long as it's still the active tool. If you come back to the Smart Brush after using another tool, then you need to click the pin shown in Figure 7-4 before you can invert the selection, thus inverting the area covered by the effect.

5. **Once you like the selection, you can adjust the effect if you want.**

   The Smart Brush gives you several ways to change what it's done:

   • **Change what happens to the selected area.** While the selection is active, just head to the Options bar, and choose a different Smart Paint adjustment. Elements automatically updates your image.

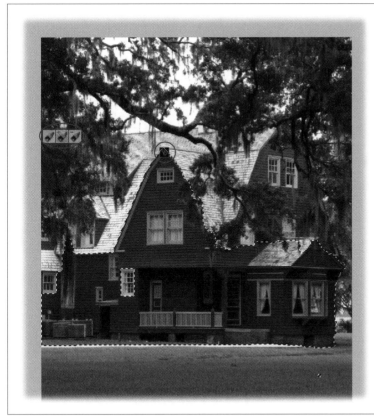

Figure 7-4:
Once you've used the Smart Brush, a pin (circled, right) appears in your photo to let you know that the selected region is now under the power of the Smart Brush. Click the pin and you see a trio of icons (circled, left) that let you edit the selected area. From left to right the icons mean New Selection, "Add to Selection", and "Remove from Selection". If you're pressed for time, there's an even quicker way to modify your selection: Just drag again to add to the area affected by the Smart Brush (or to use the same adjustment on another part of your photo), or Alt-drag to remove changes from an area. You see the pin anytime the Smart Brush is activated again, even after you've closed and saved your photo.

- **Add a different kind of Smart Paint.** At the left end of the Options bar, click the tiny triangle and choose Reset Tool. Then the Smart Brush puts down an *additional* adjustment when you use it, instead of just changing what you've already done. You can also use this to double-up an effect—to add Lipstick twice, for instance, if you thought the first pass was too faint. Each Smart Brush adjustment gets its own pin, so if you have two Smart Brush adjustments in your photo, then you'll have two pins in it, too. (Each pin is a different color.)

- **Change the settings for Smart Paint you've already applied.** Rather than adding another Smart Paint layer to increase the effect, you can just adjust the settings for the changes you've already made. Right-click the pin in your image, and then choose Change Adjustment Settings to bring up a dialog box where you can adjust the effect you're brushing on. The Smart Brush uses Adjustment layers to make its changes, so the available settings are the same as they would be if you created a regular Adjustment layer. For example, if you're using the Brighter option, as shown in Figure 7-4, then you get the settings for a Brightness/Contrast Adjustment layer.

6. **When you're happy with what you have, you're done.**

You can always go back to your Smart Paint changes again. Just activate the Smart Brush (click it in the Tools panel or press F) and the pin(s) appear again, to let you easily change what you've done. You can eliminate Smart Brush changes by right-clicking the adjusted area, and then choosing Delete Adjustment (the Smart Brush needs to be active), or by going to the Layers panel and discarding their layers (you can do this anytime, whether the Smart Brush is active or not). You can also edit a Smart Brush adjustment's layer mask the way you'd edit any other layer mask, as described on page 329. But usually it's easier just to click the pin and then adjust your selection.

The Smart Brush is especially handy for projects like creating images that are part color and part black-and-white, or even for silly special effects like making one object from your photo look like it's been isolated on a '60s-style psychedelic background.

The Smart Brush has several Options bar settings, but you usually don't need to use them:

- **New selection.** Click the left brush icon to add the same effect elsewhere in your photo. (Just clicking someplace else with the brush actually does the same thing.)

- **Add to selection.** Click this next brush icon to put the Smart Brush in add-to-selection mode, but again, the brush does that automatically even if you don't click this icon.

- **Remove from selection.** Did the Smart Brush take in more area than you wanted? Click this final brush icon before brushing away what you don't want, or just Alt-drag.

- **Brush characteristics.** You can change the size, hardness, spacing, angle, or roundness of the brush here.

- **Inverse.** If you want to apply the correction to the area you *didn't* select with the Smart Brush, then just turn on this checkbox to invert the selection.

- **Refine Edge.** Use this if you want to make the edges of your effect sleeker. See page 145 for details.

- **Smart Paint.** Click this thumbnail image for a pop-out menu of all the possible Smart Brush adjustments, grouped into categories. (If you hover your cursor over the thumbnail, the tooltip that appears says "Choose A Preset", but Adobe calls these settings Smart Paint in the Help files and elsewhere.)

If you like the idea of the Smart Brush but never seem to find exactly the adjustments you want, or if you always want to change the settings you apply, then you can create your own Smart Paint options, as described in the box on page 216.

Controlling the Colors You See

You want your photos to look as good as possible and to have beautiful, breath-taking color, right? That's probably why you bought Elements. But now that you've got the program, you're having a little trouble getting things to look the way you want. Does the following sound familiar?

- Your photos look great onscreen, but your prints are washed out, too dark, or the colors are all a little wrong.

- Your photos look just fine in other programs like Word or Windows Explorer, but they look just awful in Elements.

What's going on? The answer has to do with the fact that Elements is a *color-managed* program. That means Elements uses your monitor info when deciding how to display images. Color management is the science of making sure that the color in your images is always exactly the same, no matter who opens your file or what kind of hardware they're viewing it on or printing it from. If you think of all the different monitor and printer models out there, you get an idea of what a big job this is.

Graphics pros spend their whole lives grappling with color management, and you can find plenty of books about the finer points of it. At its most sophisticated level, color management is complicated enough to make you curl up in the fetal position and swear never to create another picture. Luckily, Elements makes color management a whole lot easier. Most of the time, you have only two things to deal with: your monitor calibration and your color space. The following pages cover both.

> NOTE   There are a couple of other color-related settings for printing, too, but you can deal with those when you're ready to print. Chapter 16 explains them.

Calibrating Your Monitor

Most programs pay no attention to your monitor's color settings, but color-managed applications like Elements rely on the *profile*—the information your computer stores about your monitor's settings—when it decides how to print or display a photo onscreen. If that profile isn't accurate, neither is the color in Elements.

So, you may need to *calibrate* your monitor, which is a way of adjusting its settings. A properly calibrated monitor makes all the difference in the world in getting great-looking results. If your photos look bad only in Elements, or if your pictures in print don't look anything like they do onscreen, you can start fixing the problem by calibrating your monitor.

Making Smart Paint

While the Smart Brush offers a lot of different Smart Paint choices (the various settings for correcting and enhancing your photos), you may find it slightly frustrating that Elements doesn't have a setting for the particular corrections you use most frequently. No problem—as long as you can use Adjustment layers (page 193) to achieve the effect you want, you can create your own Smart Paint presets, and they'll appear in the menus right along with the ones from Adobe.

To get started in Windows Vista, go to *C:\ProgramData\Adobe\Photoshop Elements\8.0\Photo Creations\adjustment layers.* (In XP, it's *C:\Documents and Settings\All Users\Application Data\Adobe\Photoshop Elements\8.0\Photo Creations\Adjustment Layers.*) These files are hidden, so you need to turn on viewing hidden files to see them (the box on page 556 tells you how). You see three files for each Smart Paint preset:

- **A PSD file** that contains the actual settings for the preset.

- **A thumbnail file,** which you need if you want to have a little preview in the menu.

- **An XML file** that tells Elements where in the menus to display the preset, whether to show it in "Black and White" or in Lighting, for instance. These XML files all have the word "metadata" in their names, so they're easy to find.

Basically, you need to edit *copies* of these files to make new ones for each preset you want to add. Here's how:

1. **Open one of the PSD files in the Editor.** To start with, pick the one that's the closest to what you want. Notice how the file is put together: It's a 160-pixel square PSD file with an Adjustment layer on it. Save the file with a new name so you don't mess up the original.

2. **Change the settings.** In the Layers panel, click once on the Adjustment layer to select it, then—in the Adjustments panel—tweak the settings. Then save the file.

3. **Create a new thumbnail.** You can just save the original thumbnail with a new name. (Thumbnails are 74-pixel square JPEGs, in case you want to make a new one from scratch.)

4. **Create a new XML file.** For most people, this is the trickiest part. Open the XML file and do a Save As, changing the name to that of the new Smart Paint choice you just created. (You can open XML files with Windows' Notepad text editor. In the "Save as" dialog box, choose All Files in the "Save as type" menu.) Then look at the contents of the file (most of it won't make much sense if you're not a geek). You're looking for a line like this:

```
<name value="$$$/content/adjustmentlayers/
ContrastHigh=Contrast High" />
```

In this example, you'd be adapting the Contrast High preset, so you just find the two instances of the name (note that there's no space in the first one), and then change them to the name of your new preset. If you're ambitious, you can also edit the text for tooltips (the text that appears when you hover your cursor over the thumbnail) and the category (you can use an existing category or create a new one). When you're finished making changes, save the file. Name it *my effect.metadata* (replace "my effect" with the actual name you gave your new preset). Make sure all three files are in the Adjustment Layers folder. The next time you start Elements, you should see your new Smart Paint right there along with the ones that came with Elements.

If you make a mistake creating your preset, and don't catch it till after starting the Editor again, to correct it, in Vista go to *C:\ProgramData\Adobe\Photoshop Elements\8.0\Locale\en_US* (this path is different if you aren't in the United States), and delete *MediaDatabase.db3* to refresh the list of presets. In XP, it's in *C:\Documents and Settings\All Users\Application Data\Adobe\Photoshop Elements\8.0\Locale\en_US* (or your location).

Getting started with calibrating

Calibrating a monitor sounds intimidating, but it's actually not that difficult—some people think it's even kind of fun. And it's worth it, because afterward your monitor may look about a thousand times better than you thought it could. Calibrating may even make it easier to read text in Word, for instance, because the contrast is better. Your calibrating options, from best to only okay, are:

- **Use a colorimeter.** This method may sound disturbingly scientific, but it's actually the easiest. A *colorimeter* is just a device with special software that does the calibration for you. Using such a device is much more accurate than calibrating by eye. For a long time, only pros could afford colorimeters, but these days if you shop around, you can find the Pantone Huey or the Spyder2Express for about $70 or less. More professional models calibrators like the Eye One Display 2 or the Monaco Optix Spyder are about $200 or less. If you're serious about controlling your colors in Elements, this is by far your best option for calibrating.

    NOTE Your calibration software probably asks you to set the brightness and contrast before you begin, even though most LCD monitors don't have adjustable dials for these settings. If you're happy with your monitor's current brightness and contrast, you can safely ignore this step. And unless you have a reason to use different settings, for an LCD monitor, you usually want to set the white point to 6500 (Kelvin) and your gamma to 2.2.

- **Software.** There's a good chance that the drivers (software) for your graphics card include some kind of calibration tool. Figure 7-5 shows a typical example. Right-click anywhere on your desktop, and choose Display Settings → Color Management (in Windows XP: Display → Properties → Settings → Advanced) to see what you have.

- **Adobe Gamma.** If you have an older version of Elements (Elements 5 or earlier), you may have this program, which used to come with Elements. It's pretty ancient, was never meant to work with anything but old CRT monitors (the big, fat ones like old-fashioned televisions), and doesn't work in Vista. If you happen to have Adobe Gamma, it's better than nothing, but it's probably less useful than any other program you might have for adjusting your display.

If your photos still look a little odd even after you've calibrated your monitor, you may need to turn on the Ignore EXIF setting in the Editor's preferences; see Figure 7-6.

Choosing a Color Space

The other thing you may need to do to get good color from Elements is to check which *color space* the program is using. Color spaces are standards Elements uses to define your colors. Color spaces can seem pretty abstruse the first time you hear about them, but they're simply ways of defining what colors mean. For example, when someone says "green," what do you envision: a lush emerald color, a deep forest green, a bright lime, or something else?

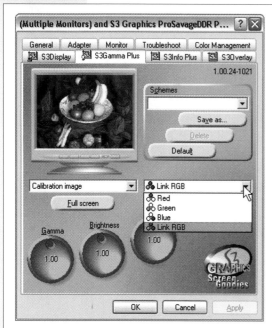

Figure 7-5:
This computer has an old, fairly basic graphics card; the video driver includes several tools to help get more accurate color, including this calibration window.

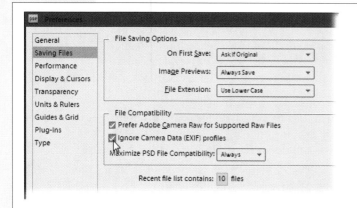

Figure 7-6:
If all the images from your digital camera have a funny color cast (usually red or yellow), go to Edit → Preferences → Saving Files, and turn on "Ignore Camera Data (EXIF) profiles". Some cameras embed nonstandard color information in their files, so this setting tells Elements to pay no attention to it, which should make your photos display and print properly.

Choosing a color space helps make sure that everything that handles a digital file—Elements, your monitor, your printer, and so on—sees the same colors the same way. Over the years, the graphics industry has agreed on standards so that everyone has the same understanding of what you mean when you say "red" or "green"—as long as you specify which color space (set of standards) you're using.

Elements gives you only two color spaces to pick from: *sRGB* (also called *sRGB IEC61966-2.1* if you want to impress your geek friends) and *Adobe RGB*. When you choose a color space, you tell Elements which set of standards you want it to apply to your photos.

If you're happy with the colors you see on your monitor in Elements and you like the prints you're getting, you don't need to make any changes. If, on the other hand, you aren't satisfied with what Elements is showing you, you'll probably want to modify your color space, which you can do in the Color Settings dialog box (Figure 7-7). Go to Edit → Color Settings or press Shift+Ctrl+K. Here are your choices:

- **No Color Management.** Elements ignores any information that your file already contains, like color space data from your camera, and doesn't attempt to add any color info to the file. (When you do a Save As, there's a checkbox that offers you the option of embedding your monitor profile. Don't turn on this checkbox, since your monitor profile is best left for the monitor's own use, and putting the profile into your file can make trouble if you ever send the file someplace else for printing.)

- **Always Optimize Colors for Computer Screens.** This option uses the sRGB color space, which is what most web browsers use; this is a good choice when you're preparing graphics for the Web. Many online printing services also prefer sRGB files. (If you've used an early version of Elements, this is the same as the old Limited Color Management option.)

- **Always Optimize for Printing.** This option uses the Adobe RGB color space, which is wider than sRGB, meaning it allows more color gradations than sRGB. This is sometimes your best choice for printing—but not always. So despite the note you'll see in the Color Settings dialog box about "commonly used for printing," don't be afraid to try one of the other settings instead. Many home inkjet printers actually cope better with sRGB or no color management than with Adobe RGB. (For Elements veterans, this setting used to be called Full Color Management.)

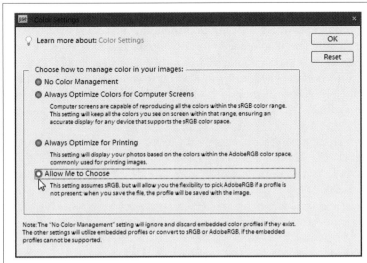

Figure 7-7:
If you select the "Allow Me to Choose" option here, you see the Missing Profile dialog box each time you open a previously untagged image.

• **Allow Me to Choose.** This option assumes that you're using the sRGB space, but lets you assign either an Adobe RGB tag, an sRGB tag, or no tag at all (color tags are explained in a moment). After you select this option, each time you open a file that isn't sRGB, you see the dialog box shown in Figure 7-8, which you can use to assign a different profile to a photo. Just save it once without a profile (turn off the ICC [International Color Consortium] Profile checkbox in the Save As dialog box), and then reopen it and choose the profile you want from the dialog box. Or, the box below explains an easier way to convert a color profile if you need to make a change.

So what's your best option? Once again, if everything looks good, leave it alone. Otherwise, for general use, you're probably best off starting with No Color Management. Then try the others if that doesn't work for you.

POWER USERS' CLINIC

Converting Profiles in Elements

If you're a color-management maven, Elements gives you a feature you'll really appreciate—the ability to easily convert an image's ICC profile from one color space to another. If you've been working in, say, sRGB, and now you want your photo to have the Adobe RGB profile, you can convert it by going to Image → Convert Color Profile and choosing Apply Adobe RGB Profile from the pop-out menu.

You can choose to remove a profile or convert to sRGB or Adobe RGB; your current color profile choice is grayed out.

This is a true conversion: Your photo's colors don't shift the way they might if you were just to tag a photo with a different profile. Why would you want to do such a conversion? If, for example, you use Adobe RGB when editing your photos, but you're sending your pictures to an online printing service that wants sRGB instead, then you may want to think about converting.

If you choose one of the other three options, when you save your file, Elements attempts to embed the file with a *color tag,* info about the file's color space—either Adobe RGB or sRGB. (This kind of tag *isn't* related to the Organizer tags you read about in Chapter 2.) If you don't want a color tag—also known as an *ICC Profile*—in your file, just turn off the checkbox before you save your file. Figure 7-8 shows where to find the profile information in the Save As dialog box, and how to turn the whole process off.

> **NOTE**   Elements automatically opens files tagged with a color space other than the one you're working in without letting you know what it's just done, so you won't know that there's a mismatch between the file's ICC profile and your working color space in Elements. (If you try to open a file in a color mode that Elements can't handle, like CMYK, then Elements offers to convert it to a mode you can use.) So, if you have an Adobe RGB file and you're working in "Always Optimize Colors for Computer Screens", Elements doesn't warn you about the profile mismatch the way early versions of the program did—it just opens the file. If you consistently get strange color shifts when you open your Elements-edited files in other programs, check to be sure there isn't a profile mismatch between your images and Elements.

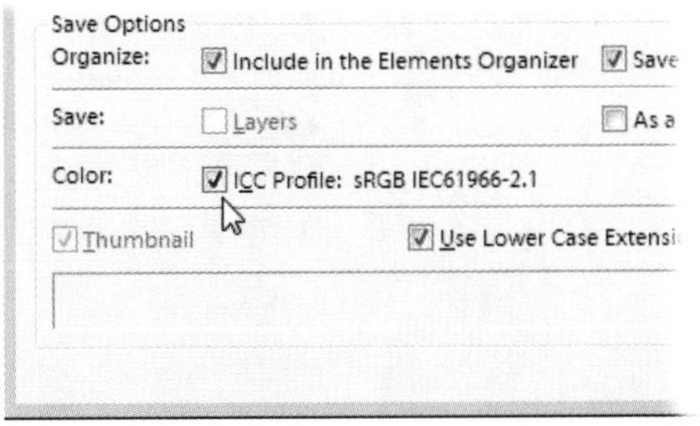

Save Options
Organize: ☑ Include in the Elements Organizer   ☑ Save
Save: ☐ Layers   ☐ As a
Color: ☑ ICC Profile: sRGB IEC61966-2.1
☑ Thumbnail   ☑ Use Lower Case Extensi

Figure 7-8:
When you save a file, Elements offers to embed a color tag in it. You can safely turn off the ICC Profile checkbox and leave the file untagged. (Assigning a profile is helpful because then any program that sees your file knows what color standards you're working with. But if you're new to Elements, you'll usually have an easier time if you don't start embedding profiles in files without a good reason.)

Using Levels

People who've used Elements for a while will tell you that the Levels command is one of the program's most essential tools. You can fix an amazing array of problems simply by adjusting the level of each *color channel*. (On your monitor, each color you see is composed of red, green, and blue. In Elements, you can make very precise adjustments to your images by adjusting these color channels separately.)

Just as its name suggests, Levels adjusts the amount, or level, of each color within an image. You can make several different adjustments by using Levels, from generally brightening your colors to fixing a color cast (page 227 has more about color casts). Many digital photo enthusiasts treat almost every picture they take to a dose of Levels, because there's no better way to polish up the color in a photo.

The way Levels works is fairly complex. Start by thinking of the possible ranges of brightness in any photo on a scale from 0 (black) to 255 (white). Some photos may have pixels in them that fall at both those extremes, but most photos don't. Even the ones that do may not have the full range of brightness in each individual color channel. Most of the time, you'll find some empty space at one or both ends of the scale.

When you use Levels, you tell Elements to consider the range of colors available in *your* photo as the *total* tonal range it has to work with. Elements redistributes your colors accordingly. Basically, you just get rid of the empty space at the ends of the scale of possibilities. This can dramatically change the color distribution in your photo, as you can see in Figure 7-9.

It's much, much easier to *use* Levels than to understand it, as you know if you've already tried Auto Levels in Quick Fix (page 125). That command is great for, well, quick fixes. But if you really need to massage your image, Levels has a lot more under the hood than you can access in Quick Fix. The next section shows you how to get at these settings.

Understanding the Histogram

Before you get started adjusting Levels, you need to understand the heart, soul, and brain of the Levels dialog box: the Histogram, shown in Figure 7-10. (You can call up this dialog box by pressing Ctrl+L.)

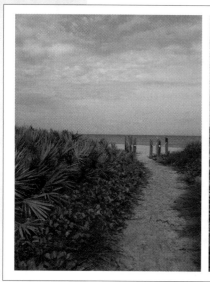 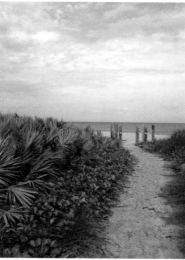

Figure 7-9:
A simple Levels adjustment can make a huge difference in the way your photos look.

Left: The gray-green cast to this photo makes everything look dull.

Right: Levels not only got rid of the color cast, but also helps make the photo look like it has better contrast and sharpness.

The Histogram is the black bumpy mound in the window. It's really nothing more than a bar graph indicating the distribution of the colors in your photo. (It's a bar graph, but there's no space between the bars, which is what causes the mountainous look.)

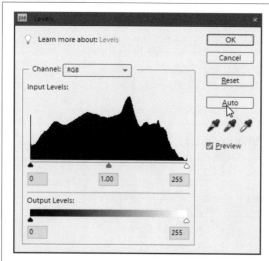

Figure 7-10:
One of the scariest sights in Elements, the Levels dialog box is actually your friend. If it frightens you, take comfort in knowing that you can always click the Auto button here, which is the same Auto Levels command as in Quick Fix. But it's worth persevering: The other options here give you much better control over the end results.

From left to right, the Histogram shows the brightness range from dark to light (the 0 to 255 mentioned earlier in this section). The height of the "mountain" at any given point shows how many pixels in your photo have that particular brightness. You can tell a lot about your photo by where the mound is before you adjust it, as demonstrated in Figure 7-11.

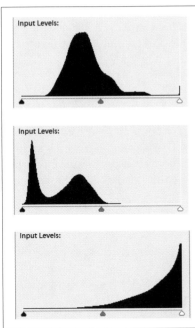

Figure 7-11:

Top: If the bars in your Histogram are all smooshed together, your photo doesn't have a lot of tonal range. As long as you like how the photo looks, that's not important. But if you're unhappy with the color in the photo, it's usually harder to get it exactly right in that kind of photo compared with one that has a wider tonal range.

Middle: If the mound is bunched up on the left side, your photo is underexposed.

Bottom: If you just have a big lump on the right side, your photo is overexposed.

Above the Histogram is a Channel menu that says "RGB". If you click it, you can choose to see a separate Histogram for each individual color. You can adjust all three channels at once in the RGB setting, or change each channel separately for maximum control of your colors.

The Histogram contains so much info about your photo that Adobe also makes it available in the Full Editor in its own panel (Figure 7-12), so you can always see it and use it to monitor how you're changing the colors in an image. Once you get fluent in reading Histogramese, you'll probably want to keep this panel around.

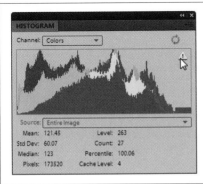

Figure 7-12:

If you keep the Histogram on your desktop, you can always see what effect your changes are having on the color distribution in your photo. To get this nifty Technicolor view, go to Window → Histogram and then choose Colors from the panel's pull-down menu. To update the Histogram, click the upper-right triangle as shown here. If you're really into statistics, there are a bunch of them at the bottom of this panel, but if you're not a pro, you can safely ignore these numbers.

The Histogram is just a graph, and you don't do anything to it directly. When you use Levels, you use the Histogram as a guide so that you can tell Elements what to consider the black and white points—that is, the darkest and lightest points—in your photo. (Remember, you're thinking in terms of brightness values, not shades of color, for these settings.)

Once you've set these end points, you can adjust the *midtones*—the tones in between that would appear gray in a black-and-white photo. If that seems complicated, it's not—at least, not when you're actually doing it. Once you've made a Levels adjustment, the next time you open the Levels dialog box, you'll see that your Histogram now runs the whole length of the scale because you've told Elements to redistribute your colors so that they cover the full dark-to-light range.

The next two sections show you—finally!—how to actually adjust your image's Levels.

> **TIP** Once you learn how to interpret the Histograms in Elements, you can try your hand with your camera's histogram (if it has one). It's really hard to judge how well your picture turned out when all you have to go by is your camera's tiny LCD screen, so the histogram can be a big help. By looking at your camera's histogram, you can tell how well exposed your shot was.

Adjusting Levels: The Eyedropper Method

One way to adjust Levels is to set the black, white, and/or gray points by using the eyedroppers in the Levels Adjustments panel. It's quite simple—just follow these steps:

1. **Bring up the Levels Adjustments panel by selecting Layer → New Adjustment Layer → Levels.**

   If you don't want a separate layer for your Levels adjustment, go to Enhance → Adjust Lighting → Levels or press Ctrl+L instead. (You'll get a dialog box instead of the panel, but it works exactly the same way.) But making the Levels changes on an Adjustment layer gives you more flexibility for making future changes.

2. **If necessary, move the Adjustments panel or the Levels dialog box out of the way so you have a good view of your photo.**

   The dialog box loves to plunk itself down smack in the middle of the most important part of your image. Just grab it by the top bar and drag it somewhere else.

3. **In the Adjustments panel or the Levels dialog box, click the black eyedropper.**

   In the Adjustments panel, from top to bottom, the eyedroppers are black, gray, and white. In the dialog box they're arranged from left to right instead.

4. **Move your cursor over your photo, and click an area of your photo that should be black.**

Should be, not *is.* That's a mistake lots of people make the first time they use the Levels eyedroppers: They click a spot that's the same color as the eyedropper rather than one that *ought to be* that color. For instance, if your photo includes a wooden carving that looks black right now, but you know it *should* be dark brown, that's a bad place to click. Try clicking a black coffee mug or belt, instead. This is called "setting a black point."

5. **Repeat with the other eyedroppers for their respective colors.**

Now find a spot that should be white (like maybe a cloud that's a little off-white now) and one that should be gray to set your white and gray points. That's the way it's supposed to work, but you can't always use all the eyedroppers in a given photo. Experiment to see what gives you the best-looking results.

NOTE   You don't always need to set a gray point. If you try to set it and think your photo looked better without it, just skip that step.

6. **If you're using the dialog box, when you're happy with what you see, click OK.**

If you're working with the Adjustments panel, you don't have to do anything: Elements has already applied your changes, so you're done.

See, it's not so hard. If you mess up, just click the dialog box's Reset button to start over again. (In the Adjustments panel, click the square made of four horizontal lines at the panel's upper right, and then choose Reset from the drop-down menu.)

Adjusting Levels: The Slider Controls

The eyedropper method works fine if your photo has spots that should be black, white, or gray, but a lot of the time, your picture may not have any of these colors.

Fortunately, the Levels sliders give you yet another way to apply Levels, and it's by far the most popular method, giving you maximum control over your colors.

Right below the Histogram are three little triangles called *Input sliders.* The left slider sets the black point in your photo, the right slider sets the white point, and the middle slider adjusts the midtones (gray). You just drag them to make changes to the color levels in your photo, as shown in Figure 7-13.

When you move the left Input slider, you tell Levels, "Take all the pixels from this point down and consider them black." With the right slider, you're saying, "Make this pixel and all higher values white." The middle slider adjusts the brightness values that are considered medium gray. All three adjustments improve the contrast of your image.

Levels Before Curves

I never know where to start adjusting the colors in my photos. Some photo mavens talk about using Levels, others about Curves. Which should I use?

Elements includes a much-requested feature from Photoshop—*Color Curves*. Despite the name, the Curves tool isn't some kind of arc-drawing tool. It a sophisticated way of adjusting the colors in your photos. Curves works something like Levels, but with many more points of correction.

In Elements, you get a simplified version of Photoshop's Curves dialog box, with a few preset settings. Because the Elements version doesn't have quite as many adjustment points, you get much of the advanced color control of Curves without all the complexity.

Generally speaking, a quick Levels adjustment is usually all you need to achieve good, realistic color. If you still aren't satisfied with the contrast in your image, or you want to create funky artistic effects, check out page 302, which explains Color Curves in detail.

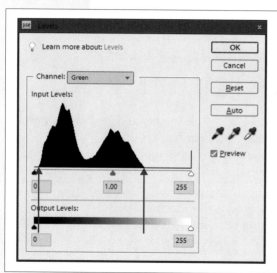

Figure 7-13:
To use the Levels Input sliders, simply drag the left and right sliders from the ends of the track until they're under the outer edges of the color data in the graph. The red arrows in this figure show where you'd position the left and right sliders for this particular photo. If there's empty space on the end of the graph, just move the slider until it's under the first mound of data.

NOTE If there are small amounts of color data—you see a flat line—at the ends of the Histogram, or if all the data is clumped in the middle of the graph—watch your photo as you move the left and right sliders to decide how far in you should bring them. Moving them all the way in may be too drastic. Your own taste should always be the deciding factor when you're adjusting a photo.

The easiest way to use the Levels sliders is to:

1. **Bring up the Levels dialog box or the Levels Adjustments panel.**

   Use one of the methods described in step 1 of the Eyedropper method (page 224). If necessary, move the dialog box or Adjustments panel so you've got a clear view of your photo.

2. **Grab the black Input slider.**

That's the one below the left end of the Histogram.

3. **Slide it to the right, if necessary.**

Move it over until it's under the farthest left part of the Histogram that has a mound in it. If you glance back at Figure 7-13, you'd move the left slider just a tiny bit, to where the left red arrow is. (Incidentally, although you're adjusting your image's colors, the Levels Histogram is always black and white no matter what you do—you don't see any color in the dialog box itself.)

You may not need to move the slider at all if there's already a good bit of data at the end of the Histogram. It's not mandatory to adjust all the sliders for every photo.

4. **Grab the white slider (the one on the right side) and move it left if necessary.**

Bring it under the farthest right area of the Histogram that has a mound in it.

5. **Now adjust the gray slider.**

This is the *midtones* slider, and it adjusts the midtones of your photo. Move it back and forth while watching your photo until you like what you see. This slider has the most impact on the overall result, so take some time to play with it.

6. **If you're using the dialog box, click OK.**

You can adjust your whole image at once or each color channel individually. The most accurate way is to open the Levels dialog box and to choose each color channel separately from the Channel drop-down menu. Adjust the end points for each channel, and then choose RGB from the menu and tweak just the midtones (gray) slider.

> **TIP**   If you know the numerical value of the pixels you want to designate for any of these settings, you can type that information into the Input Levels boxes below the Histogram. You can set the gray value from .10 to 9.99 (it's set at 1.00 automatically). You can set the other two boxes anywhere from 0 to 255.

The last control you may want to use in the Levels dialog box is the Output Levels slider, which works roughly the same way as the brightness and contrast controls on your TV. Moving this slider makes the darkest pixels darker and the lightest pixels lighter. Image pros call this "adjusting the tonal range of a photo."

Adjusting Levels can improve almost every photo you take, but if your photo has a bad *color cast*—if it's too orange or too blue, say—you may need something else. The next section explains how to get rid of color like that.

Removing Unwanted Color

It's not uncommon for an otherwise good photo to have a *color cast*—that is, to have all its tonal values shifted so it's too blue, like Figure 7-14, or too orange.

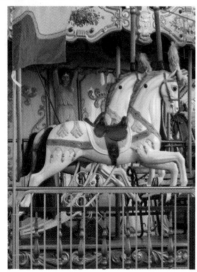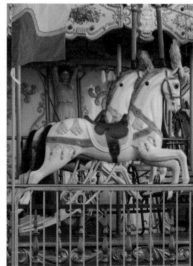

Figure 7-14:
Left: You may wind up with photos like this every once in a while if you forget to change your camera's white balance— a special setting for the type of lighting conditions you're shooting in (common settings are daylight, fluorescent, and so on). This is an outdoor photo taken with the camera set for tungsten indoor lighting.

Right: Elements fixes that wicked color cast in a jiffy. The photo still needs other adjustments, but the color is back in the right ballpark.

Elements gives you several ways to correct color-cast problems:

- **Auto Color Correction** doesn't give you any control over the changes, but it often does a good job. To use it, go to Enhance → Auto Color Correction or press Ctrl+Shift+B.

- **The Raw Converter** may be the easiest way to fix problems, though it works only on Raw, JPEG, and TIFF files. Just run your photo through the Raw converter (page 248), and adjust its white balance there.

- **Levels** gives you the finest control of all. You can often eliminate a color cast by adjusting the individual color channels (as explained in the previous section) till the extra color is gone. The drawbacks are that Levels can be very fiddly for this sort of work; sometimes this method doesn't work if the problem is severe, and it can take much longer than the other methods.

- **Remove Color Cast** is a command designed specially for correcting a color cast with one click. The next section explains how to use it.

- **The Color Variations** dialog box can help you figure out which colors you need more or less of, but it has some limitations. It's covered on page 229.

- **The Photo Filter** command gives you much more control than the Remove Color Cast command, and you can apply Photo Filters as Adjustment layers, too. Photo Filters are covered on page 273.

- **The Average Blur Filter,** used with a blend mode, lets you fix a color cast. As you'll read on page 417, it's something like creating a custom photo filter.

• **Adjust Color for Skin Tone** makes Elements adjust your photo based on the skin colors in the image. In practice, this adjustment is often more likely to introduce a color cast than to correct one, but if your photo has a slight bluish cast that's visible in the subject's skin (as explained on page 134), it may do the trick. This option works best for slight, annoying casts that are too subtle for the other methods in this list.

You can use any of these methods, but usually you'd start with Levels and then move on to the Remove Color Cast or Photo Filter command. To practice any of the fixes you're about to learn, download the photo *carousel.jpg* from the Missing CD page at *www.missingmanuals.com*.

The Remove Color Cast Command

This command uses an eyedropper to adjust the colors in your photo based on the pixels you click. With this method, you show Elements where a neutral color should be. As you saw with the carousel in Figure 7-14, Remove Color Cast can make a big difference with just one click. To use it:

1. **Go to Enhance → Adjust Color → Remove Color Cast.**

   Your cursor should change to an eyedropper when you move it over your photo. If it doesn't, go to the dialog box and click the eyedropper icon.

2. **Click an area that should be gray, white, or black.**

   You only have to click once in your photo for this feature to work. As with the Levels eyedropper tool, click an area that *should be* gray, white, or black (as opposed to looking for an area that's *currently* one of these colors). If the image has several of these, you can try clicking different spots in your photo. Just click Reset in between each sample until you find the spot that gives you the most natural-looking color.

3. **Click OK.**

Remove Color Cast works pretty well if your image has areas that should be black, white, or gray, even if they're tiny. The tricky thing is when you have an image that doesn't have a good area to sample—when there isn't any black, white, or gray anywhere in the picture. If that's the case, consider using the Photo Filter command (page 273) instead.

> **TIP** If you generally like what Auto Levels does for your photos, but feel like it leaves behind a slight color cast, a click with the Color Cast tool may be just the right finishing touch.

Using Color Variations

The Color Variations dialog box (Figure 7-15) appeals to many Elements beginners because it gives you visual clues about how to fix the color in your photo. You just click the little preview thumbnail that shows the color balance you like best, and Elements applies the necessary change to make your photo look like the thumbnail.

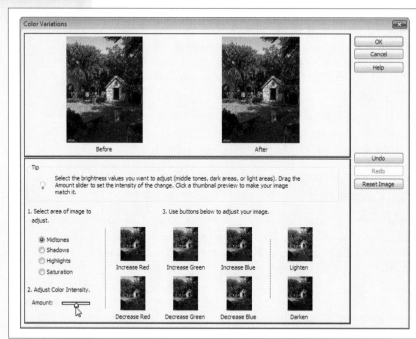

Figure 7-15:
A lot of the time, you'll do better using the Quick Fix window to make the kinds of changes you can make with Color Variations, but Color Variations comes in handy because you can see exactly what your photo needs—in this case, a little less red and a bit more lightness. (The effect is a bit exaggerated here so that you can see it easily.) The after photo is bluer than you'd probably want it to be. If that happens to you, click Reset and move the slider in the lower-left corner of this dialog box to the left a bit before you try again.

But Color Variations has some pretty severe limitations, most notably the microscopic size of the thumbnails. So it's hard to see what you're doing, and even newcomers can usually get better results in Quick Fix (page 115).

Still, Color Variations is useful when you know something isn't right with your photo's color, but you can't quite figure out what to do about it. And because it's adjustable, Color Variations is good for when you do know what you want, but want to make only a tiny change to your photo's color. To use Color Variations:

1. **Open a photo.**

   You may want to make a duplicate layer (page 177) for the adjustments, so that you'll have the option of discarding your changes if you're not happy with them. If you decide not to work on a duplicate, remember that you won't be able to undo these changes after you close the file.

2. **Go to Enhance → Adjust Color → Color Variations.**

   Elements displays the dialog box pictured in Figure 7-15.

3. **Under "Select area of image to adjust", click a radio button to choose whether to adjust midtones, shadows, highlights, or saturation.**

   Color Variations automatically selects Midtones, which is usually what you want. But experiment with the other settings to see what they do. The Saturation button works just like Saturation in Quick Fix (page 128).

4. **Use the slider at the bottom of the dialog box to control how drastic the change should be.**

   The farther right you drag the slider, the more dramatic the change. Usually, just a smidgen is enough to make a noticeable change.

5. **Below where it says "Use buttons below to adjust your image", click one of the thumbnails to make your photo look like it.**

   You can always click the Undo or Redo buttons on the right side of the window, or click Reset Image to put your photo back to where it was when you started.

6. **When you're happy with the result, click OK.**

Choosing Colors

So far, the color corrections you've been reading about in this chapter have all done most of the color assigning for you. But a lot of the time, you want to *tell* Elements what colors to work with—like when you're selecting the color for a Background or Fill layer (page 195), or when you want to paint on an image.

Although you can use any of the millions of colors your screen can display, Elements loads only two colors at a time. You choose these colors using the Foreground and Background color squares at the bottom of the Tools panel (see Figure 7-16).

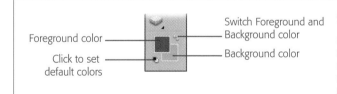

Foreground color

Click to set default colors

Switch Foreground and Background color

Background color

Figure 7-16:
The top square displays the Foreground color (here, that's blue); the bottom square displays the Background color (green). To quickly switch to the standard colors—black and white—either click the two tiny squares at the bottom left or press D. Click the curved double-headed arrow or press X to swap the Foreground and Background colors.

Foreground and Background mean just what they sound like—use the Foreground color with Elements' tools like the Brush or the Paint Bucket, and the Background color to fill in backgrounds. You can use as many colors in your images as you want, of course, but you can only use two at any given time.

The color-picking tools at the bottom of the Tools panel let you control the color you're using in a number of different ways:

- **Reset default colors.** Click the tiny black and white squares to return to the standard settings: black for the Foreground color and white for the Background color.

- **Switch Foreground and Background colors.** Click the little curved two-headed arrow above and to the right of the squares, and your Background color becomes the Foreground color, and vice versa. This is helpful when you've inadvertently made your color selection in the wrong box. (Say you set the Foreground color to yellow, but you actually meant to make the *Background* color yellow; just click these arrows and you're all set.)

- **Change either the Foreground or Background color to whatever color you want.** You can choose any color you like for either color square. Click either square to call up the Color Picker (explained below) to make your new choice. There's no limit on the number of colors you can select in Elements. Well, *technically* there is, but it's in the millions, so you should find enough choices for anything you want to do.

You have a few different ways to select your Foreground and Background colors. The next few sections show you how to use the Color Picker, the Eyedropper tool (to pick a color from an existing image), or the Color Swatches panel.

When working with some of Elements' tools, like the Type tool, you can choose a color in the tool's Options bar. Adobe knows that, given a choice, most people prefer to work with either Color Swatches or the Color Picker, so they've come up with a clever way to accommodate both camps, as shown in Figure 7-17.

Click here for the   Click here for the
Color Picker   Color Swatches

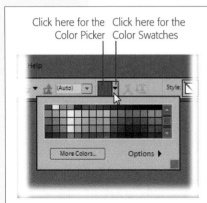

Figure 7-17:
Whether you prefer using Color Swatches or the Color Picker, you can choose your favorite (for most tools) in the Options bar. Click the color sample in the box to bring up the Color Picker, or, if you're a Swatcher, click the arrow to the right of the box to reveal the Color Swatches panel.

The Color Picker

Figure 7-18 shows the Color Picker. It has an intimidating number of options, but, most of the time, you don't need them all. Picking a color is as easy as clicking wherever you see the color you want.

The Color Picker is easy to use:

1. **Click the Foreground or Background color square in the Tools panel.**

   Elements launches the Color Picker. Some tools—like the Paint Bucket (page 378) and the Selection brush's mask color option (page 146)—use the Color Picker. It works the same way no matter how you get to it.

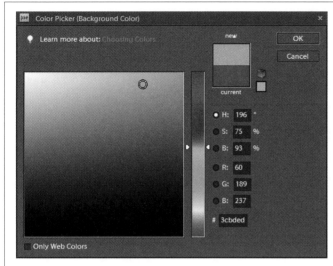

Figure 7-18:
For many beginners, the most important parts of Elements' Color Picker are the vertical rectangular slider in the middle (called, appropriately enough, the Color Slider), and the big square box, called the Color Field. Use the slider to get the general color you want, and then click in the field to pick the exact shade.

2. **Choose the color range you want to select from.**

   Use the vertical Color Slider in the middle of the Color Picker to slide through the spectrum until you see the color you want in the big, square Color Field.

3. **Click the spot in the Color Field where you see the exact shade you want.**

   You can keep clicking around and watch the color in the top box in the window change to reflect what you click. The bottom box shows your original color for comparison.

4. **Click OK.**

   The color you selected now appears in the Foreground or Background square in the Tools panel (depending on which one you clicked in step 1).

That's the basic way to use the Color Picker. The box on page 236 explains how to enter a numeric value for your color if you know it, or how to change the shades the Color Picker offers you.

> **TIP**   You're not limited to Elements' Color Picker. You can use the Windows Color Picker instead, if you prefer (maybe you're used to working with the Windows Picker, for example). To change the Color Picker, in the Elements Editor, go to Edit → Preferences → General. At the top of the dialog box, choose Windows from the Color Picker menu. Now when you click a color square, the Windows Color Picker opens up looking pretty feeble, with just a few colored squares and some white ones. But if you click Define Custom Colors, it expands, giving you access to most of the same features as in the Adobe picker. (The plain white squares are like little pigeonholes where you can save your color choices.)

The Eyedropper Tool

If you've ever repainted your house, you've probably had the frustrating experience of spotting the *exact* color you want somewhere—if only there were a way to capture that color. That's one problem you'll never run into in Elements, thanks to the handy Eyedropper tool. It lets you sample any color you see on your monitor and make it your Foreground color in Elements. If you can get a color onto your computer, Elements can grab it.

Sampling a color (that is, snagging it for your own use) couldn't be simpler with the Eyedropper. Just move your cursor over the color you want and click. It even works on colors that aren't even in Elements, as explained in Figure 7-19. Sampling is perfect for projects like scrapbook pages, where you might want to use, say, the color from an event program cover as a theme color for the project. Just scan the program and sample the color with the Eyedropper.

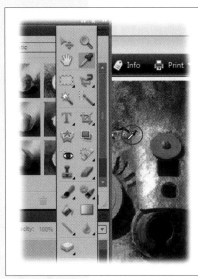

Figure 7-19:
To use the Eyedropper tool to sample colors outside of Elements, start by clicking anywhere in your Elements file. Then, while still holding your mouse button down, move your cursor over to the non-Elements object (a web page, for instance), until it's over the area you want to sample. When you let go, the new color appears in Elements' Foreground color square. If you let go before you get to the non-Elements object, this trick won't work. Here, the Eyedropper (circled) is sampling the teal color from a photo in Vista's Windows Photo Gallery. If you don't have a big monitor, it can take a bit of maneuvering to get the program windows positioned so that you can perform this procedure.

By now, you may think that Elements has more eyedroppers than your medicine cabinet. But this is the *official* Elements Eyedropper tool that has its own place in the Tools panel. It's one of the easiest tools to use:

1. **Click the Eyedropper in the Tools panel or press I.**

   Your cursor changes into a tiny eyedropper.

2. **Move the Eyedropper over the color you want to sample.**

   If you want to watch the color change in the Foreground color box as you move the Eyedropper around, hold the mouse button down as you go.

3. **Click when you see the color you want.**

Elements loads your color choice as your Foreground color so it's ready to use. (To set the Background color instead, Alt-click the color you want.)

If you want to keep your new color around so you can use it later without having to get the Eyedropper out again, you can save it in the Swatches panel. Then you can quickly choose it again anytime you want. The next section teaches you how to do this.

> **TIP** Since there may be some slight pixel-to-pixel variation in a color, you can set the Eyedropper to sample a little block of pixels and average them. In the Eyedropper's Sample Size setting in the Options bar, you can choose between the exact pixel you click (Point Sample), a 3-pixel square average, or a 5-pixel square average. Oddly enough, this Eyedropper setting also applies to the Magic Wand (page 149). Change it here and you change it for the wand, too.

The Color Swatches Panel

The Color Swatches panel holds several preloaded libraries of sample colors for you to choose from. Go to Window → Color Swatches to call up the panel. You can park it in the Panel bin just like any other panel, if you like, or leave it floating on your desktop. When you're ready to choose a color, just click the swatch you want, and it appears in the Tools panel's Foreground color square or in the color box of the tool you're using.

The Color Swatches panel is really handy when you want to keep certain colors at your fingertips. For instance, you can put your logo colors into it, and then you always have those colors available for any graphics or ads you create in Elements.

Elements starts you off with several different libraries (groups) of Color Swatches. Click the pull-down menu on the Swatches panel to see them all. A swatch you create appears at the bottom of the current library, and you can save it there, or create your own swatch libraries.

Using the Color Swatches to select your Foreground or Background color is as easy as using the Eyedropper tool. Figure 7-20 shows you how.

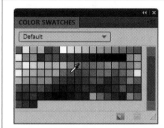

Figure 7-20:
When you move your cursor over the Color Swatches panel, it changes to an eyedropper. Simply click to select a color. If you're using a preloaded color library, you'll see labels appear as you move over each square.

You can use the Color Swatches panel:

- **To pick a Foreground color,** by just clicking the color you want.

- **To pick a Background color,** by Ctrl-clicking a color so Elements makes it the Background color.

Paint by Number

The Elements Color Picker includes some sophisticated controls that most folks can ignore. But in case you're curious, here's what the rest of the Color Picker does:

- **H, S, and B buttons.** These numbers determine the hue, saturation, and brightness of your color, respectively. They control pretty much the same values as the Hue/Saturation adjustment. (See page 306 for more about hue and saturation.)

- **R, G, and B buttons.** These buttons let you specify the amount of red, green, and blue you want in the color you're picking. Each button can have a numerical value anywhere from 0 to 255. A lower number means less of the color, a higher number means more. For example, 128 R, 128 G, 128 B is neutral gray. By changing the numbers, you can change the blend of the color.

- **# (Hex number).** Below the radio buttons is a box that lets you enter a special six-character *hexadecimal* code that you use when you're creating web graphics. These codes tell web browsers which colors to display. You can also click a color in the window to see the hex number for that shade.

- **Only Web Colors checkbox.** Turning on this box ensures that the colors you see in the main color box are drawn only from the 216 colors that antique web browsers can display. For example, if you're creating a website and you're really worried about color compatibility with Netscape 4.0, this box is for you. If you see a tiny cube just to the right of the color sample box (as in Figure 7-18), the color you're using isn't deemed web safe.

You can change the way the Color Swatches panel displays swatch information, as explained in Figure 7-21.

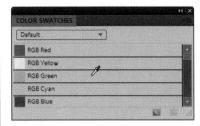

Figure 7-21:
On the Color Swatches panel, click the four-line square to the right of the panel's name and select Small List. Depending on the library you're using, you'll see the names or hex numbers for each color in addition to a small thumbnail of the color. (Some Elements tools, like the Type tools, bring up these choices via an Options button below the swatch samples, instead of having a four-line square.)

Saving colors in the Swatches panel

You can save any colors you've picked using the Color Picker or Eyedropper tool as swatches. If you don't save them, you lose them as soon as you select a different library or close the panel.

To save a swatch, you can do one of two things:

- Click the New Swatch icon at the bottom of the Color Swatches panel. (It's the same square that stands for "new" in the Layers panel.)

- Click the little square with lines on it at the panel's upper right and choose New Swatch.

In either case, you get a chance to name and save the new swatch. The name shows up as a pop-up label when you hover your cursor over the swatch in the panel. (When you save the swatch, Elements picks a spot to save it; don't change that location if you want Elements to recognize what you're saving as a swatch.) Your swatch appears at the bottom of the current swatch library. To delete a swatch that you've saved, drag it to the Trash icon in the Color Swatches panel, or Alt-click the swatch.

You can create your own swatch libraries if you want to keep your swatches separate from the ones Elements gives you. Click the Color Swatches panel's four-line square at upper right and pick Save Swatches. Then give your new library a name and save it.

> NOTE   When you save a new swatch library, it doesn't show up in the list of libraries until the next time you start Elements.

Sharpening Images

Digital cameras are wonderful, but often it's hard to tell how well-focused your photos are until you download them to your computer. And because of the way cameras' digital sensors process information, most digital image data needs to be *sharpened.* Sharpening is an image-editing trick that makes your pictures look more clearly focused.

Elements includes some almost miraculous tools for sharpening your images. (It's pretty darned good at blurring them, too, if you want; see page 415.)

> NOTE   If you've used early versions of Elements, you may be searching the Filter menu in vain looking for the Sharpen filters. It's true—your old friends Sharpen and Sharpen More are gone. In their place, Adjust Sharpness appears at the bottom of the Enhance menu, along with Unsharp Mask. (Both of these features are explained in the following sections.) If you miss the one-click ease of Sharpen and Sharpen More, just head over to Quick Fix and use its Auto Sharpen button (page 129) to get the same effect or go to Enhance → AutoSharpen.

Unsharp Mask

Although it sounds like the last thing you'd ever want to use on a photo, Unsharp Mask reigned as the Supreme Sharpener for many generations of image correction, despite it having the most counterintuitive name in all of Elements.

To be fair, it's not Adobe's fault. *Unsharp Mask* is an old darkroom term, and it actually does make sense if you know how our film ancestors used to improve a picture's focus. (Its name refers to a complicated darkroom technique that involved making a blurred copy of the photo at one point in the process.)

For several versions of Elements, Unsharp Mask ranked right up there with Levels as a contender for most useful tool in Elements, and some people still think it's the best way to sharpen a photo. Figure 7-22 shows how much a little Unsharp Mask can do for your photos.

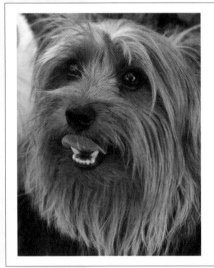
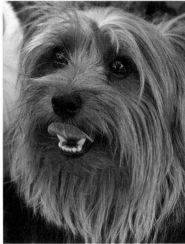

Figure 7-22:
Left: The photo as it came from the camera.

Right: The same photo treated with a dose of Unsharp Mask. Notice how much clearer the individual hairs in the dog's coat are and how much better defined the eyes and mouth are.

To use Unsharp Mask, first finish all your other corrections and changes. A good rule of thumb for sharpening is "last and once." Unsharp Mask (or any sharpening tool) can undermine other adjustments you make later on, so always make sharpening your last step. And repeatedly applying sharpening can degrade your image's quality.

> NOTE   An exception to the rule about sharpening only once is when you're converting Raw images (page 248): You can usually sharpen both in the Raw converter and then again as a last step without causing problems.

If you're sharpening an image with layers, be sure the active layer has something in it. Applying sharpening to a Levels Adjustment layer, for example, won't do anything. Also, perform any format conversions (page 75) before applying sharpening. Finally, you may want to sharpen a duplicate layer just in case you want to undo your changes later. Press Ctrl+J to create the duplicate layer.

NOTE   It's helpful to understand just exactly what Elements does when it "sharpens" your photo. It doesn't magically correct the focus. As a matter of fact, it doesn't really sharpen anything. What it does is deepen the contrast where colors meet, giving the *impression* of crisper focus. So while Elements can dramatically improve a shot that's a little soft, even Elements can't fix that old double exposure or a shot where the subject is just a blur of motion.

When you're ready to apply Unsharp Mask:

1. **Go to Enhance → Unsharp Mask.**

   You can use Unsharp Mask in either Full Edit or Quick Fix.

2. **Adjust the settings in the Unsharp Mask dialog box until you like what you see.**

   Move the sliders until you're happy with the sharpness of your photo. (The following list explains what each slider does.) In the Preview window, you can zoom in and out and grab the photo to adjust which part you see. It's also a good idea to drag the dialog box off to the side so that you can watch your actual image for a more global view of the changes you're making. You get the most accurate look at how you're affecting the image if you set the view to 100% (or Actual Pixels—see page 100).

3. **When you're satisfied, click OK.**

The Unsharp Mask sliders work much like other tools' sliders:

- **Amount** tells Elements how much to sharpen, in percent terms. A higher number means more sharpening.

- **Radius** lets Elements know how far from an edge it should look when increasing the contrast.

- **Threshold** controls how different a pixel needs to be from the surrounding pixels before Elements considers it an edge and sharpens it. If the threshold is left at zero—which is the standard setting—Elements sharpens *all* of the image's pixels.

There are many, many different schools of thought about where to move the sliders or which values to plug into each box. Whatever works for you is fine. The one thing you want to watch out for is *oversharpening*. Figure 7-23 tells you how to know if you've gone too far.

You'll probably need to experiment a bit to find out which settings work best for you. Photos you plan to print usually need to be sharpened to an extent that makes them look oversharpened on your monitor. So you may want to create separate versions of your photo (one for onscreen viewing and one for printing). Version sets (page 68) in the Organizer are great for keeping track of multiple copies like this.

Adjust Sharpness

Unsharp Mask has been around since long before digital imaging. A lot of people (including the folks at Adobe) have been thinking that, in the computer age,

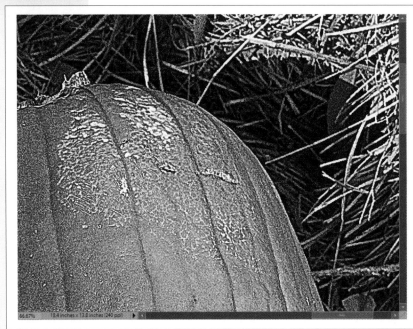

Figure 7-23:
The perils of oversharpening. This is just a normal pumpkin, not a diseased one, but oversharpening gives it a flaky appearance and makes the straw in the background look sketched in rather than real. The presence of halos (as you see along the edge of the pumpkin) is often your best clue that you've oversharpened an image.

there's got to be a better way to sharpen, and now there is. The latest tool in the war on poor focus is Adjust Sharpness.

The Unsharp Mask tool helps boost a photo's sharpness by a process something like reducing Gaussian blur (page 415). Problem is, Gaussian blurring is rarely the cause of your picture's poor focus, so there's only so much Unsharp Mask can do. In real life, blurry photos are usually caused by one of two things:

- **Lens blur.** Your camera's prime focal point isn't directly over your subject. Or perhaps your lens isn't quite as sharp as you'd like it to be.

- **Motion blur.** You moved the camera—or your subject moved—while you pressed the shutter.

Adjust Sharpness is as easy to use as Unsharp Mask, and it gives you settings to correct all three kinds of blur—Gaussian, lens, and motion. When you first open the Adjust Sharpness dialog box, its settings are almost identical to those of Unsharp Mask. It's the *extra* things Adjust Sharpness can do that make it a more versatile tool. Here's how to use it:

1. **Make sure the layer you want to sharpen is the active layer.**

   See Chapter 6 if you need a refresher on layers.

2. **Go to Enhance → Adjust Sharpness.**

   You can reach this menu item from either Full Edit or Quick Fix.

3. **Make your changes in the Adjust Sharpness dialog box.**

As shown in Figure 7-24, the dialog box gives you a nice big preview. It's usually best to stick with 50 or 100 percent zoom (use the plus and minus buttons below the preview to zoom) for the most accurate view. The settings are explained in detail in the list below.

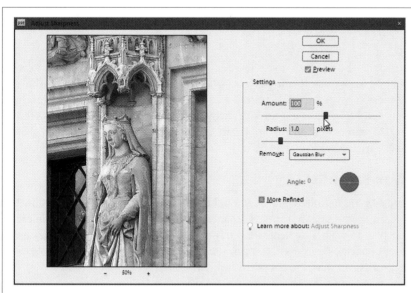

Figure 7-24:
The Adjust Sharpness dialog box shows you a good-sized preview of your image. But it helps if you position the dialog box so you can see the main image window, too, so you can keep an eye on any changes happening in areas outside the preview's frame.

4. **When you like the way your photo looks, click OK.**

The first two settings in the Adjust Sharpness dialog box, Amount and Radius, work exactly the same way they do in Unsharp Mask (page 239). Adjust Sharpness also has a few additional settings of its own:

- **Remove.** Here's where you choose what kind of fuzziness to fix: Gaussian, lens, or motion blur, as explained on page 240. If you aren't sure which you want, try all three and see which works best.

- **Angle.** In a motion blur, you can improve your results by telling Elements the angle of the motion. For example, if your grip on the camera slipped, the direction of motion would be downward. Move the line in the little circle or type a number in degrees to approximate the angle. (It's awfully tricky to get the angle exactly right, so you may find it easier to sharpen without messing with this setting.)

- **More Refined.** Turn on this checkbox and Elements takes a tad longer to apply sharpening since it sharpens more details. Generally you'll want to leave this setting off for photos with lots of little details, like leaves or fur (and people's faces, unless you like to look at pores). But you might want it on for bold desert landscapes, for example, or other subjects without lots of fiddly small parts.

Noise, artifacts, and dust become much more prominent when you turn on More Refined, since they get sharpened along with the details of your photo. Experiment, and watch the main image window as well as the preview, to see how this setting affects your photo.

NOTE   Although Amount and Radius mean the same things as they do in Unsharp Mask, don't assume that you can just plug your favorite Unsharp Mask settings into the Adjust Sharpness dialog box and get the same results. Don't be surprised if you prefer very different numbers for these settings for the two tools.

Many people who've used Smart Sharpening in the full-featured Photoshop swear they'll never go back to plain Unsharp Mask. Try out Adjust Sharpness—the Elements version of Smart Sharpening—and see if you, too, like it better than Unsharp Mask. To give you an idea of the difference between the two methods, Figure 7-25 shows the dog from Figure 7-22 again, only this time with Adjust Sharpness instead of Unsharp Mask.

The High-Pass Filter

Unsharp Mask is definitely the traditional favorite, and Adjust Sharpness is the latest thing in sharpening, but there's an alternative method that many people prefer because you do it on a dedicated layer and can lessen the effect later by adjusting the layer's opacity. Moreover, you can use this method to punch up the colors in your photo as you sharpen. It's called *high-pass sharpening*.

All sharpening methods have their virtues, and you may find that you choose your technique according to the content of your photo. Try the following procedure by downloading the photo *waterlillies.jpg* from the Missing CD page at *www.missingmanuals.com*:

1. **Open your photo and make sure the layer you want to sharpen is the active layer.**

2. **Duplicate the layer by pressing Ctrl+J.**

   If you have a multilayered image and you want to sharpen all the layers, first flatten the image or use the Stamp Visible command (see the box on page 192) so everything is all in one layer.

3. **Go to Filter → Other → High Pass.**

   Your photo now looks like the victim of a mudslide, buried in featureless gray. That's what you want for right now.

4. **In the High Pass dialog box, move the slider until you can barely see the outline of your subject.**

   Usually that means picking a setting roughly between 1.5 and 3.5. If you can see colors, your setting is too high. (If you can't quite eliminate every trace of color without totally losing the outline, a tiny bit of color is OK.) Keep in mind that the edges you see through the gray are the ones that will get sharpened the most. Use that as your guide for how much detail to include.

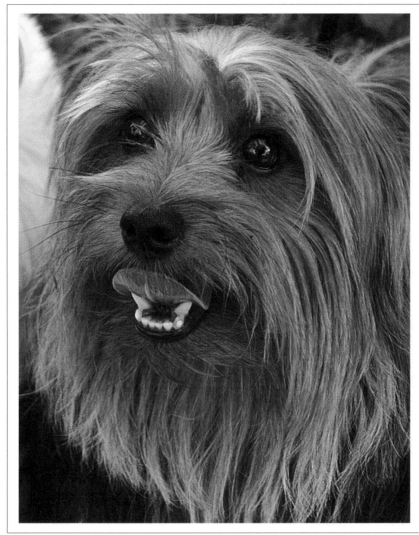

Figure 7-25:
Here's the terrier from page 238, only this time he's been sharpened using Adjust Sharpness. Notice how much more each hair in his coat stands out, and how much more detail you can see in his nose and mouth.

5. **Click OK.**

6. **In the Layers panel, set the blend mode for the new layer to Overlay.**

Ta-da! Your subject is back again in glowing, sharper color, as shown in Figure 7-26.

TIP   There's yet another way to create "pop" in your photos: the Clarity setting in the Raw converter (page 261), which sharpens and enhances contrast at the same time. (If you know what "local contrast enhancement" means, this setting does something similar.) You can use it on Raw, JPEG, and TIFF files. It's especially useful for clearing haze from your shots.

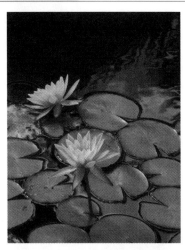

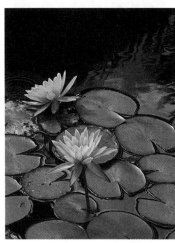

Figure 7-26:
Top: The original photo.

Bottom: High-pass sharpening using the Vivid Light blend mode makes the colors in this photo more vivid, but the ripples are much harder-edged than they were in the original. For high-pass sharpening, you can use any of the blend modes in the group with Overlay, except Hard Mix and Pin Light. Vivid Light can make your colors pop, but watch out for sharpening artifacts, since they'll be more vivid, too. Overlay gives you a softer effect.

The Sharpen Tool

Elements also gives you a dedicated Sharpen tool. It's a special brush that sharpens the areas you drag it over; Figure 7-27 shows it in action. To get to it, go to the Blur tool or press R, and then choose the Sharpen tool from the pop-out menu.

The Sharpen tool has some of the same Options bar settings as the Brush tool (see page 369 for more about brush settings). It also has a couple of settings all its own:

- **Mode** lets you increase the visibility of an object's edge by choosing from several different blend modes; Normal typically gives the most predictable results.

- **Strength** controls how much the brush sharpens what it passes over. A higher number means more sharpening.

- **Sample All Layers** makes the Sharpen tool work on all the visible layers in your image. Leave it off if you want to sharpen only the active layer.

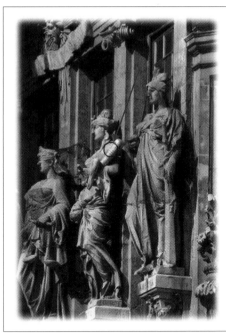

Figure 7-27:
The Sharpen tool isn't meant to sharpen a whole photo, but it's great for sharpening details. Here, it's being used to touch up the details in the middle statue. (The red arrow helps you find the circular cursor.) Approach this tool with caution: it's super easy to overdo it. One pass too many or too high a setting, and you start seeing artifacts right away.

Elements for Digital Photographers

If you're a fairly serious digital photographer, you'll be delighted to know that Adobe hasn't just loaded Elements with easy-to-use features aimed at beginners. Elements is also brimming with a collection of pretty advanced tools pulled straight from the full-featured Photoshop.

Number one on the list is the Adobe Camera Raw Converter, which takes Raw files—a format some cameras use to give you maximum editing control—and lets you convert and edit them in Elements. In this chapter, you'll learn lots more about Raw, and why you may or may not want to use it in your own photography. Don't skip to the next chapter if your camera shoots only JPEGs, though: You can use the Raw Converter to edit JPEG and TIFF images as well as Raw files, which can come in really handy, as you'll see shortly.

> **NOTE** Whereas JPEG and TIFF are acronyms for technical photographic terms, the word Raw— which you may occasionally see in all caps (RAW)—actually refers to the pristine, unprocessed quality of these files.

You'll also get to know the Photo Filter command, which helps adjust image colors by replicating the old-school effect of placing filters over a camera's lens. And Elements also has some truly useful batch-processing tools, including features that help you rename files, perform format conversions, and even apply basic retouching to multiple photos.

The big news for digital photographers is the new Exposure Merge feature, which lets you combine different versions of your photo to create a single image with a higher dynamic range (a wider range of correctly exposed areas) than you can get from a single shot. Read on to learn about it.

The Raw Converter

Probably the most useful thing Adobe has done for photography buffs is to include the Adobe Camera Raw Converter in Elements. For many people, this feature alone is well worth the price of the program, since you just can't beat the convenience of being able to perform conversions in the same program you use for editing.

If you don't know what Raw is, it's just a file format (a group of formats, really, since every camera maker has its own Raw format with its own file extension). But it's a very special one. Your digital camera actually contains a little computer that does a certain amount of processing to your photos right inside the camera itself. If you shoot in JPEG format, for instance, your camera makes some decisions about things like sharpness, color saturation, and contrast before it saves the JPEG files to your memory card.

But if your camera lets you shoot Raw files, then you get the unprocessed data straight from the camera. Shooting in Raw lets you make your *own* decisions about how your photos should look, to a much greater degree than with any other format. It's something like getting a negative from your digital camera—what you do to it in your digital darkroom is up to you.

That's Raw's big advantage—total control. The downside is that every camera manufacturer has its own proprietary Raw format, and the format varies even among models from the same manufacturer. No regular graphics program can edit these files, and very few programs can even view them. Instead, you need special software to convert Raw files to a format you can work with. In the past, that usually meant you needed software from the manufacturer before you could move your photo into an editing program like Elements.

Enter Adobe Camera Raw, which lets you convert your files right in Elements. Not only that, but the Adobe Camera Raw plug-in that comes with Elements lets you make sophisticated corrections to your photos before you even *open* them. Many times, you can do everything you need right in the Converter, so that you're done as soon as you open the converted file. (You can, of course, still use any of Elements' regular tools once you've opened a Raw file.) Using Adobe Camera Raw saves you a ton of time, and it's compatible with most cameras' Raw files.

> **TIP** Adobe regularly updates the Raw Converter to include new versions produced by different cameras, so if your camera's Raw files don't open, check for a newer version of the plug-in. You can download the latest one by going to *www.adobe.com/downloads*, and scrolling down to the section for Photoshop Elements for Windows. (Elements and Photoshop use the same plug-in, but you don't see all the features in Elements.) You'll also find a standalone version of the DNG (digital negative) Converter there, which you can use without launching Elements; see page 265.

Using the Raw Converter

For all the options it gives you, the Raw Converter is really easy to use. Adobe designed it so that it *automatically* calculates and applies what it thinks are the correct settings for exposure, shadows, brightness, and contrast. You can accept the Converter's decisions or override them and do everything yourself—it's your call.

While you may find all the Converter's various settings, tools, and tabs a little overwhelming at first, it's really laid out quite logically. Here's a quick overview of how to use it (you'll get details in a moment):

1. **Open your file in the Raw Converter.** You can call up the Raw Converter from either the Organizer or Full Edit just by opening a Raw file.

2. **Adjust your view and do any rotating, straightening, or (if you wish) cropping.** The Raw Converter has its own tools for all these tasks, so you don't need to go into the Editor for any of them.

3. **Adjust the image settings.** This is the best part of shooting Raw format images: You can tweak settings for things like lighting and color. The Converter also lets you apply final touchups: noise reduction, sharpening, and so on.

4. **Leave the Converter, go to the Editor.** The Raw Converter is a powerhouse for improving your photo's fundamental appearance, but to perform all the other adjustments Elements lets you make—applying filters, adding effects, and so on— you need to move your image to the Editor, which is also where you save the file in the standard graphics format of your choice (like TIFF, PSD, or JPEG).

If you'd like some practice with the Converter, you can find a sample image (*Raw_practice.mrw*) on the Missing CD page at *www.missingmanuals.com*, but be warned: It's a big file (7.2 MB).

To start converting your Raw file, in the Organizer, highlight the file, and then click Editor → Full Edit (or press Ctrl+I) to bring up the Converter window. (If you select multiple files from the Organizer and the Converter doesn't open automatically, then find your files in the Project bin by choosing Show Files From Organizer. Select them all, and then double-click one thumbnail to display them in the Converter.) If you're starting from the Editor, just go to File → Open. You can work with multiple files in the Raw Converter, as Figure 8-1 explains.

> **NOTE** You may not be able to open your Raw files by double-clicking them outside Elements (from the Windows desktop, for instance). You'll probably get a message to the effect that your computer has no idea what program to use to open that file. To make sure that your computer always uses Elements to open Raw files, follow the steps on page 48. (Windows may also offer to take you to a website where you can download the files necessary to let Windows display your Raw photos.)

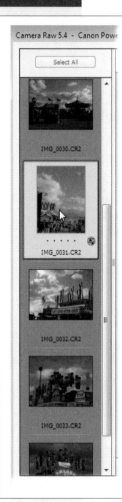

Figure 8-1:
When you open a bunch of files at once in the Raw Converter, you get a handy filmstrip view down the left side of the window. You can select a single image from the group by clicking it, and then your changes apply only to that file. Shift-click or Ctrl-click to select multiple files (or use the Select All button at the top of the list), and your selected files get changed along with the one in the main preview area. When you finish and click Open, all the selected files appear in the Project bin. If you want to save a group of them in another format, then use Process Multiple Files (page 274).

One important point about Raw files: Elements never overwrites your original file. As a matter of fact, Elements can't in any way modify the original Raw file. So your original is always there if you want to try converting it again later using different settings. It's something like having a negative from which you can always get more prints. This also applies to any image you edit in the Raw Converter, not just Raw files. You can crop a JPEG file here, for instance, and your original JPEG doesn't get cropped—only the copy you open from the Converter. There's more on working with non-Raw files in the Converter on page 264.

To Shoot in the Raw or Not

Should I shoot my pictures in Raw format?

It depends. Using Raw format has its pros and cons. You may be surprised to learn that some professional photographers choose not to use Raw. For example, many journalists don't use it, and it's not common with sports photographers, either. Here's a quick look at the advantages and disadvantages, to help you decide if you want to get involved with Raw.

On the plus side, you get:

- **More control.** With Raw you have a lot of extra chances to tweak your photos, and you get to call the shots, instead of your camera making the processing choices.

- **More fixes.** If you're not a perfect photographer, Raw is more forgiving—you can fix a lot of mistakes in Raw, although even Raw can't make a bad photo great.

- **No need to fuss with your white balance all the time while shooting.** However, you'll get better input if your camera's white balance settings are correct.

- **Nondestructive editing.** The changes you make in the Raw Converter don't change your original image one jot. It's always there for a fresh start if need be.

But Raw also has some significant drawbacks. For one thing, you can't just open a file and start editing it the way you do with JPEG files. You always have to convert it first, whether you use the Elements Converter or one supplied by the manufacturer. Other disadvantages include:

- **Larger file size.** Raw files are smaller than TIFFs, but they're usually much bigger than the highest quality JPEGs. Consequently, you need bigger (or more) memory cards if you regularly shoot Raw.

- **Slower speed.** It generally takes your camera longer to save Raw files than JPEGs—something to keep in mind when you're taking action shots. Most cameras these days have a buffer that holds several shots and lets you keep shooting while the camera is working, but you may hit the wall pretty quickly if you're using burst (rapid-advance) mode, especially with a pocket-sized point-and-shoot camera that uses Raw. In that case, you just have to wait. (Most digital single-lens reflex cameras are pretty fast with Raw these days, but they're generally even faster with JPEG.)

- **Worse in-camera preview.** For older cameras, you have some pretty significant limitations for digitally zooming the view in the viewfinder when using Raw, and Windows may not be able to show previews of your Raw files, either, without a special browser.

You may want to try a few shots of the same subject in both Raw and JPEG to see whether you notice a difference in your final results. Generally speaking, Raw offers the most leeway if you want to make significant edits, but you need to understand what you're doing. JPEG is easier if you're a beginner.

It's really your call. Some excellent photographers wouldn't think of shooting in anything *but* Raw, while others think it's too time-consuming.

NOTE   The Organizer can store your Raw files with no problems, but the Photo Downloader tends to be very slow about importing them, and has been known to choke when working with Raw files. You may well find you prefer to get your Raw photos into Elements by using one of the other methods discussed on page 46. If you shoot Raw + JPEG (the camera takes one photo and saves it as both a Raw file and a JPEG file), then you definitely don't want to use the Downloader, since it finds this scenario completely confusing.

Adjusting the view

When the Raw Converter opens, you see something like Figure 8-2. Before you decide whether to accept the automatic settings that Elements offers or to do your own tweaking, you need to get a good close look at your image. The Converter makes it easy to do this by giving you a large preview of your image, and a handful of tools to help adjust what you see:

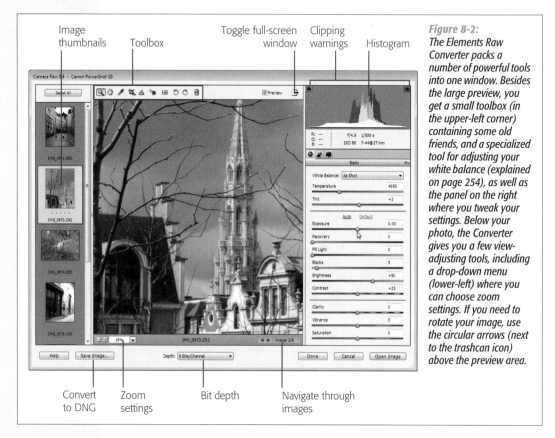

Image thumbnails   Toolbox   Toggle full-screen window   Clipping warnings   Histogram

Convert to DNG   Zoom settings   Bit depth   Navigate through images

Figure 8-2:
The Elements Raw Converter packs a number of powerful tools into one window. Besides the large preview, you get a small toolbox (in the upper-left corner) containing some old friends, and a specialized tool for adjusting your white balance (explained on page 254), as well as the panel on the right where you tweak your settings. Below your photo, the Converter gives you a few view-adjusting tools, including a drop-down menu (lower-left) where you can choose zoom settings. If you need to rotate your image, use the circular arrows (next to the trashcan icon) above the preview area.

- **Hand and Zoom tools.** These are in the toolbox above the upper-left corner of the Converter window. You use them here exactly the same way you do anywhere else in Elements. (You'll find more about the Hand tool on page 102; the Zoom tool is described on page 102.) The keyboard shortcuts for adjusting the view (page 102) and scrolling (page 102) also work in the Raw Converter.

- **View percentage.** You get a pop-up menu with preset sizes below the lower-left corner of the preview window. Just choose the size you want, or click the + or – buttons to zoom in or out.

  NOTE   Some adjustments and some of the special views, like the mask views for sharpening, aren't available unless you zoom to 100 percent or more.

- **Full Screen.** If you click the icon that looks like a page with a double-headed arrow on it, just to the right of the Preview checkbox above the image area, then you can put the Raw Converter window into full-screen view. Click it again to toggle back to the normal view.

- **Histogram.** In the upper-right corner of the Converter is a histogram that helps you keep track of how your changes affect the colors in your photo. (Flip back to page 221 for more on the fine art of reading histograms.)

> **TIP** Another handy feature in the Raw Converter is the panel just below the Histogram, where you can see important shooting information about your photo, like the aperture and ISO speed (*ISO* is a digital camera's version of film speed). If you hover your cursor over a pixel in the image, the RGB values for that pixel appear here as well.

Once you've gotten a good close look at your photo, you have a decision to make: Did Elements do a good enough job of choosing the settings for you? If so, you're done. Just click the Open Image button, and Elements opens your photo in the Editor, ready for any artistic changes or cropping. If you prefer to make adjustments to your photo in the Converter, read on. (If you're happy with Elements' conversion, but you want to sharpen your picture, then skip ahead to page 261.)

> **NOTE** Everyone gets confused by the Save Image button. That button is actually the DNG Converter (see page 265), and all you can do when you click it is create a DNG file. To save your edited Raw file, click Done if you just want to save the changes without actually opening the file, or click Open Image and then save in the format of your choice in the Editor.

Rotating, straightening, and cropping

Before tweaking your settings, you can make the following basic adjustments to your photo right in the Converter:

- **Rotate it.** Click one of the rotation arrows above the image preview.

- **Straighten it.** The Raw Converter has its own Straighten tool, which you use just like the one in the Editor's Tools panel (page 86), although it has a different icon and cursor. (It's just to the right of the Crop tool in the Raw Converter's toolbox.) However, you don't see your photo actually straighten out in the Converter— Elements just shows you the outline of where the edges of your straightened photo will be. Opening the photo in the Editor applies the straightening.

- **Crop it.** The Raw Converter has the same Crop tool as the Editor (page 89). You can crop to a particular aspect ratio (page 89) here if you want. Just right-click your photo when the Crop tool is active for a list of presets to choose from. If you want to crop to a particular size, choose Custom from the menu, and then, in the dialog box that appears, enter the numbers you want. (You also need to select inches or pixels.) Your crop information gets saved along with the Raw file, so the next time you open the file in the Converter, you see the cropped version.

As with straightening, Elements just draws a mask over the cropped area in the Converter; you can still see the outline of the whole photo. To adjust your crop, in the Raw Converter's toolbox, just click the Crop tool again, and then drag one of the handles that appear around the cropped area. To revert to the uncropped original later, right-click the Raw Converter's Crop tool and choose Clear Crop.

TIP   You can also fix red eye in the Raw Converter. The Red Eye tool is in the toolbox just to the right of the Straighten tool, and it works the same way it does everywhere else in Elements (page 121).

Adjusting White Balance

The long strip down the right side of the Raw Converter gives you lots of ways to tweak and correct the color, exposure, sharpness, brightness, and noise level of your photo. The strip is divided into three tabs. Start with the one labeled "Basic", which contains the, well, *basic* settings for the major adjustments.

First, check your White Balance setting, which is at the top of the settings in the Basic tab. Adjusting white balance is often the most important change when it comes to making your photos look their best.

The White Balance control adjusts all the colors in your photo by creating a neutral white tone. If that sounds a little strange, stop and think about it for a minute: The color you think of as *white* actually changes depending on the lighting conditions. At noon there's no warmth (no orange/yellow) to the light because the sun is high in the sky. Later in the day when the sun's rays are lower, whites are warmer. Indoors, tungsten lighting is much warmer than fluorescent lighting, which makes whites rather bluish or greenish. Your eyes and brain easily compensate for these changes, but sometimes your camera may not, or may overcompensate, giving your photos a color cast. The Raw Converter's White Balance setting lets you create more accurate color by neutralizing the white tones.

Most digital cameras have their own collections of white-balance settings. Typical choices include Auto, Daylight, Cloudy, Tungsten, Fluorescent, and Custom. When you shoot JPEGs, picking the correct setting here really matters, because it's tough to readjust white balance, even in a program like Elements. (Unless, of course, you tweak your JPEG with the Raw Converter, and even then the results may not be what you want.) With Raw photos, you can afford to be a little sloppier about setting your camera's white balance, because you can easily fix things in the Raw Converter.

Getting the white balance right can make a very big difference in how your photo looks, as you can see in Figure 8-3.

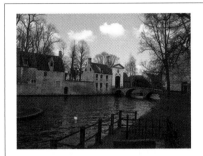 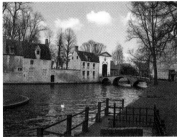

Figure 8-3:
Left: The lighting in this shot has a bluish cast that makes the scene look chilly.

Right: A single click on the swan with the White Balance tool makes the whole photo appear warmer. (It could stand a little additional tweaking, but already the better white balance makes the photo more vivid and improves its contrast.)

The Raw Converter gives you several ways to adjust your image's white balance:

- **Pull-down menu.** The White Balance menu just below the Histogram starts out by displaying As Shot, which means Elements is showing you your camera's settings. You can use the menu to change this setting, choosing from Auto, Daylight, Cloudy, and other options. It's worth giving Auto a try because it picks the correct settings surprisingly often.

- **Temperature.** Use this slider to make your photo warmer (more orange) or cooler (more blue). Moving the slider to the left cools your photo; moving it to the right warms it. You can also type a temperature in the box in degrees Kelvin (the official measurement for color temperature), if you're experienced in doing this by the numbers. Use the Temperature slider and the Tint slider (described next) together for a perfect white balance.

- **Tint.** The tint slider controls the green/magenta balance of your photo, pretty much the way it does in Quick Fix (see page 128). Move it to the left to increase the green in your photo, and to the right for more magenta.

- **White Balance tool.** The Raw window has its own special Eyedropper tool—the White Balance tool up in the toolbox. Activate it and then click any white or light gray spot in your photo, and Elements calculates the white balance based on those pixels. This is the most accurate method in this list, but you may have a hard time finding neutral pixels on which to use it.

If you're a good photographer, then much of the time a good white balance and a little sharpening may be all your photo needs before it's ready to go out into the world.

Adjusting Tone

The next group of six sliders—from Exposure down through Contrast—helps you improve your image's exposure and lighting (also known as "tone"). If you like Elements to make decisions for you, click Auto, and the program selects what it thinks are the best slider positions for each of the six settings. If you don't click anything, then Elements starts you off with the Default settings. Here's the difference between Auto and Default:

- **Auto.** Elements automatically adjusts your photo, using the same software-powered guesswork behind the other Auto buttons throughout the program, as explained in Figure 8-4.

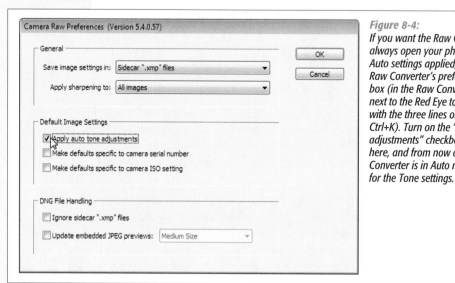

Figure 8-4:
If you want the Raw Converter to always open your photos with the Auto settings applied, then open the Raw Converter's preferences dialog box (in the Raw Converter's toolbox, next to the Red Eye tool, click the icon with the three lines on it, or press Ctrl+K). Turn on the "Apply auto tone adjustments" checkbox, as shown here, and from now on, the Raw Converter is in Auto mode, at least for the Tone settings.

- **Default.** The Raw Converter has a database of basic tone settings for each camera model. If you choose Default, then you see the baseline settings for your camera, and it's up to you to make further adjustments to your photo. If you want, you can set your own camera *defaults* (where the sliders are when your photo opens), too, as explained on page 259. If you don't like what you got with Auto, then just click Default to send your photo back to where it was when you opened it.

After you've clicked Auto or Default, you can override any setting by moving that slider yourself. If you go to the trouble of shooting Raw, then you may well prefer to do so, as Figure 8-5 demonstrates.

Here's a blow-by-blow of each of the six settings:

- **Exposure.** A properly exposed photo shows the largest possible range of detail. Shadows contain enough light to reveal detail, and highlights aren't so bright that all you see is white. Move the slider to the left to decrease exposure and to the right to increase it. (Note to photo veterans: The values on the scale are equivalent to f-stops.) Too high a choice here will *clip* some of your highlights (meaning they'll be so bright you won't see any detail in them). Figure 8-6 explains more about clipping.

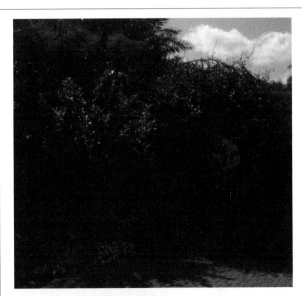

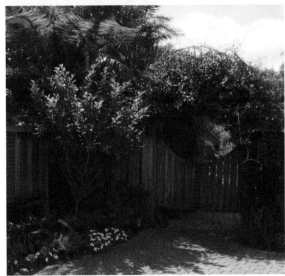

Figure 8-5:

Top: The Raw Converter's suggested Auto settings for this backlit image.

Bottom: With a little bit of manual adjustment, the photo reveals that the camera actually captured plenty of details. (Note that the sky is a bit washed out now. This image would be a great candidate for the new Exposure Merge feature, discussed on page 267.)

- **Recovery.** This clever slider brings down overexposed highlights, recovering the details that were lost without underexposing the rest of the photo. Be careful when using it, though—a little goes a long way.

- **Fill Light.** If your subject appears backlit, move this slider to the right to lighten up the shadowed areas, just the way a photographer's fill light does. Elements' Fill Light is clever enough to bring up the shadowed areas without clipping the highlights in your photos.

- **Blacks.** This slider increases the shadow values and determines which pixels become black in your photo. Increasing the Blacks value may give an effect of increased contrast in the image. Move the slider to the right to increase shadows or to the left to decrease them. A very little change here goes a long way: Move too far to the right, and you clip your shadows. (In other words, they become plain black, with no details, and your colors may become funky, too.)

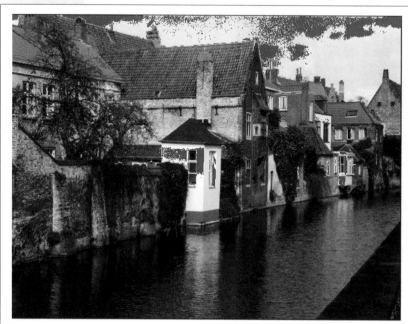

Figure 8-6:
To help you get the Tone settings right, Elements includes two triangles above the ends of the Histogram. Use these to turn on special "clipping warnings" that reveal where your highlights (in red) or your shadows (in blue) lose detail at your current settings. If the photo contains no clipped areas, then the triangle for that end of the Histogram is dark. If the triangle is white or colored, then you have a problem; click the triangle to turn the mask on to see the clipping. As you change your settings in the controls, the clipping mask changes to show the current state of your corrections. In this photo, Elements is warning you that the red and blue speckled areas will be clipped when you open the photo unless you adjust your settings.

- **Brightness.** This is somewhat similar to Exposure in that moving the slider to the right lightens your image, and moving it to the left darkens it. But this slider doesn't clip your photo the way the Exposure setting may. Use this slider to set the overall brightness of your image after you've used the Exposure, Recovery, and Blacks sliders to set the outer brightness value limits of your photo.

- **Contrast.** The Contrast slider adjusts your image's midtones. Move this slider to the right for greater contrast in those tones, and to the left for less. People usually use this slider last.

Most of the time, you'll want to use several of these sliders to get a perfectly exposed photo. Once you get things adjusted the way you want, you can go on to the lower group of settings and adjust the clarity, vibrance, and saturation of your photo. But if you want, you can also save custom settings for use with other photos, or undo all the changes you've made, as explained in the next section. If you don't have anything to save or undo, skip ahead to page 260.

Saving your settings

Most of the time, you'll probably want to use only the adjustments you're making on the particular photo(s) you're editing right now. But Elements gives you a bunch of ways to save time by saving your settings for future use. Just below the Histogram, to the right of the word "Basic", are three tiny lines with a minute arrow at their bottom right. Click that button for a pull-down menu. Whatever you choose in this menu determines how Elements converts your photo. Here's a look at what the choices mean:

- **Image Settings.** This is the "undo all my changes" option. In other words, if you've made some changes to your photo in the Converter but you want to revert to the settings Elements originally presented you with, then choose this option.

- **Camera Raw Defaults.** The Raw Converter contains a profile of normal Raw settings for your camera model that it uses as its baseline for the adjustments it makes. That's what you get when you pick this option. In Elements 8, you can add your own camera profiles, too (see page 266).

- **Previous Conversion.** If you've already processed a photo and want to apply the same settings to the photo you're currently working on, then choosing this setting applies the settings from the last Raw image you opened (but only if it's from the same camera).

- **Custom Settings.** Once you start changing settings, this becomes the active choice. You don't need to select it—Elements turns it on automatically as soon as you start making adjustments.

Since individual cameras—even if they're the same model—may vary a bit (as a result of the manufacturing process), the Camera Raw Defaults settings may not be the best ones for your camera. You can override the default settings and create a new set of defaults for any camera. Here's how:

- **To change your camera's settings:** If you know that you *always* want a different setting for one of the sliders—like maybe your Shadows setting should be at 13 instead of the factory setting of 9—move any or all of the sliders to where you want them, and then choose Save New Camera Raw Defaults from the menu discussed above. From now on, Elements opens your photos with these settings as your starting point.

• **To revert to the original Elements settings for your camera:** If you want to go back to the way things were originally, then click the Settings button (the one with the three lines on it), and choose Reset Camera Raw Defaults.

> **TIP** You can apply the same changes to multiple photos at once. See page 250 to learn how to do this.

The Raw Converter's preferences include a couple of special settings that may interest you. To bring up the Raw Converter's Preferences dialog box, in the Raw Converter's toolbox, click the icon with three lines. These preferences can be really useful, especially if you have more than one camera:

• **Make defaults specific to camera serial number.** Turn this on if you have more than one of a particular camera model; for instance, if you carry two bodies of the same model with different lenses when you shoot, or if both you and your spouse have the same camera model. This setting lets you have a different default for each camera body.

• **Make defaults specific to camera ISO setting.** Since you may shoot very differently at different ISO settings (ISO is equivalent to film speed), you can use this setting to create a default that applies only to photos shot at ISO 100, or at ISO 1600, and so on.

> **TIP** If you regularly share photos with people using other programs, you'll be pleased to know that the Elements Camera Raw preferences let you choose whether your settings get saved in the Camera Raw database or in a sidecar XMP file that goes along with the image. If you choose the XMP file, then your settings become portable along with your photo—that is, if you send the file to someone else, the settings travel along with the photo, as long as you send the XMP file, too.

You don't have to create default settings to save the changes you make to a particular photo. If you just want to save the settings for the photo or group of photos you're working on right now without having to open them all in the Editor and save them in another format, make your changes, and then click Done to update the settings for the image file(s).

> **TIP** You can also add a whole new profile for your camera for the Raw Converter to use as a basis for adjusting your photos. Page 266 explains how.

Adjusting Vibrance and Saturation

The final group of settings on the Raw Converter's right-hand section controls the vividness of your colors. Most Raw files have lower saturation to start with than you'd see in the same photo shot as a JPEG, so people often want to boost the saturation of their Raw images a bit. Move the sliders to the right for more intense color, and to the left for more muted color. If you know you'll *always* want to change the intensity of the color, then you can change the standard setting by moving the slider until you have the intensity you want, and then creating a new camera default setting, as described on page 259.

Here's what each of the three sliders does:

- **Clarity.** This slider is a bit different from the other two. Clarity isn't strictly a color tool, although it is an absolutely amazing feature. If you're an experienced Elements sharpener, you may have heard of the technique called *local contrast enhancement,* where you use the Unsharp Mask (page 237) with a low Amount setting and a high Radius setting to eliminate haze and bring out details. That's sort of what Clarity does: Through some incredibly sophisticated computing, it creates an edge mask for your photo that it uses to increase detail. It can do wonderful things for many—maybe even most—of your photos by improving contrast and adding punch. Give it a try, but be sure to look at your photo at 100 percent magnification (or more) so you can see how you're changing things. For some cameras, you may find that the details in the converted photos look rather blocky when viewed at near 100 percent size. If that happens, open the file in the Raw Converter again, and choose a lower Clarity setting this time.

- **Vibrance.** While Saturation (explained next) adjusts all colors equally, the Vibrance slider is much smarter: It increases the intensity of the duller colors, while holding back on those colors that are already so vivid they may oversaturate. If you want to adjust saturation to make your photo pop, then try this slider first; it's one of the handiest features in the Raw Converter.

- **Saturation.** This slider controls how vivid your colors are by changing the intensity of *all* the colors in your photo by the same amount.

Adjusting Sharpness and Reducing Noise

Once you've got your exposure and white balance right, you may be almost done with your photo. But in most cases, you still want to click over to the Raw Converter's Detail tab to do a little sharpening (above the word "Basic", click the icon that looks like two triangles).

Two other important adjustments are available on this tab as well: *Luminance* and *Color* (both described in a moment), used for reducing noise in your photos. None of the adjustments on this tab have Auto settings, although you can change the standard settings by moving their sliders where you want them and then creating a new camera default (page 259).

Sharpening increases the edge contrast in your photo, which makes it appear more crisply focused. The sharpening tools in the Raw Converter are a bit different from those in the Editor. But some of the sliders should look familiar if you've sharpened before, since they're similar to the settings for Unsharp Mask (page 237) and Adjust Sharpness (page 239):

- **Amount** controls how much you want Elements to sharpen. The scale here goes from zero (no sharpening) to 150 (way too much sharpening).

- **Radius** governs how wide an area Elements considers an edge to sharpen. Its scale goes from .5 pixels to 3 pixels.

- **Detail** controls how the sharpening is applied to your image. At 100—the right end of the scale—the effect is most similar to Unsharp Mask (in other words, you can overdo it if you aren't careful). At zero, you shouldn't see any sharpening halos at all.

- **Masking** is a very cool feature that reduces the area where sharpening takes place so that only edges get sharpened. If you find that you're sharpening more details than you like, then use this slider to create an Edge Mask that keeps Elements from sharpening areas inside the edges. The farther you move the slider to the right, the more area is protected from sharpening. Masking is doing some amazing behind-the-scenes calculations, so don't be surprised if there's a little lag in the preview when you use this slider.

Masking and Detail work together to perform really accurate sharpening, which is why the sliders go so high—you won't like the effect from just one of them set all the way up, but by experimenting with using both sliders, you can create excellent sharpening in your photo.

You get an extremely helpful view of your image if you hold the Alt key as you move the sliders, as explained in Figure 8-7 (but only if the view is set to at least 100%).

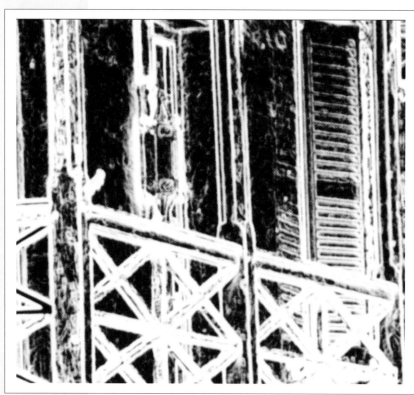

Figure 8-7:
If you've tried high-pass sharpening (page 242), then you won't have any trouble understanding this helpful view of your image. Set the view to 100 percent or higher, and then Alt-drag any of the sharpening sliders to see this black-and-white view of your image. Omitting the color makes it easy to focus on what you're doing to the edge sharpness in your photo, so you get a highly accurate view of exactly what you're doing as you manipulate the sliders.

If you're not planning on making any further edits to your photo when you leave the Raw Converter, then go ahead and sharpen it here. On the other hand, some people prefer to wait to sharpen until they finish all their other adjustments in Full Edit mode, so they skip these sliders. But you can usually sharpen here, and then sharpen again later outside the Converter, without any problems.

The final two settings on this tab (under Noise Reduction) work together to reduce *noise* (graininess) in your photo. Noise is a big problem in digital photos, especially with 5-plus megapixel cameras that don't have the large sensors found in single-lens reflex cameras. The Raw Converter gives you two adjustments here that may help:

- **Luminance.** This setting reduces grayscale noise, which causes an overall grainy appearance to your photo—something like what you see in old newspaper photos. The slider is always at zero to start with, since you don't want to use more than you need, because moving it to the right reduces noise, but it also softens the detail in your photo.

- **Color.** If you look at what should be evenly colored areas of your photo and you see obvious clumps of different-colored pixels, this setting can help smooth things out. Drag the slider to the right to reduce the amount of color noise.

In most cases, it may take a fair amount of fiddling with these sliders to come up with the best compromise between sharpness and smoothness. It helps if you zoom the view up to 100 percent or more when using these sliders.

Choosing bit depth: 8 or 16 bits?

Once you've got your photo looking good, you have one more important choice to make: Do you want to open it as an 8-bit or a 16-bit file? *Bit depth* refers to the number of pieces of color data, or *bits*, that each pixel in your image can hold. A single pixel of an 8-bit image can have 24 pieces of information in it—8 for each of the three color channels (red, green, and blue). A 16-bit image holds far more color info than an 8-bit photo. How much more? An 8-bit image can hold up to 16 million colors, which may sound like a lot, but a 16-bit image can hold up to 281 *trillion* colors.

> **NOTE** You can adjust 16-bit images with microscopic precision, but in the real world, your home printer prints in only 8-bit color anyway. If you want to do all your editing (or at least 90 percent of it) in 16-bit color, then consider upgrading to Photoshop.

Most digital cameras produce Raw files with 10 or 12 bits per channel, although a few can shoot 16-bit files. You'd think it makes perfect sense to save your digital files at the largest possible bit depth. But you'll find quite a few restrictions on how much you can do to a 16-bit file in Elements. You can open it, make some corrections, and save it, but that's about all. You can't work with layers or apply the more artistic filters to a 16-bit file, but you can use many of Elements' Auto commands. If you want to work with layers on a 16-bit file, then you need to upgrade to Photoshop.

Non-Raw Files in the Raw Converter

If your camera shoots JPEG files and you've always been curious about what this Raw business is all about, you can find out for yourself—sort of. You can open JPEG, PSD, or TIFF files with the Raw Converter, and then process them there. (If you want to try another kind of file, save it as a TIFF, and then open it with the Raw Converter. That way you can take advantage of the special tools in the Converter, like Vibrance or Clarity, for any photo.)

To open non-Raw formats in the Editor, just use File → Open As, and then choose Camera Raw (*not* Photoshop Raw) as the format. Your file opens in the Converter, and you can work on it just like a real Raw file. Actually, it's more accurate to say, "almost like a real Raw file." The thing about using other formats in the Converter is this: When your camera processed the JPEG file that it wrote to your memory card, it tossed out the info it didn't need for the JPEG, so Elements doesn't really have the same amount of information to work with that it has for a true Raw file. The Converter even lets you create a DNG—digital negative—file (page 265) from a JPEG if you want, but it can't put back the info that wasn't included in the JPEG, so this feature isn't really very useful for most people.

This means that your results can be iffy. You may find that the Raw Converter does a bang-up job on your photo, or you may find that you liked it better before you started messing with it. There are so many variables involved that it's really hard to predict the results you'll get. But it's definitely worth giving it a try.

If you find you like using the Raw Converter for JPEGs, then you might want to experiment with reducing the saturation, contrast, and sharpening in the camera if you have settings that let you do so. You're more likely to get good results from the Raw Converter if your image is fairly neutral to start with.

John Ellis has created a script for sending JPEG files straight to the Raw Converter from the Organizer (without having to use Open As in the Editor). Currently it's for Elements 7, but it's worth seeing if it works with Elements 8. You can find it at *http://johnrellis.com/editinacr*.

NOTE Your scanner may say it handles 24-bit color, but this is actually the same as what Elements calls 8-bit. Elements goes by the number of bits per color channel, whereas some scanner manufacturers try to impress you by giving you the total for all three channels ($8 \times 3 = 24$). When you see really high bit numbers—assuming it isn't a commercial printer—you can usually get the Elements equivalent by dividing by three.

Once you've decided between 8- and 16-bit color, just make your selection in the Depth drop-down menu at the bottom of the Raw Converter window. The Raw bit-depth setting is "sticky," so if you change it, all your images open in that color depth until you change it. If you ever forget what bit depth you've chosen, your image's title bar or tab tells you, as shown in Figure 8-8.

Figure 8-8:
You can always tell an image's bit depth by looking in the top bar or tab of its image window. This is an 8-bit image.

TIP   If you do decide to create a 16-bit image and later become frustrated by your lack of editing choices, then you can convert your image to 8-bit by choosing Image → Mode → 8 Bits/Channel. (You can't convert an 8-bit image to 16 bits, however.)

If you want to take advantage of any 16-bit files you have, you may want to use either Save As or the Organizer's version set option (see page 68) for the copy you plan to convert to 8-bit. That way you still have the 16-bit file for future reference. Incidentally, your Save options are different for the two bit depths: JPEG, for instance, is available only for 8-bit files, because JPEGs are *always* 8-bit files.

A popular choice when you're thinking about your order of operations (*workflow,* in photo industry–speak) is to first convert your Raw file as a 16-bit image to take advantage of the increased color information while making any basic corrections, and then convert to 8-bit for the fancy stuff like the artistic filters or layer creation.

Finishing Up

Now that you've got your photo all tweaked and sleeked and groomed to look exactly the way you want, it's time to get it out of the Raw Converter. To do that, click the Open Image button, which sends your photo to Full Edit, where you can save it in the format of your choice (TIFF or JPEG, for instance). Everyone gets confused by the Raw Converter's Save Image button—that's actually a link to the DNG Converter, discussed in the next section. If you just want to save your changes without actually opening the file, then you don't need to do anything: The next time you open the Raw file, the Raw Converter will remember where you left off.

Converting to DNG

There's been a lot of buzz lately about Adobe's DNG (digital negative) format, and if you shoot Raw, you should know what it is. As you learned at the beginning of this chapter, every manufacturer uses a different format for Raw files. Even the formats for different cameras from the same manufacturer differ. It's a recipe for an industry-wide headache.

Adobe's solution is the DNG format, which the company envisions as a more standardized alternative to Raw files. Here's how it works: If you convert your Raw file to a DNG file, then it still behaves like a Raw file—you can still tweak your settings in the Converter when you open it, and you still have to save it in a standard image format like TIFF or JPEG to use it in a project. But the idea behind DNG is that if you keep your Raw files in this format, then you don't have to worry about whether Elements version 35 can open them. Adobe clearly hopes that all camera manufacturers will adopt this standard, putting an end to the mishmash of different formats that make Raw files such a nuisance to deal with. If all cameras used DNG, then every time you bought a new camera you wouldn't have to worry whether your programs could view the camera's images.

Working with Profiles

The Raw Converter has another trick up its sleeve. It's one you can safely ignore if you're a beginner, but for Raw experts it's a very big deal indeed. The Raw Converter has a third tab: Camera Calibration. If you click it, all you see is a pull-down menu that seems to imply you're using an older version of Adobe Camera Raw. What's the point of this cryptic tab?

You can now create and edit your own camera profiles, and install them in Elements for the Converter to use. If you've ever thought, "Darn, I wish my Raw files opened looking as good as the JPEGs I shoot with my camera," or if you've stuck with another Raw converter (like the ones from Nikon or Canon) because you just can't get the same results with Adobe's Converter, then this tab's for you.

You can't actually create or edit profiles in Elements, but Adobe has developed a standalone profile editor, along with profiles for many, many cameras. They plan to eventually have profiles for every camera that shoots Raw, but they started with Nikon and Canon (since those are the most popular brands).

Editing camera profiles is beyond the scope of this book, but you can download the DNG Profile Editor and the initial set of camera profiles at *http://labs.adobe.com/wiki/index.php/DNG_Profiles*. There's also an excellent tutorial at *www.luminous-landscape.com/reviews/accessories/dng-profiles.shtml*.

If you create and install profiles, then they appear in the pull-down menu on the Camera Calibration tab, and you can select the one you want to use as the basis for all your setting changes in the Raw Converter. If you haven't done this and you're wondering why the list shows older Adobe Camera Raw versions like 4.2, that's because the list shows the version numbers for when the built-in Adobe Camera Raw profiles were last updated. So if you've been thinking, "You know, I think I liked the way my Raw files looked better a couple of versions ago," no problem. You can choose the older profile version for your camera from the list, and use that instead of the newest one.

You can create DNG files from your Raw files right in the Converter. At the bottom left of the window, just click the Save Image button, and you see the DNG Converter, shown in Figure 8-9. Choose a destination, and then select how you want to name the DNG file. You get the same naming options as in Process Multiple Files (page 274), but since you convert only one file at a time here, you may as well keep the photo's current name and just add the .dng extension.

Of course, the jury is still out on whether DNG is going to become the industry standard, although it does seem to be gaining popularity. People have had other good ideas over the years like the JPEG 2000 format (see page 74) that never really took off. Whether you create DNG files from your Raw files is up to you, but for now, it's probably prudent to hang onto the original Raw files as well, even if you decide in favor of DNG.

> **TIP** If you want to convert a group of your Raw files to DNG in one batch, the easiest way is to go to Adobe's website (*www.adobe.com/downloads*), search for "DNG", and then download the standalone DNG Converter, which you can leave on your desktop. Then just drop a folder of Raw images onto its icon, and the DNG Converter lets you process the whole folder at once. The standalone Converter is part of the Raw Converter update (page 248). If your Raw Converter is already up to date, just remove the DNG Converter and discard the rest of the download. You can also batch-save images in the Raw Converter itself by highlighting them in the list on the left side of the window, and then clicking Save Images.

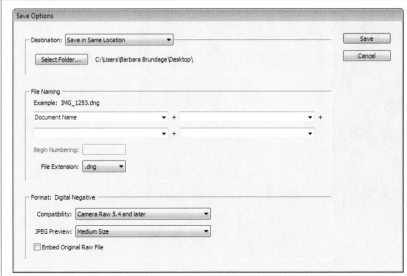

Figure 8-9:
The DNG Converter. The bottom section of this window lets you choose whether to compress the file, how to handle the image preview, and whether to embed your original Raw file in the new one. Generally, you're best off leaving the settings in this section the way they're shown here.

Blending Exposures

If you've been using a digital camera for any length of time, you're aware of what a juggling act it can be to get a photo that's properly exposed throughout its entire range, from the deepest shadows to the brightest highlights. With most digital cameras, you're likely to hit the clipping point (page 256) in an image much sooner than you want to: If you up the exposure so that the shadows are nice and detailed, then about half the time you blow out the highlights. On the other hand, if you adjust your exposure settings down to favor the highlights, then your shadows are murkier than an old Enron annual report. Figure 8-10 shows the problem.

Digital blending is a technique photographers use to get around these limitations. To use it, you *bracket* your shots, meaning you take two or more identical photos of your subject at different settings—one exposed for shadows and one for highlights—and then combine them, choosing the best bits of each one. People who are fanatical about a truly perfectly exposed photo may combine several different exposures.

That technique is great for landscapes. But if you're shooting hummingbirds, roller-skating chimps, or toddlers, you know it's just about impossible to get two identical shots of a moving subject. And if you're like many people, you may not realize you didn't capture what you wanted until you see the shot on your computer at home. But even if you only have one photo of that perfect moment, you can sometimes cheat a bit and get a similar result from processing your photo twice in the Raw Converter, once to favor the shadow areas, and once for the highlights, as was done in Figure 8-10, so that you wind up with two exposures. The problem is how to combine them into one great image.

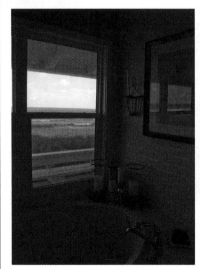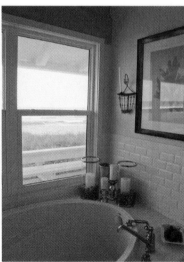

Figure 8-10:
Here's a classic example of the kind of image that can benefit from exposure merging. This is the same Raw photo processed twice.

Left: To get the beautiful ocean view properly exposed means making the interior much too dark.

Right: Correctly exposing the fancy bath area reduces the view outside to a bright blur.

In previous versions of Elements you had to either manually layer two exposures together and get busy erasing the bad spots on the top layer, or else use expensive third-party plug-ins to blend exposures. But one of the highlights of Elements 8 is a super easy way to do this. It's called Photomerge Exposure, and it's as easy to use as any of the program's other photomerge features (see Chapter 11 for more about those). It can even be a one-click fix, if you want. Elements gives you several ways to blend your photos. Your main choice is between an automatic merge, where Elements makes most of the decisions for you, and a manual merge, which gives you more control, but requires a little more effort, too.

> **NOTE** Exposure merging isn't meant for blending two totally different photos together, like replacing the blown out sky in your photo of the Eiffel tower with a good sky from a photo of your dude-ranch trip. To use Photomerge Exposure, your photos should be pretty much identical except for the exposure. Use images you took using your camera's exposure bracketing or even one shot you've processed twice or more to get one good version with properly exposed highlights, one with good shadows, and so on.

Automatic Merges

It's incredibly easy to combine your photos using the Automatic Merge option. Elements makes most of the decisions for you. (If that's not for you, you can click the Exposure Merge window's other tab and opt for a manual merge, where you call the shots, as explained in the next section.) Here's what you do:

1. **Prepare, open, and select your images.**

   You can start with two or more photos where you used exposure bracketing in your camera, or with one image that you developed in two different ways in the Raw processor (page 248), once favoring the shadows and once the highlights.

You can use up to 10 photos, so you can create as many different versions as you need to make sure every part of the image is properly exposed. Just select the photos you want to work with in the Project bin, and you're ready for the next step.

2. **Call up the Photomerge Exposure window.**

   In Full Edit, go to File → New → Photomerge Exposure, or go to Guided Edit → Photomerge → Exposure.

   The Photomerge Exposure window opens. It's a lot like the windows for Group Shot, Faces, and Scene Cleaner, if you've used any of those before, and it works much the same way.

3. **Choose to make an automatic merge.**

   If the Exposure Merge window doesn't open with the Automatic tab active, simply click the tab. (It's easy to tell which tab is active even without looking over at the right side of the window: in Automatic mode you only see one image in the preview area on the left of the screen, while in Manual mode you see two.)

4. **Select a merge option, and make any adjustments, if you wish.**

   You have two options to choose between:

   • **Simple Blending.** Elements does everything. All you have to do is click Done.

   • **Smart Blending.** If you pick this option, you can use the three sliders on the right side of the window to adjust what Elements does. (The sliders are explained below.) Elements uses a different kind of analysis on your photo here than it does for the Simple merge, so don't be surprised if the values in your image shift a bit when you click this radio button.

   NOTE The sliders won't do anything if you have Simple Blending turned on. They only become active when you switch over to Smart Blending.

5. **When you're happy with what you see, click Done.**

   Elements blends the photos as a separate file so that your originals aren't changed. Don't forget to save the blended image.

That's all there is to it. Elements does a pretty good job, as shown in Figure 8-11, depending on your photos, but you can help the program by nudging the Smart Blending sliders if you aren't quite satisfied with what Elements proposes for your image. Here's what each slider does:

• **Highlights** controls the way Elements blends the bright areas of the two images.

• **Shadows** adjusts the blend for the darker areas.

NOTE   If you've used Shadows/Highlights (page 209), you know everything you need to know about these two sliders.

• **Saturation** adjusts the color intensity, which is handy if the blend made your photo look a little drab or oversaturated. It's pretty much like the Saturation slider in Quick Fix (page 128).

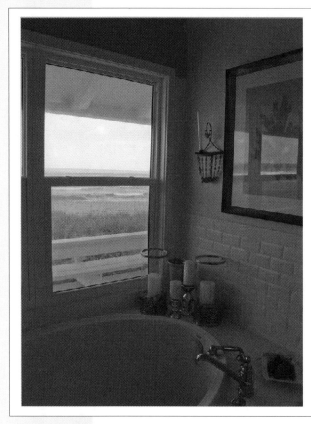

Figure 8-11:
Here's what Elements proposes as a Simple Merge for the photo shown in Figure 8-10. You'd probably want to tweak it some in the Editor, but overall, Photomerge Exposure did a pretty good job. You can do even better by making a manual merge, where you have more control over how the images blend together. The sky is still a tad light in this version, for instance.

If you prefer to have more control over what Elements does, you can opt to combine your photos manually instead, as explained next.

Manual Merges

Automatic merges are super easy to do, even for a beginner, but sometimes Elements just doesn't get it right. Or maybe you just like telling Elements what to do rather than accepting its judgment about your images. In either case, manual merges are what you want.

You begin a manual merge the same way as an automatic one (follow steps 1 and 2 on page 268). Here's what you do once you have the Photomerge Exposure window open:

1. **Choose to make a manual merge.**

   Click the Manual tab if it's not already active. Elements displays a window with spaces for two photos, exactly like the windows for Photomerge Faces, Group Shot, or Scene Cleaner (all described in Chapter 11).

2. **Choose a background photo.**

   This is the photo that is going to be the basis of your merge, the one you'll blend bits of other photos into. Usually this would be the photo with the largest area of correct exposure. (You can use up to ten photos in a manual merge, but you only work with two at a time.) Drag your background photo into the right-hand slot.

   TIP   If you're blending several exposures, you may get the best results if you choose the photo with the best midtones as your background photo, even if that's not the photo with the largest properly exposed area. That's because Elements likes to start from the middle and work out when blending several images.

3. **Choose a foreground photo.**

   This is the photo you'll copy bits from to put in the background photo. Double-click it to tell Elements it's the one you want to use. It appears in the left-hand slot.

4. **Tell Elements what to copy.**

   Click the Selection Tool button on the right side of the window (the one with the pencil on it) and drag over the areas in the foreground photo that you want to move to the background photo. This selection tool works pretty much like the Quick Selection tool (page 143) in that it automatically expands the selection from the line or dot you make. If it selects too much or if you drag over something by mistake, use the Eraser tool to remove some of your marks. See Figure 8-12.

5. **Align the photos if you need to.**

   If you find that your copied material is slightly out of alignment with the background photo (common if you used exposure bracketing for live subjects), scroll down in the Manual tab until you see Advanced Option; click those words, and then click the Alignment Tool button. When you do, three little target marks appear in each preview when you move your cursor over the photo. Drag the marks so they're in the same spot in each photo (like over a tiger's eyes and mouth in bracketed wildlife photos), and then click Align Photos. Elements figures out the difference in perspective between the two images and correct for it.

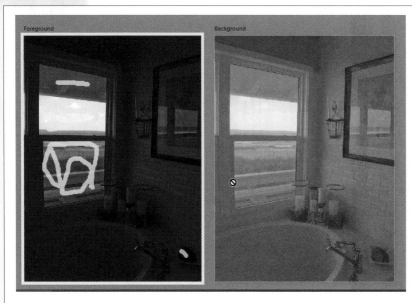

Figure 8-12:
Here's the midpoint of creating a manual merge for the image from Figure 8-10. (Show Regions is turned on here to make it easier to see what Elements is doing.) You can see the selection went a tad too far to the left, and Elements is bringing over the underexposed window frame, too. Look where the cursor is in the right-hand photo. It's the No symbol—a black circle with a slash through it— there because you always use the tools on the foreground photo, not the background photo. Erasing the frame in the foreground photo will fix this.

6. **Tweak the blending.**

    You may be horrified by how crudely the images blend at first, but that's okay. There are two settings in the Manual tab that you can use to fix things:

    - **Transparency.** Use this slider to adjust the foreground image's opacity for a more realistic effect.

    - **Edge Blending.** Turn on this checkbox and Elements automatically refines the edges of the blend to avoid that cut-and-paste look. (This one appears second in the list, but try it first.)

7. **When you like what you see, click Done.**

    As with an automatic merge, Elements creates a new layered file for the blended image so your originals are still untouched.

    NOTE If you want to add details from another image that you preselected, drag it to the foreground image slot, and repeat the process before you click Done. You can repeat this process to combine a total of 10 images if you want. Each additional photo gets a different colored marker to help you keep track of what came from which photo.

If you need to adjust the view while you're working, Elements gives you some help:

- **Zoom and Hand tools.** Your old friends the Hand (page 102) and Zoom (page 100) tools live in the little toolbox on the left of the images. They work the same way here as everywhere else in Elements.

- **Show Strokes.** This checkbox in the Merge tab lets you show or hide the marks you make with the Selection tool.

- **Show Regions.** Turn this on and Elements displays a blue mask over the background photo, with yellow over the areas where it's blending in material from the foreground photo, as you can see in Figure 8-12. The window area is yellow because that's what's coming over from the foreground photo. (If you add more photos, each gets a mask colored to match its marker color.)

NOTE   Photomerge Exposure is fun, but you may find you want something a bit more powerful. In that case you need to explore HDR (High Dynamic Range) programs and plug-ins. A good place to start is *www.hdrlabs.com*.

Photo Filter

The Photo Filter feature gives you a host of nifty filters to work with. These filters are the digital equivalent of those lens-mounted filters used in traditional film photography. They can help you correct problems with your image's white balance, and perform a bunch of other fixes from the seriously photographic to the downright silly. For example, you can correct bad skin tone or dig out an old photo of your fifth-grade nemesis and make him green. Figure 8-13 shows the Photo Filter feature in action.

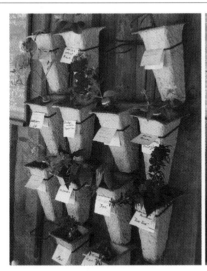 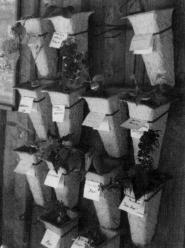

Figure 8-13:
You can use the Photo Filter to correct the color casts caused by artificial lighting or reflected light.

Left: This photo had a strong warm cast from nearby incandescent lighting.

Right: The filter named "Cooling Filter (LBB)" took care of it. Use one of the warming filters to counteract the blue cast from fluorescent lighting.

Elements comes with 20 photo filters, but for most people, the top six are the most important: three warming filters and three cooling filters. You use these filters to get rid of color casts caused by poor white balance (see page 254).

The filters sometimes work better than the Color Cast eyedropper (page 229) because you can control the strength with which you apply them (using the Density slider, explained in a moment). You can also apply them as Adjustment layers (page 193), so you can tweak them later on.

To apply a photo filter:

1. **Open the Photo Filter dialog box, or create a new Adjustment layer.**

   Go to Layer → New Adjustment Layer → Photo Filter, or Filter → Adjustments → Photo Filter. Either way, you see the Photo Filter adjustment controls. If you go the Adjustment-layer route, the controls appear in the Adjustments panel after you click OK. If you're applying the Photo Filter directly to your image, you get a dialog box instead, but both offer exactly the same controls.

2. **Choose a filter from the drop-down list, or click the Color radio button.**

   The drop-down list gives you a choice of filters in preset colors. (The numbers following the names of some filters represent the numbers of the glass filters you'd use on a film camera.) If you want to pick your own custom color, then click the Color button instead.

3. **If you chose the Color button, then click the color square next to it to bring up the "Select filter color" dialog box—which is really just the Color Picker (page 232)—and choose the shade you want.**

   You can also sample a color from your image. Your cursor turns to an eyedropper when you move it from the dialog box into your photo. Just click the color you want for your filter, and that color appears in the dialog box's color square. Elements applies the color you select to your image, so you can decide whether you like it. When you've got the color you want, click OK to close the dialog box.

4. **In the Adjustments panel or the dialog box, move the Density slider to adjust the intensity of the filter.**

   Moving the slider to the right increases the filter's effect; moving it to the left decreases it. If you leave the Preserve Luminosity checkbox turned on, then the filter doesn't darken your image. Turn off the checkbox and your photo gets darker when you apply the filter. Watch your image to see the effect.

5. **When your photo looks good, save it.**

Processing Multiple Files

If you're addicted to batch-processing your photos, then you'll love the Elements equivalent: Process Multiple Files. In addition to renaming your files and changing their formats, you can do a lot of other very useful things with this tool, like adding copyright information or captions to multiple files, or even using some of Quick Fix's Auto commands.

To call up the batch-processing window, in Full Edit, go to File → Process Multiple Files. You see yet another headache-inducing, giant Elements dialog box. Fear not—this one is actually pretty easy to understand. If you look closely, you see that the dialog box is divided into sections, each with a different specialty (see Figure 8-14).

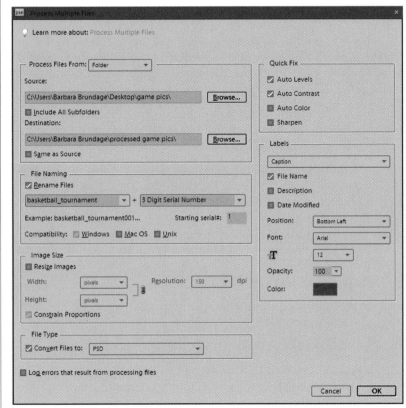

Figure 8-14:
You could call Process Multiple Files "Computer: Earn Your Keep", because it can make so many changes at once. This dialog box is set up to apply the following changes: Rename every file (from things like PICT8983 to basketball_ tournament001, basketball_ tournament002, and so on), change the images to PSD format, apply Auto Levels and Auto Contrast, and add the filename as a caption. You make all that happen just by clicking the OK button.

TIP Process *Multiple* Files is the name of the command, but you can run it on just one photo if you want, although you'll usually find it easier just to do a regular Save As (see Chapter 2 for more about saving files). Just open your photo, go to File → Process Multiple Files, and then choose Opened Files as your source. You can even opt to save the new version to the desktop without overwriting your original.

The following sections cover each part of the Process Multiple Files dialog box. You *have* to use the first section (which tells Elements which files you want to process), but you'll probably want to make use of only one or two of the other sections at any one time. (Of course, you can use them all, as shown in Figure 8-14.)

TIP   If you're working in the Organizer, then you can do some batch-processing without going to the Editor. Select the files you want, and then go to File → Export As New File(s) (or press Ctrl+E). You get a dialog box that lets you change the format, choose a new size from a list of presets, set a destination for the new images, and choose a new "common base name" if you want. If you choose this last option, then your files get the new name plus a sequential number. (By the way, this export feature is a great way to create a folder of JPEGs to send to an online photo service.)

Choosing Your Files

The upper-left section of the dialog box is where you identify the files you want to convert, and then tell Elements where to put them once it's processed them. You have several options here, which you pick from the Process Files From drop-down menu: the contents of a folder, files you import, or your currently open files.

Choosing the Import option brings up the same options you get when selecting File → Import. Use this option to convert files as you bring them into Elements—from a camera or scanner, for example.

If you want to include files scattered around in different locations on your hard drive, then speed things up by opening the files first or gathering them into one folder. If you have a couple of folders' worth of photos to convert, save time by putting all those folders into one folder and using the "Include All Subfolders" option explained in a moment. That way all the files get converted at once.

Here's a step-by-step tour of the process:

1. **Choose the files you want to convert.**

   Use the Process Files From pull-down menu to select which kind of files you want: a folder, files imported from your camera or scanner, or opened files.

2. **If you chose Folder, then tell Elements which folder you want.**

   Click the Browse button and, in the dialog box that appears, choose a folder. Files you want to process have to be in a folder if they aren't already open.

   If you have folders *within* a folder and you want to operate on all those files, then turn on the Include All Subfolders checkbox. Otherwise, Elements changes only the files in the top-level folder.

3. **Pick a destination.**

   This is when you decide where the files will end up after Elements processes them. Most of the time, you'll want a new folder for this, so click Browse, and then, in the window that opens, click New Folder. Or you can choose an existing folder in the Browse window, but a word of warning if you go this route: Be careful about choosing "Same as Source", as Figure 8-15 explains.

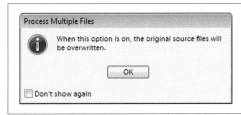

Figure 8-15:
If you turn on the "Same as Source" checkbox, then Elements warns you that it's going to replace your originals with the new versions. That's a timesaver, but it's dangerous, too—if something goes wrong, then your originals are toast. Bottom line: Don't turn on the "Same as Source" checkbox unless you have backup copies someplace else.

Renaming Your Files

Being able to rename a group of files in one fell swoop is a very cool feature, but it has a few limitations. If you think it means you can give each photo a unique name like "Keisha and Gram at the Park", followed by "Fred's New Newt", and so on, you're going to be disappointed. Instead, what Elements offers is a quick way of applying a similar name to a group of files. That means you can easily transform a folder filled with files named *DSCF001.jpg, DSCF0002.jpg,* and so on, into the slightly friendlier *Keisha and Gram001.jpg, Keisha and Gram002.jpg.*

To rename your files, turn on the Process Multiple Files dialog box's Rename Files checkbox. Below it are two text boxes with drop-down menus next to them (a + sign separates the menus). You can enter anything you like in these boxes, and it replaces every filename in the group. Or you can choose any of the options in the menus. (Both menus are the same.)

The menus offer you a choice of the document name (in three different capitalization styles), serial numbers, serial letters, dates, extensions, or nothing at all (which gives you just the trailing numbers without any kind of prefix). Figure 8-16 shows the many choices you get.

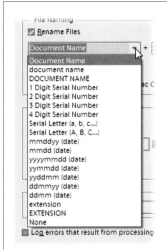

Figure 8-16:
Elements offers loads of naming options. If you select Document Name, for example, your photos retain their original names (plus whatever you choose from the right-side drop-down menu). DOCUMENT NAME gets you the same filenames in all capital letters. "1 Digit Serial Number" starts you off with the number 1, and so on.

NOTE   If you want to add serial numbers, you can designate the starting number in the "Start-ing serial#" box. Your first choice is always 1, which actually shows up as 001 because your com-puter needs the leading zeros to recognize the file order. The tenth figure in your batch would be numbered 010, the hundredth would be 100, and so on.

So if you type *tongue_piercing_day* in the text box and choose the three-digit serial number, then Elements names your photos *tongue_piercing_day001.jpg, tongue_ piercing_day002.jpg,* and so on.

NOTE   If you turn on "Same as Source", then the Rename Files option is grayed out. If you want to put your renamed files in the same folder with the originals, then leave "Same as Source" turned off, but select the same folder as the destination in the top part of the dialog box. That way Elements places your renamed files in the same folder as the originals.

You also get to designate which operating systems' naming conventions Elements should use when assigning the new names, as explained in Figure 8-17. If you send files to people or servers that run other operating systems, then you know how important this is. If you don't, then play it safe and turn on all three checkboxes. You never know when you may need to send a photo to your nephew who uses Linux.

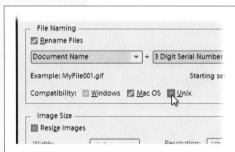

Figure 8-17:
The Compatibility checkboxes tell Elements to watch out for any characters that would violate the naming conventions of the operating systems you check. This is handy if, say, your website is hosted on a Unix server and you want to be sure your filenames don't create a problem for it. You can choose to be compatible with either or neither of the other operating systems, but the Windows checkbox is always turned on.

Changing Image Size and File Type

The Image Size and File Type sections of the Process Multiple Files dialog box let you resize your photos and change your images' file formats. The Image Size set-tings work best when you're trying to reduce file sizes (say you've got a folder of images that you've converted for Web use but found are still too big).

NOTE   Before you make any big changes to a group of files, it's important for you to under-stand how changes to an image's resolution and file size affect its appearance. See page 103 for a refresher.

To apply image size changes, turn on the Resize Images checkbox, and then adjust the Width, Height, and Resolution settings, all of which work the same way as those described on page 109.

In the File Type section, you can convert files from one format to another. This is probably the most popular batch-processing activity. If your camera creates JPEGs and you want TIFFs for editing work, then you can change a whole folder at once. From the drop-down menu, just select the type of files you want to create.

The final setting in the left half of the dialog box is the checkbox for logging errors in processing your files. It's a good idea to turn this checkbox on, as explained in Figure 8-18.

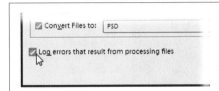

Figure 8-18:
If you turn on the "Log errors that result from processing files" checkbox, then Elements lets you know if it runs into any problems while converting the files. You'll find a little text log file in the folder with your completed images, whether there were problems or not. (If nothing went awry, it's blank.)

Applying Quick Fix Commands

In the upper-right corner of the Process Multiple Files dialog box are some of the same Quick Fix commands you have in the regular Quick Fix window. If you consistently get good results with the Auto commands there, then you can run them on a whole folder at once here.

You can run Auto Levels, Auto Contrast, Auto Color, Auto Sharpen, or any combination of those commands that you like on all the files in your folder. (If you don't see the list, then click the flippy triangle next to Quick Fix to expand it.) If you need a refresher on what each one does, then see Chapter 4, beginning on page 125.

Unfortunately, you can't batch-run the Auto Smart Fix command from this dialog box. If that's what you wanted to do, or if your only reason for bringing up the Process Multiple Files dialog box is to use any of the editing options, then you can save time by selecting your photos in the Organizer and running those commands right from the Organizer's Fix tab, as explained on page 116.

TIP   Don't forget that you can also batch-process corrections in the Raw Converter (see page 250). Then open the files and use Process Multiple Files to save all the changed files at once.

Attaching Labels

The tools in the Labels section let you add captions and copyright notices, which Elements calls *watermarks,* to your images (see Figure 8-19). Watermarks and captions get imprinted right onto the photo itself. The process is the same for creating both; only the content differs. A watermark contains any text you choose, while a caption is limited to your choices from a group of checkboxes.

First, you need to choose between a watermark and a caption (choose from the drop-down menu right below the Labels tab). You can't do both at once, so if you want both, add one, run Process Multiple Files, and then add the other and run

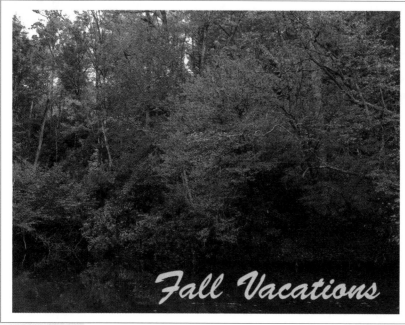

Figure 8-19:
Adobe calls the "Fall Vacations" custom text in this image a watermark. Elements is very flexible about the fonts and sizes you can choose for a watermark or caption, but you don't get much say in where it goes on your photo if you use Process Multiple Files. For maximum flexibility, use the Type tool, as explained on page 282. The drawback: You can't batch-process using that method.

Process Multiple Files again on the resulting images. You can download *fall.jpg* from the Missing CD page at *www.missingmanuals.com* if you want to practice adding your own watermarks and captions.

Watermarks

To create a watermark, you enter some text in the Custom Text box. Then choose the position and appearance of your text as explained in a moment.

Text you enter here gets applied to every photo in the batch, so this is a great way to add copyright or contact info that you want on every photo. If you want different text on each photo, check out the Description option for captions, as shown in Figure 8-20.

> **TIP** If you want to include the copyright symbol (©), hold Alt while typing *0169* (on the number pad, not the top row of the keyboard). Or you can use the Character Map (Start → All Programs → Accessories → System Tools → Character Map).

Adding captions

For a caption, you can choose any of the following, separately or in combination:

• **File Name.** You can choose to show the file's name as the caption. If you decide to run the rename option at the same time, then you get the new name you're assigning.

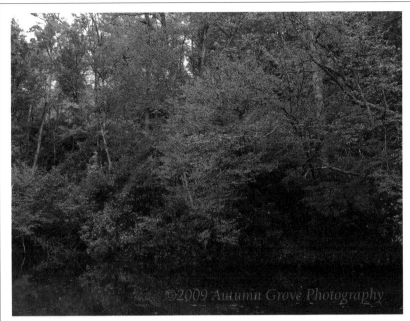

Figure 8-20:
You just can't beat Process Multiple Files for quickly adding copyright info to your photos, although some other methods give a more sophisticated look, as described in the Tip on page 282.

- **Description.** Turn this checkbox on to use any text you've entered in the Description section of the File Info dialog box (File → File Info) as your caption. This option is your most flexible one for entering text, and the only way to batch different caption text for each photo. Just enter the text for each photo in File → File Info → Description.

- **Date Modified.** This is the date your file was last changed. In practice, that usually means today's date, because you're modifying your file by running Process Multiple Files on it.

Once you've decided what you want your caption to say, you need to make some choices about its position and size. These options are the same whether you're adding a watermark or a caption, and if you switch from one to the other before actually running Process Multiple Files, then your previous choices appear:

- **Position.** This tells Elements where to put your caption. Your options are Bottom Left, Bottom Right, or Centered. Centered doesn't mean "bottom center"—it puts the text smack in the middle of your image.

- **Font.** From the drop-down menu, choose any font on your computer. (Chapter 14 has tons more info about fonts.)

- **Size.** This setting (whose icon is two Ts) determines the size of your type. Click the menu next to the two Ts to choose from several preset sizes, up to 72 point.

- **Opacity.** Use this to adjust how solidly your text prints. Choose 100 percent for maximum readability, or click the down arrow and move the slider to the left for watermark type that lets you see the image underneath it.

- **Color.** Use this setting to choose your text color. Click the box to bring up the Color Picker (page 232) and make your choice.

NOTE   If you want to use a logo as a watermark, the Process Multiple Files command can't help you. But there is a way to apply a logo to a bunch of images: First, create your logo on a new layer in one of the images. Adjust the opacity with the slider in the Layers panel until you like the results, and then save the file. Now you can drag that layer from the Layers panel onto the image window for each photo where you need it. (If you Shift-drag the layer, then it goes to exactly the same spot on each image, assuming they're all the same size.) You can also do this with Adjustment layers (page 193) to give yourself a sort of batch-processing capability for applying the same adjustments to multiple files. Another option is to create a custom brush from your logo (page 376) and use that, and then adjust the opacity or apply a Layer Style (page 423) for a truly custom look.

Retouching: Fine-Tuning Your Images

Basic edits like exposure fixes and sharpening are fine if all you want to make are simple adjustments. But Elements also gives you the tools to make sophisticated changes that aren't hard to apply and that can make the difference between a ho-hum photo and a fabulous one. This chapter introduces you to some advanced editing maneuvers that can help you rescue damaged photos or give good ones a little extra zing.

The first part of the chapter shows how to get rid of blemishes—not only those that affect skin, but also dust, scratches, stains, and other photographic imperfections. You'll also learn some powerful color-improving techniques, including the Color Curves tool, which is a great way to improve your image's contrast and color.

Then you'll learn to use the exciting new Recompose tool, which lets you change the size and shape of your photos, eliminate boring empty areas between subjects in an image, and even get rid of unwanted elements in your pictures, all without distorting the parts you want to keep. This amazing feature does it all so well that nobody seeing your photo would ever suspect it wasn't originally shot that way.

Fixing Blemishes

It's an imperfect world, but in your photos, it doesn't have to be. Elements gives you some amazing tools for fixing your subject's flaws: You can erase crow's feet and blemishes, eliminate power lines in an otherwise perfect view, or even hide objects you wish weren't in your photo. Not only that, but these same tools are great for fixing problems like tears, folds, and stains—the great foes of photo-scanning veterans. With a little effort, you can bring back photos that seem beyond help.

Figure 9-1 shows an example of the kind of restoration you can accomplish with Elements and a little persistence.

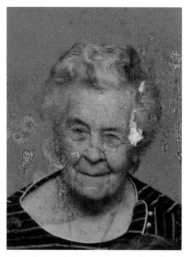

Figure 9-1:
Top: Here's a section of a water-damaged family portrait. The grandmother's face is almost obliterated.

Bottom: The same image after being repaired with Elements. It took a lot of cloning and healing to get even this close, but if you keep at it, you can do the kind of work that would have required professional help before Elements. If you're interested in restoring old photos, check out Katrin Eismann's books on the subject (Photoshop Restoration and Retouching [New Riders, 2006] is a good one to start with). They cover full-featured Photoshop, but you can adapt most of the techniques for Elements. You might also want to investigate The Photoshop Elements 5 Restoration and Retouching Book (Peachpit, 2007) by Matt Kloskowski. (Although it's for Elements 5, you can still use the techniques in Elements 8.)

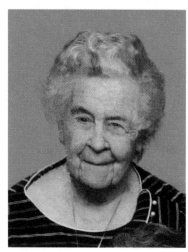

Elements gives you three main tools for this kind of work:

- **The Spot Healing brush** is the easiest way to repair photos. Just drag over the area you want to fix, and Elements searches the surrounding area and blends that info into the troubled spot, making it indistinguishable from the background. This brush usually works best on small areas, for the reasons you'll learn later in this chapter.

- **The Healing brush** works much like the Spot Healing brush, only you tell the Healing brush which part of your photo to use as a source for the material you want to blend in. This makes the Healing brush better suited to large areas, because you don't have to worry about inadvertently dragging in unwanted details.

- **The Clone Stamp** works like the Healing brush in that you sample a good area and apply it to the area you want to fix. But instead of blending in the repair, the Clone Stamp actually covers the bad area with the replacement. The Clone Stamp is best for situations when you want to *completely* hide the underlying area, as opposed to letting any of what's already there blend into your repair (which is how things work with the Healing brushes). This tool is also your best option when you want to create a realistic copy of a detail that's elsewhere in your photo. You can clone over some leaves to fill in a bare branch, or replace a knothole in a fence board with good wood, for instance.

All three tools work similarly: You just drag each tool over the area you want to change. It's as simple as using a paintbrush. In fact, each of these tools requires you to choose a brush like the ones you'll learn about in Chapter 12. But brush selection is pretty straightforward; in this chapter, you'll learn everything you need to make basic brush choices.

> **TIP** If you want to smooth out blotchy or blemished skin, check out the Surface Blur filter, explained on page 418. It's good to try if you want to do minor touchups that affect large areas. In contrast, the tools described in this section are better for fixing individual imperfections.

The Spot Healing Brush: Fixing Small Areas

The Spot Healing brush excels at fixing minor blemishes: pimples, lipstick smudges, stray lint, and so on. Simply paint over the area you want to repair, and the Spot Healing brush automatically searches the surrounding area and blends it into the spot you're brushing. Figure 9-2 shows what a great job this tool can do. (Download the file *peppers.jpg* from the Missing CD page at *www.missingmanuals. com* if you'd like to do some experimenting with this tool.)

The Spot Healing brush's ability to borrow information from surrounding areas is great in some scenarios, but a drawback in others. The larger the area you drag the brush over, the wider Elements searches for replacement material. So if there's contrasting material too close to the area you're trying to fix, it can get pulled into the repair. For instance, if you're trying to fix a spot on an eyelid, you may wind up with some of the color from the eye itself mixed in with your repair.

You get best results from this brush when you choose a brush size that just barely covers the spot you're trying to fix. If you need to drag to fix an oblong area, use the smallest brush width that covers the flaw. The Spot Healing brush also works much better when there's a large surrounding area that looks the way you want your repaired spot to look.

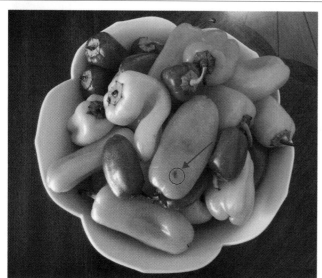

Figure 9-2:
The trick to using the Spot Healing brush is to work on very tiny areas. If you choose too large a brush or drag over too large an area, you're more likely to pick up undesired shades and details from the surrounding area.

Top: So you want to show off your garden's pepper crop, but there's a blemish on the largest pepper? No problem.

Bottom: One click with the Spot Healing brush (with a brush setting slightly larger than the bruise), and you've got a truly invisible fix.

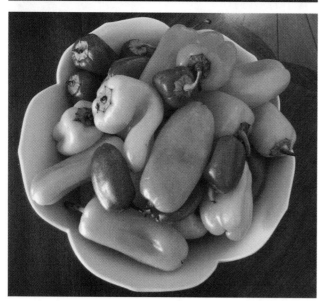

The Spot Healing brush has only four Options bar settings:

- **Brush.** Use the drop-down menu to choose a different brush style if you want (see Chapter 12 for lots more about brushes), but generally, you're best off sticking to the standard brush that Elements starts out with and just changing the size, if necessary.

- **Size.** Use this box to set the brush's size.

- **Type.** Use these radio buttons to adjust how the brush works. Proximity Match tells it to search the surrounding area for replacement pixels, and Create Texture tells it to blend only from the area you drag it over. Generally speaking, if Proximity Match doesn't work well, you'll get better results by switching to the regular Healing brush than by choosing Create Texture.

    TIP   Adobe suggests that you may like the results you get from Create Texture better if you drag over a spot more than once.

- **Sample All Layers.** Turn on this checkbox if you want the brush to look for replacement material in all your photo's visible layers. If you don't turn it on, Elements only chooses material from the active layer. (Another reason to turn this on: if you created a new, blank layer to heal on so that you can blend your work in better later by adjusting the healed area's opacity.)

You won't believe how easy it is to fix problem areas with the Spot Healing brush. All you do is:

1. **Activate the Spot Healing brush.**

    Click the Healing brush icon (the Band-Aid) in the Tools panel, and then choose the Spot Healing brush—the one with the dotted circle—from the pop-out menu. (Keyboard shortcut: J.)

2. **Choose a brush size just barely bigger than the flaw.**

    You can choose your brush size from the Options bar Size slider or by pressing] (the close bracket key) for a larger brush or [(the open bracket key) for a smaller brush.

3. **Click the bad spot.**

    If the brush doesn't quite cover the flaw, drag over the blemished area.

4. **When you release the mouse button, Elements repairs the blemish.**

    You won't see any change to your image while you drag—only after you let go.

Sometimes you get great results with the Spot Healing brush on larger areas if they're surrounded by a field of good material that's similar in tone to the spot you're trying to fix. Most of the time, though, you're better off using the regular Healing brush for large areas and for flaws whose replacement material isn't right next to the bad spot. Read on to learn how.

The Healing Brush: Fixing Larger Areas

The Healing brush lets you fix much bigger areas than you can usually manage with the Spot Healing brush. The main difference between the two tools is that with the regular Healing brush, *you* choose the area that gets blended into the repair. The blending makes your repair look very natural. Figure 9-3 shows what great results you can get with this tool.

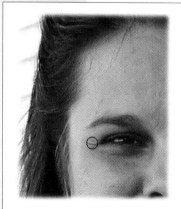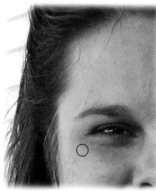

Figure 9-3:
The Healing brush is especially remarkable because it also blends the textures of the areas where you use it.

Left: This photo shows the crow's-feet at the corner of the woman's eye.

Right: The Healing brush eliminates them without creating a phony, airbrushed effect.

The repair material doesn't have to be nearby; in fact, you can sample from a totally different photo if you like. To sample material from another photo, just arrange both photos on the desktop so you can easily move your cursor from one to the other.

The basic procedure for using the Healing brush is similar to that for the Spot Healing brush: Drag over the flaw you want to fix. The difference is that with the Healing brush, you first Alt-click where you want Elements to look for replacement pixels.

GEM IN THE ROUGH

Dust and Scratches

Scratched, dusty prints can create giant headaches when you scan them. Cleaning your scanner's glass helps, but lots of photos come with plenty of dust marks already in the print, or in the file itself if the lens or sensor of your digital camera was dusty.

A similar problem is caused by *artifacts*, blobbish areas of color caused by JPEG compression. If you take a close look at the sky in a JPEG photo, for instance, you may see that instead of a smooth swath of blue, you see lots of little distinct clumps of each shade of blue.

The Healing brushes are usually your best first line of defense for fixing these problems, but if the specks are widespread, Elements offers a couple other options.

The first is the JPEG artifacts option in the Reduce Noise filter (page 412). If you're lucky, that will take care of things.

If it doesn't, other possible solutions include the Despeckle filter (Filter → Noise → Despeckle). And if that doesn't get everything, undo it and try the "Dust and Scratches" filter (Filter → Noise → "Dust and Scratches"), or the Median filter (Filter → Noise → Median). The Radius setting for these last two filters tells Elements how far to search for dissimilar pixels for its calculations; keep that number as low as possible. The downside to the filters in this group is that they smooth things out in a way that can make your image look blurred, so it's usually better to make a selection first to confine their effects to the areas that need repair. Despeckle is generally the filter that's least destructive to your image's focus.

You might also want to try creating a duplicate layer (Layer → Duplicate), running the Surface Blur filter (page 418) on it, and then, in the Layers panel, reducing the opacity of the filtered layer.

The Healing brush offers you quite a few choices in the Options bar:

- **Brush.** Click the brush thumbnail for a pop-out palette that lets you customize the size, shape, and hardness of your brush (see page 369). But generally, the standard brush works well, so you don't have to change things other than the size if you don't want to. If you have a graphics tablet (page 549), the menu at the bottom of the palette lets you choose to have how hard you press on the stylus or the stylus's scroll wheel control the brush size as you work.

- **Mode.** You can pick from a few blend modes (page 382) here, but most of the time, you want one of the top two options: Normal and Replace. Normal is usually your best choice. But if your replacement pixels make the area you work on show a visibly different texture than the surrounding area, choose Replace instead, which preserves the grain of your photo.

- **Source.** You can choose to sample an area to use as a replacement, or you can blend in a pattern. Using the Healing brush with patterns is explained on page 295.

- **Pattern thumbnails.** If you decide to use a pattern, this box becomes active. Click it to select a pattern.

- **Aligned.** If you turn on this checkbox, Elements keeps sampling new material in your source as you use the tool. The sampling follows the direction of your brush. Even if you let go of the mouse button, Elements continues to sample new material as long as you continue brushing. If you leave Aligned turned off, all the material comes from the area where you first defined your source point.

  Generally, for both the Healing brush and the Clone Stamp, it's easier to leave Aligned turned off. You can still change your source point by Alt-clicking another spot, but you often get better results if *you* make the decision about when to move on to another location rather than letting Elements decide.

- **Sample All Layers.** This checkbox tells Elements to sample from all the visible layers (page 180) in the area where you set your source point. You'd also use it if you wanted to heal on a new blank layer. Leave it turned off and Elements samples only the active layer.

- **Overlay Options.** Click this icon (the little gray overlapping squares) for a pop-out menu that lets you turn on and adjust a visible overlay for your photo. It allows you to see a floating ghostly overlay of the source area where you're sampling in relation to your original, so you can see exactly how things line up to help you do really accurate healing. You can also adjust the opacity of the overlay or invert it (make the light areas dark and the dark areas light so that you can see details better, if necessary) for a better view. Turning on the Auto Hide checkbox causes the overlay to disappear at the moment you click, so it's not in your way as you work. The Clipped option pins the overlay to your current brush so that you only see a brush-sized piece of overlay rather than one that covers the whole image. (If you notice strange gray circles following your brush around, this setting is turned on.)

If you're a beginner, you'll probably want to leave the overlay off, but advanced healers may find it very useful. It's also available for the Clone Stamp, and the settings you choose for one tool appear when you switch to the other tool.

It's almost as simple to use the Healing brush as it is to use the Spot Healing brush:

1. **Activate the Healing brush.**

   Click the Healing brush icon (the Band-Aid) in the Tools panel, and choose it from the pop-out menu. (Keyboard shortcut: J.)

2. **Find a good spot you want to sample to use in the repair and then Alt-click it.**

   When you Alt-click the good spot, your cursor temporarily turns into a circle with crosshairs in it to indicate that this is the point from which Elements will retrieve your repair material. (If you want to use a source point in a different photo, both the source photo and the one you're repairing have to be in the same *color mode*—see page 51.)

3. **Drag over the area you want to repair.**

   You can see where Elements is sampling the repair material from because it displays a cross in that spot.

4. **When you release the mouse button, Elements blends the sampled area into the problem area.**

   Often you don't know how effective the brush was until Elements is through working its magic, because it may take a few seconds for the program to finish its calculations and blend in the repair. If you don't like what Elements does, press Ctrl+Z to undo it and try again.

You can also heal on a separate layer. The advantage of doing this is that if you find the end result is a little too much—your granny suddenly looks like a Stepford wife, say—you can back things off a bit by reducing the opacity (page 180) of the healed layer to let the original show through. This is also a good plan when using the Clone Stamp (explained next). Just press Ctrl+Shift+N to create a new layer, and then turn on Sample All Layers in the Options bar.

The Clone Stamp

The Clone Stamp is like the Healing brush in that you add material from a source point that you select. The main difference between the two tools is that the Clone Stamp doesn't *blend in* when the new material is applied; instead, it simply covers up the underlying area completely. This makes the Clone Stamp great for when you don't want to leave any trace of what you're repairing. Figure 9-4 shows an example of when cloning is a better choice than healing.

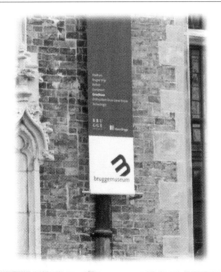

Figure 9-4:
Here's an example of when you'd choose cloning over healing.

Top: Say you want to get rid of the distracting white bottom part of this banner.

Bottom left: Using the Healing brush leaves a chalky whiteness from where it's blended the sign and the replacement brick.

Bottom right: The Clone Stamp works much better. Only the lower-right portion has been fixed, but you can see how much better the Clone Stamp covers up the banner.

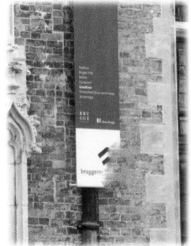

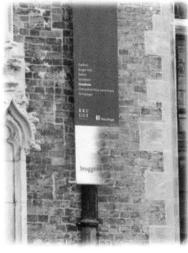

The choices you make in the Options bar for the Clone Stamp are really important in getting the best results possible:

- **Brush.** Use this drop-down menu to select a different brush style if you want (see Chapter 12 for more about brushes), but the standard brush style usually works pretty well. If the soft edges of the cloned areas bother you, you may be tempted to switch to a harder brush. But that usually makes your photo look like you strewed confetti on it, because hard edges don't blend well with what's already in your photo.

- **Size.** Choose a brush that's just big enough to get your sample without picking up a lot of other details that you don't want in your repair. While it may be tempting to clone huge chunks at once to get things done faster, most of the time you'll do better using the smallest brush that gets the sample you want.

- **Mode.** You can choose any blend mode (page 382) for cloning, but Normal is usually your best bet. Other modes can create interesting special effects.

- **Opacity.** Elements automatically uses 100-percent opacity for cloning, but you can reduce this setting to let some details from your original show through.

    TIP You gain more control by placing your clone on another layer (see page 175) than by adjusting the Clone Stamp's opacity.

- **Aligned.** This setting works exactly the way it does for the Healing brush (described earlier in this chapter). Turn it on and Elements keeps sampling at a uniform distance from your cursor as you clone. Turn it off and you keep putting down the same source material. Figure 9-5 shows an example of when you'd turn on Aligned. (If you drag rather than click with the Clone Stamp, Elements turns the Aligned checkbox on automatically.)

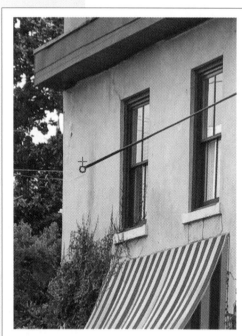

Figure 9-5:
If you want to get rid of the power line in this photo, one way is to use the Clone Stamp's Alignment option. Here the line starts in the trees at the left (if you look closely, you can see a bit of it at the left edge of the photo). By choosing a brush just barely larger than the power line and sampling just above it, you can replace the whole thing in one long sweep, despite the many changes in the background as you go.

• **Sample All Layers.** When you turn on this checkbox, Elements takes its samples from all the visible layers in the area where you set your source point. When it's off, Elements samples only the active layer.

• **Overlay Options.** Click this icon (the two overlapping rectangles) and choose Show Overlay to turn on a pale overlay that shows the clone source area floating over the original, so you can see precisely how your possible source material aligns with the original. This technique is a little confusing at first, but once you get the hang of it, it's really helpful when cloning precise patterns. If you've ever used the Clone Stamp before and accidentally cloned from the wrong spot or dragged in detail you didn't mean to grab, you'll love this feature. The options for adjusting the overlay are the same as for the Healing brush (page 289), which shares this feature: Settings you choose here will appear when you use the Healing brush and vice versa.

WORKAROUND WORKSHOP

Repairing Tears and Stains

With Elements, you can do a lot to bring damaged old photos back to life. The Healing brush and Clone Stamp are major players when it comes to restoring pictures. It's fiddly work and takes some persistence, but you can achieve wonders if you have the patience.

That said, if you're lucky enough to have good-sized useable replacement sections elsewhere in your photo, you can use the Move tool to copy the good bits into the problem area. First, select the part you want to copy. Then press M to activate the Move tool and Alt-drag the good piece where you want it. (Page 165 has more about the Move tool.)

You can use the Rotate commands to flip your selection if you need a mirror image. For example, if the left leg of a chair is fine but the right one is missing, try selecting and Alt-dragging the left leg with the Move tool. When it's where you want it, go to Image → Rotate → Flip Selection Horizontal to turn the copied left leg into a new right leg.

If you don't need to rotate an object, you may be able to just increase the Clone Stamp's brush size and clone the object where you need a duplicate. Cloning objects works well only when the background is the same for both areas.

The Clone Stamp shares its space in the Tools panel with the Pattern Stamp, which is explained on page 296. (You can tell which is which because the Pattern Stamp icon has a little blue checkerboard to its left.) Using the Clone Stamp is a lot like using the Healing brush, only the result is different:

1. **Activate the Clone Stamp.**

   Click its icon (the rubber stamp) in the Tools panel, and then choose it from the pop-out menu. (Keyboard shortcut: S.)

2. **Find the spot in your photo that you want to repair.**

   You may need to zoom way, way in to get a good enough look at what you're doing. Page 100 tells you how to adjust the view.

3. **Find a good spot to sample as a replacement for the bad area.**

You want an area that has the same tone as the area you're fixing. The Clone Stamp doesn't do any blending the way the Healing brush does, so tone differences are pretty obvious.

4. **Alt-click the spot you want to clone from.**

When you click, the cursor turns to a circle with crosshairs in it, indicating the source point for the repair. (Once you're actually working with the Clone Stamp, you see a cross marking the sampling point.)

5. **Click the spot you want to cover.**

Elements puts whatever you just selected on top of your image, concealing the original. You can drag with the Clone Stamp, but it acts like it's in Aligned mode (described in the previous list) when you do, so often it's better to click several times for areas that are larger than your sample. (The only difference between real Aligned mode and what you get from dragging is that with dragging, when you let go of the mouse, your source point snaps back to where you started. If you turn on Aligned, on the other hand, your source point stays where you stopped.)

6. **Continue until you've covered the area.**

With the Clone Stamp, unlike the Healing brush, what you see as you click is what you get—Elements doesn't do any further blending or smoothing.

The Clone Stamp is a really powerful tool, but it's crotchety, too. See the box on page 295 for some suggestions on how to make it behave.

You can clone on a separate layer, just as you can use the Healing tool on a dedicated layer. This lets you adjust the opacity of your repair afterward. Press Shift+Ctrl+N to create a new layer, and then turn on Sample All Layers in the Options bar. It's almost always a good idea to clone on a separate layer when you can, since cloning is so much more opaque than healing. If you use a separate layer, you can adjust the opacity of the cloned area afterward for a more subtle blend, if necessary.

Applying Patterns

In addition to solid colors, Elements lets you add patterns to your images, too. Quite a few patterns come with Elements, and you can download more from online sources (see page 551) or create your own. You can use patterns to add interesting designs to your images, or to give more realistic textures to certain repairs.

You can use either the Healing brush or the Pattern Stamp to apply patterns. The Healing brush has a pattern option in the Options bar. The Pattern Stamp shares a Toolbox slot with the Clone Stamp, and it works very much like the Clone Stamp, but puts down a preselected pattern instead of a sampled area.

Keeping the Clone Stamp Under Control

The Clone Stamp is a great tool, but it sometimes has a mind of its own.

If you suddenly see spots of a different shade appearing as you clone, take a look at the Options bar's Aligned box. It has a tendency to insist on staying turned on, and even if you turn it off, it can turn itself back on.

Once in a great while, the Clone Stamp just won't reset itself when you try to select a new sampling point. Try clicking the tiny down arrow on the left end of the Options bar and choosing the Reset Tool option, as shown

in Figure 9-6. If that doesn't work, exit the Editor and restart it (go to the Welcome window to restart it, if necessary) and delete Elements' preferences file. Here's how: hold down Ctrl+Alt+Shift immediately after launching the Editor. You get a dialog box asking if you want to delete the Elements settings; click Yes. This returns all your Elements settings to where they were the first time you launched the program. (Resetting the preferences cures about 80 percent of the problems you may run into in Elements.)

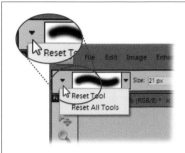

Figure 9-6:
You can reset the Clone Stamp (or, for that matter, any Elements tool) by clicking this tiny arrow at the left end of the Options bar, and then choosing Reset Tool. (If you want to reset the whole Tools panel, choose Reset All Tools.) This clears up a lot of the little problems you may have when trying to make a tool behave correctly.

NOTE Elements actually gives you lots of ways to use patterns, including creating a Fill layer that's covered with the pattern you choose. Page 195 explains Fill layers.

The tool you use to apply a pattern makes a big difference, as you can see from Figure 9-7. The next two sections explain how to use both tools.

The Healing Brush

The Healing brush's Pattern mode is great for things like improving the texture of someone's skin by applying skin texture from another photo.

Using patterns with the Healing brush is just as easy and works the same way as using the brush in normal healing mode: Just drag across the area you want to fix. The only difference is that you don't have to choose a sampling point, since the pattern is your source point. When you drag, the pattern blends into your photo.

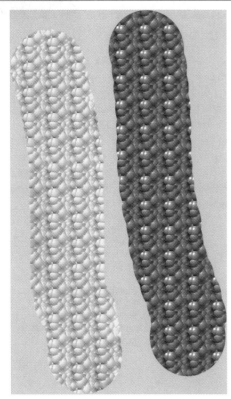

Figure 9-7:
The same pattern applied with the Healing brush (left) and the Pattern Stamp (right). The Healing brush blends the pattern into the underlying color (and texture, if there is any), while the Pattern Stamp just plunks down the pattern as it appears in the pop-out palette. (To get a softer edge on the Healing Brush's pattern, choose a softer brush from the pop-out palette.)

After activating the Healing brush, click the Pattern radio button in the Options bar, and then choose a pattern from the palette. You can see more pattern libraries if you click the right-facing arrow on the palette, or you can create and save your own patterns. Figure 9-8 explains how to create custom patterns for use with either the Healing brush or the Pattern Stamp.

> **TIP** You can create some interesting effects by changing the blend mode (page 182) when using patterns.

The Pattern Stamp

This tool is just like the Clone Stamp, only instead of copying sampled areas, it puts down a predefined pattern that you select from the Pattern palette. The Pattern Stamp is useful when you want to apply a pattern to your image without mixing it in with what's already there. For instance, if you want to see what your patio would look like if it were a garden instead, you could use the Pattern stamp to paint a lawn and a flower border on a photo of your patio.

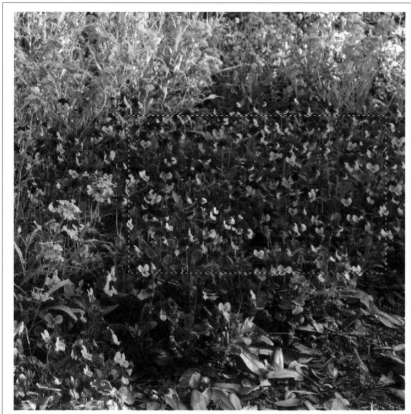

Figure 9-8:
You can easily create your own patterns. On any image, make an unfeathered, rectangular selection, and then choose Edit → "Define Pattern from Selection". Your pattern appears at the bottom of the current Pattern palette, and a dialog box pops up so you can type in a name for the new pattern. To use the whole image, don't make a selection—just go to Edit → Define Pattern. To rename or delete a pattern later, right-click it in the Pattern palette and make your choice. You can also download hundreds of different patterns from various online sources (see page 551).

To get started, click the Clone Stamp in the Tools panel, and then choose the Pattern Stamp from the pop-out menu. Click the pattern thumbnail in the Options bar. The Pattern palette opens so you can choose a pattern. The other options for this brush, like the size, hardness, and so on, are the same as for the Clone Stamp. The one extra option is Impressionist checkbox, which is mostly useful for creating special effects (see Figure 9-9).

Once you've selected a pattern, just drag in your photo where you want the pattern to appear.

Recomposing Photos

The previous sections have taught you how to remove flaws and objects you don't want in your photos by manually covering them up, bit by bit. But maybe you're thinking, "It seems so last century to have to drudge away like that. There's got to be an easier way!" You're right—there is.

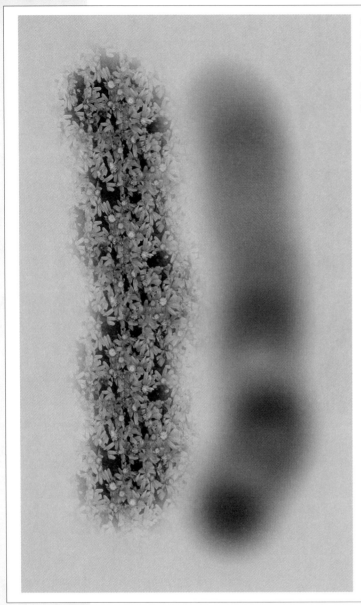

Figure 9-9:
If you turn on the Options bar's Impressionist checkbox, Elements blurs your pattern, giving an effect vaguely like an Impressionist painting. Here, you see a pattern put down with the regular Pattern Stamp (left) and the Impressionist stamp (right).

One of the coolest new features of Elements 8 is the Recompose tool, which lets you eliminate unwanted objects and people from your photos by just scribbling a line over them to tell Elements that they have to go, and then pushing the edges of your photo to reshape it. Amazingly, Elements can figure out how to keep the details you want undistorted as it makes unwanted objects vanish. Take a look at Figure 9-10 to see an example of what this tool can do. Want to get rid of your daughter's ex-boyfriend in that group shot? Just drag a line on him in the photo, push the image's edges closer together, and he's history. Couldn't get your feuding coworkers to stand close enough together not to spoil the holiday party photo? No problem—you can easily take out that empty space between them.

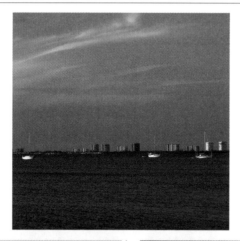

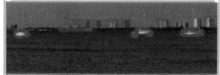

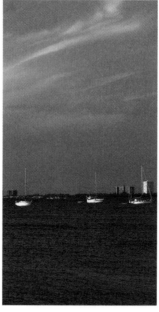

Figure 9-10:
Top: What do you do if you have a wide photo of your sailboat and you'd like to bring it closer to the other boats (and also moor it off an island with less condo sprawl)?

Bottom left: Just make a few marks on it with the Recompose tool (the green marks mean "Keep this" and the red ones "Lose this"), and then drag one edge toward the middle of the photo.

Bottom right: The end result: a narrow photo of the boats with fewer buildings in the background. (A little cloning took care of a couple of artifacts left over from the removed buildings.)

You can also use the Recompose tool to alter the shape of your photo without cropping it. Got a landscape-oriented photo that you wish were portrait-oriented instead? Recompose can fix that. There are limits to how far you can push this feature, but with a suitable photo, you can just shove it into the proportions you want, and everything will still look perfectly normal and not distorted at all.

It takes an awesome amount of computer intelligence to make this tool work, but for you, it's one of the easier tools in Elements:

1. **Open a photo and call up the Recompose tool.**

   Adobe thinks this tool is so useful that there are several ways to get at it:

   • **From the Tools panel.** In Full Edit, the Recompose tool shares a slot with the Crop tool. Their keyboard shortcut is C.

   • **From the Image menu.** Go to Image → Recompose, or press Alt+Ctrl+R.

   • **In Create projects.** Right-click inside any of the Content panel frames, and you see Recompose Photo as one of your choices, whether you're in Create or in the Editor.

2. **Tell Elements which parts of your photo you *don't* want to change.**

   You use the Protect brush to drag over the areas you want preserved. (To select this brush, click the leftmost icon on the Options bar—the green paintbrush and lock.) This is something like using the Quick Selection tool in that you don't have to select everything; just make enough marks for Elements to know which objects you mean. However, you're likely to find that this brush is a bit more literal-minded than the Quick Selection tool, so you may need more marks when using it (see Figure 9-11).

   TIP The Recompose tool has a hidden menu to speed things up. Right-click your photo when the tool is active, and you can choose Quick Highlight, which makes the whole process of telling Elements what to keep and what to eliminate go much faster. You tend to get better results with this method, too.

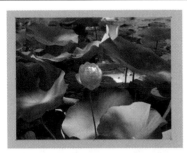

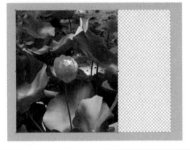

Figure 9-11:
Recomposing can help you change the aspect ratio of a photo, like this lotus image, which is too wide for its frame.

Top: A quick scribble over the flower tells Elements that's the important part of the photo, so the program knows not to change it. (Notice that there aren't any Removal marks in this image.)

Bottom: When you activate the Recompose tool, Elements put tiny square handles around your image. Drag one of these handles toward the middle of the photo and Elements squishes the photo down to size without distorting the background leaves in any obvious way.

TIP   In the Options bar, click the "Highlight Skin tones" icon (the little green man) to select the people in your photo automatically.

3. **Tell Elements what you want to get rid of.**

If there are specific objects or areas that you want to delete, drag over them with the Removal brush. (Click the Options bar icon that looks like a red paintbrush and an X.)

NOTE   You don't always need to use both brushes with the Recompose tool. You can try using it without marking anything at all, but you'll likely get better results if you give Elements at least a little guidance. If you make a mistake with either brush, use the matching eraser (the icon just to the brush's right) to remove the stray marks.

4. **Recompose your photo.**

Once you're through marking up your photo, you can use the bounding box with handles that outlines your image to resize it. It works just like the Move tool's bounding box: Just grab a square handle or a corner and drag left, right, up, or down to change the shape of your image. There are several Options bar settings that can help you out if you need to make the photo a specific size; they're explained below.

NOTE   If you want to make your image wider or taller than it is now (to make a portrait-orientation photo into a landscape one, for example), you need to add canvas (page 111) before you start, in order to give the new width or height someplace to go.

Watch as the unwanted areas disappear as you drag the edges closer together. (The disappearing part doesn't work so well when you're making the image larger rather than smaller.)

5. **Finish up.**

When you're happy with your image, click the Commit button (the green checkmark) that appears or press Enter. If you decide you don't want to recompose your photo after all, or if you need to go back and adjust the marks you made, click the red Cancel button to cancel. When you're done, crop off any extra blank space that's left over on the edges of your photo. (Page 89 covers cropping.)

NOTE   You may find that some small remnants of removed objects tend to reappear after you press Enter. Just use the Clone Stamp (page 290) or the Healing brush (page 285) to get rid of them.

The Recompose tool has several Options bar settings to make your job even easier:

• **Brushes.** There are four brush icons (from left to right): Protect brush, "Erase highlights marked for protection" (the eraser for Protect marks you don't want), Removal brush, and "Erase highlights marked for removal" (the eraser for Remove marks you made by mistake).

- **Brush size.** This is just like the size setting for any brush tool: enter a size in pixels, scrub on the Options bar, or use the bracket key shortcuts to change the size. (Chapter 12 covers brushes in detail.)

- **Highlight Skin tones.** Click this icon and, if you're lucky, Elements automatically selects the people in your photo. It's kind of dicey, though—you may find Elements prefers other objects to the folks in your pictures, but this icon is worth a click, since you can always undo Elements' selections if it chooses poorly (go to Edit → Undo Highlight Skin Tones or press Ctrl+Z).

- **Preset.** Normally this option is set to No Restriction, which lets you drag any way you like, but you can also choose to restrict your dragging to the photo's current aspect ratio or to one of several popular photo paper sizes.

- **W (width) and H (height).** If you want to enter a custom size, you can do that in these fields. Click the arrows between the boxes to swap the numbers, just like with the Crop tool.

- **Amount.** This tells Elements how much you want to protect the details from distortion. Leave it at 100%.

What's most amazing about this tool is the way your background still looks real when you're done. Someone seeing your Recomposed photo would never guess that it didn't start out looking just like it does now. Recomposing doesn't work for every photo, but when it does, the results are almost magical.

Color Curves: Enhancing Tone and Contrast

If you hang around photo-editing veterans, you'll hear plenty of talk about how useful the Curves tool is. Contrary to what you might expect, Curves isn't a drawing tool. Instead, it works much like Levels (page 221), but with many more points of correction. Adobe calls the Elements version of this tool *Color Curves* to remind you what it's for. Unlike Levels, which lets you set your entire photo's white point, black point, and gamma settings, Curves lets you target specific tonal regions. For instance, with Curves, you can make only your shadows lighter or only your highlights darker. Maybe that's why some pros say, "Curves is Levels on steroids." (For advice on when to use Levels and when to use Color Curves, see the box on page 226.)

Elements' Color Curves tool is a stripped-down version of its counterpart in the full version of Photoshop, which is just called Curves. With the more powerful Curves tool, you can work on each color channel separately, as you do in the Levels dialog box. You can also drag any point on the Curves graph (like the one you see Figure 9-12) to manipulate it directly. For example, you can drag to adjust just the middle range of your greens. Elements doesn't give you that kind of flexibility.

Since Curves, in its original-strength version, is a pretty complicated tool, Adobe makes it easier to use in Elements. To start with, you get a group of preset adjustments to choose from (see Figure 9-12). These presets are shortcuts to the types of basic enhancements you'll use most often. Just click one to try it. If you like what it does, you're done. But if you aren't quite satisfied with any of the presets, you can

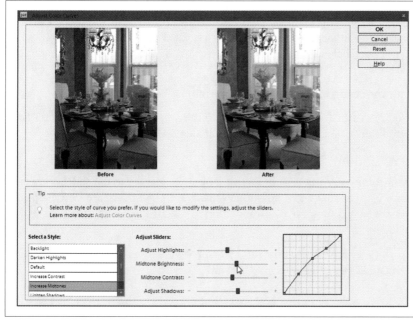

Figure 9-12:
The Adjust Color Curves dialog box gives you a good look at what you're doing to your photo with these large before and after previews. Start by clicking around in the list of preset styles in the lower-left side of the window, and then use the sliders in the middle of the lower section to fine-tune the effect if you need to.

easily make adjustments in the Adjust Color Curves dialog box's advanced options, to the right of the presets.

Here's how to improve a photo's appearance with Color Curves:

1. **Open your photo and make a duplicate layer.**

   Elements doesn't let you use Color Curves as an Adjustment layer (unlike Photoshop), so you're safer applying it to a duplicate layer in case you want to change something later. Press Ctrl+J or go to Layer → Duplicate Layer to create one.

   If you want to restrict your adjustment to a particular area of your photo, select it first so that Color Curves changes only the selected area. For instance, if you're happy with everything in your shot of Junior's Little League game except the catcher in the foreground, select him, and you can do a Color Curves adjustment that affects only him and not the rest of the photo. (See Chapter 5 if you need a refresher on selections.)

2. **Go to Enhance → Adjust Color → Adjust Color Curves.**

   Elements opens the Adjust Color Curves dialog box, where you see your original image in the preview on the left.

3. **Choose a Color Curves preset.**

   Scroll through the list in the window's lower left, and click the preset that seems closest to what you want your photo to look like. Feel free to experiment by clicking different presets. (As long as you're just clicking in the list, you don't need to click Reset between each one, since Elements starts from your original each time you click.)

The dialog box gives you a decent-sized look at how you're changing your image, but for important photos, you can also preview the effect right in your image. To do that, drag the dialog box out of the way, and check your actual photo to get a closer look at how you're changing things before you make your final choice.

4. **Apply the changes, or tweak them some more.**

If you're satisfied, click OK. If not, go to the next step. (And if you don't want to apply any Color Curves adjustments at all, click Cancel.)

5. **Make any further adjustments.**

If you think your photo still doesn't look quite right, use the sliders shown in Figure 9-13 to make any additional changes. (The sliders are described in a moment.) Click Reset if you want to undo any of the changes you make with the sliders.

Easy does it here. Notice how subtle the preset curves are. A tiny nudge of these sliders makes a big difference, so be gentle.

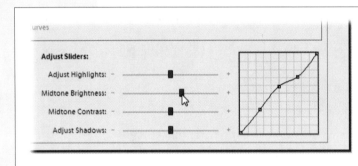

Figure 9-13:
The graph on the right side of this figure is where the Color Curves feature gets its name. When you first open the Adjust Color Curves dialog box, with no adjustments at all, the graph is a straight diagonal line. The adjustments you make cause the points on the graph to move, resulting in a curved line. Click Reset (not shown) to go back to the straight line again, or click Default in the list of presets.

6. **When you're happy with your photo's new look, click OK.**

Don't forget to save your changes. If you used the duplicate layer, you can always change your mind about them later on and start over on a fresh layer.

NOTE   If you've used Curves add-ons in an old version of Elements (like those from Richard Lynch or Grant Dixon, for example), or if you've used the Photoshop Curves Adjustment Layers (you power user, you!), the Color Curves tool may take some getting used to. You may prefer the more fully featured, free add-on Curves tool for Elements at *http://free.pages.at/easyfilter/curves.html*.

Once you've got some Color Curves experience under your belt, you probably won't be satisfied with the results you get from the presets. So don't hesitate to use the sliders to adjust different tonal regions in your photo:

• **Adjust Highlights.** Move the slider to the left to darken your photo's highlights, or to the right to lighten them.

- **Midtone Brightness.** If you'd like the middle range of colors to be darker, move this slider to the left. Move it to the right to make the midtones brighter.

- **Midtone Contrast.** This slider works just like the one in the Shadows/Highlights feature (see page 210). Move it to the right to increase your photo's contrast, and to the left to decrease it.

- **Adjust Shadows.** If you want to lighten shadows, move this slider to the right. To darken shadowy areas, move it to the left.

As you move the sliders, you can see the point you're adjusting move on the graph and watch the curve change shape. Although it's fun to see what's going on in the graph, you should pay more attention to what's happening in your photo.

Color Curves is such a potent tool that it can change your photo in ways you don't intend. Rather than using Color Curves to make huge adjustments, try another tool first. Then come back and use Color Curves for the final, subtle tweaks. On the other hand, you can also use Color Curves to create some wild special effects, if that's what you're after. See Figure 9-14 for an example.

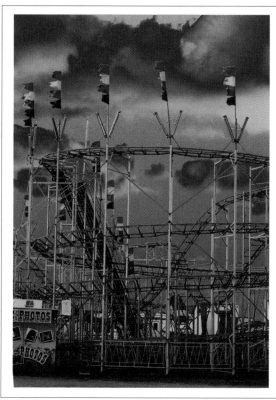

Figure 9-14:
Many people prefer to use Color Curves for artwork and special effects rather than for adjusting photos. Jimi Hendrix fans may like the Solarize preset, which Adobe includes to give you a starting point for funky pictures like this one. (Others say this preset should serve as a warning about going overboard with this tool.)

TIP   You can also apply the Solarize adjustment to part of your photo by using the Smart Brush tool (page 211). But if you use the brush method, you can't edit the settings afterward, so you may prefer to apply Solarize using Color Curves on a duplicate layer.

Making Colors More Vibrant

Do you drool over the luscious photos in travel magazines, the ones that make it look like the world's full of vivid destinations that make regular life seem pretty drab in comparison? What *is* it about those photos that makes things look so dramatic?

Often the answer is the *saturation,* or intensity, of the colors. Supersaturated color makes for darned appealing landscape and object photos, regardless of how the real thing may rate on the vividness scale.

There are various ways to adjust the saturation of your photos. Some cameras offer to help control it, but Elements lets you go even further. For example, by increasing or decreasing a photo's saturation, you can shift the perceived focal point, change the mood of the picture, or just make it more eye-catching.

By increasing your subject's saturation and decreasing it in the rest of the photo, you can focus your viewer's attention, even in a crowded photo. Figure 9-15 shows a somewhat exaggerated use of this technique; you can download the photo (*jars.jpg*) from the Missing CD page at *www.missingmanuals.com* to try it out for yourself.

It's super easy to change saturation. You might want to start out with the Raw Converter's Vibrance slider—remember that you can open other image formats there besides Raw files. If that doesn't work well, try using either of the more traditional methods: the Hue/Saturation dialog box or the Sponge tool, which are explained in the following sections. For big areas, or when you want a lot of control, use the Hue/Saturation dialog box. If you just want to quickly paint a different saturation level on a small spot in your photo, the Sponge tool is faster.

TIP   Many consumer-grade digital cameras are set to crank the saturation of your JPEG photos into the stratosphere. That's great if you love all the color. But if you prefer not to live in a Technicolor universe, you can desaturate your photos in Elements to remove some of the excess color.

The Hue/Saturation Dialog Box

Hue/Saturation is one of the most popular commands in Elements. If you aren't satisfied with the results of a simple Levels adjustment, you may want to work on the hue or saturation as the next step toward getting really eye-catching color.

Hue simply means the color of your image—whether it's blue or brown or purple or green. Most people use the saturation adjustments more than the hue controls, but both hue and saturation are controlled from the same dialog box, where you can adjust both or just one.

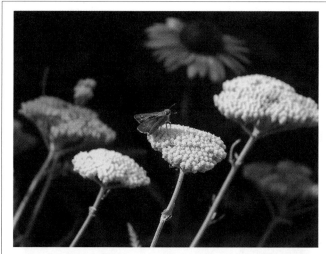

Figure 9-15:
Top: All the yellow flowers in this image are equally bright, including those in the background, so you might miss the butterfly on the front blossom.

Bottom: To make the butterfly and its flower stand out from the crowd, desaturate the rest of the image. The effect is exaggerated here, but a subtler use of this technique can work wonders for spotlighting objects in your photos.

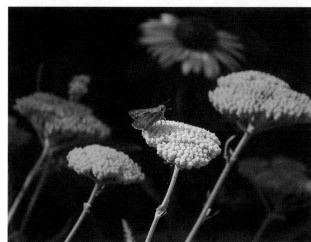

In Elements, you can use the Hue slider to actually change the color of objects in your photos, but you'll probably want to adjust saturation far more often than you want to shift the hue of a photo.

When you use Hue/Saturation, it's a good idea to first make the most of your other corrections—like Levels or exposure corrections (see page 206). When you're ready to use the Hue/Saturation command, just follow these steps:

1. **If you want to adjust only part of your photo, select the area you want.**

   Use whatever selection tool(s) you prefer. (Chapter 5 explains all about making selections.)

2. **Call up the Hue/Saturation dialog box.**

   Go to Enhance → Adjust Color → Adjust Hue/Saturation, or Layer → New Adjustment Layer → Hue/Saturation. As always, if you don't want to make changes that you can't easily reverse, use an Adjustment layer instead of working directly on your photo. (If you choose the layer, you make your changes in the Adjustments panel—page 193—rather than in the dialog box, but your options are exactly the same.)

3. **Move the sliders until you see what you want.**

   If you want to adjust only saturation, just ignore the Hue slider. Move the Saturation slider to the right to increase saturation (more color) or to the left to decrease it. If necessary, move the Lightness slider to the left to make the color darker, or move it to the right to make the color lighter. Incidentally, you don't have to change *all* the colors in your photo equally. Figure 9-16 explains how to focus on individual color channels.

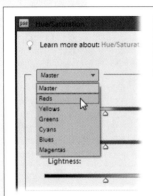

Figure 9-16:
The Hue/Saturation dialog box has a drop-down menu like the Levels dialog box that lets you adjust individual color channels. If only the reds are excessive (a common problem with digital cameras), you can lower the saturation only for the reds without changing the other channels.

> **TIP**   Generally speaking, if you want to change a pastel to a more intense color, you'll need to increase the saturation *and* reduce the lightness (move the Lightness slider to the left) if you don't want your color to look radioactive.

Adjusting Saturation with the Sponge Tool

The Sponge tool gives you another way to adjust saturation. Even though it's called a sponge, this tool works like any other brush tool in Elements. Choosing the size and hardness are just the same as choosing them for any other brush (see page 369).

> **TIP**   Although the Sponge tool is handy for working on small areas, all that dragging gets old pretty fast when you're working on a large chunk of your image. For those situations, use the Hue/Saturation dialog box instead.

The Sponge has a couple of unique settings all its own:

- **Mode.** Choose here whether to saturate (add color) or desaturate (remove color).

- **Flow.** This option governs how intense the effect is; a higher number means more intensity.

To use the Sponge tool, drag over the area you want to change. Figure 9-17 shows the kind of work the Sponge does.

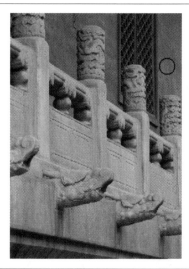

Figure 9-17:
Here, the Sponge tool was used on the upper-right part of the wall, increasing the color saturation and bringing out the reddish paint colors. Approach the Sponge tool with caution: It doesn't take much to degrade in your image, especially if you've made lots of other adjustments to it. So if you start to see noise (graininess), undo your sponging and try again at a reduced Flow setting.

You may want to create a duplicate layer (Ctrl+J) before using the Sponge. Then you can always throw out the duplicate layer later on if you don't like the changes. Here's how to use this tool:

1. **Activate the Sponge tool.**

   Press O or click its icon in the Tools panel, and then choose the sponge from the pop-out menu. Choose the brush size and the settings you want in the Options bar.

2. **Drag in the area you want to change.**

   If you aren't seeing enough of a difference, increase the Flow setting a little. If it's too strong, reduce the Flow number.

   TIP   If you have a hard time coloring (or decoloring) inside the lines, select the area you want before starting with the sponge. Then the tool won't do anything outside the selection, so you can be as sloppy as you like.

Changing an Object's Color

In Chapter 4, you saw one way to change the color of an object—select it and use the Hue and Saturation sliders in Quick Fix. Elements also gives you a few other ways to do this: You can use an Adjustment layer, the Replace Color command, or the Color Replacement tool. And the Smart Brush tools (page 211) have a whole menu full of color changes, too.

The method you choose depends on your photo and your preference. Using an Adjustment layer gives you the most flexibility if you want to make other changes later on. Replace Color is the fastest way to change one color that's widely scattered throughout your whole image, and the Color Replacement tool lets you quickly brush a replacement color over the color you want to change. Whichever method you choose, Figure 9-18 shows the kind of complex color change you can make in a jiffy using any one of these methods.

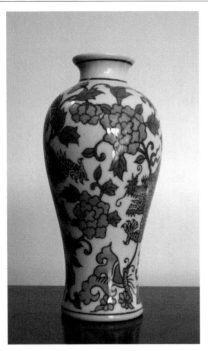
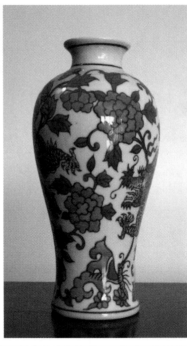

Figure 9-18:
What if you have a green-and-white vase, but you really want a red-and-white one? Just call up the Replace Color tool. (Elements gives you several ways to make complicated color substitutions like this one, all of which are covered in this section.)

NOTE   The Smart Brush lets you target the area you want to change and make a quick color adjustment, but the color presets are pretty limited (and pretty ugly). Also, the Smart Brush doesn't just apply a single color, but uses gradient maps (page 438) instead. If you can get the effect you like using the Smart Brush, go for it. But it's much harder to adjust the color with this tool by changing the settings, since you have to pick a different gradient or edit the gradient the Smart Brush used (page 432 tells you how). On the whole, the methods described in the following pages are much simpler to control.

Using an Adjustment Layer

You can use a Hue/Saturation Adjustment layer to make the same kind of color changes you saw on page 310. The advantage of using an Adjustment layer is that you can change the settings or the area affected by the layer later on (as opposed to changing your whole image). The process is exactly the same as the one described on page 306, only this time, you start by selecting what you want to change:

1. **Select the object whose color you want to change.**

   Use any of the Selection tools (see Chapter 5). If you don't make a selection before creating the Adjustment layer, you'll change your whole photo.

2. **Create a new Hue/Saturation Adjustment layer.**

   Go to Layer → New Adjustment Layer → Hue/Saturation. The new layer affects only the area you selected.

3. **Use the Adjustment panel's sliders to tweak the color until you see what you want, and then click OK.**

   Use the Hue slider first to pick the color you want. When you've gotten close to the desired color, use the Saturation slider to adjust the new color's vividness and the Lightness slider to adjust the darkness.

This method works fine if it's easy to select the area you want to change. But what if you have a bunch of different areas, or you want to change one shade everywhere it appears in your photo? For that, Elements offers the Replace Color command.

Replacing Specific Colors

Take a look at the green-and-white vase in Figure 9-18 again. Do you have to tediously select each green area one by one if you want to make it a red-and-white vase?

You *can* do it that way, but it's far easier to use the Replace Color command. It has one of those dialog boxes that look a bit intimidating, but it's a snap to use once you understand how it works. Replace Color changes every instance of the color that you select, no matter how many times it appears in your image.

You don't need to start by making a selection when you use this command. As usual, if you want to keep your options for future changes open, make a duplicate layer (Ctrl+J). Before you start, make sure your active layer isn't an Adjustment layer, or Replace Color won't work. Then:

1. **Open the Replace Color dialog box.**

   Go to Enhance → Adjust Color → Replace Color. The Replace Color dialog box in Figure 9-19 appears.

   TIP   If you want to protect a particular area of your chosen color from being changed, paint a mask on it by using the Selection brush in Mask mode (page 147) before you start.

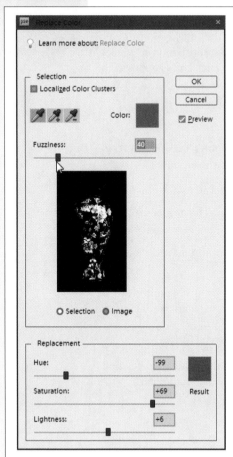

Figure 9-19:
Behold the Replace Color dialog box. The funny area that looks like a negative shows you where the sliders will affect the color. Use the Hue/Saturation sliders to adjust the replacement color (shown in the bottom-right color square) the way you would with a regular Hue/Saturation adjustment. Fuzziness works a little like a Tolerance Setting for the Magic Wand, as explained in Localized Color Clusters is something like Contiguous for the Magic Wand—it restricts the selection to colors in the immediate area of your click.

2. **Move your cursor over your photo.**

   The cursor changes to an eyedropper. Take a moment to confirm that the left-most eyedropper in the Replace Color dialog box is the active one (the one without a plus or minus sign).

3. **Click an area of the color you want to replace.**

   Elements has selected all the areas matching that particular shade, but you won't see the marching ants in your image the way you do with the Selection tools. If you click more than once, you *change* your selection instead of adding to it, the way you would with any of the regular Selection tools. To add to your selection (that is, to select additional shades), Shift-click in your photo.

   Another way to add more shades is to select the middle eyedropper (the one with the + sign next to it) and click in your photo again. To remove a color, select the right eyedropper (with the – sign) and then click. Alternatively, Alt-click with the first eyedropper to remove the shade you click from the selection.

If you want to start selecting all over again, Alt-click the Cancel button to turn it to a Reset button.

4. **When you've selected everything you want to change, move the sliders to replace the color.**

The Hue, Saturation, and Lightness sliders work exactly the way they do in the Hue/Saturation dialog box (explained earlier in this chapter). Move them and watch the color box in the Replace Color dialog box to see what color you're concocting. You can also click the color box to bring up the Color Picker (page 232) and choose a shade there. If you need to tweak the area of color you're changing, the Fuzziness slider adjusts the range of colors that Color Replacement affects, as shown in Figure 9-20.

Take a look at your photo after you've chosen your replacement color. If the preview doesn't show the color in all the areas you want, just click the missing spots with the middle eyedropper to fix them.

5. **Click OK and you're done.**

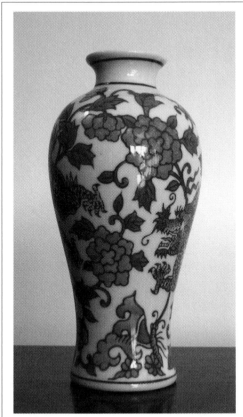

Figure 9-20:
Fuzziness is similar to the Magic Wand's Tolerance setting (page 150). Look at the red areas of the vase. There's still a lot of green in the center of some of them. Set Fuzziness higher to include more pixels than you've previously been changing (in this image, that change would make all the green center spots turn red). If you find you're picking up little bits of areas you don't want, set Fuzziness lower. Move the slider to the right for more fuzziness and to the left for less.

The Color Replacement Tool

Besides the Smart Brush, Elements gives you yet another way to brush on a color change—the Color Replacement tool. It lets you brush a different color onto the area you want to change without changing any colors besides the one you target. Figure 9-21 shows the Color Replacement tool in action.

The Color Replacement tool shares a Tools panel slot with the Brush tool. To activate it, press B or click the Brush tool, and then choose the Color Replacement tool from the pop-out list.

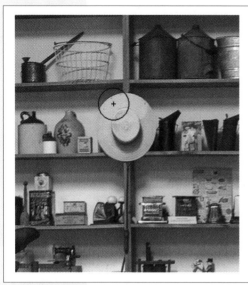

Figure 9-21:
If you'd like to put some zip into this photo by coloring the hat, the Color Replacement tool is one way to do it. Although the sampled color was actually dark teal green, the Color Replacement tool in Hue mode brushes on a pale but vivid aqua. Keeping the crosshairs inside the hat ensures that only the hat gets changed.

The Options bar settings make a big difference in how the Color Replacement tool works:

- **Brush options.** These settings (size, hardness, angle, and so on) work the same way they do for any brush. See Chapter 12 for more about brushes.

- **Mode.** This controls the tool's blend mode (page 382). Generally you want Color or Hue, although you can get some funky special effects with Saturation.

- **Limits.** This setting tells Elements which areas of your photo to look at in its search for color. Contiguous means only areas that touch each other get changed. Discontiguous means the tool changes *all* the places it finds a color—whether they're touching one another or not.

- **Tolerance.** This is just like the Magic Wand's Tolerance setting: The higher the number, the more shades of color are affected. Getting this setting right is the key to getting good results with this tool.

- **Anti-alias.** This setting smooths the edges of the replacement color. It's best to leave it turned on.

Using the Color Replacement tool is straightforward:

1. **Pick the color you're going to use as a replacement.**

   Elements uses the current Foreground color as the replacement color. To choose a new color, click the Foreground color square in the Tools panel, and then choose one from the Color Picker (page 232).

2. **Activate the Color Replacement tool and pick a brush size.**

   Click the Brush tool in the Tools panel, and then choose the Color Replacement tool from the pop-out menu. (Keyboard shortcut: B.) See Chapter 12 for help using brushes. Generally for this tool, you want a fairly large brush, as shown in Figure 9-21.

3. **Click or drag in your photo to change the color.**

   Elements targets the color that's under the crosshairs in the center of the brush cursor.

The Color Replacement tool is okay for changing large areas of color to an equivalent tone, but if you want to replace dark red with pale yellow, you probably won't like the results, because it's not great for colors where the lightness is very different. This tool hasn't been as useful in the past couple of versions of Elements as it once was, but you may still sometimes find that it's the best tool for the job.

> **TIP**   You may want to use the Color Replacement tool on a duplicate layer (Ctrl+J) so that you can adjust the layer opacity to control the effect.

Special Effects

Elements gives you some other useful ways of drastically changing the look of your image. You can apply these effects as Adjustment layers (Layer → New Adjustment Layer) or by going to Filter → Adjustments (there's much more about filters in Chapter 13). Either method gives you the same setting options. You can see them in action in Figure 9-22.

In most cases, you use these adjustments as steps along the way in a more complex treatment of your photo, but they're effective by themselves, too. Here's what each one does (listed in the order you see them in the Filter menu):

- **Equalize** makes the darkest pixel black and the lightest one white, and redistributes the brightness values for all the colors in that photo to give them all equal weight. When you have an active selection, you see a dialog box that lets you choose between simply equalizing your whole photo and equalizing it based on a selection. It doesn't always work, but sometimes Equalize is great for bringing up the brightness level of a dim photo. (This choice isn't available as an Adjustment layer, only as a filter.)

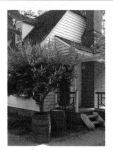
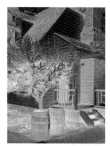
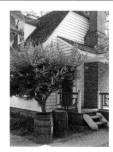

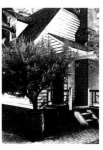
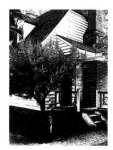

Figure 9-22:
You can get some interesting special effects with the Adjustment commands, whether you apply them as filters or Adjustment layers. (If you want to use them as filters, it's not a bad idea to start with a duplicate layer.)

Top row (left to right): The original photo, Invert, Equalize.

Bottom row (left to right): Posterize and Threshold.

- **Gradient Map** is pretty complicated. According to Adobe, it "maps the grayscale range of an image to the colors of a specified gradient fill." If you want to know what the heck *that* means, turn to page 438. Basically, a gradient map lets you apply a gradient based on the light and dark areas of your photo. The gradient colors replace the existing colors in your photo. There's a lot more to it than that, though.

- **Invert** makes your photo look like a negative. It's so useful in doing artistic effects that Elements also lets you invert in the Editor anytime just by pressing Ctrl+I. (If you want to invert just part of an image, check out the Smart Brush tools [page 211], which have some interesting variations on inversion in their Special Effects menus.)

NOTE   If you think choosing the Invert option sounds like a great way to get your negatives scanned in with a basic flatbed scanner and turned to positive images, sorry, but that won't work. Color negatives have an orange mask on them that Elements can't easily undo. You're best off with a dedicated film scanner that's designed to cope with negatives, or at least with a scanner that has software designed to deal with the mask. Invert is great for use with black-and-white negatives, though: It lets you make them into positive images you can print or use in projects.

- **Posterize** reduces the total number of colors in your photo, giving a less detailed, more poster-like effect. The lower the number you enter in the dialog box, the fewer colors you'll get and the more extreme the result. If you want blocky, poster-like edges in your photo, try Filter → Artistic → Poster Edges instead of—or in addition to—this.

- **Threshold** turns every pixel in your photo to pure white or pure black. You won't find any shades of gray here. Figure 9-23 explains how to adjust the settings for this feature.

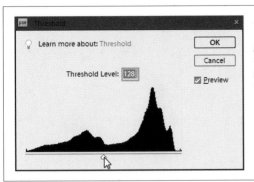

Figure 9-23:
This slider controls the dividing point between black and white pixels in a Threshold adjustment. Slide to the left if you want more white pixels, and to the right for more black ones. The graph is a histogram (page 221) showing the light-to-dark distribution of the pixels in your image.

- **Photo Filter** makes color corrections, like removing color casts from your photos. You can read about it in detail on page 283.

Removing and Adding Color

If you love classic black-and-white photography, or if you yearn to be the next Ansel Adams, then you'll be over the moon with the high-quality black-and-white conversions Elements can do. If you can't imagine why anyone would willingly abandon color, consider that in a world crammed full of eye-popping colors, black and white really stands out. Or you may be planning to have something printed where you can't use color illustrations. And, of course, for artistic photography there's still nothing like black and white, where tone and contrast make or break the photo, without any colors to distract you from the picture's underlying structure.

In this chapter, you'll learn how to make a color photo black and white, and how to create images that are partly in color and partly in black and white. You'll also learn how to colorize black-and-white images, and, along the way, how to use and edit *layer masks,* an important technique for advanced Elements work.

Method One: Making Color Photos Black and White

A stunning black-and-white image is so much more than just a color photo without color. Generally, just removing the color from a photo produces a pretty flat-looking, uninteresting image. A good black-and-white photo usually needs more contrast. You can create very different effects and totally different moods in your photo, depending on what you decide to emphasize in the black-and-white version.

Black-and-white conversion has traditionally been a pretty complicated process. If you search on Google, you can find dozens of different recipes for making conversions. Fortunately for you, Elements makes it really easy to perform these conversions, and even to do sophisticated tweaking of the different color channels. Just follow these steps:

1. **Open the photo you want to convert.**

   If the photo has multiple layers, then flatten it (Layer → Flatten Image), or make sure the layer you want to convert is the active layer (click it in the Layers panel). If you want to convert only a part of your photo, select the area you want to make black and white. As always, it's best to do this on a copy, not on your original photo.

2. **Go to Enhance → "Convert to Black and White", or press Alt+Ctrl+B.**

   The "Convert to Black and White" dialog box appears. It includes helpful before and after previews of your image, and the controls shown in Figure 10-1.

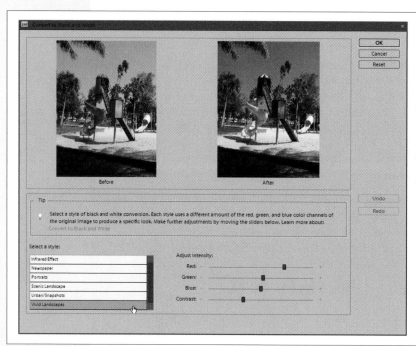

Figure 10-1:
The "Convert to Black and White" dialog box makes it really easy to create effective transformations, even if you don't have any idea what you're doing. First, choose a conversion style from the list in the bottom left, and then use the sliders to tweak the result, if necessary.

3. **Choose a conversion style.**

   Elements gives you various preset styles for the conversion. Click a style in the list to apply it to your photo. Try different styles to see which suits your photo best.

4. **Tweak the conversion, if necessary.**

Use the Adjust Intensity sliders (Red, Green, and so on) below the preview area
to increase or decrease the prominence of each color channel (page 221). (You
don't need to understand color channels to do this; just move the sliders
around and see what creates the effect you like.) Watch the preview to see how
you're changing your photo. Go gently—it doesn't take much to make quite a
difference in your image.

Once you move a slider, the right-hand Undo and Redo buttons become click-
able. Use them to step backward and forward through your changes. If you
want to start from scratch, then click Reset.

5. **When you're satisfied with how your photo looks, click OK.**

Be sure to carefully examine your actual image—don't rely on just the smallish
preview window. Move the dialog box around your screen so you can see your
whole photo before you accept the conversion. If you change your mind about
creating a black-and-white image, then click Cancel.

TIP   You may want to emphasize certain details in your photo without making additional
changes to the overall tonality. To do that, use the Dodge and Burn tools (page 380) once you've
completed your conversion.

While the different conversion styles have descriptive names, like Portraits and
Scenic Landscape, don't put too much stock in those names. They're basically just
a less intimidating way of describing preset collections of settings to the color
channels in your photo. Be sure to test out the various styles to see which works
best on your photo. For instance, you may vastly prefer the way Uncle Julio looks
when you choose the Newspaper style instead of the Portraits style.

But wait a minute, changes to the color channels? That's right. Back in Chapter 7,
you read about how your photo consists of three separate color channels: red, blue,
and green. In your camera's original file, each of these channels is recorded merely
as variations in light and dark tones; in other words, as a black-and-white image.
The file tells the computer or printer to render a particular channel as all red, blue,
or green, and the blending of the three monotone channels makes all the colors
you see.

When you convert your photo back to black and white, each of these channels
contains varying amounts of details from your photo, depending on the color of
your original subject. So, the green channel might have more detail from your subject's eyelashes, while the red channel may have more detail from the bark on the
tree she's standing under. (Remember, the color channels don't necessarily corre-
spond to the color of the objects you see in your final photo. Or, put another way:
Your camera uses a mixture of red, blue, and green to create what looks like bark
to us humans.) And noise (graininess) often happens much more in one channel
than the others.

The Adjust Intensity sliders (Red, Green, and so on) in the "Convert to Black and White" dialog box let you increase or decrease the presence of each color channel. So you can adjust how prominent various details in your photo are by changing the importance of that color channel in the complete photo. These adjustments can greatly change the appearance of the final conversion. The Contrast slider adjusts the contrast (page 126) for the combined channels.

That's the theory behind those color channel sliders, but fortunately you don't have to understand it to use them effectively. Just be sure you have a good view of your photo (zoom and, if necessary, move the dialog box around), and adjust the sliders till you're happy with what you see. If you plan to print your converted photo, read the box on page 324 for some tips on how to get a good black-and-white print from a color inkjet printer.

> **TIP** Elements gives you an even easier way to convert your photo to black and white, but it's an all-or-nothing scenario—you can't adjust the tones in your image. The Effects panel includes a very nice black-and-white tint effect. Go to the Effects panel (Window → Effects if it's not already visible), and then choose Photo Effects (it's the third icon from the left at the top of the panel). From the drop-down menu, choose Monotone Color, and then double-click the black-and-white apple to apply the effect. Also, some frames in the Frames section of the Content panel (page 474)—like a few of the Color Tint frames—automatically convert your photo to black and white when you place it in the frame. Page 465 explains how to use these frames.

Method Two: Removing Color from Photos

Since one size never fits all, Elements gives you a few other, fundamentally different ways to remove the color from your image. The instructions in the preceding section are usually your best bet when you want to convert a whole photo to black and white. But if you want to drain color from just part of your photo, or if you're looking to do something artistic, like changing a color photo into a drawing or a painting, then you can try one of these three methods:

- **Convert mode.** You may remember from page 51 that you need to choose a color mode for your images: RGB, Bitmap, or Grayscale. You can remove the color from your photo by changing its mode to Grayscale: Choose Image → Mode → Grayscale. This method is quick, but it's also a bit destructive, since you can't apply it to a layer—your entire photo is either grayscale or not.

- **Remove Color.** You can keep your photo as an RGB file and drain the color from it by going to Enhance → Adjust Color → Remove Color (or pressing Shift+Ctrl+U). This command removes the color only from the active layer, so if your photo has more than one layer, then you need to flatten it first (Layer → Flatten Image), or the other layers keep their color.

Remove Color is really just another way to completely desaturate your photo—just as you might when using the Hue/Saturation command (described next). Remove Color is faster, but you don't get as much control as with the Hue/Saturation command. Figure 10-2 shows the difference between applying the Remove Color command and converting your image to grayscale.

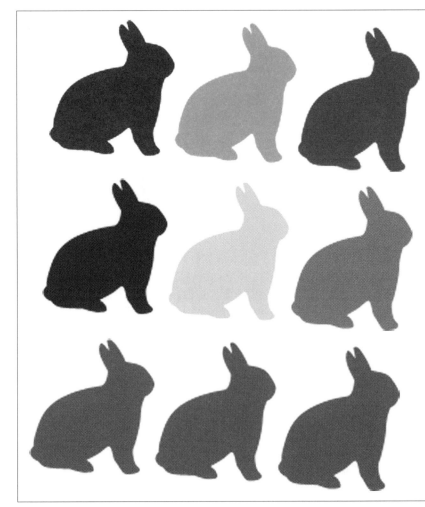

Figure 10-2:
Uncoloring your photo can generate very different results depending on the method you use.

Top: Each of these rabbits has a pure color value of 255. In other words, you're looking at rabbits that are 100 percent blue, green, and red (respectively), with zero as the value for the other two channels.

Middle: The same images converted to grayscale (Image → Mode → Grayscale).

Bottom: Using the Remove Color command gives you a very different result.

- **Hue/Saturation.** Another option is to call up the Hue/Saturation dialog box (page 306) and move the Saturation slider all the way to the left, or type *–100* into the Saturation box. The advantage of this method is that if you don't care for the shade of gray you get, then you can desaturate each color channel separately by using the drop-down menu in the dialog box. With this method, you can tweak your settings a bit to eliminate any color cast you may get from your printer.

Digital Black and White

If you love black-and-white photography, there's good news for you in the digital world: The quality of digital black-and-white printing is improving by leaps and bounds, and now you can get decent black-and-white photos from even some of the lowest-priced printers.

For all the wonders of digitizing, though, there's still nothing that can exactly duplicate the effect of a traditional silver print—although digital printing has made great strides in the past few years.

If you want to print lots of black-and-white photos, you may want to look into buying a photo printer that lets you substitute several shades of gray for your color cartridges. These special inks are constantly improving, and you can get much better prints now than you could even a year or two ago. You can buy special grayscale ink cartridge sets for even inexpensive inkjet printers, and more and more printer drivers have settings for grayscale printing. (Printer driver controls appear when you launch the Elements Print dialog box, as explained on page 488.)

TIP   If you're planning to print the results of your conversion, the paper you use can make a *big* difference in the gray tones you get. If you don't like the results from your usual paper, try a different weight or brand. You'll need to experiment because the inks for different printer models interact differently with different brands of paper.

Creating Spot Color

Removing almost all the color from a photo but leaving one or two objects in vivid tones, called *spot color*, is a very effective artistic device that's long been popular in the print industry. (In the commercial printing business, the term "spot color" refers instead to the use of special inks for a particular color in a multicolor image.)

Figure 10-3 shows an example of spot color. To practice the maneuvers you're about to learn, download the photo (*caboose.jpg*) from the Missing CD page at *www.missingmanuals.com*.

This section walks you through four of the easiest methods to create spot color. (The fifth way, explained earlier in this chapter [page 319], is to select the area you want to make black and white, and then to use the "Convert to Black and White" feature.) You can paint out color, erase your way back to color, change only a selected area to black and white, or use an Adjustment layer. With that last method, you'll also learn how to edit the Adjustment layer's layer mask so you can control which area the adjustment affects.

The end result looks the same no matter which method you choose. Just pick the one you find easiest for the particular photo you want to change.

TIP   If you have a newish digital camera, check your special effects settings for a spot or accent color setting. Many cameras can now create a black-and-white image with only one shade left in color.

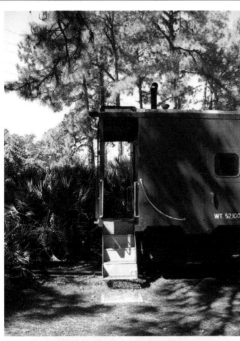

Figure 10-3:
With Elements, you can easily remove color from only part of an image.

Top: Here, the photo is a regular color image.

Bottom: The color is gone from everything except the caboose. This section teaches you four easy methods for removing color.

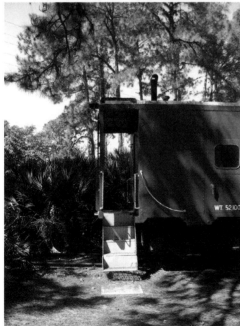

Brushing Away Color

Creating black-and-white areas in a color photo is super easy in Elements. You can use the Smart Brush to convert an area to black and white while making your selection (see Figure 10-4). In other words, you paint the object you want to make black and white, and Elements selects and converts it—all while preserving the color in the rest of your photo. If you want to keep most of your image in color while converting only small portions of it to black and white, or vice versa, definitely try this method first.

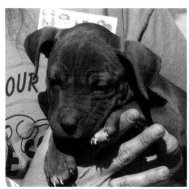 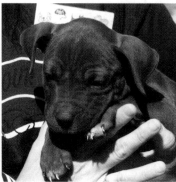

Figure 10-4:
With the Smart Brush, converting part of your photo to black and white is as simple as making a selection.

Left: The puppy is really cute, but the bright blue shirt draws your eye away from him.

Right: Drag over the puppy with the Smart Brush with the Inverse option turned on, and he stays in color while the rest of the photo turns black and white.

To paint away color with the Smart Brush:

1. **Open a photo in Full Edit mode, and then activate the Smart Brush.**

   Press F, or click its icon in the Tools panel, and then choose the brush from the pop-out menu. The Smart Brush puts its changes on their own layer, so you don't need to create a duplicate layer before using it.

   NOTE   You can also do this in Quick Fix, but you don't get a choice of styles, so skip step 2 if you do it there. (You also can't edit the settings later for conversions made in Quick Fix. If you try to do that, Elements displays an error message.)

2. **Choose the style of black-and-white conversion you want.**

   In the Options bar, at the right end of the Smart Brush's options, you'll see a small thumbnail. This is actually the pop-out menu for the Smart Brush presets (which Adobe calls Smart Paint). Click the thumbnail and then, in the preset palette that appears, click the drop-down menu and choose "Black and White". Then click the thumbnail that looks most like what you want. (If you don't like it once it's applied, you can always change it later.) Elements has a number of different conversion styles, and the names don't mean much, really. It's best to go by the thumbnail preview when choosing a style.

3. **Drag over the object that you want to make black and white.**

The Smart Brush should select the object and convert it, all in one go. If you have a hard time getting a good selection, then go back to Elements' main Tools panel and use the Detail Smart Brush (page 211) instead. (That one works like the regular Selection brush, changing only the area directly under the cursor, so you have to do more work, but you get a more accurate selection.)

That's all there is to it. If you don't like the conversion style you've chosen, or want to change the area the brush affects, just click the pin that appears when the Smart Brush is active, and then make your changes. (See page 212 for more about how to fine-tune Smart Brush edits.) You can also adjust the affected area by editing the Smart Brush's layer mask, as explained on page 329.

The Smart Brush is great when you want a photo that's mostly in color with only a small area of black and white. If you want the opposite—a photo that's mostly black and white with only a small area of color—brush over the area you want to keep in color and then, in the Options bar, turn on the Inverse checkbox, which reverses the area changed by the effect. The part of your image you made black and white gets recolored, while the rest of the photo (where you didn't brush) turns black and white. You can also use one of the methods listed in the following sections.

NOTE   The black-and-white conversion settings aren't always editable. Instead, you may see a confusing message that the Adjustment layer was created in Photoshop, even though you just created it in Elements. Adobe uses the Smart Brush to make some Photoshop-only conversion styles available to you so you can apply them but not tweak them once you're done, because Elements can't edit those styles.

Erasing Colors from a Duplicate Layer

You can also easily remove colors from parts of your image with the Eraser tool. (See page 387 for more about Elements' different erasers.) Using this method, you place a color-free layer over your colored original, and then erase bits of the top layer to let the color below show through. Here's how:

1. **Make a duplicate layer.**

Press Ctrl+J or go to Layer → Duplicate Layer. This layer is going to be black and white.

2. **Remove the color from the new top layer.**

Make sure the top layer (the new one you just created) is the active layer, and then go to Enhance → "Convert to Black and White", or to Enhance → Adjust Color → Remove Color. You should now see only a black-and-white image.

3. **Erase the areas on the top layer where you want to see color.**

Use the Eraser tool (page 387) to remove parts of the top layer so the colored layer underneath shows through. Usually you'll get the best results with a fairly soft brush.

If you want an image that's mostly colored with only a few black-and-white areas, then reverse this technique: Remove the color from the bottom layer and leave the top layer in color; then erase as described above.

When you're finished, you can flatten the layers if you want. But by keeping them separate, you still have the option of going back and erasing more of the top layer later on, or of starting over by trashing the layer you erased and making a new duplicate of the bottom layer.

Removing Color from Selections

If you don't want to have multiple layers, you can also make a selection and then use the Enhance menu's "Convert to Black and White" option or the Remove Color command. Just make sure you save your image as a version (page 68) or perform this technique on a copy if your photo isn't in the Organizer—you don't want to risk wrecking your original photo.

While the Smart Brush is the handiest tool for uncoloring small areas, as explained above, the method described here is best if you don't like any of the Smart Paint presets or if you're dead set against having a new layer.

The process for changing a selected area to black and white is simple:

1. **Mask out the area of your image where you want to keep the color.**

   Use the Selection brush in Mask mode (see page 147) to paint a mask over the area where you want to *keep* the color, to protect it from being changed in step 2. In other words, you'll make everything black and white *except* where you paint with the Selection brush.

   If you want to keep color in most of your photo and remove color from only one or two objects, then paint over them with the Selection brush in Selection mode instead, or use the Quick Selection tool.

2. **Remove the color from the selected area.**

   Go to Enhance → "Convert to Black and White", or to Enhance → Adjust Color → Remove Color, or press Shift+Ctrl+U. The color disappears from the areas not protected by the mask, but the area under the mask is untouched. (You can also perform this step by going to Enhance → Adjust Color → Adjust Hue/Saturation, and then moving the Saturation slider all the way to the left.)

You should see a photo with color only in the areas that you didn't select. This method is the least flexible of all the ones described in this chapter because once you close your image, the change is permanent. That's why you don't want to use this method on your original photo.

Using an Adjustment Layer and the Saturation Slider

If you want to keep your options open so you can change your mind about which areas to keep in color, and you don't like any of the Smart Brush presets, you can remove color with a Hue/Saturation Adjustment layer. This method is the most flexible (though it doesn't offer you the tone adjustments you can make with the Enhance menu's "Convert to Black and White" option). Using an Adjustment layer lets you both add and subtract areas of color later if you like. Here's what you do:

1. **Select the area where you want to remove the color.**

   Use any Selection tool you like (see Chapter 5 for more about Selection tools). If you think it would be easier to select the area where you want to keep the color, do that and then press Shift+Ctrl+I to invert your selection so the area that's going to lose the color is selected instead.

2. **Create a Hue/Saturation Adjustment layer.**

   Go to Layer → New Adjustment Layer → Hue/Saturation, or click the Layers panel's New Adjustment Layer icon (the half-black, half-white circle), and then choose Hue/Saturation.

3. **In the Hue/Saturation dialog box that appears, remove the color.**

   Move the Saturation slider all the way to the left to remove the color.

Why is this method better? For one thing, you can always discard the Adjustment layer if you change your mind. But that's not all: You can also edit the Adjustment layer's layer mask (see page 196 for more about layer masks) to change which parts of the photo are in color, even days or weeks later.

Remember the caboose image from Figure 10-3 (page 325)? Say you drained the color from everything except the caboose itself by using a Hue/Saturation Adjustment layer. But then you change your mind and want to leave the trees in color. Or maybe you wish you'd made the stairs black and white. You can easily fix all that by editing the layer mask. The next section tells you how.

Editing a layer mask

Elements lets you make changes to an Adjustment layer's layer mask anytime—as long as the layer hasn't been merged into another layer and the image hasn't been flattened. For example, you may want to edit your layer mask if you think your original selection needs some cleaning up, or if you want to change which area the Adjustment layer affects. You can use this same technique to change the area affected by a Smart Brush adjustment, too, although usually it's simpler just to click the pin in the image and activate the layer mask that way (see page 213 for more details on how all *that* works).

> **NOTE**   Remember that masking something means it *won't* be affected by a change. So the area that shows up in black or red on your layer mask is the area that isn't going to be changed by your adjustment. If you don't see any black or red when looking at a layer mask, then the Adjustment layer is going to change your whole photo.

You can work on the mask by painting directly in the image window, or make the layer mask visible and work in either of two special mask views, which are sometimes helpful when you have tricky edges, or if you need to check for missed spots. Here's the simplest way to make changes to the area covered by a layer mask:

1. **Make sure the Adjustment layer is the active layer.**

   If it isn't, then click it in the Layers panel. (This step is important: If the Adjustment layer isn't the active layer, you may wind up just adding paint to the actual image.)

2. **Set your Foreground and Background colors to black and white.**

   Just press D and Elements makes black the Foreground color and white the Background color. If you want to paint with white, press X to swap the colors so that white (the Background color) becomes the Foreground color.

3. **Paint directly on your image.**

   Use the Brush tool to paint on the image. Paint an area black to *keep* it from being affected by the adjustment. Paint an area white to include it in the area affected by the adjustment. In other words, black masks an area, while white increases your selected area.

   You can also use the Selection tools (the same way you would on any other selection) to change the mask's area. Just keep in mind that what's selected gets changed by the adjustment, while what's not selected doesn't change. (See Chapter 5 if you need help making selections.) If you watch the layer mask's thumbnail in the Layers panel, then you'll see that it changes to show where you've painted.

To make a layer mask visible, click it in the Layers panel. Elements gives you a choice of two different ways to see the masked area, as shown in Figure 10-5. Just Alt-click the right-hand thumbnail (the one *without* the gears on it) for the Adjustment layer in the Layers panel to see the black layer mask (instead of your photo) in the image window. Add the Shift key when you click to see a red overlay on the photo instead of the black-and-white view. Press the same keys again to get back to a regular view of your image.

The black mask view shows only the mask itself, not your photo beneath it. This is a good choice when checking to see how clean the edges of your selection are. But if you're adding or subtracting areas of your photo, then choose the red overlay view so you can see the objects in your photo as you paint over them. You can use the method described above to paint in either view.

That's all there is to it, though you can also edit a layer mask in other ways: You can use shades of gray to adjust the *transparency* of the mask. When you paint on your mask with gray, you can change the opacity of the changes made by the Adjustment layer. So you can let a little color show through the mask, for instance, without letting the full vividness of the color come through. Figure 10-6 shows an example of how you'd use this technique. The lighter the shade of gray you use, the more color shows through.

Figure 10-5:
Elements lets you edit your layer mask and gives you two different ways to see it. Here are two different views of the layer mask from Figure 10-3.

Top: To see the masked area in black, Alt-click the layer's right-hand thumbnail in the Layers panel.

Bottom: To see the masked area in red instead, Alt-Shift-click the layer's right-hand thumbnail.

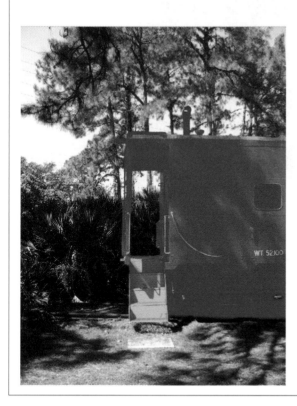

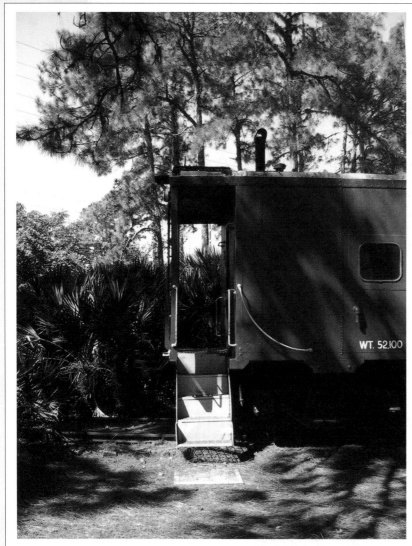

Figure 10-6:
By painting with different shades of gray on the layer mask, you can make the effect of the adjustment partially transparent. Here, a fairly light gray was used to paint over the trees and ground on the left side of the image so that a little green and brown shows through, but it's not the bright, saturated color of the original photo. (Only the left side of the image was painted so you can see the contrast with what was there before.)

Colorizing Black-and-White Photos

So far, you've read about ways to make all or part of a color photo black and white. But what about when you've got a black-and-white photo and you want to add color to it? Elements makes that easy (or at least possible). For instance, you can give an old photo the sort of hand-tinted effect you sometimes see in antique prints, as shown in Figure 10-7.

You can easily color things with Elements. But before you start tinting a photo, first make any needed repairs. See page 293 for repair strategies. For fixes to the exposure, see page 207.

Hints for Coloring Old Photographs

If you want to add some color to an antique black-and-white image, it's easier to put each part of a face that you're going to color—lips, eyes, cheek color, skin—on a separate layer than to try to control different shades on one layer. That way, you can change just one color later without a lot of hassle. (You can always merge the layers—Layer → Merge Visible, or Merge Down—later when you know for sure that you're done.) Here are some other tips when you're aiming for that 19th-century look:

- If you want to create the effect of a photo that was hand-colored a century ago, paint at less than 100-percent opacity—the tinting on old photos is very transparent.

- If you select the area before you paint, then you don't have to worry about getting color outside of where you want it, because your paint is confined to your selection.

- Skin colors are really hard to create in the Color Picker. Try sampling skin tones from another photo instead. If it's a family photo, the odds are good that the current generation's basic skin tones are reasonably close to Great Granddad's. (If you're comfortable using Elements' more advanced features, a gradient map [page 438] can be an excellent way to create realistic skin shading, although it usually takes plenty of gradient editing to get things just right.)

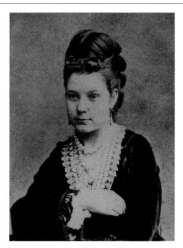 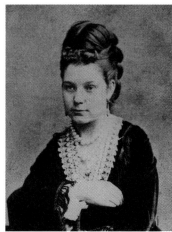

Figure 10-7:
Left: If you decide to color an old black-and-white or sepia photo, put each color on its own layer. That way you can adjust the transparency or change the hue or saturation of one color without changing the other colors, too.

Right: A very low opacity is enough for really old photos like this one if you want to give the impression of a print that was hand-colored.

Once your image is in good shape, here's how to color it:

1. **Make sure your photo is in RGB mode.**

   Go to Image → Mode → RGB Color. Your photo has to be in RGB mode or you can't color it.

2. **Create a new layer in Color blend mode.**

   Go to Layer → New → Layer and select Color as the layer's mode. With the layer in Color mode, you can paint on the layer, and the image's details still show through.

3. **Paint on the layer.**

   Use the Brush tool (page 369) and choose a color in the Tools panel's Foreground color square (page 231). Keep changing the foreground color as much as you need to. If the coverage is too heavy, then in the Options bar, reduce the brush's opacity.

You can also paint directly on the original layer (try switching the brush's blend mode to Color for this). But with that method, you'll find it far more difficult to fix things if you make a mistake when you're well into your project. Using the original layer also doesn't give you much of an out if you decide that the lip color you painted first doesn't look so great with the skin color you just chose.

The methods just described are handy for when you want to add lots of different colors to a photo, but if you want to add only a single color to part of the photo, the easiest way is to use the Smart Brush:

1. **Be sure your photo is in RGB mode.**

   Go to Image → Mode → RGB Color. (If you're photo *isn't* in RGB mode, the Smart Brush only paints in shades of gray rather than in the color you select.)

2. **Activate the Smart Brush, and then choose a color to paint with.**

   Press F or click the Smart Brush in the Tools panel, and then go to the Smart Paint setting in the Options bar (click the thumbnail to the right of Refine Edge) and then, on the palette that appears, choose the Color drop-down menu. Look through the menu thumbnails, and select the color you want.

3. **Drag over what you want to color.**

   The Smart Brush automatically creates your selection and colors it. If you don't get a good selection with the regular Smart Brush, switch to the Detail Smart Brush.

4. **Tweak the effect.**

   The color choices tend to be pretty heavy, so you may prefer to go to the Layers panel and reduce the opacity of the Smart Brush layer (see page 180 for more about layer opacity).

The Smart Brush works well if you happen to like one of the available color choices. But if you don't like any of the colors it offers, then use the new layer method described earlier in this section, which is much more flexible, since you can choose any color you want.

Tinting a Whole Photo

You can give an entire photo a single color tint all over, even if the original is a grayscale photo. Tinting is a great way to create a variety of different moods.

You have two basic ways to tint photos. (Actually, there are a lot more than two, but two should get you started.) The first method described here (Layer style) is faster, but the second (Colorize) lets you tweak your settings more. Figure 10-8 shows the result of using the Layer style method on a color photo. (For a more subtle effect, you can also use Photo Filters, described on page 273.) Photo Effects also has some terrific monotone tint effects that are explained on page 420.

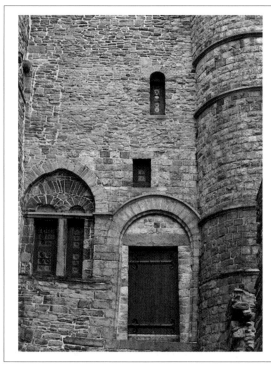

Figure 10-8:
You can most easily create a monochrome color scheme for your photo with the Photographic Effects Layer styles, which are explained in Chapter 13. This image had the Teal Tone style applied to the original color photo. Elements removed the existing color and recolored the image in one click. The downside is that you can't edit the color once you're done if you decide you'd rather have, say, orange instead.

For either method, if you want to keep the original color (or lack thereof) in part of your photo, then use the Selection brush in Mask mode (page 147) to mask out the area you don't want to change.

> **TIP** Some of the frame effects in the Content panel automatically add a tint to your photo when you apply them. The Effects panel also has some handy monochrome tint effects in its Photo Effects section.

Using a Layer style

Although many people never dig down far enough to find them, Adobe gives you some Photographic Effects Layer styles that make tinting a photo as easy as double-clicking. You'll learn more about Layer styles on page 423, but this section tells you all you need to know to use the Photographic styles. It's a simple process:

1. **Create a duplicate layer.**

   Go to Layer → Duplicate Layer or press Ctrl+J. (If you don't create a duplicate layer and your original has only a Background layer, then you'll get asked to convert it to a layer when you apply the style; click Yes.)

2. **If necessary, change the image's mode to RGB.**

Go to Image → Mode → RGB Color. With this method, it doesn't matter if your original is in color or not. The Layer style gets rid of the original color and tints the photo all at the same time.

3. **Choose a Layer style.**

Go to the Effects panel and, at the top of the panel, click the Layer Styles icon, which looks like two overlapping rectangles. Then, from the panel's drop-down menu, choose Photographic Effects. Double-click the color square you like, and drag it onto the photo; or click it once in the panel, and then click the Apply button. You can click around and try different colors to see which you prefer. Undo (Ctrl+Z) after each style that you try.

4. **When you like what you see, you're done.**

The drawback to this method is that you can't easily go back and edit the color you get from the Layer style. Even if you call up the Style Settings dialog box (see page 426), you don't get any active checkboxes, because these styles don't use those settings. Instead, you'd need to use a Hue/Saturation adjustment (see page 306) or Color Variations (page 229) to go back later and change the Layer style's tint color.

The Content panel's tint effects

The Content panel includes some frames that automatically apply a tint to your photo, as shown in Figure 10-9. These range from simple all-over colors like Sepia to fading gradients. (Page 427 has more about gradients.)

You can read more about using the Content panel's frames on page 465. To tint your photo, choose Type → Frames, and then scroll down toward the bottom of the list of thumbnails.

The Photo Effects section of the Effects panel also has some very effective color tints. Page 420 tells you how to apply Effects.

Using Colorize

You can use the Colorize checkbox in the Hue/Saturation dialog box or Adjustments panel settings to add a color tint to a grayscale photo or to change the color of a photo that already has color in it. With this method, you can choose any color you like, as opposed to the limited color choices of the Layer styles explained in the previous section. You can also adjust the intensity of the color with the Saturation slider once you've selected the shade you want.

Figure 10-10 explains how the Colorize setting changes the way the Hue/Saturation command works.

Here's how to work with the Colorize checkbox:

1. **Make sure your photo is in RGB mode.**

Go to Image → Mode → RGB Color.

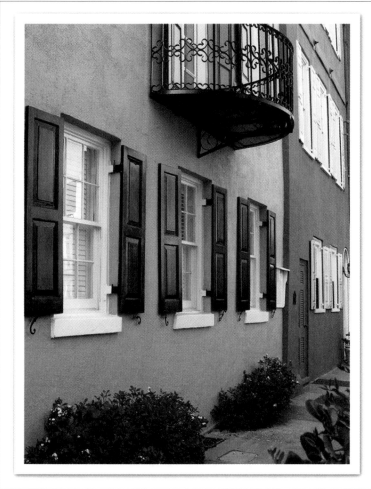

Figure 10-9:
Using the Content panel, you can apply elaborate effects, like this fading gradient, drop shadow, and frame, with just a double-click. The effect used here is the Color Tint Blue Fadeout 20px.

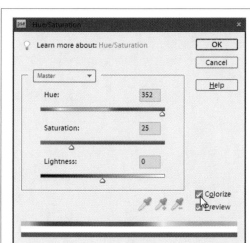

Figure 10-10:
If you want to color something that doesn't have any color information in it, like a white shirt or a grayscale image, then in the Hue/Saturation dialog box, turn on Colorize (where the cursor is here) to add color to the image. If you don't turn on the Colorize checkbox, then you can adjust the hue, saturation, and lightness of white all day long—all you'll do is go from white to gray to black because there's no color info there for Elements to work with. Also, if something is pure white (that is, contains no color info at all), then you may need to darken it by moving the Lightness slider to the left before any color shows up.

2. **Remove the photo's color, if necessary.**

   Press Shift+Ctrl+U to remove the color. Do this if the photo has become yellowed or discolored from age, for example. If your whites are really dingy, then you might want to make a Levels adjustment (page 221) to brighten them back up before removing the color.

3. **Colorize your photo on a new layer.**

   Go to Layer → New Adjustment Layer → Hue/Saturation, and then, in the Adjustments panel, turn on the Colorize checkbox. When you turn this setting on, your image gets filled with the current Foreground color. If you don't like it, that's fine—you're going to change it right now.

4. **Adjust the color until it looks the way you want it to.**

   Move the Hue, Saturation, and Lightness sliders until you find the look you want, and then click OK. Figure 10-11 shows the results.

   TIP Want to turn a full-color photo to a monotone image in a hurry? Just turn on the Colorize checkbox—you don't need to remove the color first. Colorize automatically reduces your photo to just one color. The advantage to using this method rather than a layer style is that you can use the sliders to pick any color you want.

If you selected and masked an area, then that part should still show the original color.

You can change your mind about the colorizing by double-clicking the layer's leftmost icon (the one with the gears on it) in the Layers panel. That brings up the Hue/Saturation dialog box again so you can change your settings. And you can also edit the layer mask, as described on page 329, if you want to change the area that's affected by the Adjustment layer.

When you're done, if you merge layers (or press Ctrl+Alt+Shift+E to produce a new merged layer above the existing layers), then you can use Levels (page 221), Color Variations (page 229), and the other color-editing tools to tweak the tint effect.

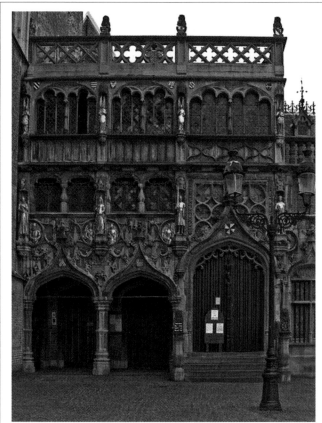

Figure 10-11:
This photo was tinted purple by turning on the Colorize checkbox in the Hue/Saturation dialog box. The gold ornaments were masked out so that they stay in full color.

Photomerge: Creating Panoramas, Group Shots, and More

Everyone's had the experience of trying to photograph an awesome view—a city skyline or a mountain range, say—only to find the whole scene won't fit into one picture because it's just too wide. Elements, once again, comes to the rescue. With the Photomerge command, you can stitch together a group of photos you shot while panning across the horizon to create a panorama that's much larger than any single photo your camera can take. Panoramas can become addictive once you've tried them, and they're a great way to get those wide, wide shots that are beyond the capability of your camera lens.

Elements includes the same great Photomerge feature that's part of Photoshop, which makes it incredibly easy to create super panoramas. Not only that, but Adobe also gives you a couple of fun twists on Photomerge that are unique to Elements: Faces and Group Shot, which let you easily move features from one face to another and replace folks in group photos. And Elements has yet another kind of merge: Scene Cleaner, for all those times when your almost-perfect vacation shot is spoiled by strangers walking into your perfectly composed scene.

> **NOTE**   Elements 8 includes yet another kind of merge: Photomerge Exposure, which lets you blend differently exposed versions of the same scene (like photos taken using your camera's exposure bracketing feature) to create one image that's perfectly exposed from the deepest shadows to the brightest highlights. You can learn all about it on page 267.

If you're into photographing buildings (especially tall ones), then you know that you often need some kind of perspective correction: The building appears to lean backward or sideways as a result of distortion caused by your camera's lens. This chapter teaches you how to use the Correct Camera Distortion filter to straighten things. You'll also learn how to use the Transform commands to adjust or warp your images.

Creating Panoramas

It's incredibly simple to make fabulous panoramas in Elements. (If you're upgrading from Elements 5 or earlier, then you know that lots of other programs made better, easier panoramas than Elements used to. Not anymore: Elements' Photomerge feature does an amazing job, totally automatically.) To make a panorama in Elements, just tell the program which photos you want to use, and Elements automatically stitches them together into a perfect panorama (this works about 99 percent of the time). Figure 11-1 shows what a great job it does.

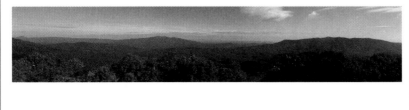

Figure 11-1:
For subjects like the Smoky Mountains, you can never capture the whole scene in one shot. Here's a six-photo panorama made with Photomerge. The individual photos had huge variations in exposure and were taken without a tripod. Elements took the images—straight from the camera with no adjusting—and blended them seamlessly.

Elements can merge as many photos as you want to include in a panorama. The only real size limitation comes when you want to print your compositions: If you create a five-photo horizontal panorama but your paper is letter size, then your printout will only be a couple of inches high, even if you rotate the panorama to print lengthwise. However, you can buy printers with attachments that let you print on rolls of paper, so that there's no limit to the longest dimension of your panorama. (These printers are very popular with panorama addicts.) You can also use an online printing service, like the Kodak EasyShare Gallery, to get larger prints than you can make at home. See page 484 for more about how to order online prints via the Organizer.

You'll get the best results creating a panorama if you plan ahead when shooting your photos. The pictures should be side by side, of course, and they should overlap each other by at least 30 percent. Also, you'll minimize the biggest panorama problem—matching the color in your photos—if you make sure they all have identical exposures. While Elements can do a lot to blend exposures that don't match well, for the best panorama, adjust your photos *before* you start creating a panorama, as explained in Figure 11-2. (The box on page 347 has more tips for taking merge-ready shots.)

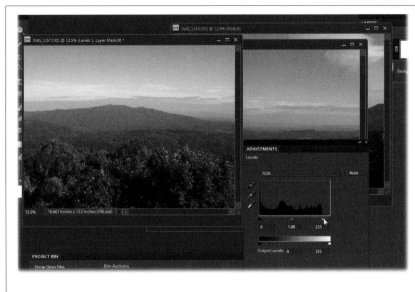

Figure 11-2:
While Elements did a very credible job with the panorama in Figure 11-1, if you look closely, you can see there's some variation in lighting between the end photos and the middle section. For even better results, use Elements to correct your photos so that the colors are as close as possible before beginning your panorama. It helps to keep them side by side so you can compare them as you work. (See page 97 to learn how to arrange your photos on the Elements desktop.)

When you've got all the photos you want to combine looking good, you're ready to create a panorama. Just follow these steps:

1. **Start your merge.**

   In the Editor, go to File → New → Photomerge Panorama. The Photomerge dialog box appears.

2. **Choose your photos.**

   If the photos you want to include are already open, then just click the Add Open Files button. Otherwise, in the drop-down menu, choose Files or Folder; then click the Browse button to navigate to the ones you want. As you click them in the window that appears, Elements adds them to the list in the Photomerge dialog box. Add more files by clicking Browse again. To remove a file, click it in the dialog box's list, and then click the Remove button.

   NOTE   You can merge directly from Raw files, although you don't have any controls for adjusting the file conversions. Photomerge works only with 8-bit files, so if you have 16-bit files, it asks if you want to convert them when it begins merging. For faster Raw merges, set the Raw converter to 8 bits (page 263) before you start.

3. **From the Layout list on the left side of the dialog box, choose a merge style.**

   Usually all you need to do is choose Auto, the first Layout option. When you click OK, your completed panorama is darned near perfect. You also get some other merge style choices for use in special situations:

   • **Perspective.** Elements adjusts the other images to match the middle image by using such methods as skewing and other Transform commands to create a realistic view.

- **Cylindrical.** Sometimes when you adjust perspective, you create a panorama shaped like a giant bow tie. Cylindrical mapping corrects this distortion. (It's called "cylindrical" because it gives an effect like looking at the label on a bottle—the middle part seems the largest, and the image gets smaller as it fades into the distance, similar to the label wrapping around the sides of the bottle.) You may want this style for really wide panoramas.

NOTE   If you choose Auto, then Elements may use either Perspective or Cylindrical mapping when it creates your panorama, depending on what it thinks will do the best job for your photos.

- **Reposition Only.** Elements overlaps your photos and blends the exposure, but it doesn't make any changes to the perspective of the images.
- **Interactive Layout.** This style lets you position your images manually. It takes you to a window that's similar to the old Photomerge window in early versions of Elements; the next section explains it in detail.

4. **Click OK to create your panorama.**

Elements whirls into action, combining, adjusting, looking for the most invisible places to put the seams, and whips up a completed panorama for you. That's all there is to it.

NOTE   Elements has a lot of complex calculations to make when creating a panorama, especially if you have lots of images or if there are big exposure differences between the photos, so it may take awhile. Don't assume that Elements is stuck; give it time to think about what it's doing. It may need a few minutes to finish up.

You'll probably want to crop your panorama (page 89), but otherwise, you're all done. You can use any of Elements' editing tools on the final panorama once Photomerge is through, if you like. You can do anything to a panorama that you can do to any other photo. The new Recompose tool (page 297) is especially useful for adjusting the proportions of panoramas, if you need to do that.

NOTE   Elements has a quirk that may cause the program to give you an out-of-memory error message when you try to save a panorama. If you run into this, just flatten your panorama (Layer → Flatten Image), and you should be able to save it.

Manual Positioning with Interactive Layout

If you need to do some manual positioning of your photos, choose Interactive Layout from the Photomerge dialog box's Layout list. When you click OK, Elements does its best to combine your photos and presents them to you in the window shown in Figure 11-3.

Here you can help Elements blend your photos better. Your panorama in its current state appears in the large preview area, surrounded by special tools to help you get a better merge. On the left side of the window is a special toolbox. The Lightbox, which contains any photos that Elements couldn't figure out how to place, is across the top, and there are special controls down the right side. You can use any combination of these features to improve your panorama.

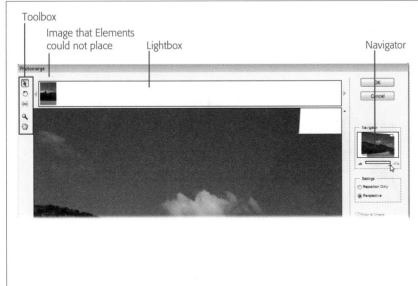

Toolbox

Image that Elements could not place

Lightbox

Navigator

Figure 11-3:
You don't often need to intervene when Elements makes a panorama, but if you want to control the process yourself, Interactive Layout lets you position your photos manually. Note how obvious the differences in exposure are in the merged photos in the graphic. Elements applies Advanced Blending only after you click OK to create your final panorama. Then the obvious exposure banding you see here disappears so you get a smooth merge.

You can manually drag files from the Lightbox into the merged photos, and reposition photos already in your panorama. Just grab them with the Select Image tool (explained below), and then drag them to the correct spot in the merge.

If you try to move a photo and it keeps jumping away from where you've placed it, turn off "Snap to Image" on the right side of the Photomerge window. Then you should be able to put the photo exactly where you want it. However, Elements isn't doing the figuring for you anymore, so use the Zoom tool to get a good look at the alignment afterward. You may need to micro-adjust the photos' exact positions.

There's a little toolbox at the top left of the Photomerge window. Some tools are familiar, and others are unique to panoramas:

- **Select Image.** Use this tool to move individual photos into or out of your merged photo or to reposition them. When the Select Image tool is active, you can drag photos into or out of the Lightbox. Press A or click the tool to activate it.

- **Rotate Image.** Elements normally rotates images automatically when merging them, but if it doesn't or if it guesses wrong, press R to activate this tool, and then click the photo you want to rotate. You see handles on the image, just the way you would with the regular Rotate commands (page 89). Just grab a corner and turn the photo until it fits in properly. Usually, you don't need to drastically change a photo's orientation, but this tool helps you make small changes to line things up better.

• **Set Vanishing Point.** To understand what this tool does, think of standing on a long, straight, country road and looking off into the distance. The point at which the two parallel lines of the road seem to converge and meet the horizon is called the *vanishing point*. Elements' Vanishing Point tool tells Photomerge where you want that point to be in your finished panorama. Knowing the vanishing point helps Elements figure out the correct perspective. Press V to activate this tool. Figure 11-4 shows an example of how it can change your results.

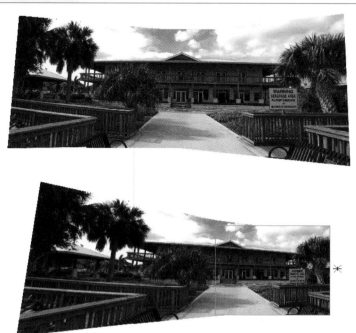

Figure 11-4:
You can radically alter the perspective of your panorama by selecting a vanishing point.

Top: The result of clicking the merge's center photo.

Bottom: The result of clicking the right-hand photo. Note that the tool selects only a particular image in the merge group, not an actual point within that image. You can click any photo to put your vanishing point there, but then if you try to tweak it by clicking a higher or lower point within the same photo, nothing happens. To change the vanishing point you've set, just click a different photo.

• **Zoom tool.** This is the same Zoom tool (page 100) you find everywhere else in Elements. Click the magnifying glass in the Toolbox or press Z to activate it.

• **Move View tool.** You use this tool exactly the way you use the Hand tool (page 102) when you need to scoot your *entire* panorama around to see a different part of it. Click the hand icon in the Toolbox or press H to activate it. (If you want to move just one photo within your panorama, use the Select Image tool instead.)

To control your onscreen view of your panorama, use the Navigator on the right side of the Photomerge window. It works just like the regular Navigator described on page 103. Move the slider to resize your view of the panorama. Drag to the right to zoom in on one area, or to the left to shrink the view so that you can see the whole thing at once. If you want to target a particular spot in your merge, then drag the Navigator's red rectangle to control the area that's onscreen.

Also, at the bottom and right side of the edge of the preview are two tiny arrows. Click one to move in the direction the arrow's pointing (for example, click the right-facing arrow to slide your image to the right). At certain view sizes, you'll also see a square, something like a checkbox, at the bottom or right side of the image. You can drag that like a handle to manipulate the view, too.

IN THE FIELD

Shooting Tips for Good Merges

The most important part of creating an impressive and plausible panorama starts before you even launch Elements. You can save yourself a lot of grief by planning ahead when shooting photos you want to combine.

Most of the time, you know *before* you shoot that you'll want to merge your photos. (You don't often say, "Wow, I can't believe I've got seven photos of the SpongeBob SquarePants balloon at the Thanksgiving Day parade that just happen to be exactly in line and have a 30-percent overlap between each one! Guess I'll try a merge.")

So, before you take pictures for a panorama, set your camera to be as much in manual mode as possible. The biggest headache in panorama making is trying to get the exposure, color, brightness, and so on to blend seamlessly. (Elements is darned good at blending the outlines of the objects in your photos.) So lock your camera settings to make the exposure of each image as similar as possible. Even on small digital cameras that don't have much in the way of manual controls, you may have some kind of panorama setting, like Canon's Stitch Assist mode, that does the same thing.

(Your camera may actually be able to make merges that are at least as good as what Elements can do, because the camera does the image-blending internally. Check out whether your model has a panorama feature.)

The more your photos overlap, the better. Elements does what it can with what you give it, but it's really happy if about a third of each image overlaps with the next.

Use a tripod if you have one, and *pan heads* (tripod heads that let you swivel your camera in an absolutely straight line) were made for panoramas. Actually, as long as your shots aren't wildly out of line, Elements can usually cope. But you may have to do quite a bit of cropping to get even edges on the finished result if you don't use a tripod.

Whether you use a tripod or not, keep the camera—rather than the horizon—level to avoid distortion. In other words, focus your attention more on leveling the body of the camera than what you see through the viewfinder. Use the same focal length for each image, and try not to use the zoom, unless it's manual, so that you can keep it exactly the same for every image.

Below the Navigator box are two radio buttons—Reposition Only and Perspective—that you can use to adjust the viewing angle of your panorama:

- **Reposition Only.** This button merely overlaps the edges of your photos, with no changes to the perspective. If you don't like the way the angles in your panorama look, try clicking Perspective instead.

- **Perspective.** If you click this button, Elements tries to apply perspective to your panorama to make it look more realistic. Sometimes the program does a bang-up job, but usually you get better results if you set a vanishing point, as explained earlier (page 346). If you still get a totally weird result, just create the panorama anyway. Then correct the perspective yourself afterward by using one of the Transform commands covered in the next section.

Once you get your photos arranged to your satisfaction, click OK, and Elements creates your final panorama.

> **NOTE** Elements always creates layered panoramas. If you're sending your panorama out for printing, flatten it (Layer → Flatten Image) before doing so, since most commercial printers don't accept layered files. Also, if you enlarge the view of your layered panorama and zoom in on the seams, you may see what look like hairline cracks. Merging or flattening the layers gets rid of these cracks.

Merging Different Faces

Merging isn't just for making panoramas. One of the Elements-only tools that Adobe gives you is Faces, a fun (okay, let's be honest—silly) feature that lets you merge parts of one person's face with another person's face. You can use it to create caricature-like photos, or for things like pasting your new sweetie's face over your old sweetie's face in last year's holiday photo. Figure 11-5 shows an example of what Faces can do. (Elements' other special tools, Group Shot and Scene Cleaner, are explained later in this chapter.)

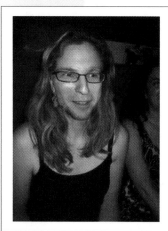

Figure 11-5:
Faces is really just for fun. You can create composite images like this one, and then use the Editor's other tools to make your photo even sillier.

Although you'd be hard pressed to think of a serious use for Faces (it *may* work for something like copying a smile from one photo to another image of the same person with a more serious expression, but the end result may not be top quality), it's fun and simple to use:

1. **Choose the photos to combine.**

   You need to have at least two photos available in the Project bin before you start.

2. **Call up the Faces feature.**

   You can get to it either from File → New → Photomerge Faces, or from Guided Edit → Photomerge → Faces.

A dialog box asks you to choose the photos you want to include. In the Project bin, Ctrl-click to select the photos you want to use, or choose Open All from the dialog box. Elements then opens the Faces window, which has a preview area on the left and an instruction pane on the right.

3. **Choose a Final photo.**

   This photo is the main image into which you're going to paste parts of the face from one or more photos. Just drag a photo from the bin into the Final image area (on the right-hand preview).

4. **Choose your Source photo.**

   This is the photo from which you're going to copy part of the face to move to the Background Image. Double-click it in the Project bin, and it appears in the left-hand preview area. You can copy from many different photos, but you can work only with one Source photo at a time. (When you're done working with one photo, just double-click the next one you want. This way you can use the ears from one photo, the nose from another, and so on.)

5. **Align your photos.**

   This step is important because Elements can't adjust for any differences in size or angle between the two shots. Click the Alignment tool button in the Faces pane, and the three little targets shown in Figure 11-6 appear in each image.

   Position the markers over the eyes and mouth in each photo, and then click the Align Photos button. (If you need help seeing what you're doing, there's a little toolbox on the left with your old friends the Zoom [page 100] and Hand [page 102] tools, so you can reposition the photo for the best view.)

   Elements adjusts the photos so they're the same size and sit at the same angle to make a good blend.

6. **Tell Elements what features to move from the Source image to the Final image.**

   Click the Pencil tool in the Faces pane and, in the Source photo, draw over the area you want to move. In a few seconds, you see the selected area appear in the Final photo. You only need to draw a quick line—don't try to accurately color over all the material you want to move. In the Options bar, you can adjust the size of the Pencil tool if it's hard to see what you're doing, or if it's grabbing too much of the surrounding area.

   If Elements moves too much material from the Source photo, use the Faces Eraser tool to remove part of your line. Watch the preview in the Final image to see how you're changing the selection. If you want to start over, then scroll to the bottom of the right-hand pane and click the Reset button.

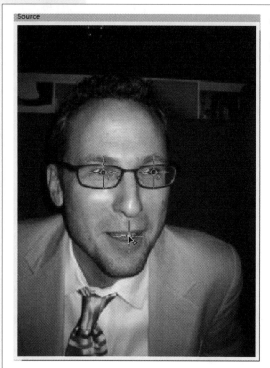

Source

Figure 11-6:
To tell Elements how to align your photos, just drag one of these three little targets over each eye and the mouth in each photo.

7. **When you're happy, click Done.**

Elements creates your merge as a layered file. Now you can edit it using any of the Editor's tools, if you wish. You may want to clean up the edges a bit or to manually clone (page 290) a little more material than Elements moved. And you can make your image even sillier with the Transform commands (page 359), the Liquify filter (page 453), and so on.

You can adjust two settings in the Faces pane:

- **Show Strokes.** If you want to see what you're selecting, then leave this checkbox on.

- **Show Regions.** Turn this on to see a translucent overlay over the Final image, which makes it easier to tell which regions you're copying over from your Source photo. It's something like the overlay option for the Healing brush (page 289) and the Clone Stamp (page 290).

It would be nice if you could use this feature to merge things besides faces, but it doesn't do a very good job of that. Even for faces, if you're doing something important, like repairing an old photo with parts from another picture of the same person, then you may prefer to make your own selections, and to manually move and adjust things (see page 197). But the Faces feature's alignment tools can simplify the process enough that it's worth giving it a try to see if it can do what you want.

Arranging a Group Shot

Have you ever tried taking photos of a whole group of people? Almost every time, you get a photo where everything is perfect—except for that one person with his eyes shut. In another shot, that person is fine, but other people are yawning or looking away from the camera. You probably thought, "Dang, I wish I could move Ed from that photo to this one. Then I'd have a perfect shot."

Adobe hears your wishes, and Group Shot is the result. It's specifically designed for moving one person in a group from one photo to another, similar photo.

You launch Group Shot by going to File → New → Photomerge Group Shot, or Guided Edit → Photomerge → Group Shot. The steps for using Group Shot are the same as for Faces, except that you don't normally need to align the photos, since Group Shot is intended for those situations where you were saying, "Just one more, everybody—and hold it!" as opposed to moving people from photos taken at different times with different angles and lighting.

But if you do need to align your photos, you can do that with the advanced options (click Advanced Options in the right-hand panel to get to them). Just place the markers the same way you do in Faces (see Figure 11-6). Another advanced option is Pixel Blending, which adjusts the moved material to make it closer in tone to the rest of the Final image.

> **NOTE** It would be great if you could use Group Shot for things like creating a photo showing many generations of your family by combining images from photos taken over many years. However, Group Shot moves someone from the Source photo and pastes that person into the same spot in the Final photo, and then creates a composite layer in the completed merge. That means the relocated person is merged into the Background image, and isn't left as an extracted object, which makes it impossible to put that person in a completely different spot. You need to do that the old-fashioned way: by moving each person onto a separate layer (see page 175) and then repositioning everybody where you want them.

Tidying Up with Scene Cleaner

With Scene Cleaner, you can eliminate unwanted people or elements in your photos. Think of all those travel magazine photos that show famous sights in their lonely glory, without any tourists hanging around to clutter up the scene. If you've ever waited patiently for what seems like hours, trying to get a shot of a famous landmark, only to give up as busloads of tourists arrive, you'll appreciate Scene Cleaner.

Or you've probably had this experience when showing your vacation photos: "Here's a shot of Jodi and Taylor at the rim of the Grand Canyon…Oh, those other people—no, no idea who they are. They just got in front of the camera somehow." Scene Cleaner was made to fix photos like those.

Scene Cleaner is easy to use, but you'll get better results if you can plan ahead when taking your photos. To get a people-less landscape, you need to shoot multiple photos from nearly the same angle. All the areas you want to feature should be uninhabited in at least one photo. So, for instance, if you can get one shot of the Statue of Liberty where all the tourists are in the left side of her crown and one where they're in the right side, you're all set. Then, to use Scene Cleaner to create a more perfect world:

1. **In the Editor, open the photos you want to combine.**

   In addition to being taken from nearly the same vantage point, the images should have similar exposures. If a cloud was passing, for instance, so that one photo is bright and one is shadowy, then you'll have to do some fancy touch-ups afterward to blend the tones together. It's usually easier to do this before-hand. Chapter 7 has the full story on exposure correction.

2. **Call up Scene Cleaner.**

   In Full Edit, go to File → New → Photomerge Scene Cleaner, or go to Guided Edit → Photomerge → Scene Cleaner. In either case, you wind up in Guided Edit to create your merged image. Elements automatically aligns your photos, so there may be a slight delay before you see the Scene Cleaner window.

3. **Choose a Final image.**

   This is the base image into which you want to put parts of your other photo(s). Drag the photo you choose from the Project bin into the Final preview area (the right-hand slot).

4. **Choose a Source image.**

   Look through your photos to find a one that has an empty area where the people or objects you want to remove from the Final photo are. Click that photo in the Project bin, and it appears in the Source preview area (the left-hand slot). (As with Faces, you can use many Source images, but you work with only one at a time—move on to the next Source photo when you're done.)

5. **Align your photos manually, if necessary.**

   Usually you don't need to do this, but if Elements didn't do a good job of automatically aligning your photos, click the flippy triangle next to Advanced Options in the right-hand pane (you may have to scroll down to see it), and then click the Alignment tool. You see the three markers described in the section on Faces (page 349). This time, instead of placing them over eyes and mouth, place them over three similar locations in each photo, and then click Align Photos.

6. **Tell Elements what you want to move.**

   If the Pencil tool isn't active, click it in the window's right-hand pane. Then, in the Source image, draw over the area you want to move to the Final photo. Just draw a quick line—Elements figures out the exact area to move. (You can also go to the Final preview, and draw over the area you want to cover—Elements can figure it out either way.)

7. **Adjust the areas if needed.**

   Use the Pencil tool again to add more areas, or the Eraser tool to remove bits if you moved too much. You can use the Eraser in either preview—Source or Final. If you have more than two photos to work with, in the Project bin, click another photo to move it to the Source slot, and then select the area you want. If you need to see the edges of the areas that Elements is moving, then turn on Show Regions, as explained in Figure 11-7.

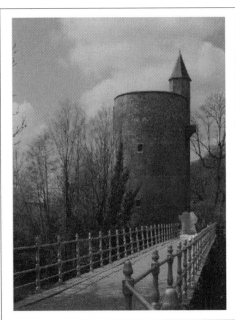

Figure 11-7:
When you turn on the Show Regions checkbox, your photo gets covered with this mask. Here the blue shows the original area from the Final photo, and the yellow represents the section (without tourists) brought over from the Source photo. The mask is helpful if you have a hard time getting exactly the amount of source material you want. (If you look very closely, you still see a bit of an arm left uncovered, since the pencil tool didn't make quite a large enough selection.) With the overlay, you get a better idea of where to erase or add material if you need to.

   If the exposures don't blend well, go the Advanced Options section of the right-hand pane, and turn on the Pixel Blending checkbox for a smoother merge.

8. **When you're happy, click Done.**

   Don't forget to save your work. If you want to start over, click Reset. If you decide to give up on the merge, then click Cancel.

Most of the time, you need only the Pencil tool and the Eraser, but Adobe gives you some additional options to help you out:

- **Show Strokes.** Leave this turned on or you can't see where you're drawing with the tools.

- **Show Regions.** Scene Cleaner actually brings over chunks of the Source image. If you turn on this option, you see a blue-and-yellow overlay showing the exact size of the material you're moving (see Figure 11-7).

- **Alignment Tool.** This lets you manually set the comparison points. Use these points if you don't like Elements automatic choices. Step 5 above explains how to use the Alignment tool.

- **Pixel Blending.** Just as in Faces, you turn on Pixel Blending when there's a discrepancy in color or exposure between your photos, so they combine more seamlessly.

It's not always easy to get enough clear areas to blend, even with multiple photos, but when you have the right kind of source photos, you can create the impression that you and your pals had a private tour of your favorite places.

Correcting Lens Distortion

If you ever photograph buildings, then you know that it can be tough getting good shots with a fixed-lens digital camera. When you get too close to the structure, your lens causes distortion, as shown in Figure 11-8. You can buy special perspective-correcting lenses, but they're expensive (and if you have a pocket camera, they aren't even an option). Fortunately, you can use Elements' Correct Camera Distortion filter to fix photos after you've taken them. It's another very popular Photoshop tool that Adobe transferred over to Elements, minus a couple of advanced options.

Correct Camera Distortion is a terrifically helpful filter, and not just for buildings. You can also use it to correct the slight balloon effect you sometimes see in close-ups of people's faces (especially in shots taken with a wide-angle setting). You can even deploy the filter for creative purposes, like creating the effect of a fisheye lens by pushing the filter's settings to their extremes.

Here are some telltale signs that it's time to summon Correct Camera Distortion:

- You've used the Straighten tool (page 86), but things still don't look right.

- Your horizon is straight, but your photo has no true right angles. In other words, the objects in your photo lean in misleading ways. For instance, buildings lean in from the edges of the frame, or back away from you.

- Every time you straighten to a new reference line, something else gets out of whack. For example, say you keep choosing different lines in your photo that ought to be level, but no matter which one you choose, something else in the photo goes out of plumb.

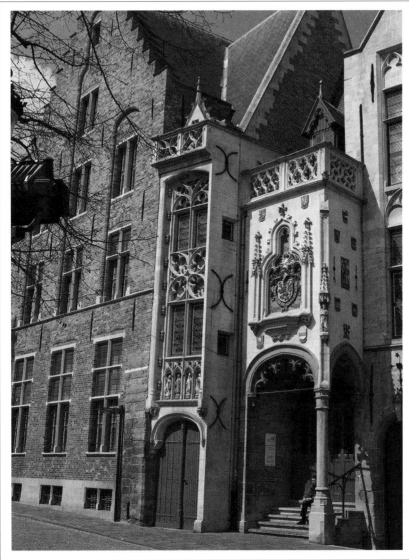

Figure 11-8:
Here's a classic example of a candidate for Elements' Correct Camera Distortion filter. This type of distortion is common when you're using a point-and-shoot camera in a narrow space that doesn't let you get far enough away from your subject. You can fix such problems in a jiffy with the help of this filter.

- If you have a problem with vignetting—a dark, shadowy effect in your photo's corners—you can fix that with Correct Camera Distortion, too. You can also *create* vignetting for special effects.

Adobe's made this filter extremely easy to use. Just follow these steps:

1. **Open a photo, and then go to Filter → Correct Camera Distortion.**

   The large dialog box shown in Figure 11-9 appears.

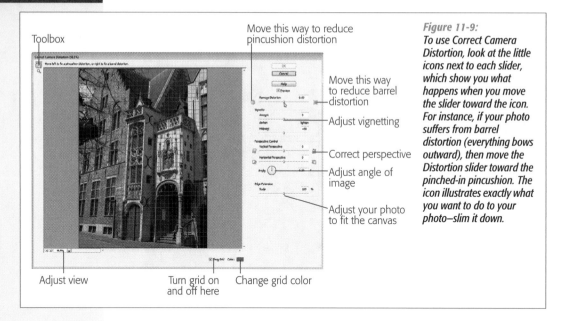

Toolbox

Move this way to reduce pincushion distortion

Move this way to reduce barrel distortion

Adjust vignetting

Correct perspective

Adjust angle of image

Adjust your photo to fit the canvas

Adjust view

Turn grid on and off here

Change grid color

Figure 11-9:
To use Correct Camera Distortion, look at the little icons next to each slider, which show you what happens when you move the slider toward the icon. For instance, if your photo suffers from barrel distortion (everything bows outward), then move the Distortion slider toward the pinched-in pincushion. The icon illustrates exactly what you want to do to your photo—slim it down.

NOTE   Even though Correct Camera Distortion is in the Filter menu, you can't reapply it using the Ctrl+F keyboard shortcut the way you can with most other filters. You always have to select it from the Filter menu.

2. **If necessary, use the Hand tool (page 102) to adjust your photo in the window.**

You want a clear view of a reference line—something you know you want to correct, like the edge of a building.

If the distortion is really bad, this mission may be impossible, but try to find at least one line as closely aligned to the grid as you can, so you have a reference for changing the photo. You can also use the usual view adjustment controls (including zoom in and out buttons) in the dialog box's lower-left corner. The Hand tool adjusts both your photo and the grid. That means you can't use it to position your photo *relative* to the grid. Also, the Hand tool doesn't do anything unless you set the view to more than 100%.

The Show Grid checkbox lets you turn the grid on and off, but since you're going to be aligning your image, you'll almost always want to keep it on. To change the color of the grid, click the Color box next to the Show Grid checkbox.

3. **Make your adjustments.**

This filter lets you fix three different kinds of problems: barrel/pincushion distortion, vignetting, and perspective problems. These errors are the ones you're most likely to run into, and correcting them is as easy as dragging sliders around. The small icons on each side of some of the sliders show you how your photo will change if you move in that direction. You may need to make only one adjustment, or you may need many (the bulleted list that follows helps you decide which controls to use).

Watch the grid carefully to see how things are lining up. When you get everything straightened to your satisfaction, you're done. If you want to start over, Alt-click the Cancel button to change it to a Reset button and return your photo to the state it was in when you summoned this filter.

4. **Scale your photo, if you wish.**

As you make your adjustments, you'll probably notice some empty space appearing on either side of your canvas (the background area of your file). This often happens when Elements pinches and stretches your photo to correct the distortion. To make things right, you've got two options. You can click OK now, and then crop the photo yourself (using any of the options you learned about back on page 89). Or, you can stay here and use the Edge Extension slider to enlarge your photo so that it fills up the window. If you use this second method, then Elements crops some of the photo.

Edge Extension is handy, but gives you little control over how the photo gets cropped. After all the effort you put into using this filter, you may as well do your own cropping to get the best possible results.

5. **Click OK to apply your changes.**

If you don't like the way things are turning out, then you can reset your photo by Alt-clicking the Cancel button. If you just want a quick look at where you started from (without undoing your work), then toggle the Preview checkbox on and off.

The Correct Camera Distortion filter gives you a few different ways to adjust your image. Your choices are divided into sections according to the different kinds of distortion they fix:

- **Remove Distortion.** Use this slider to fix *barrel distortion* (objects in your photo balloon out, like the sides of a barrel, as shown in Figure 11-10), and its opposite, *pincushion distortion* (your photo has a pinched look, with the edges of objects pushing in toward the center). Move the slider to the right to fix barrel distortion, and to the left to fix pincushion distortion.

   TIP   Barrel distortion is usually worst when you use wide-angle lens settings, while pincushion distortion generally appears when a telephoto lens is fully extended. Barreling's more common than the pincushion effect, especially when you use a small point-and-shoot camera at a wide-angle lens setting. You can often reduce barrel distortion in a small camera by simply avoiding your lens's widest setting. For instance, if you go from f2.8 to f5.6, you may see significantly less distortion.

- **Vignette.** If you see dark corners in your photo (usually caused by shadows from the lens or lens hood), then you need to spend time with these sliders.

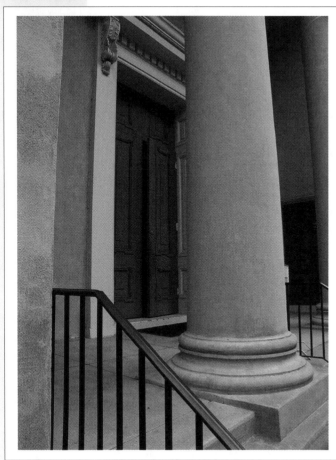

Figure 11-10:
A classic case of barrel distortion. This photo has already been straightened with the Straighten tool (page 86), but things are still pretty out of plumb here. Notice how the columns and walls lean in toward the top of the photo. You can even see a bit of a curve in the pillar on the far right. Barrel distortion is the most common kind of lens distortion, but fortunately, you can easily fix it with the Correct Camera Distortion filter.

Vignetting typically afflicts owners of digital single-lens reflex cameras, or people who use add-on lenses with fixed-lens cameras. Move the Amount slider to the right to lighten the corners, and to the left to darken them. The Midpoint slider controls how much of your photo is affected by the Amount slider. Move it to the left to increase the area (to bring it toward the center of the photo), or to the right to keep the vignette correction more toward the edges. Also consider turning off the Show Grid checkbox so that you have an unobstructed view of how you're changing the lightness values in your photo. Turn it back on again if you have other adjustments to make afterward.

- **Perspective Control.** Use these sliders to correct objects like buildings that look like they're tilted or leaning backward. It's easiest to understand the sliders by looking at the icons at both ends; each icon shows you the effect you'll get by moving the slider in that direction. The Vertical Perspective slider spreads the top of your photo wider as you move the slider to the left, and makes the bottom wider as you move it to the right. (If buildings seem like they're leaning backward, move it to the left first.) The Horizontal Perspective slider is for when your subject doesn't seem to be straight on in relation to the lens (for example, if it appears rotated a few degrees to the right or left). Move the slider to the left to bring the left side of the photo toward you, and to the right to bring the right side closer.

- **Angle.** You can rotate your entire photo by moving the line in this circle to the angle you want, or by typing a number into the box. A very small change here has a huge effect. The circle tool is easy to work with, but if you prefer, you can type a precise angle, in degrees. Here's how it works: There are 360 degrees in a circle. Your photo's starting point is 0.00 degrees. To rotate your photo to the left (counterclockwise), start from 0.01, and then go up in small increments to increase the rotation. To go clockwise, start with 359.99, and then reduce the number. In other words, 350 is further to the right than 355.

> **TIP** Each of the adjustment settings is accompanied by a box where you can type a number instead of using the sliders. If you want to make the same adjustments to several photos, take note of the numbers you used to fix the first photo, and then just plug them into the boxes for the other photos.

- **Edge Extension.** As explained in step 4 above, when you're done fixing your photo, you're likely to end up with some blank areas along the edge of your photo's canvas. Move the Scale slider to the right to enlarge your photo and get rid of the blank areas. Moving the slider to the left shrinks your photo and enlarges the blank areas, but you'll rarely need to do that.

  The Scale slider changes your actual photo, not just your view of it (as would be the case when using the Zoom tool). When you click OK, Elements resizes and crops your photo. So if you want the objects in your photo to stay the same size they were, then don't use this slider. Instead, just click OK, and then crop using any of the methods discussed starting on page 89.

The most important thing to remember when using Correct Camera Distortion is that a little goes a long way. For most of the corrections, start small and work in small increments. These distortions can be very subtle, and you often need to make only subtle adjustments to correct them.

> **TIP** The Correct Camera Distortion filter isn't just for corrections. You can use it to make your sour-tempered boss look truly prune-y, for example, by pincushioning him (just make sure you do this at home). Or, you can add vignettes to photos for special effects. You can also use the filter on shapes (simplify them first [page 395]), artwork, or anything else that strikes your fancy.

Transforming Images

You'll probably end up using the Correct Camera Distortion filter, explained in the previous section, for most of your straightening and warp-correction needs. But Elements also includes a series of Transform commands that you can use, as shown in Figure 11-11. For example, Transforming comes in handy when you want to make a change to just *one* side of a photo, or for final tweaking to a correction you made with Correct Camera Distortion. You can also apply these commands just for fun to create wacky photos or text effects.

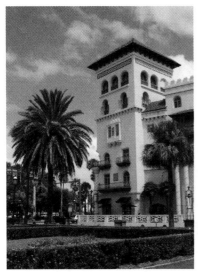 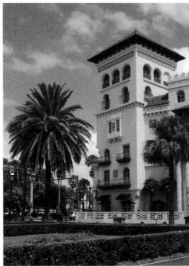

Figure 11-11:

Left: While you might use Correct Camera Distortion (page 354) to straighten a slanting building like this, you can also use the Transform commands, a better choice when you only need to adjust one side, as in this image.

Right: Here, it took only a dose of Skew and a bit of Distort to pull the building straight and make it tall again.

Skew, Distort, and Perspective

Elements gives you four commands, including three specialized ones—skew, distort, and perspective—to help straighten up the objects in your photos. While they all move your photo in different directions, the way you use them is the same. The Transform commands have the same box-like handles that you see with the Move tool, for example. You choose the command you want, and then the handles appear around your photo. Just drag a handle in the direction you want your photo to move. Figure 11-12 shows how to use the Transform commands.

To see the list of Transform commands, go to Image → Transform. The first one, Free Transform, is the most powerful because it includes all the others. (The next section has more about Free Transform—see page 363.)

> **NOTE** Transform works only on layers or active selections. If you have just a Background layer, then Elements offers to turn it into a regular layer so that you can use Transform.

The other Transform commands, which are more specialized, are:

- **Skew** slants an image. If you have a building that looks like it's leaning to the right, then you can use Skew to pull it to the left and straighten it back up again.

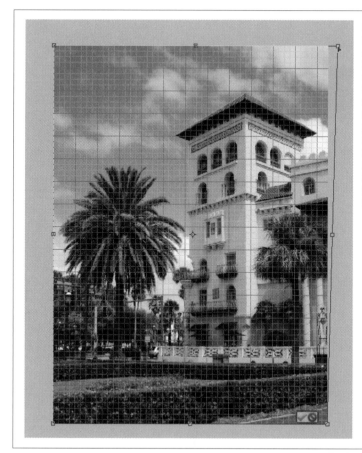

Figure 11-12:
Here's an example of how you'd use the Skew command to pull a building upright. To apply the Transform commands, make sure you can reach the handles on the corners. It helps to enlarge your image window far beyond the size of the actual image to give yourself room to pull. If you're using the tabbed image view (page 29), you don't need to do anything, because you've already got plenty of space around the image. With floating windows, just drag the lower-right corner to enlarge the window.

- **Distort** stretches your photo in the direction you want to pull it. Use it to make buildings (or people) taller and skinnier, or shorter and squatter.

- **Perspective** stretches your photo to make it look like parts are nearer or farther away. For example, if a building in your photo looks like it's leaning away from you, then you can use Perspective to pull the top back toward you.

Although Free Transform is the most versatile command, it can also be trickier to use. You may find it easier to use one of the one-way commands from the previous list so you don't have to worry about inadvertently moving a photo in an unwanted direction.

> **TIP** If you have an active selection in your image, then you can apply the Transform commands just to the selection, as long as you're not working on a Background layer.

All the Transform commands, including Free Transform, have the same Options bar settings, shown in Figure 11-13.

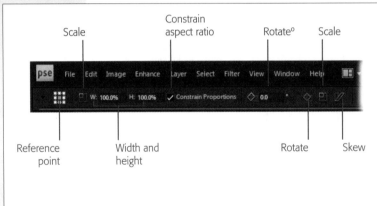

Figure 11-13:
The Options bar for the Transform commands. The W (width) and H (height) boxes let you manually specify dimensions when resizing your image (click the Scale button to their left once you're done entering the numbers). To scale by dragging, click the Scale button toward the right side of the tool options, and then drag any of the scaling handles (not shown) that appear on the bounding box surrounding your image.

From left to right, the Options bar settings control:

- **Reference point location.** This strange little doodad (shown in Figure 11-14) lets you tell Elements where the fixed point should be when you transform something. It's a miniature cousin of the placement grid you see in the Canvas Size dialog box (page 111). The reference point starts out in the image's center, but you can tell Elements to move everything using the upper-left corner or the bottom-right corner as the reference point instead. To do that, click the square you want to use as the reference.

Figure 11-14:
This nine-box icon in the Options bar is where you set the reference point for transformations, which tells Elements the central point for rotations. For example, if you want your photo to spin around the lower-left corner instead of the center, then click the lower-left square. For the Transform commands, this also tells Elements the point to work from.

- **Scale.** You can resize your image by dragging, or enter a percentage in the W or H box here. Turn on the Constrain Proportions checkbox to keep the original proportions of your image.

- **Rotate °.** The box next to the little rotated squares (to the right of Constrain Proportions) lets you enter the number of degrees to rotate your image or selection.

- **Rotate.** Click this next pair of rotated squares, and you can grab a corner of your image to make a free rotation (see page 89).

  TIP   If you Shift-drag when turning your image, then you force it to turn in 15-degree increments.

- **Scale.** Click here if you want to resize your image by dragging—as opposed to entering numbers in the Scale boxes to the left on the Options bar.

- **Skew.** Click here and then pull a corner of your image to the left or right, the way you do with the Skew command.

In most cases, you can transform your object without paying much attention to these settings. Truly, you can most easily transform your photo when you grab a handle and drag. Here's how you proceed:

1. **Position your image to give yourself room to work.**

   You need to position your photo so that you have room to drag the handles far beyond its edges. Figure 11-12 is a good example of an image window that's expanded enough to make lots of transformations. (If you're using tabbed windows [page 29], you probably have plenty of room.)

2. **Choose how you want to transform your image.**

   Go to Image → Transform, and then select the command you want. It's not always easy to tell which is best for a given photo, so you may want to try all three in turn. You can always change your mind and undo your changes by pressing Esc before you accept a change, or undo using Ctrl+Z after you've made the change.

   You can apply Transform commands only to layers, so if your image has only a Background layer, the first thing Elements does is ask you to convert that layer to a regular layer. Just click Yes and move on. Once the Transform command is active, you see the handles around your image. (You can apply Transform commands to a *selection* on a Background layer without converting it to a regular layer, though.)

3. **Transform your image.**

   Grab a handle, and then pull in the direction you want the image to move. You can also switch to another handle to pull in a different direction. If you change your mind, just press Esc to return to your original photo.

4. **When you're happy with how your photo looks, accept the changes.**

   Click the Commit button (the green checkmark) in your photo, or press Enter. Click the Cancel button (the red circle) instead if you decide not to apply the transformation after all.

   TIP Before clicking the Commit button, you can switch to another Transform command and add that transformation to your image, too.

Free Transform

Free Transform combines all the other Transform commands into one and lets you warp your image in many different ways. If you aren't sure what you need to do, then Free Transform is a good choice.

You use Free Transform exactly the same way as the other Transform tools, following the steps listed earlier in the previous section. The difference is that with Free Transform, you can pull in *any* direction, using keyboard-drag combinations to tell Elements which kind of transformation you want to apply. Each of the following transformations does exactly the same thing it would if you selected it from the Image → Transform menu:

- **Distort.** To make your photo taller or shorter, Ctrl-drag any handle. Your cursor turns into a gray arrowhead.

- **Skew.** To make your photo lean to the left or right, Ctrl+Shift-drag a handle in the middle of a side. You cursor turns into a gray arrowhead with a tiny double-arrow attached to it.

- **Perspective.** To correct the way an object appears to lean away from or toward you, press Ctrl+Alt+Shift and drag a corner. You see the same gray arrowhead cursor as when you're distorting.

Free Transform is the most powerful of all the Transform commands, but when you're pulling in several different directions, it's tricky to keep your photo from getting distorted. Consequently, some people prefer to use the simpler Transform commands, and apply multiple transformations instead.

> TIP   If you want to transform only a selected area, check out the new Transform Selection command (page 161), which lets you make any of these changes to a selection's outline without calling up Free Transform. To change the *contents* of the selection, use the tools covered in this chapter.

Part Four: Artistic Elements

4

Drawing with Brushes, Shapes, and Other Tools

If you're not artistically inclined, you may feel tempted to skip this chapter. After all, you probably just want to fix and enhance your photos—why should you care about brush techniques? Surprisingly enough, you should care quite a lot. In Elements, brushes aren't just for painting a moustache and horns on a picture of someone you don't like, or for blackening your sister's teeth in that old school photo.

Lots of Elements' tools use brushes to apply their effects. So far, you've already run into the Selection brush, the Clone Stamp, and the Color Replacement brush, to name just a few. And even with the Brush tool, you can paint with lots of things besides color—like light or shadows, for example. In Elements, when you want to apply an effect in a precise manner, you often use some sort of brush to do it.

If you're used to working with real brushes, their digital cousins can take some getting used to, but there are many serious artists now who paint primarily in Photoshop. With Elements, you now have access to most of the same tools as in the full Photoshop, if not quite all the settings available for each tool. Figure 12-1 shows an example of the detailed work you can do with Elements and some artistic ability.

This chapter explains how to use the Brush tool, some of the other brush-like tools (like the Erasers), and how to draw shapes even if you can't hold a pencil steady. You also get some practical applications for your new skills, like dodging and burning your photos to enhance them, and a super easy way to create sophisticated artistic crops for your photos—a favorite feature of scrapbookers.

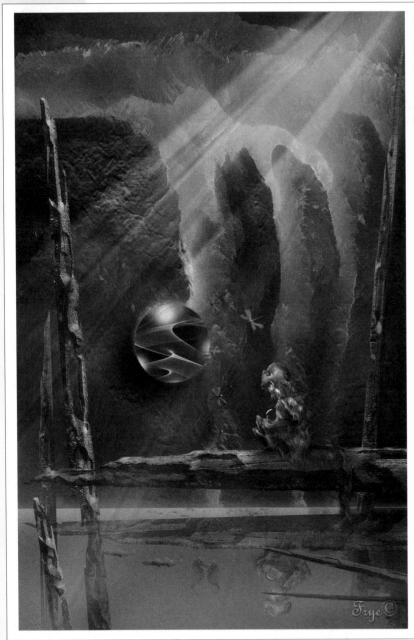

Figure 12-1:
*This complex drawing by
artist Jodi Frye was done
entirely in Elements. If
you learn to wield all the
drawing power in
Elements, you can create
amazingly detailed
artwork.*

Picking and Using a Basic Brush

If you look at the Tools panel, you'll see the Brush tool icon below the Eraser (in a single-column Tools panel) or below the Clone Stamp (in a two-column Tools panel). Don't confuse it with the Selection brushes, which are up above the Crop or Type tool, or the Smart Brush [page 211], which is below the regular Brush tool or to the right of it, depending on whether you have one or two columns of tools. To activate the Brush tool, click its icon or press B.

The Brush is one of the tools that include a pop-out menu—you can choose between the Brush, the Impressionist brush, the Color Replacement tool, and the Pencil tool. You can read about the Impressionist brush and the Pencil tool later in this chapter, and about the Color Replacement tool on page 314. This section is about the regular ol' Brush tool.

The Options bar (Figure 12-2) gives you lots of ways to customize the Brush tool.

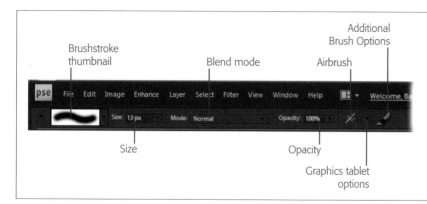

Figure 12-2:
The Brush tool's Options bar. By changing the settings shown here, as well as the hidden settings—revealed when you click the Additional Brush Options button—you can dramatically alter the behavior of any brush.

Here's a quick rundown of the available Brush options (from left to right):

- **Brushstroke thumbnail.** The Options bar displays a thumbnail of the stroke you'd get with the current brush. Click the thumbnail to view the complete Brush palette. Elements gives you a bunch of basic brush collections, which you can view and select here. You can also download many more from various websites (see page 551).

  If you click the drop-down menu, you'll see that you get more than just hard or soft brushes of various sizes (see Figure 12-3). You also get special brushes for drop shadows, brushes that are sensitive to pen pressure if you're using a graphics tablet (you can also use them with a mouse, but you don't have as many options), and brushes that paint shapes and designs. (Page 549 explains graphics tablets.)

  NOTE   One very cool feature of Elements' brushes is that any changes you make to a brush are reflected in the little brushstroke thumbnail that appears in the Brush palette.

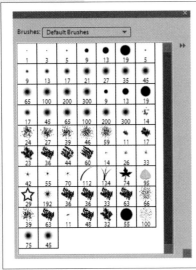

Figure 12-3:
Elements gives you a pretty good list of different brushes to choose from, and you can add your own. Here you see just one of the many brush libraries included with Elements, the Default Brushes. Page 376 tells you how to make your own brushes.

- **Size.** This slider lets you adjust the size of your brush—anywhere from 1 pixel up to sizes that may be too big to fit on your monitor. Or you can just type in a size. Figure 12-4 shows you an easy way to adjust settings like brush size using your mouse. As you're working, you can press the close bracket key (]) to quickly increase brush size, or the open bracket key ([) to decrease it.

Figure 12-4:
You don't need to open drop-down menus like the one shown here that says "98%". Just move your cursor over the word "Opacity", and the cursor changes into a pointing hand with a double-headed arrow. Now you can "scrub" (click and drag) back and forth right on the Options bar to make the changes—left for smaller, right for larger. This trick also works anywhere you see a numerical pop-out slider (as in the Layers palette's Opacity menu, for example).

- **Mode.** Here's where you choose the brush's blend mode. The mode you choose determines how the brush color interacts with what's in your image. For example, Normal simply paints the current foreground color (more about all the mode choices later).

- **Opacity.** Here's the way to control how thoroughly your brushing covers what's beneath it. You can use the drop-down menu's slider or type in any percentage you like, from 1 to 100. The maximum—100 percent—gets you total coverage (at least in Normal mode). Or you can scrub, as shown in Figure 12-4.

- **Airbrush.** Clicking the little pen-like brush just to the right of the Opacity control lets you use the brush as an airbrush. Figure 12-5 shows you how this works.

- **Graphics Tablet Options.** Click the tiny arrow to the right of the airbrush to see a bunch of checkboxes. If you use a graphics tablet, you can use these settings to tell Elements which brush characteristics should respond to the pressure of your stroke. Page 549 has more about graphics tablets.

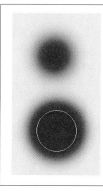

Figure 12-5:
As with real airbrushes, Elements' airbrush continues to "spray" paint as long as you hold down the mouse button, regardless of whether the mouse is moving or not.

Top: Here's what you get with one click with the brush in Regular mode.

Bottom: Here's the effect of one click with the same brush in Airbrush mode. See how far the color has spread beyond the cursor (the circle)? Not every brush offers the airbrush option.

- **Additional Brush Options.** Clicking this icon (which looks just like the Brush tool's icon) brings up the Additional Brush Options palette, which offers oodles of ways to customize your brush, all of which are covered in the next section. If you're using your brush for artistic purposes, it pays to familiarize yourself with these settings, since this is where you can set a chiseled stroke or a fade, for example.

> **TIP** If you ever want to return a brush to its original settings, click the Reset button (the tiny black arrow) on the left end of the Options bar, and then choose Reset Tool from the pop-up menu.

To actually use the Brush, enter your settings—make sure you've selected the color you want in the Foreground color square (page 231)—and then just drag across your image wherever you want to paint.

> **TIP** If you're used to painting with long, sweeping strokes, keep in mind that in Elements, that technique can be frustrating. That's because when you undo a mistake (by pressing Ctrl+Z), Elements undoes *everything* you've done while you've been holding down the mouse button. In tricky spots, you can save yourself some aggravation by using shorter strokes so you don't have to lose that whole long curve you painstakingly worked on just because you wobbled a bit at the end. (The Eraser tool [page 387] is handy for tidying up in these situations, too.)

One of the biggest differences between drawing with a mouse and drawing with a real brush is that, on a computer, it doesn't matter how hard you press the mouse. But if you've got a *graphics tablet,* an electronic pad that causes your pen movements to appear onscreen instantly, you can replicate real-world brushing, including pressure effects. Page 549 tells you all about using a tablet.

> **TIP** To draw or paint a straight line, hold down the Shift key while moving your cursor. If you click where you want the line to start, and press and hold Shift, and then click at the end point, Elements draws a straight line between those two points. Remember to click first and *then* press Shift, or you may draw lines where you don't want them.

Modifying Your Brush

When you click the Additional Brush Options button in the Options bar, you'll see a palette that lets you customize the brush. You'll run into a version of this palette for some of the other brush-like tools, like the Healing brush. The palette lets you change the way your brush behaves in a number of sophisticated and fun ways. Mastering these settings goes a long way toward getting artistic results in Elements.

TROUBLESHOOTING MOMENT

What Happened to My Cursor?

One thing that drives newcomers to Elements nuts is having the Brush cursor change from a circle to little crosshairs, seemingly spontaneously. This is one of those "It's not a bug; it's a feature" situations. Many tools in Elements offer you the option of what's called the *precise cursor,* shown in Figure 12-6. There are situations where you may prefer to see those little crosshairs so that you can tell *exactly* where you're working.

You toggle the precise cursor by pressing the Caps Lock key. So if you press that key by accident, you may find yourself in precise cursor mode with no idea of how you got there. Just press Caps Lock again to turn it off.

There's one other way you may wind up with the precise cursor, and this time you have no choice in the matter. It happens when your image is so small in proportion to the cursor that Elements *has to* display the crosshairs to show the brush in the right scale for your image. Zooming in usually gets your regular cursor back, unless you're working with a 1-pixel brush, which always uses crosshairs.

You can also elect to always see the crosshairs within the regular cursor circle if you want. In the Preferences dialog box, at the bottom of the list of painting cursors, turn on the "Show Crosshair in Brush Tip" checkbox, and you'll always have a mark for the exact center of your brush.

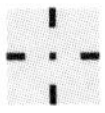

Figure 12-6:
Adobe calls these crosshairs the precise cursor. Elements sometimes makes your cursor look like this when you're zoomed way out on an image. To get the normal cursor back, you can zoom in some, and read the box above for further advice.

- **Fade** controls how fast the brushstroke fades out—just the way a real brush does when you run out of paint. A lower number means it fades out very fast (very few steps), while a higher one means the fade happens later (more steps). (Counterintuitively, zero is no fading at all—the stroke is the same at the end as it is at the beginning.) You can pick a number up to 9,999, so with a little fiddling, you should be able to get just what you want.

  If the brush isn't fading fast enough, decrease the number. If it fades too fast, increase it. A smaller brush usually needs a higher number than a larger brush does. You may find that you need to set the brush spacing (see below) up into the 20s or higher to make fading show any visible effect.

- **Hue Jitter** controls how fast the brush switches between the background and foreground colors. Some brushes, especially the ones that you'd use to paint objects like leaves, automatically vary the color for a more interesting or realistic effect. The higher the number (percentage) here, the faster the color moves from foreground to background. A lower number means the brush takes a longer distance to get from one color to the other. Brushes that acknowledge hue jitter don't put down only the two colors, but a range of hues in between. Not all brushes respond to this setting, but for the ones that do, it's a pretty cool feature. Figure 12-7 shows how it works.

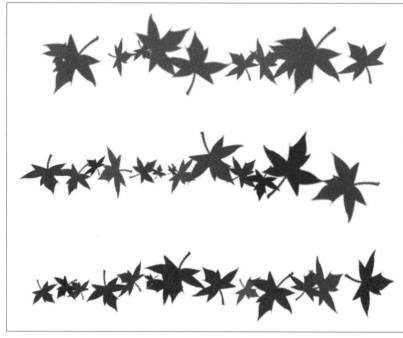

Figure 12-7:
Top: A brushstroke with no hue jitter.

Middle: The same brushstroke with a medium hue jitter value.

Bottom: The same brushstroke with a high hue jitter value. The foreground/ background colors here are red and blue. Notice how the brush automatically does a little shading, even without allowing for jitter. It takes a fairly high number to get all the way to blue in a stroke this short.

- **Scatter** means just what it says—how far the marks get distributed in your brushstroke. (When you paint with an Elements brush, you're actually putting down many repetitions of the brush shape rather than an actual line.) If you set scatter to a low number (percentage), you get a dense, line-like stroke, whereas a higher value gives an effect more like random spots.

- **Spacing** controls how far apart the brush marks get laid down when you paint. A lower number makes them close together, a higher number farther apart, as shown in Figure 12-8.

Figure 12-8:
The same brushstroke with the spacing set at 5 percent, 75 percent, and 150 percent (respectively, from top to bottom). You may have wondered why some of the brush thumbnails look like long caterpillars, when the brush should paint an object, like a star or leaf. The reason? Cramped spacing: The thumbnail shows the spacing as Elements originally sets it. Widen the spacing to see separate objects instead of a clump.

- **Hardness** controls whether the brush's edge is sharp or fuzzy. This setting isn't available for all brushes, but when it is, you can choose any value between zero and 100 percent. 100 percent is the most defined edge, zero the fuzziest.

- **Angle and Roundness.** If you've ever painted with a real brush, you should understand these settings right away. They let you create a more chiseled edge to your brush and then rotate it so that it's not always painting with the edge facing the same direction. Painters don't use only round brushes, and you don't have to in Elements, either.

There are some brushes in the libraries that aren't round, like the calligraphy and chalk brushes. But you can adjust the roundness of any brush to make it more suitable for chiseled strokes, as shown in Figure 12-9.

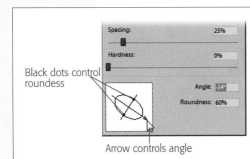

Black dots control roundess

Arrow controls angle

Figure 12-9:
Here's the bottom of the Additional Brush Options palette. To adjust a brush's angle and roundness, push the black dots to make the brush rounder or narrower, and then grab the arrow and spin it to the angle you want. You can also type a number directly into either the Angle or Roundness box.

There's also a checkbox (called Keep These Settings For All Brushes) you can turn on if you want to make all brushes behave exactly the same way. The checkbox only keeps the settings that appear *above* it in the palette, though, not the ones below it (spacing, hardness, angle, and roundness).

Saving Modified Brush Settings

If you modify a brush and like your creation, you can save it as a custom brush. You can alter any of the existing brushes and save the result—a great feature if you're working on a project that's going to last awhile and you don't want to keep modifying the settings. (Don't worry: When you modify an existing brush, Elements preserves a copy of the original.) To create your own brush, just:

1. **Choose a brush to modify.**

   Select a brush in the Brush palette. You can customize any of the brushes.

2. **Make the changes you want.**

   Change the brush settings until you get what you're after. Watch the brush thumbnail in the Options bar as you go. It changes to reflect your new settings.

3. **Tell Elements you want to keep the new brush.**

   Click the double arrows in the upper-right corner of the brush thumbnails palette and choose Save Brush. Elements asks you to name it; you don't absolutely have to, but naming brushes makes them easier to keep track of. The name will appear as pop-up text when you hover over the brush's thumbnail in the pop-out palette.

4. **Click OK.**

   The brush shows up at the bottom of your current list of brushes. If you make lots of custom brushes, you may want to create a special set for them. The Preset Manager (page 553) can help you do that.

Deleting brushes is pretty straightforward. You can select the brush in the Brush palette, and then click the double arrows on the palette's right side and choose Delete Brush from the pop-out menu. Or you can Alt-click the brush's thumbnail in the palette. The cursor changes into a pair of scissors when you hold down the Alt key; simply clicking with the scissors deletes the brush.

You can also make a selection from an image and save it as a brush (the next section explains how). Just remember, though, that brushes by definition don't have color, so you save only the *shape* of the selection, not the color of it. The color you get is whichever color you choose to apply. If you want to save a color sample, try saving your selection as a pattern (page 297), or just use the Clone Stamp (page 290) repeatedly.

The Specialty Brushes

So far you've learned about brushes that behave pretty much as brushes do in the real world—they paint a stripe of something, whether that's color, light, or even transparency.

But in the digital world, a brush doesn't have to be just a brush. With some of Elements' brushes, you can paint stars, flowers, disembodied eyeballs, gravel, or even rubber ducks with just one stroke, as shown in Figure 12-10.

If you click the arrow next to the brush's thumbnail in the Options bar, you'll see the list of brushes in the current category and a pull-down menu that lets you investigate Elements' other brush sets. The brushes used in Figure 12-10, for example, came from several different categories. Most brushes are sensitive to your pen pressure if you're using a graphics tablet (page 549).

The Specialty brushes respond readily to changes in the Additional Brush Options palette's settings (covered earlier in this chapter). Your choices there can make a huge difference in the effect you get—whether you're painting swaths of smooth grass like a lawn, or scattered sprigs of dune grass, for instance.

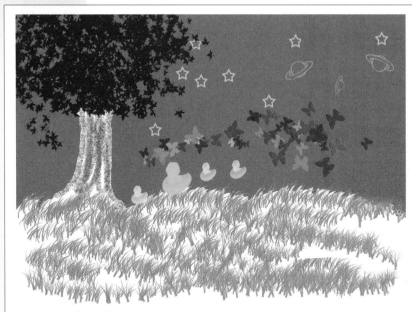

Figure 12-10:
You can digitally doodle using brushes, even if you can't draw a straight line. Everything in this lovely drawing was done with brushes that come with Elements. The leaves were painted with a brush that paints leaves; the yellow ducks come from a brush that paints ducks, and so on.

TIP   If you've tried some of the special effects brushes and found the results rather anemic, you can always go back once you've painted and punch up the color with a Multiply layer, just as you would for an overexposed photo (see page 207).

Making a Custom Brush

You can turn any picture, or selection within a picture, into a brush that paints the shape you've selected. Figure 12-11 shows what a cluster of flowers looks—and behaves like—when it's been turned into a brush.

It's surprisingly easy to create a custom brush from any object you have a picture of:

1. **Open a photo or drawing that includes what you want to use as a brush.**

   You can choose an area as large as 2500 pixels square. (Remember, you can resize your selection once it's a brush, just the way you can resize any other brush, so don't worry if it's a big area. That said, of course, if you choose a tiny size for a super-detailed brush, you may lose some definition when you use it.)

2. **Select the object or region you want.**

   Use any of the Selection tools to do this. It's a good idea to inspect your selection with the Selection brush in Mask mode as a last step (page 147), because any stray areas you included by mistake get painted with each stroke—just as if you wanted them there.

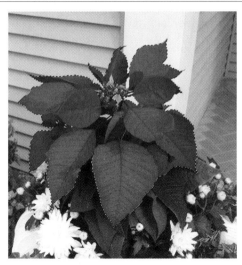

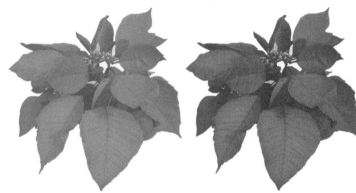

Figure 12-11:
Top: If you want to make a brush that draws poinsettias, just select one in a photo and save it as a brush.

Bottom: You can paint better than you thought! And with the brush, your poinsettias can be any color you like.

3. **Create your brush.**

   Go to Edit → "Define Brush from Selection". A dialog box appears showing the selection's shape and asking you to name the new brush. Check the thumbnail to be sure it's exactly what you had in mind. If not, click Cancel and try again. If you like it, click OK.

The new brush shows up at the bottom of your currently active list of brushes. If you want to get rid of it, Alt-click the brush's thumbnail or highlight the thumbnail, click the double arrows on the right side of the palette, and then choose Delete Brush.

The Impressionist Brush

When you paint with the Impressionist brush, you blur and blend the edges of the objects in your photo, just like in an Impressionist painting. At least that's what's *supposed* to happen. This brush is very tricky to control, but you can get some really interesting effects with it, especially if you paint on a duplicate layer and play with the Opacity setting (page 180). Usually you want a really low opacity with this brush, or some of the curlier styles will make your image look like it's made from poodle hair. Changing the Mode (page 382) can also help to control the effect.

To activate the Impressionist brush, press B or click the Brush tool's Tools panel icon, and select it from the pop-out menu. This brush has most of the same options as the regular Brush, but if you click the More Options button (the icon to the right of the Opacity setting), you'll see three new settings:

- **Style** determines what kind of brushstroke effect you want to create.
- **Area** tells Elements the diameter of the painting area.
- **Tolerance** is how similar in color the pixels have to be before they're affected by the brush.

If you really want to create a hand-painted look, you may prefer the brushstroke filters (Filter → Brush Strokes); page 405 explains how to use them. The Impressionist brush isn't really the best tool for creating true Impressionist effects, although its blurring qualities can sometimes be useful because it covers large areas faster than the Blur tool. The Smudge tool (page 385) is another excellent, though time-consuming, way to create a painted effect.

The Pencil Tool

Basically just another brush, the Pencil tool shares the Brush tool's slot in the Tools panel. Choose the Pencil from the pop-out menu or press N to activate it.

The Pencil has many of the same settings as the Brush—like size, mode, and opacity—but it offers only hard-edged brushes. In other words, you can't draw fuzzy lines with the pencil, not even the kind of lines you'd sketch with a soft pencil. The Pencil's lines are always well defined. It's especially useful when you want to work on a pixel-by-pixel basis.

You use the Pencil tool the same way you use any other brush. The big difference is the Auto Erase checkbox in the Options bar. This setting makes the Pencil paint with the Background color over areas that contain the Foreground color. But if you start dragging in an area that doesn't include the Foreground color, it paints with the Foreground color instead. This is really confusing until you try it. Take a look at Figure 12-12 for some help understanding this setting, or better yet, create a blank file (page 50) and try it yourself.

The Paint Bucket

When you want to fill a large area with color in a hurry, the Paint Bucket is the tool for you. It's right below the Brush in the Tools panel if you have two rows of tools,

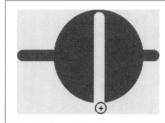

Figure 12-12:
The slightly confusing Auto Erase option was used to create two lines: a horizontal one of the Foreground color (purple) and a vertical one of the Background color (light green). The horizontal line was drawn by starting with the cursor in the background (so the Pencil erased the green, leaving a purple line across the circle). The vertical line was drawn by starting inside the purple circle, causing the Background color to be exposed.

or below the Smart brush if you have a single row. If you click it (keyboard short-cut: K) and then click in your image, all the available area (either your whole image or the current selection) gets flooded with color. It works something like the Magic Wand: Just as the Magic Wand selects only the color you click, the Paint Bucket fills only the color you click.

NOTE   Make any Options bar setting adjustments, discussed next, before clicking in your photo.

Most of the Paint Bucket's Options bar settings are probably familiar:

- **Pattern.** Normally the Paint Bucket fills the area with the Foreground color (page 231). But turn on this checkbox, and it uses a pattern (page 294) instead. Choose an existing pattern (listed in the Pattern drop-down menu on the Options bar) or create your own, just as you would with the Pattern Stamp (page 296).

- **Mode.** You can use the Paint Bucket in any blend mode, as explained later in this chapter (page 382).

- **Opacity.** One hundred percent opacity gives you total coverage: nothing shows through the paint you put down. Lower the percentage for a more transparent effect.

- **Tolerance.** This setting works the same way it does for the Magic Wand (page 150). The higher the number, the more shades the paint fills.

- **Anti-alias.** This setting smoothes the edges of the fill. Leave it turned on unless you have a specific reason not to.

- **Contiguous.** This is another familiar option from the Magic Wand (page 150). If you leave this checkbox on, you change only areas of the chosen color that touch each other. Turn it off, and all areas of the color you click get changed, whether they're contiguous or not.

- **All Layers.** Fills *any* pixels that meet your criteria, no matter what layer they're on. (The Paint Bucket actually paints on the active layer, but with this check-box turned on, it looks for pixels to change based on all the layers in your image.) To exclude just one layer, click the eye icon on the Layers panel for that layer. Don't forget that you can lock the transparent and translucent parts of layers in the Layers panel (see page 181).

You can undo a Paint Bucket fill with the usual Ctrl+Z.

TIP   You can sometimes improve blown-out skies by using the Eyedropper to select an appropriate shade of blue from another photo and then filling the blown-out areas of your sky using the Paint Bucket at a very low opacity.

Dodging and Burning

Like Unsharp Mask, dodging and burning are old darkroom techniques used to enhance photos and emphasize particular areas. Dodging *lightens* and brings out hidden details in the range you specify (midtones, shadows, or highlights), and burning *darkens* and brings out details in a given range. Both tools live with the Sponge tool in the Tools panel.

You may think that, given the Shadows/Highlights command, you don't need these tools. But they still serve a useful purpose because they let you make *selective* changes, rather than affecting the whole image or requiring tedious selections the way Shadows/Highlights does. When you dodge or burn, you just paint your changes. Figure 12-13 shows an example of when you might need to work on a particular area. Of course, you can also make a selection and then use Shadows/Highlights just on that, which you may want to try as well as dodging and burning.

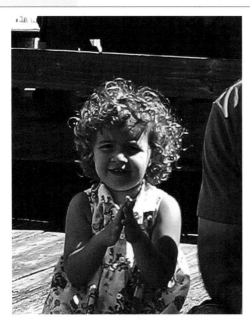

Figure 12-13:
Although the overall shadow/highlight balance of this photo is about right, the detail in the face of this little concertgoer is obscured by backlighting and by her father's shadow. Careful dodging and burning can really help with these problems, as you can see in Figure 12-14.

Skillful use of dodging and burning can greatly improve your photos, although it helps to have an artistic eye to spot what to emphasize and what to downplay. Use these tools along with the black-and-white conversion feature (page 319) to emphasize certain areas of your photos. Masters of black-and-white photography, like Ansel Adams, relied heavily on dodging and burning (in the darkroom, in those days) to create their greatest images.

Both the Dodge and Burn tools are really just variants of the Brush tool, except they don't apply color directly—they just affect the colors and tones that are already present in your photo. Adobe refers to these two as the "toning tools."

One word of warning about these tools: Unless you use them on a duplicate layer, you can't undo the effect once you close your photo. So be careful how you use them. Many people prefer to dodge and burn using the method described in the box on page 385, rather than with the actual Dodge and Burn tools, unless they're working on a black-and-white photo.

> **TIP** You may also want to try some of the Smart Brush's (page 211) lighting settings for making selective adjustments to just part of your photo. A little experimenting will give you a sense for which tools you prefer to use in different situations.

Dodging

Use the Dodge tool to lighten areas of your image and to bring out details hidden in shadows. It's a good idea to create a separate layer (Layer → Duplicate Layer or Ctrl+J) when using this tool to preserve your image if you go overboard. (Be sure you apply the Dodge tool to a layer that has something in it, or nothing happens.) Here's how to use it:

1. **Activate the Dodge tool.**

   Click the Sponge tool in the Tools panel or press O, and then choose the Dodge tool (the lollipop-like paddle) from the pop-out menu. You'll see the usual brush options, but with two differences: a Range setting that determines whether the tool works on highlights, midtones, or shadows; and an Exposure setting, which determines the strength of the effect.

2. **Drag over the area you want to change.**

   Choose a low Exposure setting for the Dodge tool (and the Burn tool as well) and drag more than once to get a more realistic result (see Figure 12-14). After you're done, if you think the tool's effect is still too strong, you can always reduce the layer's opacity (as long as you're working on a duplicate layer).

Burning

The Burn tool works just like the Dodge tool, but does exactly the opposite: It darkens. Use the Burn tool to uncover details in your highlights. (Of course, there have to be *some* details there for the tool to work.) If your photo's highlights are blown out (see page 209), you won't get any results, no matter how much you

---

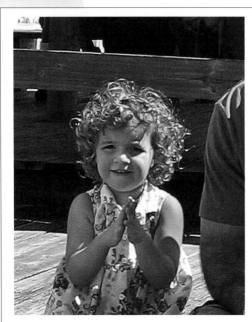

Figure 12-14:
Figure 12-13 after a dose of the Dodge and Burn tools. The girl's features are much easier to see, but if you look closely, the colors in her face are a bit flat. See page 385 to learn a different method for selectively adjusting highlights and shadows. Both methods have advantages and disadvantages. (The effects are deliberately a bit too strong in both figures to show you the perils of getting overzealous with either method.)

apply the tool. The Burn tool is grouped with the Sponge and Dodge tools. Its icon is a curled hand.

Most of the time, you'll probably want to use the Dodge and Burn tools in combination. They can help draw attention to specific parts of your photo, but they work best for subtle changes. Applying them too vigorously—especially on color photos—creates an obviously faked look. Black-and-white photos (or color images converted to black and white) can generally stand much stronger contrasts.

Blending and Smudging

You can control how Elements blends the color you add to an image with the colors that are already there. This section takes a look at two different blending methods—using *blend modes* to determine how the colors you paint change what's already in your image, and using the Smudge tool to literally mix parts of your image together. Blend modes are almost limitless in the ways they can manipulate images.

Blend Modes

Blend modes control how the color you add when you paint reacts with the existing pixels in an image—whether you just add color (Normal mode), make the existing color darker (Multiply mode), or change the saturation (Saturation mode).

Image-editing experts have found plenty of clever ways to use blend modes for some really sophisticated techniques. Thorough coverage of these maneuvers would turn this into a book the size of the Yellow Pages, but Figure 12-15 shows a few examples of how simply changing a brush's blend mode can radically change your results.

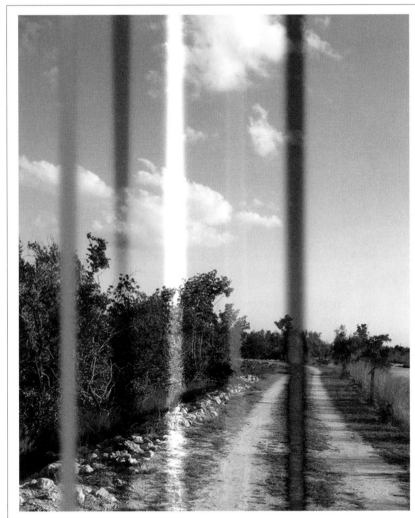

Figure 12-15:
This photo shows the effect of some of the different blend modes when used with the Brush tool. The same color was used for each of the vertical stripes— you can see how different the result is from just changing the mode. From left to right, the modes are: Normal, Color Burn, Color Dodge, Vivid Light, Difference, and Saturation.

There are so many ways to combine blend modes that even Elements pros can't always predict the results, so experimenting is the best way to learn about them.

Elements groups the blend modes according to the effects they have. You won't always see every group or all the choices, but generally speaking, in Elements menus (such as the Options bar menu for the Brush tool, for example) the top group includes what you might call painting modes, followed by modes for darkening, lightening, adjusting light, special effects modes, and adjusting color.

Keep in mind that the modes work quite differently with layers than with tools. In other words, painting with a brush in Dissolve mode produces an effect quite different than creating a layer in Dissolve mode and painting on it, as shown in Figure 12-16.

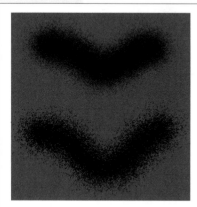

Figure 12-16:
Blend modes behave differently when used in layers than they do when using a tool that's set to the same mode. Both these strokes were done using Dissolve mode in pure black at 100-percent opacity. The difference is that the top stroke is painted with the Brush tool in Dissolve mode, while the bottom one is a brushstroke in Normal mode on a Dissolve layer.

Modes are really cool and useful once you get used to them, but if you're just starting out in Elements, there's no need to worry about them right away.

TIP   If you'd like to learn more about how each mode works, you can find a lot of useful tutorials on the Web. A good place to start is *www.photoshopgurus.com/tutorials/t010.html*. (Ignore the section "Additional blend mode information"—that's only for Photoshop folks.)

The Smudge Tool

The Smudge tool does just what you'd think: You can use it to smear the colors in your image, as if you were rubbing them with your finger. You can even "finger paint" with this tool, if you feel the call of your inner preschooler. Adobe describes the effect of the Smudge tool as being "like a finger dragged through wet paint." It's sort of like a cousin to the Liquify filter (page 453), but without as many options.

If you want to turn your photos into paintings (Figure 12-18), the humble Smudge tool is your most valuable resource. For artistic smudging, you need a graphics tablet so you can vary the stroke pressure. You can use the tool without a tablet, but you won't get nearly as good an effect. If you'd like to learn more about this kind of smudging, you can find some excellent tutorials in the Retouching forum at Digital Photography Review (*www.dpreview.com*; search for *smudging*). The forums at *www.retouchpro.com* are also a favorite hangout for expert smudgers.

Blend Modes Instead of Dodge and Burn

You can do a lot in Elements without ever touching blend modes. But if you take a little time to familiarize yourself with them, you might find they become a regular part of your image-editing toolkit. For instance, you may prefer the effect you get using a layer in Overlay mode to that of the Dodge and Burn tools.

To adjust a photo using a layer in Overlay blend mode, first make basic adjustments like Levels or Shadows/Highlights. Then, when you're ready to fine-tune your photo by painting over the details you want to enhance, here's what you do:

1. **Create a new layer.** Go to Layer → New → Layer or press Shift+Ctrl+N.

2. **Before dismissing the New Layer dialog box, choose the Overlay blend mode.** Select Overlay from the Mode menu, and turn on the checkbox that says "Fill with Overlay-neutral color (50% gray)." You won't see anything happen yet.

3. **Set the Foreground and Background colors to black and white, respectively.** Press D to set the Foreground and Background squares to black and white.

4. **Activate the Brush tool.** Choose a brush (set to Normal mode), and set the opacity very low, maybe 17 percent or even less. (You'll need to experiment a bit to see how low a setting is low enough.)

5. **Paint on the areas you want to adjust.** Paint with white to bring up the detail in dark areas and with black to darken overly light areas. (Remember that you can switch from one to the other by pressing X.) The detail on your photo comes up just like magic.

Figure 12-17 shows the results of using Overlay mode on the image from Figure 12-13 so you can compare the results. This method has the added advantage of being adjustable by changing the opacity of the Overlay layer. You can carry this technique to extremes for really interesting effects when you want an artistic rather than realistic result.

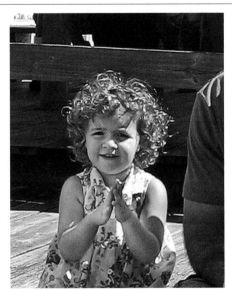

Figure 12-17:
Here's the little girl from Figure 12-13 again, this time after using Overlay blending, as described in the box above. Unlike the results of using the Dodge and Burn tools (Figure 12-14), the color isn't grayish—as dodging made it—but the contrast where shadowed areas meet bright ones still needs some work.

TIP   If you're serious about smudging, check out Scott Deardorff's online classes at *www. digitalartacademy.com*. (Most of the classes there are for a different program, Corel Painter, but his smudging classes cover Photoshop and Elements.) Scott is one of the most talented smudgers out there. Visit his website at *www.scottdeardorffportraits.com* to see some outstanding examples of what skilled hands can accomplish with the humble Smudge tool.

A warning: If you have a slow computer, there's quite a bit of lag between when you apply the Smudge tool and when the effect actually shows up. This delay makes the tool tricky to control, because you have to resist the temptation to keep going over the area until you see results.

You'll find the Smudge tool hidden under the Blur tool in the Tools panel. Click the Blur tool or press R and, from the pop-out menu, choose the Smudge tool (its icon, not surprisingly, is a finger that looks like it's painting).

The Smudge tool has mostly the same settings as a regular brush, but it also includes the Sample All Layers checkbox (page 289), just like the Healing brush and the Clone Stamp. It also has two additional settings: Strength and Finger Painting.

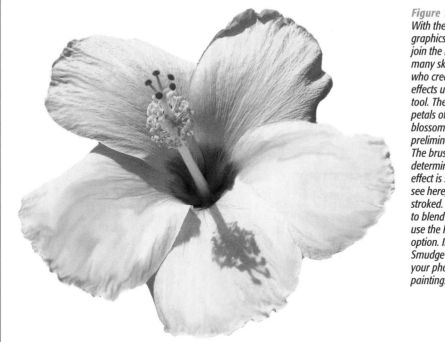

Figure 12-18:
With the help of a graphics tablet, you can join the ranks of the many skilled smudgers who create amazing effects using only this tool. The bottom three petals of this hibiscus blossom show preliminary smudging. The brushes you use determine whether the effect is smooth, as you see here, or more heavily stroked. When you want to blend in other colors, use the Finger Painting option. In effect, the Smudge tool lets you turn your photo into a painting.

• **Strength.** This setting means just what it says—it controls how hard the tool smudges the colors together. A higher number results in more blending.

• **Finger Painting.** Turning on this checkbox makes the Smudge tool smear the Foreground color at the start of each stroke. When this box is turned off, the tool uses the color that's under the cursor at the start of each stroke. Figure 12-19 shows the difference. This option is useful for creating artistic smudges. If you want a bit of a contrasting color to help your strokes stand out more, choose a Foreground color (page 231) and turn this checkbox on.

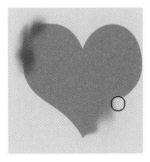

Figure 12-19:
The Smudge tool smears colors together. The strokes on the left were done with the Finger Painting checkbox turned on, which lets you introduce a bit of the Foreground color (orange, in this case) into the beginning of each stroke. This technique is really useful for shading or when you need to mix in just a touch of another color. The smudging on the right was done with Finger Painting turned off, so it uses only the colors that are already in the image.

TIP   Use the Eyedropper (page 234) to sample other areas of your image to add Finger Painting colors that harmonize well with the area you're smudging.

Once you've chosen your settings, smudge away.

NOTE   When using the Smudge tool, you only see results where two colors come together. It blends together the pixel colors where edges meet. If you use Smudge in the middle of an area of solid color, nothing happens unless you've turned on Finger Painting.

The Eraser Tool

Everyone makes mistakes. Adobe has thoughtfully included three different mistake-fixers. If you click and hold the Eraser icon in the Tools panel, you'll see the Eraser, the Magic Eraser, and the Background Eraser. (You can also activate the Eraser by pressing E.) You'll probably use all three at one time or another. This section covers all your options.

Using the Eraser

The Eraser is basically just another kind of brush tool, only instead of adding color to your image, it removes color from the pixels. How it works varies a little depending on where you use it.

If you use the Eraser on a regular layer, it replaces the color with transparency. On a Background layer, or one in which transparency is locked, it replaces whatever color is there with the Background color (see Chapter 6 for more about how layers work).

The Eraser's settings are pretty much the same as for any other brush—including brush style, size, and opacity—but with the Eraser a couple of them work differently:

- **Mode.** For this tool, Mode doesn't have anything to do with blend modes (page 382), but rather tells Elements the shape of the eraser you want to work with. Your choices are Brush, Pencil, and Block.

  You can see the difference in how the Eraser is going to work by watching the brush style preview in the Options bar as you change modes. Picking Brush or Pencil mode lets you use the Eraser as you would those tools—in other words, you can choose any brush you like. The Brush option lets you make soft-edged erasures, while Pencil mode makes only hard-edged erasures. Choosing Block mode changes the cursor to a square, so that you can use it as you would an artist's erasing block—sort of.

- **Opacity** determines how much color gets removed—at 100 percent, it's all gone (or all replaced with the background).

To use the Eraser:

1. **Activate the Eraser.**

   Click the Eraser tool in the Tools panel (keyboard shortcut: E). Its icon is a pink eraser, so it's easy to find.

2. **Choose your settings.**

   Choose a size, mode, and opacity. (As noted earlier, the mode and opacity settings work differently here than they do for regular brushes.)

3. **Drag anywhere in your image to remove what you don't want.**

   You may need to change the size of the Eraser a few times. It's usually easiest to use a small Eraser (or the Background Eraser—page 389) to accurately clear around the edges of the object you want to keep, as shown in Figure 12-20. Then you can use a larger brush size to get rid of the remaining chunks, once you don't have to worry about accidentally going into the area you want to keep.

   TIP   You can use a selection (see Chapter 5) to limit where the Eraser operates.

It's tedious to erase around a long outline or to remove entire backgrounds, so Elements has two other kinds of Erasers for those situations.

The Magic Eraser

Once you try it, you're likely to wonder why the heck Adobe gave this pedestrian tool such an intriguing name. What's so magic about the Magic Eraser?

Well, not much, really. It's called "magic" because it works a lot like the Magic Wand tool (page 149), in that you can use it to select pixels of a single color or range (depending on the tolerance settings). It even has the same little sparklies as the Magic Wand does in its icon to remind you of the relationship.

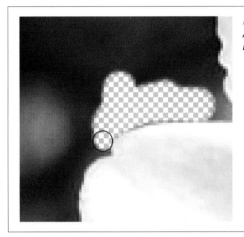

Figure 12-20:
Accurate erasing around an object usually means zooming way, way in so you can control which pixels the Eraser is changing.

The problem, as Figure 12-21 shows you, is that the Magic Eraser isn't as clean in its work as the other erasers. Still, it can be a big help in eliminating large chunks of solid color. Moreover, if you're lucky, you may be able to clean the edges right up with Refine Edge (you'll need to make a selection to use it) or the Defringe command (Enhance → Adjust Color → Defringe Layer). To use Refine Edge, you'll need to select the layer's contents, or click in the empty background area with the Magic Wand (page 149), and then choose Select → Invert. (There's more about Refine Edge on page 145 and about Defringing on page 390.)

It's usually best to use the Magic Eraser in combination with at least one of the other erasers if you're looking to achieve really clean results. One sometimes-useful side effect of the Magic Eraser is that when you click your photo with it, Elements automatically turns your Background layer into a regular layer, just the way the Background Eraser does. So if you want to do something to the remaining object that requires a regular layer—applying a Layer style (page 423), for instance—you save yourself a step.

The Background Eraser

Lots of people think *this* eraser deserves the name "Magic" much more than the Magic Eraser tool. The Background Eraser is a tremendous help when you want to remove all the background around an object.

The Background Eraser erases all the pixels under the brush (but outside the edges of the object) and renders the area it's used on transparent, even if it's a Background layer. (If you click with it on a Background layer, your computer may hesitate for a sec because it's busy transforming your Background to a regular layer.)

Here's how to use it:

1. **Select the Background Eraser.**

   Press E or, in the Tools panel, click the Eraser icon. Then choose the Background Eraser from the pop-out menu. (Its icon is an eraser with a pair of scissors next to it.)

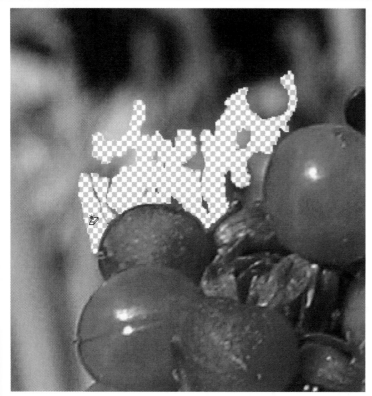

Figure 12-21:
This figure gives you a closeup look at the Magic Eraser at work on the background behind a cluster of berries. A couple of clicks with the Magic Eraser got rid of a bunch of the background, and setting the tolerance higher would've gotten even more. But if you look closely, you can see the disadvantage of this tool: The edges of the berries are fringed with dark, ragged areas it didn't eliminate. You may be able to clean up the edges with Enhance → Adjust Color → Defringe Layer (page 160), or Refine Edge (page 145), but those methods aren't always 100 percent successful.

2. **In the Options bar, choose a brush size.**

   The cursor turns into a circle with crosshairs in it. These crosshairs are important: They're the Background Eraser's "hot spot." Elements turns any color that you drag them over into transparency. The circle size changes depending on how large a brush you choose, but the crosshairs stay the same size. As you can see in Figure 12-22, with a large brush, there may be a lot of space around the crosshairs. That makes it easy to remove big chunks of the background at once, since everything in the circle gets eliminated.

   TIP   If you start seeing *all* your brushes (not just the Background Eraser) as crosshairs, the box on page 372 tells you how to get back to your regular cursor.

3. **Drag in your photo.**

   Move around the edge of the object you want to keep, being careful not to let the crosshairs move into the object, or else you'll start erasing that, too. If you make a mistake, just use Ctrl+Z to undo.

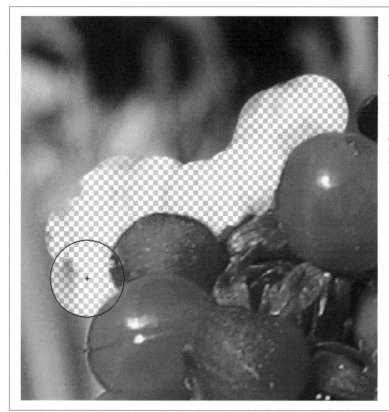

Figure 12-22:
The Background Eraser does a very careful job of separating the berries from their background. Just be sure to keep the little crosshairs away from the color you want to keep. Here, because the crosshairs are outside the red, only the background is getting removed. But if you moved the crosshairs over a berry, you bite chunks out of it.

The Background Eraser has three Options bar settings to help refine how it works:

- **Brush.** If you want a different brush style, choose it from this pull-down menu.

- **Limits.** Do you want the Background Eraser to remove only contiguous color, or all the patches of a certain color? This works exactly like the Contiguous setting for the Magic Wand (page 150).

- **Tolerance.** This setting tells the Background Eraser how similar colors must be for it to remove them, again it's just like the Magic Wand setting (page 150).

You may not need to change any of these settings to get the results you want.

If you want to remove the background around an object, you may find it most effective to start with the Background Eraser around the edge of the object, and then to use the other Erasers to clean up. The advantage of this method is that you don't have to clean up junk left over from the Magic Eraser. It's also easier to maneuver the Background Eraser than the regular Eraser, especially if you don't have a graphics tablet.

Drawing with Shapes

Wow, so many brush options and Adobe still isn't done—there's yet another way to draw things in Elements. The program includes the Shape tool (which is actually a group of tools that share one slot in the Tools panel), which lets you draw geometrically perfect shapes, regardless of your artistic ability. And not just simple shapes like circles and rectangles: You can draw animals, plants, starbursts, picture frames—all sorts of things, as shown in Figure 12-23. This tool should appeal to anyone whose grade-school masterpieces always got put up on the wall behind the piano somewhere.

Figure 12-23:
Here are just a few of the shapes that you can draw with Elements, even if you flunked elementary school art class. These objects look even more impressive once you gussy them up with Layer styles (page 423).

Turning yourself into an artist by using Elements' Shape tool is easy. Just follow these steps:

1. **Open an image or create a new one.**

   You can add shapes to any file you can open in Elements.

2. **Activate the Shape tool.**

   Click the Shape tool in the Tools panel or press U. The Shape tool is sometimes a little confusing to newcomers to Elements, because its icon reflects the shape that's currently active—so you may see a rectangle, a polygon, or a line, for instance. (You see a blue rectangle before you've used this tool for the first time.)

3. **Select the shape you want to draw.**

   Use the Tools panel menu to choose a rectangle, a rounded rectangle, an ellipse, a polygon, a line, or a custom shape. (If you choose the custom shape, you have lots of shapes to choose from. Click the Shape pull-down menu in the Options bar to pick the one you want.) All the shapes, and their accompanying options, are described in the following sections.

4. **Adjust your settings in the Options bar.**

   Choose a color by clicking the color square in the Options bar or use the Foreground color (page 231). Clicking the Options bar's color square brings up the Color Picker (page 231). If you click the arrow to the right of the square, you get the Color Swatches panel instead (page 235).

   If you have special requirements, like a rectangle that's exactly 1"×2", click the downward-facing arrow just to the right of the shape's thumbnail to open the Custom Shape Options panel, where you can enter the size of your shape.

   There's also an Options bar setting that lets you apply a Layer style (see page 423) as you draw your shape. Just click the downward-facing arrow on the right side of the Style box, and then choose the style you want from the pop-out panel. To go back to drawing without applying a style, choose the rectangle with the diagonal red line through it.

5. **Drag in your image to draw the shape.**

   Notice that *how* you drag the cursor affects the final appearance of the shape. For example, the way you drag determines the proportions of your figure. If you're drawing a fish, you can drag so that it's long and skinny or short and fat. Even with practice, it can take a couple of tries to get exactly the proportions you want.

   > **TIP**   If you're trying to create exact copies of a particular shape you've already drawn, use the Shape Selection tool (page 398) to create duplicates of the first shape.

The Shape tool automatically puts each shape on its own layer. If you don't want it to do that, or need to control how shapes interact, use the squares in the middle of the Options bar. With one exception (Exclude Overlapping Shape Areas), they're the same as the ones for managing selections (page 141). Use them to add more than one shape to a layer, subtract a shape from a shape, keep only the area where shapes intersect, or exclude the areas where they intersect.

> **TIP**   If you want to draw multiple shapes on one layer, click the Options bar's "Add to Shape" rectangle. Then, everything you do is on the same layer. (Shapes don't have to touch or overlap to use this option.)

You can turn any shape from a *vector image* (infinitely resizable) into a *raster image* (drawn pixel by pixel) by clicking the Simplify button in the Options bar. The box on page 395 tells you everything you need to know about the difference between vector and raster images.

You can also add custom shapes by choosing them in the Content panel (page 474). In the panel, just double-click the shape you want, or click the shape's thumbnail and then click Apply.

The following sections describe all the main shape categories and their special settings.

Rectangle and Rounded Rectangle

The Rectangle and Rounded Rectangle tools work pretty much the same way and are really popular for creating web page buttons. With either tool active, in the Options bar, you can click the blue version of the shape to display a menu (the name of the menu depends on which shape tool you're using; for simplicity's sake, this section calls it the "Shape Options" menu) where you'll find the following settings:

- **Unconstrained.** Elements selects this option automatically unless you change it. It lets you draw a rectangle with whatever dimensions you want—how you drag determines the proportions.

- **Square.** To draw a square instead of a rectangle, click this radio button before you start, or just hold down the Shift key as you drag.

- **Fixed Size.** This setting makes Elements draw your shape the size you specify. Just enter the dimensions you want in inches, pixels, or centimeters.

- **Proportional.** Use this setting if you know the proportions you want your rectangle to have, but not the exact size. Just type in the proportions. For example, if you enter a width of 2 and a height of 1, no matter where you drag, the shape is always twice as long as it is high.

- **From Center.** This setting lets you draw your shape from its center instead of from a corner. It's useful when you know where you want the shape but aren't sure how big it needs to be.

- **Snap to Pixels.** This checkbox makes sure that the edge of your rectangle falls exactly on the edge of a pixel. You'll get crisper-looking edges with this setting turned on. It's available only for the Rectangle and Rounded Rectangle tools.

Most of the Shape tools have similar options. The Rounded Rectangle has one Options bar setting of its own, though: *Radius,* which is the amount (in pixels) that the corners are rounded off. A higher number means more rounding.

TIP Looking to add a simple, empty rectangle, square, circle, or ellipse? See the box on page 399.

Rasterizing Vector Shapes

Back in Chapter 3, you read about how the majority of your images (definitely your photos) are just a bunch of pixels to Elements. These images are known as *raster* images. The shapes you draw with the Shape tools work a little differently; they're called *vector* images.

A vector image is made up of a set of directions specifying what kind of geometric shapes your computer should draw. The advantage of vector images is that you can size them way up or down without producing the kind of pixelation you get when you resize a raster image too much.

Your shape keeps its vector characteristics until you *simplify* the layer that it's on. Simplifying, also called *rasterizing,* just means that Elements turns your shape into regular pixels (in other words, a raster image). Once you simplify, you have the same limitations on resizing as you do for a regular photo. For example, you can make your image smaller, but you can't make it larger than 100 percent without losing quality. Sooner or later, you may want to transform your vector image to a regular raster image so that you can do certain things to it, like add filters or effects.

If you try to do something that requires simplifying a layer, Elements generally asks you to do so via a dialog box. To rasterize your shape, just click OK, or click the Simplify button in the Options bar. Remember that once you've rasterized a shape, if you try to resize, you won't get the clean, unpixelated results that you got when it was a vector image. If you need to resize a shape, it's easiest to start over with a new shape—if that's feasible (yet another good reason to use layers).

Also, before you simplified the layer, you could change the shape's color by clicking the Options bar's color box, but now the shape totally ignores what you do in the Options bar. Simplifying always affects the *whole* layer—everything on it is simplified, or nothing on it is. Once you simplify a shape, you have to select it and change its color the way you would on any detail in a photo.

The Content panel brings yet another wrinkle to the raster/vector situation—Smart Objects. The items in the Content panel (the frames, backgrounds, and other doodads) act as vector objects, except that they may seek out a particular place in the layer stack. (Page 472 has more on Smart Objects.)

Ellipse

The Ellipse tool has the same Shape Options settings as the Rectangle tool. The only difference is that you can opt for a circle instead of a square. You can also draw a circle by pressing the Shift key while you drag.

Polygon

You can draw many kinds of regular polygons with this tool. Use the Options bar to set the number of sides. The Shape Options menu's choices are a bit different for this tool:

- **Radius.** This setting controls the distance from the center to the outermost points.

- **Smooth Corners.** If you don't want sharp edges at the corners, turn on this checkbox.

- **Star.** This setting inverts the angles to create a star-like shape, as shown in Figure 12-24.

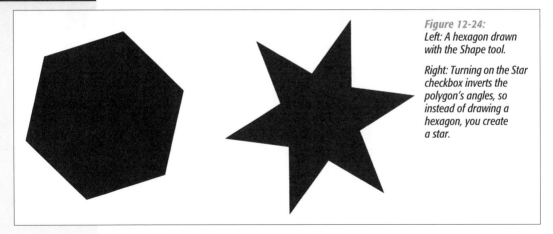

Figure 12-24:
Left: A hexagon drawn with the Shape tool.

Right: Turning on the Star checkbox inverts the polygon's angles, so instead of drawing a hexagon, you create a star.

- **Indent Sides By.** If you're drawing a star, this sets how much (in a percentage) you want the sides to indent.

- **Smooth Indents.** Turn this checkbox on if you don't want sharp *interior* angles on your star.

Line Tool

Not surprisingly, you use this tool for drawing straight lines and arrows. Specify the weight (width) of the line in pixels in the Options bar. If you want an arrowhead on your line, the Shape Options menu lets you control what it looks like:

- **Start/End.** Do you want the arrowhead at the start or the end of the line you draw? Tell Elements your preference by turning on the appropriate checkbox.

- **Width and Length.** These settings determine how wide and how long the arrowhead is. The measurement unit is the percentage of the line width, so if you enter a number lower than 100, your arrowhead is narrower than the line it's attached to. You can pick values between 10 and 5,000 percent. If your length setting is too low, you get a shape that looks more like a T than an arrow.

- **Concavity.** Use this setting if you want the sides of the arrowhead indented. The number determines the amount of curvature on the widest part of the arrowhead (see Figure 12-25). Pick a setting between –50 percent and +50 percent.

TIP   If you prefer fancier arrows, you'll find some in the Custom Shape tool, explained next.

The Custom Shape Tool

This tool lets you draw a huge variety of different objects, as you can see in Figure 12-26. Its Tools panel icon is the little blue heart. Click it or press U and then choose the Custom Shape tool from the pop-out menu.

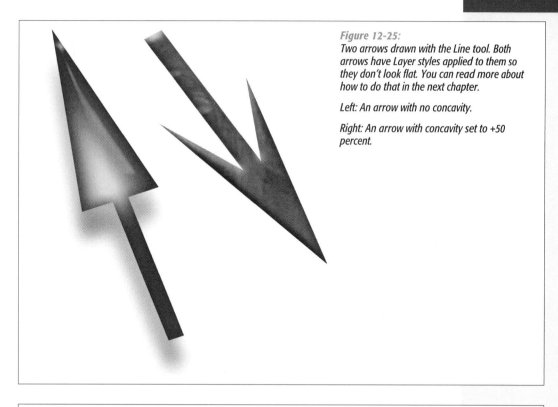

Figure 12-25:
Two arrows drawn with the Line tool. Both arrows have Layer styles applied to them so they don't look flat. You can read more about how to do that in the next chapter.

Left: An arrow with no concavity.

Right: An arrow with concavity set to +50 percent.

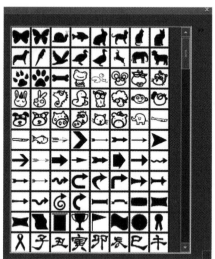

Figure 12-26:
Here's just a small part of the shape library you can choose from in the Shape Picker.

Once the Custom Shape tool is active, the Options bar displays a little thumbnail labeled "Shape" with a drop-down arrow next to it. Click this arrow to bring up the Shape Picker. Various shapes automatically appear, but if you click the double arrows in the upper-right corner of the window, you see a menu with lots more choices. To scroll through them all, choose All Elements Shapes.

> **TIP** There's a copyright symbol shape if you want something official-looking that's easy to size way up for use as a watermark on your photos.

The Custom Shape tool also has a few Shape Options settings:

- **Unconstrained.** This setting lets you control the proportions of your shape by the way you drag.

- **Defined Proportions.** The shape keeps the proportions that the designer who created the shape gave it.

- **Defined Size.** The shape is always the size it was originally created to be—dragging won't make it bigger or smaller. It just plinks out at a fixed size that you can't control (except by resizing after the fact).

- **Fixed Size.** Enter the dimensions you want in inches, pixels, or centimeters.

- **From Center.** Lets you start drawing in the center of the object.

> **NOTE** Note: You can add shapes to Elements (page 556 explains how), but they appear in the Content panel, not the Shape Picker. Look for files that end in *.csh* when you're downloading new shapes.

The Shape Selection Tool

The gray, upward-pointing arrow icon in the Options bar (just to the left of any Shape tool's icon) is the Shape Selection tool. This is a special kind of Move tool (page 165) that works only on shapes that haven't been simplified yet (page 395), as explained in Figure 12-27. (You can also activate the Shape Selection tool from the Tools panel pop-out menu.)

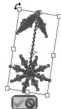

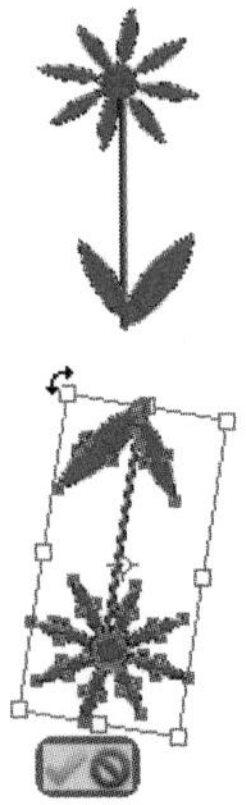

Figure 12-27:
The Shape Selection tool gives you the same kind of bounding box as the Move tool, and it works the same way, but only on shapes that haven't been simplified. You can also apply transformations like skewing and rotating (page 359) when the Shape Selection tool is active. Once you simplify a shape's layer, you have to use the regular Move tool to move it around. You can always use the Move tool, even on shapes that haven't been simplified, where you could use the Shape Selection tool instead.

This tool may seem unnecessary, but if you're working with lots of shapes, it saves tons of time not to have to keep switching tools when you want to move a shape. Just click the Shape Selection tool and then move your shape. (The shape doesn't have to be on the active layer.) You can also use this Selection tool to combine multiple shapes into one by clicking the Options bar's Combine button. You also have the other options that you have when using any of the shape tools: add, subtract, intersect, and exclude.

The Shape Selection tool works just like the Move tool: You can drag to move, hold down Alt to copy (instead of moving) the original shape, drag the handles to resize the shape, and so on. Unfortunately, you can't align and distribute shapes with this tool the way you can with the Move tool. If you need to line things up, use the regular Move tool instead.

WORKAROUND WORKSHOP

Drawing Outlines and Borders

If you've played around with the Shape tool, you may have noticed that you can't draw shapes that are just outlines (that is, that aren't filled with color). No matter what you do, your shape is always a solid shape (except for the frame shapes). Even if you haven't ever touched the Shape tool, you may be wondering how the heck to get a simple, plain-colored border around a photo.

The easiest way to create an outline is to make a selection using the Marquee tool or another selection tool and then select Edit → Stroke (Outline) Selection. The Stroke dialog box pops up and lets you enter the width of the line in pixels and choose a color.

You'll also see choices for Location, which tell Elements where you want the line—around the inside edge of the selection, centered on the edge of the selection, or around the outside. (If you're bordering an entire photo, don't choose Outside, or the border won't show up because it's off the edge of your image.)

You can also choose a blend mode (page 382) and set the opacity. Using a mode can give you a more subtle edge than a normal stroke does. The Preserve Transparency checkbox just ensures that any transparent areas in your layer stay transparent. When you're finished adjusting the Stroke dialog box's settings, click OK and then deselect (press Ctrl+D or just click someplace else in the image) to turn off your Marquee, and you've got yourself an outlined shape.

Be sure to also check out some of the simpler frame designs in the Content panel (page 474). They let you apply a simple border with just a double-click.

The Cookie Cutter Tool

At first glance, you may think the Cookie Cutter is a pretty silly tool. But actually, it's a really handy tool that you may use all the time once you understand it. The Cookie Cutter creates the same shapes as the Custom Shape tool, but you use it to crop a photo to the shape you chose. Want a heart-shaped portrait of your sweetie? The Cookie Cutter is your tool. If you're a scrapbooker, with a couple of clicks you can get results that would have taken ages and a bunch of special scissors to create with paper.

If you're not into that sort of thing, don't go away, because hidden in the shapes library are some of the most sophisticated, artistic crop shapes you can find. You can use them to get the kinds of effects that people pay commercial artists big bucks to create—like abstract crops that give a jagged or worn edge to your photo (great for contemporary effects).

You can also combine the result with a stroked edge, as explained in the box on page 399, and maybe a Layer style (page 423). Even without any additional frills, your photo's shape will appear more interesting, as shown in Figure 12-28.

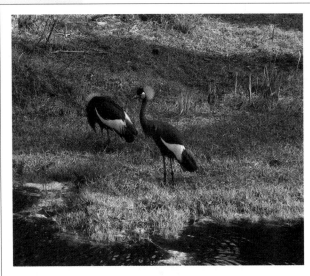

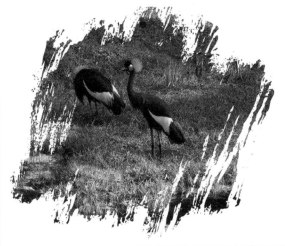

Figure 12-28:
A quick drag with the Cookie Cutter is all it took to create the bottom graphic from the top photo. If you want to create custom album or scrapbook pages, you can rotate or skew your crops before you commit them. Page 359 explains how to rotate and skew your images.

Elements also gives you a couple of other ways to create cutouts and fancy edge effects. If you plan to print your cropped photo for use in a scrapbooking project, for example, check out the Picture Package (page 500). The frames there include some shape crops, and you can do everything right in the Organizer Print dialog box, if those shapes work for you. (Despite the name, you can make a Picture Package with only one photo.) And the Frames section of the Content panel (page 474) includes a bunch of crops, ranging from simple shapes like stars to elaborate edges that make your photo look like a half-completed jigsaw puzzle.

You use the Cookie Cutter just like the Custom Shape tool, but you cut a shape from a photo, instead of drawing a shape:

1. **Activate the Cookie Cutter tool.**

   Click the Cookie Cutter in the Tools panel (its icon is like a star), or press Q.

2. **Select the shape you want your photo to be.**

   Choose a shape from the Shapes panel by clicking the down arrow next to the shape displayed in the Options bar. You have access to all the Custom Shapes, but pay special attention to the Crop Shapes category. Click the double arrows on the Shape Picker to see all the shape categories, or choose All Elements Shapes.

3. **Adjust your settings, if necessary.**

   You have the same Shape Options described earlier for the Custom Shapes (page 398), so you can set a fixed size or constrain proportions if you want. Click the Shape Options button to see your choices.

   You can choose to feather the edge of your shape, too. Just enter the amount in pixels. (See page 151 for more about feathering.) The Crop option crops the edges of your photo so they're just large enough to contain the shape.

4. **Drag in your photo.**

   A mask appears over your photo, and you see only the area that will still be there once you crop, surrounded by transparency.

5. **Adjust your crop if necessary.**

   You can reposition the shape mask or drag its corners to resize it. Although the cropped areas disappear, they'll reappear as you reposition the mask if you move it so that they're included again.

   Once you've created the shape, you'll see the Transform options (page 359) in the Options bar (which means that you can skew or distort it if you want) until you *commit* your shape, as explained in the next step. You can drag the mask around to reposition it, or Shift-drag a corner to resize it without altering the proportions. It may take a little maneuvering to get exactly the parts of your photo that you want inside the crop.

6. **When you've got everything lined up the way you want, click the Commit button (the green checkmark) in the image window or just press Enter.**

If you don't like the results, click the Cancel button (the red circle) or press Esc. Once you've made your crop, you can use Ctrl+Z if you want to undo it to try something else.

NOTE   The Cookie Cutter replaces the areas it removes with transparency. If the transparency checkerboard makes it too hard for you to get a clear look at what you've done, temporarily create a new white or colored Fill layer (page 195) beneath the cropped layer. You can delete it once you're sure you're happy with your crop.

Filters, Effects, Layer Styles, and Gradients

There's a popular saying among artistic types who use software in their studios: *Tools don't equal talent.* And it's true: No mere program is going to turn a klutz into a Klimt. But Elements has a few special tools—filters, effects, and Layer styles—that can sure help you fool a lot of people. It's amazing what a difference you can make to the appearance of any image with only a couple of clicks.

Filters are a jaw-droppingly easy way to change the appearance of your images. You can use certain filters for enhancing and correcting images, but Elements also gives you a bunch of other filters that are great for unleashing all your artistic impulses, as shown in Figure 13-1. You'll find the original photos (*rooftops.jpg* and *bauhinia.jpg*) on the Missing CD page at *www.missingmanuals.com*, if you want to play around with these images yourself.

Most filters have settings you can adjust to control how the filter changes your photo. Elements has more than a hundred different filters, so there isn't room in this chapter to cover each one individually. But you'll learn the basics of applying filters, and get in-depth coverage of some of the filters you're most likely to use frequently.

Effects, on the other hand, are like little macros or scripts designed to make elaborate changes to your image, such as creating a 3-D frame around it or making it look like a pencil sketch or an oil pastel. They're super easy to apply—you just double-click a button—but you can't tweak their settings as easily as you can with filters, since effects are programmed to make very specific changes. (Adobe calls them Photo Effects, but you can apply them to any kind of image, not just photos.)

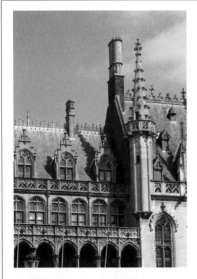

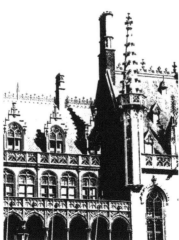

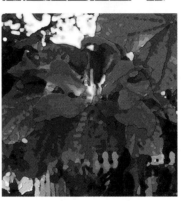

Figure 13-1:
*Elements' filters let you add all
sorts of artistic effects to your
photos. Here you see two plain
photos on the left, and on the
right two examples of how you
can transform them with filters.*

*Top: These figures show how
you can make a photo
resemble a colored-steel
engraving.*

*Bottom: These figures show
how you can create a
watercolor look. For both
images, several filters were
applied to build up the effect.*

If you've used Elements before, then you may know that the effects are also called *actions*. Full-featured Photoshop lets you record and save your own actions, and install actions created by others. Elements has an Action Player, so you can use certain Photoshop actions in Elements. You can't *create* actions in Elements, but you can run them once someone creates them for you.

Layer styles change the appearance of just one layer of your photo (see Chapter 6 for more about layers). They're great for creating impressive-looking text, but you also can apply them to objects and shapes. Most Layer styles include settings you can easily modify.

You can combine filters, effects, and Layer styles on the same image if you like. And you can spend hours trying different groupings, because it's addicting to watch the often-unpredictable results you get when mixing them up.

The last section of this chapter focuses on *gradients*. A gradient is a rainbow-like range of color that you can use to color in an object or a background. You can also use gradients and *gradient maps*—gradients that get distributed according to the brightness values in your photo—for precise retouching effects.

Using Filters

Filters let you change the look of your photos in complex ways, and using them is as easy as double-clicking a button. Elements gives you a ton of filters, grouped into categories so it's easier for you to choose the one that does what you want. This section offers a quick tour through the filter categories and some info about using some of the most popular filters, like Noise and Blur.

To make it easy to work with filters, Elements lets you apply them from two different places: the Filter menu, where you choose them from the list that appears, and the Effects panel. (The Filter menu is the only place where you can see *every* filter. Some filters, like the Adjustment filters, don't appear in the panel.) Elements also has a Filter Gallery, a great feature that helps you get a good idea of how your photo will look when you apply the artistic filters. The next part of this section explains how to use all three methods.

Applying Filters

In the Filter menu, you choose a filter from the list by category and then by name. In the Effects panel, thumbnail images give you a preview of what the filters do by showing how they affect a picture of an apple. Filters do the same thing whichever way you choose them.

The Filter Gallery gives you a preview of what a filter looks like when applied to *your* image. Some filters automatically open the Filter Gallery when you choose them from the menu or the panel. Or you can call up the Gallery (without first choosing a filter) by going to Filter → Filter Gallery. You can't apply every filter from the Gallery—only some of the ones with adjustable settings.

> TIP   You can easily apply the same filter repeatedly: Press Ctrl+F, and Elements automatically applies the last filter you used, with whatever settings you last used. The top listing in the Filter menu also shows the name of this same filter (selecting it has the same effect as the keyboard shortcut: Elements applies it with the same settings you just used). Press Ctrl+Alt+F to bring up the dialog box the for last filter you used, so you can change your settings.

Filter menu

The Filter menu groups filters into 14 categories (Correct Camera Distortion [page 354] is all by itself at the top of the list, not in a category). You'll also see a divider below the bottom category (Other). When you first install Elements, the Digimarc filter is the only filter below this line, but other filters you download or purchase will appear here, too.

When you choose a filter from the list, one of three things happens:

- **Elements applies the filter automatically.** This happens if the filter's name doesn't have an ellipsis (…) after it in the list. Just look at the result in your photo, and then undo it (Ctrl+Z) if you don't like the effect. (You can't adjust settings for these filters to tweak their effects.) If you do like it, then you're done.

- **You see a dialog box.** Elements filters that have adjustable settings have an ellipsis (…) after their names. Some of them (mostly corrective filters) open a dialog box where you can tweak their settings. Adjust the settings while watching the small preview in the dialog box to see what you're doing, and then click OK.

- **You see the Filter Gallery.** Some of the more artistic, adjustable filters automatically call up the Filter Gallery so you can get a nice, big preview of what you're doing and rearrange the order of multiple filters before applying them. Applying filters from the Gallery is explained on page 407.

Regardless of how you apply the filter, once you're done, you can always undo it (Ctrl+Z) if you're not happy with the effect. If you like it, then there's no need to do anything else except save your image.

> **TIP** Since you can't undo filters after you've closed your image, many people apply filters to a duplicate layer. Press Ctrl+J to create a duplicate layer.

Effects panel

If you're more comfortable with visual clues when choosing a filter, then you can find most filters in the Effects panel (Figure 13-2), which is, logically enough, also where you apply effects (page 420).

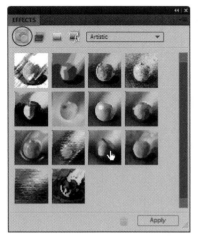

Figure 13-2:
The Effects panel gives you a preview of what every filter looks like when applied to the same picture of a green apple. Click the Filters button (circled), and then, from the drop-down menu (the one that says "Artistic" here), choose a category. If you know what you want a filter to do, but don't know what it's called, scrolling through these thumbnail images should help you find the one you want. To apply a filter from the panel, double-click the thumbnail, or click the thumbnail once and then click Apply. You can also drag the filter's thumbnail from the panel onto your image.

The Effects panel is one of the panels in the Panel bin the first time you launch Elements. If it's not there waiting for you, go to Window → Effects, and then click the Filters button (circled in Figure 13-2). Choose a category from the drop-down menu or choose Show All. The categories are the same as in the Filter menu, except that Adjustments is available only in the menu, and Sharpen appears in the panel but not in the menu.

To apply a filter from the panel, double-click its thumbnail or drag the thumbnail onto your image. If the filter has adjustable settings, Elements displays the same dialog box or Filter Gallery window you'd see when applying the filter from the Filter menu, as described earlier.

One small drawback to applying filters from the panel is that you can't tell from the thumbnail whether a filter is one that applies automatically, with no adjustable settings. Elements doesn't give you any clue like an ellipsis (…) to tell you which group a filter falls into.

Filter Gallery

The Filter Gallery (Filter → Filter Gallery), shown in Figure 13-3, is one of Elements' more popular features. It gives you a big preview window, a look at all the green-apple thumbnails so you have a visual guide to what each filter will do, and, most importantly, it lets you apply filters like layers—you can stack them up and change the order in which Elements applies them to your image. Changing the order can make some big differences in how filters affect your image. For example, you get very different results if you apply Ink Outlines *after* the Sprayed Strokes filter compared to the opposite order. The Gallery makes it easy to play around and see which order gives you the look you want. The layer-like behavior of the filters in the gallery is only for previewing, though—you don't end up with any new layers after you apply the filter(s).

The Gallery is more for artistic filters than corrective filters. You can't apply the Adjustment or Noise filters from here, for instance. The Gallery's filters are from the artistic, brushstroke, distort, sketch, stylize, and texture categories. (See the next section for an overview of all the filter categories.)

The Filter Gallery window is divided into three panes. On the left side is a preview of what your image will look like when you apply the filter. The center holds the thumbnails for the different filters, and the right side contains the settings for the currently chosen filter. Your *filter layers* are at the bottom of the settings pane. You can see what filters you've applied, add or subtract filters, and rearrange their order here.

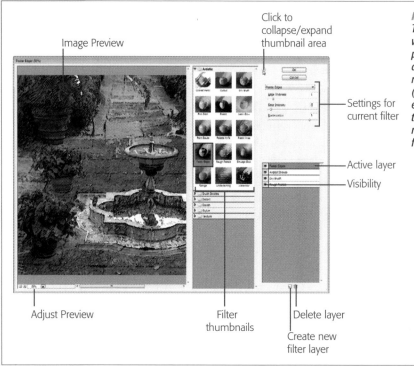

Click to
collapse/expand
thumbnail area

Image Preview

Settings for
current filter

Active layer

Visibility

Adjust Preview

Filter
thumbnails

Delete layer

Create new
filter layer

Figure 13-3:
The Filter Gallery. If you
want an even larger
preview, then click the
double arrow in the top-
right part of the window
(labeled "collapse/
expand") to collapse the
thumbnail area and
regain that whole section
for preview space.

NOTE   You don't create any new, permanent layers when you use the Filter Gallery. Filter layers work something like regular layers (see Chapter 6), but they're what you might call "working
layers": They help you figure out which order to apply filters in; they don't actually create new layers in your image. In other words, you have separate filter layers only until you click OK in the
Filter Gallery. Then all your chosen filters get applied to your image at once. You can't apply the filters, close your photo, come back later, and still see the filters as individual, changeable layers. And
most importantly, your filters become part of the layer to which you apply them.

If you've used a recent version of full-featured Photoshop, then be aware that Elements doesn't
create editable smart filters the way Photoshop does—it handles filters the way earlier versions of
Photoshop (Photoshop CS2 and earlier) did. This trait is good to keep in mind if you're trying to
do something based on instructions written for Photoshop (a tutorial you've found online, say).

In addition to letting you adjust the settings for a given filter, the Filter Gallery lets
you perform a few other tricks:

- **Adjust the preview magnification of your image.** In the Gallery's lower-left corner, click the percentage or the arrow next to it to bring up a list of preset views
  to choose from. You can also click the + and − buttons to zoom in or out. Easier still, use the Ctrl+= (the Ctrl key plus the equal sign key) and Ctrl+− (the
  Ctrl key plus the minus key) shortcuts to zoom in and out from the keyboard.

- **Choose a new filter.** Click a filter's thumbnail once, and you see the settings for the new filter and the preview image updates right away—usually. (The box on page 411 has details.)

- **Add a new filter layer.** Each time you click the New Filter Layer icon (see Figure 13-4), you add another filter layer to the ones you already have.

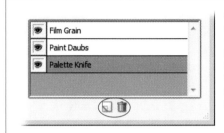

Figure 13-4:
If you've used layers before (see Chapter 6), then these little icons (circled) should look familiar. In the Filter Gallery, they make new filter layers instead of regular layers. Click the square icon to add a new filter layer to your image. Click the trashcan icon to delete a filter layer. The eye icons next to your filter layers turn visibility on and off just as they do in the Layers panel. Remember, filter layers don't show up as real layers in the Layers panel—only in the Filter Gallery.

- **Change the position of filter layers.** Just drag them up and down in the stack to change the order Elements will apply them to your image.

- **Hide filter layers.** Click the eye next to a filter layer in the filter layer panel to turn off its visibility, just like in the regular Layers panel (page 180).

- **Delete filter layers.** Highlight any filter layer by clicking it, and then click the trashcan icon to delete it.

- **Change the content of a layer.** You can change what kind of filter is in a particular layer. For instance, if you applied the Smudge Stick, and you like all your other changes but wish you had used the Glass filter instead, then you don't have to delete the Smudge Stick layer. Just highlight the Smudge layer, and then click the Glass filter button to change that layer's contents.

TIP   If you press Ctrl+F using the Filter Gallery, Elements reapplies all the filters that were in your last gallery set. Ctrl+Alt+F brings up the dialog box for the last filter so you can change your settings before you apply it again.

Filter Categories

Elements divides filters into categories to help you more easily track down the one you want. Some of the categories, like Distort, contain filters that vary hugely in what they do to your photo. Other categories, like the Brush Stroke filters, contain filters that are all pretty obviously related to one another. Here's a quick breakdown of the categories:

- **Correct Camera Distortion.** This isn't really a category, just a single filter that lets you correct perspective distortion (think: tall buildings) as well as vignetting (shadows) caused by your camera's lens. It's explained in detail on page 354.

- **Adjustments.** These filters apply some photographic, stylistic, and artistic changes to your photo. Most of the adjustments are explained on page 315; the Photo Filters are covered on page 273.

- **Artistic.** This is a huge group of filters that do everything from give your photo a cut-from-paper look (Cutout) to make it resemble a quick sketch (Rough Pastels). You generally get the best effects with these filters by using multiple filters or applying the same one several times.

- **Blur.** The blur filters let you soften focus and add artistic effects. They're explained later in this chapter (page 415).

- **Brush Strokes.** These filters apply brushstroke effects and create a hand-painted look.

- **Distort.** These filters warp images in a variety of ways. The Liquify filter is the most powerful, and you'll find a tutorial for using it on page 453.

- **Noise.** Use these filters to add or remove grain. They're explained on page 413.

- **Pixelate.** These filters break up your image in different ways, making it show the dot pattern of a magazine or newspaper's printed image (Halftone), or the fragmented look you see on television when a show is concealing someone's identity.

NOTE The Color Halftone filter makes your image look like it's made of many dots of color, like a magazine or other printed illustration, or comic-style pop art. However, it's not the same as true halftone screening, which Elements can't do. If the print shop you're working with needs a halftone, you have to either use the full-featured Photoshop or ask the printer to do the conversion for you.

- **Render.** This group includes a pretty diverse bunch of filters that let you do things like create a lens flare effect (Lens Flare), transform a flat object so it looks 3-D (3D Transform), and make your image look like fibers (Fibers) or clouds (Clouds). The Lighting Effects filter, a powerful but confusing filter that's like a whole program in itself, helps you change the way lighting appears in your image. For a full rundown on what this filter does and how to use it, check out the Missing CD page at *www.missingmanuals.com*.

- **Sharpen.** This category, which only contains the Unsharp Mask filter (page 237), appears in the panel but not the Filter menu. (The sharpening commands are in the Enhance menu instead.)

- **Sketch.** These filters can make your photo look like it was drawn with charcoal, chalk, crayon, or some other material, or make the photo look like it was embossed in wet plaster, photocopied, or stamped with a rubber stamp.

- **Stylize.** These filters create special effects by increasing the contrast in your photo and displacing pixels. You can make your photo look radioactive or like it's moving quickly, or reduce it to outlines.

- **Texture.** These filters change the surface of your photo to look like it was made from another material. Use them to create a crackled finish (Craquelure), a stained-glass look (Stained Glass), or a mosaic effect (Mosaic Tiles).

- **Video.** These filters are for creating and editing images for (and from) videos.

- **Other.** This is a group of fairly technical, highly customizable filters. The High Pass filter is explained on page 242. You can use Offset to shift an image or a layer a little bit, or to position tiled image layers.

- **Digimarc.** Use this filter to check for Digimarc watermarks in photos. Digimarc is a company that lets subscribers enter their info in a database so that anyone who gets one of their photos can find out who holds the copyright.

You can find a number of filter plug-ins online, ranging from free to very expensive. Page 551 suggests some places to start looking. Once you've installed new filters, you access them in the Filter menu, at the bottom of the list.

NOTE Filters are platform specific, so you can't use plug-ins written for the Mac version of Elements if you're running Windows. Only Windows plug-ins work with the Windows version of Elements.

UNDER THE HOOD

Filter Performance Hints

If Elements could speak, it would say, "Easy for *you*," when it comes to filters and effects. Although you don't have to do much to apply them, the program has a huge amount of work to do on its end. Elements is pretty fast, but if your computer is slow or memory-challenged, it can take a long time to apply filters and even to update the preview. You can speed things up by applying filters to a selection for previewing. Filters that have their own dialog boxes—as opposed to the Filter Gallery—display a flashing line under the size percentage (below the preview area) to show their progress.

Here are few other filter-related tips worth remembering:

- Filters don't do anything if they don't have pixels to work on, so be sure you're targeting a layer with something in it—not an Adjustment layer.

- If you apply a filter to a selection, you'll probably want to feather (page 151) or refine (page 145) the edges to help blend the filtered edges into your photo.

- Alt-click the Cancel button in the Filter Gallery or in any filter dialog box to turn it into a Reset button. Clicking Cancel makes the window go away, while Reset lets you start over without having to call up the filter again.

- If your filters are grayed out in the Filter menu, check to be sure you're not in 16-bit mode (page 263) or in grayscale, bitmapped, or index color (all these color modes are explained on page 51).

Useful Filter Solutions

This section shows how to use some of Elements' most popular and useful filters to correct your photos and create special effects. For instance, you'll learn how to modify graininess to create an aged effect or to smooth out a repair job. And you'll find out how to blur photos to create a soft-focus effect, or to make subjects look like they're moving.

Removing noise: Getting rid of graininess

Noise, undesired graininess in an image, is a big problem with many digital cameras, especially those with small sensors and high megapixel counts. It's rare to find a fixed-lens camera with more than 5 megapixels that doesn't have some trouble with noise, especially in underexposed areas.

If you shoot using the Raw format, then you can correct a fair amount of noise right in the Raw Converter (page 263). But the Raw Converter may produce unpredictable results if you use it on JPEGs. And even Raw files may need further noise reduction once you've edited a photo after converting it.

Elements includes the Reduce Noise filter, which is designed specifically to help get rid of noise in your photos. To get to it, go to Filter → Noise → Reduce Noise. You get a dialog box with a preview window on the left and settings on the right. To use the filter, first use the controls below the preview to set the view to at least 100 percent, or preferably even higher. You need to see the pixels in your photo so you can tell how the filter is changing them as you adjust the settings.

You get three settings, each of which you control by a slider:

- **Strength.** This setting controls the overall impact of the filter. It reduces the same kind of noise as the Luminance Smoothing setting in the Raw converter (page 263). The higher this setting is, the greater the risk of softening your photo.

- **Preserve Details.** Using noise reduction can soften the appearance of your photo. This setting tells Elements how much care to take to preserve details.

- **Reduce Color Noise.** This control adjusts uneven color distribution in your image. You can set the slider pretty high without harming your photo.

The Remove JPEG Artifact checkbox tells Elements to minimize *JPEG artifacts*—the uneven areas of color caused by JPEG compression (see page 73). A mottled pattern in what should be a clear blue sky is one classic example of JPEG artifacting. Turn on the checkbox to help smooth things out.

For each setting, move the slider to the right if you want more and to the left if you want less. Watch the effect in the preview window to see how you like the changes. You may notice a little lag time before the preview updates. When you see what you want, click OK to apply the filter.

The Reduce Noise filter does an OK job on areas with a small amount of noise, like the sky in many JPEG photos, but it's not one of Element's strongest tools. If your camera has major noise problems, you may need special noise reduction software. Some of the most popular programs are Noise Ninja (*www.picturecode.com*), Neat Image (*www.neatimage.com*), and Noiseware (*www.imagenomic.com*). All have demo versions you can download to try out the programs. If you search on Google for "noise reduction software," you'll get a variety of other options as well, including several free programs.

Adding noise: Smoothing out repair jobs

Elements also gives you a filter for *creating* noise. Why do that when most of the time you try so hard to get rid of noise? One reason is when you're trying to age your photo: If you want to make it look like it came from an old newspaper, for instance, you'd add some noise.

The other most common use for noise is to help make repaired spots blend in with the rest of an image. If you've altered part of a photo in Elements, especially by painting on it, odds are the repaired area looks perfectly smooth. That's great if the rest of the photo is noise free. But if the photo is a little grainy, that smooth patch is going to stand out like a sore thumb. Add a bit of noise to make it blend in better, as shown in Figure 13-5. Also, if you see color banding when you print, adding a little noise to the photo may help fix that in your next print.

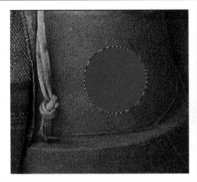
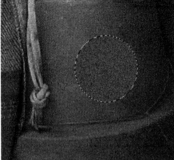

Figure 13-5:
Left: If you use the Average Blur filter in a repair on this noisy photo, the blended area stands out, making the repair obvious.

Right: By adding some noise, the change becomes much less noticeable.

To add noise to a photo, start by selecting the area where you want to add noise. Using a duplicate layer (Ctrl+J) for the noise is a good idea, since you can always undo changes if you've got them on their own layer. Here's what you do:

1. **Call up the Add Noise filter.**

   Go to Filter → Noise → Add Noise to bring up the filter's dialog box.

2. **Adjust the settings to your liking.**

   The settings are explained in the following list. Use the dialog box's preview window to check how the changes are affecting your photo.

3. **When you're satisfied, click OK.**

You have three options in the Add Noise dialog box:

• **Amount.** This option controls how heavy the noise is going to be. Just drag the slider to the right for more noise or to the left for less. You can also type in a number; a higher percentage means more noise.

- **Uniform or Gaussian.** These buttons let you control how the noise gets distributed through your image. Uniform is just what it says—the same all over. Gaussian produces a more speckled effect.

  If you're adding noise to duplicate existing noise in a grainy photo, then you probably want Gaussian distribution. For an old newspaper photo look, try Uniform. In either case, experiment until you get what you want.

- **Monochromatic.** This setting limits you to grayscale noise. Take a look at the middle image in Figure 13-6, and notice how many more colors you can see in the noise, compared to the solid red of the original. The bottom-left bell's noise was applied with the Monochromatic setting turned off.

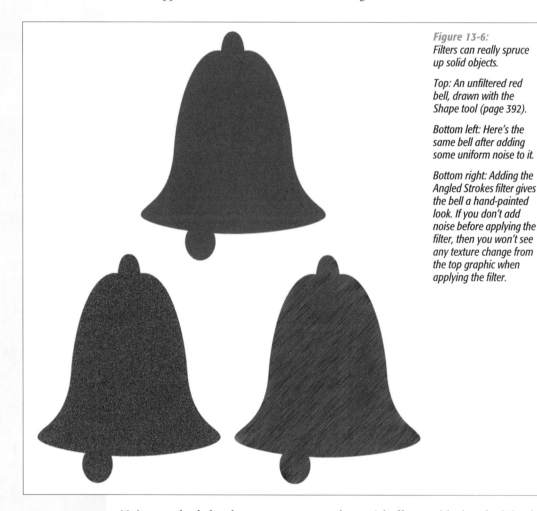

Figure 13-6:
Filters can really spruce up solid objects.

Top: An unfiltered red bell, drawn with the Shape tool (page 392).

Bottom left: Here's the same bell after adding some uniform noise to it.

Bottom right: Adding the Angled Strokes filter gives the bell a hand-painted look. If you don't add noise before applying the filter, then you won't see any texture change from the top graphic when applying the filter.

Noise can also help when you want to apply special effects to blocks of solid color, as shown in Figure 13-6. If you try to apply the Angled Strokes filter to a solid color, then you don't see the strokes. Adding noise gives the filter something to work on.

Gaussian Blur: Drawing attention to an object

Probably the most frequently used of the Blur filters, Gaussian Blur (Filter → Blur → Gaussian Blur) lets you control how much an image is blurred. Besides using it to blur large areas, like the background in Figure 13-7, bottom, you can apply the Gaussian Blur filter at a very low setting to soften lines—useful when you're going for a sketched effect. If you'd like to try out the different blurs, download the hawk photo (*yellowbeak.jpg*) from the Missing CD page at *www.missingmanuals.com*.

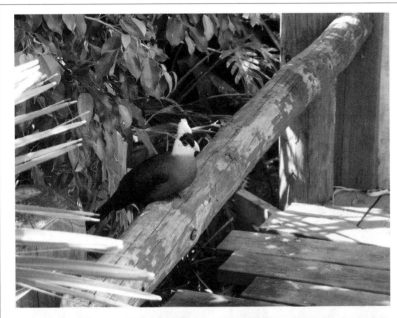

Figure 13-7:

Top: This little guy felt well enough hidden to let the camera get pretty close, and he was almost right: it's hard to focus on him with all the stuff in the background. Blurring the background will center the focus on the bird rather than the distracting details.

Bottom: Applying the Gaussian Blur to the background makes the bird the clear focal point.

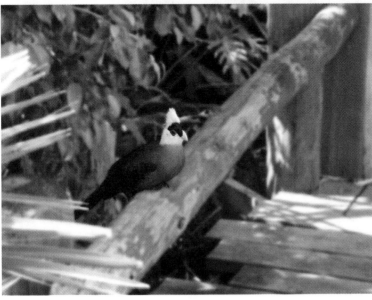

When using the Gaussian Blur, you have to set the *radius,* which controls how much the filter blurs things. A higher radius produces more blurring; use the filter's preview window to see what you're doing.

Radial Blur: Producing a sense of motion

As you can see in Figure 13-8, the Radial Blur filter really creates a sense of motion. It has two styles: Zoom, which is designed to give the effect of a camera zooming in, and Spin, which produces a circular effect around a center point you designate.

The Radial Blur dialog box may look a bit complicated, but it's really not. (Call it up by going to Filter → Blur → Radial Blur.) Unfortunately, you don't get a preview with this filter, because it drains so much processor power. That's why you have a choice between Draft, Good, and Best Quality. Use Draft for a quick look at roughly what you'll get. Then, most of the time, choose Good for the final version. Good and Best aren't very different except on large images, so don't feel like you always have to choose Best for the final version.

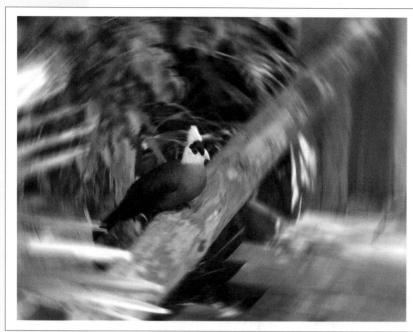

Figure 13-8:
A Radial Blur applied in Spin mode. As you can see, this filter can produce an almost vertiginous sense of motion. If you don't want to give people motion sickness, go easy on the Amount setting. This is a setting of 5, but unless you're looking for a psychedelic '60s effect, 1 or 2 is usually plenty.

Once you've chosen your method (Zoom or Spin), set the Amount, which controls how intense a blur Elements applies. Next, click inside the Blur Center box to tell Elements where you want the blur centered, as shown in Figure 13-9. Finally, click OK when you're finished.

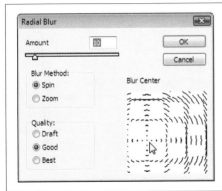

Figure 13-9:
The Blur Center box lets you identify the center point of the Radial Blur's effect (whether you've chosen Zoom or Spin mode). Drag the ripple drawing inside the box in any direction; here, the center point has been moved just to the left and down from its original position in the center of the box.

Color correcting with the Average Blur filter

If you've already given the Average Blur filter a whirl, then you may be wondering what on earth Adobe was thinking when they created it. If you use the filter on a whole photo, then your image disappears under a hideous soup, something like what you'd get by pureeing together all the colors in your photo. Oddly enough, this effect makes the filter a great tool for getting rid of color casts (page 227). You can use the Average Blur to create a sort of custom Photo Filter (page 273) toned specially for the image you use it on. The secret is in using blend modes (page 182). Here's how:

1. **Open your image and make a duplicate layer.**

   Press Ctrl+J or go to Layer → Duplicate Layer.

2. **Apply the Average Blur filter.**

   Make sure your duplicate layer is the active layer (click it in the Layers panel if it isn't), and then go to Filter → Blur → Average. Your photo disappears under a layer of (probably) very unpleasing solid color, but you'll fix that next.

3. **Change the blur layer's blend mode.**

   In the Layers panel, from the Mode drop-down menu, choose Color. Already things are starting to look better.

4. **Invert the blur layer.**

   Press Ctrl+I to invert the colors.

5. **Reduce the blur layer's opacity and do any other necessary tweaking.**

   Use the Layers panel's opacity slider. Start with 50 percent. By now, the color should look right—no more color cast. Tweak if necessary, and then save your work.

   TIP   You may want to add a Hue/Saturation layer (page 196) if you find that no matter how you adjust the opacity slider, the photo still looks a little flat.

The Average Blur filter is a particularly good way to color-correct underwater photos, where it's hard to get a realistic white balance using your camera's built-in settings.

Improving skin texture with the Surface Blur filter

Elements gives you yet another way to blur your photos—the Surface Blur filter. At this point you may be thinking that you have enough ways to eliminate details in your photos, but Surface Blur is actually very handy, especially if you take pictures of people. This filter is smart enough to avoid blurring details and areas of high contrast, which makes it very handy for fixing skin. If you want to eliminate pores, for instance, or reduce the visibility of freckles, this is your tool, as shown in Figure 13-10, and it's pretty simple to use, too:

1. **Open your image, and then make a duplicate layer.**

   Press Ctrl+J or go to Layer → Duplicate Layer.

   > **TIP** For best results, you may want to start by selecting the area you want to blur (see Chapter 5 for help with selections). Then make your duplicate layer from the selection, in order to maintain maximum detail in the areas you aren't trying to fix. For example, select only the skin areas of your subject's face, leaving out the mouth and eye areas so they won't be affected by the blur.

2. **Apply the Surface Blur filter.**

   Make sure your duplicate layer is the active layer (click it in the Layers panel if it isn't), and then go to Filter → Blur → Surface Blur. Move the dialog box out of the way, if necessary, so that you can watch what you're doing in the main image window and in the dialog box's preview area.

3. **Tweak the filter's settings till you like the effect.**

   The sliders are explained below. Be cautious—it doesn't take much to make your photo start to look like a painting. Click OK when you've got the flaws concealed as much as possible without losing important details like eyelashes.

4. **If you want, change the blend mode and/or the opacity for the duplicate layer.**

   Use the Layers panel's sliders for this step. If you want to eliminate skin blemishes, try Lighten blend mode, for example.

The Surface Blur filter isn't hard to understand, but you usually have to do a fair amount of fiddling with the sliders to get the best balance for the blur effect. Here's what the sliders do:

- **Radius.** As with other filters, this setting controls how far Elements should blur your image. Move the slider to the left for a smaller blur, and to the right for a wider blur.

- **Threshold.** This slider controls the level at which Elements begins to blur. A low setting means you see less blurring; a higher setting means more blurring.

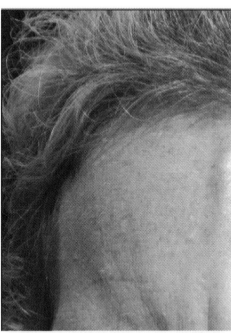

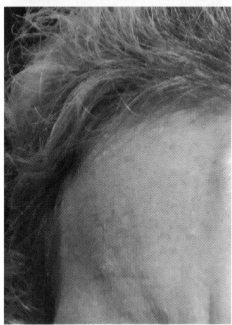

Figure 13-10:
The Surface Blur filter is handy for creating better-looking skin, minimizing lines and flaws, or reducing the visibility of pores.

Top: The original photo.

Bottom: A dose of Surface Blur evens out fine lines in the skin and preserves individual hairs that have good definition. But if you look closely, the areas of hair with less definition got blurred along with the skin. In cases like that, use a selection to limit where the blur gets applied.

TIP   When you have to do a lot of experimenting, sometimes it's easier just to highlight the number in each setting's box, and then use the up and down arrow keys to adjust the effect.

Adding Effects

Like filters, effects give you loads of ways to modify your photo's appearance—from adding lizard-skin textures to surrounding your image with a classy picture frame. Although you apply effects with a simple double-click, these clicks trigger a series of changes. Some effects involve many complex steps, but Elements works so quickly you might not even notice all the changes it makes.

NOTE   You usually can't customize or change an effect's settings–they're an all-or-nothing deal. For example, if you use one of the Frame effects, then you either take the frame size as Elements applies it to your image, or you don't; you can't adjust the scale of the frame relative to your photo. This quality is why most of the frames are now Smart Objects (page 472) that you apply from the Content panel, rather than effects–you have more control over Smart Objects.

You'll find effects in a few different spots in Elements:

- **The Effects panel** is home to most photo effects—things like photo tinting (Figure 13-11)—and a few frames. The panel is explained after this list.

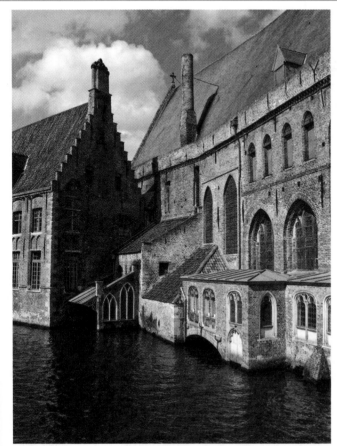

Figure 13-11:
The Effects panel's Photo Effects section lets you age a photo by applying an antique look to it, as shown here. This was a color photo until the Vintage Photo effect was applied to it.

• **The Content panel** houses some effects intended primarily for text, but sometimes you can use them for other purposes. They create cool results with shapes, too, for instance. Page 474 has the full scoop.

• **Guided Edit.** Elements has a few effects that Adobe included as part of its let-us-show-you-how section; you'll find them at the very bottom of the list of tasks, and Guided Edit walks you through applying them. (Page 32 tells you more about using Guided Edit.)

To apply an effect from the Effects panel, choose Window → Effects, and then click the Photo Effects button (it shows a rectangle with little sparkles around it). Just as with filters, use the panel's drop-down menu to see all your choices, or pick from only one category. The thumbnail images give you a preview of how each effect changes your image.

To apply an effect, in the Effects panel, double-click its thumbnail, or click the thumbnail once, and then click Apply. You can also just drag the thumbnail onto your photo. That's all there is to it. If you don't like the result, press Ctrl+Z to undo it, since you can't do much to tweak it.

Here are a couple effects-related tips to help you get the most out of these nifty-but-quirky features:

• A few effects flatten (page 193) or simplify (page 395) your image, so it's usually best to make a copy of your image, or wait until you're done making all your other edits, before applying an effect.

• Many effects create new layers; check the Layers panel once you're done applying them. You may want to flatten your image to reduce the file size before printing or storing it. (See Chapter 6 if you need a refresher on layers.)

Using Actions

If you hang around people who use Photoshop, then you'll hear a lot of talk about *actions* and how useful they are. An action is a little script, like a macro in a program like Word, that automates the steps for doing something, which can save you tons of time. For example, imagine an action that applies your favorite filter and crops a photo to a certain size, or one that creates a complicated artistic effect, like a colorful watercolor look that would take many steps to do manually. Wouldn't it be great to be able to use actions in Elements?

Well, in a way Elements has always been able to use actions—under the hood, effects are really actions. And you could always add some Photoshop actions to Elements, although the process used to be pretty complicated. But not anymore: Recent versions of Elements include the Action Player, which lets you run many Photoshop actions right in Elements.

It's quite easy to use actions in Elements. Adobe gives you a few useful ones to get you started, and you can add your own, as explained later in this section. To run an action:

1. **Open a photo in the Editor, and then go to the Action Player.**

   Click the Edit tab → Guided → Automated Actions → Action Player.

2. **From the first drop-down menu, choose the Action set you want.**

   Action sets are groups of related actions. The sets that come with Elements let you choose between actions to add captions (and canvas to display the captions), trim weight from your subjects, resize and crop your photos, or apply special effects to them.

3. **From the second drop-down menu, choose the specific action you want to use.**

   You can choose how much thinner to make someone with the Lose Weight actions, for example, or what color canvas (white, gray, or black) to add for a caption.

4. **Run the action.**

   Just click Play Action, and Elements does its thing. If you don't like the results, click Reset or press Ctrl+Z to undo the action, and then try another action instead. (You can't step backward in the Elements Action Player.)

   The actions that come with Elements all happen pretty much instantly, but if you add actions from other sources, then you may see pop-up dialog boxes to adjust settings for some steps. Just make any changes, click OK, and the action resumes and completes itself automatically.

5. **When you like the results, click Done.**

   If you decide you don't want to use an action after all, click Cancel instead.

One of the best things about the Action Player is that you can easily add more actions to it. You can't *create* new actions in Elements—you need Photoshop for that—but you'll find thousands of free actions on the Internet that you can download and add to Elements. Page 551 suggests some places to look for them.

Once you download an action, if you're using Vista, just save it in *C:\Program-Data\Adobe\Photoshop Elements\8.0\Locale\en_US\Workflow Panels\Actions* (the "en_US" part is different if you aren't in the United States). For Windows XP, it's *C:\Documents and Settings\All Users\Application Data\Adobe\Photoshop Elements\ 8.0\Locale\en_US\Workflow Panels\Actions* (ditto). (You need to turn on hidden folder viewing for either operating system, since these are hidden files; the box on page 556 tells you how.) The next time you start Elements, you'll see your action in the drop-down menu shown in Figure 13-12.

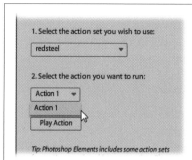

Figure 13-12:
If you add an action that isn't part of an action set, then you still have to make a choice in both Guided Edit panel menus. Just choose its name in the first menu, and then, in the Action menu, choose Action 1 as shown here.

Redsteel is an action that contains the steps used to create the building image in Figure 13-1. You can download it from the Missing CD page at www. missingmanuals.com if you want to try installing actions. It works best on photos with lots of detail. On images with large blocks of color, the effect is more like pop art than a colored steel engraving.

It's important to understand a few differences between actions in Photoshop and in Elements. Photoshop can run an action on a whole folder of images at once. In Elements, you're restricted to one photo at a time. Also, Elements can't completely perform actions that invoke Photoshop-only commands. For example, if you run an action that includes creating a history snapshot, then you see the dialog box shown in Figure 13-13.

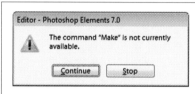

Figure 13-13:
When you run an action in Elements, you may see lots of dialog boxes asking for your input as the action works through the steps. However, if you see this dialog box, then you're trying to run an action that includes a step that Elements can't do. You don't have to stop the action, but be aware that you won't get the same results as you would in Photoshop.

If you like to play it safe, you can find a number of actions written specifically for Elements. Page 551 tells you where to look for them.

NOTE   While the Action Player is great, there's one disadvantage to having it in Guided Edit: You can't access the Layers panel, which is annoying if you're running an action that requires you to choose a layer mid-action, because you can't select a particular layer without the Layers panel. The good news is that you can install actions in the Effects panel. This lets you use actions in Full Edit, where you can get to the Layers panel anytime an action requires it. By installing actions in the Effects panel, you can still use the various add-on tools to Elements that are actually actions like the various free toolsets available online. You'll find much more about downloading and installing these in Chapter 19.

Adding Layer Styles

Like filters and effects, Layer styles let you transform objects by giving them new characteristics such as drop shadows. Layer styles are especially useful for modifying individual objects like text and buttons, because you can edit the text and change the button's shape even *after* you've applied the Layer style.

Layer styles, as their name suggests, work on the contents of one layer—rather than on your whole image. That's important. A Layer style affects *everything* on a layer. If you want to apply a Layer style to just one object in your picture, select the object, and then put it on its own layer by pressing Ctrl+J (or going to Layer → New → "Layer via Copy") or Ctrl+Shft+J (or going to New → "Layer via Cut"). Figure 13-14 shows what you can do with Layer styles.

You apply Layer styles from the Effects panel (Window → Effects). Click the Layer Styles button (which has two overlapping squares on it) and then—from the drop-down menu—choose a category or Show All. Finally, select the layer you want to modify (by highlighting it in the Layers panel), and then double-click the thumbnail for the Layer style you want to use, or click it once and then click Apply. (You can also drag a style's thumbnail to a layer to apply it.) The box on page 426 shows you how to modify any style's settings once you've applied it.

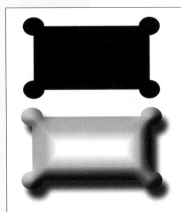

Figure 13-14:
Layer styles are great for making fancy buttons for websites. Changing this plain black Custom Shape was as simple as double-clicking the Star Glow Layer style (in Complex Styles). If you want to change something like the drop shadow, it's easy to do that once you've applied the style. (Keep reading to learn how to edit Layer styles.)

NOTE   Some tools, like the Type tool (see page 441), have an Options bar setting that lets you choose a Layer style.

Here's a quick rundown of the choices available in each Layer style category:

- **Bevels** give objects a 3-D look by making them appear raised from the page or embossed into it. Figure 13-15 shows how combining a bevel and a drop shadow can add a lot of dimension to even a simple shape.

- **Complex** includes a variety of elaborate styles that make objects look like they're made from metal, cactus, or several other materials. These styles are particularly useful for applying to type.

- **Drop Shadows** adds shadow effects that make your object look like it's floating above the page.

  NOTE   To add a drop shadow to an entire photo, you have to also add canvas (see page 111) to give the shadow someplace to fall.

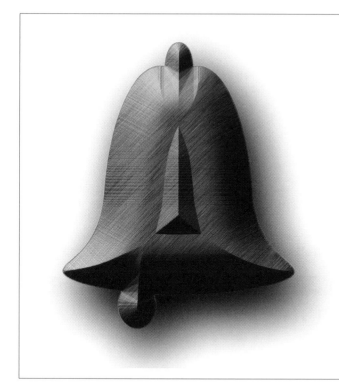

Figure 13-15:
Here's the bell image from earlier in this chapter. Adding a bevel and a drop shadow gives it much more dimension and depth.

- **Glass Buttons** are supposed to make objects look like, well, glass buttons, but many people think they look more like plastic. They're useful for creating web page buttons.

- **Image Effects** give you a wealth of ways to transform your photo, including fading it and making it look like the pieces of a puzzle or a tile mosaic.

- **Inner Glows** add light around the inside edge of your object.

- **Inner Shadows** give your image a hollow or recessed look by casting a shadow within the object, rather than outside it the way drop shadows do.

- **Outer Glows** create the same kind of light effects that Inner Glows do, only they go around the outer edge of your image.

- **Patterns** apply an overall pattern to your image. Want to make something look like it's made from metal or dried mud, or to fill in a dull background with a really vivid pattern? You'll find lots of choices here.

- **Photographic Effects** include several favorite traditional photographic techniques. You can add a variety of monochrome effects, like good old-fashioned sepia.

- **Strokes** let you put a black or colored border around the edge of a layer, or an object on its own layer. They're great for making outlined text, too.

• **Visibility** changes the opacity and visibility of your layer. Use these styles to create a ghosted effect, or when you're applying multiple Layer styles and you want to use an object's outline without having the object itself visible.

• **Wow Chrome, Neon, and Plastic** styles make objects look like they're made from shiny chrome, outlined in neon, or made from plastic.

NOTE   You can apply Layer styles only to regular layers. If you try to apply one to a Background layer, Elements asks you to convert it to a regular layer before the style can take effect.

If someone sends you a file made using Layer styles that you don't have, then you can snag them for your own use by highlighting the layer with the styles on it, and then going to Layer → Layer Style → Copy Layer Style. Then, in an image where you want to use the styles, click the layer you want to modify, and then choose Layer → Layer Style → Paste Layer Style. This command applies all the styles used in the original image to the layer you targeted.

POWER USERS' CLINIC

Editing Layer Styles

You can create highly customized Layer styles in Elements (see Figure 13-16). Start by applying a Layer style, and then you can edit it as much as you like. Just double-click the Layer Styles icon in the Layers panel (the little italic "fx" to the right of the layer's thumbnail) or select Layer → Layer Style → Style Settings.

Once the Style Settings dialog box appears, you can edit your style in many different ways:

• **Drop Shadow.** You can change the shadow's direction, distance, opacity, or even its color. When the Style Settings dialog box is open, you can drag the shadow around right in your image window until it's positioned where you want it.

• **Glow.** You can set the color, size, and opacity for both inner and outer glows, and turn each one on or off individually.

• **Bevel.** Change the size or direction of the bevel.

• **Stroke.** A *stroke* is a border around the edge of the style (like a line). You can change the color, size, and opacity of the stroke.

You can customize styles in so many ways that you can practically make your own style from an existing one. There's only one hitch: You can't change the standard settings for each style or save your custom style, so any changes you make affect the style only as you're currently applying it.

To remove a Layer style, in the Layers panel, right-click the layer, and then choose Clear Layer Style, or go to Layer → Layer Style → Clear Layer Style. These commands are all-or-nothing: If your layer has multiple styles, they all go away at once. To remove one style at a time, use the Undo History panel (page 36).

TIP   If you want to see what your image looks like without the styles you've applied to it, then go to Layer → Layer Style → Hide All Effects.

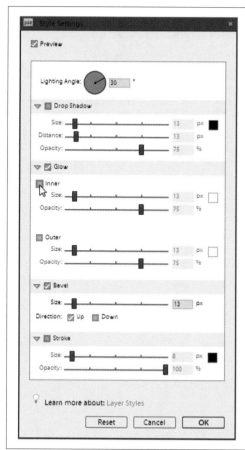

Figure 13-16:
The Style Settings dialog box gives you a lot of choices. Use the flippy triangles on the left to see the settings for a particular style characteristic or to collapse the ones you don't need now. To apply a new characteristic to a style (like adding a glow to a style that doesn't already have one), just turn on its checkbox. Click the color squares to the right of a slider to bring up the Color Picker (see page 232), and then choose a new color for that setting.

You can download hundreds of additional Layer styles from the Web (see page 551 for tips on where to look and how to install them). It's easy to get addicted to collecting Layer styles because they're so much fun to use. You've been warned.

Applying Gradients

You may have noticed that a few of the Layer styles and Photo Effects apply a color tint that fades away at the edges of your layer or image. In fact, Elements lets you fade and blend colors in almost any way you can imagine by using *gradients*. With gradients, you can create anything from a multicolor rainbow extravaganza to a single color that fades away into transparency. Figure 13-17 shows you a few examples of what you can do with gradients. The only limit is your imagination.

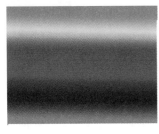

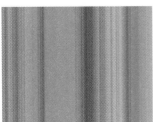

Figure 13-17:
Here are three examples of gradients drawn with the Gradient tool.

Top: This figure shows a gradient that creates a rainbow effect.

Middle: If you play with the Gradient Editor (page 432), you can create all sorts of interesting effects. Here's the gradient from the top figure again, only this time it's applied left to right instead of top to bottom. It looks so different because the noise option was used (see page 436). Click the Randomize button a couple of times for this effect.

Bottom: This figure shows a gradient you can create if you want a landscape background for artwork.

You can apply gradients directly to your image using the Gradient tool, or you can create *Gradient Fill layers,* which are whole layers filled with—you guessed it—gradients. You can even edit gradients and create new ones by using the Gradient Editor. Finally, there's a special kind of gradient called a *gradient map* that lets you replace the colors in your image with the colors from a gradient. This section covers the basics of using all these tools and methods.

The Gradient Tool

If you want to apply a gradient to a particular object in your image, then the Gradient tool is the fastest way to do so. This tool may seem complicated when you first see it, but it's actually pretty easy to use. Start by activating the Gradient tool (the yellow-and-blue rectangle) in the Tools panel or by pressing G. Figure 13-18 shows the Gradient tool's Options bar.

Using the Gradient tool is as easy as dragging. Click where you want the gradient to start, and then drag to the point where you want it to stop (you'll see a line connecting your beginning and ending points). When you release the mouse, the gradient covers the whole available space.

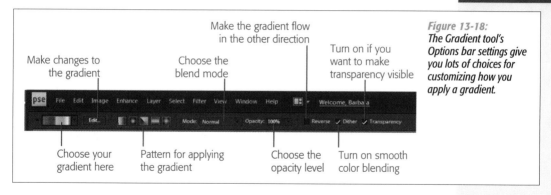

Make changes to the gradient

Make the gradient flow in the other direction

Choose the blend mode

Turn on if you want to make transparency visible

Figure 13-18:
The Gradient tool's Options bar settings give you lots of choices for customizing how you apply a gradient.

Choose your gradient here

Pattern for applying the gradient

Choose the opacity level

Turn on smooth color blending

For example, say you're using a yellow-to-white gradient. If you click to end the gradient one-third of the way into your photo, the yellow stops transitioning at that point, but the remaining two-thirds of your photo are covered with white. (In other words, something put down by the tool covers the entire space—your whole photo, in this case. Clicking stops the color *transition*—no more yellow beyond that point—but the gradient's end color [white] fills in everyplace else.) Drag the gradient within a selection if you want to confine the area it covers (see Chapter 5 if you need a refresher on making selections) so that the whole photo or layer isn't affected by the gradient's colors.

> **TIP** The Gradient tool puts the gradient on the same layer as the image you apply it to, which means that it's hard to change anything about a gradient after you apply it. If you think you might want to alter a gradient, use a Gradient Fill layer (page 431) instead.

Some of Elements' gradients use your Foreground and Background colors as the two colors that generate the gradient. But Elements also offers a number of preset gradients with different color schemes that Adobe has created for you.

Click the arrow to the right of the gradient thumbnail in the Options bar, and you see a little panel of different gradients, some of which use your selected colors, and others that have their own color schemes. The gradients are grouped into categories. In the upper-right corner of the gradient thumbnails panel, click the double arrow to see all the gradient categories. Choose one, and the available gradients change to reflect those in the new category. You can work only with the gradients in one category at a time.

You can also download gradients from the Web and add them to your library using the Preset Manager (see page 553), or create your own gradients from scratch. (See page 551 for some suggestions of where to look for new gradients.) Creating and editing gradients is explained later in this chapter, in the section about the Gradient Editor.

To apply a gradient with the Gradient tool, first make a selection if you don't want to see the gradient in your whole image. Then:

1. **Choose the colors you want to use for your gradient.**

   Click the Foreground and Background color squares (page 231) to choose colors. (Some gradients ignore these colors and use their own preset colors instead.)

2. **Activate the Gradient tool.**

   Click it in the Tools panel or press G.

3. **Select a gradient.**

   Go to the Options bar, click the Gradient thumbnail, and then choose the gradient style you want. Then make any other necessary changes to the Options bar settings, like reversing the gradient. (Your Options bar settings are explained in a moment.)

4. **Apply the gradient.**

   Drag in your image to mark where the gradient should run. If you're using a linear gradient, then you can make it run vertically by dragging up or down, or make it go left to right by dragging sideways. For Radial, Reflection, and Diamond gradients (see Figure 13-19), try dragging from the center of your image to one edge. If you don't like the result, press Ctrl+Z to undo it. Once you like the way the gradient looks, you don't need to do anything special to accept it, except of course to save your image before you close it.

You can customize gradients in several ways, even without using the Gradient Editor. When the Gradient tool is active, the Options bar offers the following settings:

- **Gradient.** Click the arrow to the right of the thumbnail to choose a different gradient from the one displayed.

- **Edit.** Click this button to bring up the Gradient Editor (page 412).

- **Gradient types.** Use these five buttons to determine the way the colors flow in your gradient. From left to right, your choices are Linear (in a straight line), Radial (a sunburst effect), Angle (a counterclockwise sweep around the starting point), Reflected (from the center out to each edge in a mirror image), and Diamond. Figure 13-19 shows what each one looks like.

- **Mode.** You can apply a gradient in any blend mode (see page 182).

- **Opacity.** If you want your image to be visible through the gradient, then reduce the opacity here.

- **Reverse.** This setting changes the direction in which the colors are applied so that, for example, instead of yellow to blue from left to right, you get blue to yellow.

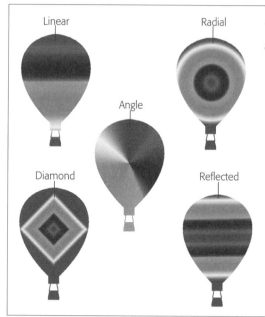

Linear   Radial   Angle   Diamond   Reflected

Figure 13-19:
The same gradient pattern applied using the different gradient types: Linear, Radial, Angle, Diamond, and Reflected.

- **Dither.** Turn on this checkbox, and Elements uses fewer colors, but simulates the full color range using a noise pattern. This can help to prevent banding of your colors, making smoother transitions between them.

- **Transparency.** If you want to fade to transparency anywhere in your gradient, then turn on this checkbox. Otherwise, the gradient can't show transparent regions.

Gradient Fill Layers

You can also apply a gradient using a special Fill layer. Most of the time, this method is better than the Gradient tool, especially if you want to be able to make changes to your gradient later on.

To create a Gradient Fill layer, go to Layer → New Fill Layer → Gradient. The New Layer dialog box appears so you can set the layer's opacity and blend mode (page 182). Once you click OK, the new layer fills with the currently selected gradient, and the dialog box shown in Figure 13-20 pops up. You can change many of the settings for your gradient here or choose a different gradient.

The settings in the Gradient Fill dialog box are pretty much the same as those in the Options bar for the Gradient tool:

- **Gradient.** To choose a different gradient, click the arrow next to the thumbnail to see the gradient thumbnails panel. To choose from a different gradient category, click the double arrows in the panel's upper right, and then choose the category you want.

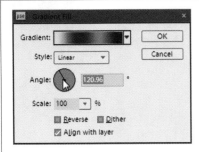

Figure 13-20:
The Gradient Fill dialog box gives you access to most of the same settings you find in the Options bar for the Gradient tool. The major difference is that in the Fill layer, you set the direction of your gradient by typing in a number for the angle or by changing the direction of the line in the circle as shown here (the cursor is pointing to the line that you drag to change the angle). With a Gradient Fill layer, you don't get a chance to set the direction by dragging directly in your image as you do with the Gradient tool, but while the dialog box is on your screen, you can drag the gradient in your image to change where it transitions.

- **Style.** You get the same choices you do for the tool (for example, Linear, Diamond, and so on). In this dialog box, you see only the name of the style, not a thumbnail of it. Choose a different style and Elements previews it in the layer itself.

- **Angle.** This setting controls the direction the colors will run. Enter a number in degrees or spin the line in the circle by moving it with your cursor to change the direction of the flow.

- **Scale.** This setting determines how large your gradient is relative to the layer. 100 percent means they're the same size. If you choose 150 percent, then the gradient exceeds the size of your layer, which means you see only a portion of the gradient in the layer. For example, if you had a black-to-white gradient, you'd see only shades of gray in your image. If you turn off the "Align with layer" checkbox, you can adjust the location of the gradient relative to your image by dragging the gradient.

- **Reverse.** Turn on this checkbox to make colors flow in the opposite direction.

- **Dither.** Use this setting to avoid banding and create smooth color transitions.

- **Align with layer.** This setting keeps the gradient in line with the layer. Turn it off and you can pull the gradient around in your image to place it exactly where you want it. At least, that's how it's supposed to work. Usually you can drag while the dialog box is visible but not after you click OK.

When you've gotten the gradient looking the way you like, click OK to create the layer. You can edit it later by double-clicking its left icon (the one with the gradient on it) in the Layers panel. That brings up the Gradient Fill Layer dialog box again, so you can change its settings or even choose a different gradient.

Editing Gradients

Elements' Gradient Editor lets you create gradients that include any color combination you like. You can even make gradients in which the color fades to transparency, or modify existing gradient presets. For instance, you can easily make a two-color gradient where the fade is very one-sided, if you want a large, plain area where you can put text (the plain area helps keep the text readable).

The Gradient Editor isn't the easiest tool in the world to use. This section will give you the basics you need to get started. Then, as happens so often with Elements features, a little bit of playing around with the Gradient Editor will help you understand how it works.

The Gradient tool has to be active to launch the Gradient Editor. In the Options bar, click the Edit button to see the Gradient Editor (see Figure 13-21).

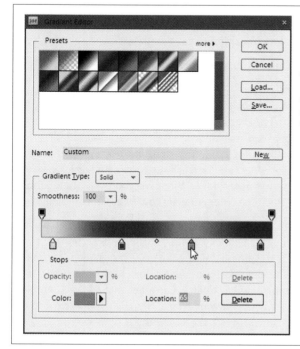

Figure 13-21:
The powerful and complex Gradient Editor. Here, the orange-colored stop (where the cursor is) has been clicked to make it active. The colored triangle on the stop is Elements' way of telling you it's the active stop. The two tiny diamonds on either side of the active stop mark the midpoint of the transition between the selected color and its neighbors. You can move these diamonds to change the midpoints.

The Gradient Editor opens showing the currently selected gradient. You can choose a different gradient by picking from the thumbnails at the top of the Gradient Editor window, or by clicking the "more" button to the right, and then choosing a new category from the list. You'll learn how to save your gradients later in this chapter.

To get started using the Gradient Editor, first choose your gradient's type and smoothness settings:

- **Gradient Type.** Your choices are Solid or Noise. Solid gradients are the most common; they let you create transitions between solid blocks of color. Noise gradients, which are covered later in this section, produce bands of color, as you might see in a spectrometer.

- **Smoothness.** This setting controls the evenness of the transitions between colors.

Most of the work you do in the Gradient Editor takes place in the *Gradient bar,* the long colored bar where your chosen gradient is displayed. The little boxes (also called *stops*) and diamonds surrounding the Gradient bar let you control the color and transparency of your gradient.

For now, you care only about the stops *beneath* the Gradient bar. Each one is a *color stop;* it represents where a particular color falls in the gradient. (You always need at least two color stops in a gradient.) If you click a stop, then the pointed end becomes colored, letting you know that it's the active stop. Anything you do at this point is going to affect the area governed by that stop. You can slide the stops around to change where the colors transition in your gradients.

The color stops let you customize your gradient in lots of different ways. Using them, you can:

- **Change where the color transitions.** Click a color stop and you see a tiny diamond appear under the bar. The diamond is the midpoint of the color change. Diamonds always appear between two color stops. You can drag the diamond in either direction to skew the color range between two stops so that it more heavily represents one color over another. (You know you've successfully grabbed the diamond when it shows color.) Wherever you place the diamond tells Elements the point at which the color change should be half completed.

- **Change one of the colors in the gradient.** Click any color stop, and then click the Color square (at the bottom of the Gradient Editor, in the Stops section) to bring up the Color Picker (page 232). Choose a new color, and the gradient automatically reflects your change. You can also pick a new color by moving your cursor over the Gradient bar. The cursor turns to an eyedropper that lets you sample a color from the bar or from anywhere in your image. If you click the arrow to the right of the Color square, you can select the Foreground or Background color without having to go to the Color Picker. (The User Color option just means the normal behavior, where moving over the bar brings up the eyedropper.)

- **Add a color to the gradient.** Click just below the bar to indicate where you want the new color to appear. You see a new color stop where you clicked. Next, click the Color square at the bottom of the window to bring up the Color Picker so you can choose the color you want to add. The new color appears in the gradient at the new stop. Repeat as many times as you want, adding a new color each time. If you want to duplicate an existing color from your gradient, click its stop, and then click below the bar where you want to use that color again.

- **Remove a color from a gradient.** If a gradient is *almost* what you want, but you don't like one of the colors, you don't have to live with it. You can remove a color by clicking its stop to make it the active color. Then click the Delete button at the bottom right of the Gradient Editor to remove that color, or just drag its stop downward off the bar. (The Delete button is grayed out if no color stop is active.)

Transparency in gradients

You can also use the Gradient Editor to adjust the transparency in a gradient. Elements gives you nearly unlimited control over the transparency in gradients, and the opacity of any color at any point in the gradient. Adjusting opacity in the Gradient Editor works very much like using the color stops to edit the colors, but instead of color stops, you use *opacity stops.*

> **NOTE** Transparency is particularly nice in images for web use, but remember that you need to save in a format that preserves transparency, like GIF, or you lose the transparency. If you save your file as a JPEG, the transparent areas become opaque white. See page 503 for more about file formats for the Web.

The opacity stops are the little boxes *above* the Gradient bar. You can move an opacity stop to wherever you want, and then adjust the transparency by using the settings in the Gradient Editor's Stops section. Click the Gradient bar wherever you want to add an opacity stop (click above the Gradient bar, rather than in it). The more opacity stops your Gradient bar has, the more points where you can adjust the gradient's opacity.

Here's how to add an opacity stop and then adjust its opacity setting:

1. **Click one of the existing opacity stops.**

   If the little square on the stop is black, it means the stop is completely opaque. A white square is totally transparent. The new stop you're about to create will have the same opacity as the stop you click, but you can adjust the new stop once you create it. (You can actually skip this step if you want, but it lets you predetermine the opacity of your new stop.)

2. **Add a stop.**

   Click anywhere just above the Gradient bar where you want to add a stop. If you want your gradient to be precisely positioned, then you can enter numbers (indicating percentage) in the Location box below the Gradient bar. For example, 50 percent positions a stop at the bar's midpoint.

3. **Adjust the new stop's opacity.**

   Go to the Opacity box below the Gradient bar, either enter a percentage or click the arrow to the right of the number, and then move the slider to change the opacity setting. If you want to get rid of a stop, click its tab, and then press Delete, or drag it upward away from the bar.

By adding stops, you can make your gradient fade in and out, as shown in the background of Figure 13-22, which has a simple vertical blue-to-transparent linear gradient that's been edited so that it fades in and out a few times.

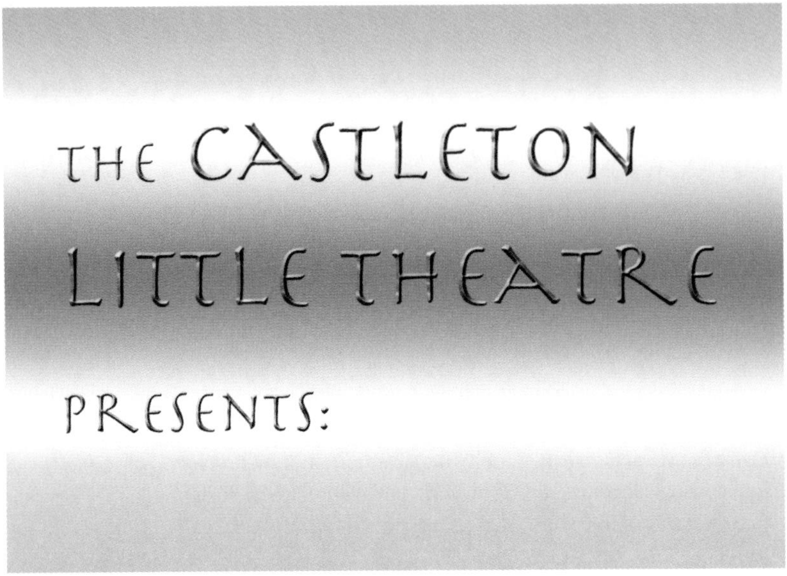

Figure 13-22:
You can make a gradient fade in and out like this background by adding more opacity stops and reducing the opacity of each stop.

Creating noise gradients

Elements also lets you create what Adobe calls *noise gradients.* A noise gradient isn't speckled like you might expect if you're thinking of camera noise (page 413). Instead, noise gradients randomly distribute their colors within the range you specify, giving a banded or spectrometer-like effect to the gradient. The effect is interesting, but noise gradients can be a bit unpredictable. The noisier a gradient is, the more stripes of the colors you see, and the greater the number of random colors.

With the Gradient tool active, you can create a noise gradient by going to the Options bar and clicking the down arrow to the right of the gradient's thumbnail. This opens the gradient thumbnail panel. Click the panel's double arrows at the upper right, and then, in the pop-out list of categories, select Noise Samples, You can edit them by clicking the gradient thumbnail in the Options bar to bring up the Gradient Editor. Or you can click the Edit button to bring up the Gradient Editor, and then choose Noise from the Gradient Type menu, if you want to start without a Noise Sample preset.

Noise gradients have some special Gradient Editor settings of their own:

- **Roughness** controls how often the gradient transitions (see Figure 13-23).

- **Color Model** determines which color mode you work in—RGB or HSB. RGB gives you red, green, and blue color sliders, while HSB lets you set hue, saturation, and brightness (see page 236 for more about these settings).

Figure 13-23:
The amount of noise in a gradient can make quite a difference in the effect you get.

Top: Here's a solid gradient.

Middle: A gradient with the same colors and 50 percent noise.

Bottom: A gradient with the same colors and 90 percent noise.

- **Restrict Colors** keeps your colors from getting too saturated.

- **Add Transparency** puts random amounts of transparency into your gradient.

- **Randomize.** Click this button to add random colors (and transparency, too, if you turned on that checkbox). Keep clicking the Randomize button until you see an effect you like.

Saving Gradients

After all that work, you probably want to save your gradient so you can use it again. You have two ways to save a gradient from the Gradient Editor:

- **Click the New button.** In the Name box, enter a name for your new gradient. Your gradient gets added to the current category. Elements creates a new preset gradient for you that's available in the gradient thumbnails panel, in the currently visible set of gradients.

    TIP   If you forget and click the New button before naming your gradient, or if you just want to change its name, in the Gradient Editor right-click the gradient's thumbnail, and then choose Rename Gradient.

- **Click Save.** The Save dialog box appears, and Elements asks you to name the gradient. You'll save the new gradients in a special Gradients folder, which Elements automatically takes you to in the Save dialog box. This method saves the whole set of presets that's visible when you create your gradient. When you want to use the gradient again, click the Gradient Editor's Load button, and then select it from the list of gradients that appears. The new set appears at the bottom of the list.

    TIP   You can also save and load gradients from the Options bar's gradient thumbnail panel's More menu.

Gradient Maps

Gradient maps let you use gradients in nonlinear ways. So instead of a rainbow that shades from one direction to another, in a gradient map, the gradient colors are substituted for the existing colors in your image. You can use gradient maps for funky special effects or for serious photo corrections.

When you create a gradient map, Elements plots out the brightness values in your image and then applies those values to a gradient (light to dark). Then Elements replaces the existing colors with the gradient you choose, using the lightness values as a guide for which color goes where.

That sounds complicated, but if you try it, you'll quickly see what's going on. Take a look at Figure 13-24, for instance. Applying a gradient map dramatically livens up this dull photo, but that's not all gradient maps are good for. Gradients and gradient maps can also be valuable tools for straight retouching. See the box on page 440 to learn how to use gradients to fix the color in your photo.

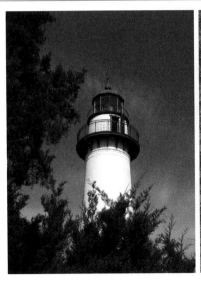 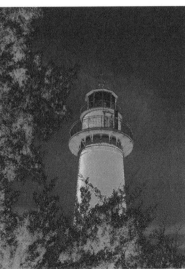

Figure 13-24:
Left: A very ordinary shot of a lighthouse.

Right: The image becomes something altogether different when you apply a gradient map adjustment.

You can apply a gradient map directly to your image by going to Filter → Adjustments → Gradient Map. (You can also apply a gradient map with the Smart Brush [page 211]; in the Options bar's Smart Paint setting, choose Special Effects → Rainbow Map.) But most times, for maximum control you'll want to use a Gradient Map Adjustment layer, because it's easier to edit after you've created the layer.

Here's how to apply a Gradient Map Adjustment Layer:

1. **Create a Gradient Map Adjustment layer.**

   Go to Layer → New Adjustment Layer → Gradient Map. The New Layer dialog box appears so that you can choose a color mode and opacity for your new layer, and name it if you want. Click OK, and a gradient map appears in your photo, but don't worry if it's not at all what you had in mind. You can modify it by going to the Adjustments panel, shown in Figure 13-25.

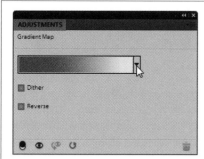

Figure 13-25:
The Adjustments panel for a Gradient Map Adjustment layer. Clicking the tiny arrow to the right of the thumbnail (where the cursor is here) displays a drop-down menu showing the available gradient patterns. Click in the pattern preview area to bring up the Gradient Editor (page 432) if you want to make changes to the gradient you've chosen.

2. **Choose a gradient.**

   In the panel, you see a gradient whose colors are based on your current Foreground and Background colors (see page 231). That gradient is the map of the lightness/darkness values that Elements has made for your image. If you want your image to show color, then you need to choose a color gradient rather than a black- or gray-to-white one. At the right of the gradient thumbnail, click the arrow, and then choose a color gradient.

   The Dither checkbox adds a little random noise to make the gradient's transitions smoother. The Reverse checkbox switches the direction in which Elements applies the gradient to the map. For example, if you chose a red-to-green gradient, then reversing it would put green where it would have previously put red, and vice versa. It's worth giving this setting a try—you can get some very interesting effects.

3. **Keep editing until you're satisfied with the result.**

   Elements automatically replaces the colors in your image with the equivalent values from the gradient you chose, so you can watch each one as you click around in the gradient libraries. When you like what you see, just save your image. You can also edit your gradient map layer by clicking it in the Layers panel, as explained in Figure 13-25.

Remember that you don't have to use your gradient in Normal blend mode—you can use any layer blend mode (page 182). You can spend hours playing around with the different effects you can get with the gradient map. Other filters and adjustments can produce unexpected results when used with it.

TIP   Try equalizing your image (Filter → Adjustments → Equalize) after applying a Gradient Map adjustment. The colors can shift quite dramatically. Equalizing is a good thing to try if you find that your gradient map makes your image look dull or dingy. However, you may need to merge the image's layers (page 191) to get this command to work, since you can't equalize an Adjustment layer. (See page 315 for more about the Equalize command.)

POWER USERS' CLINIC

Using Gradients for Color Correction

If you just want to use Elements for enhancing and correcting your photos, then you may think that all this gradient business is big waste of time. But keep in mind that gradients and gradient maps aren't just for introducing lurid colors into your photos—they're also powerful tools that can help you correct your photographs.

For instance, say you've got a photo where one side is much darker than the other, and you want to apply an Adjustment layer so it affects only the dark side of the image. You can pull off this trick by bringing up the Adjustment layer's layer mask (see page 196), and then applying your gradient directly to the mask.

You can also use Gradient Map Adjustment layers in different blend modes to help balance out the colors in your photos, although you may need to use the Gradient Editor to play with the distribution of light and dark values to get the best effect.

Gradient maps are also useful for colorizing skin in black-and-white photos. Set up a gradient based on three or more skin tones, and you can get a more realistic distribution of color tones than you could get by painting.

Text in Elements

If you want to add text to your images, Elements makes it easy. You can quickly create all kinds of fancy text to use on greeting cards, as newsletter headlines, or as graphics for web pages.

Elements gives you lots of ways to jazz up your text: you can apply Layer styles, effects, and gradients to it, or warp it into psychedelic shapes. And the Type Mask tools let you fill individual letters with the contents of a photo. Best of all, most Type tools let you change your text with just a few clicks (see Figure 14-1). By the time you finish this chapter, you know all the ways that Elements can add pizzazz to your text.

Adding Text to an Image

It's a cinch to add text to an image in Elements. Just select the Type tool, choose a font from the Options bar, and type away. The Type tool icon in the Tools panel is easy to recognize: a capital T. Elements actually gives you four different Type tools, all of which are hidden behind the Type tool icon's pop-out menu: the Horizontal Type tool, the Vertical Type tool, the Horizontal Type Mask tool, and the Vertical Type Mask tool.

You'll learn about the Type Mask tools later in this chapter (see page 456). To get started, you'll focus on the regular Horizontal and Vertical Type tools. As their names imply, the Horizontal Type tool lets you enter text that runs left to right, while the Vertical Type tool is for creating text that runs down the page.

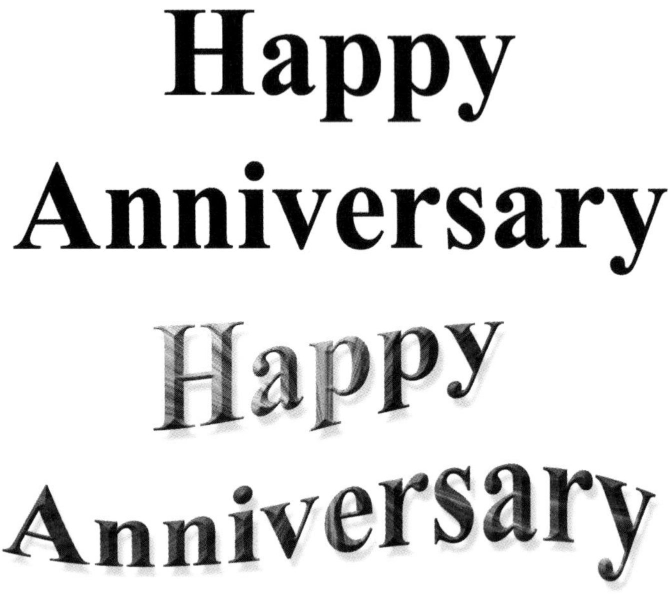

Happy Anniversary

Happy Anniversary

Figure 14-1:
With Elements, you can take basic text and turn it into the kind of snazzy headlines you see on greeting cards and magazine covers. It took only a couple of clicks—a couple of Layer styles (Angled Spectrum and a bevel) and some warping—to turn the plain black letters (top) into an extravaganza (bottom).

When you use the Type tools, Elements automatically puts your text on its own layer, which makes it easy to throw out what you've typed and start over again. When the Type tool is active, Elements creates a new Text layer each time you click in your image.

TROUBLESHOOTING MOMENT

Why Does the Type Tool Turn My Photo Red?

If your image gets covered with an ugly reddish film every time you click it with the Type tool, that means you've activated one of the Type *Mask* tools rather than one of the regular Type tools. (Type masks, covered later in this chapter, are useful when you want to create text that's cut from an image.)

To switch over to the regular Type tools, just click the Type tool icon in the Tools panel and use the pop-out menu to select either of the regular Type tools (horizontal or vertical).

Text Options

Whether you select the Horizontal or Vertical Type tool, take a look at the many Options bar settings (Figure 14-2). These choices let you control pretty much every aspect of your text, including font selection, font color, and alignment.

Your choices from left to right are:

- **Font Family.** Choose your font, listed here by name. Elements uses the fonts installed on your computer.

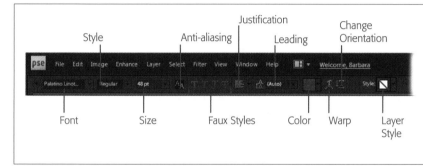

Figure 14-2:
The Type tool's Options
bar lets you control lots
of different settings, most
of which are pretty
standard, like the font
and the size of the letters.
The choices toward the
right end of the bar—like
Warp and Layer style—
are where the fun begins.

TIP   The font family menu displays the word "Sample" in the actual fonts to make it easier for you to find the one you want. To see all your fonts, in the Options bar, click the down arrow to the right of the font name box for a pop-out menu. You can adjust the size of the preview samples by going to Edit → Preferences → Type.

- **Font Style.** Here's where you select the styles available for your font, like Bold or Italic.

- **Size.** This is where you choose how big the text should be. (Text is traditionally measured in *points*.) You can choose from the list of preset sizes in the drop-down menu, or just type in the size you want. You aren't limited to the sizes shown in the menu—you can enter any number you want. See the box on page 444 for help understanding the relationship between points and actual size in Elements.

  If points make you nervous, you can change the Type measurement unit to millimeters or pixels by going to Edit → Preferences → Units & Rulers.

- **Anti-aliased.** This setting smoothes the edges of your text. Turn it on or off by clicking the little square with the two *A*s on it. Anti-aliasing is explained later (page 449), but usually you want it turned on.

- **Faux Styles.** Faux as in "fake." If your chosen font doesn't have a bold, italic, underline, or strikethrough version, you can tell Elements to simulate that style here by clicking the appropriate icon. (This option isn't available for some fonts.)

- **Justification.** This drop-down menu tells Elements how to align your text, just like in a word-processing program. If you enter multiple lines of text, this is where you tell Elements whether you want it lined up left, right, or centered (for horizontal text). If you select the Vertical Type tool, you can align along the top, bottom, or middle.

TIP   If you choose the Vertical Type tool, your columns of text run from right to left (each time you start a new column) instead of left to right. If you want vertical text columns to run left to right, you need to put each column on its own layer and position them manually. You can use the Move tool's Distribute option to space them evenly (page 186).

TROUBLESHOOTING MOMENT

How Resolution Affects Font Size

It's easy enough to pick a font size in the Text tool's Options bar. But you may find that what you thought would be big, bold, headline-size text is so tiny in your image that you can hardly see it. What gives?

In Elements, the actual size of text in your image is tied to the image's resolution. So, if you thought that choosing 72-point text would give you a headline that's an inch high, it will do so only if the *resolution* of your file is 72 pixels per inch (ppi). The higher the resolution, the smaller that same text is going to be. So if the resolution is 144 ppi instead, your 72-point text prints half an inch high. In a 216 ppi image, it'll be one-third of an inch high, and so on.

If you're working with high-resolution images, you have to increase the size of your fonts to allow for the extra pixel packing that comes from increased resolution. It's not

uncommon to have to choose sizes that are *much* higher than anything listed in the Options bar's size menu. Don't be afraid of really big sizes if you need them—just keep entering larger numbers in the size box until the text looks right in proportion to your image.

Another thing about text in Elements that can be confusing is that the program creates text based on the *actual* size of your image, not the view size. So if you're zoomed way in on your image and you add some text that looks like it's a reasonable size, it may be much smaller when you see the image at actual size or print it. People often try to put very small text on a very big image and wonder why it's so hard to read. If you aren't sure about the actual size of your document, try going to View → Print Size before typing. This view offers only an approximation, but it helps you get a better idea of what your text will look like.

- **Leading (rhymes with "bedding").** This setting controls the spacing (measured in points) between the lines of text. For horizontal text, leading is the difference between the baselines (the bottom of the letters) of each line. For vertical text, leading is the distance from the center of one column to the center of the column next to it. Figure 14-3 shows what a difference leading can make. The first setting you'll always see here is Auto, which is Elements' guess about what looks best. You can change the leading by choosing a number from the list or by entering the amount you want (in points, unless you changed the measurement unit in Elements' preferences).

- **Color.** Click this square to bring up the Color Picker (page 232) to set the color of your text. Or click the arrow to the right of the color square to bring up Color Swatches (page 234). When you've made your selection, the Foreground color square (page 231) changes to the new color.

  NOTE   When the Type tool cursor is active in your image, you can't use the keyboard commands to reset Elements' standard colors (black and white) or to switch them. You have to click the relevant buttons in the Tools panel instead.

- **Warp.** The little T over a curved line hides a bunch of options for distorting your text in lots of interesting ways. There's more about this option on page 449. (The Warp Text command is also available from Layer → Type → Warp Text.) This is grayed out until you actually type something.

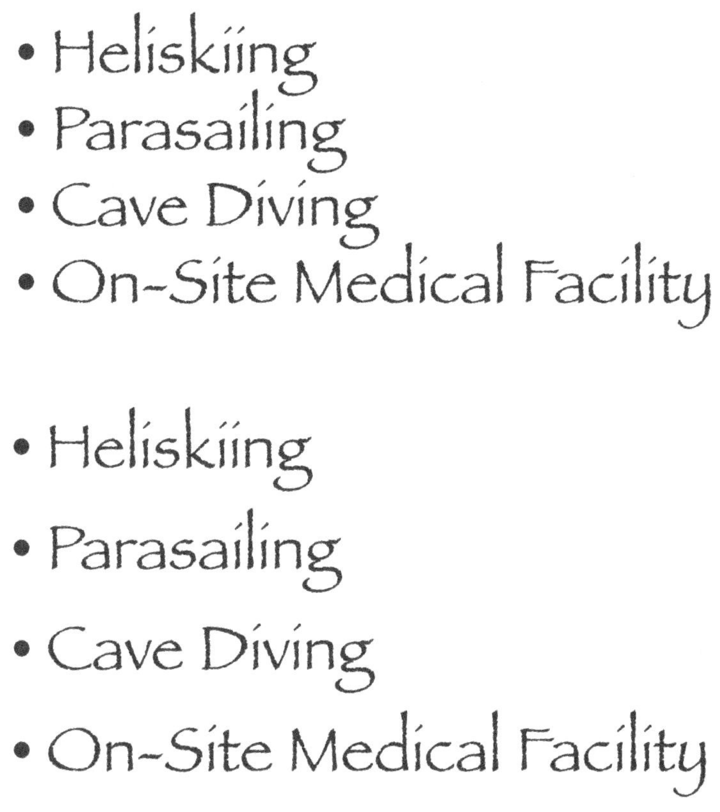

- Heliskiing
- Parasailing
- Cave Diving
- On-Site Medical Facility

- Heliskiing
- Parasailing
- Cave Diving
- On-Site Medical Facility

Figure 14-3:
Leading is the space between lines of text.

Top: A list of four items with Auto leading.

Bottom: The same list with the leading number set a bit higher. (If you adjust the leading of vertical text, you change the space between the columns, rather than the space between letters within a column. See the box on page 448 to learn how to tighten up the space between letters that are stacked vertically.)

- **Orientation.** This button that shows a T with two arrows next to it changes your text from horizontal to vertical, or vice versa. You can also change text orientation by going to Layer → Type → Horizontal or Vertical. You can't change the orientation of text till you have some text, so this setting is also grayed out until you create some text.

- **Style.** You can add funky visual effects to your text with Layer styles (page 423). First, enter some text and then, on the Options bar, click the Commit button (the green checkmark). Next, click the Style box and choose a Layer style from the pop-out palette. If you want to remove a style that you've just applied, click the double arrows on the upper-right corner of the palette and choose Remove Style from the pop-out menu, or go to Layer → Layer Style → Clear Layer Style.

These two choices don't show up at all until you've typed something:

- **Cancel.** When you add text to your image, Elements automatically places the text on its own layer. Click the Cancel button (the red circle with a slash) to delete this newly created text layer. This button works only if you click it *before* you click the Commit button (described next). To delete text after you've committed it, drag its layer to the Trash in the Layers panel.

- **Commit.** Click this green checkmark after you type on your image to tell Elements that yes, you want the text to stay the way it is.

If you see either of these buttons in the Options bar, that means you haven't committed your text, and many menu selections and other tools aren't available until you do. When you see these buttons, you're in what Elements calls *Edit mode*, where you can make changes to your text, but most of the rest of Elements features aren't available to you. Just click Commit or Cancel to get the rest of the program's options back.

Creating Text

Now that you're familiar with the choices in the Options bar, you're ready to start adding text to your image. You can add text to an existing image or start by creating a new file (if you want to create text to use as a graphic by itself, say). To use either the Horizontal or Vertical Type tools, just follow these steps:

1. **Activate the Type tool.**

   Click the tool in the Tools panel or press T, and then select the Horizontal Type tool or the Vertical Type tool from the pop-out menu.

2. **Modify any settings you want to change on the Options bar.**

   See the list in the previous section for a rundown of your choices. You can make changes after you enter the text, too, so your choices aren't set in stone yet. Elements lets you edit your text until you simplify the Text layer. (See page 395 for more about what simplifying a layer means.)

3. **Enter your text.**

   Click in your image where you'd like your text to go and start typing. Elements automatically creates a new layer for your text when you use the Type tools. If you're using the Horizontal Type tool, the horizontal line you see is the baseline your letters sit on. If you're typing vertically, the vertical part of the cursor is the centerline of your characters.

   Type the way you would in a word processor, pressing Enter to create new lines. If you want Elements to *wrap* your text (adjust it to fit a given space), drag with the Type tool in your image to create a text box before you start typing. Otherwise, you need to insert returns manually. If you create a text box, you can resize it to adjust the text's flow by dragging the handles after you finish typing. (This won't work anymore after you simplify the layer.)

   As noted earlier, if you want to use the Vertical Type tool, you can't make the columns of text run left to right. So if you need several vertical columns of English text, enter one column and then click the Commit button. Then start over again for the next column, so that each column is on its own layer.

NOTE   Be careful about clicking when the Type tool is active. Each mouse click starts a new layer. That's great if you're creating lots of separate text boxes to position individually, but it's easy to create a layer when you don't mean to. If you accidentally make a new layer, just delete it in the Layers panel, or merge it (page 191) with your existing Text layer.

4. **Move your text if you don't like where it's positioned.**

Sometimes the text doesn't end up exactly where you want it. As long as you haven't committed the text, you can move it with the Type tool—just grab the little black square at the beginning of the baseline and drag. If you have trouble moving your text, try the Move tool, but note that switching to the Move tool automatically commits your text (see step 5). If you need to move vertical columns of text, wait until you've committed the text to rearrange the columns.

5. **If you like what you see, click the checkmark in the Options bar to commit the text.**

When you commit your text, you tell Elements that you accept what you've created. The Type tool cursor is no longer active in your photo once you commit. If, on the other hand, you don't like what you typed, click the Cancel button in the Options bar, and the whole Text layer goes away.

Once you've entered text, you can modify it using most of Elements editing tools—add Layer styles (page 423), move it with the Move tool (page 165), rotate it, make color adjustments, and so on.

TIP   If you try to paste text into Elements by copying it from your word processor, the results can be unpredictable. Sometimes things work fine, but you may find the text comes in as one endlessly long line of words. If that happens, it's often easier to type your text in Elements from scratch than to try to reformat the text.

Editing Text

In Elements, you can change your text after you've entered it, just like in a word processor. Elements lets you change not only words, but the font and its size, too, even if you've applied lots of Layer styles. You modify text by highlighting it and making the correction or by changing your settings in the Options bar. Figure 14-4 shows you the easy way to highlight text for editing.

TIP   As mentioned earlier, you can see the word "Sample" in the menu displayed in the actual fonts themselves. Even better, Elements also gives you a quick way to preview what your actual text will look like in other fonts. First, select the text, and then click in the Options bar's Font box. Use the up and down arrow keys to move around in the font list. Elements changes the words in your document so they appear in each font you choose as you go through the list.

Using Asian Text Options to Control Spacing

Getting letters spaced correctly when using the Vertical Type tool can be tough. Elements lets you set the leading (page 444), but with vertical text, the leading affects the spacing between *columns* of letters, not between the letters within a column. Also, sometimes you may want to adjust the spacing between letters written in horizontal text. Elements lets you make either of these fixes, but you need to enlist the help of the program's Asian Text Options—even if you're writing in English.

To get started, go to Edit → Preferences → Type, and turn on the Show Asian Text Options checkbox. Now, the next time you click in an image with the Type tool, you'll see an Asian character in the Options bar just to the left of the Cancel button.

Click the character to see a pop-out menu with three options: *Tate-Chuu-Yoko, Mojikumi,* and a pull-down menu

with percentages on it. You want the pull-down menu, which is for *Tsume,* a setting that reduces the amount of space around the characters or letters you apply it to.

To apply Tsume, just highlight the characters you want to change in your image, and then select a percentage from the pull-down menu. The higher the percentage, the tighter the spacing.

You can select a single letter or a whole word when using Tsume. Since it reduces the space all the way around each letter you apply it to, you can use it for either vertical or horizontal text, although for horizontal text, you'd be most likely to use it to tidy up the spacing of just one or two letters. For vertical text, Tsume is a great way to tighten up the spacing of all the characters.

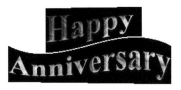

Figure 14-4:
If you change your mind about what you want to say, no problem. Here, the text is highlighted so that the words can be changed. The best part is that you can change the text to say anything, and all the formatting stays exactly the same. (You can't do this after you simplify a Text layer, though.) If you find it hard to highlight your text by dragging, go to the Layers panel and double-click the layer's text icon (the white rectangle with the T in it). When you do, the text on that layer becomes highlighted and ready for any changes.

You can make all these changes as long as you don't *simplify* your text. Simplifying is the process of changing text from a vector shape that's easy to edit to a rasterized graphic (see the box on page 395 for details). In this respect, text works just like the shapes you learned about in Chapter 12: Once you simplify text, Elements doesn't see it as text anymore, just as a bunch of regular pixels.

You can either simplify text yourself (by selecting Layer → Simplify Layer), or wait for Elements to prompt you to simplify, which it'll do when you try to do things like apply a filter or add an effect to your text.

NOTE   While the text effects included with Elements don't simplify your text, it's possible that effects you download may automatically simplify your text without asking first. So make sure you've made all the edits you want to your text before using any effects you've downloaded.

Smoothing text: anti-aliasing

Anti-aliasing smoothes the edges of your text. In Chapter 5 (page 151), you read about anti-aliasing for graphics; anti-aliasing has a similar effect on text: It gets rid of any jaggedness by blending the edge pixels on letters to make the outline look even, as shown in Figure 14-5.

Elements always starts you off with anti-aliasing turned on, and 99 percent of the time you'll want to keep it on. The main reason to turn it off is to avoid *fringing*—a line of unwanted pixels that make text look like it was cut out from an image with a colored background.

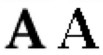

Figure 14-5:
An extremely close look at the same letter with and without anti-aliasing. The left A has anti-aliasing turned on, making the edges smooth (well, smoother). The edges on the right A are much more jagged and rough looking.

You turn anti-aliasing on and off by clicking the Options bar's Anti-aliased button (the two *A*s). The button has a dark outline when anti-aliasing is on. You can also turn anti-aliasing off and on by going to Layer → Type → Anti-Alias Off or Anti-Alias On. Once you simplify text, you can't change its anti-aliasing setting.

> **TIP** If you're seeing really jagged text even with anti-aliasing turned on, check your resolution. Text often looks poor at low resolution settings—just as photos do. See page 103 for more about resolution.

Warping Text

With Elements, you can warp the shape of your text in all sorts of fun ways. You can make it wave like a flag, bulge out, twist like a fish, arc up or down, and lots more. These complex effects are really easy, too, and best of all, you can still edit the text once you've applied these effects. Figure 14-6 shows just a few examples of what you can do. If you add a Layer style (explained on page 423) too, warping is even more effective.

To warp text, follow these steps:

1. **Enter some text.**

   Use the Move tool (page 165) to reposition the text, if necessary.

2. **Select the text you want to warp.**

   Make sure the Text layer is the active layer, or you won't be able to select what you typed. Click the Text layer in the Layers panel if it's not already highlighted there.

3. **Click the Create Warped Text button in the Options bar.**

   The Type tool has to be active for the Create Warped Text button (the T with a curved line under it) to appear. The Warp Text dialog box, shown in Figure 14-7, appears.

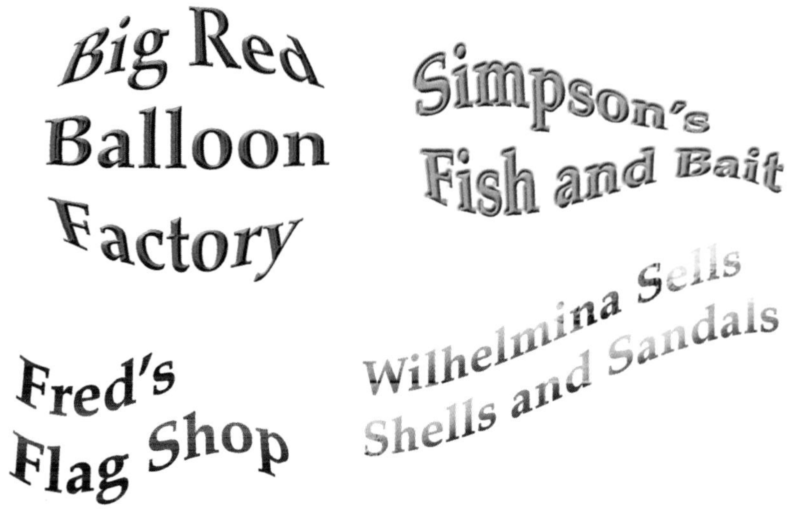

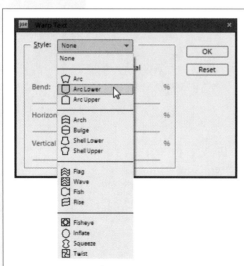

Figure 14-6:
Elements gives you oodles of ways to warp your text. Here are just a few of the basic warps, applied using their standard settings. Clockwise from the upper left: Inflate, Fish, Rise, and Flag. You can tweak these effects endlessly using the sliders in the Warp dialog box. (These examples also have Layer styles applied to them.)

Figure 14-7:
As you can see, you have lots of ways to warp your text. Once you choose a warp style, Elements displays sliders in the dialog box that you can use to customize the effect.

4. **Tell Elements how to warp your text.**

   Select a warp from the Style drop-down list. Next, make any changes you want to the sliders or the horizontal/vertical orientation of the warp (tweaking these settings can radically alter the effect). Push the sliders around to experiment.

   You can preview the results right in your image. Your options are described in more detail in a moment.

5. **When you come up with something you like, click OK.**

NOTE   You can't warp text that has the Faux Bold style applied to it (you can warp the other styles to your heart's content). If you forget and try to do so, Elements politely reminds you. The program even offers to remove the style and continue with your warp.

Elements gives you lots of different warp styles to choose from, and you can customize the look of each style by using the settings in the Warp Text dialog box, which comes up when you click the Create Warped Text button. The settings are pretty straightforward:

- **Style.** This is where you choose among all the warping patterns, like Arc, Flag, and so on. To help you select, Elements includes thumbnails in the list that show the general shape of each warp.

- **Horizontal/Vertical.** These radio buttons control the orientation of the warping. Most of the time, you'll want to leave the button the same as the text's orientation, but you can get interesting effects by warping the opposite way. A vertical warp on horizontal text gives more of a perspective effect, like the text is moving toward you or away from you. You can get some really funky effects by putting a horizontal warp on vertical text.

- **Bend.** This is where you tell Elements how much of an arc you want, if you'd like to change it from Element's standard setting. Type a percentage in the box or just move the slider until you get what you want. A higher positive percentage makes a bigger warp. A negative number makes your text warp in the opposite direction. For example, if you want an inverted arc, choose the Arc style and then move the slider to the left into the negative region.

- **Horizontal/Vertical Distortion.** These settings control how much your text warps in the horizontal or vertical plane. Moving the sliders gives you precise control over just how and where your text warps. They work pretty much the same way as the Bend setting—type a negative or positive percentage or move the sliders.

The best way to find the look you want is to experiment. It's lots of fun, especially if you apply a Layer style first (page 423) to give your text a 3-D look before warping it.

TIP   Many of the warps look best on two lines of text, so that the lines bend in opposite directions. However, you can also get really interesting effects by putting two lines of text on separate layers and applying different warps to each.

To edit your warp after it's done, double-click the Text layer's Warp thumbnail icon in the Layers panel (it's a T with a curved line under it). Doing that automatically makes the text layer active and highlights the text. Then, click the Create Warped Text button in the Options bar to open the Warp dialog box showing your current settings. Make any changes you want or set the style to None to get rid of it.

Adding Special Effects

Besides warping your text, you can apply all kinds of Layer styles, filters, and special *text effects* to give text a more elaborate appearance. You can change the color of your text, make the letters look 3-D, add brushstrokes for a painted effect, and so on. (There's more about Layer styles, filters, and effects in Chapter 13.)

Elements gives you lots of different ways to add special effects to your text. The following sections demonstrate three of the most interesting: applying text effects, using a gradient to make rainbow-colored text, and using the Liquify filter to warp text in truly odd ways.

Text Effects

The Content panel (page 474) has a whole category dedicated to effects for text (Figure 14-8). You apply text effects just the way you apply any other effect: Make the Text layer active and then double-click the effect you want.

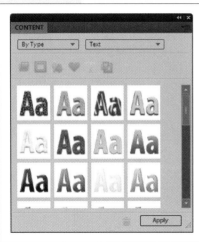

Figure 14-8:
The Content panel includes a whole section of text effects. Most, like Animal Fur Zebra and Denim, are unique to this section. Others, like Bevel, are just shortcuts for effects you could also achieve using Layer styles, gradients, or other Elements tools.

If you already have Layer styles on your text, it's hard to predict how much these effects will respect the existing Layer styles. Some effects build onto the changes you've previously made with Layer styles; most undo anything you've done before. Experimenting is the best way to find out what happens when you combine Layer styles and effects.

Text Gradients

Gradients fill your text with a spectrum of color. The simplest way to get these rainbow effects is to apply one of the Layer styles or text effects that include a gradient. But those methods don't give you any control over the colors or direction of the gradient. If you have a specific look in mind, you may have to start from scratch and do it yourself. The easiest way is to start with a type mask, as explained on page 457. But if you already have some existing text, as long as you haven't simplified it, you can easily fill it with a gradient.

> **TIP** Heavier, chunkier fonts show off gradients better than thin, spidery ones. Fonts with names that end in Extended, Black, or Extra Bold are good, like Arial Black or Rockwell Extra Bold.

First, make sure you've got some text in your image, and then follow these steps:

1. **Create a new layer for your gradient directly above your Text layer.**

   You're going to group the two layers (page 188), which is why they need to be next to each other. To create the new layer, press Ctrl+Shift+N or go to Layer → New → Layer. In the New Layer dialog box, turn on the "Use Previous Layer to Create Clipping Mask" checkbox.

   Look at the Layers panel to be sure the new layer is the active layer and that it's right above the Text layer. If it isn't active, give it a click in the Layers panel to highlight it. If it's not above the Text layer, drag it to the right spot.

2. **Activate the Gradient tool.**

   Click the Gradient tool in the Tools panel (or press G), and then choose a gradient style in the Options bar. (See page 427 for more about how to select, modify, and apply gradients.)

3. **Drag across your new layer in the direction you want the gradient to run.**

   Because the layers are grouped, the gradient appears only in your text. If you don't like the effect, press Ctrl+Z and drag again until you like what you see. That's all you have to do, except of course save your work if you want to keep it. (You can also activate the Move tool [page 165] and drag the gradient layer around till your text shows the color range you wanted. You won't see the gradient layer itself as you move it, but the colors of your text will change.)

> **TIP** You may have noticed that the Smart Brush tool (page 211) includes Rainbow Map as one of the adjustments you can brush onto your image. Sounds like it might be just the ticket for avoiding all this layer creation, and so on, doesn't it? Unfortunately, it applies a gradient *map* (see page 438), not a regular gradient, to your image. Because text is all the same tonal level, you'll just get a one-color result on the letters with the Smart Brush's Rainbow Map, not a rainbow at all.

> However, there are a couple of gradients in the text effects, so you might want to check out the Content panel before trying the steps above. If you find an effect that's exactly what you want, you'll save yourself some effort.

Applying the Liquify Filter to Text

The Options bar's Create Warped Text button (explained earlier on page 449) gives you lots of ways to reshape your text. But there's an even more powerful way to warp text: the Liquify filter (see Figure 14-9).

NOTE   You can use the Liquify filter to warp *anything* in an image—not just text. Use it to alter objects in photographs and drawings, for example: Fix someone's nose, make your brother look like E.T., give a scene a watery reflection, and so on.

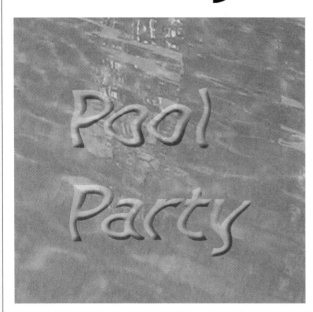

Figure 14-9:
The Liquify filter can reshape text in many different ways, including making text undulate like it's underwater (as shown here), making letters twirl around on themselves, or adding a flame-like effect.

Top: Plain black text.

Bottom: After adding a Wow Plastic Layer style, you can use the Liquify filter's Turbulence tool to make your letters look like they're swimming.

To use the Liquify filter, you first need to simplify the layer your text is on (Layer → Simplify Layer, or click OK when the Liquify filter asks if you want to simplify; just remember that you can't edit text once you simplify it.) Then, call up the Liquify dialog box by going to Filter → Distort → Liquify. You can also open it by double-clicking the Liquify filter's thumbnail in the Distort section of the filters in the Effects panel.

Up pops yet another large Elements dialog box. Like most of them, it's fairly straightforward once you learn your way around it. In the upper-left corner is a little toolbox with some very special tools in it (see Figure 14-10).

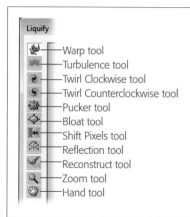

Figure 14-10:
The Liquify dialog box has its own toolbox. Along with the standard Hand and Zoom tools to help you adjust the view as you work, you get highly specialized tools found nowhere else in Elements.

Each tool has its own keyboard shortcut that works only in this window (given here in parentheses after the tool's name). From top to bottom they are:

- **Warp tool (W).** This lets you push the pixels of your image in any direction you want, although it usually takes a fair amount of coaxing to create much of an effect.

- **Turbulence tool (A).** You can use this tool to create clouds and waves. Its effect depends on the Turbulent Jitter setting on the right side of the dialog box (explained later); a higher number creates a smoother effect.

- **Twirl Clockwise tool (R).** Click your image and hold down the mouse button, and the pixels under your cursor spin clockwise. The longer you apply this tool, the more extreme the spin effect.

- **Twirl Counterclockwise tool (L).** The opposite of the Twirl Clockwise tool, this one makes the pixels under the cursor spin counterclockwise.

- **Pucker tool (P).** This tool makes the pixels under the cursor move toward the center of the brush.

- **Bloat tool (B).** The opposite of the Pucker tool, this one makes pixels move *away* from the center of the brush.

- **Shift Pixels tool (S).** The pixels you drag this tool over move perpendicularly in relation to the direction of your stroke. For example, if you drag from the top of an image straight down, the pixels you pass over move to the right. Alt-drag to make them shift the opposite way.

- **Reflection tool (M).** Drag to create a reflection of the area the tool passes over. Overlapping strokes create a watery effect.

- **Reconstruct tool (E).** Pass this wonderful tool over areas where you've gone too far, and you selectively return them to their original condition without wrecking the rest of your changes.

- **Zoom (Z)** and **Hand (H) tools.** These are the same Zoom (page 100) and Hand (page 102) tools you find elsewhere in Elements.

Your image appears in the preview window in the center of the dialog box. You can adjust the view with the Zoom tool or by using the magnification menu in the lower-left corner of the dialog box.

> **TIP** It often helps to zoom in really close when using the Liquify filter. If you've added text to a large image, select the text with the Marquee tool (page 139) before activating the Liquify filter. Then you'll see only the selected area in the filter's dialog box, which makes it easier to get a high zoom level.

On the right side of the dialog box are the filter's Tool Options settings:

- **Brush Size.** You can enter a number as low as 1 pixel or as large as 600 here.

- **Brush Pressure.** This is how much the brush affects the pixels you drag over. The range is from 1 to 100. The higher the pressure, the stronger the effect of the brush. If you're using a graphics tablet, turn on the Stylus Pressure checkbox so that the harder you press, the more effect you get.

- **Turbulent Jitter.** This controls how smooth your changes look. The higher the number, the smoother the effect.

- **Stylus Pressure.** Turn this on if you're using a graphics tablet (page 549) and you want the tool to be sensitive to how hard you press.

To use the filter, just pick your tool, modify your Tool Options (if you want), and then drag across your image. This is a processor-intense filter, so there may be a fair amount of lag time before you see results, especially if your computer's slow. Give Elements time to work.

If you like what you see in the preview, click OK and wait a few seconds while Elements applies your transformations. You're done. But if you don't like what you see, you can always have another go at it. Click the Filter dialog box's Revert button, which returns your image to the condition it was in before you started using the Liquify filter. Another option is Alt-clicking the Cancel button to turn it to a Reset button that resets the tool settings *and* your image.

Type Masks: Setting an Image in Text

So far in this chapter, you've read about how to create regular text and how to glam it up by applying Layer styles and effects. But in Elements, you can also create text by filling letters with the contents of a photo, as shown in Figure 14-11. (You'll find *sunset.jpg*, the photo used as the basis for Figures 14-11 and 14-12, on the Missing CD page at *www.missingmanuals.com.*)

The Type Mask tools work by making a selection in the shape of your letters. Essentially, you're creating a kind of stencil that you'll place on top of your image.

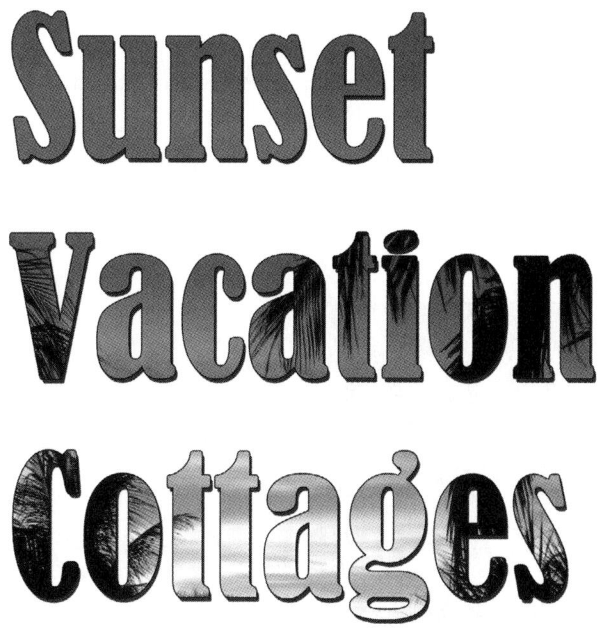

Sunset
Vacation
Cottages

Figure 14-11:
Using the Type Mask tools, you can create text that's made from an image. You can also use these tools to emboss text into your photo (see Figure 14-12).

Once you've used the type mask to create text-shaped selections, you can perform all sorts of neat modifications to your text: emboss the text into your image (which makes it looks like it's been stamped there); apply a stroke to the outline of your text (useful if the font doesn't have a built-in outline option); or copy and move the text to another document entirely.

Using the Type Mask Tools

Here's how to create a type mask and lay it over an image so that the letters are filled with whatever's in your image:

1. **Open the image that you want to use as your source for creating the text.**

2. **Activate one of the Type Mask tools.**

   Click the Type tool in the Tools panel or press T. Then select the Type Mask tool you want—horizontal or vertical—from the pop-out menu. The Type Mask tools behave just like the regular Type tools—a horizontal mask goes across the page, a vertical mask goes up and down. The Type Mask tools also have the same Options bar settings as the regular Type tools, except for Color and Style.

3. **Click your image and start typing.**

   When you click, a red film covers your image. The red indicates the area that *won't* be part of your letters. By typing, you're going to cut a visible selection through the red area (see Chapter 5 if you need a refresher on selections).

When you type, instead of creating regular text, you're creating a text-shaped selection. You can see the shape of the selection as you type.

It's important to choose a very blocky font for the type mask, since you can't see much of the image if you use thin or small text.

It's hard to reposition the words once you've committed them, so take a good look at what you've got. While the mask is active, you can move the mask by dragging it, as explained in Figure 14-12.

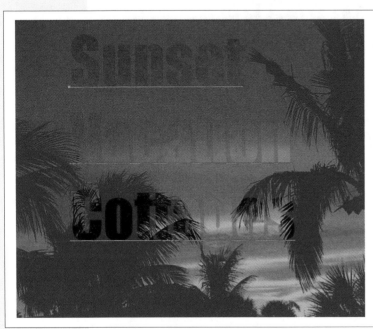

Figure 14-12:
Once you've activated the Type Mask tool and clicked on your image, you'll see a red mask appear over your picture. As you start typing, your text appears, as shown here. As long as you haven't committed the text yet, you can easily move it around by holding down Ctrl and dragging it. But as soon as you let go of your mouse, Elements turns the text into a text-shaped selection.

4. **Don't click the Commit button until you're satisfied with what you have.**

   Once you click the Commit button (the green checkmark on the right side of the Options bar), you can't alter your text as easily as you can with the regular Type tool. That's because the regular tools create their own layers, while the Type Mask tools just create selections. Once you commit, your text is just like any other selection—Elements doesn't see it as text anymore, so you can no longer change its size by highlighting it and picking a different size, for example. If you drag your selection when the mask is active, Elements automatically commits your text when you let go of the mouse button.

5. **When you're happy with your selection, click the Commit button.**

   Once you click the Commit button, you see the outline of your text as an active selection. You can move the selection outline by nudging it with the arrow keys, and you can use the Transform selection command (page 161) to scoot it around in your image or to resize, transform, or rotate it. (This can make the letters look a little strange, though, so watch the effects carefully.)

6. **Remove the nontext portion of your image.**

Go to Select → Inverse and then press Backspace to remove the rest of the image. Or you can copy and paste the selection into another document. If you want a transparent background, double-click your Background layer to turn it to a regular layer before you remove the background.

Figure 14-13 shows the effect of pressing Ctrl+J and placing a type mask selection on a duplicate layer of its own, and then adding Layer styles (page 423) to the new layer.

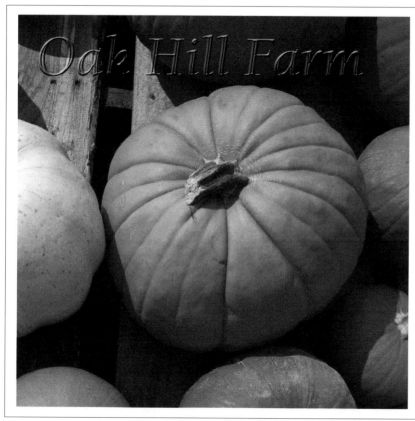

Figure 14-13:
By copying text to another layer, you can bevel or emboss it into your photo. This photo shows something you need to watch out for—text that's kind of hard to see because it blends right into the image. You may need to place your text a few times before you get it positioned correctly. Or you can add a colored outline to make it stand out more, as described in the next section.

Creating Outlined Text

If the font you're using doesn't come with a built-in outline style, there are three ways to create outlined text in Elements. The text effects in the Content panel (page 474) include an outlined text effect that you can apply with just a double-click. If you don't like what you get with that, you can also use the Stroke Layer styles or the Type Mask tools to outline text. Both these methods (which are explained in this section) are easy, but they require a bit more time than using the Content panel. The tradeoff is that you have more control over the result. Use the Layer styles method if you want your text outline to be filled in, since the type mask gives you an empty outline.

Using the Stroke Layer style

To add an outline to text:

1. **Open your image or create a new one, and then activate the Type tool.**

   Click the Type tool icon in the Tools panel or press T until you get either the Horizontal or Vertical Type tool (not the Type *Mask* tool).

2. **Choose your Options bar settings.**

   Select the font, size, style, and so on.

3. **Enter the text and commit it.**

   After you type your text, press Enter or click the checkmark in the Options bar.

4. **Apply a Stroke Layer style.**

   Go to the Effects panel → Layer styles → Strokes, and then double-click the style you want. If you don't like any of the Stroke styles, you can edit the result in the next step.

5. **Edit the outline if you wish.**

   In the Layers panel, double-click the text layer's Layer style icon (the little "fx" to the right of the layer's name) to bring up the Style Settings dialog box, where you can change the width and color of the stroke (see page 426).

Using the Type Mask tool

To make a text outline like the one shown in Figure 14-14:

1. **Open your image or create a new one (if you just want the text by itself), and then activate the Type Mask tool of your choice.**

   Click the Type tool or press T, and then select either of the Type *Mask* tools.

2. **Choose your font and size.**

   Use the Options bar's settings to pick a font you like, determine its size, and so on. Outlined text works better with a fairly heavy font rather than a slender one. Bold fonts also work well here, rather than regular fonts.

3. **Enter your text.**

   Click in your image where you want the text to go, and then type away. If you want to warp your text, do it now, before you commit it.

4. **Click the Options bar's Commit button (the checkmark).**

   Be sure you like what you've got before you do, because once you commit the text, it changes into a selection that's hard to edit. If you'd rather start over, click the Cancel button (the red circle with a slash) instead.

5. **Add a stroke to your outline.**

Be sure the text selection is active, and then go to Edit → "Stroke (Outline) Selection". Choose a line width in pixels and the color you want, and then click OK. (There's more about your other choices in the Stroke dialog box on page 399.) Your selection turns into an outline of the text you typed.

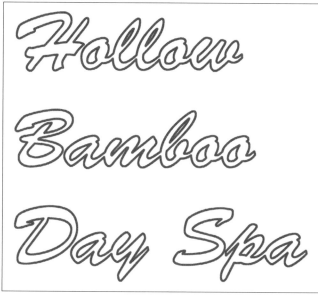

Figure 14-14:
By using the Type Mask tools, you can create outlined text almost as quickly as ordinary text.

NOTE   You can also create a hollow outline using the Stroke Layer styles: After you type some text, simplify the Text layer (Layer → Simplify). Next, go to the Effects panel and choose a stroke Layer style in a contrasting color. Then select the color of the text itself (as opposed to the outline) with the Magic Wand (page 149; be sure to turn off Contiguous), and delete that color. The downside to this approach is that you can't edit the text once you simplify it.

Part Five:
Sharing Your Images

5

Creating Projects

If you're into making scrapbooks, greeting cards, or other photo concoctions, Elements is perfect for you. You can dress up your pictures in all sorts of creative ways without any other software. Elements is crammed with add-on graphics, frames, and other special effects; you can even create multipage documents.

This chapter kicks off with an in-depth look at how to create a photo collage. Once you've got those steps under your belt, all the other projects (summarized starting on page 479) use the same basic method. You'll also learn how to create photo books and calendars using Kodak Gallery and Shutterfly, Adobe's online photo-printing partners.

> **NOTE** You can also create online albums (photo-filled web pages) and slideshows in Elements. You'll learn all about those projects in Chapter 18.

Photo Collages

The Create tab (in both the Editor and the Organizer) helps you make fancy pages featuring your photos, which you can then share as either printouts or digital files. Although Elements gives you lots of preset layouts to start from, you can customize every aspect of them to create projects that are totally your own.

A *photo collage* is a page displaying one or more of your photos, with or without a themed background. (Flip ahead to Figure 15-3 to get a glimpse of what Elements can help you do.) Elements' *wizards* (a series of guided questions that lead you from start to finish) all begin with one or more suggested photo placeholders, but you can add or remove photos at will. You can also change the background, frame styles, and other details.

NOTE   Photo collages, like all the printable projects on the Create menu, start off at a resolution of 220 ppi. That's perfectly fine print quality for most people's taste. But if you want a higher resolution, your best bet is to cook up your own project from scratch, since increasing the resolution of a prebuilt Elements project often throws the layout out of whack. (Kodak Photo Books are a little different. If you try to print a single, double-paged spread, it prints at 72 ppi—meaning poor quality—unless you first save your book as a PDF. The "Print with Local printer" option produces a 220 ppi file like the other Create projects.)

To create a photo collage:

1. **Open some photos in the Editor or select them in the Organizer.**

   This step is optional, but if you preselect photos, Elements can automatically place them into your layout for you.

2. **Go to Create → Projects → Photo Collage.**

   If you start from the Organizer, Elements bounces you over to the Editor to create your collage. The panel shown in Figure 15-1 appears.

3. **Choose your page size from the Page Size drop-down menu.**

   If you don't like the units of measurement listed in the Page Size menu, you can change them. Go to Edit → Preferences → Units & Rulers, and change the Photo Project Units setting to inches or centimeters.

4. **If you want, select a theme from the "Choose a Theme" section.**

   Themes give you coordinated backgrounds and frames for your photos. (You can always choose a different background later if you don't like the one that comes with the frame, or a new frame to replace the one that comes with the background.) Click a theme's thumbnail to select it, and a larger thumbnail appears, giving you a closer look at your choice.

   If you pick a theme and then decide you don't want any theme at all, click the upper-left thumbnail in the list of thumbnails to choose No Theme. If you go themeless, you just get a blank background, but you can always add backgrounds from the Content panel later.

5. **Choose a Layout style.**

   Scroll through the thumbnails and click the one you like. You can rearrange your layout after you've chosen it by adding, removing, and rotating the images, among other things. The layouts are arranged from one picture per page at the start of the list, to many pictures at the bottom of the list.

6. **Choose from the Additional Options settings, if you like.**

   If you turn on the "Auto-Fill with Project Bin Photos" checkbox, the pictures you chose in the Organizer or Project bin automatically appear in your collage when Elements creates it. If you want to determine which photos go into which slots in the layout yourself, turn off this checkbox.

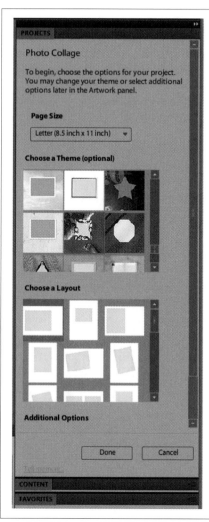

There's also a checkbox for having captions you've added to your photos (page 69) appear in the collage. (You can add text or edit the captions later, so you're not tied to what's in the Caption field.) This checkbox is grayed out if you haven't selected any photos with captions.

If you selected some photos before you started, the "Number of Pages" box tells you how many pages long your creation will be. This number updates to reflect your current Layout choice. So, for example, if you select three photos in the Organizer and choose a single photo per page, the number in this box is 3. If you click a layout that uses three photos per page, the number changes to 1. (If you haven't selected any photos, you can specify how many pages you want by typing in a number.)

7. **When you've made all your choices, click Done.**

Elements gets to work creating your collage. It puts each image in the collage on its own layer. If you preselected photos and left the Auto-Fill checkbox turned on, Elements puts your photos into the frames for you. Your document will have as many pages as needed to place all your photos in the layout you chose. If you didn't select any photos, you see the text "Click here to add photo or Drag photo here" inside each frame. That's fine, because you can add photos in the next step.

8. **Adjust your photos.**

If you haven't already picked photos for your project, click an empty frame in the collage and then choose a photo from the dialog box that appears, or drag a photo from the Project bin to a frame. (To add photos to a frame in Full Edit, click the Move tool first.)

Regardless of how you get photos into the collage, you can make a number of adjustments to them once they're in. Click once to resize the frame, or double-click any photo to bring up the controls shown in Figure 15-2, which let you make tweaks without changing the frame's size. Click the Commit button (the green checkmark) to apply your changes, or the red Cancel button to get rid of them.

You can also change a frame's style by choosing a new style from the Content panel (page 474). To change to the new frame, double-click the new style, or drag it to the photo. You can also click it once and then click Apply.

9. **Customize your collage.**

Here's the fun part. Click a photo in your collage, and drag it into a different position. Drag in art from the Content panel; these graphics are vector images (page 395), which means they'll look great no matter how big or small you make them. You can also add text to your collage (find out how to do that in Chapter 14), and change the background by selecting a new one in the Content panel (page 474). You can even flatten your image and use filters on the entire page. Figure 15-3 shows an example of what you can do with a photo collage.

NOTE   Elements' new guides feature (page 87) is especially handy for aligning new additions to your project.

If you click back to the Editor, you can use any tool or filter on your collage, but you may need to simplify a layer (page 395) or flatten your image first, so save that step till you're sure you like your collage. You can use the Move tool to rearrange your collage's layers after you simplify them, but once you simplify layers, you can't enlarge their contents without losing quality, just like with any normal photo.

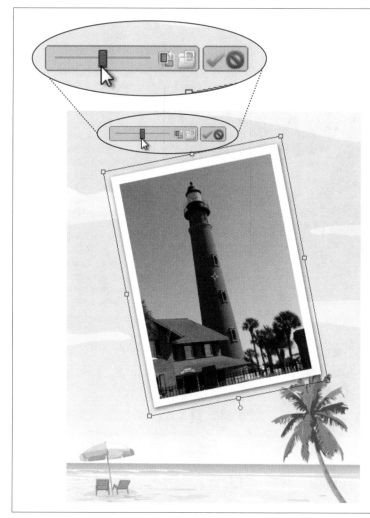

Figure 15-2:
When you double-click a photo, you get these controls for adjusting it. To resize your picture, move the slider to the left (smaller) or right (larger). Rotate your photo by clicking the blue rectangles (next to the slider), or click the folder icon to choose a different photo. You can also drag a handle of the photo's bounding box to resize your photo or do a manual rotation, just the way you'd use the Move tool (page 165).

10. **Save your collage.**

    When finished, press Ctrl+S to name your project and save it. You can save it in any standard file format if it's a one-page collage, but if you have more than one page, you have to save it as a PSE file, which is a special format just for multi-page Elements documents (see the box on page 474 for details), or as a PDF file.

There's almost no limit to what you can do in a photo collage. Anything you've read in the other chapters of this book works here, too. Plus, you can do a few special things with photos in a collage:

- **Remove a photo from your collage.** Right-click the photo and then choose Clear Photo. To remove the photo's placeholder and frame as well, choose Clear Frame instead.

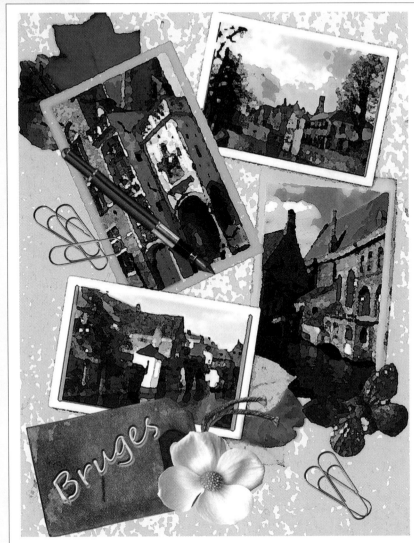

Figure 15-3:
This composition was created as a photo collage. All the artwork except for the photos themselves came from the Content panel. The photos and some of the background graphics (like the leaves) were added first, the file was flattened, and then several filters were applied to give it a painted effect (see Chapter 13 for more about filters). Finally, the remaining graphics (the pen, the flower, and the paperclips) were added to make them look like they're lying on a painted page.

- **Make your photo appear without a frame.** Right-click and then choose Clear Frame.

- **Resize a frame.** You can resize a frame either before or after you put a photo into it. Click once on the frame to bring up handles, and then drag a corner of the frame to make it larger. You can also rotate a framed photo using these handles.

- **Resize the frame to fit the photo.** If you want to make the frame fit the photo, instead of the other way around, right-click the photo and then choose "Fit Frame to Photo".

- **Recompose the photo to fit the frame.** You can use the Recompose tool (page 297) right in your photo collage. For instance, you might have a landscape-orientation photo and a portrait-orientation frame you want to use. Just recompose your photo so you don't have to crop it.

  TIP   You can do all of the above in Full Edit, too, once your collage is complete, but you need to activate the Move tool first, or you won't see correct options when you right-click.

- **Add another photo.** Just drag a frame from the Content panel to a blank area in your collage. If you get too close to an existing frame, the new frame may replace the one on an existing photo. If that happens, just press Ctrl+Z to undo it and drag again, more carefully, to the blank spot. You can also drag a photo into your collage from the Project bin.

- **Change your theme.** If you wish you'd gone with a different theme after you've already created your collage, go to the Content panel and select By Type from the first drop-down menu and Themes from the second to see a list of all the Create themes. Double-click a theme's thumbnail or drag it onto your collage, or click the thumbnail once and then click Apply. Presto—you've got your existing layout with new frames and background.

- **Edit a frame's Layer style.** Most of the frames have a Layer style applied to them. Right-click the frame and choose Edit Layer Style to change things like the size of the frame's drop shadow. You can also edit the styles from the Layers panel in Full Edit the same way you'd edit any Layer style. (See page 426 for more about editing Layer styles.)

You can also add and delete *pages* from photo collages, as explained in the next section.

TIP   You can apply artwork from the Content panel to any image, not just those in photo collages and other Create projects.

Creating Multipage Documents

Elements makes it easy to create a file that's more than one page long. A photo collage automatically starts with as many pages as it needs to hold all your preselected photos, but you can add pages to any of the Create projects anytime—and remove them, too. (You can also add and remove pages from any Elements file, not just the Create projects.)

The size and resolution of your existing page determines the size and resolution of pages you add. In other words, if your current file is just a single 3"×5" photo and you add a page to it, you get a new 3"×5" page. If you want to add a letter-size page to a small photo file, you first have to add canvas to the photo (page 111) or resize it. (But check out page 110 to see why resizing a small photo to letter size probably won't work well.)

Smart Objects

Smart Objects are one of the ways Adobe makes Elements projects so fun and easy. Like their big-shot cousins in the full version of Photoshop, these objects seem to know where they are and what you're trying to do–and behave accordingly. Here are some of the things that make Smart Objects so smart:

• When you apply a new background from the Content panel, it immediately zooms down to the bottom of the layer stack to replace the existing background, without any assistance from you.

• The frames in the Content panel automatically target your photos. Want to frame an image? Just go to the Content panel and double-click a frame. It automatically appears in your image, though you may need to adjust its size or the area that it frames once it's in your photo.

• You can resize, transform, and distort objects from the Content panel's graphics section as much as you want without affecting the image quality. This behavior is something like how vector art works, but what's going on under the hood is quite a bit different. (The preview may appear pixelated if you enlarge a graphic a *lot*, but the actual object should be okay once you click the green checkmark Commit button.)

Anything you put into an Elements file by using File → Place in Full Edit becomes a Smart Object (you can resize it to any size, for instance). Also, anything you drag into one of the Create projects (photos, graphics, whatever) becomes a Smart Object.

However, there are a few things you can do to Smart Objects only if you simplify them (page 395). For example, if you try to paint on a Smart Object in Elements, you just get the dialog box shown in Figure 15-4.

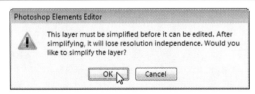

Figure 15-4:
You can enlarge, reduce, transform, and distort Smart Objects, but if you try to paint on them or to apply filters or effects to them, you get this message. It's fine to click OK, but once you do, your formerly Smart Object will behave like any other object. (You can't increase its size to more than 100 percent, for instance, or it'll go all pixely on you.)

To add a new page to your document, go to the Editor's Edit menu, and choose one of the following commands:

• **Add Blank Page (keyboard shortcut: Alt+Ctrl+G).** This command creates a new, totally empty page with the same dimensions and resolution as your existing page.

• **Add Page Using Current Layout (Alt+Shift+Ctrl+G).** When you choose this option, Elements creates a page that's exactly like the current state of your existing page, including any changes you've made, except that instead of photos, there are placeholders for you to fill in. So, for example, if you've changed frame styles and dragged a photo to another position, the new frame and positioning (without the photo) appears in your new page. Any graphics you've added from the Content panel show up as well. This option is a big help when you're making photo books or scrapbooks.

You can navigate through all the pages in your document using the Project bin, as shown in Figure 15-5. If you decide you've got too many pages, go to Edit → Delete Current Page, and the currently active page is history. You can also add and delete pages right from the Project bin by right-clicking and choosing what you want to do from the pop-out menu, a big help when you're editing a multipage project.

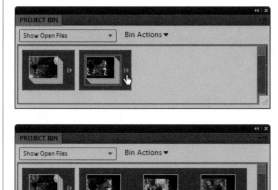

Figure 15-5:
You can expand and collapse the pages of your file so they don't hog the Project bin.

Top: A collapsed photo book and a multipage photo collage in the Project bin. (Note how each type of project reflects the project's page shape and even shows its theme.) Collapsed multipage documents have a special outline in the bin to make them easy to recognize.

Bottom: Here's the expanded thumbnail for the collage, so you can select a single page to edit. Click the arrow (where the cursor is) again to collapse the thumbnail.

No matter what kind of file you start with—whether it's a Create project or just a regular JPEG—you have to save your file as a PSE or PDF format file if you add pages to it. Elements reminds you with the dialog box in Figure 15-6. While it's *really* nice to be able to create multipage documents in Elements, the PSE format has some drawbacks, too, as explained in the box on page 474.

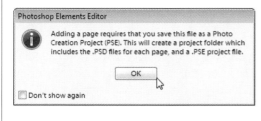

Figure 15-6:
You can't save a document with multiple pages in common file formats like TIFF or PSD. Your only option is PSE, as this dialog box reminds you whenever you add a second page to a document. See the box on page 474 to learn why PSE format is a mixed blessing. (Actually, this message isn't totally true—you also get the option to save as a PDF file, but your options for editing a PDF are limited, so do that last, when you're sure you're done making any changes.)

Working with the Content and Favorites Panels

Adobe gives you a ton of artistic goodies to use for customizing your projects, and a special panel just to hold it all: the Content panel. You also get a Favorites panel, where you can keep the items you use most often from the Content panel (and from the Effects panel, too).

About PSE Files

Anytime you create a multipage document in Elements, you get one file format choice when it's time to save—PSE. This special format has both advantages and disadvantages.

When you create a PSE file, you actually create a *folder* containing a separate .psd file for each page (or for each double-page spread if you're creating a photo book), and the PSE *project file*, which contains all the info Elements needs to reassemble your document the next time you open it. That's handy when you're working in Elements, but the drawback is that hardly any other program can read these files. PSE files work just fine if you print at home or use Kodak Gallery for online printing. You can send PSE files to Kodak Gallery as easily as you send JPEGs.

The rub comes if you want to use a different printing service. If you make, say, a book that you want to print at Lulu.com or MyPublisher.com, they can't work with your PSE file—at least not at this writing. Most printing services require PDF files. Fortunately, Elements can save your multipage PSE file as a multipage PDF that you can upload to your printing service of choice. (Be aware, though, that Elements creates huge PDF files.) Usually you wait till you're through editing to create your PDF. Keep the file as a PSE file as long as you still have work to do.

The Content Panel

This panel holds backgrounds, frames, graphics, shapes, text effects, and themes to use in projects. The Content panel works something like the Effects panel, with menus and a row of little icons for each of its major categories (see Figure 15-7). Here's how it works:

1. **Make the Content panel visible.**

   This panel is always visible in Create, but you can make it visible in Full Edit by going to Window → Content. (The Content panel still appears in Create, even when you make it visible in the Editor. You can't remove it from Create.)

2. **Choose how you want to search.**

   In the left-hand drop-down menu, choose to search by type (like backgrounds, frames, and so on), or choose Show All to see everything in the panel.

3. **Refine your search.**

   In the right-hand drop-down menu, choose what you specifically want. What's in this menu changes depending on your choice in the left-hand menu. So if

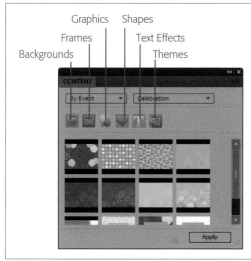

Graphics   Shapes
Frames   Text Effects
Backgrounds   Themes

Figure 15-7:
Once you've winnowed down your choices by selecting from the two drop-down menus shown here, use these little category icons (labeled) to further control which thumbnails appear in the Content panel. Elements starts you off by including all the categories (a gray outline around a button means it's active and that its category is included in your search). Click any of the buttons to turn them off and exclude that category from your search. So here you see the results of searching By Event → Celebration. And since the Graphics button is turned off, no graphics appear in the thumbnail area.

you choose By Type on the left, you see Backgrounds, Frames, Graphics, and so on in this menu. If you choose By Mood on the left instead, the right-hand menu offers you choices like Active, Adventurous, Fun, Romantic, and Thoughtful.

4. **If you like, filter your results.**

    Here's where those category buttons below the menus come into play. (From left to right the buttons are Backgrounds, Frames, Graphics, Shapes, Text Effects, and Themes.) You may still get an awful lot of results from some of your menu choices, so you can use the buttons to filter out items you don't want. If you chose By Seasons and Winter in the menus, respectively, but don't want to see frames, just turn off the Frames button (click it to get rid of the gray highlight around it), and Elements excludes frames from your results.

    You can turn on and off as many buttons as you want in order to include or exclude various kinds of content. To bring something you've excluded back into your search results, click its button again to turn it back on. If you're like a lot of people, most of the time you'll want to stick with By Type and choose the category you want. In that case, the buttons are dimmed.

5. **Add your choice to your image.**

    To use anything from the Content panel, double-click its thumbnail or drag it onto your image. (You can also click your selection once and then click Apply.)

    To remove what you've added, press Ctrl+Z if you just added it, or click the object with the Move tool and then press Backspace. If you use the Backspace key, Elements asks if you want to "Delete the Layer"—you do.

A word of warning: Don't use the Content panel's trashcan icon to delete an object from your project. That seems like a logical thing to do—after all, that's how it works in the Layers panel. But with the Content panel, the trashcan deletes the graphic, frame, or whatever from the *panel*, not just from your image. Only use the trashcan for Content panel items you never want to use again. For example, if you've downloaded and installed a frame (as described on page 556) and know you won't use it again, then it's time to use the trashcan. If that seems like a lot of navigation, check out the Favorites panel (described in the next section) for a faster way to reach Content panel items you use a lot.

TIP   One advantage of signing up for a Photoshop.com account (page 20) is that the Content panel displays a lot of extra items you can download. Free downloads display a blue banner across the corner of their panel thumbnail, while items only available for those with paid accounts have a gold banner.

The Favorites Panel

If you use the same effects, graphics, and styles over and over, you may find it tedious to keep navigating to them in the Content or Effects panels. Simplify things by saving your Content and Effects standbys in the Favorites panel. Then you can get to these items with just a click or two.

To see the Favorites panel, click the Create tab, and you should see the Favorites panel at the very bottom of the Panel bin. To see the Favorites panel in the Editor, go to Window → Favorites to bring it up.

To add an item to the Favorites panel, right-click its thumbnail in the Content or Effects panel, and then choose "Add to Favorites", or just drag its thumbnail to the Favorites panel.

To delete a favorite, right-click its thumbnail and then choose "Remove from Favorites", or click it once to highlight it, and then click the trashcan icon at the bottom of the panel (unlike with the Content panel, trashing something here just removes it as a favorite, not from Elements altogether). If you forget what a thumbnail is for, right-click it and choose Details to see a description of it.

Photo Books

Elements lets you create several sizes of pages to use in a bound book of photos—a popular gift item. Go to Create → Projects → Photo Book, and you'll see several different ways of creating photo books with Elements:

• **Print with Local Printer.** If you want to print your book at home or take or send it to a print shop, this option lets you create a standard photo book that you can save as a PDF, which is the preferred format for most print shops. The steps for creating a book this way are described in detail after this list.

- **Create Photo Books at Shutterfly.** In the Organizer, you select the photos you want to include and then click this button. Elements uploads your images to Shutterfly, and you choose the kind of book you want and use the wizard on their website to complete and order it. (Page 486 explains how to create a Shutterfly account.)

- **Create Digital Scrapbooks at Shutterfly.** This works exactly the same way as creating a Shutterfly photo book. While Shutterfly's photo books put your images into their templates, digital scrapbooks have blank pages. You create pages of your own design on your computer, then upload your finished work to Shutterfly.

- **Create a Photo Book—Kodak Gallery.** This works almost exactly like the "Print with Local Printer" option. You get a chance to select your title-page photo, though, and when you're done, you can upload your completed book file to the Kodak Gallery for printing. (See page 486 for more on creating a Kodak Gallery account.) You can also save a book created this way as either a PSE or PDF file, so this is another option you can use if you want to print the book at home or send it elsewhere for printing. If you create your book using this wizard, it has to be at least 20 pages long, but not more than 80. When you view your completed book in Elements, you see blue lines near the edges of the pages. These are guidelines to show you the boundaries of the printed area of your photos.

Creating a photo book is something like creating a collage (page 465). Elements walks you through the process with plenty of handholding:

1. **If you want, choose your photos.**

   If you want Elements to automatically lay out your photos in the book, make sure you have them open in the Project bin and in the correct order before you start. Or you can wait and add each picture manually after you create the book's layout.

   NOTE Photo books usually have a cutout cover through which you can see one large image on the title page. This page has a different layout from the rest of the book. If you're using photos in the Project bin, drag the photo you want for the title page so that it's the first one in the lineup. Or you can wait and choose your title page photo after you complete the book layout.

2. **Start your book.**

   In either the Editor or the Organizer, go to Create → Projects → Photo Book. Elements switches over to the Editor, if you aren't there already. Choose the kind of book you want to make from the list, as explained above. Elements then presents your first set of choices for the book.

3. **Choose a page size.**

   Use the drop-down menu to pick dimensions for your pages. You can select several different sizes, but 10.25" × 9" is the one most commonly used by online services.

4. **Choose a layout.**

You have two options:

- **Random Photo Layout.** Elements makes the decisions for you about how many photos will be on each page; every page may be different. It's best to avoid this option unless you have a *lot* of photos, since some of the layouts have as many as 20 tiny photos on a page—although, of course, you can edit things later.

- **Choose Photo Layout.** Click this option and Elements presents you with a long list of page-layout thumbnails. Click a thumbnail to select it. You need to pick left- and right-hand page layouts, which can be the same or different, as you prefer. Click Next to select a theme.

5. **Choose a theme.**

If you picked "Choose a Photo Layout", then you'll see themes on the next screen. (If you're using a random layout, just scroll down in the same screen.) When you click a thumbnail in the theme list, Elements takes a few seconds, and then displays a little thumbnail showing the selected theme's style.

Your other choices here are the same as for a photo collage (page 466). If you plan to send the book out for printing, usually you need a minimum of 20 pages.

6. **Create your book.**

Click Create, and Elements creates and opens a PSE file for you. You can edit anything in the file exactly the same way you can change things in a photo collage. Elements gives you some special controls for navigating through the layout, as explained in Figure 15-8.

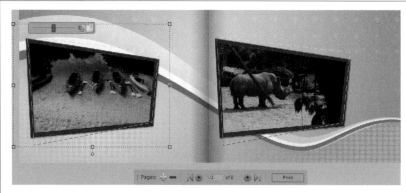

Figure 15-8:
When you click Create, Elements gives you a helpful double-page view of your book so you can edit the pictures or change the layout. The control strip shown here below the book lets you move through the pages to see each double-page spread, or add or remove pages. You can drag the strip anywhere in the work area so it doesn't cover up your photos. Here you see the controls for adjusting the left photo and frame so they match up better.

Don't forget to save the PSE file. If you used the Kodak Gallery book wizard, then you're ready to print. You can upload the book to Kodak for printing (page 486) right from the Editor by clicking the Order button that appears in the control strip. If you don't want to order from Kodak, you can save your book as a PDF file to send to some other photo-book publisher (see the box on page 546).

You can also create a book of photos without using the Elements' Photo Book feature at all. Just connect to the Kodak Gallery or Shutterfly website, upload your photos (as explained on page 486), and then have the company print them in its own style of photo book. (You don't get any page decorations or layout choices when you use the Kodak wizard, though.) One thing to keep in mind if you're getting a bound photo book: Whether you order from Kodak or another publisher, almost all books use only a single photo for the first page because that's what shows through the cover cutout.

Greeting Cards

Adobe calls them "greeting cards", but they're more like what most people call postcards. An Elements Greeting Card is a 4"×6" or 5"×7" single-sided page rather than a folded card. To create one, go to Create → Projects → Greeting Card to get started.

First, either choose to create a card to print yourself, or go to Shutterfly or Kodak Gallery to create your card online; just click the appropriate button. Or if you want to print the card yourself, click "Print with Local Printer".

> **NOTE** If you want to create cards online, it's best to start from the Organizer and select the photo(s) you want to use before you begin, or you may find that Elements wants to use *all* the photos currently visible in the Organizer. If you're going to print them yourself, it doesn't matter whether you start in Organizer or Editor.

If you choose one of the online options, Elements prepares your photos and whisks you off to the corresponding website. Log into the site, or create an account if you don't have one, then use the site's online wizard to create and order your cards. (There's more about online creations on page 481.)

If you choose "Print with Local Printer", Elements bounces you over to the Editor to create your card. The layout and template choices are identical to those for photo collages, and the process is exactly the same, so just follow the steps on page 466.

> **NOTE** You may find you have more size and layout choices using the websites. Shutterfly also lets you use your photos on other kinds of stationery.

CD/DVD Jackets

Elements lets you create CD jewel case inserts and DVD inserts, which appear on the front and back of the case. To make a CD insert in either the Editor or the Organizer, just go to Create → Projects → More Options → CD Jacket; you get a variety of different templates, all the right size to fit in a CD case.

The steps for creating a CD jacket are the same as for a photo collage (page 466), but the layout choices, of course, are different. Pay special attention to the photo placement when choosing your layout: The right side of the layout is the front cover. Turn the "Auto-Fill with Project Bin Photos" checkbox off or on to suit you. (If you have five photos in the Project bin, you don't want to get a five-page CD jacket, which is what may happen. If there aren't enough slots on one page for all the open photos, Auto-Fill just makes extra pages to place the open images. So turn Auto-Fill off if you don't want Elements to use all your open photos.)

Unfortunately, only the "2 Centered" CD-insert layout even approximately marks out the general spine area, where most CDs display their titles. If you decide to enter text that you want to appear on the spine, click the Horizontal Type tool (page 441), type away, and then go to Image → Rotate → Layer 90° Left. Then use the Move tool to place the text where you want it. (You could also use the Vertical Type tool, but usually it's quite a job to get the type to look good, and most English speakers find it easier to read horizontally typed text sideways than to read long columns of vertical text.)

> **TIP** If you use a theme (page 466) and want to add spine text, remember that home inkjet printers don't do a good job printing small, white type on a dark background. You're better off going with dark type on a light background.

The DVD Jacket wizard (Create → Projects → More Options → DVD Jacket) is identical except for the layout choices.

CD/DVD Labels

You can create stick-on labels for CDs and DVDs with Elements (Create → Projects → More Options → CD/DVD Label) and print them on blank label sheets from any office supply store. Elements gives you templates that create a single-label layout. When you're done, you need to place your work into the template that goes with your specific brand of labels. (Most CD or DVD labels print two to a page.) The major brands, like Avery (*www.avery.com*) and Neato (*www.neato.com*), have free downloadable templates on their websites to help you position the labels properly on the page.

> **NOTE** While labels make your discs look great, it's risky to put a stick-on label on any disc you'll use in a computer. If the label gets stuck in the disk drive, you may have to replace the drive. Consider using a marker to label discs for computer use, or buying printable discs if you have a printer that will take them.

Online Creations

Besides what you can do in Elements, you can create a handful of projects online at Shutterfly or Kodak Gallery (page 486). For example, you can order greeting cards using their formats and templates instead of Elements Greeting Card choices. First, select your photos in the Organizer, or open them in the Editor. Then go to Create → Greeting Card. Elements automatically uploads your photos, and you see them in the Kodak or Shutterfly wizard, which walks you through creating and ordering cards. You need to set up an account the first time you use either of these sites. Setting up an account and using the sites are explained on page 486.

You can also create calendars online. Before you start, you have to select 12 photos in the Organizer. Then go to Create → Photo Calendar, and Elements whisks you off to Kodak Gallery or Shutterfly. (You can access the Photo Calendar menu choice from either the Organizer or the Editor, but it's the photos you've selected in the Organizer that get uploaded.) If you select fewer than 12 photos, the Kodak wizard nags you to add more, and you don't have the option of using the same photo for each month. (Elements doesn't include templates for creating calendars to print at home or to take to your local print shop.) Shutterfly offers a variety of different calendar types, including 18-month calendars, collage calendars where you can use multiple photos on one page, and calendars that show the whole year on one page.

Element's doesn't have a built-in way to create a calendar to print at home, but if you look around online, you can usually find calendar templates you can open in Elements, add your own photos, and print yourself. Another online ordering option (if you're in the United States) is PhotoStamps. This is real, legitimate postage that features the photo of your choice. If you've always wanted to be immortalized on a stamp, here's your chance. Select one or more photos, and then go to Create → More Options → PhotoStamps. Elements automatically uploads your photos to Stamps.com, where you can create an account and then order away.

> **NOTE** While PhotoStamps are fun, they're a bit pricey, so you may want to save them for special occasions, like sending wedding announcements. Before you spend a lot of time preparing photos, check the price list to see whether you really think the stamps will be worth the cost. (Image files you use on stamps have to be less than 5 megabytes in size.)

Printing Your Photos

Now that you've gone to so much trouble to make your photos look terrific, you probably want to share them with other people. This chapter and the next two look at the many different options Elements gives you for sharing your photos with the world at large.

This chapter covers the traditional method: printing your photos. You can print them at home on an inkjet printer, take them to a kiosk at a local store, or use an online service. Elements makes it especially simple to use Shutterfly and Kodak Gallery, Adobe's online printing partners. You also get an easy connection to several other popular online photo services (page 546). The best thing about using an online service is that you're not limited merely to ordinary prints: You can create hardcover books, calendars, embarrassing t-shirts—you name it.

> **TIP** If you create online albums at Photoshop.com (page 519), you can let friends order prints directly from your Photoshop.com web page. (Those prints come from Shutterfly.)

Getting Ready to Print

Whether printing at home or sending photos to a printing service, you need to make sure your image file is set up to give you good-looking prints.

The first thing to check is your photo's resolution, which controls the number of pixels per inch (ppi) in your image. If you don't have enough pixels in your photo, then your print will look grainy and pixelated. Most photo aficionados consider 300 ppi ideal; a quality print needs a resolution of at least 150 ppi to avoid the grainy look you see in low-resolution photos. See page 107 for more on reviewing and setting your photo's resolution.

TIP   Be sure to set your resolution to a whole number—decimals may cause black lines on your prints with some printers. In other words, 247 ppi is fine, but you may have problems if the ppi is 247.32. Older printers are most likely to have problems with decimals.

When printing on photo paper or sending your photos out for printing, make sure that your images are cropped to fit a standard paper size. (Cropping is covered starting on page 89.) When printing at home, the paper and ink you use make a big difference in the color and quality of your printed photo. It may seem like a marketing scam, but you really will get the best results by using your printer manufacturer's recommended paper and ink.

Ordering Prints

You don't even need to own a printer to print your photos. There's no shortage of companies hoping you'll choose them for that privilege. You can order prints online or use a print kiosk at a local store. Elements makes it really easy to prepare your photos for printing either way. Just save your photos in a compatible file format (see page 71 for more about picking a file format). JPEG format is usually your best bet, but always check with the service you plan to use to see if it has any special requirements.

If you plan to physically take your photos in for printing (as opposed to ordering them online), burn the photos to a CD to take in. Use the Organizer to export your photos to the desktop, as explained in Figure 16-1. Then use your computer's CD-creation program to burn your exported photos to a disc, or just copy the exported photos to a memory card or portable USB drive.

NOTE   You can also burn a CD from within Elements (in the Organizer go to the Share tab, and click the "Burn data CD/DVD" button). That works fine as long as your photos are in the correct format and you don't include any photos from stacks (page 46) or version sets (page 68). Stacks and version sets may cause problems for commercial printers and kiosks, which don't understand them.

Adobe has partnered with the popular online service Shutterfly and with Kodak's online photo-printing service, Kodak Gallery, to make it simple to upload photos directly from Elements. You can order prints, books, or any of the other photo-bearing items that they would love to sell you. Of course, you're free to use any other online printing service (see page 546 for some suggestions), but the process for using them isn't integrated right into Elements the way it is with these two.

NOTE   If you've ordered online from an early version of Elements but haven't done so recently, Kodak Gallery is the current name for what used to be Ofoto.com. If you have an Ofoto account, then you can still use it with Kodak Gallery. (There are a couple of places in Elements where Kodak Gallery is referred to as Kodak EasyShare Gallery, another former name, but it's all the same service.)

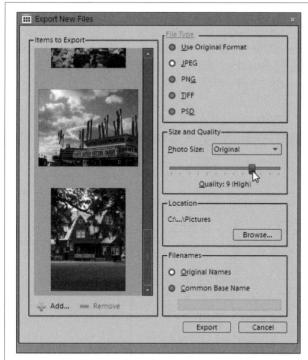

Figure 16-1:
Use the Export New Files dialog box to get your images ready for in-store printing (at a kiosk, for example). First, in the Organizer's Media Browser, select your photos. Then choose File → Export As New File(s) to send them to your desktop so you can burn them to a CD. In the dialog box that appears, pick a new file format in the dialog box's File Type section, if necessary (you have TIFFs and the store wants JPEGs, for example). For printing, always choose maximum quality (the Quality slider becomes active only when you choose to export as JPEGs). In the Location section, click the Browse button to choose the desktop. File renaming is up to you. When everything looks good, click Export to do just that.

Once you've edited your photos and are ready to place your order, just follow these steps:

1. **Select the photos you want to have printed.**

   Open them in the Editor, or click to select them in the Organizer. (Your photos don't have to be in the Organizer if you start from the Editor, and they aren't added to the Organizer automatically when you order prints.)

2. **Connect to the service you want to use.**

   You can order prints from Shutterfly or Kodak Gallery from either the Editor or the Organizer:

   • **File menu.** Go to File → Order Prints, and select the service you want to use.

   • **Create tab.** Go to Create → Photo Prints, and choose Shutterfly or Kodak Gallery from the list of options that appears.

   If you start from the Create tab, click the button for the online service you want to use. (The process is very similar for either.) Regardless of where you start, Elements brings the Organizer forward, prepares your photos, and connects to the service.

3. **The online prints wizard opens.**

The details differ slightly depending on whether you're using Kodak or Shutterfly, but the general process is the same. You need to log in before you can order, or to create an account if it's the first time you're using either service. An easy-to-follow *wizard* (a series of guided question screens) appears to help set up your account and complete your order. Figure 16-2 shows the Shutterfly wizard.

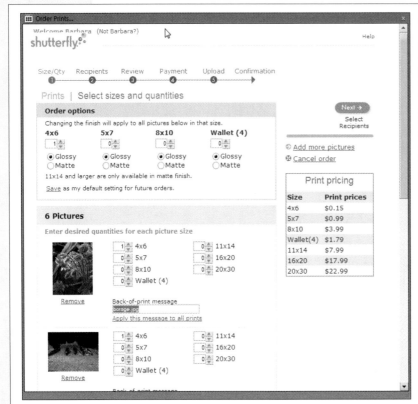

Figure 16-2:
You can choose from many different sizes, and order as many of each photo as you like. As you can see here, you can even choose to add the name of the image or a text message to the back of each print. This is Shutterfly's online wizard, but the one for Kodak Gallery is very similar.

4. **Order your prints.**

The wizard lets you add or subtract photos, choose how many of each and which size, the finish you want, etc. Then you enter info about the recipients (their names and addresses). Both companies' wizards remember who you've sent photos to with previous orders, so you don't have to reenter Aunt Suzie's address each time. When your order is all set, enter your payment information, and you'll receive an envelope of prints in the mail in a few days.

TIP   Elements automatically checks for updates to these services, and automatically notifies you about special promotions the sites are offering. You can stop it from doing either by, in the Organizer, going to Edit → Preferences → Adobe Partner Services and turning off the appropriate checkboxes in the "Check for Services" section. You can also tell Elements how to handle updates when it finds them by opening the Organizer and going to Help → Updates → Preferences, where you can choose whether Elements should check for updates and install them automatically, or ask before it installs anything. To see the Updates Preferences, you have to first let the Updater run. Then the Preferences button appears in the window Elements displays when the Updater finishes.

Even though Elements makes ordering prints from Kodak or Shutterfly really convenient, you can use either service without going through Elements, and you can use other online print services like Snapfish (*www.snapfish.com*). The real advantage of ordering from Elements is the convenience of being able to work right in the Organizer.

TIP   If you use Shutterfly, you can start your order right from Full Screen view (page 56). The Quick Edit panel there has a "Mark for Printing" button. Click it when you see photos you want to print. Then, when you return to the Media Browser from Full Screen view, a pop-up window offers you the choice of printing the photos at home or ordering prints. Click Order Prints, and Elements prepares your photos and opens the Shutterfly wizard for you.

If you're using Adobe's Photoshop.com service (page 20), then you can connect to many popular online print services right from the personal web page you get as part of your Photoshop.com account. And when you share an album online there, you can let friends order prints of your photos right from your web page. See page 519 for more details.

Printing at Home

If you prefer to do your own printing at home, one of the new features in Elements 8 is a redesigned Print window, which looks the same whether you call it up from the Editor or the Organizer. Adobe wanted to make it quick and easy to create the kind of prints you'd order online (as described on page 484) or get from a store kiosk—prints on typical photo-sized paper. It's still possible to do more elaborate printing from Elements, but the workflow is a bit different in Elements 8.

In earlier versions of Elements, printing was quite different depending on whether you were printing from the Editor or the Organizer. In Elements 8, printing from either spot is quite similar, but printing from Elements 8 differs quite a bit from printing in any previous version of Elements. It may take you a little while to get used to it.

Before you go to print, it's really important to be sure the resolution (ppi) of your print is what you want (see page 107 for more about resolution), and it's a good idea to do any cropping of your photo (page 89) before you call up the Print window. You can start from either the Editor or the Organizer, and once you're in the

Print window, you can choose to create individual prints, a contact sheet of small thumbnails of all your photos, or a picture package of several sizes of prints.

Making Individual Prints

The basic process of printing from Elements 8 is the same no matter where you start or what you're printing. (You'll see a few differences if you're printing contact sheets or picture packages, which are covered later in this chapter.) This section is about making individual prints (one photo per page) from the Editor, since that offers the most options. To learn about the minor differences between printing from the Editor and from the Organizer, see the box on page 491. Once you understand making single prints from the Editor, you won't have any trouble with other kinds of printing:

1. **Choose the photo(s) you want to print.**

   Select your photos in the Project bin if you want to print more than one photo. Otherwise Elements prints only the active photo, or if you haven't selected a photo, it prints everything in the bin. (You can add or remove photos once you're in the Print window, too—if the photos are already in the Organizer, as explained in Figure 16-3.) You can also choose to print all your open photos by going to the Project bin's Bin Actions menu and selecting Print Bin Files.

2. **Go to File → Print.**

   The Print window appears. It's divided into three main sections: On the left is a filmstrip-like view where you can add or remove to print (Figure 16-3). In the middle is a preview area, where you see the image you're going to print and some controls for rotating and adjusting the image (there's a blue outline around the area that's going to print). And on the right is a strip of numbered controls, listed in the order in which you need to make your choices.

3. **Choose the printer you want to use.**

   Select it from the drop-down menu on the right side of the window (Step 1 listed there).

4. **Choose your printer settings.**

   Under Step 2 (Printer Settings), check to see what Elements proposes as far as the type of paper and the print quality. Click Change Settings if you don't like what you see; make any changes in the window that opens, and click OK. (There's a setting here to change the print size, but you don't need to use it—you'll do that in the main Print window in the next step.) Depending on your printer, you may have other options here, like which paper tray you want the printer to use. If your printer lets you make borderless prints, you see a checkbox for that, too. Turn it on, and you'll only see borderless choices in the next step.

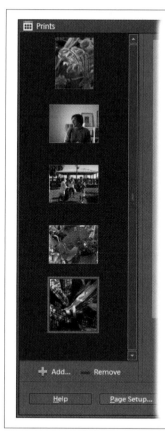

Figure 16-3:
In the left side of the Print window, you can add more photos to print, but only if they're already in the Organizer. Click the green + button, and a window opens that lets you browse through all your Organizer photos to choose which to add. If you want to print photos that aren't in the Organizer, open them in Elements and select them in the Project bin before you start. If you decide not to print one of the photos in the list, click its thumbnail, and then click the red − button.

5. **Select your paper size.**

Click the Select Paper Size menu (step 3 in the window) for a list of the sizes of paper available for your printer. What's available is determined by the printer you chose in Step 1, and by whether you turned on Borderless in the Printer Settings (there's no checkbox for Borderless if you have a printer that can't make borderless prints).

6. **Choose what kind of prints you want to make.**

In the Print window's Step 4, choose whether to make individual prints, a contact sheet, or a picture package. In this example, you're making individual prints (one photo per page), so choose that. (If you want to make a contact sheet or picture package, flip to page 499.)

7. **Select a print size.**

Use the Step 5 drop-down menu. If your print isn't one of the preset sizes, choose Actual Size or Custom. If you choose Custom, you see a window with the Custom Size choices from the More Options window, which is explained on page 493. Enter your choices and click OK.

If you turn off the "Crop to Fit" checkbox, Elements prints your whole image as large as it can be within the Print Size you chose, even if that means leaving empty space at some of the edges. If you want to make your image fill the available space, leave "Crop to Fit" turned on and Elements trims your image to fit the print size you chose. Figure 16-4 shows the difference this setting makes.

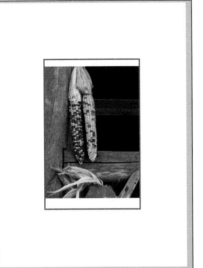

Figure 16-4:
Top: Here's how the photo will print with "Crop to Fit" turned off. Notice the white space at the top and bottom of the blue bounding box.

Bottom: Leave "Crop to Fit" turned on, and Elements enlarges your photo enough to fill all the space before cropping off the excess.

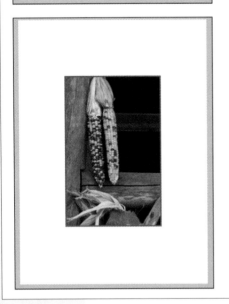

8. **Choose how many copies of each page you want to print.**

If you want to make more than one copy of each print, enter the number of copies of each you want in the box below the "Crop to Fit" checkbox. (Elements prints this many copies of *every* print in this batch—you can't make three copies of one photo and two of another, for example.)

9. **Print your photos.**

Click Print, and the Windows Print dialog box opens. Click Print there, and Elements prints your photos. If you change your mind, click Cancel or close the Print window instead.

That's the basic process for printing in Elements 8. If you're in a hurry or not fussy, you can have a handful of prints in short order. But odds are that you're using Elements just because you *are* fussy about your photos, and you may want to tweak several other settings. The next sections cover all the ways you can customize things like how your photo sits on the page, its color management, and so forth.

THE SIMPLE LIFE

Printing from the Organizer

In Elements 8, the process for printing individual images is exactly the same whether you start from the Editor or the Organizer except for three details, which all involve clicking the Print window's More Options button:

- **Image positioning.** The Editor always prints one photo per page, regardless of the relative sizes of the photos and your paper, while the Organizer may place more than one photo on a page if there's room. If you want to restrict the Organizer to placing only one image on a sheet, click the More Options button → Printing Choices, and turn on "One Photo Per Page."

- **Max Print Resolution.** When you go to More Options → Custom Print Size, the Organizer has a box with this label (while the Editor's Print window just lists your image's print resolution in pixels per inch). If you don't make a change here,

anything you print from the Organizer will print at 220 ppi or less (see page 107 for more about resolution and why this may matter).

- **Color Management.** Instead of the many options you find in the Editor when you go to More Options → Color Management (see page 495), the Organizer just presents you with the current color space for your image and a drop-down menu set to "Same as Source". Leave that setting as is.

You begin by selecting the photos you want to print in the Organizer's Media Browser rather than in the Project bin, but otherwise the whole process is identical from either the Editor or the Organizer. You can also mark photos for printing from Full Screen view (page 56). When you return to the Media Browser, a pop-up window gives you the option of printing your photos or ordering prints online (page 484).

NOTE The Print window isn't *color managed* (page 215), which means that what you see in the window isn't necessarily the same as the colors you'll get when you print; the preview is just meant to show you where your photo is going to print.

Positioning Your Image

There are two main ways to adjust the relationship between your image and the paper you print it on. Elements' Print window has some controls for rotating and sizing your image, which is normally all you'll need. You can even scoot your photo around within the preview area to determine which part of it is going to print, if you don't want to print the entire image. And if you want, you can also call up the Windows Page Setup dialog box, which is the same for all programs on your computer. The following sections explain your options.

Print window settings

When you open Elements' Print window, you see your photo surrounded by a blue outline (called a *bounding box)* in a white preview area. The white area is your paper, and the blue box represents the printing boundaries of your photo. (The blue outline doesn't get printed. Incidentally, Adobe's official name for the area surrounded by the blue outline is the Print Well, in case you run into it in any tutorials.) Your first impulse may be to grab the box and try to adjust the placement of your photo on the page. But if you do this, rather than moving the blue box, you just move your image *within* the box.

If you've used a previous version of Elements, you may be looking for where to turn off the Center Image setting. (In older versions of Elements, turning off this setting let you move your photo around on the page to position it wherever on the paper you wanted it to print.) Unfortunately, in Elements 8, there's no such setting. You can't move the blue box: it's *always* where Elements decides it should be on the page, even if you're printing, say, a 4"×6"-photo on a letter-sized piece of paper. Its location depends on the size of the print relative to the paper, but wherever it appears, it's fixed in place. Elements may choose to show you only one image per page, or it may fit more than one if your chosen print size is small enough and you started printing from the Organizer rather than the Editor, but it's not for you to say—Elements is in charge in the Print window. (If this news makes your blood pressure rise, head over to the box on page 494 for a workaround.)

Though you can't move the bounding box, there are several ways to change how your image appears within it.

- **Rotate your photo.** Below the preview area are the same rotation icons you see elsewhere in Elements. Click one to rotate your photo within the bounding box. (You may need to go to Page Setup—see page 493—if you want to rotate the box on the page, and then it may or not change when you alter the page orientation.)

- **Resize your photo.** If you don't want to print the whole image, you can zoom in on part of your photo by using the slider below the preview to control which part of it appears in the box, Be careful with this feature: You can easily enlarge your image beyond a reasonable pixel density. (When you click Print, Elements will warn you if the image is going to print at less than 220 ppi, but as a general rule it's best to take care of any resizing *before* you open the Print window.)

- **Reposition your photo in the box.** You can drag your image around in the pre-view area to determine which part of it will print. (You can also accidentally drag your image almost out of view. If that happens, just choose a different print size in the right-hand part of the window, and then switch back to the original size. Elements recenters your image in the Print Well each time you change this setting.)

> **NOTE** If you turn on the "Crop to Fit" checkbox, Elements crops based on the *original* position of your image; it doesn't take into account any dragging that you do. In other words, you can't control the part of your photo that gets printed if you use "Crop to Fit".

- **Make your image and the print size the same.** If you decide to make a 4"×6" print of an image that's the right aspect ratio (shape) for a 5"×7" print, for exam-ple, you'll have some empty space on the edges because the print size and the aspect ratio aren't equivalent. There are two ways around this. First, you can turn on "Crop to Fit", and Elements will chop off the extra edges of your photo. Or, in the Select Print Size menu, choose Actual Size if you've already cropped your image to a photo-paper size. You can also use a Custom size, as explained next.

- **Custom Print Size.** Either choose Custom from the Print window's Select Print Size menu, or click the More Options button and click Custom Print Size to call up the Custom Print Size dialog box. There you can type in the exact height and width you want to print, in inches, centimeters, millimeters, points, or pixels. Below the Height, Weight, and Unit boxes, Elements lists the pixel resolution you'll have at that size (see page 107 for more about resolution).

- **Make your image fill the paper.** If you click the More Options button and then click Custom Print Size, you can turn on the "Scale to Fit Media" checkbox, and Elements makes your image larger or smaller so that all of it fits into your desired page size. You may need to use Windows' Page Setup dialog box (described below) to change the paper orientation after choosing this.

Of course, none of these options will let you print your image at the upper-right corner of the page, or put more than one photo on a page. Use the workaround in the box on page 494 to do that, or use a picture package (page 500) to print multi-ple photos on one page.

Windows' Page Setup dialog box

In the lower-left corner of Elements' Print window, there's a Page Setup button. Click it to bring up the Windows Page Setup dialog box. Normally, you don't need to use this dialog box at all in Elements 8—choosing your printer in the window's Step 1 area takes care of things. But once you've got everything set up in Elements' Print window, you can use Page Setup to override Elements' settings. So, for exam-ple, if you want to rotate the paper 90 degrees relative to the blue bounding box, this is where you do it. You can also select a printer here, but normally choosing a printer in the Print window changes Page Setup to match.

Placing Your Photo Where You Want It

As explained on page 492, Elements' automatically decides where on the page to print your photos. Adobe seems to think that most people don't really care where on the page their photos print as long as they print, or that you like the idea of letting Elements call the photo-placement shots for you. That's fine if you agree, but if you're of the "It's my darned photo on my darned paper in my darned printer" school of thought, or if you don't wanting every print centered on the page, you may not appreciate this new feature. Don't worry—there's a way around it, and it only adds one more step to printing. Before you print your image:

1. **Create a new, blank document the same size as your paper.** Go to File → New → Blank File. Choose a white or transparent background, and set the resolution to 300 ppi or whatever you normally use for printing. (See page 103 if you need help choosing a resolution.) Save the blank file with a name like Printing Template.

2. **From now on, when you want to print an image on a particular part of the page, open this file and copy and paste your photo(s) into it.** Then use the Move tool (page 165) to position them wherever you like.

If you have trouble getting photos centered on the page because of the way your printer feeds the paper (some printers have to hang on to one end of the sheet and always put a wider margin there because of that) you can use Elements' new guides feature (page 87) to put a non-printing guideline as a mark in the blank document to remind you where the effective end of the printable area of the page is, so you know what your real boundaries are. You can even use this method to create your own picture package for multiple prints, as explained on page 502.

Finally, if you print a lot and just can't deal with all these workarounds, check out Qimage (*www.ddisoftware. com/qimage/*), a popular program just for printing and resizing images.

Additional Print Options

Elements includes a number of other useful ways to tweak your photo, like putting a border around it, printing crop marks as guides for trimming the printed photo, or even flipping it for printing as an iron-on transfer. You'll find these by clicking the Print window's More Options button and then, on the dialog box's left, clicking Printing Choices:

- **Photo Details.** You can print the image's filename, shot or creation date, and/or caption on the page with your photo by turning on the relevant checkbox here. (The image preview area shows where your text will get printed.) Caption text is what you entered in the Organizer (see page 69), or you can go to File → Info in the Editor to add a caption in the relevant field.

- **Border.** If you want to add a border to your photo, turn on the Thickness checkbox, and enter the size you want for your border (in inches, millimeters, or points). Elements shrinks your photo to accommodate the border, even if there's plenty of empty space around the picture, so you may need to enlarge the photo a bit before printing to get the size you originally chose. Click the white square that appears to bring up the Color Picker (see page 232) so you can choose a border color. If the page has empty space you want to fill with a background color, then turn on the Background checkbox, and click its color square to bring up the Color Picker.

- **Trim Guidelines.** The Print Crop Marks checkbox lets you print guidelines in the margins of your photo to make it easier to trim exactly. Crop marks are useful mainly for trimming bordered photos so that the borders are exactly even.

- **Iron-on Transfer.** Turn on the Flip Image checkbox to horizontally reverse your image. You'd use this when printing transfers for projects like t-shirts.

Color Management

In the Editor, Elements gives you several advanced color-related settings if you click the Print window's More Options button and then click Color Management on the left side of the dialog box. If you're content with the way your prints look without adjusting these settings, just be happy and ignore them. But if you don't like the color you're getting from Elements, then use these advanced controls to make adjustments.

> **NOTE** Color management can be a dauntingly complicated subject to understand. The advice in the following pages should be enough to get you started, but if you're determined to learn more, a good place to start is Brad Hinkel's *Color Management in Digital Photography* (Rocky Nook, 2007). It covers Photoshop but many of its explanations are suitable for Elements users as well.

You may remember from Chapter 7 that Elements is a *color-managed* program, which means it tries to coordinate the color settings used by various devices and programs: your photo file (which may retain color settings applied by your camera), your monitor, your Elements settings, and your printer. Sometimes you need to step in and help Elements decide which settings are best, since different devices and programs can have different interpretations of what certain colors look like.

WORKAROUND WORKSHOP

Economical Print Experiments

If you've just gone out and bought top-quality photo paper, you may be suffering from a bit of sticker shock and perhaps are even thinking, "Oh yeah, great. Now I'm supposed to use this stuff up experimenting? At that price?"

The good news is, while you have to bite the bullet and sacrifice a sheet or two, you don't need to waste the whole box. Try this: First follow the directions in the box on page 494 for creating a blank file so that you can put your image where you want it on the paper. Next, make a small selection somewhere in a photo you want to print, press Ctrl+C, and then make your blank file the active file and paste your selection into it (Ctrl+V). You now have a file with only a small piece of your photo in it.

This is your test print. Use the Move tool (page 165) to drag your small photo to the large page's upper-left corner. Now, try printing the page using Elements' standard settings. If your print looks good, then you're ready to print the whole photo.

On the other hand, if you don't like the result, try again. This time, move your test print over to the right a little bit using the Move tool. Change your settings (keeping note of the changes you've made), and then print again on the same piece of paper. Your new test prints out beside the first one. Keep moving the test area around on the page, and you can try out quite a few different combinations of settings, all on the same sheet of paper.

Color management may sound intimidating, but you already took the first steps there when you chose your paper type and print quality. Now your most important decision is whether you want Elements or your printer to manage your photo's color settings. (You can let Elements *and* your printer have a say in color management, but that almost always mucks things up.) The good news is that Elements does its best to keep you from double-managing your color, and it tries to make managing the color in your prints as painless as possible.

You have four main color-management choices to make in the More Options dialog box:

- **Color Handling.** Here's where you decide who's going to be in charge: Elements (Photoshop Elements Manages Colors), your printer (Printer Manages Colors), or nobody (No Color Management). The choice you make here determines your options in the rest of the settings. Elements also gives you some hints about your printer settings, as you can see in Figure 16-5.

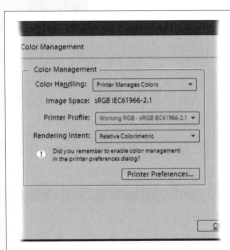

Figure 16-5:
Elements thoughtfully reminds you to turn your printer's color management feature off when you choose Photoshop Elements Manages Colors or No Color Management. Click the Printer Preferences button shown here to adjust your printer's settings.

- **Image Space.** This setting shows you which, if any, color space your file is tagged with (for example, sRGB or Adobe RGB). You don't actually choose a setting here; this line just lets you know the color space associated with your file. See page 217 for more about color spaces.

- **Printer Profile.** This setting is grayed out unless you chose Photoshop Elements Manages Color in the Color Handling menu. If Elements is managing the color, then you can choose the profile you want from a list of all the profiles Elements can find on your computer.

- **Rendering Intent.** Use this setting to tell Elements what to do if your photo contains colors that fall outside the color range of the print space you're using; your choices are explained in the box on page 498. (When you choose No Color Management for your Color Handling setting, this option isn't available.)

The easiest way to set up color management, and a good way to start, is to choose Printer Manages Color. This means that Elements hands your photo over to your printer and lets your printer take care of the color management duties. Then all you need to do is select the proper paper profile and settings for your printer.

Selecting a paper profile may sound kind of technical, but actually, you've probably already done it, back in Printer Settings → Change Settings (step 4 on page 488). It's usually as simple as choosing, say, Photo Paper Plus Glossy from the list of options there. If you chose a paper type and print quality already in the Elements Print window, your printer preferences should have changed to reflect them. However, your printer may give you some additional choices that are worth exploring. Just click the Printer Preferences button below the Source Space area to get to these settings, or, in Elements' Change Settings window, click the Advanced Settings button. The exact wording in the dialog box that appears differs depending on what kind of printer you've got, but Figure 16-6 shows a typical printer's settings.

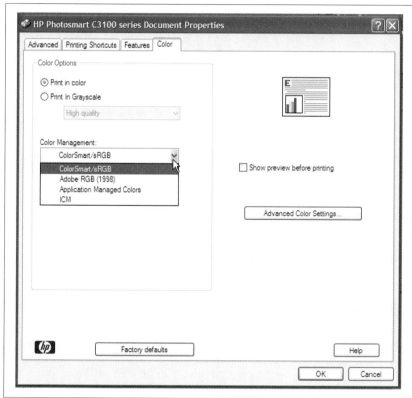

Figure 16-6:
If you're not sure how to set up color management in your printer's settings, it's easy. In this example, just leaving this menu set to ColorSmart/sRGB is all it takes. If you plan to let Elements manage color, choose "Application Managed Colors" instead. Different brands of printers have different names for their color management systems, of course, but it's usually pretty simple to figure out which option you want.

TIP   If your camera takes photos in sRGB, and you've been editing them in No Color Management or "Always Optimize Colors for Computer Screens", then don't alter your workflow by choosing Adobe RGB for the printer profile, as your colors may shift drastically. If for some reason you want to change the color space for the printer, first go to Image → Convert Color Profile, and then apply the Adobe RGB profile to your photo. If you aren't absolutely sure that your printer understands Adobe RGB (many inkjets don't), and you don't have a compelling reason for changing this setting, then it's best to leave things alone.

You can configure Elements' color settings in a zillion different ways, and you may need to experiment a bit to find what works best for you. (See the box on page 495 for advice on how to cheaply test out a bunch of different print settings.) If you go looking around for more info, you'll find that this subject is very controversial—everyone has a different approach that's the "right" one. In fact, you have many options that can lead to good results.

UNDER THE HOOD

What's Your Intent?

For most people, the Rendering Intent setting in Elements' Print window is the most confusing of the color-management options. Here are the basics you need to know to choose a setting:

Sometimes your photo may contain colors that fall outside the color boundaries of the print space you're using; those are colors that the print space can't properly display. The Intent setting tells Elements what to do if that happens. You have four choices:

• **Perceptual** tells Elements to preserve the relationship between the colors in your image—even if that means it has to visibly shift some colors to make them all fit.

• **Saturation** makes colors very vivid—but not necessarily very accurate. This setting is more for special effects than for regular photo printing.

• **Relative Colorimetric** tries to preserve the colors in both the source and the output color spaces by shifting things to the closest matching color in the printer profile's space. This is Elements' standard setting, and it's usually what you want because it keeps your colors as close as possible to what you see onscreen.

• **Absolute Colorimetric** lets you simulate another printer and paper. This setting is for specialized proofing situations.

Printing Multiple Photos

Elements also lets you print from the Organizer, which gives you many more output options than the Editor, including the ability to print several photos on one page. You can create *contact sheets* of thumbnails and *picture packages* (like you'd order from a professional photographer), and easily add all kinds of fancy borders to your photos in the Organizer. (In Elements 8, you can begin creating a contact sheet or a picture package from the Editor, but Elements bounces you over to the Organizer for your actual printing.)

Contact Sheets

Contact sheets show thumbnail views of multiple images on a single page. They're great for creating a visual reference guide to the photos you've archived on a CD, for instance. Or you may want to print a contact sheet of all the photos on a memory card as soon as you download the photos to your computer, even before you edit them (see Figure 16-7).

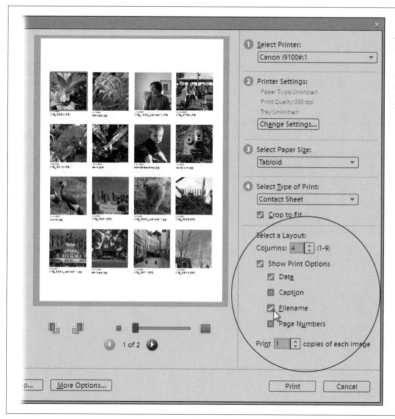

Figure 16-7:
An Elements contact sheet. In the "Select a Layout" section (circled), the Columns menu lets you decide how many columns of images appear on your contact sheet.

To print a contact sheet, in the Print window, go to the "Select Type of Print" menu and choose Contact Sheet. The window changes to show a "Select a Layout" section, and you can use the following settings to customize your contact sheet:

- **Columns.** Here's where you decide how many vertical rows of photos to have on a page (up to nine). The more columns you have, the smaller your thumbnails. Even if you have only one image currently chosen, increasing the number of columns shrinks the thumbnail.

- **Show Print Options.** Turn on this checkbox and you can decide whether to have Elements print the image's date, caption (any text in the image's caption field), and/or filename below each thumbnail. You can also add page numbers if you're printing multiple pages. (If all your photos fit on one page, Page Numbers is grayed out.)

You can add and remove images as explained earlier, and you can click on a photo in the layout and use the slider to zoom, just as you can with individual prints. When you like your layout, click Print.

Picture Package

Elements' Picture Package tool lets you print several images on one sheet. You can print a package that's one photo printed repeatedly, or create a package that includes multiple photos.

To get started, press Ctrl+P to call up the Print window. Go to "Select Type of Print" and choose Picture Package. Next, under "Select a Layout", pick which composition style you want (choices include four 3"×5" photos, two 5"×7" photos, and so on). Then choose a frame, if you'd like one, by picking from the "Select a Frame" menu. Add photos to your package by clicking the Add button in the lower-left corner of the window.

> **NOTE** You can also start a picture package in either the Editor or the Organizer by going to the Create tab → Photo Prints → Picture Package. The only real advantage to starting there is that the Print window opens with "Picture Package" preselected in Step 4.

Figure 16-8 shows you how to change the layout of your photos once they're on the page. If you turn on the Fill Page With First Photo checkbox, then you get an whole page dedicated to each photo showing multiple sizes of the image, instead of various photos on each page.

Elements crops your photos to fit their slots if you turn on the "Crop to Fit" checkbox, but you're probably better off doing that yourself in the Editor (page 89) before you start. You can select a photo in the layout and then use the rotation buttons and the zoom slider to tweak it. When you've got your photos arranged the way you want them, click Print.

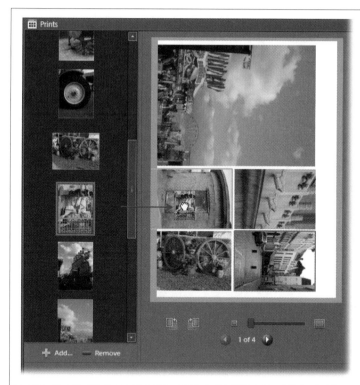

Figure 16-8:
Reorganizing your picture package is drag-and-drop easy. If you have empty space in your layout and want to fill it, or you want to change the photo in a particular slot, just drag a thumbnail from the filmstrip on the left into the slot where you want to use the photo. (You can't drag images between slots, only from the thumbnails on the left.) To remove a photo from the package, click it on the left side of the main window and then click the red Remove button.

Creating Your Own Package

You may find that you want a layout for your picture package that's different from any of the choices Elements offers. You can easily make your own picture package from scratch:

1. **Save all the photos you want to use at the same resolution.**

2. **In the Editor, create a new document (Ctrl+N or File → New).** Make sure it's the size you want your finished package to be, and that it has the same resolution as your photos. (See page 51 for more about setting a file's resolution.) You can save time by choosing the Letter preset size from the New dialog box's Size menu; that size is already set to 300 ppi.

3. **Bring each photo into your new file.** Press Ctrl+A to select all your photos, and then copy (Ctrl+C) and paste (Ctrl+V) them into your new document. You can also drag photos from the Layers panel (page 197), and then position them as you wish, if you're using floating windows (page 29).

Once the photos are in your new document, you can use the Move tool (page 165) or Scale command (page 359) to resize them.

When you have all your photos positioned and sized to suit you, save the combined file, and then print it. You can make the file smaller by flattening it first (Layer → Flatten Image), but only flatten it if you don't think you'll want to tweak your layout later.

You can also create new layouts for yourself in the Organizer. Go to C:\Program Files\Adobe\Elements Organizer 8.0\Assets\locale\en_US \layouts (the "en_US" part will be different if you aren't in the United States). Choose the layout that's closest to what you want. Open it in the text editor of your choice, save it with a new name, and then make your changes. When you're done, save your changes, and then put the new file into the same folder as the original. If you're not sure about what to change, the layouts folder has a helpful ReadMe file that explains what to do.

Email and the Web

Printing your photos is great, but it costs money, takes time, and doesn't do much to instantly impress faraway friends. And to many people, printing is just so 20th century. Fortunately, Elements comes packed with tools that make it easy to prep your photos for onscreen viewing and to email them in a variety of crowd-pleasing ways.

Image Formats and the Web

Back in the Web's early days, making your graphic files small was important because most Internet connections were as slow as snails. Nowadays, file size isn't as crucial; your main obligation when creating graphics for the Web is ensuring they're compatible with the web browsers people use to view your web pages. That means you'll probably want to use either of the two most popular image formats, JPEG or GIF:

- **JPEG** (Joint Photographic Experts' Group) is the most popular choice for images with lots of detail, and where you need smooth color transitions. Photos are almost always posted on the Web as JPEGs.

    NOTE   JPEGs can't have transparent areas, although there's a workaround for that: Fill the background around your image with the same color as the web page you want to post it on. That way, the background blends into the web page, giving the impression that your object is surrounded by transparency. See Figure 17-4 (page 508) for details on how this trick works.

- **GIF** (Graphics Interchange Format) files are great for images with limited numbers of colors, like corporate logos and headlines. Text looks much sharper in GIF format than it does as a JPEG. GIFs also let you keep transparency as part of your image.

- **PNG** (Portable Network Graphic) is a web graphics format that was created to overcome some of the disadvantages of JPEGs and GIFs. There's a lot to like about PNG files: They can include transparent areas, and the format reduces the file size of photographs without losing data, as happens with JPEG files (see page 73 for more about that). PNG files' big drawback is that only newer web browsers deal with them well. Older versions of Internet Explorer are notorious for not supporting the PNG format, so if you've got potential viewers with ancient computers, then you probably don't want to use PNG.

Elements makes it a breeze to save your images in any of these formats using the Save For Web dialog box, covered in the next section.

Saving Images for the Web or Email

If you plan to email your photos or put them up on your website, Save For Web is a terrific feature that takes any open image and saves it in a web-friendly format. It also gives you lots of options to help maintain maximum image quality while keeping file size to a minimum. Save For Web aims to create as small a file as possible without compromising the image's onscreen quality.

Save For Web creates smaller JPEG files than you get by merely using Save As, because it strips out the EXIF data, the information about your camera's settings (see page 69). To get started with Save For Web, go to File → "Save for Web" or press Alt+Shift+Ctrl+S. The dialog box shown in Figure 17-1 appears.

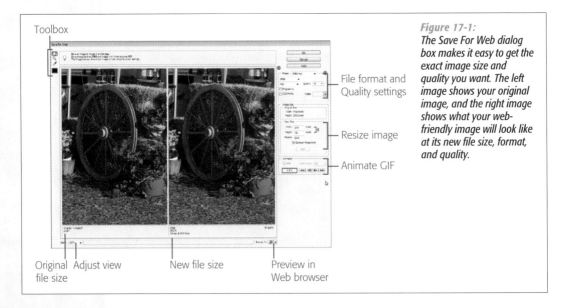

Toolbox

File format and Quality settings

Resize image

Animate GIF

Original file size   Adjust view   New file size   Preview in Web browser

Figure 17-1:
The Save For Web dialog box makes it easy to get the exact image size and quality you want. The left image shows your original image, and the right image shows what your web-friendly image will look like at its new file size, format, and quality.

The most important point to remember when saving images for the Web is that the resolution (measured in pixels per inch, or ppi) is completely irrelevant. You just care about the image's pixel dimensions, such as 400×600. If you're working with a photo that you've optimized for print, you almost certainly want to downsize it; Save For Web makes that a snap.

Elements gives you a lot of useful tools in the Save For Web dialog box, like the Hand (page 102) and Zoom (page 100) tools for adjusting your view. But the main attraction is the before-and-after image preview in the two main preview panes. On the left is your original and on the right is what the image will look like after saving.

The file size is listed below each image preview. Below the right preview, you see the estimated download time, which you can adjust by modifying your assumptions about your recipient's Internet connection speed, as shown in Figure 17-2. You can also change the zoom percentage (using the Zoom menu in the bottom left of the dialog box), but you should usually stick with 100 percent because that's your image's size on the Web.

The upper-right corner of the window has your file format and quality choices (what you see varies a bit depending on which format you've chosen). Below that are your options for resizing your image. If you want to create animated GIFs (those tiny moving images you see on web pages), then set up the animation at the bottom of the settings area. Creating animated GIFs is explained later (page 511).

Using Save For Web

When you're ready to use Save For Web, follow these steps:

1. **Open the image you want to modify.**

2. **Launch the Save For Web dialog box.**

   Go to File → "Save for Web" or press Alt+Shift+Ctrl+S. The Save For Web dialog box appears.

   NOTE   If you're working with a large file, you may see a dialog box stating that "The image exceeds the size Save for Web was designed for", along with dire-sounding warnings about slow performance and out-of-memory errors. Just click Yes to tell Elements that you want to continue anyway. Unless you're running on really antique hardware, you won't have any problems.

3. **Choose the format and quality settings you want for your web image.**

   Use the drop-down menu below the word "Preset" to choose a format. Your choices are explained in the following section.

4. **If necessary, resize your image's dimensions.**

   If you want to make sure that anyone can see the whole image, no matter how small his monitor, enter 650 pixels or less for the longest side of your photo in the New Size area. (About 650 pixels is the largest size that fits on small monitors without scrolling. If your friends all have big, new monitors, you can go much larger.) As long as the Constrain Proportions checkbox is turned on, you don't have to enter the dimension for the other side of your photo. Remember, if any of your friends don't have broadband, large photos can take a long time to download on dial-up connections. Elements helps you out by telling you the download times for various connections, as explained in Figure 17-2.

   You can also resize your image by entering a percentage (for example, entering *90* shrinks your image by 10 percent). When you're finished entering the new dimensions, click Apply.

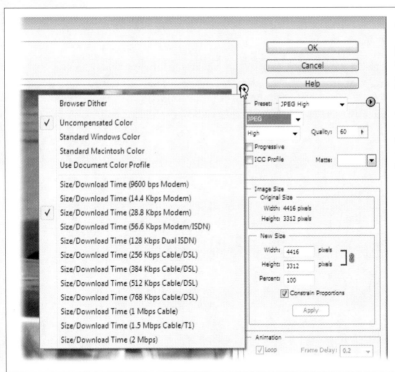

Figure 17-2:
The Save For Web dialog box gives you an estimate of how long it'll take to download your image. If you want to change the download settings (for example, the speed of the Internet connection), go to the upper-right corner of the preview area and click the arrow button to call up this pop-out list.

5. **Check your results.**

   Look at the file size again to see if it's small enough, and take a close look at the image in the right-hand preview area. Use Elements' file size optimization feature (explained in Figure 17-3), if necessary. You can also preview your image in your actual web browser (see page 509).

6. **When everything looks good, click OK.**

Name the new file, and then save it wherever you like. There's no Undo option in the Save For Web dialog box, but you can Alt-click the Cancel button to change it to a Reset button. If you're processing several photos with the same settings, Press the Alt key to change the Help button to a Remember button, and then click it. That way, the next time you open Save For Web, it'll have your current settings preselected.

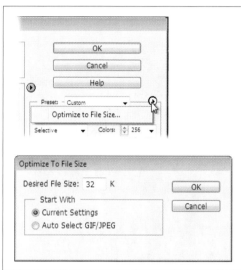

Figure 17-3:
Save For Web's file-size optimization feature is helpful when you need to send a file someplace that puts limits on your total file size.

Top: When you click the triangle next to the Preset menu and then choose "Optimize to File Size", Elements displays a dialog box where you can enter your desired file size.

Bottom: Use K (kilobytes) as your unit of measurement in the Optimize To File Size dialog box. Picking Current Settings tells Elements to start with whatever settings you've entered in the main Save For Web window, like the format and quality. Auto Select GIF/JPEG means you want Elements to decide between GIF and JPEG for you. Once you've finished making your selections, click OK, and Elements shrinks your image to the size you requested.

Save For Web file format options

You can reduce file size by changing the length and width of your image, as explained in Step 4. But you can also make your file smaller by adjusting the quality settings. The quality options you see in the Save For Web dialog box vary depending on which format you choose to save the file as:

- **JPEG.** Elements offers you a variety of basic JPEG quality settings: Low, Medium, High, Very High, and Maximum. You can then fine-tune the quality by entering a number in the Quality box on the right (not surprisingly, a higher number means higher quality). Generally, Medium is usually enough if you're saving for web use. If you're using Save For Web to make JPEG files for printing, then use Maximum instead.

    If you turn on the Progressive checkbox, then your JPEG loads from the top down. This option was popular for large files when everyone had slow dial-up connections, but it makes a slightly larger file, so it's not as popular today. Using the ICC Profile checkbox, you can keep a color space profile embedded in your image. (See page 217 for more about color spaces.)

With the Matte menu, you can set the color of any area that's transparent in your original (see Figure 17-4). If you don't set a matte color, Elements uses white. By choosing a matte color that matches the background of your web page, you can make it *look* like your image is surrounded by transparency. In Elements, you have three ways to select your color: Click the arrow on the right side of the Matte box, and then choose from the drop-down menu; click the arrow on the right side of the Matte box, and then sample a color from your image with the Eyedropper tool; or click the Matte box's color square to call up the Color Picker. (See page 232 for more about using the Color Picker.)

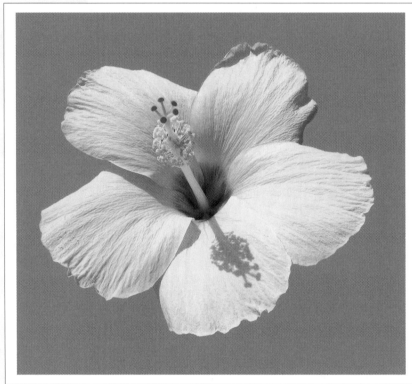

Figure 17-4:
JPEG format doesn't preserve transparent areas when you save your image, but Elements helps you simulate transparency by letting you choose a matte color, which replaces the transparency. When you choose a matte color that's identical to your web page's background, you create a transparent effect. The purple matte around this hibiscus blossom will blend into the purple background of the page it goes on.

- **GIF.** The fewer colors a GIF contains, the smaller the file. In Elements, the GIF format names in the Preset menu tell you the number of colors that will be in your GIF. For example, GIF-128 means 128 colors, and GIF-32 means 32 colors. You can also use the Colors box to set your own number of colors. Use the arrows on the left edge of the box to scroll to the number you want, or just type it in the box.

If you turn on the Interlaced checkbox, then your image downloads in multiple passes (sort of like an image that's slowly coming into focus). With today's computers, interlacing isn't as useful as it used to be on slower machines. If you want to keep transparent areas transparent, then leave the Transparency checkbox turned on. If you don't want transparency, then choose a matte color the way you do for a JPEG (see the previous bullet point). If you're creating a GIF that you plan to animate, turn on the Animate checkbox. (You need a layered file to make an animated GIF; page 511 has more about animating GIFs.)

Dither is an important setting. The GIF format works by compressing and flattening large areas of colors. When you use dithering, Elements blends existing colors to make the image look like it has more colors than it actually has. For instance, Elements may mix red and blue pixels in an area to create purple. You can choose how much dither you want by entering a percentage. Depending on your image, you may not want any dithering; in that case, set the Dither field to 0%.

- **PNG-8.** The more basic of your PNG choices in Elements, PNG-8 gives you pretty much the same options as you get with GIF.

With both PNG-8 and GIF, you get advanced options for how to display colors (to have Elements generate the color lookup table if you're a web-design maven). The menu below the file-format menu lists your options (Elements chooses Selective unless you change it). You can safely ignore this menu, but if you're curious, here are your choices: Selective, the standard setting, favors broad areas of color and keeps to web-safe colors; Perceptual favors colors to which the human eye is more sensitive; Adaptive samples colors from the spectrum appearing most commonly in the image; and Restrictive keeps everything within the old 216-color web palette.

- **PNG-24.** This is the more advanced level of PNG. Technically, both PNG formats let you use transparency, but more web browsers understand transparent areas in PNG-24 than in PNG-8. Your save options are the same as some of those for JPEG files.

TIP   The Elements Color Picker lets you limit your choices to web-safe colors, if you turn on the Only Web Colors checkbox in its lower-left corner. But do you *have* to stick to this limited color palette for web graphics? Not really. You need to be seriously concerned about keeping to web-safe colors only if you know the majority of people looking at your image will be using *very* old web browsers. All modern browsers have been able to cope with a normal color range for many years now.

Getting colors to display consistently in all browsers is another kettle of fish entirely. See the next section for details.

Previewing Images and Adjusting Color

Elements gives you a few different ways to preview how your image will look in a web browser. You can start by looking at your image in any browser you have on your computer (see Figure 17-5).

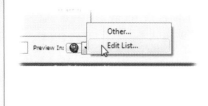

Figure 17-5:
To preview your image in a web browser, click the Preview In icon in the Save For Web dialog box's bottom right to launch your computer's standard web browser. (The icon on your screen might look different from the globe-and-question-mark one you see here because Elements displays your chosen browser's icon, or the last browser you used for previewing in Elements.) Or you can click the arrow and choose a browser from the list. The first time you click this arrow, you may need to pick Edit List, as shown in the figure, and then click Find All to use the browser you want. Elements sniffs out every browser on your computer and adds what it finds to the list of available browsers. (Sometimes Elements only finds Internet Explorer, and you have to add other browsers, like Firefox, manually via the Add button in the Browsers window.)

To add a new browser, in the Save For Web dialog box, click the Preview In drop-down list, and then choose Edit List. Then, in the Browsers dialog box that appears, click the Add button and navigate to the one you want. If you want to have *all* your browsers listed, then click Find All. From now on, you can pick any browser from the list. When you do, Elements launches the browser with your image in it.

If you want to get a rough idea of how your image will look on other people's monitors, click the arrow next to the upper-right corner of the right-hand preview window. The list that appears includes the following color options:

- **Browser Dither.** If an image contains more colors than a web browser can display, the browser uses dithering (see page 509) to create the additional colors. Select this option to get an idea of how your image will look if a browser has to dither the colors.

- **Uncompensated Color.** This option shows colors the way they normally appear on your monitor, so it doesn't adjust the color—it just displays what you usually see.

- **Standard Windows Color.** This option displays colors the way they should look on an average Windows monitor.

- **Standard Macintosh Color.** This option shows colors the way they should look on an average Mac monitor.

- **Use Document Color Profile.** If you kept the image's ICC profile (page 217), then this setting tries to match how your image will look as a result.

Keep in mind that these are all only rough approximations. You need only take a stroll down the monitor aisle at your local electronics store to see what a wacky bunch of color variations are possible. You really can't control how other people will see your image, unless you go to their homes and adjust their monitors for them.

NOTE   Changing any of these color options affects only the way the image displays on your monitor in Save For Web; it doesn't change anything in the image itself or the way it displays in other parts of Elements.

Creating Animated GIFs

With Elements, it's easy to create *animated GIFs,* those little illustrations that make web pages look annoyingly jumbled or delightfully active, depending on your tastes. If you've ever seen a strip of movie film or the cels for a cartoon, Elements creates a similar series of frames with these specialized GIFs.

Animated GIFs are made up of layers. (If you download an animated GIF and open it in Elements, it appears as a multilayered image.) When you create an animated GIF, you make a new layer for each frame. Save For Web creates the actual animation, which you can preview in a web browser.

> **NOTE**   It's a shame that you can't easily animate a JPEG the way you can a GIF. Most elaborate web animations involving photographs are done with Flash, which is another program altogether. (You can learn a little more about Flash on page 519; if you want the full story, pick up a copy of *Flash CS4: The Missing Manual.*) But Elements offers another option if you want to make a stand-alone animation as opposed to an animated graphic for a web page: *flipbooks* (page 539), cartoon-like Windows Media format animations.

The best way to learn how to create an animated GIF is to make one. Here's how to make twinkling stars:

1. **Set your Background color to black and your Foreground color to some shade of yellow.**

   See page 231 if you need help setting your Foreground and Background colors.

2. **Create a new document.**

   Press Ctrl+N. Set the size to 200 pixels×200 pixels, choose RGB for the color mode, and then choose Background Color for your background contents. (Set the resolution to 72 ppi.)

3. **Activate the Custom Shape tool (page 396) and choose your star shape.**

   In the Options bar, click the down arrow to the right of the Shape field to open the Shapes palette. Then click the arrow in the palette's upper right and, from the menu, select Nature. Click the Sun 2 shape, which is in the top row, second from the left.

4. **Draw some stars.**

   Drag to draw one yellow star, and then, in the Options bar, click the "Add to shape area" button before drawing four or five more stars. (This step puts all the stars on the same layer, which is important, since then you won't have a bunch of layers to merge.)

5. **Merge the star layer and the Background layer.**

   Choose Layer → Merge Down. You now have one layer containing yellow stars on a black background, like the bottom layer shown in Figure 17-6.

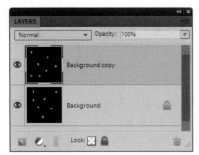

Figure 17-6:
This animated GIF has only two frames, which makes for a pretty crude animation. The more frames you have, the smoother the animation. But more frames make a bigger file, too. On a tiny image like this one, size doesn't matter, but with a larger image, your file can get huge pretty fast.

6. **Duplicate the layer.**

   Choose Layer → Duplicate Layer. You now have two identical layers.

7. **Rotate the top layer 90 degrees.**

   Click any other tool in the Tools panel, and then go to Image → Rotate → Layer 90° Left (if the Shape Selection tool is active, then the Rotate command doesn't work). You should now have two layers with stars in different places on each one.

8. **Animate your GIF.**

   Go to File → Save For Web, and in the dialog box that appears, turn on the Animate checkbox. (If you don't see the Animate checkbox, make sure GIF is listed in the box below the word "Preset"; if it's not, select it from the drop-down menu.) In the Animation section of the dialog box, you can adjust the time between frames if you want. Leave the Loop checkbox turned on so the animation repeats over and over. (If you turn it off, your animation plays just once and stops.)

9. **Preview your animation.**

   You can use the arrows in the Animation section to step through your animation one frame at a time, but for a more realistic preview, view the image in a web browser as explained in the previous section. The stars should twinkle. Well, OK, they flash off and on—think of twinkle lights. Save your animation, if you like, by clicking OK.

Emailing Photos

Elements makes emailing your photos a piece of cake. With just a few clicks, Elements preps your image, fires up your email program, and attaches your image to an outgoing email. (Of course, you can also email images without Elements' help, and you may prefer that method since you get more freedom to specify settings like file size.)

Creating Web Buttons

Elements makes it a snap to create buttons to use on web pages. Here's what you do:

1. **Create a new blank file (File → New → Blank File).** In the New dialog box's Preset menu, choose Web and pick a size you like; from the Background Contents menu, choose Transparent. Then click OK.

2. **Set the Foreground color square to the color you want to use for your button, and use the Shape tool to draw the shape you want.** (It helps to choose Actual Pixels for your view size when doing web work, because that shows you the same size you'll see in a web browser.)

3. **Apply one or more Layer styles (page 423) to make your button look more 3-D.** Bevels, some of the Complex Layer styles, and the Wow Layer styles are all popular choices.

4. **Add any necessary text using the Type tool (page 441).** You may want to apply a Layer style to the text, too.

5. **Save as a GIF.**

Easy, huh?

NOTE Elements can prep your image and automatically launch your email program only if you're using Vista's Windows Mail, Outlook Express, Outlook, or Adobe's own mail server. The first time you use one of Elements' email features, you get a pop-up window asking you to choose one of these programs. If you want to change the program later, in the Organizer, go to Edit → Preferences → Sharing.

Elements' email features don't work with other email programs like Yahoo Mail or Thunderbird. If you want to use a different email program, just use that program's Attach button instead. (You can export your image from the Organizer to your desktop to make it easier to find.)

The Share tab gives you an almost bewildering array of formatting choices for emailing photos. You can send simple attachments or prearranged groups of photos, frame the photos, change the background color, and so on. Here are your main choices:

• **E-mail Attachments.** This is the most traditional option, where you send each photo as a standard attachment.

• **Photo Mail.** Elements lets you send emails formatted in *HTML,* the programming language used to create web pages. This option gives you all kinds of fancy design choices, and your photo gets embedded in the body of the email—it's basically like emailing someone a custom-built web page featuring your image.

The catch is that the recipient has to be using a mail program that understands HTML. Most newer email programs fit the bill, but if you're emailing someone who uses ancient software like AOL 4, then your email formatting doesn't appear correctly. An even larger problem, though, is that if your recipient has her email program's HTML option turned off, then your email doesn't appear with all its formatting intact. Page 514 has more info about Elements' Photo Mail options.

- **PDF Slide Show.** This option creates a basic PDF-format slideshow of all your images. All you have to do is name the slideshow (see page 517).

You need to choose the kind of email you want to send before you start. To pick, click the one you want in the Share tab. You can start from either the Editor or the Organizer, although you get sent over to the Organizer to actually create your mail. The basic process is pretty similar for all three types and is explained in detail below. There's one really annoying aspect of sending images from the Organizer, though: The messages you send include an ad for Elements.

> **TIP** Don't want to be in the advertising business? To get rid of the Adobe ad at the bottom of your messages, highlight it in the message, and then press Backspace. Or, if you want to eliminate it from *all* your Elements emails, go to *C:\Program Files\Adobe\Elements Organizer 8.0\Assets\locale\en_US\email\signatures* (the "en_US" part is different if you live outside the U.S.). Open the files you find there using a text editor like Notepad, and remove the advertising lines. Save the change, and from now on, your Elements emails will be ad free.

Individual Attachments

To send your files as regular email attachments, just follow these steps:

> **NOTE** If you want to email photos that aren't already in the Organizer, open them in the Editor before you start, and then choose Share → E-Mail Attachments.

1. **In the Organizer, select your photos, and then go to Share → E-Mail Attachments.**

   You can preselect photos before you start, or add or change them once the E-mail panel appears. Figure 17-7 explains how. (You can also start from the Editor, if you want. Elements includes your open photos when it whisks you off to the Organizer to create your email, so you can email images not already in the Organizer. Elements automatically adds your selected images to the Organizer if they aren't there already. Once you get to the E-mail panel, you can only add Organizer photos.)

   In the E-mail window, below the image thumbnails, you see some info that can help you decide how many photos to send and how large to make them:

   - **Number of Items.** Indicates how many photos you've selected to send.

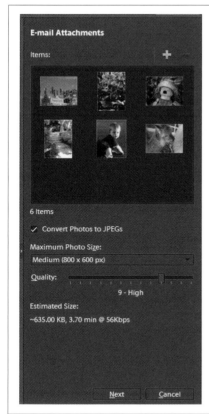

E-mail Attachments

Items:

6 Items

☑ Convert Photos to JPEGs

Maximum Photo Size:

Medium (800 x 600 px)

Quality:

9 - High

Estimated Size:

~635.00 KB, 3.70 min @ 56Kbps

Next   Cancel

Figure 17-7:
The Organizer's E-mail window is pretty easy to use. You can start with one photo or a group, as shown here. To send more photos, just drag the photos' thumbnails from the Media Browser into the E-mail window. You can also highlight the photos in the Media Browser, and then, at the top of the E-mail window, click the Add button (the green + sign). Remove photos you don't want by highlighting them, and then clicking Delete (the red – sign, which is grayed out in this image). Drag your photos in the pane to change their order.

- **Convert Photos to JPEGs.** JPEG is the best format for emailing photos, so you can turn on this checkbox to have Elements make JPEG versions of all your photos. (If your photos are already JPEGs, then the option is grayed out.) If you just want to convert some of your photos to JPEGs, select their thumbnails before you turn on this checkbox.

- **Maximum Photo Size.** This sets how large you want your emailed photos to be. Remember that it can take a really long time to download a large image with a dial-up connection, and many email providers have a 10 MB limit per mailbox. If you need to change the size, then use this drop-down menu to choose a new size.

- **Quality.** If you're just emailing photos for viewing onscreen, then you can get away with a lower-quality setting than you can for photos that the recipient is going to print.

Finally, below these settings you see Elements' calculation of how large the attachment will be and how long it'll take to download with a dial-up connection (a useful warning if you're sending to people with slow Internet connections). When you're satisfied with your attachment, click Next.

2. **Type in a message (optional).**

In this pane, you can change or remove the message that automatically comes up, which says, "Here are the photos that I want to share with you." To remove or change this message permanently, follow the steps listed on page 514 for changing the signature (the message is in the same folder).

3. **Address your email (optional).**

Decide whether you want to enter an email address now. You can:

- **Do nothing.** Wait until Elements is through, and then type the address in the completed email before you send it.

- **Select Recipients.** Elements keeps a Contact Book—a list of people you regularly email—so you can simply select names from the list. (Read more about it in the box on page 517.) If you haven't used the Elements email feature before, then start by clicking the Edit Contacts button (the little silhouette just above the Select Recipients window) and entering your recipient's contact info.

- **Edit Contacts.** If you want to enter a new recipient or change the information for someone in your list, then click the Edit Contacts button (the silhouette), and enter the new info in the Contact Book.

4. **To finish, click Next.**

Elements launches your email program, creates a new message, and attaches the files for you. You can make any changes to the message or recipient in your email program now. (If your files are pretty big for emailing, then Elements displays a warning and suggests burning a CD instead.)

Photo Mail

Elements also gives you a ton of options for gussying up your photos if you choose Photo Mail, which is actually HTML mail. When you send HTML mail, your message gets formatted using a *template,* a stationery design in which your photo appears.

The process for sending Photo Mail is pretty much the same as for regular attachments, but in the first panel you can choose whether to display captions along with your photos.

When you click Next in Step 4, the Stationery & Layouts wizard (a series of guided question screens) presents a long list of stationery theme categories with several choices in each. The preview window updates to show each one as you click it. You can add a caption to any photo in this window by highlighting the text below the photo and typing what you want. When you find a style you like, click Next to go to the next window.

ORGANIZATION STATION

The Contact Book

The Organizer makes it easy to call up the addresses of people you regularly email by keeping a Contact Book. Anytime you send email to a new recipient, you first have to add the address to the Contact Book by clicking the Edit Contacts button (the silhouette) in the E-mail window. (You can also get to the Contact Book by choosing Edit → Contact Book in the Media Browser or Date view.)

Once you've got the Contact Book open, click the New Contact button to add an address. Then you can enter a name, email address, phone number, and other contact info. To edit or delete a contact, just highlight it in the list, and then click the relevant button.

You can also create groups of names in the Contact Book, for times when you want to send the same photo to several people at once. To do this, click New Group, enter a name for the group, select entries in the Contact Book, and then click Add. The people's names go into the Members

list. To remove a name from the group, highlight it in the Members list, and then click Remove.

Elements makes it easy to coordinate the Contact Book with your existing address book. You can choose to import addresses from Vista's Windows Mail, Microsoft Outlook, or Outlook Express, as well as any that you saved as V-cards (a digital business card format) in other programs. Just click Import and choose your source. You can also export your Contact Book addresses as V-cards to use them in other programs.

If you have a Photoshop.com account (see page 20), then your Contact Book is stored online, so Elements nags you to connect to Photoshop.com if you try to use it when you aren't connected to the Internet. If you don't use Photoshop.com, then your Contact Book is stored on your computer and should always be available to you.

When you're mailing more than one photo, you have a choice of several different page layouts. Below the layouts, you can choose a typeface from a list of five common fonts. Click the box to the right of the font name to choose a color for the text. You can also customize the frame or border around your photos, as shown in Figure 17-8. Each time you make a change in the left pane of the window, Elements updates the preview so you can see just what you're getting.

When you've adjusted everything to your liking, click Next. (Click Cancel if you don't want to send the email after all, or Previous if you want to go back and choose a different theme.) Elements creates your ready-to-send email. You can make any changes to the message and address just as you would to any other email—and send it off like any other email, too.

PDF Slideshows

You can also email a group of your photos as a slideshow. Elements uses the popular PDF format, which lets your recipients page through each slide using the free, ubiquitous Adobe Reader program. They just open the PDF and view the photos one by one. You can create a PDF slideshow from the Share tab in either the Editor or the Organizer if you don't want to deal with the Slide Show Editor (covered in more detail on page 529).

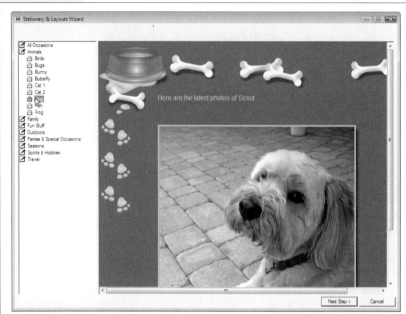

Figure 17-8:
The Stationery & Layouts wizard lets you choose from various frame styles. If you pick a frame style that leaves empty space around the photo, then you can customize the background color of your email. For some styles, you can adjust the padding (the matte-like space between the photo and the frame) and the frame's size.

To create a slideshow, select your photos as described earlier, and then in the Organizer go to Share → More Options → PDF Slide Show, or in the Editor go to Share → PDF Slide Show. (If you start from the Editor, Elements sends you over to the Organizer to create your slideshow.) In the PDF Slide Show panel that appears, Elements offers you a choice of sizes and quality, just as you have for sending regular email attachments. Name the slideshow, and then click Next. In the next panel, enter a message or recipients if you like, and then click Next. Elements tells you the size of your slideshow and suggests that if it's going to be larger than a megabyte, you should consider another route, like burning a CD or using Photoshop.com. Click OK, and Elements generates a standard email message with the slideshow attached.

Online Albums and Slideshows

Last chapter, you learned how to email your photos. But what if you've got legions of friends—do you have to email your pictures to everyone individually? Not with Elements, which makes it incredibly simple to post photos online, thanks to Photoshop.com, a one-stop shop where you share your photos and back them up online. You can create fancy online albums complete with professional-looking effects, courtesy of *Flash*, the ubiquitous Adobe program that's responsible for zillions of nifty online animations.

Elements can also help you put together elaborate slideshows, complete with slick between-photo transitions like wipes and dissolves, clip art, and even audio. And for the perfect combination of high-tech wizardry and old-school charm, you can make digital *flipbooks*, simple slideshows that are easy to share with friends. Like the flipbooks of yore, these little shows can make a series of still photos appear to move, like a cartoon. Finally, Adobe has teamed up with Yahoo to give photo-taking map lovers a way to indulge both passions: customizable Yahoo maps sprinkled with photos detailing your latest road trip. In this chapter, you'll learn the ins and outs of all these ways of sharing your photos.

Online Albums

Adobe calls these "albums," but the online albums you create from Elements aren't just boring, grid-like rows of photos like you see on most photo websites. Instead they're elaborate, Flash-based displays in which your photos do things like appear in an animation of old-fashioned slides dropped onto a table, and your friends sift through the pile and click the slides they want for a closeup view. And you can choose whether to share your album with the whole world or to limit viewing to your family and friends.

Sharing a New Album

If you use Photoshop.com (page 20), Adobe makes it super easy to share your albums there, right as you create them. Follow the steps on page 62 for creating and naming an album, and then, before you click Done:

> **NOTE** This section describes using the Organizer's Album panel, but you can also start a new online album from the Share tab in either the Organizer or the Editor, as explained later in this chapter (page 523). The process is very similar; the only difference is that you choose a sharing method when you start, and then click Next to go to the Album Details panel.

1. **In the Organize bin's Album Details panel, click the Sharing tab.**

   On the left side of the window, you see a preview of your slideshow, and on the right side, you see a list of options for sharing to Photoshop.com. (If you decide you want to change the order of your photos, or add or delete photos, you can click back to the Content tab to rearrange them at any time.)

2. **If you wish, change the template.**

   Elements starts you off by displaying your photos in a slideshow on the left side of the window. If you want something different, go to the "Select a Template" menu above the preview area, and choose a template category, and then double-click the various template thumbnails that appear below the menu. Use the slider below the thumbnails to move back and forth through the category's available slideshows. The left side of the window displays a large preview of what your photos will look like in the selected template, and there's also a description of the template below the thumbnails.

   > **NOTE** In the template list, you see the same little blue and gold banners on some thumbnails that you see in the Content panel (page 474). They mean the same thing here: If a template has a blue banner, you can download it for free (if you have a Photoshop.com account). If the banner is gold, you need a Plus account (the paid version) to download it. Once you download a template, you won't see the banner on it anymore.

   Some templates play as a slideshow automatically, and others are interactive, as explained in Figure 18-1. (Elements applies the last template style you clicked when you create your album.)

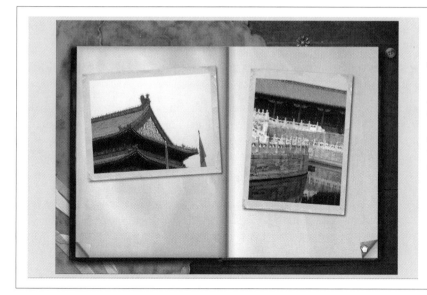

Figure 18-1:
Some of the album styles automatically start playing their slideshows, while others, like the Scrapbook template shown here, are interactive. Your friends "turn" the pages of the book to go backward and forward through your album.

3. **Change any settings for the album.**

Some albums have "ghosted" settings panels that come into focus when you move your cursor over them. Others have tabs you can click within the preview to make changes. The settings you can change depend on the template: You may only be able to tweak the title that appears, or to do things like changing the number of burning candles on a cake.

TIP   Some templates have a checkbox for sound effects. Sound effects are fun, but remember that before viewers can start watching, the audio files have to load. If your friends have slow Internet connections, you may want to leave sounds turned off.

4. **Choose the album options you want in the Sharing pane.**

Your choices are explained in detail below, but this is where you choose who gets to see your album and, if you want to, personalize the notification message they receive when your album appears on Photoshop.com.

5. **Click Done.**

If you aren't signed into Photoshop.com, the login window appears. Once you log in, your album uploads to the site, and the people you specified in step 4 receive an email with a link to your photos. (If you decide not to create an Online Album after all, click Cancel instead.)

The Sharing pane gives you several choices for who gets to see your albums and what they can do with the photos:

- **Share to Photoshop.com.** Turn on this checkbox to make the options below it available.

- **Display in My Gallery.** If you turn this on, your album becomes public. Any-one browsing Photoshop.com can see it (and comment on it, if you don't change that setting on your Photoshop.com account page).

- **Message.** If you want to include a personal message in the album notification email, type it here.

- **Send E-mail To.** Click the Contacts button (the one with the head and shoulders of two people on it) to choose your recipients. You can select all your contacts, none, or open the Contact Book (page 517) to add people. The names appear in a list; just turn off the checkboxes next to the names of people who shouldn't receive a notification.

    TIP   If you don't want to hassle with creating contacts every time you invite different people to view an album, just send the invitation to yourself, copy the link in the email you receive, and then paste that into a regular email to send to your recipients. Or, once the album is posted on Photo-shop.com, just copy the URL from your web browser's address bar.

- **Allow Viewers to.** Here's where you can choose to let your friends download your photos or order prints of them (or both), if you like.

- **View Online.** Click this button to see your completed album at Photoshop.com.

You can go back to the Sharing pane at any time to add new recipients or to change your album's content or template. To do that, click the Edit Album button at the top of the Albums panel in the main Organize bin, or just click the Share button to the right of the album's name. To stop sharing an album and to remove it from Photoshop.com, click the Stop Sharing button (the red circle with a slash).

But your sharing isn't limited to Photoshop.com. If you know you know you don't want to use Photoshop.com, you can start your album from the main Share tab by clicking the Online Album button, which lets you choose a sharing method. Alter-natively, if you're using the process described in the above list, just don't turn on the Sharing pane's "Share to Photoshop.com" checkbox when you create your album; click Done, and then follow the instructions for sharing existing albums in the next section. (The other sharing options are explained in detail below.)

    NOTE   If you aren't in the United States, then when you create an online album, you do so at Adobe's Photoshop Showcase website (page 21) rather than on Photoshop.com. The process is exactly the same, and so are the templates available. However, your options for downloading and sharing the photos from the completed album may be different.

You have a few drawbacks to posting your album to Photoshop.com. For one thing, it's not really private—anyone who can figure out your Photoshop.com web address can see your albums, whether you invite them or not. And if you have friends with dial-up Internet connections, the online albums will take forever to load for them. Fortunately, Adobe gives you other ways to share your albums, as the next section explains.

Other Ways to Share

You don't have to decide whether to share an album while you're creating it. Even if you don't sign up for a Photoshop.com account, you can still create the same kinds of albums and impress friends with them, since you can also upload them to your own website via FTP (File Transfer Protocol, the way you'd send any other files to your site), or you can just burn a CD or DVD.

It's also easy to share your existing albums, either from the Share tab or from the Organize tab's Albums panel:

- **Share tab.** In either the Organizer or the Editor, click the Share tab and select Online Album. Elements sends you over to the Organizer, where you can create a new album or choose an existing album from the list, and then select how you want to share it. The rest of the process is the same as the one for sharing a new album (page 520).

- **Edit Album.** In the Organizer's Albums panel, you can select an album, and then click the Edit Album button (the pencil at the top of the panel). This method offers you only the same Photoshop.com options you get when creating a new album, though—you can't share to FTP or DVD this way.

- **Album name.** In the Albums panel, right-click an album's name, and then choose to export to FTP, a CD or DVD, or to your hard disk. (Photoshop.com isn't an option here.)

The process for any of these options is similar to the one described in the previous section. You can change templates, rearrange your photos, add or remove photos, and so on, exactly the way you would when creating a new album. The main difference is your sharing options:

- **Export to FTP.** Choose this option and the Album Details panel's Sharing tab presents you with fields where you can enter the FTP address of your web server (get this from the company that hosts your site if you don't know it), your user-name and password, and the name of the folder where you want Elements to put the gallery.

  Then click Done, and Elements builds your album and sends it to your server. If all goes well, you'll have the same album on your site that you could have built at Photoshop.com. (The only options missing are the ones for printing and downloading.)

TIP   If you want to check to be sure that Elements can "see" your server, click the Album Details panel's "Test Access to Server" button. Elements contacts your web host and presents you with a window where you can watch the steps as it tries to log on and upload the file. As it completes each step, a green checkmark appears. If you see the red No symbol, it means there was a problem with that step and you have to figure out what went awry.

- **Export to CD/DVD.** The Sharing tab gives you the same options for renaming and changing the template that it does for an FTP export, but instead of entering server information, you choose the drive to use to burn the disc, and enter a name for the CD or DVD. When you click Done, Elements asks you to insert a disc. Put one in, and then click OK. Elements burns the disc, and then asks if you want to verify it. You do. Finally, it reminds you to label the completed disc before it ejects it.

  Discs made this way play in a computer, not in a DVD player. If your friends use Windows, the disc should play automatically when they put it into their computer. If that doesn't work (sometimes the loading animation loops endlessly and the slideshow never runs), or if they're using Macs, tell them to open the disc, navigate to the Root folder, and then double-click the index.html file inside that. The slideshow plays in their web browser.

- **Export to Hard Disk.** Elements saves your album to a folder on your hard drive. In the Album Details panel's Sharing tab, click the Browse button to choose the location for your album and then click Done. This way you can create an "online" album that plays right on your own computer, even when you aren't connected to the Internet. To play the slideshow, open the folder and double-click the file named *index.html*. Your web browser opens and the slideshow runs in it.

You can share albums this way even if you also uploaded them to Photoshop. It's a really handy way to make a fancy slideshow.

Slideshows

Online albums are about the easiest way you'll find to make fancy slideshows to share with people in other places, but maybe you want more control than they give you, or maybe you want to add features like music or panning and zooming over your photos, à la Ken Burns. Elements makes it easy to create very slick little slideshows—some even with music and transitions between the images—that you can play on your PC or send to your friends.

By using the Slide Show feature, you can make really elaborate slideshows. If you prefer the simple life, you can quickly create a plain-vanilla PDF slideshow in about as much time as it takes to email a photo.

PDF slideshows are really straightforward to create, and look quite impressive, but you can't add audio to them or control how your slides transition. On the plus side, you can send a PDF slideshow to anyone, regardless of what operating system that person uses. As long as your recipients have Adobe Reader or another PDF-viewing program, they can watch your show.

The Slide Show Editor, on the other hand, lets you indulge your creativity big time. You can add all sorts of snazzy transitions, mix in sound (background music or narration), add clip art, pan around your slides, and more. It's a bit more complex to work with the Slide Show Editor than to make a PDF, but the real drawback to the Slide Show Editor comes in your choices for the final output. The slideshow file you create isn't as universally compatible as PDF slideshows, as explained later in this chapter.

The easiest slideshow of all, though, is the one you make in the Organizer's Full Screen view, where it's a snap to create a full-featured slideshow with just a couple of quick settings adjustments. But you can only show this kind of slideshow to people who can see your computer monitor—you can't save it and send it away or post it on the Web.

> TIP   If you plan to create a simple PDF slideshow, then you need to do all your photo editing beforehand. Full Screen view and the Slide Show Editor, on the other hand, let you edit as much as you like before you finalize your slideshow.

Full Screen View

Elements 8 gives you a really easy way to create an impressive little slideshow to play on your computer, which could come in handy if you want to play a retrospective of Mom and Dad's life together during their 50th wedding anniversary party at your house, for example. You do this via the Organizer's newly gussied-up Full Screen view, and you have all kinds of options for music and fancy transitions between the slides.

To get started:

1. **In the Organizer, select the photos and videos you want to use in your slideshow, and then go to Full Screen view.**

    Press F11 or click the Full Screen button (the little computer-monitor icon between the thumbnail size slider and the view order button). If you want your photos in a particular order, put them into an album (page 62) and rearrange them there.

2. **In Full Screen view, adjust the settings for your slideshow.**

    Use the control strip across the bottom of the screen (shown in Figure 18-2) to control how Elements presents your slideshow. (Your options are explained below.) You can't change background color in these slideshows—it's always black.

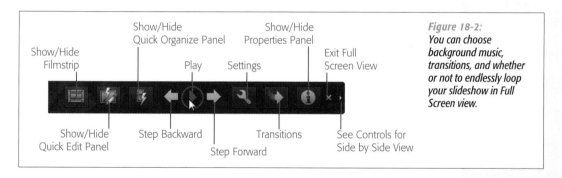

Figure 18-2:
You can choose background music, transitions, and whether or not to endlessly loop your slideshow in Full Screen view.

3. **Run your slideshow.**

    Press the Play button or tap the spacebar to start your slideshow. To pause it, press the Pause button or press the spacebar again. To exit Full Screen view and get back to the Organizer, click the X button at the right end of the control strip or press Esc.

You probably won't use all the options in the control strip (Figure 18-2). For instance, it's unlikely that you'd want to see the Quick Edit or Organizer panels while showing off your photos to your friends. The two most important buttons are the ones just to the right of the playback controls:

- **Settings.** Click this button and you can choose which music you want to add to your slideshow (or choose None if you don't want any). If you don't see the audio file you want to use, click the Browse button to find it. You can opt to play audio captions you've recorded in the Slide Show Editor (page 535), display captions, or allow Elements to resize your photos and videos so they fit onscreen (yes, videos play here, too, if you include them in your show).

    You can also choose to display a filmstrip of thumbnails of all your photos down the right edge of the screen (the control strip button does the same thing), or to have the show start automatically when you enter Full Screen view. Use the Page Duration box to determine how long your photos stay on the screen. Just pick a duration from the drop-down menu, or type a number (in seconds) into the box.

- **Transitions.** You can choose from among four kinds of transitions between your slides: Classic (one photo simply gives way to the next), Fade In/Out, Pan & Zoom (Elements pans across each slide as it displays), or 3D Pixelate, which makes a glittery dissolve between each one. Move your cursor over each thumbnail to see a demo of each transition, and then click the radio button under the one you want.

It hardly takes any time to set up a slideshow this way, and all you have to do once you get it going is to stand back and accept compliments for your nifty display. The disadvantage to this kind of slideshow, obviously, is that you can't share it with anyone who doesn't have access to your computer. But Elements gives you a bunch of ways to make slideshows to send to other folks.

> **TIP** If you want a fancier slideshow than you can create in Full Screen view, you can create an online album (see page 519) and export it to your Hard Disk. To play it there, open the folder and double-click the file named *index.html.*

PDF Slideshows

Elements gives you two ways to create a PDF slideshow. The first, the Simple PDF slideshow, is very basic, just a quick run-through of the photos you choose. But if you make a PDF in the Slide Show Editor, you can create something slightly more elaborate.

Simple PDF slideshow

You can start a PDF slideshow from either the Editor or Organizer, although you always *create* your show in the Organizer. In the Editor go to the Share tab → PDF Slide Show. In the Organizer, it's hiding under Share → More Options → PDF Slide Show. Once you find it, it's as easy as sending an email. You can read more about it on page 517. This slideshow has no transitions, no clip art, and no custom type, but it's the most compatible kind of slideshow you can make in Elements, which means that almost anyone you send it to will be able to view it. And you can easily create a reasonable-sized file so anybody can watch it, no matter how underpowered their computer.

Making a PDF in the Slide Show Editor

The other way to create a PDF slideshow isn't as intuitive as the method just described. When you create a show in the Slide Show Editor as explained in the next section, you can choose between saving it as a Windows Media Video (WMV) file or a PDF. If you want to preserve your show's multimedia bells and whistles, then you need to choose WMV. But then there's that tantalizing PDF option. You may think this PDF slideshow sounds like the best of both worlds—a very compatible format and all the fancy effects you created with the Slide Show Editor.

Unfortunately, that's not quite how it works. When you create a PDF this way, you lose the pan-and-zoom feature (page 536), the audio, and the transitions that you set. You do keep any custom slides, text, and clip art that you added, though. On the whole, it's best to use this feature when you've created a full-scale slideshow but one or two of the people you want to send it to can't open Windows Media files. The people who get the PDF can't see everything the WMV recipients do, but it's faster than trying to recreate a separate version for the WMV-challenged.

To create a PDF using the Slide Show Editor, just follow the instructions in the following section for creating a slideshow. When you're ready to create your PDF, click Output, and in the Slide Show Output dialog box that opens, choose "Save As a File". On the right side of the Slide Show Output dialog box, click the PDF File button. This step brings up a series of settings just for your PDF:

- **Slide Size.** This setting starts out at Small. If you're going to burn a CD, then you can choose a larger size. But if you want to email the final file, then choose Small or Very Small. You also have a Custom choice for when you want to create a size that's different from one of the presets.

- **Loop.** Turn this on, and the slideshow repeats over and over until your viewer stops it by pressing Esc.

- **Manual Advance.** If you want recipients to be able to click their way through the slideshow instead of having each slide automatically advance to the next one, turn this on.

- **View Slide Show after Saving.** Turn this on, and as soon as Elements is through creating your slideshow, it launches Adobe Reader so you can watch the results of your work.

TIP   To make a PDF from an existing slideshow file, in the Media Browser, right-click the slide-show's thumbnail, and then choose Edit. Once the Slide Show Editor opens, click Output → "Save As a File".

When you've got everything set the way you want it, click OK to bring up the Save As dialog box. Name your file, and then save it.

DECISIONS, DECISIONS

Choosing a Slideshow

A couple of versions ago, people sometimes slammed Elements for not offering much in the way of slideshows. Now Elements gives you so many slideshow options you might get overwhelmed trying to decide which one to choose. Here are some suggestions to help you out:

- **Slideshows on your computer.** The fastest way to create a slideshow to display on your computer screen is to use the Organizer's Full Screen view, as explained on page 525.

- **Slideshows for the Web.** If you want to share your slideshow on the Internet, create an online album (page 519).

- **Slideshows with audio.** If you want a narrated soundtrack for your slideshow, use the Slide Show Editor to create your show, and then burn it to a disc to share with friends, who can watch the show on their computers using Windows Media Player.

- **Slideshows to view on TV.** If you have Vista Home Premium or Ultimate, or Windows Media Center Edition, use the Slide Show Editor, and choose "Send to TV" as your output choice. If you want to send a slideshow to someone else to watch on her TV, you can try a VCD. But frankly, you'd be better off using another program

like Adobe's Premiere Elements or any other DVD-authoring software to create a true DVD, if your computer has a DVD burner.

- **Slideshows for people uncomfortable with technology.** You've got two options here, neither of which is guaranteed to prevent Uncle Joe from badgering you that he can't see pictures of his new grandniece. You can create an online album (page 519) and send a disc or email a link, but recipients need a web browser with Flash installed. The simple PDF slideshow (page 517) is also pretty straightforward, but your recipients have to have Adobe Reader or another PDF viewer to watch it. If you know they don't have Reader and won't know how to install it, try a flipbook [page 539] at the slowest setting. For the severely techno-challenged, consider a photo book, described on page 476.

Finally, if you still don't think Elements offers enough choices for you, ProShow Gold from Photodex (*www.photodex.com*) is probably the most popular slideshow program for Windows. And if you don't like the Elements photo albums, JAlbum (*http://jalbum.net*) is a popular free alternative, although these days many people just use one of the photo-sharing services mentioned on page 546 to create their slideshows online.

Using the Slide Show Editor

The Slide Show Editor lets you add audio, clip art, and nifty slide-to-slide transitions. You also get several different ways to share your completed slideshow, including making a Video CD (VCD) or—if you also have Premiere Elements—a DVD that your friends can watch in a regular DVD player. If your operating system is Vista (Home Premium or Ultimate) or Windows Media Center Edition, then you can even send your slideshow to your TV and watch it there (as long as the TV is hooked up to your computer, Xbox 360, or other device that can play WMV files).

To get started, from the Organizer, select the images you want to include. You may want to set up an album (page 62), which lets you control the order of your images. (You can change the order once they're in the Slide Show Editor, but for large shows, you save time if you have things arranged in pretty much the correct order when you start.) You can also start with a single photo and, once you're in the Slide Show Editor, click the Add Media button to add more photos. In any case, once you've got your photos selected, go to Create → Slide Show.

Slide Show Preferences

Once you choose to create a slideshow, Elements presents you with the Slide Show Preferences dialog box before you get to the actual Slide Show Editor. You can click right past this dialog box if you like, but it gives you some useful options for telling Elements how you want it to handle certain aspects of all your shows, like the duration of each slide and the background color. (You can change these settings for a particular show in the Slide Show Editor itself.)

In the Slide Show Preferences dialog box, you can adjust:

- **Static Duration.** This determines how long each slide displays before it moves on to the next one.

- **Transition.** This setting tells Elements how to move from one slide to the next. You get many different styles to choose from, like a pinwheel effect or having the next slide move into view from the side. If you choose a different transition from the pop-out menu, then you can audition it in the little preview area at the right of the window, as explained in Figure 18-3.

- **Transition Duration.** Use this to set how fast you want the transitions to happen.

- **Background Color.** If you want a different background color, click this color square to bring up the Color Picker (page 232).

- **Apply Pan & Zoom to All Slides.** If you set up the Pan & Zoom feature (explained later in this chapter) for one slide, turn this on and the camera swoops around *every* slide.

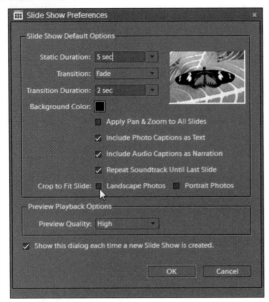

Figure 18-3:
You can set the slide duration and background color for all your slideshows in the Slide Show Preferences window. It's also a great place to audition different transitions. If you want to see what a particular transition does, select it from the Transition drop-down menu, and Elements plays it in the little preview area on the right. If you choose a transition here, then Elements automatically applies it to every slide. But you can override this setting for individual slides in the Slide Show Editor's storyboard by clicking the transition you want to change and choosing a different one.

- **Include Photo Captions as Text.** If you want to display a photo's Caption field, turn on this checkbox. (This works in reverse, too—you can hide your captions by turning off this checkbox.)

- **Include Audio Captions as Narration.** If you've recorded audio captions for your slides (page 535), leave this checkbox turned on if you want your audience to hear them.

- **Repeat Soundtrack Until Last Slide.** Leave this checkbox turned on, and if you run out of music on your soundtrack, Elements repeats your song(s) as many times as necessary.

- **Crop to Fit Slide.** Turn on either of these checkboxes (for landscape- and portrait-oriented photos), and, if your image is too large for the slide, then Elements chops off the excess for you. However, it's best to do any cropping (page 89) yourself before starting your slideshow.

- **Preview Playback Options.** Choose the quality for previewing your show while you're working on it. This setting doesn't affect the quality of the final slideshow.

Once you're through setting these preferences, click OK. If you don't want to see the preferences every time you start a new show, then just turn off the "Show this dialog each time a new Slide Show is created" checkbox. You can call up the dialog box again anytime you're in the Slide Show Editor by going to Edit → Slide Show Preferences.

Creating slideshows with the Slide Show Editor

After you click OK in the Slide Show Preferences dialog box, Elements launches the Slide Show Editor. It's crammed with options, but everything is laid out logically—in fact, it's pretty similar to the Full Edit window. You get a menu bar across the top of the window, but most of the commands here are available elsewhere via a button or a keystroke (like Ctrl+Z to undo your last action).

On the left side of the window, in the preview area, you see the slide you're currently working on. A Panel bin (called a "Palette bin" in the View menu) is on the right side of the screen, and you can collapse it just like the Full Edit Panel bin, by clicking its left edge to get it out of your way. (Collapsing the bin makes the preview space expand across the window.) You click the hidden Panel bin's edge again to bring it back.

At the bottom of the window is a strip called the *storyboard*, where you see your slides and the transitions between them. (If you didn't preselect any photos, the storyboard just says "Click Here to Add Photos to Your Slide Show".) Click a slide or transition here, and its properties (duration, background color, pan-and-zoom settings) appear in the Panel bin. To hide the storyboard, go to the Slide Show Editor's View menu, and turn it off by removing the checkmark next to its name. You can turn it back on again there, too.

> **TIP** If you want to add photos to your slideshow, click the Add Media button at the top of the Slide Show Editor's preview window. The advantage to bringing photos in this way (as opposed to selecting them before you start creating your slideshow) is that you can pick photos, videos, and audio clips that *aren't* in the Organizer, by clicking the Add Media button and then choosing either the "Photos and Videos from Folder" or the "Audio from Folder" option and then navigating to the files you want. You can even edit your photos right in the Slide Show Editor. The disadvantage is that you have to choose each photo separately, or you have no control over the order in which Elements brings them into the show.

The Slide Show Editor lets you finesse your show in lots of different ways. For instance, you can:

- **Edit your slides.** You can make changes to your photos right here in the Slide Show Editor. In the preview window, just click your image, and then, using the choices that appear in the Properties panel (Figure 18-4), you can rotate your slide, resize it, crop it, and apply the Auto Smart Fix (page 123) and the Auto Red Eye Fix (page 121). If you want to do more substantial editing, then just click the More Editing button, and Elements whisks your slide over to Full Edit.

- **Change durations.** In both the storyboard and the Properties panel, Elements lists a duration number indicating how long a slide appears onscreen before it transitions to the next slide. Click the number for a pop-up menu that lets you change how long that slide appears onscreen (pick Custom if you want to enter

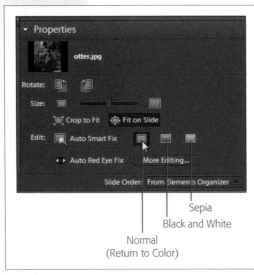

Figure 18-4:
The three little rectangles to the right of the Slide Show Editor's Auto Smart Fix button let you change your photo to black-and-white, to sepia, or back to color again, if you change your mind. To change your slide to black-and-white or sepia, just click the button for the effect you want. To undo a color change you make here, click the Normal button. The changes you make with these buttons affect only the photo on your slide, not the original image.

Sepia

Black and White

Normal
(Return to Color)

your own duration rather than selecting from the menu). You can assign different durations to each slide, if you want. You can also use the pull-down menu next to the slide's thumbnail in the Properties panel, but only if you want to choose a duration between 3 and 7 seconds.

• **Pick transitions.** Elements gives you lots of different ways to get from one slide to the next. These transitions appear in the storyboard and are represented by small thumbnail icons between the two slides they connect. (The icon changes to reflect the current transition style when you choose a new one.)

On the right side of the storyboard transition icon, if you look very hard, you see a tiny black triangle. (If you mouse over it, it lights up to make it easier to see.) Click it to see a pop-out menu listing all of Elements' transitions, and then choose the one you want.

Transitions have their own Properties panels, which appear when you click a transition in the storyboard. You can choose how long a transition takes and, for some transitions, the direction in which you want the transition to move.

If you like to make long slideshows, you'll appreciate the Quick Reorder feature, explained in Figure 18-5. When you switch over to the Quick Reorder window, you see all your slides in a view that looks like a contact sheet, making it easy to reposition slides that would be annoyingly far apart if you had to move them in the storyboard. In Quick Reorder, you just drag them to another spot in the lineup without the hassle of scrolling.

You can also change the order of all your slides by using the Slide Order drop-down menu above the right side of the storyboard, although your choices there are limited. If you start a slideshow by first selecting your photos from the Organizer, then the Slide Order menu reads From Organizer, but you can choose Date (Oldest First),

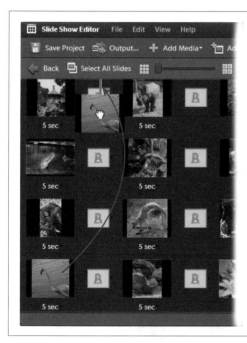

Figure 18-5:
You can reorder slides by dragging them in the storyboard, but if you have more than a few slides, all that scrolling is a pain. Elements makes it easier with the Quick Reorder window. Just click the Quick Reorder button in the lower-left corner of the Slide Show Editor (just above the storyboard) to bring up what looks like a contact sheet of your slides. Then drag any picture to its new location. You see a vertical blue line (the arrow points to one), indicating a photo's new position. When you're done, in the window's upper-left corner, click Back to return to the main editing window.

Date (Newest First), Random, Folder Location, Custom (this is what you see if you manually drag slides to new locations), and Reset (which puts your photos back in the order they were in when you first brought them into the Slide Show Editor).

Adding special effects

Elements gives you all kinds of ways to gussy up your slideshow, including adding clip art, text, and sound. If you want a slide that lists credits, for instance, start by creating a blank slide. (Click the slide right before the spot where you want the blank slide, and then, above the preview area, click the Add Blank Slide button.) Elements adds a blank slide to the right of the slide you selected, to which you can then add whatever you like—like credits, for instance. Here's a rundown of what you can add to your blank slide (or to any of your slides, for that matter, as shown in Figure 18-6). Just click the relevant button (Graphics, Text, or Narration) in the Extras section at the top of the Slide Show Editor's right-hand panel to see your options.

- **Graphics.** Elements gives you a whole library of clip art you can add to your slides. The art is divided into categories: animals, backgrounds, costumes, flowers, food, frames, holidays and special occasions, home items, miscellaneous, ornaments, scrapbooks, sports and hobbies, and thought and speech bubbles.

  Use the backgrounds on a blank slide, because they cover a whole slide, but you can add the rest of the clip art to slides that already have something on them. To add a piece of clip art to a slide, just double-click the clip art's thumbnail in the panel.

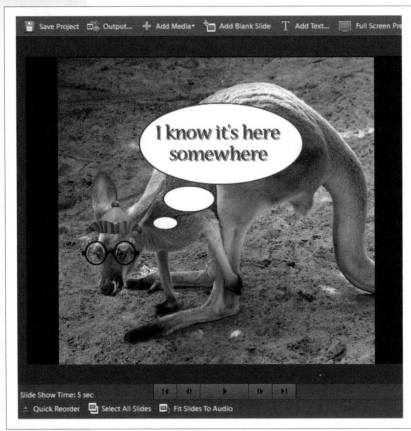

Figure 18-6:
You can add all sorts of clip art to your slides, as well as create slides that include only art or text. If you'd like to angle clip art (like the hat and glasses here) to make it fit your subjects better, see the Tip below.

It appears on your slide surrounded by a frame. You can grab the corners of the frame and drag them to resize the clip art to the size you want, or use the Size slider in the Properties panel. You can also reposition the art by dragging it. To remove it, right-click it, and then choose Delete.

TIP   If you play around with Elements' clip-art costumes (hats, outfits, and glasses that you can paste onto your friends' pictures), you may notice that you can't rotate the clip art on the slide. If you want to adjust the angle for any of the clip art, here's a workaround. All the art lives in *C:\Program Data\Adobe\ Elements Organizer\8.0\Slideshow Graphics* if you have Vista. In Windows XP it's *C:\Documents and Settings\All Users\Application Data\Adobe\ Elements Organizer\8.0\ Slideshow Graphics.* (Program Data and Application Data are hidden folders, so you need to turn on hidden folder viewing to see them—see the box on page 556.) Open your slide in Full Edit, and then add the clip art there (by importing it from the Graphics folder listed in the previous sentence). Then, use the Move tool (page 165) to place the clip art just so, and use the transform commands (page 359) to adjust the shape as needed. When you're done, you can re-import your image into the Organizer as a version (page 68), and use that version in your slideshow. You can also open the clip-art images themselves, change them, and then save them as PNG files under a new name in the same folder as the originals; they appear right in the Slide Show Editor's clip-art section along with the originals.

- **Text.** You can add text to your slides, and apply a number of fancy styles to your text. Click the Text button at the top of the panel (the T), and then double-click the text style you like. The Edit Text window pops up. Type in the words you want to add to your slide and then click OK. The text appears in your slide, surrounded by a blue bounding box, which you can use to place the text where you want it. You can also drag a text style to the slide and then, in the Properties panel, click the Edit Text button to enter your words.

TIP   When the Edit Text window is active, you can't click OK by pressing Enter. You just create a line break in your text. You need to actually click the OK button.

At the same time, the Text Properties panel appears at the lower-right of the Slide Show Editor, where you can change the text's font, size, color, and style. You can even choose a different drop-shadow color here if you're using shadowed text. If you want to edit text later on, just click the letters on the slide to bring back the bounding box and the Text Properties panel.

- **Narration.** You can record narration for your slideshow by clicking the slide you want to add your voice to, and then, in the Extras panel, clicking the Narration button (the blue microphone). Elements displays the recording window shown in Figure 18-7. (Of course, you need to have some kind of microphone hooked up to your PC to record your voice.)

- **Music.** You can add a full-scale soundtrack to your slideshow if you want. To do that, click the bottom of the Slide Show Editor where it says, "Click Here to add Audio to Your Slide Show". In the window that opens, navigate to the audio file you want, and then click Open. You can choose from any MP3, WAV, AC3, or WMA files on your PC.

TIP   If you use iTunes, then you need to convert your iTunes AAC files to one of these formats before Elements acknowledges their existence. To do so, follow the instructions at *http://support. apple.com/kb/HT1550*.

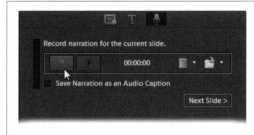

Figure 18-7:
Adding narration to your slides is pretty simple. Just click the red Record button and start talking, and then click it again when you're done. Click the Play button to preview what you've got. If you don't like how things turned out, click the trashcan icon, and then choose Delete This Narration. If you want to permanently save your narration as an audio caption for the original photo, then turn on the "Save Narration as an Audio Caption" checkbox. You can also click the folder icon to the right of the recording controls to import an existing audio caption to use with this slide.

You can make your slideshow fit the duration of the music, if you like. At the top of the storyboard, click "Fit Slides to Audio", and Elements adjusts the duration of your slideshow to last the length of the song. Or, if you'd rather repeat a short audio clip over and over, go to Edit → Slide Show Preferences, and then turn on "Repeat Soundtrack Until Last Slide". If you don't choose either one, then Elements doesn't make any attempt to synchronize the length of the soundtrack and the length of the slideshow.

TIP   If you have problems getting the Organizer to play one of your MP3 files, then you may find you have better luck if you use an audio program to re-encode your MP3 as a variable bit-rate MP3 file. Check the audio program's options or help files for instructions on how to do this.

• **Pan & Zoom.** Filmmaker Ken Burns popularized this technique, where the camera moves around a still photo, giving the impression of motion. To create this effect in Elements, just click the slide you want to pan over and then, in the Properties panel, turn on the "Enable Pan & Zoom" checkbox.

TIP   If you've lost the Pan & Zoom properties because you clicked over to the slide's Edit or Text properties, then you can get back to Pan & Zoom by clicking once in the preview area outside the slide itself.

The Properties panel has two little thumbnails, labeled "Start" and "End". Click the Start thumbnail to choose where to begin panning over your photo. The green pan frame appears in your photo, marking the spot where Elements will begin panning over your slide. To change the starting point for your pan, drag the frame to another place on the slide, or drag a corner to resize the frame.

Then, click the End thumbnail in the Properties panel, and repeat the process with the red frame to set the end point for panning and zooming. If you decide you want to edit the effect, just click either thumbnail again to bring back the pan frame. You can also click the buttons between the thumbnails to swap where you start and end.

You can control the zoom level by how large you make your start and end frames. A small frame means the camera has to zoom in to fill the slide; an end frame that's larger than the start frame makes the camera zoom out.

NOTE   Panning and zooming usually looks pretty jerky when you preview your slideshow, but don't worry about that—it should be smooth in the final slideshow.

You can also pan more than once on a slide. To do that, click "Add Another Pan & Zoom to This Slide". If you want all your slides (or selected slides) to show the same pan and zoom you just set up, go to the Edit menu, and choose what you want to do: "Apply Pan & Zoom to Selected Slide(s)" or "Apply Pan & Zoom to All Slides".

TIP   While Elements doesn't give you a way to create scrolling credits, you can fake them by creating a slide with a list of people you want to credit, and then applying the pan-and-zoom effect to
the slide multiple times.

Saving and sharing your slideshow

After all the work you've done creating your slideshow, needless to say, you want
to save it. (If you forget, Elements reminds you to do so when you exit the Slide
Show Editor.)

TIP   You can watch a full-screen preview of your slideshow by clicking the aptly named Full
Screen Preview button above the Panel bin, or by pressing F11. Press Esc to get back to the Slide
Show Editor window.

Before saving, you need to decide what you want to do with your slideshow: burn
it to a CD, email it as a file, and so on. It's important to remember that no matter
what you choose (except for saving as a PDF), you're going to end up with a Windows Media Video (WMV) file.

That doesn't matter as long as everyone you want to share your slideshow with is
using a computer or DVD player that uses a recent version of Windows Media
Player. (It's part of the Windows operating system [if you've disabled Windows
updates, you can download the latest version from Microsoft]; for Macs, you
can find a free plug-in at *www.microsoft.com/windows/windowsmedia/player/
wmcomponents.mspx*.) But unfortunately, that's not always the case. If you want to
send a slideshow to someone who doesn't have Windows Media Player, your options
are to create a PDF file as explained on page 526, upload your slideshow to YouTube
(*www.youtube.com*), and send a link to your friends, or use other software to change
the format to something your recipients have, like QuickTime, for example.

To see your Output options, click the Output button above the Slide Show Editor's preview window. You see the dialog box shown in Figure 18-8, where you can
choose from several ways to save and share your slideshow.

- **Save As a File.** Choose this option to save your slideshow to your hard drive as a
  PDF or WMV file. The PDF options are explained on page 527. If you choose
  WMV, you get several choices for size and quality. Select the one that best suits
  how you plan to share your slideshow. (If you're curious about the various
  choices, pick the one you want to know more about, and then click the Details
  button. Elements displays a pop-up window with info about that size and its
  suggested uses.)

- **Burn to Disc.** You can create a Video CD (VCD) using Elements. This is a disc
  that plays in a DVD player, just like a regular DVD, but you don't need a DVD
  recorder to create it (because you're just using a plain old CD). The downside is
  that VCD is a tricky format—the quality is poor, and you can expect to have
  problems getting the discs to play in some DVD players. If you want to send
  VCDs, you may want to make a short test slideshow for your friends to be sure
  they can watch one before you invest a lot of time in creating a large project.

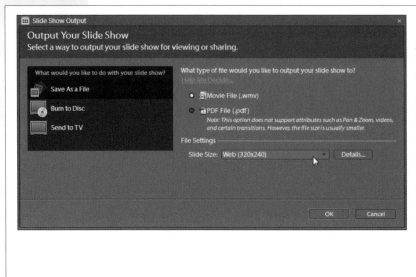

Figure 18-8:
To pick a format for your slideshow, click the Slide Show Editor's Output button to call up this dialog box. Choose what you want to do from the list on the left; the options on the right change to reflect your choice. If you're creating a WMV file, then you get a number of different slide size options. For items that offer PAL and NTSC variations, PAL is the format you should choose if you plan on viewing the slideshow in Europe or China; choose NTSC for most other areas of the world, including the United States.

TIP If you'd like to check which players can handle VCDs, or if you just want to know more about the format, head over to *www.videohelp.com/vcd*, where you'll find information and links to lists of compatible players.

You can also include other slideshows on the same disc if you turn on the "Include additional slide shows I've made on this disc" checkbox. Then click OK to bring up the "Create a VCD with Menu" window where you can choose the slideshows you want to include. In that window, you have to choose between the NTSC or PAL formats for your disc. Choose PAL if you're sending your slideshow to Europe or China; choose NTSC for most other areas, including the United States. Then click Burn to start burning the disc.

TIP If you also have Adobe's Premiere Elements program (and a drive that can create DVDs), then you can send your slideshow to Premiere Elements to make a true DVD. If you have a DVD recorder but not Premiere Elements, you can save your slideshow, and then use any other DVD-authoring software you've got loaded on your PC. If you have a DVD burner, you almost certainly got some kind of authoring software with it.

- **Send to TV.** If you have Vista Home Premium or Ultimate, or Windows Media Center Edition running on your PC and your TV is connected to your computer, or if you have a device like an Xbox 360 that can play WMV files, you can send your slideshow straight to your TV for large-screen viewing. In the Output window, click "Send to TV", and then type a name for your slideshow in the Name box. Next, choose the option in the Settings pull-down menu that correctly describes your TV, and then click OK. (If you aren't sure what to choose in the Settings menu, click the Details button to learn more about the currently selected option.)

NOTE   As long as you save your slideshow as an Organizer project file by clicking Save Project in the Slide Show Editor, you can go back and edit it whenever you like. Doing this tells the Organizer to keep an editable version of the slideshow that you can work on. To edit an existing slideshow, in the Organizer, just right-click its thumbnail, and choose Edit from the pop-up menu. Elements opens your show in the Slide Show Editor so that you can make your changes. If you want to work on your slideshow again, then you need to save the actual Slide Show file, too, in addition to your PDF or WMV file, if you created one. (You can't edit PDFs or WMVs in the Slide Show Editor.) If you don't save the project file, you don't have an editable slideshow anymore.

Flipbooks

In some ways, a *flipbook* is like a very simple slideshow without any transitions, audio, or fancy panning and zooming. After slogging through the last section, you may be thinking you've had enough slideshow options in Elements, thank you very much. But all that's different about a flipbook is the speed at which the images appear. A flipbook's *frame rate* (how fast one image appears and disappears) is very fast. When you put a stack of photos you took with your camera set to burst mode into a flipbook, you can create an animation where the images change so fast it appears that your subject is moving.

TIP   Flipbooks are great for creating a time-lapse effect. For instance, if you take a photo of the building progress of your new house each day from the exact same spot, you can combine all the photos and watch your house go from an empty lot to finished in just a few seconds.

The flipbook effect is similar to an animated GIF (page 511), but you can use JPEGs in your flipbook, so the image quality is much higher than with a GIF. The downside is that you can't easily include a flipbook on a web page. Your completed flipbook is a Windows Media file, so all you or your friends can do is watch it like a movie or regular slideshow. That said, Elements does give you several different output sizes, so you can pick one that's suitable for watching on a regular TV (although you need Adobe's Premiere Elements or some other video-creation program to make a version your TV understands).

You may also want to create a flipbook to use as a plain old slideshow, since they're quick to produce and easy to email. Regardless of how you plan to use your flipbook, here's how to get started:

1. **In the Organizer, select the photos you want to include.**

   You have to choose at least two photos, or you'll get a warning (instead of the Flipbook wizard) when you try to continue. You can't add or delete photos once you're in the wizard, so be sure you have *all* the photos you want before you start. You may want to make an album (page 62) to help you keep track.

The flipbook displays your photos in order based on their filenames or numbering. For example, files with names like *img_0617.jpg*, *img_0618.jpg*, and so on, appear in numerical order. The only control the Flipbook wizard gives you is that you can reverse the order of the whole group of images. (See page 277 for advice on renaming a batch of photos using a sequential number scheme.)

2. **Go to Create → More Options → Flipbook.**

The Flipbook wizard displays the window shown in Figure 18-9. You can preview your flipbook by clicking the Play button below the image area.

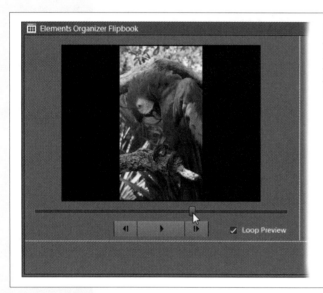

Figure 18-9:
If you want to review your photos to make sure you've included the right ones, you can do so by moving this slider. However, you can't add or remove photos once you're in the Flipbook wizard.

3. **Adjust your settings.**

You have only a limited number of options in the flipbook window. Because the images move so fast, flipbooks don't let you use transitions between slides. All you can do is choose:

- **Playback Speed.** Here's where you control the number of frames per second (each photo is one frame). One frame per second is the slowest option, and even that's pretty zippy for a regular slideshow. The more frames per second you choose, the faster and smoother the animation effect, and the shorter the total playback time.

- **Reverse Order.** If you want to see your slides from last to first, instead of first to last, then turn on this checkbox.

- **Output Settings.** These settings determine the final size of your flipbook. You get a variety of file formats to choose from. *Computer Monitor* is a good medium size that gives you a convenient balance between file size and image size. *Web* is a good size for use on a web page (assuming your viewers have broadband Internet connections). *E-mail* creates a tiny show that you can send to people with dial-up connections. You can also choose to create your flipbook as *DVD-NTSC, DVD-PAL, VCD-NTSC,* or *VCD-PAL.* NTSC is for video players in the United States and most other areas, and PAL is used in Europe and China. (If you choose any of these settings, then you need a program like Premiere Elements to create your final DVD for TV viewing. Although you can create a flipbook in a format for use on a DVD, Elements can't create the menus and extra files your DVD player needs to play the file.) Unfortunately, the VCD choices are subject to the quality limitations discussed on page 537. Figure 18-10 gives you more advice if you need help choosing a setting.

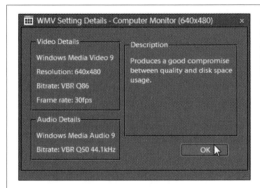

Figure 18-10:
If you're not sure which output format to use for your flipbook, click the Details button in the Photoshop Elements Flipbook window. As shown here, you get a window with more info about the size that's currently selected.

- **Loop Preview.** Turn on this checkbox and your preview plays endlessly once you click the Play button, until you stop it by clicking the Pause button.

4. **Create your flipbook.**

   When you're happy with how your flipbook performs, click Output. If you want to make big changes, like adding or removing photos, or if you decide you don't want to make a flipbook after all, then click Cancel. (You need to start from the beginning if you want to change which photos are included.)

   When you click Output, a new window opens where you can name and save your video, which automatically gets added to the Organizer. Then you're all done.

Sharing Photos with Yahoo Maps

Elements gives you another fun way to share your photos online: placing them as virtual pins stuck in a Yahoo map. Your first reaction may be a yawn and, "So what? I know where I've been." But this is actually a very cool feature.

It's great because you can choose to use a satellite view of the map, and in many places, you can zoom in to the level where you can see individual buildings. This means you can place your photos *exactly* where you took them. Want to sell your house? Find it on the map and attach your photos. Or click the mountain lodge where you spent your vacation, and then attach your photos. Trace out the route of your trip to Europe, and then place the photos of each site you visited.

Once you've created your photo-speckled map, you aren't limited to admiring your work on your own computer. You can create an online album (page 519) to post it on the Internet, where your friends can click the pins on the map to view a slideshow of your photos for that spot, or send it straight to Flickr (*www.flickr. com*)—the enormously popular photo-sharing site. Adobe has made this easy by building the map feature right into the Organizer. The Organizer even has a Map view, as explained in Figure 18-11.

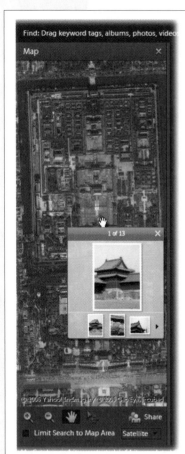

Figure 18-11:
To see the Yahoo Map pane, go to Window → Show Map, or right-click a photo or tag (label) and choose "Place on Map", and then enter the location where you want to attach the photo. Once you're in Map view, you can click a pin to see the photos attached to that spot. Click the large thumbnail on the little pop-out window for a full-screen slideshow of the pin's photos with the same options, like music and transitions, that you have for other Full Screen view slideshows (page 525). Press Esc to get back to the map.

NOTE   If your camera has built-in GPS (a Global Positioning System that always knows where the camera is), then Elements automatically reads your GPS data and places your photos on the map. The camera writes the GPS coordinates into your EXIF data (see page 69), so you don't have to do a thing except enjoy the view. At least, that's how it's supposed to work. Unfortunately, some cameras write this information in places that Elements can't find, so you may have to go back and add it manually.

To create a map with your photos, just follow these steps:

1. **Place your photos on the map.**

    You have several ways of getting photos onto the Map:

    • Right-click a photo's thumbnail, and then choose "Place on Map". You get a dialog box where you can enter the general location (London, for example, or North Carolina) or even the specific address where your photos should go.

    • Drag and drop photos where you want them when the Map pane is open. You may need to use the Map Move tool (more on how to use that in a moment) to reposition the photos exactly where you want them.

    • Assign a Place tag (page 58) to a group of photos, and then put the tag on the map using either of the two previous methods. All photos with this Place tag get positioned in the same spot on your map.

    NOTE   The map is pretty grabby. When you're dragging in a photo to a location close to a spot where you already have photos, it may get sucked into the existing group, even if that's not where you want it. Sometimes it's easier to drop a photo a ways from where you want it, and then use the Move tool to bring it to a location close to existing pins. The map tends to bog down if you stress it by putting too many photos on it. It works better if you limit the number of images you include at one time. You may find you need to remove the photos from one trip before adding the ones from the next one.

    Use the Map tools to adjust the view to your liking, and then use the Map Move tool (see Figure 18-12) to reposition your photos, if necessary. The more you zoom the view, the more accurate your placement.

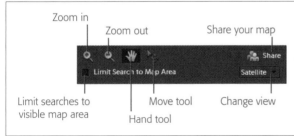

Zoom in
Zoom out
Share your map
Limit searches to visible map area
Move tool
Change view
Hand tool

Figure 18-12:
The Map pane has its own little toolbox, used only to adjust your view of the map and to rearrange your photos. To zoom in or out, click one of the Zoom tools and then click the map. The area you click becomes the center of the map. The Hand tool works just like the regular Hand tool (page 102), but it only moves the Map around. The Map Move tool lets you reposition your photos on the map.

2. **View your photos on the map.**

Click any pin to display the little pop-up window you can see in Figure 18-13. To see a particular photo, click it in the little thumbnail strip along the bottom of the pop-up window.

The pin icon is always one pin for each location, no matter how many photos you have attached there. (It would be nice if the number of pins corresponded to the number of photos, but whether you have 2 photos or 20 attached to a particular spot on the map, you just see one pin.) If you have more than one pin in an area and you're zoomed out too far to show each location, then the map shows a group of three pins, no matter how many pins are actually in the area.

3. **When you've got all your photos positioned as you want them, share your map.**

Click the Share button, and then choose how you want to share your map (your choices are explained below). If you aren't ready to share it yet, your pins stay on the map even if you don't click the Share button—you don't need to do anything special to save them for later.

The Map pane gives you three ways to view the map. If you click the Map pull-down menu, you can choose:

- **Map.** This is like a standard street map: a drawing with street names and numbers on it.

- **Hybrid.** This view combines the satellite view and the map view, so you see a satellite photo with the street names marked on it.

- **Satellite.** This is an aerial photo of the area, taken by satellite, but the level of detail is pretty amazing if you zoom it all the way in. (Not all areas have the same zoom level available; the map tells you if it can't zoom to the maximum level.)

The Map pane also includes a little toolset below the map to help you get things arranged to your liking (you can see it in Figure 18-12). The Zoom and Hand tools work like the regular Zoom (page 100) and Hand tools (page 102), but they work only on the map (not on the photos). The Map Move tool is very handy for repositioning photos. It's tough to position your photos precisely on the first try. Click the Map Move tool, and then grab a pin and drag it where you want it. If you have multiple photos on a pin and you want to move only one photo, the easiest way is to right-click it, choose "Remove from Map", and then add it in again.

> **TIP** The map can be a little cranky about scrolling long distances. If you find it's hard to maneuver the map to the spot where you want to put your photos, try right-clicking any photo in the Media Browser, choosing "Place on Map", and then entering your area in the search box. You can always remove the photo (right-click it and then select "Remove from Map") once the map shows the region you want, if that photo doesn't belong there.

If you've already placed a photo on a map, you can go right to that location by right-clicking the photo in the Media Browser and then choosing "Show on Map".

The Map pane opens, showing your photo's current location. When you want to get rid of a photo, right-click it, and then choose "Remove from Map". (You can do this in the Media Browser or from its pin in the map.)

Once you've arranged all your photos to your satisfaction, you can share your map. Click the Share button and agree to the Yahoo Map terms of use (in that window, click Share), and then choose whether to share to Photoshop.com (Photoshop Showcase if you're not in the United States) or Flickr. If you choose Photoshop. com (Photoshop Showcase), then Elements sends your map to the Album wizard (see page 520). Just name your album, and then choose whether to share to Photoshop.com, export to a CD or DVD, or export your album to send to your own website. (Online albums are covered in detail starting on page 519.) You can change from the Map template to another style of online album while you're creating the album. In the Album pane, just click the Sharing tab, and then double-click the template you want. You can also add, remove, or rearrange photos in the Content tab, just as with any other online album. Figure 18-13 shows a completed Yahoo Map online album.

TIP   When you share a map, the photo page that Elements generates automatically opens with the plain Map view showing, so you need to explain to friends how to change to one of the other views by clicking the word "Hybrid" or "Satellite", as they prefer, for a more realistic look.

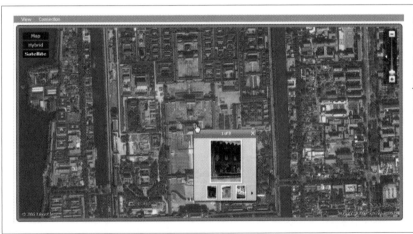

Figure 18-13:
Here's a finished Yahoo Map online album. It's a great way to share your photos with friends. They just need to click a pin to see the photos "pinned" to a particular location.

If you choose Flickr, then a wizard walks you through authorizing and uploading your photos. They'll be displayed on Flickr's map feature. (The first time you send photos, you have to create a Flickr account if you don't have one.)

Other Ways to Share

Elements makes it simple to post your photos to several other popular sites besides Photoshop.com, so your friends can view your photos online. You can quickly send photos to Kodak Gallery, SmugMug, and others, right from within Elements. (The list changes depending on Adobe's current partnerships.) Once your photos are posted, you and your friends can order not only prints, but also t-shirts, mugs, bags, and other items with your photos on them. (Merchandise options vary, depending on which service you use.) Here's a quick rundown of what you can do with each site, and what it'll cost you:

- **Kodak EasyShare Gallery.** Besides ordering prints from Kodak Gallery (page 484), you can upload your photos for your friends to view online. Once your friends set up free accounts, they can order prints directly from Kodak. This site also offers a wide variety of gift items with your photos on them, like mugs, bags, shirts, and more. It's free, except for the cost of what you order.

- **SmugMug Gallery.** SmugMug is another site that offers a lot of different gift items you and your friends can order. You can try it free for 7 days, and your friends can order prints and merchandise without a paid account. But if you want to maintain a gallery here, it's $39.95 a year for a basic account after the trial period expires.

- **Send to a CEIVA Digital Photo Frame.** It's not exactly online sharing, but if you have a CEIVA-brand digital photo frame, Elements makes it easy to send your photos to it. (The CEIVA frame is an electronic gadget that looks like a regular digital picture frame, but displays photos you send to it digitally over a phone line or via WiFi, rather than photos on a card you insert into it.) Just choose Share → More Options → "Send to CEIVA Digital Photo Frame" to connect and upload your photos. A basic CEIVA account that lets you send photos to someone's frame is free, but you have to sign up for it; the frames are pretty expensive. You can connect to the site from the Share menu or go to *www.ceiva.com* to learn more.

- **Phone/iPod.** If you have an iPhone or an iPod Touch, Elements makes it easy to share your photos that way, too. If you used your iPhone to take pictures and you want to get them into Elements or if you're using your iPod or iPhone to move photos from another device to your computer, just connect your iPhone or iPod to your computer and then use the Photo Downloader (page 42) to send them straight to the Organizer, or download them in Windows Explorer and use File → Get Photos in the Organizer.

  To send photos or albums to your iPod or iPhone, either to show them off to your friends or to transport them to another device or computer, connect the iPod or iPhone to your computer, then go to iTunes → Photos → Sync photos from → Photoshop Elements. Don't turn on "Include full-resolution photos" unless you're using the iPod to transport your pictures to another device or computer—you don't need full-resolution images if you're just going to look at them on your iPod or iPhone, and those big image files take up a lot of room.

- **Flickr.** This is a really popular photo-sharing site where you can create galleries and slideshows, or order different kinds of merchandise featuring your photos. Basic accounts are free.

To upload a photo to any of these sites, just select it in the Editor or the Organizer, click the Share tab → More Options, and then choose the one you want. (You can also select and upload more than one photo at a time.)

You're asked to sign in if you already have an account, or to create one if you don't. Each site has a simple-to-use wizard that walks you through the sign-up process, and they also have tours so you can look around before you decide to join.

If you aren't sure which one(s) to try, ask your friends which one they like. Each site has pros and cons. You may want to try them all before you decide.

Part Six:
Additional Elements

Chapter 19: Beyond the Basics

Beyond the Basics

So far, everything in this book has been about what you can do with Elements right out of the box. But as with many things digital, there's a thriving cottage industry devoted to souping up Elements. Of course, signing up for a Photoshop.com account (page 20) gives you access to a lot of extra goodies from Adobe, but a ton of other stuff is available, too. You can add new brush shapes, Layer styles, actions, and fancy filters. Best of all, a lot of what's out there is free. And many of the tools are designed to make Elements behave more like Photoshop. This chapter looks at some of these extras, how to manage the stuff you collect, and how to know when you really need the full version of Photoshop instead. You'll also learn about the many resources available for expanding your knowledge of Elements beyond this book.

Graphics Tablets

Probably the most popular Elements accessory is a *graphics tablet,* which lets you draw and paint with a pen-like stylus instead of a mouse. A tablet is like a souped-up substitute for a mouse: You control your onscreen cursor by drawing directly on the tablet's surface—an action that many artists find offers them greater control. If trying to use the Lasso tool with a mouse makes you feel like you're trying to write on a mirror with a bar of soap, then a graphics tablet is for you.

NOTE   Some deluxe-model graphics tablets act as monitors and let you work directly on your image. But you need to budget close to a thousand dollars for that kind of convenience.

Most tablets work like the one shown in Figure 19-1. You use the special pen on the tablet just as you would a mouse on a mousepad; any changes you make appear right on your monitor.

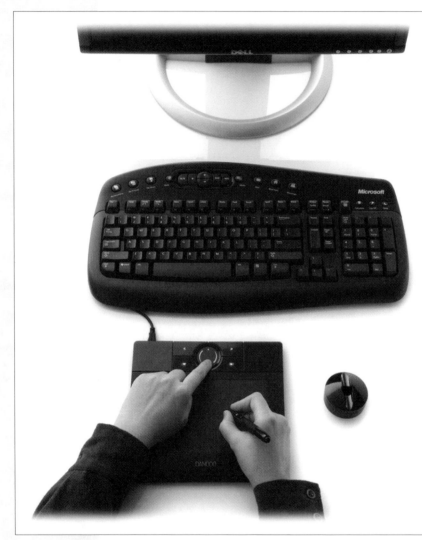

Figure 19-1:
A Wacom Bamboo tablet in action. The working area is inside the rectangle on the tablet surface. The buttons and ring let you do things like zoom and scroll. For basic photo retouching, a small tablet is usually fine once you get used to it. If you want to do more drawing and you generally use sweeping strokes when you draw, then you may want a larger model.

For most people, it's much easier to control fine motions with a tablet's stylus than with a mouse. And when you use a tablet, many of Elements' brushes and tools become *pressure sensitive*—the harder you press, the darker and wider the line becomes. The stylus lets you create much more realistic paint strokes, as shown in Figure 19-2.

When using the Brush tool, you'll see a tiny black triangle in the Options bar just to the right of the Airbrush setting; that lets you access the tool's Tablet Options.

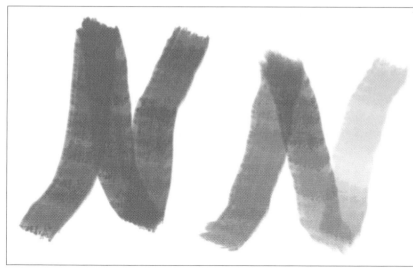

Figure 19-2:
*Two almost identical
paint strokes, starting
with fairly hard pressure
and then easing up. Both
were made using the
same brush and color
settings. The only
difference is that the
stroke on the left was
drawn with a mouse, and
the one on the right
came from a tablet. You
can see what a difference
the pressure sensitivity
makes.*

Many brushes and tools are automatically pressure sensitive when you hook up a tablet. These settings let you choose whether to let the pressure control the size, opacity, roundness, hue jitter, and scatter for your brushes. (See page 369 for more about Brush settings.)

With a tablet, you can also create hand-drawn line art—even if you don't have an artistic bone in your body—by placing a picture of what you want to draw on the surface of the tablet and tracing over it. Also, if you find constant mousing troublesome, you may have fewer hand problems when using a tablet's stylus. Most tablets come with a wireless mouse, which works only on the surface of the tablet. Or you can use your regular mouse on a mousepad or on your desk the way you always do, if you like to switch back and forth between the stylus and a mouse.

Tablets now start at less than a hundred dollars, a big drop from what they used to cost. There are lots of different models, and their features vary widely. Sophisticated tablets offer more levels of sensitivity and respond when you change the angle at which you hold the stylus.

Wacom, one of the big tablet manufacturers, has some pretty nifty tablet demos on its website (*www.wacom.com*) if you click on the various product tours. You can't actually simulate what it's like to *use* a tablet, but the animations give you a good idea of what your life would be like if you were to go the tablet route.

Free Stuff from the Internet

You have to spend some money if you want a graphics tablet, but there's a ton of free stuff—tutorials, brushes, textures, and Layer styles, for example—available online that you can add to Elements. Most of these add-ons say they work with Photoshop, but since Elements is based on Photoshop, you can use most of them in Elements, too.

Here are some popular places to go treasure hunting:

- **Adobe Exchange** (*www.adobe.com/cfusion/exchange/*). On Adobe's own website, you can find hundreds and hundreds of downloads, including more Layer styles than you could ever use, brushes, textures, and custom shapes to use with the Shape tool. Many are free, once you register. This site is one of the best resources anywhere for extra stuff. About 99 percent of the items listed are made specifically for Photoshop, but Photoshop's brushes, swatches, textures, shapes, and Layer styles work in Elements, too. See the box on page 556 for help with installing your finds in Elements.

- **MyJanee** (*www.myjanee.com*). You'll find lots of tutorials and free downloads on this site.

- **Sue Chastain** (*http://graphicssoft.about.com*). This is another site with lots of downloads and many tutorials.

- **Panosfx** (*www.panosfx.com*). Panos Efstathiadis produces some wonderful actions (see the next section for more about actions) for Photoshop, and now he's adapted many of them for Elements as well. Most are free; some cost a few dollars.

- **Optik Verve Labs** (*www.optikvervelabs.com*). This is the home of Virtual Photographer, one of the most amazing plug-ins (add-on utilities) for Elements. Best of all, it's free.

- **Hidden Elements** (*www.hiddenelements.com*). Richard Lynch has been creating wonderful add-on tools for Elements practically as long as the program has existed. Some are free, many are not, but all are worth the investment.

- **Grant's Tools** (*www.cavesofice.org/~grant/Challenge/Tools/index.html*). Here's another source of popular free tools for Elements, though it hasn't been updated since Elements 6. But the tools that work in Elements 6 mostly work in Elements 8, too.

- **Simple Photoshop** (*http://simplephotoshop.com*). The home of the popular (not free) Elements+ add-on tools, and also some tutorials.

If you're willing to pay a little bit, you've got even more choices. You can find everything from more elaborate ways to sharpen photos to really cool collections of special edges and visual effects. Prices range from donationware (pay if you like it) to some sophisticated plug-ins that cost hundreds of dollars. You can also buy books like the *Wow!* series (Peachpit Press), which have loads of illustrations showing the styles available on the included CD.

NOTE   Elements 8 is based on Photoshop CS4, so CS4 downloads are compatible. Plug-ins and other goodies designed for older versions of Photoshop or Elements usually work with newer versions, but not the other way around. For example, a brush made for Photoshop CS4 works in Elements 8 but not in Elements 3.

Mac plug-ins don't work in Windows, and vice versa, but many plug-ins offer two versions, one for each platform. When buying a plug-in, check with the developer to be sure it works with Photoshop Elements, and if you're using Windows Vista or Windows 7, check on the plug-in's compatibility with them, as well.

With so many goodies available, it's easy get overwhelmed trying to keep track of everything you've added to Elements. Your best bet is to make backup copies of anything you download, so you'll have it if you ever need to reinstall Elements.

Elements also includes a Preset Manager (Figure 19-3) that can help you keep track of certain kinds of downloads. Go to Edit → Preset Manager to launch it.

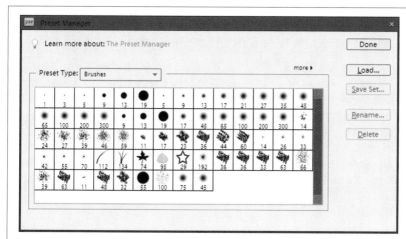

Figure 19-3:
Elements' Preset Manager is a nifty feature that lets you see all your brushes, swatches, gradients, and patterns in one place. You can use it to switch which groups are loaded, to add or remove items, and so on—the same way you do in the main brush window.

When You Really Need Photoshop

You can do a ton with Elements, but some people do need the full version of Photoshop. For example, if you want to write your own *actions* (little scripts, like macros, that automate certain things in Photoshop) or if you have to work extensively in CMYK mode, then you need Photoshop.

CMYK is the color mode used for commercial printing—it stands for Cyan, Magenta, Yellow, and blacK, which are the colors professional printers use. When you send a file to a print shop, the printer usually tells you it needs to be a CMYK file. You can't convert files to CMYK in Elements, so if you need CMYK files on a regular basis, it's worth the extra price of Photoshop to avoid the aggravation. If you only occasionally need CMYK, you might just ask your printer about converting the file for you for an additional charge.

TIP   Richard Lynch (*www.hiddenelements.com*) created a workaround for CMYK conversion for earlier versions of Elements. You may want to check his website to see what workarounds and other goodies he's come up with for Elements 8.

In Photoshop you get more of everything: more choices, more tools, more settings, more types of adjustment layers, and so on.

Beyond This Book

You can do thousands of interesting things with Elements that are beyond the scope of this book. The Elements Inspiration Browser and Help menu give you access to dozens of interesting tutorials right from Elements. Also, bookstores have loads of titles on Elements and Photoshop, and a lot of procedures are the same in both programs. And you can find all kinds of specialized books on everything from color management to making selections to scrapbooking.

POWER USERS' CLINIC

Making Elements Behave More Like Photoshop

Ever since Elements first came out, there's been quite a cottage industry devoted to figuring out ways to get Elements to behave more like Photoshop. If you've used Elements 3 or earlier versions, the odds are pretty good that you're familiar with the extra tools and action players created by Richard Lynch, Paul Shipley, Grant Dixon, and Ling Nero. Unfortunately, Adobe decided to write Elements 4 in a way that disabled the traditional route used by add-on tools to access some of the underlying Photoshop code needed for these additional features to work. That meant that many of the existing add-on tools stopped working in Elements 4.

For now, it's best to stick to actions written for Elements 4, 5, 6, 7, or 8 to be sure they'll work. (See the box on page 556 for more about installing action-based tools.) If you've been using extra tools or actions in Elements 2 or 3, then you may want to keep the older version of the program around just for them. (You can have as many different versions of Elements as you like installed on your computer, but Adobe recommends that you run only one version at a time.)

In addition, you'll find hundreds of tutorial sites on the Web. Besides those mentioned earlier in the chapter, other popular sites include:

- **Adobe** (*www.adobe.com*). You'll find plenty of free online training for Elements here.

- **Photoshop Roadmap** (*www.photoshoproadmap.com*). This site has tutorials and plug-ins for Photoshop, but there's a big section of Elements tutorials, too.

- **Photoshop Support** (*www.photoshopsupport.com/elements/tutorials.html*). Despite the name, this site isn't run by Adobe, but it has a whole section of Elements tutorials.

- **YouTube** (*www.youtube.com*). Yep, that's right: You can find videos about almost anything on YouTube, including lots of Elements tutorials.

- **Photoshop Elements User** (*www.photoshopelementsuser.com*). This is the website for a subscriber-only print newsletter, but it includes some free online video tutorials, a forum, and a good collection of links. This is the only publication especially for Elements. Their forums are hosted at *www.elementsvillage.com*.

- **Graphic Reporter** (*http://graphicreporter.com*). The website of Photoshop maven Lesa Snider includes many well-written Elements tutorials.

- **Eclectic Academy** (*www.eclecticacademy.com*). This site offers popular, inexpensive online courses in Elements.

If you search around online, you're sure to find a tutorial for any project you have in mind, although many of them are written for Photoshop. In most cases, you can adapt them for Elements. If you get stuck or need help with any other aspect of Elements, there's an active online community that's sure to have an answer for you. Besides the sites already mentioned, try:

- **Adobe Support forum** (*http://forums.adobe.com/community/photoshop_elements*). The official Adobe Photoshop Elements User-to-User forum, where you can connect with lots of helpful and friendly people. It's your best bet for getting answers without calling Adobe support.

- **Digital Photography Review** (*www.dpreview.com*). This site has a bunch of camera-specific forums. You can also get a lot of Elements answers in the Retouching forum if you specify in your question that you've got Elements rather than Photoshop.

- **RetouchPRO** (*www.retouchpro.com*). The forums here cover all kinds of retouching and artistic uses of Elements and Photoshop. They also host frequent webcasts about digital imaging.

- **Photoshop Creative Elements** (*www.photoshopcreativeelements.com*). Another forum for Elements enthusiasts.

Many sites are devoted to scrapbooking using Elements. A good place to start is Scrapper's Guide (*www.scrappersguide.com*), a commercial site run by Linda Sattgast.

No matter what you're looking for—add-ons, tutorials, communities—try a Google search, and you're sure to find a site that has what you want.

There's no question about it: Once you get familiar with Elements, it's addictive. Lots of other folks have found out how much fun this program is, so you shouldn't have any trouble finding the answer to any question you have.

The only limit to what you can do with Elements is your imagination. Enjoy!

Adding Layer Styles, Shapes, and Actions to Elements

Adding your online finds to Elements 8 is a good news/bad news situation: It's easy to add Layer styles, shapes, and actions (see the box on page 554 for more about using actions in Elements), but if you want to categorize them or have them show up in your Content panel searches, you're in for a trip through some pretty techie territory. (It's like the process for setting them up in Elements 7, if you've used that version.)

To add your extras, just put them into the following folders; the next time you launch Elements, they'll show up in the Show All section of the relevant palette:

- **Layer styles**. Put them into *C:\Documents and Settings\All Users\Application Data\Adobe\ Photoshop Elements\8.0\Photo Creations\layer styles* if you use Windows XP, or *C:\ProgramData\ Adobe\Photoshop Elements\8.0\Photo Creations\ layer styles* if you use Vista. The files should have the extension *.asl*.

- **Actions**. The easiest way to install most actions is via Guided Edit's Action Player (page 421). The drawback is that if you install an action that requires you to use the Layers panel during a step (to choose the target layer for the action's next step, for instance), you can't do that in Guided Edit. And since many add-on tools for Elements are really actions, you want to be able to use them in Full Edit. But you can't do that with actions installed in the Action Player.

If you do want to use actions in Full Edit, you can, but it's a bit more complicated. First, you need two files: one for the action itself (the .atn file) and one to use as a thumbnail so that you can find the action to launch it. The thumbnail needs to be a 64-pixel square PNG image with *exactly* the same name as the action (except for the file extension), including spacing, capitalization, and so on. Put both the thumbnail and the .atn file (individually, not in a folder) into *C:\Documents and Settings\All Users\Application Data\Adobe\Photoshop Elements\ 8.0\Photo Creations\photo effects* if you use Windows

XP, or *C:\ProgramData\Adobe\Photoshop Elements\ 8.0\Photo Creations\photo effects* if you use Vista. (In both Windows XP and Vista, you'll need to turn on hidden files to see these folders by going to Control Panel → Classic View → Folder Options → View → "Show Hidden Files and Folders".)

- **Shapes**. Put your downloaded shape files (which need to have the .csh file extension) into *C:\ Documents and Settings\All Users\Application Data\ Adobe\Photoshop Elements\8.0\Photo Creations\ shapes* in Windows XP or *C:\ProgramData\Adobe\ Photoshop Elements\8.0\Photo Creations\shapes in Vista*.

Once everything is in the right place, your Layer style or shape will show up in Show All in the Content panel. Your actions also appear in the Effects panel → Photo Effects → Show All. For mere mortals, that's all there is to it, but if you're a techie who understands XML, read on.

You can make your content appear in its own category if you also create an XML file (a little snippet of code that gives Elements directions for how to categorize the file and search for it). The easiest way to do this is to find an XML file for an existing Layer style, photo effect, or whatever you have, duplicate it, and then edit its contents. The XML files go into the same folder as the item you're adding. (Each layer style, shape, and so on, that came with Elements has one of these files.)

Regardless of whether you did the XML steps or not, to remove content you've added, just right-click it in the appropriate panel and choose Delete Content from the shortcut menu, or click the icon once and then click the trashcan icon at the bottom of the panel. If you created an XML file, go dig that out and delete it, too.

XML is pretty intimidating, but you can simplify the whole process by using something like Graffi's Add-O-Matic (www.graficalicus.com), which installs add-on content for you. As of this writing it's for Elements 5 through 7, but it's likely he'll update it for Elements 8. It costs $11, but if you're addicted to Elements add-ons, it may be worth the money.

Part Seven:
Appendixes

7

The Organizer, Menu by Menu

This appendix gives you a quick tour of the main menus in the Organizer—the ones listed at the top of the screen. The Organizer has two main views: Media Browser and Date view. Both offer the same menu choices—everything listed here is available in either view. Keyboard shortcuts and buttons in the Organizer windows give you access to many of these menu items. When you have two ways to run a command, both are mentioned here.

In addition to the main menus discussed here, the Organizer is chockfull of *short-cut menus* (also called *contextual menus*). That means you can right-click almost anywhere in the Organizer and get a menu with several options specific to the object you clicked. Right-click a tag (page 58), for instance, and you get a menu that includes choices for editing the tag or changing it to a category.

> NOTE   If you also have Premiere Elements or Photoshop installed, you'll see a few additional menu choices not listed here. This appendix covers the items that appear when you're in the Organizer and go to Edit → Preferences → Editing, and turn off "Show Premiere Elements Options".

File Menu

This menu is where you import photos, start new projects, manage catalogs, and export photos. It's also where you quit the Organizer when you're done.

Get Photos and Videos

Here's where you import photos into the Organizer. You can tell Elements to find and import photos and videos:

- **From a camera or card reader** (keyboard shortcut: Ctrl+G).

- **From a scanner** (Ctrl+U).

- **From files and folders** (Ctrl+Shift+G).

- **By searching.** This option tells Elements to search your computer for photos. You can choose to search all your hard drives (if you have more than one attached to your PC), your C: drive only, your My Documents folder, or you can browse to a particular folder or drive to search only its contents.

New

You can choose to create a new blank file (select Photoshop Elements Image File) that will appear in the Editor. (The Organizer itself doesn't create blank files.) Your other options here are:

- **Premiere Elements Video Project.** Even if you don't have Premiere Elements (Adobe's video-editing program) installed, you see this menu item. But if you click it and you don't have that program, Elements just tells you to install it.

- **Image from Clipboard.** You can copy a photo in the Organizer (Ctrl+C), and then choose this option to start a new Editor file by copying your photo from the Clipboard (the invisible file that stores what you copy until you paste it somewhere).

- **Photomerge Group Shot.** Group Shot lets you move people from one group photo to another, similar photo (page 351). You can use it to replace someone who's looking away from the camera or blinking, for example.

- **Photomerge Faces.** This one lets you combine parts of different faces, just for fun (page 348).

- **Photomerge Scene Cleaner.** This feature lets you remove unwanted people or other details from a photo by copying over bits of other photos (page 351).

- **Photomerge Panorama.** Create a panorama from files you've selected in the Organizer. Choosing this feature takes you to the Editor for the actual merge. See page 342 for more about panoramas.

- **Photomerge Exposure.** Combine two differently exposed versions of the same shot for one perfectly exposed image (page 267).

Open Recently Edited File in Editor

Choose a file from this list, and the Organizer opens it in the Editor so you can work on it there.

Catalog

This is where you manage your catalogs (page 53). A window opens where you can choose a catalog to open, repair, or optimize from a list of your existing catalogs. You can also create a new catalog, and rename, move, or delete a catalog here. Keyboard shortcut: Ctrl+Shift+C.

Burn Data CD/DVD

Use this menu option to quickly burn a project or a group of photos to a CD or DVD. Choose this for sharing photos, and use "Copy/Move to Removable Disk" (described next) when changing where you store files. Keyboard shortcut: Ctrl+Alt+C.

Copy/Move to Removable Disk

If you want to move a photo or a group of photos to a CD or DVD, choose this command. Page 75 has more info about backing up your files. Keyboard shortcut: Ctrl+Shift+O.

Backup Catalog to CD, DVD, or Hard Drive

It's wise to back up your catalog, and this command makes it easy to do so. You can choose to back up your entire catalog or just a few photos. See page 77 for detailed directions on using this command. Keyboard shortcut: Ctrl+B.

Restore Catalog from CD, DVD, or Hard Drive

Choose this option when you want to replace your catalog with an archived version, or if you accidentally delete photos or otherwise run into trouble with the current version.

Duplicate

Highlight a photo or a Create project, and choose this menu item to make a duplicate. Keyboard shortcut: Ctrl+Shift+D.

Reconnect

Sometimes your Organizer catalog (page 53) can't find a file when you ask for it. Usually this happens when you move or rename a file using something other than Elements (like Windows Explorer). This command tells the Organizer to find the file again. You can reconnect:

- **Missing File.** Choose this to reconnect one file.
- **All Missing Files.** The Organizer searches for all the files it can't find.

Watch Folders

Use this command if you regularly import photos into certain folders (see page 46). Elements monitors the folders you choose and checks for new photos, movies, or audio files stored in them. You can tell Elements to automatically place any of these it finds into your catalog. Or you can just have Elements notify you that it found new files and let you decide what to do with them.

Rename

If you want the Organizer to keep track of your photos, you need to move and rename them from within Elements (rather than using, say, Windows Explorer). So if you want to change a photo's name, choose this menu item. Keyboard shortcut: Ctrl+Shift+N.

Write Keyword Tag and Properties Info to Photos

Normally your Organizer tags exist only in your catalog's database. But if you want to make the tag info part of the photo file itself, first select the photo(s) in the Media Browser, and then choose this menu item. Elements writes your tags into the file's metadata (page 69). You can select multiple photos and use this command on the whole group at once.

Move

If you want the Organizer to keep track of your photos, you have to move them within Elements once they're in your catalog. To move a photo, choose this menu item, and then select a destination in the Folder view window that appears (see page 55). You can also move files by dragging them if you go to Display → Folder Location or press Ctrl+Alt+3. You'll see a new pane on the left of the Media Browser with a view of your hard drive's folder structure (just like you see elsewhere in Windows). You can drag your photos into the folders you want. Keyboard shortcut for Folder view: Ctrl+Shift+V.

Export As New File(s)

If you want to export a group of photos for use by another program, this is one way to do it. Choose this command from the menu, and you get a dialog box where you can pick the destination of your files and rename them if you like. You can also convert the exported files to a different format: Your choices are JPEG, PSD, TIFF, and PNG. This menu option is useful if you need to create JPEGs for printing at a store kiosk, for example. Keyboard shortcut: Ctrl+E.

Print

Choose this command, and you get Elements' Prints window, which is discussed in detail in Chapter 16. Keyboard shortcut: Ctrl+P.

Order Prints

This is one way to connect to the Shutterfly and Kodak Gallery online services to order prints or photo books. See page 484 for details on how to order online prints from the Organizer.

Exit

You can close the Organizer here or by pressing Ctrl+Q. Note that the Editor doesn't quit along with the Organizer, so if the Editor is also running, you have to exit it separately.

Edit Menu

This menu contains choices that let you make changes to your files. It's also where you can access your Elements preferences to change their settings.

Undo

You can undo your last action in the Organizer by selecting this menu item or by pressing Ctrl+Z.

Redo

If you undo something and then change your mind, select the item or press Ctrl+Y.

Copy

To copy something to the Clipboard, highlight it, and then select this menu item or press Ctrl+C.

Select All

To select all the photos in any window in the Organizer, choose this menu item or press Ctrl+A.

Deselect

To clear all selections, choose this menu item or press Ctrl+Shift+A.

Delete from Catalog

Select the photo you want to get rid of and choose this option to remove it from the catalog database. (You can press Delete to do the same thing.) If you want to remove the photo from your hard drive as well, the dialog box that appears gives you the option to do so.

Rotate 90° Left

To rotate a photo 90 degrees counterclockwise, select it, and then choose this menu item or just press Ctrl+left arrow key.

Rotate 90° Right

To rotate a photo 90 degrees clockwise, select it, and then choose this menu item or press Ctrl+right arrow key.

Auto Smart Fix

To instantly apply the Auto Smart Fix command to your photo, choose this item or press Ctrl+Alt+M. See page 123 for more about this command.

Auto Red Eye Fix

Choose this option or press Ctrl+R to automatically find and correct red-eye problems in all the selected photos. See page 121 for more about this feature.

Edit with Photoshop Elements

Choose this menu item or press Ctrl+I to send selected photos to the Editor so you can work on them.

Adjust Date and Time

If you want to change a file's date and time settings, select this item or press Ctrl+J. The dialog box that appears gives you three choices:

- **Change to a specified date and time.** This lets you adjust the date and time manually.

- **Change to match the file's date and time.** This changes the time and date to reflect the last time you modified the file.

- **Shift by a set number of hours (time zone adjust).** This lets you change the date and time of a selected group of photos. Elements applies any changes you make to all the photos you've selected. For example, if you elect to move the time back three hours (via the Time Zone Adjust dialog box), all your selected photos have their times moved back three hours.

Add Caption

To add a caption to a selected image, choose this menu item or press Ctrl+Shift+T.

Update Thumbnail

If an image's thumbnail stops displaying correctly or doesn't show the correct image, select the thumbnail by clicking it, and then choose this menu item or press Ctrl+Shift+U.

Set as Desktop Wallpaper

To use one of your photos as wallpaper for your desktop, just click its thumbnail in the Media Browser, and then choose this menu item or press Ctrl+Shift+W. If you select multiple photos, Elements arranges them like tiles so that they all appear as a sort of collage.

Ratings

Choose this menu item to assign the selected image(s) a rating of zero to five stars, so you can quickly find your favorites or sort out the duds.

Visibility

Using the pop-out menu here, you can mark photos as Hidden or Visible, or make all your hidden photos visible. See page 60 for details.

Place on Map

To stick photos onto a Yahoo map, choose this menu item, and you get a dialog box for entering the location where each photo should appear. Page 541 has more about maps.

Remove from Map

If you've put a photo on a Yahoo map and you want to take it off, choose this menu item.

Show on Map

If you've assigned a photo to a spot on a Yahoo map, choose this menu item to see the map showing the photo's location.

Stack

This is where you create and manage *photo stacks.* Stacks are groups of photos that you want to store together; only the top photo shows in the Media Browser until you expand the stack. You can create stacks from unrelated photos, unlike version sets (see the next item).

Your stacking options are:

- **Automatically Suggest Photo Stacks.** If you've taken photos using your camera's burst (rapid advance) mode or bracket mode, this menu item sorts related photos into their own stacks. Elements isn't smart enough to look through a folder and find all the photos you took of Yellowstone National Park, though. The photos have to be similar in subject and taken very close together in time—using your camera's burst mode, say—for this command to work. Keyboard shortcut: Ctrl+Alt+K.

- **Stack Selected Photos.** After you highlight your photos, choose this menu item or press Ctrl+Alt+S to put them into a stack.

- **Unstack Photos.** This modifies a selected photo stack so that the photos it includes are no longer joined together.

- **Expand Photos in Stack.** Choose this option or press Ctrl+Alt+R to see all the photos in a stack.

- **Collapse Photos in Stack.** To compress an expanded stack again, choose this command or press Ctrl+Alt+Shift+R.

- **Flatten Stack.** This reduces your stack so you see only the top photo, and not the ones below it, which no longer exist as separate images after you run this command.

- **Remove Selected Photos from Stack.** Use this item to remove one or more photos from a stack. This command and the next one appear only for expanded stacks.

- **Set as Top Photo.** Highlight a photo and choose this item to send that photo to the top of the stack. From now on, it becomes the visible photo.

Version Set

This is where you manage your *version sets*. When you make changes to a photo in the Editor, you have the option of creating a version set, as long as your photo is stored in the Organizer. In a version set, each time you save your photo, Elements saves it as a copy with a new name—that is, a different version. This lets you save many files containing your changes and go back to any one anytime. Your options here are:

- **Expand Items in Version Set.** Choose this item or press Ctrl+Alt+E to see all your versions at once.

- **Collapse Items in Version Set.** To return an expanded version set to single-image view, choose this command or press Ctrl+Alt+Shift+E.

- **Flatten Version Set.** Use this to reduce a version set to one photo—the top one.

- **Convert Version Set to Individual Items.** If you want to be able to work with the files in a version set as though they were separate photos, choose this item and, instead of a version set, Elements creates multiple individual photos.

- **Revert to Original.** This deletes later versions, leaving only your original photo as it was when you first brought it into the Organizer.

- **Remove Item(s) from Version Set.** If you find you've saved more versions than you need, highlight the ones you want to get rid of, and then choose this menu item. (You have to expand your version set to see this option.)

- **Set as Top Item.** Highlight a photo, and then choose this option to send that photo to the top of the set. From now on, it becomes the visible photo. (You only see this item for expanded version sets.)

Run Auto-Analyzer

Choose this item, and Elements examines all your photos and videos—or those you select—and applies Smart tags (page 63) to them based on what it finds. To see what Elements thinks of your photo, hover your cursor over the purple Smart tag icon attached to the photo. You may see "High Quality, In Focus", or "Medium Quality, Blurred" or any other combination of the Smart tags from the list in the tagging pane. Auto-Analyzer has its own pane in Edit → Preferences, where you can choose which qualities you it want to use as filters, like Object Motion or Blur.

Color Settings

This is where you can set your color space (page 217). You can also press Ctrl+Alt+G to bring up Elements' color settings.

Contact Book

If you want to see or edit your Contact Book of email addresses (to use when sending your photos from Elements), you can get to it here. See page 517 for more about Elements' Contact Book.

Preferences

Here's where you can make changes to your Organizer settings for things like getting and saving photos; connecting to cameras or scanners; emailing; editing; and creating tags, albums, and calendars. If you're using the online sync feature at Photoshop.com (page 75), this is where you control album syncing. You can also adjust the settings for what you want to see in Folder view (page 55), and for using the online services like Kodak Gallery and Shutterfly (page 546) here. In addition, it's where you tell Adobe whether you want to see ads for special offers.

Find Menu

This menu is really the heart of the Organizer. From it, you can search for your photos in many different ways.

Set Date Range

Choose this menu item, and a dialog box appears that lets you specify start and end dates. The Organizer shows all the photos that fall in the date range you specify. Keyboard shortcut: Ctrl+Alt+F.

Clear Date Range

After you've searched for a date range, choose this menu item or press Ctrl+Shift+F to see your complete catalog in the Media Browser again.

By Caption or Note

When you choose this item, you get a dialog box that lets you search for any text in your captions or notes (it doesn't have to be the entire caption). The Organizer finds all the photos with those words in either field. Keyboard shortcut: Ctrl+Shift+J.

By Filename

Enter part of a filename, and the Organizer finds the file for you. Keyboard shortcut: Ctrl+Shift+K.

All Version Sets

Choose this, and Elements shows you all the version sets in your catalog. Keyboard shortcut: Ctrl+Alt+V.

All Stacks

This menu item makes Elements show you all the photo stacks you've made. Keyboard shortcut: Ctrl+Alt+Shift+S.

By History

Here you can choose to find your file based on any of the following factors:

- **Imported on.** This is the date you brought your file into the Organizer.

- **E-mailed to.** You can search by the names of people you've emailed your photos to, but only if you sent the messages from the Organizer (page 517).

- **Printed on.** Search for the photos you printed from Elements on a certain date.

- **Exported on.** Search for all the photos you exported from the Organizer on a particular date.

- **Ordered Online.** Search for the photos you've ordered from Shutterfly or Kodak Gallery (page 484).

- **Shared Online.** Search for the photos you've shared on Photoshop.com (page 20) or via one of Adobe's online partners like Kodak Gallery.

- **Used in Projects.** Search for all the photos you've used in Create projects (page 465).

By Media Type

The Organizer doesn't organize only still photos—it can also keep track of movies and audio files. Here, you can search for all the files of a particular type:

- **Photos.** Find all your still photos (press Alt+1).

- **Video.** Find all your video clips (press Alt+2).

- **Audio.** Find all your audio files (press Alt+3).

- **Projects.** Find all your Create projects (press Alt+4).

- **PDF.** You can import and tag PDF files in the Organizer. If you want to see all your PDFs, choose this option or press Alt+5.

- **Items with Audio Captions.** If you've recorded captions for any of your photos (see page 535), you can search for them by choosing this menu item or by pressing Alt+6.

By Details (Metadata)

If you want to search your photos according to what's stored in their metadata, like the EXIF information (page 69) from your camera, this is where you start. See page 67 for more about how to perform these searches.

Items with Unknown Date or Time

Choose this menu item if you want to find any photos that haven't been properly tagged with the date and time. Keyboard shortcut: Ctrl+Shift+X.

By Visual Similarity with Selected Photo(s) and Video(s)

This is a very cool feature: If you want to find photos and videos that have colors and tones similar to a particular photo (or group of photos) or video, select the photo(s) and/or video(s) you want to match, and then choose this item. Elements ranks all your photos and videos by color. The closest matches appear at the top of the list.

Untagged Items

To find photos that you haven't tagged yet, choose this menu item or press Ctrl+Shift+Q.

Unanalyzed Content

If you've used the Auto-Analyzer (page 63) to apply Smart tags to some of your catalog, choose this menu item or press Ctrl+Shift+Y to see the rest of your catalog that you haven't analyzed yet.

Items Not in Any Album

Choose this menu item to find all the photos you haven't used in albums.

Find People for Tagging

Choose this item, and Elements searches your photos for pictures with people's faces in them. Elements 8 not only finds generic faces, but once you've tagged a person in one photo, it can find her in future photos. See page 61.

View Menu

This menu lets you control how the Organizer presents your photos.

Refresh

If you need to make the Organizer redraw its screen, choose this menu item or press F5. You might want to do this if your recent edits don't appear in a photo's Organizer thumbnail, for example.

Media Types

Choose this item to bring up a window where you can decide what kinds of files the Organizer displays, or you can use the keyboard shortcuts. Your choices are photos (Ctrl+1), video files (Ctrl+2), audio files (Ctrl+3), projects (Ctrl+4), and PDF files (Ctrl+5). Just turn on the ones you want, and turn off the ones you don't.

Hidden Files

Use this option to see or hide all your files with the Hidden tag (page 60).

Details

When this setting is turned on (it usually is unless you've turned it off), you see info about your photos in the Media Browser window, like the date and the tag icons. Turn this setting off to see just the thumbnails with no other information. Keyboard shortcut: Ctrl+D.

Show File Names

Turn this on to see your photos' names displayed below their thumbnails.

Show Grid Lines

Turn this on to see dividing lines between each thumbnail.

Show Borders Around Thumbnails

Although it's hard to see, Elements displays a very fine border around each thumbnail unless you turn off this setting.

Expand All Stacks

To see every photo in every stack, choose this menu item.

Collapse All Stacks

To return all your stacks to single-photo view so you see only the top photo, choose this menu item.

Window Menu

This menu is where you choose which parts of the Organizer you see. For instance, you can choose to show the Timeline (page 65) or to hide the Task pane here.

Hide Task Pane

If you want to have the entire Organizer window for viewing thumbnails, you can turn off the Task pane here, or just click its edge. (If the Task pane is hidden, this menu item reads "Show Task Pane" instead.)

Show Map

Choose this option to bring the Yahoo map into view. There's more about using Yahoo maps on page 541.

Timeline

If you turn on the Timeline, you see each group of photos as a bar on a graph across the top of the Media Browser. The height of the bar indicates how many photos are in each group. The groups are arranged according to your choice in the pull-down menu at the top of the thumbnails area. Ctrl+L is the keyboard shortcut to toggle the Timeline on and off.

Properties

To see the Properties window for a photo, select the photo, and then choose this menu item or press Alt+Enter.

Help Menu

This menu is where you find the Elements' Help files and info about the program.

Elements Organizer Help

When you select this item or press F1, Elements launches your web browser to display the Help files.

Key Concepts

Elements' Help files include a glossary of digital-imaging terms. If you're wondering what a particular term means, choose this menu item and it'll take you to the online glossary so you can look it up.

Support

Select this to go to Adobe's online Support area and knowledgebase for either Photoshop Elements or Premiere Elements.

Video Tutorials

Choose this menu item to go to the video tutorials section of Adobe's support site, where you can watch videos on how to do popular Elements tasks.

Forum

This takes you to Adobe's online support forum for either Photoshop Elements or Premiere Elements.

About Elements Organizer

Choose this to see a window with info about the version of the Organizer you've got. You'll also see a very long list of patents and credits for all the people who worked to bring you the Organizer.

Patent and Legal Notices

If you want the Organizer's patent numbers, you can view and copy them here.

System Info

Choose this item for a window showing info about Elements itself and about your Windows operating system. If you can't remember which Windows service pack you have, for instance, you can check here. There's also information about some important plug-ins. If you're not sure whether you have QuickTime, for example, you can find out here.

Updates

Select this menu item, and Elements searches for updates. You can also change your update preferences by clicking the Preferences button in the window that opens when it's done updating, searching for updates, or trying to connect to Adobe's server.

Elements Inspiration Browser

The Inspiration Browser (page 34) links you to a number of video and PDF tutorials. You can launch it from here.

Welcome Button

When you're signed on to your Photoshop.com account (page 20), you'll see the text "Welcome, <your name>". Click it to go directly to your Photoshop.com account online. If you're not signed on, you see "Sign In" here instead.

Create New Adobe ID

If you don't have an Adobe ID (which you need to use Photoshop.com), click this button to create one (you can also do this from any of the other places in Elements that take you to Photoshop.com).

Undo

Click this button or press Ctrl+Z to undo your last action.

Redo

Click here or press Ctrl+Y to redo your last action.

Display Menu

This menu lets you choose how you'd like to arrange your photos for viewing.

Thumbnail View

For the basic Media Browser view, where you see thumbnails of your photos, choose this menu item or press Ctrl+Alt+1.

Import Batch

Select this menu item to see your photos grouped according to when you imported them. Each batch is separated by a header that lists the import date and time. Keyboard shortcut: Ctrl+Alt+2.

Folder Location

Choose this option for a view of your photos grouped by the folders that contain them. You also get a folder-tree view of your computer and networked drives on the left of the window. The header for each group of thumbnails in the middle of the window gives you a button you can click to assign the name of the folder they're in as an Instant Keyword Tag. Keyboard shortcut: Ctrl+Alt+3.

Date View

Date view displays your photos on a calendar. You can switch to Date view by selecting this menu item or by pressing Ctrl+Alt+D. (If you're in Date view, this menu item reads "Media Browser", so you can get back to the usual state of the Organizer.)

View, Edit, Organize in Full Screen

Choose this menu item or press F11 to get a full-screen slideshow of your photos. Elements presents you with a floating control strip to help you navigate through the photos, but it appears only when you pass your cursor over it. It's a great way to look through a group of newly imported photos, and you can even choose music to listen to while you watch your slideshow. Pressing the Esc key takes you out of Full Screen view. In Elements 8, you can also choose to have transitions between your photos. And you can use the Quick Fix editing commands (page 116) and apply tags right in Full Screen view.

Compare Photos Side by Side

This option is similar to "View Photos in Full Screen" in that you get a full-screen view. But in this view, you get to see any two photos of your choice side by side. It's great for deciding which photos to keep or print. (You can also get this view by pressing F12.) To bring in a new photo for comparison, click the photo that you want to get rid of. Press Esc to exit this view.

Welcome Menu

Click the little blue-and-white house to bring up the Elements Welcome screen that you see when the program first launches. To the right of this icon are the standard Windows buttons for minimizing, restoring, and closing the Organizer window.

The Editor, Menu by Menu

The Editor's menus are far more complex than the Organizer's menus. All three editing modes—Full Edit, Quick Fix, and Guided Edit—have the same menus, although some choices are grayed out when you're in Quick Fix or Guided Edit mode. When you need a menu item that's not available in Quick Fix or Guided Edit, just switch back to Full Edit to use it.

Several of the menus in Elements are *dynamic*, meaning they change quite a bit to reflect the choices currently applicable to your image. That means the choices you see in this appendix represent only what you *may* see depending on the situation. The Layer menu, for instance, offers you very different options depending on the current state of your image and which layer is active.

> NOTE   If you have Adobe Premiere Elements installed, then you'll see some extra menu options not included in this basic list. Also, you may see all these choices in one menu row (in the order listed here), or you may have two rows of menu items, depending on the size of your Elements window.

System Menu

The bright blue square with "pse" on it, at the upper-left corner of the Elements window, is actually a button. Click it to get a pop-out menu for closing, moving, maximizing, and minimizing the Editor, as well as for restoring it to its original size.

File Menu

The commands listed here let you create, import, open, save, and print files.

New

Choose this menu item if you want to start a new file in Elements. Your options are:

- **Blank File** (or press Ctrl+N).
- **Image from Clipboard.** This automatically pastes into a new file anything you've copied.
- **Photomerge Group Shot.** This lets you move a person from one photo of a group into another photo of the same group (page 351).
- **Photomerge Faces.** Use this one to combine parts of different faces for caricatures and other fun effects (page 348).
- **Photomerge Scene Cleaner.** This feature lets you remove unwanted people or other details from a photo by copying over bits of other photos (page 351).
- **Photomerge Panorama.** Use this option to combine your photos into panoramas (page 342).
- **Photomerge Exposure.** This new feature lets you combine bracketed shots into one properly exposed photo (page 267).

Open

Choose this menu item or press Ctrl+O to open an existing file.

Open As

This menu option (or Alt+Ctrl+O) lets you choose the format for a file as you open it. Select it when you want to use the Raw Converter with non-Raw formats like JPEG or TIFF (page 264).

Open Recently Edited File

Here's you'll find a pop-out list of the most recent files you've had open in Elements.

Duplicate

When you need to make a copy of your photo, choose this option. Elements names the copy the same thing as the original with "copy" tacked onto the end, though you can change the copy's name in the dialog box that appears.

Close

To close the active image window, choose this menu item or press Ctrl+W.

Close All

To close all your open image windows, choose this option or press Alt+Ctrl+W.

Save

To save your work, select this option or press Ctrl+S.

Save As

To save your image under another name or in a different format, choose this command or press Shift+Ctrl+S.

Save For Web

To save an image so that it's optimized for posting on a web page or sending by email, choose this menu item or press Alt+Shift+Ctrl+S. For more on the Save For Web window, see page 504.

File Info

Choose this menu item to bring up the File Info window, which includes all sorts of information (file creation date, file format, and so on) about your image.

Place

Use this command to place a PDF, Adobe Illustrator, or EPS file into an image as a new layer. If the artwork is larger than the image you place it in, Elements automatically makes it small enough to fit. In Elements 8, anything (including objects from images in regular formats like TIFF or JPEG) that you put into a file with this command becomes a Smart Object (page 472).

Organize Open Files

Choose this menu option to add the files you have open in the Editor to the Organizer.

Process Multiple Files

This is where you batch-process files to rename them, change their format, add copyright information, and so on (see page 274 for everything that Elements lets you do to groups of files).

Import

This is where you bring certain file formats into Elements. It's also where you can connect to external devices like scanners. (They'll show up in this menu if you install their drivers.) Your basic choices before you connect or install anything are:

- **Frame from Video** (page 49)

- **WIA Support** (the built-in support for scanners that's part of the Windows operating system)

Export

This command is always grayed out. That's normal. Adobe left it in for the benefit of any third-party plug-ins that may need it—but you don't need it in Elements to use the program's standard tools and commands. (If you need to export files, you can do that from the Organizer—see page 484.)

Automation Tools

Like Export, this command is only here for a few third-party plug-ins that may need it. Normally, it's grayed out.

Print

Choose this command and you get the Print window, which is discussed in detail in Chapter 16. Keyboard shortcut: Ctrl+P.

Order Prints

This is your portal to connecting to Kodak Gallery or Shutterfly to order prints, calendars, or photo books. See page 484 for how to order prints online. Choose this item, and Elements switches you over to the Organizer, and then connects you from there.

Exit

You can close the Editor by selecting this item or by pressing Ctrl+Q. The Organizer doesn't quit along with the Editor—if the Organizer is also running, you have to exit it separately.

Edit Menu

The choices listed here let you make changes to your files. This is also where you can access your Elements preferences to change their settings.

Undo

To back out of your last action, select Undo here or press Ctrl+Z. You can keep applying this command to undo as many steps as you've set in the Undo History panel's preferences (Edit → Preferences → Performance → History States).

Redo

If you undo something and then change your mind again, redo it here or press Ctrl+Y.

Revert

Choose this command to return your image to the state it was in the last time you saved it.

Cut

To remove something from your image and store it on the Clipboard (so you can paste it into another file), choose this menu item or press Ctrl+X.

Copy

To copy something to the Clipboard, highlight it and select this menu item or press Ctrl+C. The Copy command copies only the top layer in a file with layers. To copy *all* the layers in your selected area, use Copy Merged instead.

Copy Merged

To make a single, combined copy of all the layers in the selected area to the Clipboard, choose this menu option or press Shift+Ctrl+C. To copy just the active layer to the Clipboard, use Copy instead.

Paste

Use this command or press Ctrl+V to add whatever you have cut or copied to an image.

Paste Into Selection

Use this special command for pasting something within the confines of an existing selection. See page 141 for more on how this command works. Keyboard shortcut: Shift+Ctrl+V.

Delete

This command removes what you've selected without copying it to the Clipboard—it's just gone. You can press Backspace to do the same thing.

Fill Layer, Fill Selection

Choose this menu item to fill your active layer with a color or pattern (page 294). When you make a selection in your image, this menu item changes to Fill Selection. You can also choose a blend mode and opacity for your fill.

Stroke (Outline) Selection

This command puts a colored border around the edges of a selection.

Define Brush, Define Brush from Selection

If you want to create a custom brush from your photo or from an area of your photo, choose this command. The process is explained in detail on page 376.

Define Pattern, Define Pattern from Selection

This command creates a pattern from your image or selection. See page 298 for more about applying patterns.

Clear

Use this command to permanently remove information from the Undo History panel, the Clipboard, or both (choose All). If you have a corrupt image in the Clipboard (or one that's too large), it may cause Elements to slow way down or quit on you. Once in a while, the Clipboard may get stuck, too—you try to copy and paste an item, but still get whatever you copied previously. Clear fixes such problems.

Add Blank Page

This command lets you add a new, blank page to your current project. Find out more about working with multipage files on page 471. Keyboard shortcut: Alt+Ctrl+G.

Add Page Using Current Layout

If you create a photo collage (page 465) or other elaborate layout and you want to use that page as a template for new pages, choose this command instead of Add Blank Page. Keyboard shortcut: Alt+Shift+Ctrl+G.

Delete Current Page

If you're working with a multipage document and want to get rid of your current page, choose this command.

Color Settings

Here's where you choose your color space for Elements (page 217). Keyboard shortcut: Shift+Ctrl+K.

Preset Manager

This is where you access the window that helps you manage your brushes, swatches, gradients, and patterns. See page 553 for more on how the Preset Manager works.

Preferences

This menu item gives you access to the many Elements settings you can customize. You'll find the following preference windows available from this menu (they're discussed in detail in the appropriate parts of this book):

- **General** (or press Ctrl+K)
- **Saving Files**

- **Performance** (where you set the number of history states and assign *scratch disks*—see page 608)

- **Display & Cursors**

- **Transparency**

- **Units & Rulers**

- **Guides & Grid**

- **Plug-Ins**

- **Type**

- **Organize & Share** (brings up the Organizer's preferences)

Image Menu

This menu lets you make changes to your image, like rotate it, change its shape, crop or resize it, or change its color mode.

Rotate

Use these commands to change the orientation of your image (page 84). The first group of options applies to your whole image:

- **90° Left**

- **90° Right**

- **180°**

- **Custom**

- **Flip Horizontal**

- **Flip Vertical**

The next group does the same thing but to a layer or selection. The menu choices change depending on whether you have an active selection in your image. If you have a selection, you'll see the word "Selection" instead of "Layer."

- **Free Rotate Layer**

- **Layer 90° Left**

- **Layer 90° Right**

- **Layer 180°**

- **Flip Layer Horizontal**

- **Flip Layer Vertical**

Finally you can choose to:

- **Straighten and Crop Image**
- **Straighten Image**

These last two commands are mostly for when you need to straighten whole scanned images. To straighten the *contents* of an image, use the Straighten tool (page 86).

Transform

These commands let you change the shape of your image by pulling it in different directions (they're explained in detail on page 359). Your choices are:

- **Free Transform** (Ctrl+T) incorporates the other three commands.
- **Skew** slants an image.
- **Distort** stretches your photo in the direction you pull it.
- **Perspective** stretches your photo to make it look like parts are nearer or farther away.

> **TIP** You might prefer to use the Correct Camera Distortion filter for transforming your images to correct perspective. See page 354.

Crop

Choose this menu item to crop your image to the area you've selected (page 89).

Recompose

Use this to bring up the new Recompose tool (page 297), which lets you reshape your photos without distortion and eliminate unwanted objects in them at the same time. You can also press Alt+Ctrl+R or click its icon in the Tools panel.

Divide Scanned Photos

If you place several photos on your scanner glass at once and then choose this command, Elements cuts your photos apart and straightens and crops each one. See page 81 for more about how this works.

Resize

Here's where you change the actual size of your image (as opposed to changing the size of the view on your screen). Resizing is explained in Chapter 3. Your choices are:

- **Image Size** (page 103). Keyboard shortcut: Alt+Ctrl+I.
- **Canvas Size** (page 111).

- **Reveal All.** If you drag a layer from another image into your photo and part of the layer falls outside the perimeter of the target image, use this command to see the entire dragged layer. It basically resizes the canvas to fit all of the images. Also, some versions of Photoshop hide the area outside a selection when you use the Crop tool. When someone sends you one of these images, use this command to see the area that was hidden by the crop.

- **Scale** (page 362).

Mode

This is where you can change the color mode for your image (page 51). Your choices are:

- Bitmap
- Grayscale
- Indexed Color
- RGB Color

You'll find two other commands in this menu:

- **8-bits/Channel** reduces images from 16-bit color to 8-bit (see page 263).

- **Color Table** shows you the color table (the colors of your image as swatches) for an Indexed Color image.

Convert Color Profile

If you need to change the ICC (International Color Consortium) profile of an image, you can do it from this menu, which lets you apply an sRGB or Adobe RGB profile, or you can remove the profile from an image. For more on color profiles, go to page 217.

Magic Extractor

Use this command or press Alt+Shift+Ctrl+V to call up the Magic Extractor window, which automates the process of selecting an object in your photo and removing it from the background. See page 155 for details.

Enhance Menu

This menu contains the commands you use to adjust the color and lighting of your images. The first six options apply changes automatically, and the remainder let you adjust your changes.

Auto Smart Fix

Choose this option or press Alt+Ctrl+M to have Elements adjust your image's lighting, color, and contrast at the same time (page 123).

Auto Levels

Use this command or press Shift+Ctrl+L to make Elements adjust the individual color channels of your image (page 125).

Auto Contrast

Choose this command or press Alt+Shift+Ctrl+L, and Elements adjusts the brightness and darkness of your image without changing the colors (page 126).

Auto Color Correction

Use this option or press Shift+Ctrl+B to have Elements adjust your image's color in much the same way that Levels does. Auto Color Correction looks at different information in your photo to make its decisions, though (page 127).

Auto Sharpen

This command applies the same one-click sharpening you get when you use the Auto Sharpen button in Quick Fix (page 129).

Auto Red Eye Fix

Use this command or press Ctrl+R to apply the same auto red-eye correction found in the Organizer (page 121).

Adjust Smart Fix

This command is the same as Auto Smart Fix, except you get a slider to adjust the degree of change that Elements makes to your photo. Keyboard shortcut: Ctrl+Shift+M.

Adjust Lighting

Your choices for adjusting the light and dark values in your photos are:

- Shadows/Highlights (page 209).
- Brightness/Contrast (page 207).
- Levels. You can also press Ctrl+L to bring up the Levels dialog box (page 221).

Adjust Color

With these settings you can change a color, replace a color, remove a color cast, remove all the color from your image, or add color to a black-and-white photo. Choose from:

- Remove Color Cast (page 227).
- Adjust Hue/Saturation (page 306). Keyboard shortcut: Ctrl+U.
- Remove Color (page 322). Keyboard shortcut: Shift+Ctrl+U.

- **Replace Color** (page 310).

- **Adjust Color Curves** (page 302). The Color Curves tool lets you adjust the brightness and contrast of specific tonal ranges (like highlights or midtones) in your photo.

- **Adjust Color for Skin Tone** (page 134). This setting adjusts the colors in your image based on the skin tones of someone you select in the photo.

- **Defringe Layer** (page 160). This setting gets rid of the rim of contrasting pixels you may get when you remove an object from its background.

- **Color Variations** (page 229).

Convert to Black and White

Use this menu item or press Atl+Ctrl+B to convert a color photo to a black-and-white image (page 319).

Unsharp Mask

This is the most popular traditional method for sharpening your photos (page 237).

Adjust Sharpness

Choose this menu item to use Adobe's newest sharpening tool (page 239).

Layer Menu

Here's where you'll find the commands for creating and managing layers. (Chapter 6 is all about layers.) This is the most dynamic menu in Elements—what you see at the bottom of the menu changes depending on the layers in the open image and on the characteristics of the active layer. This is a basic rundown of the main menu options you'll usually see if your open image has only a Background layer. (Sometimes you'll see choices that are visible but grayed out.) The choices for merging and combining layers change the most as your layers change.

New

This is where you create new, regular (as opposed to Adjustment) layers. Your options are:

- **Layer** (or press Shift+Ctrl+N).

- **Layer from Background.** If your image doesn't currently have a Background layer, you see "Background from Layer" instead of "Layer from Background".

- **Layer via Copy** page 179 (or press Ctrl+J).

- **Layer via Cut** page 179 (or press Shift+Ctrl+J).

Duplicate Layer

Use this command to make a copy of the active layer. As long as you don't have a selection, you can also use Ctrl+J to do the same thing.

Delete Layer

If you want to eliminate a layer, click it in the Layers panel to make it the active layer, and then choose this command.

Rename Layer

Choose this option to—you guessed it—change a layer's name. You can also double-click the layer's name in the Layers panel to rename it.

Layer Style

If a layer has a Layer style applied to it (page 423), you can adjust it here:

- **Style Settings** brings up the dialog box where you can adjust some of the Layer style's settings. Double-clicking the Layer style icon in the Layers panel (the little "fx" to the right of the layer's name) brings up the same dialog box.

- **Copy Layer Style** lets you copy to the Clipboard any styles applied to a layer, so you can apply them to another image or layer.

- **Paste Layer Style** applies your copied style to a new layer, even in a new image.

- **Clear Layer Style** removes all the styles applied to a layer.

- **Hide All Effects** hides all the styles applied to a layer so that you can see what your image looks like without them. If you hide all the styles, this menu item reads "Show All Effects" instead.

- **Scale Effects** lets you adjust the size of certain aspects of Layer styles.

New Fill Layer

Choose this option to create a layer that's filled with a color, gradient, or pattern. You can also do this from the Layers panel by clicking the Create Adjustment Layer icon (the black-and-white circle). Your options are:

- **Solid Color** (page 195)

- **Gradient** (page 431)

- **Pattern** (page 195)

New Adjustment Layer

This command, not surprisingly, creates a new Adjustment layer (page 195). The types of layers you can create are:

- Levels (page 221)
- Brightness/Contrast (page 196)
- Hue/Saturation (page 306)
- Gradient Map (page 438)
- Photo Filter (page 273)
- Invert (page 316)
- Threshold (page 317)
- Posterize (page 317)

Layer Content Options

For Fill layers, this menu item brings up the dialog box where you can adjust the active layer's settings. For Adjustment layers, it makes the Adjustments panel display the settings for the selected layer. You can also double-click the left icon for the layer in the Layers panel (the one with two gears).

Type

This command gives you ways to modify a Text layer, as long as you haven't simplified it (page 395). You can choose:

- **Horizontal.** Change vertical text to horizontal text.
- **Vertical.** Change horizontal text to vertical text.
- **Anti-Alias Off.** Anti-aliasing is explained on page 449.
- **Anti-Alias On.**
- **Warp Text.** See page 449.
- **Update All Text Layers.**
- **Replace All Missing Fonts.** If your image is missing fonts, this command replaces them, but you can't choose which font Elements uses as the replacement. It's usually just as easy to replace fonts by highlighting the text and selecting a new font in the Options bar.

Simplify Layer

This command *rasterizes* your layer, turning the layer's contents from a vector or Smart Object to one that's built pixel by pixel. See page 395 for more about the difference between vectors and pixels.

Create Clipping Mask, Release Clipping Mask

This command links two layers together so the bottom layer determines the opacity of the upper layer (page 188). If you've used earlier versions of Elements, this is the same as the old "Group with Previous" command. When you have clipped layers, this item changes to read "Release Clipping Mask" instead. Keyboard shortcut for either: Ctrl+G.

Arrange

Use these commands to change the order of layers in the layers stack, or just drag them in the Layers panel. See page 186 for details on rearranging layers. ("Front" is the top of the stack, and "Back" is directly above the Background layer.)

- **Bring to Front** (or press Shift+Ctrl+]).
- **Bring Forward** (or press Ctrl+]).
- **Send Backward** (or press Ctrl+[).
- **Send to Back** (or press Shift+Ctrl+[).
- **Reverse.** Select two or more layers, and this command reverses the order in which they appear in the layer stack.

Merge Layers

Choose this command or press Ctrl+E to combine multiple layers into one layer. You may also see Merge Down, which merges a layer with the layer immediately beneath it, or Merge Clipping Mask, which merges grouped layers.

Merge Visible

Use this option or press Shift+Ctrl+E to merge all the visible layers into one layer.

Flatten Image

This command merges all the layers into one Background layer.

Select Menu

Here's where you make, modify, and save selections in your image. See Chapter 5 for more about selections.

All

Choose this command or press Ctrl+A to select your whole image.

Deselect

Use this command or press Ctrl+D to remove all selections from your image.

Reselect

If you use the Deselect command but then want your selection back again, choose this menu item or press Shift+Ctrl+D.

Inverse

This command switches the selected and unselected areas of your image. The area that wasn't previously selected is now selected, and the previously selected area is now unselected. Keyboard shortcut: Shift+Ctrl+I.

All Layers

Use this command to select all the layers in your image, including hidden layers.

Deselect Layers

Choose this option to unselect all the layers in your image.

Similar Layers

Use this command to select all the layers of your image that are the same type, such as all Adjustment layers or all Text layers.

Feather

Choose this option or press Alt+Ctrl+D to feather (blur) the edges of a selection (page 151).

Refine Edge

This command lets you groom the edges of a selection (page 145).

Modify

These commands let you change the size or edges of your selection. They're all explained in Chapter 5.

- **Border** selects the edge of your selection (page 165).
- **Smooth** rounds the corners of selections (page 165).
- **Expand** moves the edge of your selection outward (page 163).
- **Contract** moves the edge of your selection inward (page 163).

Grow

This command expands your selection to include contiguous areas of similar color (page 163).

Similar

This option expands your selection to include more areas of similar color, but—unlike the Grow command—it doesn't restrict the growth to contiguous areas (page 163).

Transform Selection

This new command lets you adjust the size of a selection by dragging its edges (page 161). You can also reshape it with any of the Transform commands (page 359).

Load Selection

If you've saved a selection, choose this command to use it again.

Save Selection

If you want to save a selection so you can use it later without recreating it, use this command (page 167).

Delete Selection

Use this command to permanently remove a saved selection.

Filter Menu

Filters let you change the appearance of your image in all sorts of ways—Chapter 13 covers filters in detail. Elements comes with some filters that are mostly for correcting and improving your photos, while others create artistic effects. You can apply filters from this menu or from the Effects panel. The filters are grouped into categories to make it easier to find. Every image responds to filters differently, so the descriptions here are a very rough guide.

Last Filter

The top item in the Filter menu always features the last filter you applied. Choose it or press Ctrl+F to reapply that filter with the same settings you previously used. If you want to change the settings, then you need to choose the filter from its regular place in the list of filters or press Ctrl+Alt+F.

Filter Gallery

This option lets you try the effects of different filters, rearrange them, and preview what they'll look like in your photo (page 407).

Correct Camera Distortion

Use this filter to correct various kinds of lens distortion problems (page 354).

Adjustments

This group of filters is primarily (but not exclusively) for correcting and enhancing photos. The filters are discussed on page 315, unless otherwise noted:

- Equalize
- Gradient Map (page 438)
- Invert (or press Ctrl+I)
- Posterize
- Threshold
- Photo Filter (page 273)

Artistic

Use these filters to apply various artistic effects to your image, ranging from a pencil-sketch look to a watercolor effect:

- **Colored Pencil** makes your photo look like it was sketched with a colored pencil on a solid-colored background.
- **Cutout** makes your image look like it was cut from pieces of paper.
- **Dry Brush** makes your photo look like it was painted using a dry brush.
- **Film Grain** adds grain to make your photo look like old film.
- **Fresco** makes your photo look like it was painted quickly in a dabbing style.
- **Neon Glow** adds vivid color to your image while softening the details.
- **Paint Daubs** gives your photo a painted look.
- **Palette Knife** makes your photo look like you painted it with a palette knife. While you may think of a palette knife as a tool for blending heavy paint daubs, Adobe describes the effect of this filter as looking like a thin layer of paint that reveals the canvas beneath it.
- **Plastic Wrap** makes your image look like it's covered in plastic.
- **Poster Edges** gives your image accented, dark edges while reducing the number of colors in the rest of the photo.
- **Rough Pastels** makes your image look like it was quickly sketched with pastels.
- **Smudge Stick** uses short, diagonal strokes that soften the image by smearing the detail.
- **Sponge** paints with highly textured areas of contrasting color like you'd get by sponging on color.

• **Underpainting** makes your image look like it's painted on a textured background.

• **Watercolor** simplifies the details in your image the way they would be if you were creating a watercolor painting.

Blur

Soften and blur your images with these filters:

• **Average** (page 417).

• **Blur.**

• **Blur More.**

• **Gaussian Blur** (page 415).

• **Motion Blur.** You apply this pretty much the same way as the Radial blur, described on page 416, but it creates a one-way blur, like you'd see behind Road Runner when he's scooting away from Wile E. Coyote.

• **Radial Blur** (page 416).

• **Smart Blur.** This filter reduces grain and noise without affecting the edge sharpness of your photo. It's also used for special artistic effects.

• **Surface Blur.** This filter blurs without reducing edge contrast (page 418).

Brush Strokes

These filters give your image a hand-painted look:

• **Accented Edges** emphasizes the edges of objects as though they were drawn in black ink or white chalk.

• **Angled Strokes** creates diagonal brushstrokes that all run in the same direction.

• **Crosshatch** creates diagonal brushstrokes that crisscross.

• **Dark Strokes** paints dark areas of your image with short, tight, dark strokes, and paints light areas with long, white strokes.

• **Ink Outlines** makes your image look like it was drawn with fine ink lines.

• **Spatter** gives the effect you'd get from a spatter airbrush.

• **Sprayed Strokes** paints your image with diagonal, sprayed strokes in its dominant colors.

• **Sumi-e** gives the effect of drawing with a wet brush full of black ink, in a Japanese-influenced style.

Distort

These filters warp your image in a variety of ways:

- **Diffuse Glow** makes your image look as though you're viewing it through a soft diffusion filter.

- **Displace** lets you create a map to tell Elements how to distort your image.

- **Glass** makes your image look like you're viewing it through various kinds of glass, depending on the settings you choose.

- **Liquify** (page 453).

- **Ocean Ripple** gives an underwater effect by adding ripples to your image.

- **Pinch** pulls the edges of your photo toward the center.

- **Polar Coordinates** lets you create what's called a *cylinder anamorphosis*. With this kind of distortion, the image looks normal when you see it in a mirrored cylinder.

- **Ripple** creates a pattern like ripples on the surface of water.

- **Shear** distorts your image along a curve.

- **Spherize** makes your image expand out like a balloon.

- **Twirl** spins your photo, rotating a selection more in the center than at the edge, producing a twirled pattern.

- **Wave** creates a rippled pattern but with more control than the Ripple filter gives you.

- **ZigZag** creates a bent, zigzagging effect that's stronger in the center of the area you apply the filter to.

Noise

Use these filters to add *noise* (graininess) to your photos or to remove noise from them (unless otherwise specified, these filters are explained on page 288):

- **Add Noise** (page 413)

- **Despeckle**

- **Dust & Scratches**

- **Median**

- **Reduce Noise** (page 412)

Pixelate

These filters break up your photo into spots or blocks of various kinds:

- **Color Halftone** adds the kind of dotted pattern you see in things that have been color-printed by a commercial press.
- **Crystallize** breaks your image into polygonal blocks of color.
- **Facet** reduces your image to blocks of solid color.
- **Fragment** makes your image look blurry and offset.
- **Mezzotint** creates an effect something like that of a mezzotint engraving.
- **Mosaic** breaks your image down to square blocks of color.
- **Pointillize** makes your photo look like it's made of many dots of color.

Render

This is a diverse but powerful group of filters that transform your photo in many ways:

- **Clouds** covers your image with clouds made up of the Foreground and Background colors (page 231).
- **Difference Clouds** also creates clouds, but blends them in your image in Difference mode.
- **Fibers** creates an effect like spun and woven fibers.
- **Lens Flare** creates starry bright spots like you'd get from a camera lens flare.
- **Lighting Effects** is a complex filter for changing the light in your photo. For an in-depth tutorial on how to use this filter, see this book's Missing CD page at *www.missingmanuals.com*.
- **Texture Fill** lets you use a grayscale image as a texture for your photo.

Sketch

Here's another group of artistic filters. Most of them make your image look like it was drawn with a pencil or graphics pen:

- **Bas Relief** gives your photo a slightly raised appearance, as though it's carved in low relief.
- **Chalk & Charcoal** makes your photo look like it was sketched with a combination of chalk and charcoal.
- **Charcoal** gives a smudgy effect to your image, like a charcoal drawing.
- **Chrome** is supposed to make your image look like polished chrome, but you might prefer the Wow Chrome Layer styles in the Effects panel (page 423).

- **Conté Crayon** makes your image look like it was drawn with Conté crayons (a drawing medium originally made of graphite and wax, now made from chalks, that's used for making bold strokes) using the Foreground and Background colors.

- **Graphic Pen** makes the details in your image look like they were drawn with a fine pen using the Foreground color, with the Background color for the paper color.

- **Halftone Pattern** gives the dotted effect of a halftone screen, like you see in printed illustrations. The effect only *looks* like a halftone—this filter doesn't create a true halftone that your print shop might request.

- **Note Paper** makes your image look like it's on handmade paper. The Background color shows through in spots in dark areas.

- **Photocopy** makes your photo look like a Xerox copy.

- **Plaster** makes your image look like it was molded in wet plaster.

- **Reticulation** creates an effect you might get from film emulsion—dark areas clump and brighter areas appear more lightly grained.

- **Stamp** makes your image look like an impression from a rubber stamp.

- **Torn Edges** makes your photo look it's made from torn pieces of paper.

- **Water Paper** makes your photo look like it was painted on wet paper, making the colors run together.

Stylize

These filters create special effects by displacing the pixels in your image or increasing contrast:

- **Diffuse** makes your photo less focused by shuffling the pixels according to the settings you choose.

- **Emboss** makes objects in your image appear stamped or raised.

- **Extrude** gives a 3-D effect by pushing some of the pixels in your image up, something like toothpaste squeezed from a tube.

- **Find Edges** emphasizes the edges of your image against a white background.

- **Glowing Edges** adds a neon-like glow to the edges of objects in your photo.

- **Solarize** produces an effect like what you'd get by briefly exposing a photo print to light while you're developing it. It combines a negative and a positive image.

- **Tiles** breaks up your image into individual tiles. You can choose how much to offset them.

- **Trace Contour** outlines areas where there are major transitions in brightness. The result is supposed to be something like a contour map.

- **Wind** makes your image look windblown.

Texture

These filters change the surface of your photo to look like it was made from another material:

- **Craquelure** produces a surface effect like cracked plaster.

- **Grain** adds different kinds of graininess to your photo.

- **Mosaic Tiles** is supposed to make your photo look like it's made of mosaic tiles with grout between them.

- **Patchwork** reduces your image to squares filled with the image's predominant colors.

- **Stained Glass** is supposed to make your photo look like it's made of stained glass. The effect's usually more like a mosaic.

- **Texturizer** makes your photo look like it's on canvas or brick. You can select a file to use as a texture.

Video

These filters are for use with video images:

- **De-Interlace** smoothes images captured from video by removing the odd or even interlaced lines.

- **NTSC Colors** restricts your colors to those suitable for television reproduction.

Other

This is a group of fairly technical filters:

- **Custom** lets you create your own filter.

- **High Pass** is discussed on page 242.

- **Maximum** replaces pixel brightness values with the highest and lowest values of surrounding pixels. It spreads out white areas and shrinks dark areas.

- **Minimum** does the opposite of the Maximum filter: It spreads out dark areas and shrinks white ones.

- **Offset** moves your selection by the number of pixels you specify.

Digimarc

Use this filter to check for Digimarc watermarks in photos. Digimarc is a commercial system that lets subscribers enter their information in a database so that anyone who gets one of their photos can find out who the copyright holder is by searching the Digimarc database.

View Menu

This menu's commands let you choose different ways to see your image onscreen. For more details on adjusting your view, see page 96.

New Window for...

This command lets you create a duplicate window for your image so you can see it at two different magnification levels at once. The new window goes away when you close your image—it doesn't create a copy of your photo.

Zoom In

To increase the view size, you can choose this menu item or press Ctrl+=. You can also use the Zoom tool (page 100).

Zoom Out

To reduce the view size, choose this menu item or press Ctrl+–. You can also use the Zoom tool (page 100).

Fit on Screen

Use this command or press Ctrl+0 (that's the number zero, not the letter O) to make your photo as large as it can be without your having to scroll to see parts of it.

Actual Pixels

Choose this option or press Ctrl+1 to see your image in the exact size it would appear on the Web or in other programs that can't adjust view size like Elements can.

Print Size

Elements makes its best guess as to how large your image would print at its current resolution (page 107).

Selection

When this menu item is turned on, the outlines of your selections are visible. You can toggle the setting off and on here, or by pressing Ctrl+H.

Rulers

If you want to see rulers around the edges of your image window, toggle them on and off here, or by pressing Shift+Ctrl+R. You can adjust the unit of measurement in Edit → Preferences → Units & Rulers.

Grid

If you want to see a measurement and alignment grid on your photos, use this setting or press Ctrl+' (the apostrophe key) to toggle it on and off. You can adjust the grid size in Edit → Preferences → Grid.

Guides

Guides (page 87) are a new feature in Elements 8 that help you align objects in your files. If your image has guides in it, toggle viewing them off and on here, or press Ctrl+; (the semicolon key).

Notes

If you receive an image created in Photoshop that includes notes, choose this menu item to see them.

Snap to

If you want to control the Elements autogrid (a hidden system that determines how precisely you can place things when you move them in your images), use these commands.

- **Guides.** When you're working with a file that includes guidelines, this setting is where you toggle on and off whether objects you add will snap to those guidelines.

- **Grid.** When this setting is turned on, Elements automatically jumps to the nearest gridline. If the way your tools and selections keep jumping away from you bothers you, then turn off the Grid here. Then everything stays exactly where you place it. You have to make the Grid visible (View → Grid) before you can change its settings.

Lock Guides

If you've created guides (page 87) in your image and you don't want them to move, use this menu item or press Alt+Ctrl+; to lock them in place.

Clear Guides

If you have guides (page 87) in your image and you want to get rid of them, choose this menu item.

New Guide

To create a nonprinting guideline (page 87) in your image so that you can easily align objects, select this menu item.

Window Menu

This menu controls which panels and bins you see, as well as letting you adjust how your image tabs or windows display. Windows that are currently visible have a checkmark next to their names.

Images

Use these commands to control how Elements displays your images. The choices are explained in detail on page 97.

- **Tile.** Your images appear edge to edge so that all the windows or tabs are equally visible.

- **Cascade.** Your image windows appear in overlapping stacks. (Cascade is the usual view when you start Elements for the first time.) You can't choose this menu item when using tabs.

- **Float in Window.** Choose this to make the active image tab into a floating window. (You first have to turn on floating windows in Edit → Preferences → General.)

- **Float All in Windows.** If you've turned on floating windows, choose this and all your image tabs turn into windows.

- **Consolidate All to Tabs.** If you have floating windows and you want to go back to tabbed view, select this item.

- **New Window.** This is the same as the View menu's "New Window for…" command. It opens a separate view of your image, not a duplicate file.

- **Match Zoom.** Choose Match Zoom to get the same magnification level in all open windows as in the active image window.

- **Match Location.** When you have only part of a photo visible in a window, choose Match Location to make all open windows display the same part of their images, like the upper-left corner, for example.

Tools

The Tools setting hides and shows the Tools panel (page 29).

Adjustments

This shows and hides the Adjustments panel (page 195).

Color Swatches

Select this item to show or hide the Color Swatches panel (page 235).

Content

The Content panel holds frames, backgrounds, graphics, shapes, themes, and text effects to use in projects. It's always visible in Create mode, but if you want to see it in Edit mode as well, this is where you make it visible. See page 474 for more about using this panel.

Effects

This menu item shows and hides the Effects panel, from which you apply filters, photo effects, and Layer styles. See page 406.

Favorites

You can put your favorite items from the Content and Effects panels into the Favorites panel for easier access (page 476). Like the Content panel, the Favorites panel is always visible in Create mode, but you can use this menu item to make it visible in Full Edit or to hide it again once it's visible.

Histogram

Select this item to show or hide the Histogram in its own panel (page 221).

Info

Use this setting to bring up a panel with information about your photos, like the file size and color value numbers.

Layers

Make the Layers panel visible or hidden by choosing this item. See page 172.

Navigator

Turn the Navigator (page 103) off and on here. The Navigator lets you adjust which portion of a large image is visible onscreen and adjust the zoom.

Undo History

This item setting makes the Undo History panel visible or hides it. The Undo History panel shows a record of all the changes to your image up to the number of states you set in Edit → Preferences → Performance → History States. See page 36 for more about this panel.

Panel Bin

This setting minimizes (hides) and maximizes (reopens) the Panel bin (page 25). You can also just click the edge of the bin to hide or expand it.

Reset Panels

Use this command to return all panels to their original locations.

Welcome

Choose this menu item to see the Welcome screen that appears when Elements starts up.

Project Bin

This setting shows and hides the Project bin (page 28).

Image Windows/Tabs

At the bottom of the Window menu, you see a list of all the files you have open in Elements. Choose one to bring it to the front as the active window or tab.

Help Menu

The Help menu is where you find the Elements' Help files, and information about the program.

Photoshop Elements Help

When you select this menu item or press F1, your web browser launches to show you the Help files.

Getting Started

This menu item takes you to a section of Adobe's website that includes video tutorials to help newbies.

Key Concepts

Elements' Help files include a glossary of digital-imaging terms. If you're wondering what a particular term means, choose this menu item and it'll take you to the online glossary so you can look it up.

Support

Select this to go to Adobe's online Support area and knowledgebase.

Video Tutorials

Choose this menu item to go to the video tutorials section of Adobe's support site, where you can watch videos on how to do popular Elements tasks.

Forum

This takes you to Adobe's online support forum for Photoshop Elements.

About Photoshop Elements

Choose this item to see a scrolling window with info about the version of Elements you've got. You'll also see a very long list of patents and credits—an impressive testament to the complexity of Elements' engineering.

About Plug-In

Select this option for a long pop-out menu displaying all the plug-ins in your copy of Elements. Choose a plug-in from the list to see its version number and date information.

Patent and Legal Notices

This menu item displays a long list of the various patents for Elements, as well as trademark info for some of the components used in the program.

System Info

Choose this item for a window showing information about Elements itself and also about your Windows operating system. If you can't remember which service pack you have, for instance, then you can check here. You'll also find info about some important plug-ins. If you're not sure whether you have QuickTime, for example, go here to find out.

Registration

If you're not in the U.S. and you didn't register Elements with Adobe the first time you used the program, you can choose this menu item to bring up the registration window again.

Deactivate

Elements 8 includes *activation,* a process that limits the number of computers on which you can install your copy of Elements. If you need to uninstall Elements to move it to a new computer, be sure to use this command to deactivate it on the old computer so you can install it on the new computer.

Updates

This is where you check for updates to Elements components. After you select this menu item and the Updater checks in with Adobe, click the Preferences to control how Elements handles updates.

Elements Inspiration Browser

The Inspiration Browser (page 34) links you to a number of video and PDF tutorials. You can launch it from here.

Arrange Menu

This menu (whose icon is a gray square divided up into smaller squares and rectangles) lets you organize your image windows and tabs to best suit your workflow. The top part of the menu consists of thumbnails for the different ways you can tile your image views. Clicking a thumbnail puts you in a tabbed, tiled view, even if you began with floating windows. Just click the thumbnail that shows the layout you want. The large, single rectangle at the menu's upper left returns you to the basic tab view of one visible image tab with the others tucked away behind it.

> **TIP** To tile floating windows, go to Window → Images → Tile.

The bottom part of the menu rounds up several useful view commands also found in other menus:

- **Float All in Windows.** If you've enabled floating windows (page 97), choose this and all your image tabs turn into windows.

- **New Window.** This is the same as the View menu's "New Window for…" command. It opens a separate view of your image, not a duplicate file.

- **Actual Pixels.** Choose this option or press Ctrl+1 to see your image the exact size it would appear on the Web or in other programs that can't adjust view size (as Elements can).

- **Fit On Screen.** Use this command or press Ctrl+0 to make your photo as large as it can be without you having to scroll to see parts of it.

- **Match Zoom.** Choose this item to make the magnification level of all open windows match the active image window.

- **Match Location.** When you have only part of a photo visible in a window, choose this item to make all open windows display the same part of their images, like the upper-left corner, for example.

- **Match Zoom and Location.** This combines the two preceding commands.

Welcome Button

When you're signed on to your Photoshop.com account (page 20), you'll see text that says "Welcome, <your name>." Click it to go directly to your Photoshop.com account online. If you're not signed on, you see "Sign In" instead.

Create New Adobe ID

If you don't have an Adobe ID (you need one to use Photoshop.com), click this button to create one. You can also do this from any of the places in Elements that take you to Photoshop.com.

Reset Panels

With Elements' new, customizable interface, it's easy to lose track of things. Click this button to put everything back where it was the first time you started Elements.

Undo

Click this button or press Ctrl+Z to undo your last action.

Redo

Click here or press Ctrl+Y to redo your last action.

Organizer

Click here to go to the Organizer.

Welcome Screen

Click this button that looks like a little house when you want to see the Welcome screen (page 15) that appears when you first start Elements.

Installation and Troubleshooting

Elements is easy to install and is pretty trouble-free once it's up and running. This appendix not only describes some things you can do to ensure a smooth installation, but also provides cures for most of the little glitches that can crop up once you're using the program.

Installing Elements

Before you install Elements, it helps to make sure your PC is ready to receive its newest addition. First of all, if your computer's on a network, take it off the network temporarily. (You can go back on as soon as you've installed Elements.) Also, it's important to disable any antivirus software, as well as *any* products from Symantec (whose programs tend to quarrel with Adobe software during installation). You can turn any of these programs back on as soon as you've finished the installation. (Elements 8 needs to contact Adobe for *activation,* explained below, but it can wait till after you've finished installing.)

Also, you need to install Elements when you're logged into an administrative account on your computer. (If you've never done anything to change your account and you have only one account on your machine, it's almost certainly an administrative account.)

NOTE   If you have a previous version of Elements on your computer, you don't need to remove it before installing Elements 8. All versions of Elements run as separate programs, so you can keep older versions, too, if you want.

Make sure you have your Elements serial number handy. You can install Elements without a serial number, but only as a 30-day trial; when the 30 days are up, the program stops working. If you have a retail version of Elements, the serial number is on the label on the install disc's case. If you got it bundled (when you bought a scanner, for example), you'll usually find the serial number on the paper sleeve the disc is in. (It's not a bad idea to write your serial number right on the disc so you'll always have it around if you need to reinstall.)

> **TIP**   Once you install and register Elements, Adobe hangs onto a record of your serial number, so if you ever misplace the number, you can get it from Adobe. Also, when Adobe releases new versions of Elements, they usually offer a rebate for registered owners of previous versions. And if you agree to let Adobe send you email, they often offer discounts on other programs, like on the full version of Photoshop, if you want to move on later.

It's a good idea to make a complete backup of any existing Organizer catalogs before you start, just in case (see page 75 for info on backing up). After you do that, here's how to run the installer:

1. **Put the install disc in your computer's drive.**

   The disc window should open automatically. If it doesn't, then double-click the disc's icon or right-click it and choose Open. Then double-click Setup.exe to start the installer.

2. **Choose a language and then click OK.**

   This determines the language the installer uses.

3. **The installation wizard opens; click Next.**

   The installation *wizard* is a series of guided question-and-response screens.

4. **Decide whether to remove any older versions of Elements.**

   If you already have one or more versions of Elements on your computer, the installer reminds you about them, asking if you want to add the new version or get rid of the previous version(s). It's up to you whether to remove them.

   If you want to remove your older versions, click No to cancel the installation, and then remove the older versions yourself before starting the Elements 7 installer again. (In Vista, do this by going to Start → Control Panel → "Uninstall a Program". In Windows XP, it's Start → Control Panel → "Add or Remove Programs".) You can choose which versions to leave or to remove—it's not an all-or-nothing decision. You need to uninstall each version individually, if you decide to remove the old ones.

   Click Yes to keep your old versions and to continue installing Elements 8.

5. **Select the language to use for Elements and accept the license agreement.**

   Elements 8 is multilingual, so you can install different-language versions from the same installer.

6. **Enter the serial number and your location.**

If you don't have a serial number, you can only run Elements in trial mode for 30 days. Choose your country from the drop-down list, and then click Next.

7. **Choose where you want the installer to put Elements.**

Unless you have a specific reason to do so (if you install all your programs on a separate drive, for example), just agree to the location the installer suggests.

8. **Click Install to begin the installation.**

Elements installs. When the installer is done, click Finish to exit the installer, and then restart your computer. (Technically, you don't *have* to restart, but it helps to make sure that everything's tidied up, that all the processes are completed, and that Windows knows about the new program.)

9. **Register Elements.**

The installer creates a desktop shortcut to Elements. To launch Elements, double-click the shortcut or right-click it and choose Open.

The first time you start Elements, you see a button in the Welcome screen labeled "Create Adobe ID". Click it and enter your info to register Elements and sign up for your free Photoshop.com account. Elements also needs to activate itself (see page 608), but you don't have to do anything about this, except to let the program connect to the Internet at least once.

If you aren't in the U.S., it works a little differently. You get a registration screen at the end of the installation process. If you don't register, the window keeps popping up each time you start Elements, but after a few times you'll see a Never Register button at the bottom of the window. Click it to make the screen go away forever if you don't want to register. If you change your mind later, go to Editor → Help → Registration to call up that window again so you can register.

> **NOTE** Elements stores your catalog (page 53) separately from the actual program files. You can install and uninstall Elements as many times as you like without damaging or losing your existing catalog (if you have one from a previous version of Elements). However, as mentioned above, it's a good idea to back up any existing catalogs from older versions before installing Elements 8.
>
> When you first install Elements 8, if the Organizer doesn't find your existing Elements catalog, go to File → Catalog → Open. Then navigate to your catalog (usually called something like *My Catalog*) and open it. Elements automatically makes a backup copy of your catalog and adds "-1" to its name (My Catalog-1, for example). Elements 8 then uses your existing catalog (the one *without* the -1 in its name). Just remember that any changes you make in Elements 8 won't appear in the old version of the catalog (the one *with* the -1 in its name).

Activation

Elements 8 brings a new wrinkle to installation: *activation.* That's a process where Elements collects information about the computer you install it on and sends that to Adobe. Your installations are physically tied to the computers Adobe knows about. For Elements, you can install your copy on two different computers. If you want to install it on a third computer, you have to *deactivate* it on one of the first two before you can do that. This is a change from earlier versions of Elements, where your license to use the program had the same restrictions but Adobe didn't do anything to keep you from installing Elements on 20 computers.

You don't have to *register* Elements (the benefits of registering include free space on Photoshop.com and a record of your serial number [see page 20]), but you do need to *activate* it. The good news is that you don't have to do anything special to activate Elements—just let the program go online at least once. If you don't normally allow your computer online or you have a firewall that blocks outgoing connections, you need to make sure that Elements can connect or the program will stop working after 30 days. To check whether your activation was successful, go to Editor → Help and you should see a Deactivate menu item.

You can run Elements for a while without activating it, but it just runs as a trial, and when the 30 days are up, that's it unless you activate it. If you uninstall Elements, remember to deactivate it first. In the Editor, go to Help → Deactivate. After that, you can't use Elements on that machine again until you reactivate it by entering your serial number again. It's especially important to deactivate Elements if you're selling your computer or replacing your hard drive.

You *can* uninstall and reinstall Elements on the same machine without deactivating it first, but it's safest to deactivate each time you uninstall. That way, if something happens before you reinstall, like a major Windows crash that requires a hard drive replacement, you won't have any problems. The only solution for activation problems is to contact Adobe.

Scratch Disks

Elements uses a *scratch disk*—space on your hard drive—when it's busy making your photos gorgeous. The calculations Elements makes behind the scenes are very complex, and it needs someplace to write stuff down while it's figuring out how to change your image. It does so by using a scratch disk if the task at hand is too heavy-duty for your system's main memory to cope with alone.

You probably have just one hard drive in your computer, and Elements automatically uses that drive as the scratch disk. That's fine, and Elements can run very happily without a dedicated scratch disk.

TIP   You can make Elements *really* happy by keeping your hard drive defragmented and making sure there's plenty of free space available for Elements to use. To defragment in Vista, go to Control Panel → "System and Maintenance" → Administrative Tools → "Defragment your hard drive". In Windows XP, it's Control Panel → "Performance and Maintenance" → "Rearrange items on your hard disk to make programs run faster".

If you're fortunate enough to have a computer with more than one internal drive, you can designate a separate disk as your scratch disk to improve Elements performance. Your scratch disk needs to be as fast as the drive Elements is installed on, or there's no point in setting up a special scratch disk. If you have a USB external drive, for instance, forget it (USB isn't fast enough, even USB 2.0)—just leave your main drive as your scratch disk.

To assign a scratch disk, in the Editor, go to Edit → Preferences → Performance and choose your preferred disk. You can select up to four disks to use as scratch disks.

Troubleshooting

If Elements behaves badly from the moment you install it, something probably went funky during your installation. That's easy to fix. Uninstall Elements and reinstall it.

To remove Elements, first deactivate it (in the Editor, select Help → Deactivate). Then, in Vista go to Control Panel → "Uninstall a Program" (in Windows XP, Control Panel → "Add or Remove Programs") and remove Elements. Then reinstall the program.

Fortunately, Adobe makes very good software that looks after itself really well. There is, however, one simple procedure you can perform if Elements starts acting funny: delete your *preferences file,* which is where Elements keeps track of your preferred settings for the program. Deleting it fixes the overwhelming majority of problems you may develop. In Elements, you'll most likely need to delete the preferences file when dealing with Editor-related problems.

NOTE   There's one downside to throwing out your preferences file: Once Elements supplies you with a replacement (which it generates automatically), you'll have to re-enter any changes you made to things like window behavior (page 97) and other preferences. Your panels also go back to their original locations, so you'll need to rearrange them if you pulled any of them out of the bin. But deleting the preferences file doesn't affect your image files at all.

Here's how you delete the preferences file:

1. **Quit the Editor if it's currently running, and then restart the Editor.**

   Press Ctrl+Alt+Shift before you launch the program, and keep holding down those keys as you start the Editor until you see the window described in Step 2.

2. **Delete your preferences.**

A window appears asking if you want to delete the Elements settings. Click Yes. If you don't see the window, quit the Editor and try again.

It's much less common to need to reset the Organizer's preferences, but if you do want to reset the Organizer, that's easy, too: When you're in the Organizer, go to Edit → Preferences → General, and click the Restore Default Settings button at the bottom of the window.

> **NOTE** John Ellis's website is an excellent source of troubleshooting help for Organizer problems: *www.johnrellis.com/psedbtool/photoshopelements-6-7-faq.htm*. It's mostly about Elements 6 and 7, but much of the info there is useful for Elements 8, too.

Elements is usually pretty zippy, but if you find that it's really slowing things down on your computer, there are a couple of things you can do. First, go to the Organizer and select Edit → Preferences → Auto-Analyzer Options and make sure everything is turned off there. (You won't be able to use People Recognition [page 61] if you do this.) If that doesn't do it, follow the instructions in the box on page 56 for disabling the Adobe Active File Monitor in your Windows services. You'll lose the ability to use watched folders and to see added content like Layer styles and actions if you do this, but it'll speed things up.

Index

Colophon

Rachel Monaghan provided quality control for *Photoshop Elements 8 for Windows: The Missing Manual*.

The cover of this book is based on a series design by David Freedman. Karen Montgomery produced the cover layout with Adobe InDesign CS using Adobe's Minion and Gill Sans fonts.

David Futato designed the interior layout, based on a series design by Phil Simpson. This book was converted by Abby Fox to FrameMaker 5.5.6. The text font is Adobe Minion; the heading font is Adobe Formata Condensed; and the code font is LucasFont's TheSansMonoCondensed. The illustrations that appear in the book were produced by Robert Romano using Macromedia FreeHand MX and Adobe Photoshop CS.

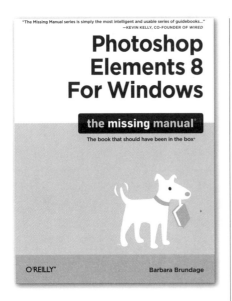
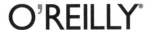